STUDIES IN EVANGELICAL HISTORY AND THOUGHT

Evangelicals and Education

Evangelical Anglicans and Middle-Class Education in
Nineteenth-Century England

STUDIES IN EVANGELICAL HISTORY AND THOUGHT

A full listing of all titles in this series
appears at the close of this book.

STUDIES IN EVANGELICAL HISTORY AND THOUGHT

Evangelicals and Education

Evangelical Anglicans and Middle-Class Education in Nineteenth-Century England

Khim Harris

Foreword by David Bebbington

Wipf and Stock Publishers
199 W 8th Ave, Suite 3
Eugene, OR 97401

Evangelicals and Education
Evangelical Anglicans and Middle-Class Education
in Nineteenth-Century England
By Harris, Khim
Copyright©2004 Paternoster
ISBN: 1-59752-730-0
Publication date 6/5/2006
Previously published by Paternoster, 2004

This Edition Published by Wipf and Stock Publishers
by arrangement with Paternoster

Paternoster
9 Holdom Avenue
Bletchley
Milton Keyes, MK1 1QR
Great Britain

STUDIES IN EVANGELICAL HISTORY AND THOUGHT

Series Preface

The Evangelical movement has been marked by its union of four emphases: on the Bible, on the cross of Christ, on conversion as the entry to the Christian life and on the responsibility of the believer to be active. The present series is designed to publish scholarly studies of any aspect of this movement in Britain or overseas. Its volumes include social analysis as well as exploration of Evangelical ideas. The books in the series consider aspects of the movement shaped by the Evangelical Revival of the eighteenth century, when the impetus to mission began to turn the popular Protestantism of the British Isles and North America into a global phenomenon. The series aims to reap some of the rich harvest of academic research about those who, over the centuries, have believed that they had a gospel to tell to the nations.

Series Editors

David Bebbington, Professor of History, University of Stirling, Stirling, Scotland, UK

John H.Y. Briggs, Senior Research Fellow in Ecclesiastical History and Director of the Centre for Baptist History and Heritage, Regent's Park College, Oxford, UK

Timothy Larsen, Associate Professor of Theology, Wheaton College, Illinois, USA

Mark A. Noll, McManis Professor of Christian Thought, Wheaton College, Wheaton, Illinois, USA

Ian M. Randall, Deputy Principal and Lecturer in Church History and Spirituality, Spurgeon's College, London, UK, and a Senior Research Fellow, International Baptist Theological Seminary, Prague, Czech Republic

To my family.

Contents

List of Illustrations		xi
Foreword		xiii
Preface		xv
Introduction		1
I	**The Church of England and Middle-Class Education in the Nineteenth Century**	**9**
1	The Church of England in the Nineteenth Century	11
	Theological Change	12
	Organizational Change	48
	Social Change	54
	Political Change	60
2	Middle-Class Education in Nineteenth-Century England	65
	The Victorian Middle Class	70
	Secondary Education	76
	High Church Schools	89
	Tractarian and Anglo-Catholic Schools	102
	Broad Church Schools	115
II	**Individual Evangelical Initiative**	**125**
3	Francis Close at Cheltenham	127
	Cheltenham College	132
	Cheltenham Grammar School	143
4	Talbot Greaves and the Founding of Weymouth College	157
	Postscript	169

| 5 | Francis Wright and the Founding of Trent College | 173 |
| 6 | Francis Pocock and the Founding of Monkton Combe School | 193 |

III Corporate Evangelical Initiative — 217

7	Evangelical Societies and Middle-Class Education	219
	The Church Association	219
	Stemma of the Church Society	223
	The Clerical and Lay Associations	234
	The Union of Clerical and Lay Associations	238
	The Church Pastoral Aid Society	250
8	The South-Eastern Clerical and Lay Church Alliance and South-Eastern College, Ramsgate	257
9	The Western District Clerical and Lay Association and Dean Close Memorial School	277
10	The Church of England Evangelical College and School Company	305

Conclusion — 327

Appendices — 333
1. Biographical Notes on Some Key Nineteenth-Century Evangelicals — 335
2. Church Association Register of Evangelical Schools — 356
3. Middle-Class Schools Referred to in this Book — 358

Bibliography — 361
Index — 417

List of Illustrations

The Revd Francis Close Perpetual Curate of Cheltenham, 1826–56 Courtesy of Cheltenham Art Gallery and Museum	130
Cheltenham Proprietary College in 1843 Courtesy of the Cheltonian Society	139
The Revd Talbot Greaves Rector of Melcombe Regis, 1856–81 After C. G. Falkner, *History of Weymouth College* Reproduced by permission, Old Weymouthians' Society	159
Photograph of Weymouth College in 1894 After *St James's Budget* 18 May 1894	167
Francis Wright Founder of Trent College National Portrait Gallery, London	175
An early picture of Trent College Courtesy of Trent College	185
The Revd Francis Pocock Headmaster of Monkton Combe School, 1868–75 After A. F. Lace, *A Goodly Heritage*	199
The Revd Alfred Peache Perpetual Curate of Mangotsfield with Downend, Bristol, 1859–74 Courtesy of St John's College, Nottingham	203
The Revd Henry Wright Honorary Clerical Secretary CMS, 1872–80 After E. Stock, *History of the CMS*, vol. 3	207
Stemma of the Church Society	223

The Very Revd Robert Payne Smith 263
Dean of Canterbury, 1871–95
National Portrait Gallery, London

South-Eastern College in 1884 269
After *The Lawrentian* centenary edition
Reproduced by permission, St. Lawrence College

The Revd Canon Edward Hoare 273
Incumbent of Holy Trinity, Tunbridge Wells, 1853–94
After J. H. Townsend, *Edward Hoare*

The Very Revd Francis Close 287
Dean of Carlisle, 1856–82
National Portrait Gallery, London

The Revd Dr W. H. Flecker 301
Headmaster, Dean Close School, 1886–1924
After R. F. McNeile, *A History of Dean Close School*
Reproduced by permission, Old Decanian Society

Dean Close School, 1886 302
After R. F. McNeile, *A History of Dean Close School*
Reproduced by permission, Old Decanian Society

The Right Revd J. C. Ryle 317
Bishop of Liverpool, 1880–1900
National Portrait Gallery, London

The Hon. Sydney Gedge 319
M.P. for Stockport and Walshall
Reproduced by permission, Birmingham Library Services

Foreword

A public school, according to E. A. Litton in 1850, "has for its special object the general education of youth"[1]. Litton, who was one of the leading Evangelical Anglican theologians of the nineteenth century, was to become Vice-Principal of St Edmund Hall, Oxford, in the following year and so possessed developed views on education. He was drawing a contrast with a university, which, in his view, was designed to provide a professional training or else to promote the learning of the whole nation. The public school, by which Litton meant a place of education for the middle classes as opposed to the masses, was to inculcate a broad body of knowledge and the capacity to reason out intellectual problems. He certainly hoped that the principles of the public schools would accord with the training in biblical Christianity that he himself provided at Oxford, where he saw Protestantism as threatened by the Catholicising movement that had grown up in the previous two decades under Newman and Pusey.[2] Litton was in favour of Evangelical public schools.

The subject of this book is the Evangelical public schools in which Litton believed. Not all English Evangelicals are considered, for Evangelical Nonconformists, who had their own institutions such as Mill Hill School, fall outside the scope of this volume; nor is all education, for the substantial contribution of Evangelical Anglicans to elementary and commercial schooling is left for others to explore. Instead Khim Harris wisely focuses on the way in which Evangelicals in the Church of England provided institutions where their sons could be sent for a sound education. Between 1860 and 1886 they founded five new schools: Weymouth College, Trent College, Monkton Combe School, St Lawrence's, Ramsgate, and Dean Close Memorial School, Cheltenham. Each is the subject of careful analysis to discover the aims of the individuals and organisations that saw them as bastions of godliness as well as good learning.

The findings are instructive. It might readily be assumed that the purpose of the schools was to protect the children who attended from High Church errors, the legacy of the Oxford Movement that Litton deplored. The Evangelical public schools would then need to be seen as a counterblast to the Anglo-Catholic public schools established from 1848 by Nathaniel Woodard. Khim Harris shows, however, that the earlier Evangelical institutions were designed not so much to combat Catholicising error as to supply a much-needed facility for the Evangelical middle classes themselves. Even when, in the later foundations, there was more of an element of defensiveness against the rising High Church presence, the aim of making provision for Evangelical families was a persistent motive. The case is argued cogently on the basis of a thorough examination of the relevant primary sources and the result is a masterly account of an educational movement that has hitherto lacked a historian. Khim Harris has authoritatively filled a major gap in the historiography of the Victorian period.

David Bebbington
University of Stirling
August 2004

---

[1] E. A. Litton, *University Reform: A Letter to the Rt. Hon. Lord John Russell, M. P., &c.*, 2nd edn London 1850, p. 9.
[2] Ibid., p. 12.

Preface

Perth, Western Australia, has been described as the most isolated city in the world, located some 3,000 kilometres from the next closest Australian city, and on a continent 15,000 kilometres from England, where this study is set. This circumstance greatly increased my dependence upon the help and forbearance of the librarians at The University of Western Australia, who over the six years duration of this study, managed to obtain something like 1,000 books and articles from around 50 different libraries. So my first acknowledgement must be to the staff of the Scholars Centre within the Reid Library, who patiently and cheerfully processed my interminable requests for what must have seemed to be some very obscure titles.

To the supervisor of this book in its initial form as a doctoral thesis, Dr Donald Leinster-Mackay, I am deeply indebted on several accounts: for his willingness to supervise me well beyond the date of his official retirement; for his infectious commitment to the protocols of scholarship and the pursuit of truth; but also and most importantly, for allowing me free access to his encyclopaedic knowledge of nineteenth-century English education. I have also benefited from the friendship of an Evangelical Anglican clergyman and enthusiastic church historian who has researched and written on nineteenth-century Evangelicalism. The Revd Dr Alan Munden has been a constant source of encouragement, and his shrewd observations and extensive knowledge of the period saved me from going wrong at a number of points.

During three research visits to the United Kingdom, it was invaluable to have access to the collections at the Cambridge University Library and the library of Ridley Hall, Cambridge; the British Library (including the Newspaper Library at Collindale); Lambeth Palace Library and Oak Hill College Library in London; as well as the Bodleian Library and Pusey House in Oxford. The staff at the Cheltenham Public Library were always patient and helpful, and I am grateful to the archivist at Lancing College, Mrs Janet Pennington, whose enthusiastic willingness in helping me find some of Nathaniel Woodard's more obscure papers, and further assistance when I had returned to Australia, were well beyond the call of duty. I am similarly grateful to the archivists of Corpus Christi College, Oxford; Homerton College, Cambridge; Weymouth College at the Weymouth Public Library; the National Society at the Church of England Record Centre in South Bermondsey; the Church Pastoral Aid Society and the Church Missionary Society at the University of Birmingham, who not only helped me when I was in their country, but also replied to later requests which were sent from mine.

I am extremely thankful to the archivists of the schools which are part of this study. Mr Roland Symons at Monkton Combe School provided valuable suggestions and managed to find some papers which were thought to have been lost. Mr Toby Leadbetter of Trent College was always helpful, and rallied from his hospital sickbed to assist me on my last visit to the school without complaint. Mr Humphrey Osmond at Dean Close School gave me the benefit of his gentlemanly erudition, which, together with his vast knowledge of the history of Dean Close School (not to mention the Church of England), is legendary among his friends and past pupils. Mrs Christine Leighton and Mr Tim Pearce of Cheltenham College were helpful in allowing me to access the school archives and the Governors' Minute Books and then later to source a good picture of the school. Dr Derek Scales of St Lawrence College was instrumental in locating the single extant copy of a report of the South-Eastern Clerical and Lay Church Alliance, and was also kind enough to meet with me, and have me stay while he was on holidays during the summer of 2001. I owe a great deal to Derek's fine scholarship and precise mind, as well as his extensive knowledge of the Protestant wing of the Church of England.

One of my research visits to England was in part made possible by a Bishop J. H. Moorman Scholarship from St Deiniol's Library at Hawarden, Flintshire, in 1998. My thanks to the Warden, the Revd Peter Francis who, as well as being a gracious host, gave me unlimited access to a library which specialises in nineteenth-century works. It was during this time, somewhat ironically, that I gained a better acquaintance with a former colleague from The University of Western Australia, Dr Patrick Armstrong. I was grateful then, for his enthusiastic encouragement of my research in a period of English history which was of mutual interest, and more recently, for his invaluable comments on a late draft of the thesis upon which this book is based. The Revd Andrew Reid, one time General Secretary of the Australian Fellowship of Evangelical Students, and the thirteenth Rector of St Matthew's Anglican Church in Shenton Park, Western Australia, was kind enough to read through a draft of the thesis, and to provide me with his typically incisive comments. Mr Trevor Hearl, a

Preface xvii

well-known educational historian, gave me some helpful early pointers; and the well-respected religious historian, Professor John Kent, provided some useful suggestions on two chapters of the thesis. I join with other historians of the period in thanking Professor Kent for locating in a second-hand bookshop in Bristol, the only surviving minute book of the Western District Clerical and Lay Association.

Finally, much gratitude is owed to my wife, Eugenie, for her unfailing patience, encouragement and support. My frequent absences abroad and the long periods of isolation while I was at my study desk, have meant that she has come to know what it is like to be a sole parent, not to mention a sole spouse. I would also like to thank my children for their willingness to put up wit17h a father who was at times present in body but annoyingly absent in mind. This book is dedicated to my fourth son, Peter, who was born two days after I had finished writing it. I hope that he will never have to hear those terrible words that his three brothers have come to dread: "Daddy's working".

For all errors, omissions, solecisms and infelicities of expression that may linger within the pages of this study, I alone am responsible and must beg, if not the indulgence, then at any rate the pardon of the reader.

Khim Harris
August 2004

Introduction

Napoleon's taunt that England was a nation of shopkeepers had, in retrospect, a great measure of truth in it, for during the first half of the nineteenth century there was enormous growth in the number, power and political influence of the middle classes. For much of this period there was very little in the way of middle-class education, since the Church, and then the state, concentrated its early educational efforts on the provision of elementary education. By the 1840s, Thomas Arnold's work at Rugby was beginning not only to influence the old upper-class boarding schools, but also to inspire the foundation of new schools, whose pupils were drawn largely from the upper middle class: well-to-do manufacturers, traders, and professionals. The first of these was Cheltenham College, whose constitution in its early years was firmly based on Evangelical principles. From around this time, a number of Anglican Churchmen also began founding schools for pupils whose families were less well-off, but still 'middle class'. Different founders reflected different theological sections within the Church, so that schools were established by High-Church Tractarians and Anglo-Catholics; by Broad Churchmen; and by Evangelicals. This study traces the development of the Evangelical provision of middle-class education, and how this was influenced—and in some cases, inspired by—the work of other Anglicans.

Like Ancient Gaul, the work is divided into three parts. The first section is a survey of the nineteenth-century Church of England and the overall provision of middle-class education during this period. It is based, of necessity, on an examination of secondary sources, although extensive use is made of (a) the minute books and reports of the National Society (1811) which are located in the Society's archives at the Church of England Record Centre in London; (b) a large number of nineteenth-century religious newspapers and periodicals, mainly located in the British Library Newspaper Library; (c) the Woodard Corporation archives located at Lancing College, Sussex; and (d) the 21 volumes of the Schools Inquiry Commission Report (1867–8), as well as other germane parliamentary statutes, papers and reports. Although the bibliography lists only those references which have been used in the writing of this book, it is by no means a complete record of all the works and sources which have been consulted.

The second section of the work explores the contribution which various individual Evangelical Anglican clergy and laymen made to the provision of middle-class education from the early 1840s to the end of the nineteenth century. It begins with the contribution of Francis Close, the influential Perpetual Curate of Cheltenham, in the second quarter of the century, and examines the work of two other clergymen, Talbot Greaves and Francis Pocock, who were also West Country clergy. The educational effort of one of the great industrialists of the period, Francis Wright, is the subject of chapter 5, and the school he founded in the Midlands provided a counterbalance to what was largely a movement amongst Evangelicals of the South and the West. This part of the study is based almost entirely on sources, both primary and secondary, located in the archives of these schools, and makes extensive use of school magazines and school council minute books, as well as what was reported by the two most important Evangelical newspapers of the period: *The Record* (1828–1948) and *The Rock* (1867–1905).

The third section of the work surveys the formation of various Evangelical societies, some of which were a response to the rise of Anglo-Catholicism, and all of which became involved in various ways in the provision of middle-class education. It is almost completely based on primary sources, as very little research has been carried out to date on any of these organizations, or the schools which they founded. These sources include (a) the minute books and papers of the Church Association, located in the Church Society archives; (b) the single surviving minute book of the South-Western Clerical and Lay Association, currently in private hands; and (c) the archives of the Church Pastoral Aid Society at the University of Birmingham. Extensive use was also made of the archives at St Lawrence College, Ramsgate, and of those at Dean Close School, Cheltenham, in order to document the early history of these Evangelical middle-class schools and the organizations which were behind their establishment. This survey of the corporate contribution of Evangelicals to middle-class education concludes with a detailed examination of a body which has been occasionally referred to, but until now, never fully documented due to lack of information. The author's re-discovery of the complete set of minute books of the Church of England Evangelical College and Schools Company at Trent College in 1997 has meant that the complete history of Evangelical involvement in middle-class schooling in the nineteenth century can now be documented.

As if to make up for the 'somnolence' of the eighteenth-century Church, the nineteenth-century Church of England was distinguished by rapid change and reform. These changes can be grouped, according to a general consensus amongst religious and social historians, into theological, organizational, social and political processes. Different theological and ecclesiastical emphases resulted in a system of parties which were a significant feature of the nineteenth-century Church, and which are still a feature of Anglicanism today. By the end of the nineteenth century, there were three distinct parties in the Church of England: High-Church Anglo-Catholic; Broad Church; and the so-called 'Low Church' Evangelicals. The significance of these different theological groupings within the Church of England is such that it has coloured the way in which the history of the Church has been described and interpreted. The predominance of Anglo-Catholic church historians has meant that much of our understanding of the Church of England during this period has been influenced by a particular understanding of the significance and effect of the Oxford Movement and other nineteenth-century developments in the Church. Recent historical surveys, largely arising out of post-graduate research that was carried out in British universities in the 1980s, have begun to redress this imbalance. These tend to utilise the approaches of social and political historians, and avoid the partisan style which characterises many of the early religious histories.

Another approach to the study of Anglican history has been through examination of the massive organizational or institutional change which resulted from legislation and internal Church reform, particularly that arising from the revival of the diocese as an administrative body, and the professionalization of the clergy. Early studies of the effect of social change within the Church of England tended to emphasise the individual rather than the corporate response to social issues of the day, and this was especially the case for Evangelicals who were very active in this area. However, the Christian Socialist movement of the 1840s, and then in the 1870s, was an important and long-lasting Broad Church response to the social problems of the nineteenth century. The idea that religion, and the religious attitudes of politicians, influenced the nineteenth-century political administration, has received welcome recent attention, and this contrasts with other approaches which tended to concentrate on the political dimensions of specifically religious issues. The importance of educational reform as a response to the social and political issues of the day has also been identified, and its significance to a work on educational history is critical. While nineteenth-century elementary education has been the focus of much prior historical research, much less is known about the Church's involvement in secondary or "middle-class" education during this period, and this becomes the subject of the second chapter of this book.

The work of sociologists, rather than educational or church historians, has been drawn upon to formulate a meaning for 'class' and a definition of 'middle class'. A three-fold class system is adopted, largely after the approach of nineteenth-century contemporaries. The hierarchical class system which was also applied to schools during this period is also examined in order to survey secondary education, which in the nineteenth century was always middle-class education. The significance of the proprietary school, a nineteenth-century educational phenomenon, is emphasised, and this provides the necessary background for the chapters which follow; as all of the Evangelical middle-class schools either began as proprietary schools, or started as private schools which were later converted to this arrangement. The prominence which was given to this type of school by the various Royal Commissions on education during this period provides another justification for this approach. John Roach's useful term, "private foundation schools", is adopted for these middle-class schools which were to later become proprietary and/or public schools. Typically, the Church of England contribution to this sector was characterised by an increasing partisan spirit, with new schools being founded by High Church, Broad Church and (significantly for this study), Evangelicals.

The first foray into middle-class education by members of the Church of England was by High Churchmen associated with the National Society in the 1830s. This led to the establishment of the diocesan Boards of Education and the founding of diocesan Training Colleges. It was followed by a series of educational initiatives which were largely motivated by the Oxford Movement. Several Churchmen associated with this new and powerful Catholic revival within the Anglican Church noticed that a large body of English children, the offspring of the people normally described as "middle-class", were practically excluded from both parochial and public schools. The most important of these Churchmen was Nathaniel Woodard, although others both preceded him and took their inspiration from his great work at Sussex in the 1840s and '50s, and later in the North and the Midlands. While Woodard could be best described as an Anglo-Catholic, other schools were founded by Anglicans who could be more accurately described as 'Tractarians'. All of these were characterised by a high level of ritual in their church services and varying levels of High Church practice such as sung liturgy, daily services, the hearing of pupils' confession. The late Brian Heeney, through his 1969 book, *Mission to the Middle Classes: The Woodard Schools 1848–1891*, contributed much to the account of this educational advance.

The significance of Broad Church clergymen in the development of middle-class education has only recently been recognized, and the influence of this group in the development of middle-class day schools and the system of Oxford and Cambridge local examinations is now well documented. In the late 1850s a system of County Schools was being established in the shires; and in the capital a movement for the provision of middle-class day schools, which started in a City parish, became the inspiration for other day school initiatives. The County School movement was responsible for the founding of a new, middle-class hall of residence in Cambridge, around the time that Anglo-Catholics were founding a similar institution in Oxford. The significance of the Broad Church involvement in middle-class education was that it resulted in Anglican institutions catering for Nonconformists for the first time. It was this fact, together with the founders' 'liberal' approach to theology, which spurred some Anglo-Catholics and Evangelicals into founding their own institutions. The late John Honey, who wrote the ground-breaking *Tom Brown's Universe: The Development of the English Public School in the Nineteenth Century* in 1977, was an early researcher of this aspect of middle-class educational provision.

Hitherto, the contribution of Evangelicals to middle-class education has been somewhat neglected. In the period 1840–1870, a number of individual Evangelicals—both clerical and lay—became involved in the provision of middle-class schools. The first of these, Francis Close of Cheltenham, was also a pioneer in infant education and teacher training. As the powerful Clerical Vice-President of Cheltenham College, he was one of the key people involved in the early development of what has been described as the first Victorian public school. He was also responsible for the re-foundation of Cheltenham's Grammar School. Three other well-known Evangelicals provided the impetus, and in some cases the finance, for the establishment of middle-class schools in the South, the West and the Midlands. Although a number of the supporters, and reporters, of these schools were clearly motivated by party feeling—the schools were perceived by some as the Evangelical response to the Oxford Movement and also to Woodard's educational initiatives—the founders themselves seemed to have been motivated simply by a desire to provide an education for the sons (and later the daughters) of the members of their own party. There is no record of any of these men making partisan statements regarding the other new middle-class schools; with the exception of Francis Close, who was a well-known anti-Catholic controversialist. In this sense, Woodard's new schools, as well as some of the schools being founded by other Anglicans, provided an example to follow rather than a system to counteract.

In the last quarter of the nineteenth century, party feeling intensified in the Church of England and this led to the formation of Evangelical societies which were designed for the support of Evangelicals and, in the case of the Church Association, the defence of Evangelicalism. By 1868 the success of the Woodard schools was causing concern among some Evangelicals. The schools were seen as a 'breeding ground' for 'Romanism', and their success also highlighted the lack of equivalent Evangelical middle-class schools. The Church Association made the first corporate Evangelical response to the Woodard schools. In 1868 it issued a paper which described and criticised these foundations, and in the following year it formed an Association for Middle-Class Schools whose aim was to raise money to set up five new Evangelical schools in different parts of the country. However, it was the regionally-based Clerical and Lay Associations, as well as the central Union of Clerical and Lay Associations, which achieved the greatest success in founding such schools. This was despite continued interest and discussion on this issue by both the Church Association and the Church Pastoral Aid Society, right throughout the nineteenth century and into the next. The South-Eastern Clerical and Lay Church Alliance was responsible for founding St Lawrence College in Ramsgate, Kent; and the Western District Clerical and Lay Association (together with the Union of Clerical and Lay Associations in London) was behind the foundation of Dean Close School in Cheltenham. In each case there was strong feeling amongst the supporters of these schools that they needed to respond to what was seen as the "Tractarian threat" being presented by the extraordinary success and growth of the Woodard schools.

The Church of England Evangelical College and School Company was founded in December 1890 in order to purchase Monkton Combe School from private ownership. This body eventually became the landlords for this school, and the owners and governors of two other Evangelical middle-class schools. The Company had originally planned to found Evangelical colleges in each of the universities, but this was later abandoned due lack of funds. This organization was the most effective and enduring response by Evangelicals to the perceived need for Evangelical middle-class schools. However, unlike the other corporate Evangelical initiatives, its board members saw the Woodard schools as an example to follow, rather than an enemy to attack. The Evangelical Church Schools Company (as it was later known) eventually divested itself of the land and buildings of Monkton Combe School (which was taken over by a local Evangelical body), but remained the owners of Weymouth College until this school closed in 1940. Its association with Trent College in Long Eaton continued until the 1960s, when legal changes to the school's constitution removed the

Introduction 7

direct link between this school and the Evangelical party in the Church of England.

After surveying the history of the Church of England and middle-class education in the nineteenth century (chapters 1–2), the approach of this study is first to examine the history of the founding of schools by four Evangelical Anglicans in the period 1840–70 (chapters 3–6); then to describe the various Evangelical organizations which appeared from 1858–90 (chapter 7); and finally to document the schools which they established or purchased from 1879–1902 (chapters 8–10). The methodology has been to base the survey of prior research and publications, outlined in part I of the book, mainly upon secondary sources; including extensive consultation of (mostly British) unpublished theses and dissertations. The rest of the study, outlined in parts II and III of the book, is almost completely based on primary sources located in the archives of the various schools, and the Evangelical organizations with which they were associated. Relevant secondary sources have also been consulted, particularly where there has been a gap in the historical record, or significant new research has been undertaken. Throughout the study, extensive use has been made of nineteenth-century periodicals and newspapers, many of which contain the most detailed (if often biased) accounts of the period. Exhaustive footnotes provide the reader with further detail and bibliographic information, the latter of which is cross-referenced in a select bibliography that appears at the end of the volume. Finally, a collection of appendices provides some short biographies of key Evangelicals who are mentioned in the work; as well as two lists of middle-class schools of the period.

The study is set between 1811, the year when the National Society was established, and 1902, when the Evangelical Church Schools Company purchased Weymouth College. It concentrates on the provision of 'middle-class education', a term which is explored in some detail in chapter 2, so that the study is limited to the schooling of children who had completed their elementary education and (depending upon their parents' income and social standing), were either preparing for 'higher education', or the workforce. This study is primarily concerned with the education of boys. However, the increasing contemporary concern about the provision of girls' education, particularly later in the nineteenth century and during the early years of the next, is reflected by frequent but limited references to this new and important educational development. Three middle-class schools for girls were founded by the Evangelical 'National Church League' in the early 1900s; and in the 1920s, 13 boys' schools were established by the ultra-Protestant 'Martyrs' Memorial and

Church of England Trust'. They provide an ideal starting point for further research into the involvement of Evangelicals in education—both for boys and for girls—in the twentieth century.

It is ironic that what was seen as the chief rival to Evangelicalism and to Evangelical schools—the Anglo-Catholic movement and the Woodard schools respectively—ultimately became the inspiration for Evangelicals to become involved in middle-class education, and the spur to found their own middle-class schools later in the century. The Evangelical schools which were established in the period 1860–1890 might never have been started, or would never have survived through their many financial crises, if Nathaniel Woodard had not established his school at Shoreham for the "sons of gentlemen of limited means, clergymen, [and] professional men" in 1848. Not so much a counterblast to Woodard, these Evangelical middle-class schools are best seen as a continuation of the same impulse, but for a different group of Anglicans. This study shows that Evangelicals responded in different ways to the challenge of providing education for a rising middle class. It also suggests that as well as responding to what was seen by some Evangelicals as an Anglo-Catholic threat, there was an independent Evangelical educational initiative that predated, and ran parallel to, Woodard's new schools.

PART I

THE CHURCH OF ENGLAND AND MIDDLE-CLASS EDUCATION IN THE NINETEENTH CENTURY

CHAPTER 1

The Church of England in the Nineteenth Century

During the nineteenth century the Church of England underwent a process of change and reform which was more rapid, more extensive and more enduring than any which it had experienced since the Reformation. The description and analysis of these changes has produced a body of literature which is characterised by its diversity of opinions, as well as by its sheer volume.[1] Surveys of Church of England hagiography are also distinguished by a wide range of approaches. For example, Frances Knight's four categories of church histories are a quite different grouping from Gerald Parsons', although they both agree that 'Church parties' and administrative/institutional reform are key types. The present study also subdivides the historiography of the nineteenth-century Established Church into four main categories, some of which are different from those which have been published by other historians. With the benefit of a little more hindsight, and the publication of several key works of Anglican[2] history since 1995, four new approaches can be discerned. Historians

---

[1] The authoritative study of the Church of England in the nineteenth century is W. O. Chadwick, *The Victorian Church*, 2 vols, London 1966, 1970. Prior to this, the standard histories were F. W. Cornish, *The English Church in the Nineteenth Century*, 2 vols, London 1933; and L. E. Elliott-Binns, *Religion in the Victorian Era,* London 1953. Recent studies are referred to below.

[2] The term 'Anglican' has been adopted in this study for the sake of convenience and clarity as a simple description of adherence to the Church of England. The word is probably an anachronism, for members of the Church of England in the nineteenth century would not have used it as a term to describe themselves: preferring instead 'churchman' or 'churchgoer'. In the 1840s the word was used pejoratively by the Tractarians to refer to the old High Churchmen. See P. Avis, "What is Anglicanism?" in S. Sykes and J. Booty (eds), *The Study of Anglicanism*, London 1988, pp. 405–24. For a discussion of nineteenth-century understanding of Anglican membership, see F. Knight, "From Diversity to Sectarianism: The Definition of Anglican Identity in Nineteenth-Century England", in R. N. Swanson (ed.), *Unity and Diversity in the Church,* Studies in Church History 32 (1996): 377–86.

have tried to document and understand the process of change in the Church of England from either a theological, organizational, social, or political framework. The survey below provides a detailed examination of the theme of theological change in the nineteenth century Church of England, thus providing the context for the rest of this examination, followed by a brief overview of the literature associated with each of the other three approaches.[3]

In his groundbreaking study of church history entitled *The Unacceptable Face*, John Kent has pointed to the problems of "historical identity", which arise from the study of an organization which has both a secular (social, economic, political) and a religious (theological) 'face'. He identifies some of the reasons why the study of Church parties is a necessary starting point for this type of enquiry. But the Church of England must also be studied as part of the history of the national religious culture, of which not only the Christian but also the Anglican tradition formed the largest, but not always the only, constituent:

> Its basic institutions—parishes, sees and so forth—have a social and economic life of their own which can be, and often is, treated historically from a purely secular point of view, but as soon as one turns to their religious purposes and to their relation to the state...one faces competing claims as to what history is about, and as to what constitutes 'Anglicanism'...These differences of interpretation are more than academic: they have been institutionalized into opposing parties.[4]

The start of this survey provides some explanation for a nineteenth-century obsession that continued well into the next century: explaining the existence and significance of these opposing parties.

Theological Change

A focus on party ideologies has completely dominated analysis of the nineteenth-century Anglican Church in the last 150 years and this approach persists today. John Wolffe has pointed out[5] that this has been based on a taxonomy of Church parties which was outlined by

---

[3] For a useful survey of the sources of the history of the Church 'in and of' England, see W. B. Stephens, *Sources for English Local History*, Cambridge 1981, ch. 8.
[4] J. Kent, *The Unacceptable Face*, London 1987, p. 96.
[5] J. R. Wolffe, "Anglicanism" in D. G. Paz (ed.), *Nineteenth-Century English Religious Traditions: Retrospect and Prospect*, London 1995, p. 1.

Revd[6] W. J. Conybeare[7] in a controversial 1853 article in *The Edinburgh Review*.[8] This has recently been re-printed and subjected to a detailed commentary by Arthur Burns.[9] Conybeare divided the clergy of the day into three main parties: High Church, subdivided into "Anglican", Tractarian, and "High and Dry"; Low Church, made up of Evangelical, "Recordite," and "Low and Slow"; and Broad Church, the descendents of the eighteenth-century Latitudinarians, which included "theoretical" and "antitheoretical" clergy.[10] Conybeare was not the first contemporary to write on the subject,[11] but his article was one of the most widely read, and continues to be today.[12] While some church historians have questioned the theological validity of party labels prior to the Tractarian era,[13] Gerald Parsons[14] and Paul Avis[15] first showed

---

[6] Throughout this book, the definite article is not included for this abbreviation, hence 'the Reverend' is written (but not read) as simply 'Revd'.

[7] William John Conybeare (1815–1857) was Principal of the Liverpool Collegiate Institute 1842–48 (see below, p. 73, fn. 58) and Vicar of Axminster, Devon 1848–54. He was part of a distinguished family of clerical academics and 'parson-naturalists'. See P. Armstrong, *The English Parson-Naturalist: A Companionship Between Science and Religion*, Leominster 2000, pp. 117–8.

[8] W. J. Conybeare, "Church Parties", *Edinburgh Review* 98, 200 (October 1853): 273–342. In 1855 Conybeare issued a revision of his article in a collection of periodical essays, *Essays Ecclesiastical and Social*, London 1855. References to Conybeare's article which follow are from this edition.

[9] A. Burns, "W. J. Conybeare: 'Church Parties'", in S. Taylor (ed.), *From Cranmer to Davidson: A Church of England Miscellany*, Woodbridge 1999.

[10] Wolffe, "Anglicanism", p. 1. The convention of using capitals when describing groups within the church reflects the author's perception that each party or school was a distinctive movement within the Church of England.

[11] The following studies of church party appeared before Conybeare's essay: R. Vaughan, *Religious Parties in England*, London 1838; W. F. Hook, *Letter to the Right Reverend the Lord Bishop of Ripon, on the State of Parties in the Church of England*, London 1841; R. Montgomery, *The Three Parties: or, Things as They are in the Church of England...*, London 1845; T. Dury, *On the Parties in the Church of England*, London 1850. Works which were published after Conybeare's article included: E. H. Plumptre, "Church Parties, Past, Present and Future", *Contemporary Review* 7 (1868); L. Stephen, "The Broad Church", *Fraser's Magazine* n.s. 1 (March 1870): 313–25; and "On the Position of the Evangelical Party in the Church of England", *Fraser's Magazine* 73 (January 1878): 22–31.

[12] It continues to be a set text for courses on Victorian church history in at least two British universities.

[13] See for example, M. Evershed, "Party and Patronage in the Church of England, 1800–1945", DPhil thesis, Oxford University 1985, p. 10.

that recognisable Church parties did exist in the pre-Tractarian Church of England, and this has been supported by more recent research by Peter Nockles[16] and Nigel Yates.[17] All have concluded that these parties were not as marked as later in the century for they were part of a broadly based theological consensus which Avis has likened to "a series of mutually overlapping circles".[18] While this approach to the history of Victorian Anglicanism has been criticised by some past[19] and recent[20] scholars as unhelpful, it continues to hold for many an almost irresistible fascination. It also goes some way to explaining the religious bias which accompanies many of the early works of Anglican history.[21]

General histories of the nineteenth-century Church published between 1960 and 2001 still maintain the 'party' framework as a powerful organizing principle. Owen Chadwick's classic and unrivalled *The Victorian Church*, a key departure point for all historians of the Church of England during this period, describes the Oxford Movement in much greater detail than, for example,

---

[14] G. Parsons, "Reform, Revival and Realignment: The Experience of Victorian Anglicanism", in G. Parsons (ed.), *Religion in Victorian Britain I: Traditions*, Manchester 1988, pp. 31–2.

[15] P. Avis, *Anglicanism and the Christian Church*, Edinburgh 1988, pp. 163–7. See also idem., "The Tractarian Challenge to the Identity of Anglicanism", *King's Theological Review* 9 (1986): 14–17.

[16] P. B. Nockles, "Continuity and Change in Anglican High Churchmanship in Britain 1792–1850", DPhil thesis, Oxford University 1982; and idem., *The Oxford Movement in Context: Anglican High-Churchmanship 1760–1857*, Cambridge 1994. See also idem., "Church Parties in the pre-Tractarian Church of England 1750–1833: the 'Orthodox'—some problems of definition and identity", in J. Walsh et al. (eds), *The Church of England c. 1689–c. 1833: from Toleration to Tractarianism*, Cambridge 1993, pp. 334–59.

[17] N. Yates, *Anglican Ritualism in Victorian Britain 1830–1910*, Oxford 1999.

[18] Avis, "The Tractarian Challenge", p. 16.

[19] Richard Wheatley devoted the whole of his 1822 Bampton Lecture to warning against the consequences of party division.

[20] See, for example, F. Knight, *The Nineteenth-Century Church and English Society*, Cambridge 1995, pp. 19–20; and S. Williams, "The Language of Belief: An Alternative Agenda for the Study of Victorian Working-Class Religion", *Journal of Victorian Culture* 1 (1996): 303–17. Both point to the irrelevance of 'churchmanship' labels for the majority of lay members of the Church of England, and suggest that the traditional ecclesiastical history is essentially a history of the institutions and the clergy, but not the 'people', of the church.

[21] For a discussion of the emerging awareness of "the influence of historians' own perspectives in both 'biasing' their accounts and defining the topics they tackle", see Burns, "W. J. Conybeare", p. 217.

Evangelicalism.[22] Chadwick's special interest in the Oxford Movement was announced in his lengthy introduction to *The Mind of the Oxford Movement*,[23] and it has remained a focus throughout his life; so much so that a collection of his writings, talks and reviews on the subject was published as recently as 1990.[24] Ann Crowther perpetuates a proud tradition of seeing nineteenth-century church history as the history of controversy,[25] and Desmond Bowen remains firmly in the mould of 'the history of the church is the history of the party'.[26] E. R. Norman provides perhaps the first truly 'modern' religious history as opposed to the older-style ecclesiastical narratives,[27] although the writing of histories of particular parties in the Church continues unabated.[28] Yates has suggested that a welcome new feature of some recent works on Anglican Evangelicalism is that they have "eschewed a narrow approach and deliberately sought to make connections and put national events into an international perspective."[29] He has even pointed out that some of the most valuable insights into both Tractarianism and Ritualism have come from historians who have been primarily concerned with Evangelicalism.[30] The most recent general history of the nineteenth-century Church, by Frances Knight, includes an examination of lay and regional religion, as well as clerical cultures.[31]

---

[22] Chadwick, *The Victorian Church*. Chadwick's interest in the Oxford Movement is also a personal one, for in later works he identifies himself as an Anglo-Catholic.

[23] O. Chadwick (ed.), *The Mind of the Oxford Movement*, London 1960.

[24] O. Chadwick, *The Spirit of the Oxford Movement*, London 1990.

[25] M. A. Crowther, *Church Embattled: Religious Controversy in Mid-Victorian England*, London 1970. For a similar approach in a collection of essays, see also A. Symondson, *The Victorian Crisis of Faith*, London 1970.

[26] D. Bowen, *The Idea of the Victorian Church*, Montreal 1968.

[27] E. R. Norman, *Church and Society in England 1770–1970*, Oxford 1976. For a discussion of the evolution of 'church historians' or 'historians of religion' into the 'mainstream' of historical research, see Burns, "W. J. Conybeare", pp. 216–7.

[28] See especially the work of Kenneth Hylson-Smith, referred to below, p. 25.

[29] Yates, *Anglican Ritualism*, p. 4. See especially I. Bradley, *The Call to Seriousness: The Evangelical Impact on the Victorians*, London 1976; D. W. Bebbington, *Evangelicalism in Modern Britain*, London 1989; and W. R. Ward, *The Protestant Evangelical Awakening*, Cambridge 1992.

[30] See, for example, J. H. S. Kent, *Holding the Fort: Studies in Victorian Revivalism*, London 1978; and P. Toon, *Evangelical Theology 1833–1856: A Response to Tractarianism*, London 1979.

[31] See also D. McClatchey, *Oxfordshire Clergy 1777–1869: A Study of the Established Church and the Role of its Clergy in Local Society*, Oxford 1960; and J. Obelkevich, *Religion and Rural Society: South Lindsey 1825–1875*, Oxford 1976.

The research upon which it is based concentrates upon "rural central England" and is an attempt to compensate for what is seen as "an overly urban approach in nineteenth-century history, which ignores the fact that, until 1850, more people lived in the country than in the town."[32] It provides a refreshing counterbalance to the Trollopian-inspired myth that the Church of England revolved around the bishop and the cathedral.[33]

Anglican historiography was dominated by a High Church, Tractarian/Anglo-Catholic tradition from the mid-nineteenth century up until the 1950s.[34] For historians working within this tradition, the Oxford or Tractarian movement was seen as both the inspiration and means by which the nineteenth-century Church reformed itself. It was almost as if the events of 1833 (the date of Keble's famous assize sermon, singled out by Newman as the origin of the Tractarian tradition in the *Apologia Pro Vita Sua*[35]) miraculously revived the Church from its 'eighteenth-century somnolence'.[36] The first generation of Anglo-Catholic historians[37] was epitomised by R. W. Church, whose book *The Oxford Movement: Twelve Years, 1833–1845* first appeared in 1891, and was reprinted with an introduction by

---

[32] Knight, *Nineteenth-Century Church*. Cf. J. H. S. Kent "The Role of Religion in the Cultural Structure of the Later Victorian City", *Transactions of the Royal Historical Society* 23 (1973): 153–173.

[33] It should be noted that Frances Knight's book is based upon her extensive research of John Kaye (1783–1853), Bishop of Lincoln 1827–53, as well as a study of local churches in the South and East Midlands. See also F. Knight, "The Influence of the Oxford Movement in the Parishes c. 1833–1860: A Reassessment" and J. Morris, "The Regional Growth of Tractarianism: Some Reflections", both in P. Vaiss (ed.), *From Oxford to the People: Reconsidering Newman and the Oxford Movement*, Leominster 1996.

[34] For a recent and exhaustive survey of High Church historiography, see Nockles, *The Oxford Movement in Context*, pp. 1–43. For a discussion of the terms, 'Anglican', and 'Anglo-Catholic', both used in the sentence above, see ibid., pp. 40–3.

[35] See J. H. Newman *Apologia Pro Vita Sua*, London 1913 (first published 1864), p. 136.

[36] Nockles has described how the Tractarians were dismissive of the eighteenth-century Church of England and its High Church tradition; Newman described it as "the last miserable century". Nockles, *The Oxford Movement in Context*, pp. 4–5.

[37] Except for the contemporaneous accounts by A. P. Perceval, *A Collection Connected with the Theological Movement of 1833*, London 1842; and W. Palmer, *A Narrative of Events Connected with the Publication of the Tracts for the Times...*, Oxford 1843. See O. Chadwick, "The Oxford Movement and its Reminiscencers", in idem. (ed.), *The Spirit of the Oxford Movement*, Cambridge 1990, ch. 7.

Geoffrey Best as recently as 1970. This was followed by J. H. Overton, who wrote a history of the nineteenth-century Church in 1894, placing the events of 1833 firmly at the centre: "The national feeling, long pent-up, depressed, despondent, had at length obtained freedom to pour forth; and the effect was amazing. The Church suddenly came to life."[38]

These early Tractarian historians set out to describe and interpret the "colourful and dramatic sequence of controversies and clashes"[39] which accompanied the development of Tractarianism. Their histories, and others, especially by S. L. Ollard,[40] were highly romantic accounts of the Church, and at least one recent scholar has purposely set out to dismantle and replace the mythology about ritualism that they generated.[41] Many Tractarian histories regressed into 'ripping yarns' in celebration of the heroes of the movement,[42] whereas others concentrated on key individuals such as Keble, Pusey, Froude and Newman.[43] Anniversaries of Keble's Assize Sermon have been the stimulus for more papers[44] and books[45] celebrating the occasion, most with a tendency to put forward the view that the Oxford Movement

---

[38] J. H. Overton, *The English Church in the Nineteenth Century (1800–1833)*, London 1894, p. 14.

[39] Burns, "W. J. Conybeare", p. 216.

[40] S. L. Ollard, *A Short History of the Oxford Movement*, London 1915. Another monocular perspective by Ollard was *The Anglo-Catholic Revival*, London 1925.

[41] Yates, *Anglican Ritualism*, pp. 4–9.

[42] Knight, *Nineteenth-Century Church*, p. 7.

[43] See Wolffe, "Anglicanism", pp. 4–5 for a review of some of this literature, and for Newman, P. B. Nockles, "Recent Studies of John Henry Newman", *Anglican and Episcopal History* 63, 1 (1994): 73–86. Key works which reassess the Movement's leaders include G. Battiscombe, *John Keble: A Study in Limitations*, London 1963; P. A. Butler (ed.), *Pusey Rediscovered*, London 1983, and S. Gilley, *Newman and His Age*, London 1990. For a recent reappraisal of both Newman and Manning, see D. Newsome, *The Convert Cardinals: John Henry Newman and Henry Edward Manning*, London 1993, especially chs 2–3.

[44] G. Rowell (ed.), *Tradition Renewed: The Oxford Movement Conference Papers*, London 1986.

[45] For the fiftieth anniversary, see especially C. P. S. Clarke, *The Oxford Movement and After*, London 1932; W. J. S. Simpson, *History of the Anglo-Catholic Revival from 1845*, London 1932; M. Donovan, *After the Tractarians*, London 1933; and F. L. Cross, *The Oxford Movement and the Seventeenth Century*, London 1933. For the hundredth: G. Rowell, *The Vision Glorious: Themes and Personalities in the Catholic Revival in Anglicanism*, Oxford 1983, and W. N. Yates, *The Oxford Movement and Anglican Ritualism*, London 1983.

had saved the Church of England.[46] One early exception to this Anglo-Catholic hagiography was the Swedish historian, Yngve Brilioth,[47] who first highlighted the 'prehistory' of the movement, including the influence of Evangelicalism and the development from the old High-Church tradition.[48] However, most histories of the movement still start with the events of 1833 and end with Newman's conversion in 1845, leaving unexplored the relationship of the Oxford Movement to Ritualism and later nineteenth-century Anglo-Catholicism. By contrast, more recent surveys by Yates, Nockles and Reed[49] give considerable attention to the events leading up to 1833 and to developments after 1845. They also focus less on the movement's "complex and powerful personalities"[50] and more on the social, spiritual, organizational or political aspects.[51]

Peter Nockles gives 'old-style' High-Churchmanship a welcome new profile and dispels the myth that it was a moribund party waiting for revival by the Oxford Movement. He points to its intellectual vitality, especially in relation to political theology, and its record in the performance of public worship, which altogether supports J. C. D. Clark's contention that revival occurred "not only by reaction against the existing order but by evolution from it".[52] Nockles suggests that the term "High Church" needs to be rescued from "the misappropriation and glosses of much post-Tractarian historiography"[53] and recognised for what it was: an independent tradition within the Church of England. Contrary to earlier understanding,[54] Nockles has shown that the theological developments of the 1830s were "far less a revival of traditional Anglican High-Churchmanship than a radical departure

---

[46] Yates, *Anglican Ritualism*, p. 7.

[47] Y. Brilioth, *The Anglican Revival: Studies in the Oxford Movement*, London 1925.

[48] Another seminal study of the influence of High Churchmanship in this period is the work of the Italian scholar, Pietro Corsi: see especially *Science and Religion: Baden Powell and the Anglican Debate, 1800–1860*, Cambridge 1988.

[49] Yates, *Anglican Ritualism*; Nockles, *The Oxford Movement in Context*; and J. S. Reed, *Glorious Battle: The Cultural Politics of Victorian Anglo-Catholicism*, London 1996.

[50] Burns, "W. J. Conybeare", p. 216.

[51] Knight, *Nineteenth-Century Church*, p. 8.

[52] J. C. D. Clark, *English Society, 1688–1832*, Cambridge 1985, p. 354. This ground-breaking, revisionist study reasserts the central role that the Church of England played in eighteenth-century politics and theology, and the importance of the 'Orthodox' tradition within Anglicanism.

[53] Nockles, "Church Parties", p. 335.

[54] See Brilioth, *The Anglican Revival*.

from it."[55] John Shelton Reed's approach is that of the sociologist, and he has based his research mostly on the surviving contemporary polemical literature, including a particularly thorough use of the Pusey House pamphlet collection. He provides some important insights into the appeal of ritualism to clergy and women, and challenges the "slum priests" myth that Ritualists exercised a special ministry to the urban working classes.[56] Nigel Yates's book is a revisionist study that seeks to reassess Anglican Ritualism. It sets out to "set events in the Church of England in the widest possible context" including architecture,[57] art, historical research, literature, philosophy and political thought. Most importantly, it considers the impact of Ritualism on the Church of England as a whole and its significance in the wider perspective of British church history in the four centuries since the Reformation.

Nockles[58] and others[59] have shown that of all the many labels descriptive of church party, "none has suffered more from over-usage and misapplication"[60] than that of 'High Church'. As mentioned above, this is partly because of the presuppositions engendered by the Oxford Movement. J. C. D. Clark has noted that "The Victorian conception of 'High Church' was one largely drawn from the Oxford Movement".[61] There are also a number of other possible reasons. First, traditional High Churchmanship and Tractarianism have often been regarded as synonymous. Again, this is largely the result of Tractarian hagiography. Secondly, there is the problem of terminology, something

---

[55] Yates, *Anglican Ritualism*, p. 2.
[56] See L. E. Ellsworth, *Charles Lowder and the Ritualist Movement*, London 1982; and comments by J. Kent, *The Unacceptable Face*, p. 89, and Wolffe, "Anglicanism", pp. 5–6.
[57] See also N. Yates, *Buildings, Faith and Worship: The Liturgical Arrangement of Anglican Churches, 1600–1900*, Oxford 1991.
[58] For a discussion of the meaning of the term, see Nockles, "Church Parties", and idem., *The Oxford Movement in Context*. Nockles has made the most substantial contribution to the study of High Churchmanship to date, and what follows is greatly indebted to his prior work.
[59] Nockles's research was preceded by G. W. O. Addleshaw, *The High Church Tradition: A Study in the Liturgical Thought of the Seventeenth Century*, London 1941; G. Every, *The High Church Party 1688–1718*, London 1956; and W. R. Fryer, "The High Churchmen of the Earlier Seventeenth Century", *Renaissance and Modern Studies* 5 (1961): 106–48. It has been followed by K. Hylson-Smith, *High Churchmanship in the Church of England, From the Sixteenth Century to the late Twentieth Century*, Edinburgh 1993, which is based upon idem., "The Evangelicals in the Church of England, 1900–1939", PhD thesis, University of London 1982.
[60] Nockles, "Church Parties", p. 334.
[61] J. C. D. Clark, *Revolution and Rebellion*, Cambridge 1986, p. 109.

which Nockles has discussed in some detail.[62] For the purposes of this survey, perhaps the most succinct definition is one which Archdeacon Daubeny gave in his influential *Guide to the Church* (1798). He defined High Church simply as "a decided and principled attachment to the Apostolic government of the Church".[63] Thirdly, there is the issue of whether High Church represents one group, or can be further subdivided into 'Orthodox' and, by implication, 'Broad' or 'Latitudinarian'.[64] Further confusion has resulted from the practice of a number of modern historians who have taken up the theological usage of the label, 'Orthodox', and used it interchangeably with 'High Church'.[65] Aspects of the role and principles of the 'Orthodox' party in the Church of England have now been elucidated by a number of recent scholars, especially Clive Dewey, Arthur Burns and Frances Knight.[66]

There is another misconception—more common in the general rather than the 'academic' community—that 'High Church' is the theological corollary to 'Evangelical'. Nockles has pointed out that it was only from the 1840s onwards that Evangelicals came to acquire the label 'Low Church', and that this was inspired by Tractarian opposition. In the early nineteenth century, the term 'Low Church' was not levelled at Evangelicals, but strictly confined to the older Latitudinarian party associated with Bishop Hoadly.[67] Before the rise of Tractarianism, Evangelicals could be as anti-'Low Church' in this sense as any High Churchman. There is even one, albeit rather obscure, example of an Evangelical bishop being described as 'High Churchman.'[68] This historical distinction between 'Evangelical' and 'Low Church', and the later, apparent fusion of the two, has been discussed elsewhere. The purpose of mentioning it here is to highlight

---

[62] See especially Nockles, "Church Parties", pp. 335–8.
[63] C. Daubeny, *A Guide to the Church* vol. 1, London 1798, xliv. Cited by Nockles, "Church Parties", p. 337.
[64] This is the subject of Nockles's article, "Church Parties".
[65] See, for example, J. M. Turner, *Conflict and Reconciliation*, London 1985, pp. 110–11; and A. M. C. Waterman, *Revolution, Economics and Religion*, Cambridge 1991, p. 196.
[66] C. Dewey, *The Passing of Barchester*, London 1991; A. Burns, *The Diocesan Revival in the Church of England*, Oxford 1999; and Knight, *Nineteenth-Century Church*.
[67] Benjamin Hoadly (1676–1761) was Bishop of Bangor from 1716; Hereford from 1721; Salisbury from 1723; and Winchester from 1734. He was a vociferous opponent of High Church 'orthodox' principles, especially the apostolic succession.
[68] Bishop Ryder was described as such by a visiting American clergyman. Nockles, "Church Parties", p. 348.

an ahistorical misuse of the term 'Low Church' amongst Anglicans today, just as High-Church Anglicans of the early 1800s were fond of using the ahistorical and sweeping sobriquet of 'Puritan' for Calvinistic Evangelicals.

The High-Church 'Hackney Phalanx'[69] or 'Clapton Sect'[70] has also suffered at the hands of historians. Eclipsed by the Evangelical 'Clapham Sect',[71] which was seen as a more prominent and significant force, and dismissed by Anglo-Catholic historians as a group of unimaginative 'High and Dry' Tories, this informal network of "conservative but conscientious clergy" exerted great influence in the pre-Tractarian Church. The Hackneyites drew from the old High-Church tradition, emphasizing the heritage of the Church and the necessity of the visible church in the scheme of salvation. They upheld the alliance of Church and State as a means of consecrating the State. The Hackney Phalanx was a major force in the rise of Church education, through their founding of the National Society in 1811,[72] and also in the church building movement through the formation of the Church Building Commission in 1818.[73] The revival of the old Church

---

[69] The term 'Hackney Phalanx' was first coined by Dr William Hales, Rector of Killesandra, Ireland, to describe "the motley group of London High Churchmen who entertained him on visits to the capital", including the Rector of Hackney, H. H. Norris. Nockles, *The Oxford Movement in Context*, p. 14, fn. 50.

[70] Named after the village of Clapton near Hackney, which later became the home of Joshua Watson and a focal point for gatherings of the Phalanx. This alternative designation was in contradistinction to the Clapham Sect of Evangelicals (see fn. 71 below).

[71] A group of influential Evangelical laymen who lived in or near the village of Clapham. They included Henry Thornton (1760–1815), James Stephen (1758–1832), Zachary Macaulay (1768–1838) and William Wilberforce (1759–1833). See J. Telford, *A Sect That Moved the World*, London 1907; M. G. James, "The Clapham Sect—its History and Influence", DPhil thesis, Oxford University 1950; E. M. Howse, *Saints in Politics*, London 1953; D. Spring, "The Clapham Sect: Some Social and Political Aspects", *Victorian Studies* 5 (1961–2): 35–48; I. C. Bradley, "The Politics of Godliness: Evangelicals in Parliament, 1784–1832", DPhil thesis, Oxford University 1974; and I. Bradley, *The Call to Seriousness: The Evangelical Impact on the Victorians*, London 1976.

[72] For a description of the formation and work of the 'The National Society for Promoting the Education of the Poor in the Principles of the Established Church throughout England and Wales', see G. C. T. Bartley, *Schools for the People*, London 1871; P. A. Welsby, *A Short History of the National Society*, London 1961; H. J. Burgess, *Enterprise in Education*, London 1958; and C. K. Francis Brown, *The Church's Part in Education 1833–1941,* London 1942.

[73] The Church Building Commission was founded in 1818 with large subscriptions from the King and Parliament; the latter gave £1,000,000 as a thanksgiving for victory at Waterloo. See M. H. Port, *Six Hundred New*

Societies[74] and the administrative reform of the Church were also part of their agenda. Despite their significance, their history remains to be written.[75]

Three of the men responsible for the day-to-day direction of the Phalanx were: the "virtual leader of the High Church party", Joshua Watson;[76] his brother, Archdeacon J. J. Watson,[77] and H. H. Norris.[78] Other leading members of the Phalanx were Charles Manners-Sutton,[79] William Van Mildert[80] and William Howley.[81] The coherence of the Phalanx was aided by their close geographical proximity to each other,[82] personal and family links,[83] patronage ties,[84] and common

---

Churches: A Study of the Church Building Commission, 1818–1856..., London 1961.

[74] The Society for Promoting Christian Knowledge (SPCK) and the Society for the Propagation of the Gospel (SPG). See below, p. 23, fns. 85 and 86.

[75] Hylson-Smith devotes a whole chapter to the Phalanx in *High Churchmanship*; however, the best accounts are in E. Churton (ed.), *Memoir of Joshua Watson*, 2 vols, London 1861; C. Dewey, *The Passing of Barchester*, 'Appendix'; E. A. Varley, *The Last of the Prince Bishops: William Van Mildert and the High Church Movement of the Early Nineteenth Century*, Cambridge 1992, ch. 3; and Nockles, *The Oxford Movement in Context*, pp. 14–8.

[76] Joshua Watson (1774–1855), a wealthy London wine merchant and contractor, was a key lay leader of the High Church party. Watson was a Church Building Commissioner from 1828 and helped found King's College, London, in 1829. See E. Churton, *Memoir of Joshua Watson*; and A. B. Webster, *Joshua Watson: The Story of a Layman, 1771–1855*, London 1954.

[77] John James Watson (1768–1839) was Vicar and later Rector of Hackney, 1799–1839, as well as Archdeacon of St Albans from 1816 and Prebend of St Paul's, 1825–39.

[78] Henry Handley Norris (1771–1850) was Perpetual Curate 1809–31 and Rector 1831–50 of South Hackney.

[79] Charles Manners-Sutton (1755–1828) was Dean of Peterborough 1792–3, Bishop of Norwich 1793–1805, and Archbishop of Canterbury 1805–28. He was "A staunch supporter of the small but very active band of High Churchmen" (i.e. the Hackney Phalanx).

[80] William Van Mildert (1765–1836) was Bishop of Llandaff 1819–26 and Bishop of Durham 1826–36. See G. F. A. Best, "The Mind and Times of William Van Mildert", *Journal of Theological Studies* 14, 2 (1963): 355–70; and E. A. Varley, *The Last of the Prince Bishops*. Van Mildert was responsible for the founding of the University of Durham in 1832 out of the revenues and property of this wealthy see.

[81] William Howley (1766–1848) was Bishop of London 1813–28 and Archbishop of Canterbury 1828–48. See C. Dewey, *The Passing of Barchester*, London 1991, p. 155 and *passim*.

[82] They were all concentrated in or near London, as well as a high concentration in Northamptonshire.

[83] See Nockles, *The Oxford Movement in Context*, pp. 15–8.

membership of various social and Church organizations. This included the SPCK,[85] the SPG,[86] the National Society[87] and the Church Building Society. Joshua Watson was Treasurer of the SPCK and active in the SPG; he was a co-founder of the National Society and its first Treasurer in 1817. He was also co-founder of the Church Building Commission and the Additional Curates Society.[88] According to the *Dictionary of National Biography* (DNB), Henry Norris "largely ruled" the SPCK from 1793–1834. Fellowship was also fostered by the publication of various periodicals. *The British Critic* was purchased by Joshua Watson in 1811, and this became the main organ of High-Church, Tory-orientated Anglicans until it was taken over by Tractarians in 1838.[89] According to Josef Altholz, *The Christian Remembrancer* (1819–68) was another product of the Hackney Phalanx, edited by Henry Norris and produced monthly. The only other 'old' High-Church periodical was the *Church of England Quarterley Review* (1837–58), which took its stand on 'Church and State', crusading against "infidelity, liberalism and popery."[90] As the century progressed, the High Church came to be identified more and more closely with the Tractarians, then Ritualism, and out of this evolved today's High-Church Anglo-Catholics.

---

[84] See especially Dewey, *Passing of Barchester*.

[85] The Society for Promoting Christian Knowledge was founded in 1699 by Lord Guilford, Sir Humphrey Mackworth, Mr Justice Hoole and Colonel Maynard Colchester. During the eighteenth century it fostered the growth of charity schools and the distribution of Bibles and Christian literature. See W. O. B. Allen and E. McClure, *Two Hundred Years: The History of The Society for Promoting Christian Knowledge, 1698–1898*, London 1898; W. K. L. Clarke, *A History of the S.P.C.K.*, London 1959; and R. W. Unwin, "The Established Church and the Schooling of the Poor: the Role of the S.P.C.K. 1699–1720", in V. Mclelland (ed.), *The Churches and Education*, 14–32, Evington, Leicester 1984.

[86] The Society for the Propagation of the Gospel in Foreign Parts was founded in 1701 by Thomas Bray and others. By the 1800s it was in urgent need of new men and new ideas, as it had degenerated into a board of management administering trust funds.

[87] For the National Society, see fn. 72 above.

[88] See below, p. 251, fn. 213.

[89] John Henry Newman became the editor in July 1838. He had been assisting the previous two editors from 1836. See E. R. Houghton and J. L. Altholz, "The British Critic, 1824–1843", *Victorian Periodicals Review* 24, 3 (1991): 111–8, and J. L. Altholz, *The Religious Press in Britain 1760–1900*, London 1989, pp. 23–7.

[90] "Introduction", *Church of England Quarterly Review* 1 (January 1837): 1. Cited by Altholz, ibid., p. 26.

Alongside the High-Church and Anglo-Catholic traditions of interpretation and subject matter, there has also been a significant Evangelical tradition of historiography. Apart from articles in periodicals,[91] the earliest of these were either apologies for the Evangelical party,[92] or highly critical histories of Tractarianism, such as Walter Walsh's 1899 "lurid polemic" in *The Secret History of the Oxford Movement*.[93] Stock's four-volume *History of the Church Missionary Society* was published in the same year, and for a book which set out to record the history of an Evangelical organization rather than the movement itself, it manages to do both successfully.[94] In the twentieth century, Evangelical histories have been few and far between, especially in comparison with the Anglo-Catholic contribution as discussed above. The most significant and enduring was G. R. Balleine's *A History of the Evangelical Party in the Church of England*, which first appeared in 1908 and went through five editions, the last of which was extended by G. W. Bromiley in 1951.[95] Balleine's aim, set out in his Preface, was "to arouse interest in a much neglected piece of church history, to clear away a few of the misconceptions that prevail about the Evangelicals, and to stir some readers to greater earnestness".[96] As Knight has suggested, it was a work to "educate and inspire his fellow Evangelicals by providing a

---

[91] See "On the Present Position of the Evangelical Party in the Church of England", *Christian Observer* 72 (1873): 83–96. Articles on the history of the Evangelical party were also being published by High Church journals: see, for example, W. E. Gladstone, "The Evangelical Movement; Its Parentage, Progress, and Issue", *British Quarterly Review* 139 (July 1879): 1–26.

[92] See W. H. B. Proby, *Annals of the "Low-Church" Party in England...*, 2 vols, London 1888.

[93] W. Walsh, *The Secret History of the Oxford Movement*, London 1899. See also idem., *The Secret Work of the Ritualists*, London 1894; and *The History of the Romeward Movement in the Church of England 1833–1864*, London 1900.

[94] E. Stock, *The History of the Church Missionary Society: its Environment, its Men and its Work,* 4 vols, London 1899–1916. My copy has written on its frontespiece, in 'copperplate' handwriting, "This is the best account of the English Evangelicals through the 19th Century."

[95] Bromiley added a brief appendix that updated the story from 1900–1950. Other early twentieth-century histories of Anglican Evangelicalism include H. C. G. Moule, *The Evangelical School in the Church of England*, London 1901; G. W. E. Russell, *A Short History of the Evangelical Movement*, London 1915 (Russell was a self-declared High Churchman of Evangelical parentage); and L. E. Elliott-Binns, *The Evangelical Movement in the English Church*, London 1928.

[96] G. R. Balleine, *A History of the Evangelical Party in the Church of England*, 3rd edn, London 1951, ix. Unless indicated otherwise, all the references to Balleine that follow are from this edition.

compelling account of the development of the party",[97] and despite some inaccuracies and exaggerations,[98] it not only fulfilled this aim, but it set a new and early standard in the use of primary sources as the basis for historical research.[99] It was criticised by the same author for "ignoring the High Church", and for its poor treatment of non-Evangelicals;[100] however, this is hardly fair for a work that was a self-declared history of just one section of the Church[101] and which suffered from every author's bugbear: the limitations of space. Valid criticism can certainly be directed at more recent attempts to do the same thing, especially if the author does not prescribe his limits: Kenneth Hylson-Smith's *Evangelicals in the Church of England 1734–1984* is one example of this approach. Hylson-Smith's self-declared attempt to "provide a replacement and updating of Balleine suffers from an overemphasis on the history of eminent Evangelical personalities. Both authors focus on the life and work of Grimshaw, Romaine, Newton, the Venns, Ryder, Simeon, Wilberforce, Bickersteth, Close, the Sumners and Ryle.[102] However, Hylson-Smith's book lacks the very thing that he extolls in his Preface: the use of "new disciplines such as sociology and the social sciences in general".[103] Unlike Balleine, Hylson-Smith's introduction provides no caveat, but instead a rope.

---

[97] Knight, *Nineteenth-Century Church*, p. 9.

[98] Knight has pointed out correctly that one of these was Balleine's assertion that "before the Evangelical revival there were no evening services of any kind whatever." Balleine, *A History of the Evangelical Party*, p. 191.

[99] Balleine studied more than a thousand eighteenth-century biographies and pamphlets and used his daily London Underground journeys to read "all the seventy-five volumes of the *Christian Observer*...[and] the back numbers of *The Record* and *The Guardian*...[as well as] Bristol, Manchester, and Liverpool newspapers". Balleine, *A History of the Evangelical Party*, viii.

[100] Knight, *Nineteenth-Century Church*, p. 9.

[101] See the Preface, where Balleine states: "I have tried to keep the book strictly within the limits of its title. It does not profess to be a complete history of the Church of England since 1729...[and] little has been said about the work of the High Church Party, except when necessary to explain the work of Evangelicals, and hardly anything at all about the work of the Broad Churchmen." Balleine, *History of the Evangelical Party*, viii.

[102] See Appendix 1 for biographical information on some of the key nineteenth-century Evangelicals who are mentioned in this book. Leading eighteenth-century Evangelicals such as William Grimshaw (1708–1763); William Romaine (1714–1795); and Henry Venn of Huddersfield (1725–1797), are not included.

[103] Hylson-Smith, *Evangelicals in the Church of England*, viii.

John Kent has made the point that the intention of Evangelical historians in the tradition of Balleine and Hylson-Smith, as well as L. E. Elliot-Binns,[104] J. S. Reynolds[105] and Michael Hennell,[106] was to "bring Evangelicalism into the foreground of the Victorian picture".[107] This was achieved by emphasizing its theological loyalty to Luther and Calvin; by showing its positive contribution to social values; and by working out for Evangelicalism a pedigree as distinguished from that of Anglo-Catholicism.[108] This pedigreed included John and Charles Wesley, the two Henry Venns,[109] Charles Simeon (1759–1836)[110] and J. C. Ryle (1816–1900).[111] As suggested above, an Anglo-Catholic equivalent list would probably include John Henry Newman (before his conversion to Rome), John Keble, Edward Pusey, Charles Gore and Henry Scott Holland.

It has also been suggested that Charles Simeon was elevated to "ecclesiastical hero" status by Evangelical historians. Even one non-Evangelical historian, Charles Smyth, described Simeon "as one of the Founding Fathers, or Remodellers of the Church of England in the nineteenth century".[112] John Kent argues that if this were true, the Evangelical party may have been better prepared for what was to happen to the Church from the 1830s: "Nothing Simeon said or did helped men in a period when Evangelicalism had come to be rejected as formal, and when religious revival meant the passionate Anglo-Catholic return to the use of images."[113] The theological limits of Evangelicalism that were set down by Simeon and his successors still pervade Evangelical/Anglo-Catholic polemic. Peter Toon's

---

[104] Elliott-Binns, *The Evangelical Movement in the English Church*, and *The Early Evangelicals: A Religious and Social Study*, London 1953.

[105] J. S. Reynolds, *The Evangelicals at Oxford 1735–1971*, Oxford 1953 (repr. 1975); See also E. J. Poole-Connor, *Evangelicalism in England*, London 1966; and J. E. Orr, *The Second Evangelical Awakening in Britain*, London 1949.

[106] M. Hennell, *Sons of the Prophets: Evangelical Leaders of the Victorian Church*, London 1979.

[107] Kent, *The Unacceptable Face*, p. 85.

[108] See D. Samuel, "Roots and Reformations", *Churchman* 104, 3 (1990): 197–213.

[109] See Appendix 1.

[110] Ibid.

[111] Ryle refers to this pedigree in his call for a return to the 'Old Paths', the title of one of his books, viz. J. C. Ryle, *Old Paths*, London 1877.

[112] C. H. E. Smyth, *Simeon and Church Order: A Study of the Origins of the Evangelical Revival in Cambridge in the Eighteenth Century*, Cambridge 1940, p. 6.

[113] Kent, *The Unacceptable Face*, p. 87.

Evangelical Theology 1833–1856: A Response to Tractarianism[114] has shown that Evangelical Anglican theologians are capable of answering Pusey successfully. However, like the frequently voiced appeal by Evangelicals to the Thirty-nine Articles,[115] these are not seen as convincing by Anglicans who put their trust in other authorities, or no authority at all.

A more sophisticated approach to the study of Evangelicalism has been evident in recent years. Evangelicals have been subjected to some new and much needed scrutiny from a variety of standpoints. Some of it has been from a cultural or literary perspective. Ian Bradley's *Call to Seriousness* is an early example of the former, and Elizabeth Jay's *Religion of the Heart*[116] looked at Evangelicalism from the context of the Victorian novel. Both suffer from the lack of a clear definition of Evangelicalism, although they throw refreshing new light on the subject.[117] John Kent put out the first of his many challenges to the traditional view of Evangelical history—and the writing of history—in 1978, although it seems to have been ignored by those who, like its title, saw their main role as *Holding the Fort*. Doreen Rosman's *Evangelicals and Culture*[118] is a social history which uses the evidence of periodical literature to show that between 1770 and 1833, Evangelicals shared the ideas and tastes of their contemporaries rather more than has been realized; although they tended to withdraw into a subculture later in the century. Boyd Hilton is the first of the new breed of historians who approaches Evangelicalism from the standpoint of an intellectual rather than an ecclesiastical or sociological study. His *Age of Atonement* comes to similar conclusions as Rosman, in emphasizing the connection between Evangelical thought and the developing culture. However, he also examines in some detail the impact of social, economic, political and even scientific theories upon Evangelical thought. Wolffe has pointed out that Hilton's argument suffers from a failure to distinguish between "Evangelical writers and

---

[114] Toon, *Evangelical Theology*, 1979.

[115] The Thirty-nine Articles of Religion are a set of doctrinal formulae "agreed upon by the Archbishops, Bishops, and the whole clergy of the Provinces of Canterbury and York, London 1562" and were regarded by Evangelicals as defining the Church of England's position in relation to dogmatic controversies.

[116] See also E. J. Jay, "Anglican Evangelicals and the Nineteenth-Century Novel", DPhil thesis, Oxford University 1975.

[117] Other studies of the clergy in fiction include C. K. Francis Brown, *A History of the English Clergy 1800–1900*, London 1953, pp. 190–214; and A. Pollard "Trollope and the Evangelicals", *Nineteenth-Century Fiction* 37 (1982): 329–39.

[118] See also D. M. Rosman "Evangelicals and Culture in England 1790–1833", PhD thesis, Keele University 1978.

non-Evangelicals who shared certain Evangelical forms of expression".[119] This is surely one of the disadvantages of a secular approach to a religious topic. Another attempt at a secular history is G. M. Ditchfield's *Evangelical Revival*. While this "introduction for all A-level and undergraduate students" suffers from being far too short for a study spanning two centuries, its undenominational and international perspective places it above some of the earlier, partisan works on the same topic.

D. W. Bebbington's important survey of Evangelicalism begins a new generation of solidly researched general interpretations of Evangelicalism along interdenominational lines. *Evangelicalism in Modern Britain* takes a completely new approach to religious historiography by emphasising the theological roots of the movement and the national and interdenominational impact. It has been suggested that his definition of Evangelicalism "is couched more in terms of style than content";[120] however, it is a definition that has now become a standard reference point for other researchers in the field. Bebbington questions the veracity of a popular and scholarly tradition which sees nineteenth-century culture as defined by Evangelicalism, and argues strongly that it was a movement which "reflected more than it defied, broader contemporary cultural trends."[121] He identifies four characteristics which were regarded as the special marks of Evangelical religion: "*conversionism*, the belief that lives need to be changed; *activism*, the expression of the gospel in effort; *biblicism*, a particular regard for the Bible; and what may be called *crucicentrism*, a stress on the sacrifice of Christ on the cross. Together they form a quadrilateral of priorities that is the basis of Evangelicalism."[122] It is a definition of Evangelicalism that will be adopted in this study. Bebbington also places nineteenth-century Evangelicalism squarely within the tradition of the eighteenth-century revival which was spearheaded by George Whitefield and John Wesley. He provides a detailed study of Evangelicals and society, and supplies a history of an important development in the later nineteenth-century: the rise of the Keswick Movement.[123]

---

[119] Wolffe, "Anglicanism", p. 9.
[120] Ibid.
[121] Ibid.
[122] Bebbington, *Evangelicalism in Modern Britain*, pp. 2–3.
[123] The non-denominational Keswick Convention was first held in July 1875. What began as a semi-private meeting of Evangelical clergy and laity rapidly developed into one of the most famous mass gatherings of Christians, attracting upwards of 10,000 people each summer. See J. C. Pollock, *The Keswick Story*,

The story of English revivalism and revival movements in general has been given a significant boost with the recent publication of *Transforming Keswick* and *Firestorm of the Lord* respectively.[124] Charles Price and Ian Randall have documented the character and teaching of Keswick as well as the influence of key players such as Evan Henry Hopkins (1837–1918)[125] and T. D. Harford-Battersby (1822–1883).[126] The importance of meetings and conferences on Anglican Evangelicalism has also been highlighted by the most recent history of nineteenth-century Evangelicalism, *Evangelical Anglicans in a Revolutionary Age* by Nigel Scotland. This ambitious attempt to survey aspects of Anglican Evangelicalism not covered by Balleine or Hylson-Smith examines important topics such as nineteenth-century Evangelical Anglican theology, culture and spirituality, as well as their role in politics and education.[127]

Gerald Parsons has argued that the creation of a distinct and more defined Evangelical identity was largely the result of the controversies with Tractarianism in the years between 1833 and, roughly, the mid-1850s.[128] The 1830s are certainly regarded as marking an important watershed in Evangelical history, and great deal of research has been centred on the period leading up to this.[129] David Newsome, drawing

---

London 1964; S. Barabas, *So Great Salvation*, London 1952; and C. I. Price and I. Randall, *Transforming Keswick*, Carlisle 2000.

[124] C. Price and I. Randall, *Transforming Keswick*, 2000; S. Piggin, *Firestorm of the Lord: The History and Prospects for Revival in the Church and the World*, Carlisle 2000.

[125] See A. Smellie, *Evan Henry Hopkins*, London, 1920.

[126] See Battersby and Battersby, eds., *Memoir of T. D. Harford-Battersby Late Vicar of St. John's, Keswick and Honorary Canon of Carlisle*, London 1890. On the Keswick Movement, see also D. W. Bebbington, *Holiness in Nineteenth-Century England*, Carlisle 2000.

[127] N. A. D. Scotland, *Evangelical Anglicans in a Revolutionary Age*, Carlisle 2004, x-xi.

[128] Parsons, "Reform, Revival and Realignment", p. 34.

[129] See G. F. A. Best "Church and State in English Politics, 1800–1833", PhD thesis, Cambridge University 1955; I. Bradley, "The Politics of Godliness: Evangelicals in Parliament 1784–1835", DPhil thesis, Oxford University 1974; W. J. C. Ervine, "Doctrine and Diplomacy: Some Aspects of the Life and Thought of Anglican Evangelical Clergy 1797–1837", PhD thesis, Cambridge University 1967; R. H. Martin, "The Pan-Evangelical Impulse in Britain 1795–1830 with special reference to four London societies", DPhil thesis, Oxford University 1974; S. C. Orchard, "English Evangelical Eschatology 1790–1850", PhD thesis, Cambridge University 1968; I. S. Rennie, "Evangelicalism and English Public Life 1823–50", PhD thesis, University of Toronto 1962; H. Van Young, Jr., "The Evangelical Clergy in the Church of England 1790–1850", PhD thesis, Brown University 1958; J. Walsh *et al.*, *The Church of*

partly on Haddon Willmer's Hulsean Prize essay, calls the first chapter of his book "The Crisis of Evangelicalism", and D. N. Hempton[130] asks the question: "What happened to evangelicalism to transform it from the enlightened and thoughtful respectability of the Clapham Sect to the bigotry of McNeile (1795–1879),[131] Cumming[132] and Drummond[133]?" Such harsh sentiments were not new, for it was F. K. Brown's thesis that "able young men and women all over England who had been brought up in the best Evangelicalism were repelled during these years by something".[134] Sir James Stephen, the son of Wilberforce's brother-in-law who was born and bred in the direct centre of the Evangelical inner circle, wrote to his wife in 1845: "Oh where are the people who were at once really religious, and really cultivated in heart and understanding—the people with whom we could associate as our fathers used to associate with each other. No 'Clapham Sect' nowadays!"[135] A generational transfer can therefore be discerned from the era of Wilberforce, Simeon and the Clapham Sect in the first quarter of the nineteenth century, to the era of Shaftesbury and McNeile in the early and middle Victorian years. A number of studies has suggested that the Evangelicalism of the second quarter of the century was characterised by a narrowing of its theology[136] as well

---

England c.1689–c.1833; and H. Willmer's 1962 Hulsean Prize essay, "Evangelicalism 1785–1835", Cambridge University. Cf. A. Burns, "The Diocesan Revival in the Church of England c.1825–1865", DPhil thesis, Oxford University 1990, and P. Toon, "The Evangelical Anglican Response to Tractarian Teaching, 1833–56", DPhil thesis, Oxford University 1977.

[130] D. N. Hempton, "Evangelicalism and Eschatology", *Journal of Ecclesiatical History* 31, 2 (1980): 179–94.

[131] See Appendix 1.

[132] John Cumming was minister of the Scotch Church, Crown Court, London.

[133] Henry Drummond (1786–1860), banker and Member of Parliament, violently shook the Evangelical fraternity in the 1830s by taking his money and some of his followers into Edward Irving's recently founded Catholic Apostolic Church (1833).

[134] F. K. Brown, *Fathers of the Victorians*, Cambridge 1961, p. 520.

[135] C. E. Stephen (ed.), *The Right Honourable Sir James Stephen...Letters with Biographical Notes*, Gloucester 1906, p. 87.

[136] In particular, an acceptance of Calvinism over Arminianism, a form of Biblical literalism, and a shift from postmillennialist to premillenialist theology. See Toon, *Evangelical Theology*; Hempton, "Evangelicalism and Eschatology"; S. C. Orchard, "English Evangelical Eschatology 1790–1850"; and E. Culbertson, "Victorian Evangelical Theology", *Churchman* 106, 4 (1992): 308–322.

as its anti-Catholicism,[137] just as the Evangelicalism of the second half of the century was distinguished by its anti-Ritualism.[138]

Wesley Balda has provided a correction to the image of doctrinally rigid Victorian low-Churchmen which has grown out of this simplistic view of Victorian Evangelicalism.[139] Taking the clergy working in Simeon Trust[140] parishes as a dependable sample of Anglican Evangelicals at mid-century, he suggests that "the activities of these men...consistently present a picture of Christian moderation within the crucible of papal intrigue and tractarian/ritualist expansion".[141] The modern idea that there was a united front to Evangelicalism during this period overlooks the dichotomies within the movement, and "incorrectly reinforces popular Victorian stereotypes as descriptive of evangelicalism as a whole".[142] Raymond Brown credits the movement with a "negative, defensive mission",[143] and Ian Bradley suggests that Anglican Evangelicalism was characterized as having "endemic narowness and oppressiveness" and that it assumed "a new obscurantism and fanaticism" in the 1840s and 1850s.[144] Ian Rennie has theorised that the diminished conflict between *The Record* and the *Christian Observer* is sufficient to indicate the disappearance of division within the movement by 1844,[145] and William Ervine also concludes that division amongst Evangelicals did not substantially

---

[137] See ch. 7 below.

[138] Ian Bradley's thesis is that Evangelical children who became Catholics or atheists in the 1840s and 1850s were reacting against this very different type of Evangelicalism. See Bradley, *Call to Seriousness*, pp. 194–202.

[139] W. D. Balda, "Simeon's 'Protestant Papists': a Sampling of Moderate Evangelicalism within the Church of England 1839–1865." *Fides et Historia* 16, 1 (1983): 55–67.

[140] Between 1816 and his death in 1836, Charles Simeon (see Appendix 1) purchased the advowson, or right of presentation, to twenty-one parishes around the country. He formed the 'Simeon Trust' in 1817 to manage the scheme. The original trustees were Lord Calthorpe, John Thornton, John Sargent, Daniel Wilson, William Carus and William Marsh. Although originally intended chiefly to prevent the appointment of 'idle' clergy, the scheme increasingly became a means of advancing Evangelical incumbents. By 1865, 44 churches belonged to the Simeon Trust. See W. D. Balda, "Spheres of Influence: Simeon's Trust and its implications for Evangelical Patronage", PhD thesis, Cambridge University 1981.

[141] Balda, "Simeon's 'Protestant Papists'", p. 55.

[142] Ibid., p. 56.

[143] R. Brown, "Evangelical Ideas of Perfection: A Comparitive Study of the Spirituality of Men and Movements in Nineteenth-Century England", PhD thesis, Cambridge University 1964, p. 177.

[144] Bradley, *Call to Seriousness*, p. 194.

[145] Rennie, "Evangelicalism and English Public Life", p. 90.

exist.[146] The unfortunate result of this viewpoint is a lack of awareness of the considerable diversity within the movement. However, it is true that Evangelicals were united on one theological point: that of anti-Catholicism.

John Wolffe and others[147] have shown that antagonism to Catholicism in both its Roman and Anglican forms led to stronger definitions of Evangelical belief on the nature of authority, salvation and the sacraments.[148] The Evangelicals saw themselves as custodians of the reformed character of Anglicanism. Even some High Churchmen resisted the Tractarian attempt to "unprotestantize" the Church of England and in so doing gave rise to the term 'Evangelical High Churchman'.[149] Some Evangelicals and Broad Churchmen also made a "pragmatic partnership" in opposition to the Tractarians. They found a range of common ground on which to oppose the Tractarian position, a theological consensus which would be unthinkable later in the century as other theological issues such as biblical criticism took centre stage.[150] In these controversies the Evangelicals deployed a variety of means to publicize and pursue their aims. They responded to Tractarian editions of the Church Fathers and the Caroline Divines with new editions of the English Reformers. The Parker Society was formed in 1840 and republished 54 volumes of the English Reformers

---

[146] Ervine, "Doctrine and Diplomacy", p. 308.

[147] The definitive study of mid-nineteenth-century British anti-Catholicism is now J. R. Wolffe, *The Protestant Crusade in Great Britain 1829–1860*, Oxford 1991. This is based upon idem., "Protestant Societies and Anti-Catholic Agitation in Great Britain, 1829–1860", DPhil thesis, Oxford University 1984. Other useful works include J. R. Wolffe, "Anti-Catholicism and Evangelical Identity in Britain and the United States, 1830–1860", in M. A. Noll, D. W. Bebbington and G. A. Rawlyk (eds), *Evangelicalism*, Oxford 1994; D. G. Paz, *Popular Anti-Catholicism in Mid-Victorian England*, Stanford, Cal. 1992; W. Ralls, "The Papal Aggression of 1850: A Study in Victorian Anti-Catholicism", in G. Parsons (ed.), *Religion in Victorian England IV: Interpretations*, Manchester 1988, pp. 115–34; W. L. Arnstein, *Protestant versus Catholic in Mid-Victorian England*, London 1982; E. R. Norman, *Anti-Catholicism in Victorian England*, London 1968; and G. F. A. Best, "Popular Protestantism in Victorian England", in R. Robson (ed.), *Ideas and Institutions of Victorian Britain*, London 1967, pp. 115–42. See J. R. Wolffe's "Historiography of anti-Catholicism" in *The Protestant Crusade*, pp. 5–6.

[148] Wolffe, "Anglicanism", p. 8.

[149] For a discussion of the difficulties of identifying members of this group, see Toon, *Evangelical Theology*, pp. 4–5.

[150] Parsons, "Reform, Revival and Realignment", p. 34.

for 1,000 subscribers between 1841 and 1853.[151] Foxe's *Acts and Monuments* appeared in a new edition in 1837 and the Calvin Translation Society commenced publication in 1843.[152] In Oxford, Charles Golightly (1807–1885), an ally of both Evangelicals and High Churchmen, was the prime instigator of the 1839–40 movement for the Oxford Martyrs' Memorial. This memorial to the Protestant martyrs of 1555–6[153] was also a means of publicizing the writings of the Reformers.[154] Notable Evangelical divines such as William Goode[155] and E. A. Litton had published responses to and criticisms of aspects of Tractarianism. Goode set out to reply systematically to Tractarian theology as a whole, and Litton published his major treatise, *The Church of Christ*, in 1851. Local Protestant societies were formed to defend Protestantism and to "keep watch on the activities of local Tractarian clergy".[156] In this way the distinction between anti-Catholicism, anti-Tractarianism and anti-Ritualism became blurred, if not in the minds of mid-nineteenth-century Anglicans, then at least in the thinking of twentieth-century historians.

The confusion between these different movements has been addressed by Yates in *Anglican Ritualism in Victorian England*. He identifies three different movements among High Churchmen in the 1830s and 1840s. Each was separate, but they were also linked even in some cases by the sharing of the same personnel. First there were the Tractarians: those who published the *Tracts for the Times* and their followers. Then there were the Ecclesiologists: those who sought to restore and rebuild churches using medieval principles of architecture.[157] The leading figure in this development was J. M. Neale (1818–1866), who founded the Cambridge Camden Society[158] in 1839 and who edited the movement's controversial and influential journal,

---

[151] It ended in 1855. For a history of the Society, see P. Toon, "The Parker Society", *Historical Magazine of the Protestant Episcopal Church* 46, 3 (1977): 323-332.

[152] Avis, "The Tractarian Challenge", p.15.

[153] Cranmer, Latimer and Ridley. The Memorial was modelled on the crosses erected by King Edward I, especially the one at Waltham. Toon, *Evangelical Theology*, p. 41.

[154] See Toon, *Evangelical Theology*, pp. 39–41.

[155] William Goode was a Cambridge graduate and son of well-known Evangelical, William Goode the elder, a contemporary of John Newton who succeeded William Romaine at Blackfriars in 1795. Toon, *Evangelical Theology*, p. 6.

[156] Parsons, "Reform, Revival and Realignment", p. 35. See Wolffe, *The Protestant Crusade*, pp. 318–9 for a useful list of these societies.

[157] Specifically, fourteenth-century Gothic, a style which the Ecclesiologists believed to be free of "late medieval corruptions".

[158] Renamed the Ecclesiological Society in 1846.

The Ecclesiologist (1841–68).[159] Lastly there were the Ritualists: those who wanted to introduce more ceremonial into the services of the church. As already noted above, there were also the old High Churchmen, "some of whom rejected all of these movements, some of whom accepted all of them, and many who accepted some but rejected others."[160] It has already been pointed out that Nockles discussed the relationship between the Tractarians and the High Churchmen. Yates has shown that the ideas of the ecclesiologists were already well established at the beginning of the nineteenth century.[161] In contrast to some recent research which implies that Ritualism is a separate and later development from Tractarianism,[162] Yates[163] and others[164] have suggested that there was considerable cross-pollination between the Tractarians, Ecclesiologists and Ritualists.

The Ritualist controversy has been studied from the perspective of ecclesiastical history,[165] historical theology,[166] politics[167] and even geography.[168] G. I. T. Machin defined Ritualism as a collective name for the general adoption by some Anglican clergy of "Catholic ceremonies and vestments, the practice of confession, and the founding of convents and monasteries".[169] Like the Tractarian ideas, the adopted rituals aroused great opposition by both clerical and lay members of a society that was still, as seen by the reaction to Catholic Emancipation

---

[159] See P. Levine, *The Amateur and the Professional: Antiquarians, Historians and Archaeologists in Victorian England, 1838–1886*, Cambridge 1986; and J. F. White, *The Cambridge Movement: The Ecclesiologists and the Gothic Revival*, Cambridge 1962.

[160] Yates, *Anglican Ritualism*, p. 48.

[161] Yates, *Buildings, Faith and Worship*, pp. 150–51.

[162] George Herring argues that Ritualism had little impact before 1860: see G. W. Herring, "Tractarianism to Ritualism: A Study of Some Aspects of Tractarianism outside Oxford, from the Time of Newman's Conversion in 1845 until the First Ritual Commission in 1867", DPhil thesis, Oxford University 1984. Wellings states that Ritualism was a separate development from the Oxford Movement dating from the 1860s; see M. Wellings, "Aspects of late Nineteenth-Century Evangelicalism", DPhil thesis, Oxford University, pp. 12–13.

[163] Yates, *Anglican Ritualism*, pp. 48–69.

[164] See especially Reed, *Glorious Battle*, pp. 15–28.

[165] See especially Yates, *Anglican Ritualism*.

[166] E. Culbertson, "Victorian Evangelical Theology", *Churchman*, 106, 4 (1992): 316–8.

[167] Yates, *Anglican Ritualism*, ch. 5: "The Attempt to Control Anglican Ritualism".

[168] Ibid., ch. 3: "The Geography and Personnel of Anglican Ritualism".

[169] G. I. T. Machin, *Politics and the Churches in Great Britain 1869 to 1921*, Oxford 1987, p. 4.

(1829) and the Maynooth Grant (1845), overwhelmingly anti-Catholic.[170] Those who criticised Ritualism felt that it was a betrayal of the Reformation, and many also thought that it was part of a secret plot to lead the English people back to the Church of Rome.[171] By the late 1840s the situation had become critical and it was thought that legislation passed by Parliament at the beginning of the decade "for better enforcing Church Discipline"[172] could be used to solve the conflict. When this proved impossible, the *Public Worship Regulation Act* of 1874 was passed in an attempt to provide a more effective remedy for the control of Ritualism.[173] This was to be equally ineffective and led eventually to the so-called "Crisis in the Church",[174] and the setting up of the Royal Commission on Ecclesiastical Discipline in 1881. The story of how the secular and ecclesiastical court systems were used to try to control Ritualism has been told elsewhere.[175] In almost every case, it did not halt or even slow down ritual innovation. However, like the anti-Catholic movement, it did lead to the formation of a number of new societies to support adherents of both sides of the cause.

The earliest of these was the Society of the Holy Cross which was established in 1855. This was a wholly clerical society, although candidates for ordination were accepted as members before they were ordained. Later Ritualist societies such as the English Church Union

---

[170] For a discussion of the Roman Catholic Emancipation Bill of 1829 and opposition to the Maynooth Grant which led to the 'Maynooth crisis' of 1845, see E. R. Norman, *Anti-Catholicism in Victorian England, passim.*; Wolffe, *The Protestant Crusade, passim.*; and G. A. Cahill, "The Protestant Association and the Anti-Maynooth Agitation of 1845", *Catholic Historical Review* 43, 3 (1957): 273–308.

[171] W. Walsh, *The Secret History of the Oxford Movement*, 5th edn, London 1899. For a reassessment of Walsh, see M. Wellings, "The Oxford Movement in Late Nineteenth Century Retrospect: R. W. Church, J. H. Rigg and Walter Walsh", *Studies in Church History* 33 (1997): 511–15.

[172] 3 and 4 Vict. 1874: Cap. 86.

[173] See G. W. Graber, *Ritual Legislation in the Victorian Church of England: Antecedents and Passage of the Public Worship Regulation Act, 1874*, New York 1993.

[174] Machin, *Politics and the Churches in Great Britain: 1869 to 1921*, pp. 234–55.

[175] See especially Yates, *Anglican Ritualism*, ch. 5; J Bentley, *Ritualism and Politics in Victorian Britain: The Attempt to Legislate for Belief*, Oxford 1978; and W. J. Fong, "The Ritualist Crisis: Anglo-Catholics and Authority, with special reference to the English Church Union 1859–1882", PhD thesis, University of Toronto 1977.

(1859),[176] the Confraternity of the Blessed Sacrament (1862) and the Guild of All Souls (1873) had a much larger membership of both clergy and laity. Yates used the membership list of the Society of the Holy Cross, which is extant for the period 1855–84, as a rough guide to the level of clerical support for Ritualism in the 1860s and 1870s.[177] One of the three Ritualist priests who founded the society was Charles Lowder, who was responsible for establishing the new church and parish of St Peter's, London Docks, between 1860 and 1866.[178] The Evangelical response to Ritualism was primarily through education and the formation of societies. In 1902 it was estimated that there were 48 Protestant or Evangelical societies,[179] and Herbert Gladstone stated that at least 51 existed in 1908.[180] Some were anti-Roman Catholic rather than specifically engaged in the battle against Ritualism. Within the loose organization of Evangelicalism, three main groups of societies with some bearing on the Ritualist controversy can be identified.[181]

---

[176] Founded by the Manchester Church Society "to defend and maintain unimpaired doctrine, discipline and ritual of the Church of England against Erastianism, Rationalism and Puritanism...". See Yates, *Anglican Ritualism*, pp. 151–2; and G. Bayfield Roberts, *The History of the English Church Union 1859–1894*, London 1895. For an Evangelical response to the formation of this society, see F. Close, *"The English Church Union": A Ritualistic Society*, London 1868; idem., *Further Evidence of the True Character of the English Church Union...*, London 1869; and chapter 7 below.

[177] Yates, *Anglican Ritualism*, pp. 71–7.

[178] Charles Fuge Lowder (1820–1880) was Curate of St Barnabas, Pimlico 1851–56, and founded the 'iron church' at St George's-in-the-East in 1856. He later moved to the new church and parish of St Peter's, London Docks, in 1866, where he was made incumbent.

[179] *Record*, 2 May 1902, p. 406.

[180] C. Mallet, *Herbert Gladstone, a Memoir*, London 1932, pp. 217–8. Members of these Protestant societies had telegraphed the King in protest of a planned procession in London of Roman Catholics celebrating the visit in July 1908 of a Papal Legate to England. W. E. Gladstone's second son, Herbert John (1854–1930), the Viscount Gladstone, was Home Secretary 1905–10.

[181] Wellings, "Aspects of Late Nineteenth-Century Evangelicalism", p. 119. Some of the ideas below were first outlined in Wellings's DPhil thesis and Wolffe's, *The Protestant Crusade*. For a brief discussion of the impact of Evangelical societies earlier in the century, see Bradley, *Call to Seriousness*, ch. 7: "The Age of Societies". For unpublished studies on the later development of Evangelical societies, see A. Bentley "The Transformation of the Evangelical Party in the later Nineteenth Century", PhD thesis Durham University 1971; and B. E. Hardman, "The Evangelical Party in the Church of England 1855–65" PhD thesis Cambridge University 1971.

The first group consisted of general Evangelical unions, conferences or meetings which occasionally turned their attention to aspects of 'Crisis in the Church'. Pre-eminent among these was the Islington Clerical Meeting, a gathering of Evangelicals held each January by invitation of the Vicar of Islington and founded in 1827 by Daniel Wilson the elder (1778–1858).[182] By 1888, when W. H. Barlow (1833–1908) was vicar,[183] attendance stood at 400, and by 1902 this figure had more than doubled.[184] The Islington Clerical Meeting had a varied programme, but the Ritual issue was very frequently an item of discussion. For example, the subject for 1900 was "The Church of England: Catholic, Apostolic, Reformed and Protestant, offering an opportunity for temperate criticism of medieval accretions by Chancellor Bernard and for a defence of Protestantism by Professor [H. E.] Ryle."[185] Regional conferences of the Clerical and Lay Associations and the Evangelical Unions also heard papers on topics relevent to Ritualism, although this was not a central part of their charter.[186]

The second group of societies comprised the older Protestant organizations which concentrated their attention primarily on Roman Catholicism. Their activities have been described in some detail by John Wolffe in *The Protestant Crusade in Great Britain 1829–1860*. The two with the longest history were the British or Protestant Reformation Society, and the National Club. The British Reformation Society was established in 1827, at the time of the agitation over Roman Catholic emancipation. It was essentially a missionary society to Roman Catholics; producing propaganda, running mission stations and organizing reply lectures to counteract Roman missions.[187] The National Club, founded in 1845, was committed to the defence of the Protestant Succession and Constitution, and, although not active in polemic, it offered a focus for Protestant meetings and political campaigns.[188] Alongside these two long-established societies were a number of more recent organizations. One of them, the Protestant

---

[182] See Appendix 1. His son, also named Daniel, was Vicar of Islington 1832–86.
[183] See Appendix 1.
[184] M. Barlow (ed.) *The Life of William Haggar Barlow*, London 1910, ch.11; and *The Record* 17 January 1902, p.61.
[185] *Record,* 12 January 1900, pp. 40–42. H. E. Ryle, Dean of Westminster, was the son of Bishop J. C. Ryle of Liverpool.
[186] Both these organizations are discussed in some detail in ch. 7 below.
[187] Its full name was The British Society for Promoting the Principles of the Reformation. See Wolffe, *The Protestant Crusade*, passim.
[188] See ibid., pp. 210–19; and R Stewart, *The Politics of Protection: Lord Derby and the Protectionist Party 1841–1852*, Cambridge 1971, pp. 31 and 109.

Alliance, was founded by Lord Shaftesbury (1801–1885)[189] in 1851. It was an interdenominational society which saw its role as opposing the spread of Romanism in Great Britain.[190] The Alliance also organized Protestant demonstrations which included attacks on Ritualism within the Church of England.[191]

The third group of societies was almost completely concerned with the issue of Ritualism. They included the Church Association, the Protestant Churchmen's Alliance,[192] and the National Church League.[193] The Church Association was founded in 1865 and initially secured considerable support from Evangelical Churchmen.[194] Problems began to develop, however, over the policy of prosecuting extreme Ritualists. The Association undertook legal proceedings in order to clarify the law, rather than to persecute Ritualists, but the refusal of Ritualist clergymen to obey the Courts placed Evangelicals in a dilemma. Some continued to support the policy of prosecution, but many regarded this approach as "morally dubious and tactically unsound."[195] The Association became more and more alienated from mainstream Evangelicalism, and was denounced as being "ultra-Protestant" by others within the party.[196] The Protestant Churchmen's Alliance (PCA) was formed after the Lincoln Judgement[197] at a meeting at Exeter Hall[198] in 1889 by representatives of the Clerical and

---

[189] See Appendix 1.

[190] *Record,* 18 December 1903, p. 1231.

[191] For example, the Great Protestant Demonstration of May 1898, about which a *Verbatim Report* was published.

[192] See N. D. J. Straton, *Why Should We Join the Protestant Churchmen's Alliance?*, London 1889.

[193] Not included here is the Protestant Truth Society, a mainly lay movement founded in 1889 by John Kensit, a Protestant book-seller. The PTS was described by one contemporary as "ultra-Protestant fanatics" and, on the whole, was not supported by the Evangelical clergy. See Machin, *Politics and the Churches in Great Britain 1869 to 1921*, pp. 239–41; and J Britten, *A Prominent Protestant (Mr John Kensit)*, London 1898.

[194] For more information on the Church Association, see below, 219–34.

[195] Bentley, "The Transformation of the Evangelical Party", p. 134.

[196] H. Lewis, "The Present Condition of the Evangelicals", *The Nineteenth Century and After* 62 (July–December 1907): 232.

[197] The case against the Ritualist Bishop of Lincoln, Edward King. See especially Bentley, *Ritualism and Politics in Victorian Britian*, pp. 114–20 and Yates, *Anglican Ritualism*, pp. 273–6. The case was regarded as a 'win' by the Anglo-Catholics over the Evangelicals.

[198] Exeter Hall was erected on the Strand in London in 1831 as a non-denominational meeting place for religious, scientific and philanthropic groups. It became the prime venue for meetings of Evangelical societies. The building was acquired by the YMCA in 1880 and demolished in 1907. Today the site is

Lay Union and other Evangelicals "who felt unable to fully support the Church Association".[199] Its other antecedents included the Protestant Association (founded 1835)[200] and the Protestant Educational Institute (1870).[201] By February 1890 it was reported that the PCA had 522 clerical members and by the following April, it had been established in 25 dioceses.[202] In 1892 the PCA joined with the Union of Clerical and Lay Associations[203] to become the National Protestant Church Union (NPCU). In 1906 this merged with the Church of England League[204] to form the National Church League, which in 1950 amalgamated with the Church Association to form today's Church Society.

The other way in which Evangelicals met the Anglo-Catholic challenge was through education. In January 1896 an article appeared in the *Churchman* entitled "The Need of Evangelical Literature of the Highest Order".[205] It covered a wide area of church life, but its main point was that Evangelicals needed to produce 'shilling primers' on doctrine, and short books that could answer the popular manuals being produced by the Ritualists. Books of this kind started to be printed by Evangelical publishers.[206] The NPCU-commissioned *English Church Teaching* by Moule, Girdestone and Drury sold 15,000 copies by 1903

---

occupied by the Strand Palace Hotel. See L. W. Cowie, "Exeter Hall", *History Today* 18 (1968): 390–7, and J. Stephens, *Essays in Ecclesiastical Biography*, 3rd edn, London 1853, p. 582.

[199] *Rock* 21 June 1889, pp. 8–9. Also see Stock, *History of the CMS*, vol. 3, p. 281.

[200] It was concerned for the "Maintenance of the Protestant character of the State". See Wolffe, *The Protestant Crusade*, pp. 90–106.

[201] Machin, *Politics and the Churches in Great Britain 1869 to 1921*, p. 179.

[202] *Record*, 28 February 1890, p. 203; and 24 April 1891, p. 395.

[203] See below, p. 238–50.

[204] The Church of England League was founded in 1904. It was formerly the Ladies' League for the Defence of the Reformed Faith of the Church of England, which was founded in 1899 by Lady Wimbourne. See Machin, *Politics and the Churches in Great Britain 1869 to 1921*, pp. 241–2. The Ladies' League was involved in the education of middle-class girls in the early years of the twentieth century. In 1900 it formed the Church Education Corporation "to establish and maintain girls' schools of an Evangelical character." Some of the early schools include Sandecotes School, Parkstone (founded 1900); Upplands School, St Leonards (1903); and Milham Ford School, Oxford (1906). See G. W. Bromiley's "Appendix" in Balleine, *History of the Evangelical Party*, 3rd ed. pp. 259–60.

[205] *Churchman* 44 (January 1896): 201–7.

[206] One such Evangelical publisher was Robert Seeley (1798–1888) of Seeley and Burnside. Seeley published the *Christian Guardian* 1802–53; *The Churchman's Monthly Review* 1841–7; all the publications of the CMS; as well as the works of Richard Cecil and biographies of John Newton, William Cowper, Henry Martyn and Hannah More. He also wrote *Essays on the Church* (1834).

and it remained a popular handbook throughout the first half of the twentieth century.[207] In 1900 the publisher Nisbet began to issue a series of 'Church of England handbooks' on topical subjects, and by 1901 there were five in this series. Other books were published in the early years of the twentieth century, including two series of 'shilling handbooks' known as the English Church Manuals and the Anglican Church Handbooks.[208] As well as these short publications, other books sought to make the Evangelical case against Ritualism at a popular level. J. C. Ryle's books, particularly *Knots Untied*,[209] which set out teaching on baptism and the Lord's Supper in the form of questions and answers, were among the most straightforward and popular. Well-known Evangelical clergymen were in high demand to give lectures and sermons which set out the Evangelical position. Some of these lectures and sermon series were eventually published.[210]

During this period, a number of Evangelical periodicals and newspapers were also being regularly published. These have been surveyed by Josef Altholz in *The Religious Press in Britain*.[211] The *Churchman* (1879–)[212] was a monthly that followed[213] the Clapham Sect's *Christian Observer* (1802–77).[214] It claimed a larger circulation than its successor, possibly because it abandoned the old-fashioned practice of anonymous writing.[215] The most notorious organ of the

---

[207] *Record*, 28 August 1903, p. 833.

[208] Wellings, "Aspects of Late Nineteenth-Century Evangelicalism", p. 139.

[209] J. C. Ryle, *Knots Untied*, London 1874.

[210] For example, F. J. Chavasse, *Plain Words on Some Present Day Questions*, London 1899.

[211] See Altholz, *The Religious Press in Britain*, ch. 3 for a brief and sometimes imprecise overview of Evangelical Anglican publications during this period.

[212] For a history of this periodical (which is still being published), see J. R. Wolffe, "The First Century of *The Churchman*", *Churchman* 102, 3 (1988): 197–214.

[213] Wolffe has pointed out that while "it clearly fitted into the gap in Evangelical literature left by the demise of the *Christian Observer*...there is no evidence of direct continuity between the two publications". Wolffe, ibid., p. 199. Cf. Altholz's suggestion that it was a "replacement"; Altholz, *The Religious Press in Britain*, p. 17.

[214] The *Christian Observer* was founded in 1802 on the initiative of the Eclectic Society. A monthly, its circulation was limited to around 1,000 copies, but it was respected as the most 'literary' of the Evangelical journals and pursued a more moderate line than *The Record*. The journal ceased publication in 1877.

[215] The editors were Walter Purton 1879–92, W. M. Sinclair 1892–1901, and Henry Wace 1902–5, who was also Dean of Canterbury 1903–24 (see Appendix 1). In 1917 the Council of the National Church League, headed by Dean Wace, purchased the *Churchman*. Since 1950 it has been published by the Church Society.

Anglican Evangelicals was not a respectable monthly but a newspaper, *The Record*. It began in January 1828 as a weekly paper "viewing the news about Church and State through moderate Evangelical eyes", but it ran into financial difficulties within a few months and was taken over by a group of Evangelical laymen. One of them was Alexander Haldane, a young barrister from Scotland who was the son and nephew of two major figures in the Scottish Evangelical Revival.[216] The paper's new owners set forth an aggressive Calvinistic Evangelicalism, Tory in outlook, and "strongly opposed to Roman Catholicism, Tractarianism, Latitudinarianism, Socialism and Chartism."[217] Their tone often upset readers, but the success of the paper suggests that it was appreciated by both clergy and laity. In 1843 it claimed that its circulation was greater than that of the *Globe* and only sixty less than the *Standard*.[218] Its main competition was *The Rock* (1867–1905), which was the organ of the "more aggressive section" of the party including the Church Association; distinguishing itself, for example, by violent attacks upon well-known Evangelicals such as Hoare and Ryle. *The Rock* changed hands in the early eighties, and "was for a while carried on upon milder lines."[219] Its earlier extreme position was replaced by the *English Churchman* (1843–), which in 1884 was transformed from a hitherto High Church publication into a vigorous and successful organ of "decided and aggressive Protestantism".[220] However, for many people "Evangelicalism meant *The Record*", and a hostile critic would speak of the "Recordite Party" as the *reductio ad absurdum* of Evangelicalism.[221]

Three other areas of education concerned Evangelical Churchmen in the second half of the nineteenth century. These were schools, universities, and the training of teachers and the clergy. In each of these areas the Anglo-Catholics seemed to have firmly established themselves. Consequently, this period witnessed attempts by

---

[216] His father was James Haldane and his uncle, Robert Haldane. They were described as "Calvinistic, aristocratic evangelists".

[217] Toon, *Evangelical Theology*, p. 7.

[218] For the full story, see J. F. Altholz, "Alexander Haldane, *The Record*, and Religious Journalism", *Victorian Periodicals Review* 20 (Spring 1987): 23–31. In 1948, *The Record* was incorporated with the *Church of England Newspaper* (1923–1948) to become *The Church of England Newspaper and The Record* (1949–1967).

[219] Stock, *History of the CMS*, vol. 3, p. 280.

[220] The *English Churchman* was founded in 1843 as the "organ of the extreme wing of the High Church-Tractarian group". In 1884 it was bought out and transformed into an Evangelical newspaper. See D. A. Scales, "Stemma of the 'English Churchman'" for an overview of its many antecedents.

[221] Altholz, *The Religious Press in Britain*, p. 18.

Evangelicals to build up their own resources within the educational system. Since the beginning of the century, concern about the lack of supply and training of men for the ministry had become an issue of increasing concern for all parties, and each had responded to the problem in different ways.[222] The first theological colleges for graduates, Chichester (1839) and Wells (1840), were both High Church foundations and it was not until later in the century that Evangelicals set up their own graduate colleges:[223] Wycliffe Hall was founded at Oxford in 1877,[224] and Ridley Hall at Cambridge in 1881.[225] There was also a growing need for teachers and schools that were seen to be supportive of the religious views of Evangelical parents. Francis Close founded an Evangelical teacher training college in Cheltenham as early as 1847[226] and he was also a leader in education for the poor[227] and middle classes.[228] Close was not the only Evangelical to make a name for himself in promoting Evangelical colleges and schools, although he was undoubtably the most successful. A discussion of Evangelical initiatives in elementary and higher education is, however, beyond the scope of this work. This

---

[222] This subject has been discussed in more detail elsewhere, notably in F. W. B. Bullock, *A History of Training for the Ministry of the Church of England and Wales from 1800 to 1874*, St Leonard's-on-Sea 1955; Crowther, *Church Embattled*, ch. 9: "Clerical Education"; and D. Dowland, *Nineteenth-Century Anglican Theological Training: The Redbrick Challenge*, Oxford 1997.

[223] See J. Bateman, *The Tractarian Tendencies of Diocesan Theological Colleges*, London 1853. Evangelical theological colleges for non-graduates included St Bees's, Cumbria (founded 1816); St Aidan's Birkenhead (1847–1970); and St John's, Highbury (1863). See Dowland, *Nineteenth-century Anglican Theological Training*; G. C. B. Davies, *Men for the Ministry*, London 1963; T. Park, *St Bees College 1816–1895*, Barrow-in-Furness 1982; F. B. Heiser, *The Story of St Aidan's College, Birkenhead 1897–1947*, Chester 1947; and A. F. Munden, *The History of St John's College Nottingham. Part One: Mr Peache's College at Kilburn*, Nottingham 1995. See also E. Royle "Evangelicals and Education" in J. Wolffe (ed.), *Evangelical Faith and Public Zeal*, London 1995, pp. 127–31.

[224] See Reynolds, *The Evangelicals at Oxford*, pp. 13–14.

[225] See F. W. B. Bullock, *The History of Ridley Hall Cambridge*, 2 vols, London 1941, 1953.

[226] See R. S. Trafford, *The Revd Francis Close and the Foundation of the Training Institution at Cheltenham 1845–78*, Cheltenham 1997, a work which borrows heavily from A. F. Munden, "The Church of England in Cheltenham 1826–1856 with particular reference to the Revd. Francis Close", MLitt thesis, Birmingham University 1980.

[227] See A. F. Munden, *A Cheltenham Gamaliel: Dean Close of Cheltenham*, Cheltenham 1997, pp. 36–8.

[228] See ch. 3 below.

study is limited to just one area of Evangelical educational endeavour: middle-class education.

There was another major grouping within the Church of England whose roots went back to an earlier period. This was the 'Broad Church', a term which came into use around 1850.[229] This group was less sharply defined than the other Church parties and was characterised by "a commitment to the tolerance of a breadth of theological opinions and to the idea of the essential comprehensiveness of the church". If the views of Thomas Arnold[230] were representative, this meant the inclusion of Dissenters within the Established Church, something which was inconceivable for the Evangelicals and the High Churchmen or Tractarians. W. J. Conybeare argued that the Broad Church "can scarcely be called a party at all",[231] but rather a set of individuals, "many of whom disagreed with each other except in the idea that the authority of the Bible and the Church might be subjected to historical and scientific criticism".[232] He said that various names were used: "Moderate, Catholic, or Broad Church, by its friends; Latitudinarian or Indifferent by its enemies."[233] More recently, Duncan Forbes used the term 'Liberal Anglicanism' as a synonym for Broad Church,[234] and while this accurately describes their attitudes towards theology, it does not mean that these men were necessarily political or

---

[229] For the origins of this term see C. R. Sanders, *Coleridge and the Broad Church Movement*, Durham, N.C., 1942, pp. 8–9. It was first used by A. P. Stanley in an article in *The Edinburgh Review* of that year. Stanley later became Dean of Westminster and was the biographer of Thomas Arnold. He "was the archetypal Victorian Broad Churchman who gloried in the Church of England as an expression of national Christianity and opposed all efforts to narrow its comprehensiveness", P. Butler, "From the Early Eighteeenth Century to the Present Day", in S. Sykes and J. Booty (eds), *The Study of Anglicanism*, London 1988, p. 36.

[230] Thomas Arnold (1795–1842) was a fellow of Oriel College from 1815 and Headmaster of Rugby School from 1828 until his death. In 1841 Arnold was appointed Regius Professor of Modern History at Oxford. Arnold's reputation as the man who reformed the public schools of England by his moral and religious example and teaching to produce truth-telling Christian gentlemen was fostered by Thomas Hughes in *Tom Brown's School Days*, London 1857. See J. J. Findlay (ed.), *Arnold of Rugby: His School Life and Contribution to Education*, Cambridge 1914; T. W. Bamford, *Thomas Arnold*, London 1960; and M. McCrum, *Thomas Arnold, Headmaster: A Reassessment*, Oxford 1989.

[231] Conybeare, "Church Parties", p. 147.

[232] Crowther, *Church Embattled*, p. 29.

[233] Conybeare, "Church Parties", p. 141.

[234] See D. Forbes, *The Liberal Anglican Idea of History*, Cambridge 1952.

social Liberals.[235] The Broad Church were the theological successors of the eighteenth-century Latitudinarians, although, as Conybeare suggested, this would have been a description used by its enemies rather than its friends.[236] The term was generally pejorative.

Conybeare identified two main groups within the Broad Church in his 1853 *Edinburgh Review* article.[237] These two groups were: "theoretical"—those who "sympathise in the love of comprehension", and "anti-theoretical". The former group included some of the leading thinkers of the age, whereas the latter included senior clergy[238] who managed to hold a number of seemingly competing views of Church order and doctrine, while avoiding public controversy by not exposing the liberal theological views of the "theoretical" school.[239] He pointed out that although the Broad Church were "destitute of...an organ in the periodical press", there was no shortage of publications by Broad Churchmen; for Broad Church clergymen "richly contributed to Classical Philology, to the Mathematical Sciences, to the Physical Sciences,[240] to Secular History, to Ecclesiastical History, to Poetry, and to general literature".[241] In a statement that came closest to identifying his own party preferences, Conybeare suggested that in theology, "the most valuable and original additions to the national stock have proceeded from [this] quarter".[242] Burns has suggested that this "wild exaggeration ignoring the important work of the clergy of other schools"[243] gave an important opening to Conybeare's critics.

M. A. Crowther described two generations of Broad Churchmen, distinguished by intellectual activity rather than chronology. The first generation included Thomas Arnold,[244] J. C. Hare,[245] F. D. Maurice,[246]

---

[235] Cf. R. Brent, *Liberal Anglican Politics: Whiggery, Religion and Reform 1830–1841*, Oxford 1987.

[236] See Conybeare, "Church Parties", p. 141.

[237] In his 1855 revised version of "Church Parties", Conybeare numerically adds these two groups together to form the "Normal type" of Broad Church, as opposed to the "Exaggerated type" ('concealed unbelievers') and the "stagnant type" (Latitudinarians). Conybeare, "Church Parties", p. 158.

[238] Conybeare used the example here of the Bishop of Lincoln and later Bishop of London, John Jackson (1811–1885). Ibid., p. 346. See Burns, "W. J. Conybeare", p. 346 fn. 240.

[239] Wolffe, "Anglicanism", p. 12.

[240] Conybeare's clerical brothers, Revd Professor John Josias Conybeare and Revd William Daniel Conybeare, were active members of the Geological Society of London (1807); Armstrong, *The English Parson-Naturalist*, p. 117.

[241] Conybeare, "Church Parties", p. 148.

[242] Ibid.

[243] Burns, "W. J. Conybeare", p. 347 fn. 241.

[244] See fn. 230 above.

Richard Whateley[247] and R. D. Hampden.[248] Hare and Maurice were 'Coleridgeans', whereas Whateley and Hampden belonged to the intellectual school known as the Oriel 'Noetics'. Arnold, who had some affinities with both groups, was enormously influential. His writings were widely read and Rugby school became a breeding ground for future Broad Churchmen: A. P. Stanley[249] and the leaders of Christian Socialism,[250] J. M. Ludlow[251] and Thomas Hughes,[252] were all pupils at Rugby under Arnold. The second generation reached the peak of its notoriety with the publication of *Essays and Reviews* in 1860.[253] Contributors like Jowett, Williams and Temple (see below) were all members of this later group. The publication of *Essays and Reviews* initiated what was arguably the greatest theological and religious controversy of the Victorian era; the book sold 15,000 copies in three months[254] and in five years went into 13 editions.[255]

Wolffe has shown that although *Essays and Reviews* revived perceptions of Broad Churchmen as theological radicals,[256] there was a continuity between some of the essays[257] and the position adopted by Arnold in his *Principles of Church Reform* in 1833. For example, each had a similar emphasis on "a comprehensive National Church in which

---

[245] Julius Charles Hare (1795–1855) was Incumbent of Herstmonceaux 1832–40 and Archdeacon of Lewes 1840–55. See A. J. C. Hare, *Memorials of a Quiet Life*, 2 vols, London 1877.

[246] Frederick Denison Maurice (1805–1872) was Professor of English Literature and History at King's College, London 1840–53. See J. Coombs, *George Anthony Denison: The Firebrand, 1805–1896,* London 1984.

[247] Richard Whately (1787–1863) was Principal of St Alban's Hall, Oxford 1825–31, and Archbishop of Dublin 1831–63.

[248] Renn Dickson Hampden (1793–1868) was Regius Professor of Divinity at Oxford 1836–47 and Bishop of Hereford 1848–68.

[249] Arthur Penrhyn Stanley (1815–1881) was Dean of Westminster 1864–1881.

[250] See below, pp. 57–60.

[251] John Malcolm Ludlow (1821–1911) was attracted by F. D. Maurice and Charles Kingsley to the Christian Socialist cause and edited their short-lived weekly newspaper, the *Christian Socialist*.

[252] Thomas Hughes (1822–1896), author of *Tom Brown's School Days*, was one of the leaders of Christian Socialism.

[253] See I. Ellis, *Seven Against Christ: A Study of 'Essays and Reviews'*, Leiden 1980.

[254] E. Williams, *The Life and Letters of Rowland Williams, DD*, London 1874, vol. 2, p. 36.

[255] Parsons, "Reform, Revival and Realignment", p. 41.

[256] Wolffe, "Anglicanism", p. 14.

[257] H. B. Wilson, "The National Church", in *Essays and Reviews*, 11th edn, London 1863, pp. 173–248.

wide freedom of opinion would be permitted".[258] B. G. Worrall in *The Making of the Modern Church* has suggested that what was new was the attempt by the essayists to respond to biblical criticism.[259] This produced a strong response from other Anglicans, as the continuing influence of eighteenth-century concepts of evidential theology[260] meant that, up until now, most Churchmen—Broad or otherwise, had held a conservative view of scripture.[261] However, the influence of new historical and scientific evidence, mostly emanating from Germany, which questioned the date and authorship of a number of the books of the Bible, was a completely new theology and initially neither Evangelicals nor the High Church had an adequate response to it.[262] As Josef Altholz has pointed out, "They were, after all, the products of a common university education, old-fashioned but not unsophisticated; and their argumentation revealed the strength and weakness of this intellectual heritage."[263]

This narrowness in the orthodox structure of reason meant that there was a lack of flexibility in Victorian theology for the views of the Broad Church. This also had ecclesiastical repercussions. Thomas Arnold, widely regarded as one of the leading Churchmen of the time, was (it was said) never offered a bishopric because of his views on a comprehensive Church that would include Dissenters. Benjamin Jowett (1817–1893) was requested by the Vice-Chancellor of Oxford to sign the Thirty-Nine Articles again. Rowland Williams (1817–1870) was arraigned in the Church courts;[264] and although Frederick

---

[258] Wolffe, "Anglicanism", p. 14.

[259] B. G. Worrall, *The Making of the Modern Church*, London 1988, p. 101.

[260] See J. L. Altholz, "The Mind of Victorian Orthooxy: Anglican Responses to 'Essays and Reviews', 1860–1864", in G. Parsons (ed.), *Religion in Victorian Britain VI: Interpretations*, p. 29; and especially, idem., *Anatomy of a Controversy: The Debate over "Essays and Reviews" 1860–1864*, Aldershot 1994, which is a very comprehensive analysis of the topic.

[261] Some eighteenth-century Latitudinarians had considered that Biblical revelation was not consistent with reason, and the Deists bypassed the scriptures altogether, seeing the universe as a sufficient revelation in itself. Unlike today's extreme liberals, they did not harbour doubts of the existence of God or the necessity of religion, but instead tried to make religion conform to their idea of reason.

[262] See Crowther, *Church Embattled*, p. 35.

[263] See Altholz, "The Mind of Victorian Orthodoxy", p. 29.

[264] Rowland Williams and Henry Wilson were charged with heresy and found guilty by the Court of Arches in 1862. They were subsequently acquitted on appeal to the Judicial Committee of the Privy Council in 1864.

Temple[265] eventually rose to be Primate, his elevation to the see of Exeter and then his translation to London aroused a great deal of anger and criticism.[266] Temple's career successes, and the rise of German liberal theology, eventually helped the essayists of 1860 gradually to receive more acceptance as the century progressed, so that by the end of it, the Broad Church was seen by many as an integral part of Anglicanism. Some have even suggested that, as a result of the stalemate between Evangelicals and Anglo-Catholics at the end of the nineteenth century, the Church of England could have been regarded as being constituted on a *de facto* Broad Church basis.[267]

The emphasis on parties and party conflict in the preceding pages presents two dangers of interpretation. The first is the idea that parties were discrete bodies in the nineteenth century, and that each of these groups kept largely to themselves. As Wolffe has stated, "Broad Churchmen and Evangelicals could show sympathy with each other against Romanizers; Evangelicals and Anglo-Catholics could both attack "liberalism"; while Broad Churchmen and High Churchmen had a shared antipathy to Evangelical "irregularity."[268] The second is to see parties as a source of revival and renewal in the Church of England. John Kent has provided a corrective to the "Anglican mythology" that the Evangelicals and the Anglo-Catholics "animated a body which was otherwise in danger of finding that it had no soul".[269] Instead, he stresses the negative impact of party conflict on the Victorian Church. He also emphasises the need to evaluate the implications of conflict and to see the Church in its wider social context. Church parties—and the theological viewpoints that each held—represent just one dimension of the nineteenth-century Church of England. The response of the Established Church to other developments in the nineteenth century is the focus of the rest of this chapter.

---

[265] Frederick Temple (1821–1902) was Bishop of Exeter 1869–85; Bishop of London 1885–96; and Archbishop of Canterbury 1896–1902.
[266] Crowther, *Church Embattled*, p. 37.
[267] Wolffe, "Anglicanism", p. 15.
[268] Ibid.
[269] Kent, *The Unacceptable Face*, p. 96.

Organizational Change

The second approach to the study of Anglican history is through examining what may be termed the Church's 'institutional' revival. During the nineteenth century, political pressures combined with social and economic change resulted in major reform of the administrative structures of the Church of England. While some historians of the nineteenth-century Church have concentrated on "the importance of Anglican theology in sustaining an *'ancien régime'* state",[270] others have contributed to our understanding of the development of the institutional presence of the Church. Clearly, an understanding of the transformation or "modernization"[271] of one of the most important institutions in the lives of the inhabitants of nineteenth-century England is vital to a proper understanding of this period.

The first historians of 'institutional' Anglicanism emphasised that the reform which the Church underwent from the 1830s onwards was part of a wider, utilitarian, government-sponsored movement to increase the efficiency of institutions, including Parliament itself.[272] Olive Brose's study of the relationship between Church and Parliament from 1828 to 1860 showed that the need for internal reform of the Established Church was analogous to the need for parliamentary reform.[273] Geoffrey Best also pointed to the fact that Church reforms were nearly all designed to enhance the parish as an effective unit of government where the clergy, many of whom were magistrates, could help in the task of maintaining law and order.[274] This co-operation between Church and State was emphasised by Brose, who suggested that Church reform was seen as a necessary prerequisite to the Church's performing its national function, and that it was a joint enterprise between Church and State.[275] This was in fact what

---

[270] Burns, *The Diocesan Revival*, p. 4.
[271] Kent, *The Unacceptable Face*, p. 95.
[272] Parsons, "Reform, Revival and Realignment", pp. 17–18. This essay remains one of the most complete surveys of this topic, especially the section entitled "The Administrative and Pastoral Revolution".
[273] O. J. Brose, *Church and Parliament: The Reshaping of the Church of England 1828–1860*, London 1959, p. 7.
[274] G. F. A. Best, *Temporal Pillars: Queen Anne's Bounty, the Ecclesiastical Commissioners, and the Church of England*, Cambridge 1964, p. 145.
[275] Brose, *Church and Parliament*, p. 20.

happened: the Ecclesiastical Commission was founded in 1835[276] by Robert Peel[277] to produce reports for improving the state of the Church, and the recommendations of these reports were enacted by Parliament.[278] Kenneth Thompson also emphasised the significance of the Ecclesiastical Commission for Church reform, and suggested that the secular administration's main interest in the Church was not religious, but rather "the Church's usefulness to society, especially in maintaining control and stability."[279]

John Wolffe has pointed to the dangers of concentrating attention on the reforms associated with the Ecclesiastical Commission, for recent work has increasingly indicated that this needs to be placed into a wider context. Peter Virgin's seminal study of eighteenth and early nineteenth-century ecclesiastical structures shows that reform of the Church's structures had begun before the 1830s, when the Queen Anne's Bounty was re-invigorated and 11 parliamentary grants from 1809–20 were used to alleviate the worst extremes of clerical poverty.[280] Thompson's thesis that the Commission's reform agenda was stymied by the decentralised nature of the parish system, and by the perceptions of Evangelicals and Anglo-Catholics that reform would not help their partisan cause,[281] provides another reason why a broader approach to administrative reform of the Church may be necessary. As John Kent has said, "Anglican history has been written on the principle...that the parochial system is the ideal-type of the ecclesia...and...[that] the...Anglican Evangelical and Anglo-Catholic parties...did not want to see the parish system modified, and put the growth of their organizations before any kind of centralizing ecclesiastical development".[282]

---

[276] For a history of the Ecclesiastical Commission, see S. C. Carpenter, *The Church and the People*, p. 98, and J. R. Brown, *Number One Millbank: The Story of the Ecclesiastical Commissioners*, London 1944.

[277] See N. Gash, *Sir Robert Peel: The Life of Sir Robert Peel after 1830*, London 1972.

[278] See N. Gash, *Reaction and Reconstruction in English Politics, 1832–1852*, Oxford 1965.

[279] K. Thompson, *Bureaucracy and Church Reform*, London 1970, p. 3.

[280] P. Virgin, *The Church in the Age of Negligence*, Cambridge 1989, p. 20. See also K. Thompson, *Bureaucracy and Church Reform*, p. 11; and F. C. Mather, "Georgian Churchmanship Reconsidered: Some Variations in Anglican Public Worship, 1714–1830", *Journal of Ecclesiastical History* 36 (1985): 255–83. For an early history, see W. R. Le Fanu, *Queen Anne's Bounty: A Short Account of its History and Work*, London 1933.

[281] Thompson, *Bureaucracy and Church Reform*, pp. 91–155.

[282] Kent, *The Unacceptable Face*, pp. 95–6.

Whereas Parsons' study of "The Administrative and Pastoral Revolution" in the Church begins in 1832,[283] and Thompson sets 1836 as his starting point,[284] other historians of institutional Anglicanism have concentrated on developments in the Church later in the Victorian period, when there were further significant changes. The Oxford episcopate of Samuel Wilberforce[285] is seen as a key development by Pugh[286] and others,[287] as they develop what Arthur Burns calls the "Wilberforce thesis".[288] Chadwick places his discussion of the episcopal development of diocesan institutions in the relevant chapter of *The Victorian Church* in *Part Two (1860–1901)*.[289] Wolffe has pointed to the significance of the new bishoprics set up by the Conservative government from 1874 to 1880.[290] A number of other studies have concentrated on the influence of "reforming" bishops:

---

[283] Parsons, "Reform, Revival and Realignment", p. 17.

[284] This was the year when church tithes were abolished, and when the Registrar-General's Office was set up. It gave people the opportunity of being married and having births and deaths recorded at a registry office or chapel, rather than in their parish church.

[285] Samuel Wilberforce (1805–1873) was Bishop of Oxford 1845–69 and Winchester 1869–73. He was a High Churchman of conservative views who attacked the authors of *Essays and Reviews* and condemned Charles Darwin's theory of evolution.

[286] R. K. Pugh, "The Episcopate of Samuel Wilberforce, Bishop of Oxford 1845–1869, and of Winchester 1869–1873, with special reference to the see of Oxford", DPhil thesis, University of Oxford 1957, and idem., *The Letter Books of Samuel Wilberforce 1843–1868*, Oxford 1969.

[287] The literature on Samuel Wilberforce is immense. Nineteenth-century biographies include those by his son, R. Wilberforce (together with A. R. Ashwell); G. W. Daniel; and J. W. Burgon, who featured Wilberforce in his *Lives of Twelve Good Men*. Twentieth-century biographies have been written by G. W. E. Russell; J. C. Hardwick; and by S. Baring Gould in *The Church Revival*. Studies of Wilberforce's bishoprics include S. Meacham, *The Lord Bishop: The Life of Samuel Wilberforce 1805–1873*; D. Bowen in *The Idea of the Victorian Church*; and D. Newsome in *The Parting of Friends*.

[288] Burns has shown that by 1845, when Wilberforce was elevated to the see of Oxford, the diocesan revival was already well established, and the claim that Wilberforce "transformed the episcopate" is an exaggerated one. Burns, *The Diocesan Revival*, pp. 10–11.

[289] Chadwick, *The Victorian Church*, part 2, pp. 328–400. See also J. R. H. Moorman, *A History of the Church in England*, 3rd edn. London 1973, p. 359; and D. L. Edwards, *Christian England*, London 1989, pp. 209–18.

[290] See Burns, *The Diocesan Revival*, ch. 8: "More Bishops and More Dioceses".

"Blomfield at Chester and London,[291] and Phillpotts at Exeter,[292] and the greatest of the Evangelical bishops, Sumner of Winchester, [who] had pioneered nearly every reform and custom which Wilberforce was to introduce."[293] However, the most comprehensive study of the institutional and administrative history of the modern Church is Arthur Burns's *Diocesan Revival in the Church of England, c1800–1870*. As the title suggests, this account of one of the main aspects of nineteenth-century Church reform is based largely on the study of changes at the diocesan, rather than the parish or governmental level.

Burns demonstrates that diocesan reform really began in the eighteenth century, when there were early efforts to develop and improve episcopal visitations, as well as to extend the responsibilities of Archdeacons and to revive the office of Rural Dean. By the 1830s, on the eve of the Oxford Movement, these early reforming moves had become much more extensive and systematic. Developments in the reform and administration of the major diocesan "officers" of the Church—bishops, archdeacons, and rural deans[294]—were paralleled by the development of other diocesan administrative structures. These included improved record-keeping and statistics; the foundation of new diocesan societies; attempts to reform the archaic disciplinary structure of the Church; moves towards the creation of new dioceses and sees; and the later appearance of diocesan representative bodies, especially ruridecanal chapters and conferences, and diocesan assemblies. By 1870, Burns concludes, "the Anglican diocese was equipped with an effective structure binding the parochial clergy (and to some extent the churchgoing laity) more tightly into the institution."[295]

The revival and development of the Church's corporate life was an important component of the administrative revival of the Church of England.[296] Historians have generally treated the campaign for

---

[291] Charles James Blomfield (1787–1857) was Bishop of Chester 1824–28 and London 1828–56. See M. Johnson, *Bustling Intermeddler? The Life and Work of Charles James Blomfield*, Leominster 2001.

[292] See W. J. Conybeare, "Bishop Phillpotts", *The Edinburgh Review* 95 (1852): 54–94; and J. R. Wolffe, "Bishop Henry Phillpotts and the Administration of the Diocese of Exeter 1830–1869", *Transactions of the Devonshire Association*, 114 (December 1982): 99–113.

[293] Pugh, "The Episcopate of Samuel Wilberforce", p. 77. For Sumner, see Appendix 1.

[294] See J. A. Atkinson, *Rural Deans and Ruri-Decanal Chapters*, Manchester 1864.

[295] Burns, *The Diocesan Revival*, p. 260.

[296] For a recent and detailed treatment of this topic, see Burns, *The Diocesan Revival*, ch. 9: "Synods and Conferences: The Revival of Diocesan Assemblies". See also Crowther, *Church Embattled*, pp. 205–18.

diocesan assemblies[297] as an adjunct of the demand for the restoration of Convocation in the 1850s.[298] Anne Crowther dismisses the first synod at Exeter in 1851 as an isolated theological protest and an early example of the use of such assemblies as an exercise in 'church defence'.[299] Owen Chadwick stresses both 'church defence' and a desire to bring clergy and bishops together in purely clerical assemblies, and he sees the incorporation of laymen as a later development which was unwelcome to some.[300] Gerald Parsons has shown how in the 1850s and the 1860s, "pressure developed for the creation of diocesan synods or conferences".[301] In 1866 the first diocesan conference met at Ely. By 1882 all but three dioceses had such conferences. In the 1860s and 1870s another important development occurred with the creation of the Church Congresses. Clergy and laity attended and participated in these annual meetings, which were chaired by the bishop of the diocese in which the Congress was being held. They quickly became "a barometer of opinion in the Church of England", and they were an important element in the continuing revival of the Church's institutional life.[302]

As well as changes to the administrative structures, the nineteenth-century Church of England also experienced a wide-ranging revival of the ordained pastoral ministry. C. K. Francis Brown provided the first history of the nineteenth-century clergy in 1953, and his biographical survey remains a rich source of information on individual clergy and the clerical profession in the nineteenth-century Church.[303] Brian Heeney—Nathaniel Woodard's publicist—was the first modern historian to examine the theory of pastoral ministry in the mid-Victorian Church, and he showed that during this period, pastoral

---

[297] The use of the term 'synod' and 'conference' to describe particular types of diocesan assemblies varied in the nineteenth century. See Crowther, *Church Embattled*, pp. 209–10.

[298] In 1854 the Convocation of Canterbury met to conduct meaningful business for ther first time since 1717. The Convocation of York did not meet until 1861 because of the opposition of the Archbishop of York to its revival. After 1861, however, both Convocations met regularly and became important arenas for the conduct of the Church of England's business, although their role remained one of debate and the formulation of policy, not the enactment of new measures which would have required the sanction of Parliament. Parsons, "Reform, Revival and Realignment", p. 28.

[299] Crowther, *Church Embattled*, pp. 206–7.

[300] Chadwick, *Victorian Church*, part 2, pp. 359–60.

[301] Parsons, "Reform, Revival and Realignment", p. 28.

[302] Ibid.

[303] See also D. McClatchey, *Oxfordshire Clergy 1777–1869: A Study of the Established Church and the Role of its Clergy in Local Society*, Oxford 1960.

theologians of all parties came to assert two fundamental principles in respect of the pastoral ideal: first, that the ordained ministry was a unique religious vocation, and second, that it therefore demanded distinctive qualities and standards of character and behaviour.[304] In a later study, which was based on a survey of the handbooks of pastoral theology, Heeney detected a shift in the understanding of the clergyman from that of being a 'professional' because of his high social status, to being so because he had adequate theological training and pastoral skills.[305]

Heeney, as well as Alan Haig in *The Victorian Clergy* and Anthony Russell in *The Clerical Profession*, was concerned with the process by which the clergy acquired certain occupational characteristics. The contention of all three authors was that during the nineteenth century the clerical profession was revolutionised. Rosemary O'Day has taken issue with this idea, suggesting that "the development of the clerical profession should be seen as a continuum stretching from the middle ages", and that there should be "no disjuncture between the nineteenth century profession and the clergy of the preceding years."[306] There is no denying, however, that there were changes in the structure and self-understanding of the clerical profession.[307] As Owen Chadwick has put it, "No one doubted in 1860, and few will doubt now, that the clergy of 1860 were more zealous than the clergy of 1830, conducted worship more reverently, knew their people better, understood a little more theology, said more prayers, celebrated sacraments more frequently, studied more Bible...".[308] Contemporary observation supported this idea. When Bishop George Selwyn returned from New Zealand to preach at Cambridge in 1854, he declared that "a great and visible change has taken place in the thirteen years since I left England. It is now a very rare thing to see a careless clergyman, a neglected parish or a desecrated church".[309] As Alan Gilbert has remarked, there was no

---

[304] B. Heeney, "The Theory of Pastoral Ministry in the Mid-Victorian Church of England", *Historical Magazine of the Protestant Episcopal Church* 42 (1974): 215–30.

[305] B. Heeney, *A Different Kind of Gentleman: Parish Clergy as Professional Men in Early and Mid-Victorian England*, Hamden 1976, pp. 4–7.

[306] R. O'Day, "The Clerical Renaissance in Victorian England and Wales", in *Religion in Victorian Britain I: Traditions*, p. 185. See also idem., "The Men from the Ministry", in *Religion in Victorian Britain II: Controversies*, Manchester 1988, pp. 259–79.

[307] Knight, *The Nineteenth-Century Church*, p. 13.

[308] Chadwick, *The Victorian Church*, part 1, p. 127.

[309] G. A. Selwyn, *The Work of Christ in the World: Four Sermons Preached before the University of Cambridge on the Four Sundays preceding Advent in the Year of Our Lord 1854*, Cambridge 1855, p. 7. Cited by A. D. Gilbert, *Religion and*

single explanation for this change.[310] However, the work of the Ecclesiastical Commission helped provide a context. The *Church Pluralities Act* of 1838 made a major impact on the problem of non-residence, while The *Church Discipline Act* of 1840 sought to limit further the possibilities of clerical excess, abuse or laxity. But legal or organizational innovations alone do not explain the changes in the expectations and behaviour of the English clergy. As Gilbert has suggested, the "metamorphosis of the religious Establishment" around the beginning of the Victorian era implicated the essential nature of Anglican religious culture, and it was based on vital changes in the role of the Church in English society.[311]

Social Change

Anglican thinking on social issues, according to John Wolffe, was reflected in a blending of pastoral responses with the influence of intellectual and theological trends. The complexity of this blend and the lack of a single Church approach to social questions has meant that few scholars have ventured into this area of Anglican church history. Edward Norman's substantial book on the subject was the first foray into this field, and examines the subject in terms of the history of ideas, giving considerable attention to the impact of the prevailing orthodoxy of 'political economy'.[312] Parsons has made a characteristically brave attempt to study the period: his contribution to the second volume in the *Religion in Victorian Britain* series is a masterly survey of research on this topic up to 1988, and is an important source of ideas for the overview which follows. John Wolffe has suggested that a number of recent studies on the complexities of Evangelical social thought may provide a basis for the re-evaluation of the wider Anglican picture. These include Boyd Hilton's *The Age of Atonement*, which examines the influence of Evangelicalism on English social and economic thought in the period 1785–1865; and the published results of a symposium of Evangelical historians at the University of York in 1992, entitled *Evangelical Faith and Public Zeal*. Earlier books on Evangelicals and social reform tended to study individual Evangelicals

---

Society in Industrial England: Church, Chapel and Social Change 1740–1914, London 1976, p. 132.

[310] Gilbert, *Religion and Society in Industrial England*, p. 132.

[311] Ibid.

[312] E. R. Norman, *Church and Society in England 1770–1970: A Historical Study*, Oxford 1976. See especially ch. 4: "The Victorian Church and the Condition of Society".

rather than their influence on social change,[313] making them of limited use to this study.

Individual differences in relation to social problems can probably be explained in terms of social background, predisposition, response to circumstances, as well as different eschatologies.[314] Just as individual Christians varied in their social attitudes and stances, so then the Church of England exhibited variations and subtleties in its approach to social issues. This is also an area where controversy between varying historical interpretations has been intense. For example, there has been ongoing debate about the role that Nonconformity[315] and the Sunday School Movement[316] played in the lives of the English working class.[317] Wolffe has pointed out the tendency of some recent commentators to misinterpret anachronistically the Christian Socialists, as well as slum ritualists such as A. H. Stanton,[318] as forerunners of collective socialism in the twentieth century.[319] Frequently held assumptions about the links between Ritualist sacramentalism and social radicalism; Evangelical social activism and paternalistic intervention; and moderate High Church responses to the 'Condition of England', all require sympathetic evaluation on their own terms. This

---

[313] J. W. Bready, *England: Before and After Wesley. The Evangelical Revival and Social Reform*, New York 1938; K. Heasman, *Evangelicals in Action: An Appraisal of their Social Work in the Victorian Era*, London 1962; and Bradley, *The Call to Seriousness*.

[314] Wolffe, "Anglicanism", p. 23. Three main eschatological schools existed from the early nineteenth century: postmillenialists, who held that the thousand years of Revelation 20 would be essentially a continuation of human history, reached through the gradual improvement and triumph of religion; premillenialists, who held that the thousand years would be preceded by a period of cataclysm and turmoil presaging the Second Coming of Christ; and amillenialists who held that good and evil would continue in the world until the Second Coming of Christ—the thousand years of Revelation 20 being a description not of a period on earth preceding Christ's return, but of the souls of dead believers reigning with Christ in Heaven. R. G. Clouse, 'Views of the Millenium' in *Evangelical Dictionary of Theology*, Cumbria 1984, pp. 714–18.

[315] See Gilbert, *Religion and Society in Industrial England*.

[316] T. W. Laqueur, *Religion and Respectability: Sunday Schools and English Working-Class Culture, 1780–1850*, London 1976.

[317] On the Church of England and the working class, see K. S. Inglis, *Churches and the Working Classes in Victorian England*, London 1963; H. McLeod, *Class and Religion in the Late Victorian City*, London 1974; J. Cox, *The English Churches in a Secular Society: Lambeth, 1870–1930*, Oxford 1982.

[318] Arthur Henry Stanton (1839–1913) was Curate of St Alban's, Holborn 1862–1913; refusing all further preferment. For 'slum ritualists', see J. S. Reed, *Glorious Battle*, ch. 8: "Ritualism and the Urban Poor".

[319] Wolffe, "Anglicanism", p. 23.

is essential for an understanding of the development of popular support for a 'social gospel' by the end of the nineteenth century.[320]

Boyd Hilton[321] and Douglas Holladay[322] have demonstrated that, by the middle of the nineteenth century, Evangelicals were divided in their approach to social issues. Richard Soloway and Brian Dickey have recently explored some of the background to this,[323] and identify J. B Sumner (1780–1862)[324] as a key Anglican proponent of the principles of political economy. His views encompassed *laissez-faire* social theory; the absolute priority of private charity in the relief of poverty; and the undesirability of state intervention and social reform.[325] On the other hand, there were Anglican Evangelicals such as the Tory Radicals and the 'Paternalists':[326] Bull, Sadler, Oastler and the most famous Evangelical of them all, Shaftesbury, were prepared to advocate a degree of state intervention in social reform—albeit only by extending their underlying concept of paternalism to encompass the state itself.[327] Dickey has shown that these different forms of social

---

[320] Wolffe, "Anglicanism", p. 24. See also G. Parsons, "Social Control to Social Gospel: Victorian Christian Social Attitudes", in G. Parsons (ed.), *Religion in Victorian Britain II:Controversies*, p. 59.

[321] Hilton, *The Age of Atonement*, pp. 15–16.

[322] J. D. Holladay, "19th Century Evangelical Activism: From Private Charity to State Intervention, 1830–50", *Historical Magazine of the Protestant Episcopal Church* 50 (1982): 53–79.

[323] R. A. Soloway, *Prelates and People: Ecclesiastical Social Thought 1783–1852*, London 1969, pp. 96–101; and B. Dickey, "'Going about and doing good': Evangelicals and Poverty c.1815–1870", in J. R. Wolffe (ed.), *Evangelical Faith and Public Zeal*, London 1995, pp. 38–58. See also R. S. Dell, "Social and Economic Theories and Pastoral Concerns of a Victorian Archbishop", *Journal of Ecclesiastical History* 16 (1965): 196–208; and N. A. D. Scotland, *John Bird Sumner: Evangelical Archbishop*, Leominster 1995, pp. 18–25.

[324] See Appendix 1.

[325] Sumner was regarded as a crucial interpreter of the arguments of Adam Smith and Thomas Malthus; his 1816 *Treatise on the Records of Creation...* being the means by which most early nineteenth-century Churchmen learned their Malthus. Soloway, *Prelates and People*, pp. 95–101; Dickey, "Evangelicals and Poverty", pp. 43–6; Scotland, *John Bird Sumner: Evangelical Archbishop*.

[326] See D. Roberts, *Paternalism in Early Victorian England*, London 1979.

[327] Lord Shaftsbury's concern for social reform, like Wilberforce's for slave emancipation, was predicated on the assumption that this was an essential preliminary for moral and spiritual transformation in the individual—that there were occasions in which the material environment was so oppressive and dehumanizing that evangelistic efforts could make little progress. Shaftsbury's premillenial eschatology also shaped his philanthropic and missionary outlook and activities: transformation of any kind was to be intiated before Christ's

involvement continued to be widespread among Evangelicals as the century progressed.[328]

The mid-century Christian Socialist movement began in April 1848, when J. M. Ludlow, Charles Kingsley[329] and F. D. Maurice met in Maurice's London house.[330] They did not call themselves 'Christian Socialists' until 1850, and in 1851 Maurice made the famous observation that their purpose was to influence "the unsocial Christians and the unChristian socialists". The movement formally lasted only until 1854, when the members realised that their practical initiatives in founding co-operative enterprises were not succeeding. However, before the movement dissolved as a distinct entity, in October 1854 it established the Working Men's College in Red Lion Square and Maurice, who had been sacked from his professorship at King's College London for not believing in hell,[331] was appointed its first principal.[332] Despite the collapse of their organization, the ideas of the Christian Socialists continued to influence Victorian social thinking and attitudes, and there are many examples of how, after 1850, "the former predominance of the values of non-interventionist

---

return. See G. B. A. M. Finlayson, *The Seventh Earl of Shaftesbury*, London 1981, pp. 183–4.

[328] Dickey, "Evangelicals and Poverty", p. 45.

[329] Charles Kingsley (1819–1875) was Rector of Eversley in Hampshire and a well-known author; writing dramatic poetry, pamphlets, articles and a series of novels including *The Water Babies* (1863). He was Professor of English Literature at Queen's College, London and then Professor of Modern History at Cambridge 1860-9, as well as being a keen naturalist. His father and namesake, Charles Kingsley (1782–1860) was the Rector of St Luke's, Chelsea 1836–60, and a noted Evangelical.

[330] For a history of the movement, see T. Christensen, *Origin and History of Christian Socialism*, Aarhus 1962, and E. Norman, *The Victorian Christian Socialists*, Cambridge 1987.

[331] See G. Rowell, *Hell and the Victorians: A Study of the Nineteenth-Century Theological Controversies Concerning Eternal Punishment and the Future Life*, Oxford 1974, pp. 62 and 84. For a brief account of Maurice's dismissal, see Chadwick, *The Victorian Church* vol.1, pp. 545–50.

[332] See F. J. Furnivall, *Early History of the Working Men's College*, London 1891; F. Maurice, *The Life of Frederick Denison Maurice...*, London 1884, vol. 2 p. 221ff. The following year the college moved to premises in Great Ormond Street where it was based until 1904, when it moved to Camden Town. Working Men's Colleges based on the London model were set up from 1855–1862 in Manchester, Salford, Ancoats, Leicester, Halifax, Liverpool, Wolverhampton, Oxford and Cambridge. See J. W. Adamson, *English Education 1789–1902*, Cambridge 1964, pp. 167–9.

evangelicalism and political economy continued to be steadily eroded by other alternative Christian social values and perceptions".[333]

Kathleen Woodroofe has shown that during this period there was a huge increase in the numbers of charitable and philanthropic bodies,[334] and Gerald Parsons cites James Fraser, who was appointed Bishop of Manchester in 1870, as an example of the increasing respectibility of more liberal Christian social attitudes in the third quarter of the century. Fraser believed that the Church should firmly support attempts to improve social conditions. He supported the Co-operative Movement and was the first bishop to address one of its congresses. He mediated, with varying success, in industrial disputes that occurred in his diocese. Desmond Bowen and Stephen Mayor document his most famous actions when in 1872 he defended the right of Joseph Arch and some agricultural workers to found a union and in 1874, during a lock-out of striking agricultural workers, he defended strikers and criticised the farmers.[335]

The re-emergence or revival of Christian Socialism in the late 1870s was another example of how Victorian Christian social attitudes were continuing to develop and diversify.[336] Beginning with the foundation of the Guild of St Matthew by Revd S. W. Headlam[337] in 1877,[338] there followed over the next three decades "a remarkable proliferation of societies, leagues and unions committed to a more or less precise and overt Christian Socialism".[339] The smaller, mostly short-lived societies like the Christian Socialist Society (1886); the Christian Socialist League (1894); and the Christian Socialist Brotherhood (1898), were interdenominational and mainly supported by Nonconformists. The largest and most influential of the societies was the Christian Social Union (CSU), which was founded in 1889 by a group of Anglo-

---

[333] Parsons, "Social Control to Social Gospel", p. 46.

[334] Between 1850 and 1860 alone, 144 new societies for social or moral improvement were founded. K. Woodroofe, *From Charity to Social Work in England and the United States*, London 1962, p. 23.

[335] Bowen, *The Idea of the Victorian Church*, pp. 274–5; S. Mayor, *The Churches and the Labour Movement*, London 1967, pp. 91–2 and 101–3.

[336] See P. d'A. Jones, *The Christian Socialist Revival, 1877–1914*, Princeton 1968.

[337] Stewart Duckworth Headlam (1847–1924) was Curate of St Matthew's, Bethnal Green, from 1873 until he was dismissed in 1878 because of his public support of theatres and music halls. His work at Bethnal Green and later at St Thomas's, Charterhouse 1879–81 and St Michael's, Shoreditch 1881–4, "convinced him of the importance of education". He was a member of the London School Board 1888–1904. R. Aldrich and P. Gordon, *Dictionary of British Educationists*, London 1989, p. 109.

[338] See Norman, *Christian Socialists*, pp. 98–120.

[339] Parsons, "Social Control to Social Gospel", p. 51.

Catholics.[340] By 1895 it had 27 branches and almost 3,000 members, and at its height it had a membership of 6,000, which included a number of bishops.[341] The CSU numbered among its leading members such well-known personalities as B. F. Wescott, Henry Scott Holland and Charles Gore. Wescott was president of the CSU until 1900, and presented a famous paper on 'Socialism' to the 1890 Church Congress at Hull. Other notable Anglicans who described themselves as Christian Socialists included leading figures in the Settlement Movement, most notably Samuel Barnett and E. S. Talbot.[342] By 1900 Christian Socialism and social Christianity were firmly established as part of the Anglican Christian experience, and members of the Church of England were more conscious of the potentially socially radical implications of Christian belief, and of the case for social mission, than their early Victorian predecessors had been.

The connection between Christan socialism and education is a close one, as illustrated by Maurice whose convictions led him from being a university professor to teacher of working class men. Education was the social issue of the nineteenth century, and Anglican involvement in education is a central theme of the significant body of literature on this topic. Wolffe has suggested that there has been a tendency by many scholars to adopt a 'Whiggish' view[343] of the development of the modern school system, where nineteenth-century Anglican attitudes are made to appear obstructive, rather than being evaluated on their own terms.[344] From an intellectual perspective, education attracted wide Anglican interest, and leading clergymen such as Thomas Arnold, Francis Close, Nathaniel Woodard, J. H. Newman, J. B. Sumner and J. C. Wigram were passionately committed to the provision of education, seeing this as central to the mission of the national Church. At the parochial level, the erection and development of schools was a central part of the Church's defence against Dissent and of its offensive on working-class irreligion.[345] Education also represented a crucial strand in the Church's counterattack against Dissent in the 1830s, and resistance to the politically-motivated Whig

---

[340] They were part of the younger and more liberal Anglo-Catholic generation which produced, also in 1889, the collection of theologically critical essays, *Lux Mundi*.

[341] d'A. Jones, *The Christian Socialist Revival*, p. 217.

[342] Parsons, "Social Control to Social Gospel", p. 52.

[343] See H. Butterfield, *The Whig Interpretation of History*, London 1951.

[344] Cf. J. Hurt, *Education in Evolution: Church, State, Society and Popular education, 1800–1870*, London 1971.

[345] See H. McLeod, *Religion and Irreligion in Victorian England: How Secular was the Working Class?*, Bangor 1993.

education programme of 1839. It is the Church's response to such political motivations which will now be examined.

Political Change

The Church of England has recently become a central focus for historians interested in the place of religion in nineteenth-century politics.[346] Two types of approaches can be discerned. The first, exemplified by G. I. T. Machin in his two-volume survey of the period from 1832 to 1921,[347] examines the political dimensions of specifically religious issues. As Wolffe has pointed out,[348] this field of investigation includes not only parliamentary politics, but also the executive action of government in such matters as patronage and the administration of the Ecclesiastical Commission.[349] Alan Gilbert has highlighted the significance of Nonconformist agitation in bringing about political and adminstrative change; what Knight has called "the alliance between Dissent and democracy".[350] Machin argued that the rapid expansion of Noncomformity led to the Church being willing (for the most part) to co-operate in government-sponsored institutional reform along the lines described by Olive Brose,[351] G. F. A. Best[352] and Kenneth Thompson.[353] Of course, as explained above, not all sections of the Church were happy with this development, as evidenced by Pusey's "gloomy prophecy":[354] "We shall live under the supremacy of the Commission, it will be our legislative, executive, the ultimate appeal of our bishops; it will absorb our Episcopate; the Prime Minister will be our Protestant Pope."[355] Although the inclusion of

---

[346] Wolffe, "Anglicanism", p. 17. Once again, I am indebted to John Wolffe for his masterley survey of the literature, and issues; and also to Frances Knight's overview in *Nineteenth-Century Church and English Society*, pp. 18–19.

[347] G. I. T. Machin; *Politics and the Churches in Great Britain, 1832 to 1868*, Oxford 1977; and *Politics and the Churches in Great Britain, 1869–1921*, Oxford 1987.

[348] Wolffe, "Anglicanism", p. 17.

[349] See D. W. R. Bahlman, "Politics and Church patronage in the Victorian Age", *Victorian Studies* 22 (1978–9): 253–95; W. T. Gibson, "Disraeli's Church Patronage, 1868–1880", *Anglican and Episcopal History* 61 (1992): 197–210.

[350] Knight, *The Nineteenth-Century Church*, p. 18.

[351] Brose, *Church and Parliament*, London 1959.

[352] G. F. A. Best, *Temporal Pillars*, London 1964.

[353] K. Thompson, *Bureaucracy and Church Reform*, Oxford 1970.

[354] Bowen, *The Idea of the Victorian Church*, p. 21.

[355] *British Critic* 23 (1838): 526, cited by D Bowen, *The Idea of the Victorian Church*, p. 21.

bishops on the Commission led some critics to soften the tone of their opposition, the resistance to this form of government interference in the affairs of the Church was great.[356]

The second approach to the study of the Church and politics is to argue that religious attitudes in general and Anglican ones in particular were key influencers in the wider formation of government policy. Perry Butler[357] and J. P. Parry[358] have taken this approach in their examination of the career of W. E. Gladstone, as has Peter Jagger.[359] Allen Warren's study of Disraeli, the Conservative Party and the Church[360] is an important reminder that it was not just the Liberals who were influenced by the Church. Richard Brent has recently attempted to apply a similar technique in his study of the politics of the 1830s; choosing to study the politics of a period of time rather personalities or parties.[361] The most significant work of this kind has been J. C. D. Clark's *English Society, 1688–1832*, which boldly argues that Anglicanism was fundamental to the defence of the pre-1832 constitution and that its redefinition was central to the "revolutionary" changes of 1828 to 1832.[362] As David Hempton has recently observed, the fact that the Anglican Church of the nineteenth century was closely bound up with the lives of its adherents is clearly the main reason why a study of the politics of the period cannot be properly investigated without reference to religion.[363]

John Wolffe, in his *God and Greater Britain*,[364] takes a similar approach as J. C. D. Clark, except that he examines the topic from a religious rather than secular point of view, and deals with a later

---

[356] See P. J. Welch, "Contemporary Views on the Proposals for the Alienation of Capitular Property in England, 1832–1840", *Journal of Ecclesiastical History*, 5 (1954): 185.

[357] P. A. Butler, *Gladstone: Church, State and Tractarianism: A Study of his Religious Ideas and Attitudes, 1809–1859*, Oxford 1982.

[358] J. P. Parry, *Democracy and Religion: Gladstone and the Liberal Party, 1867–1875*, Cambridge 1986. See also idem., "Religion and the Collapse of Gladstone's First Government", *Historical Journal* 25 (1982): 71–101.

[359] P. J. Jagger, *Gladstone, Politics and Religion*, London 1984; idem., *Gladstone*, London 1998; and idem., *Gladstone: The Making of a Christian Politician*, Alison Park, Pa., 1991.

[360] A. Warren, "Disraeli, the Conservatives and the National Church, 1837–1881", in *Parliament and the Church, 1529–1960*, pp. 96–117.

[361] R. Brent, *Liberal Anglican Politics*, Oxford 1987.

[362] Wolffe, "Anglicanism", p. 17.

[363] D. Hempton, *Religion and Political Culture in Britain and Ireland*, Cambridge 1996, p. 178.

[364] J. R. Wolffe, *God and Greater Britain: Religion and National Life in Britain and Ireland 1843–1945*, London 1994.

period: 1843–1945. Wolffe's thesis is that religion had a noticeable influence on both the substance and the style of politics, and that this influence was "most significant when it was linked with the forces of national self-assertion."[365] He approaches the topic in three main ways. First, he outlines some of the key issues and developments relating to the constitutional position of religion in order to indicate the manner in which it shaped political life. Secondly, he looks at how, at national as well as local levels, religious alignments and sentiments contributed substantially to the definition and consolidation of political loyalties. Finally, after some consideration of the situation in Wales, Scotland and Ireland, he examines the role of ritual and ceremonial based on the monarchy—a different but influential kind of politics—and how this provided support for a British identity during a period of great social and administrative change.[366]

One historian, Gerald Parsons, has identified an arena where politics and religion met, and clashed: the area of elementary education.[367] The history of elementary education in nineteenth-century England and Wales is, however, such a well-documented area of study that a detailed, or even brief survey, would seem to be unnecessary. Such works as those of Frank Smith[368] and Charles Birchenough[369] have already shown that Parsons' observations are valid. More specifically, the relationship between Evangelicals and elementary education has been the subject of a number of studies.[370] Elementary education was clearly another major area of Church involvement in the nineteenth century, but it is not one that will be discussed here.

Therefore, in both education, and in the gradual disestablishment of the privileges of the Church of England by the end of the century, the relationship between the state and religion had became less intimate and more neutral. As Gerald Parsons has suggested, there was a clear trend in the Victorian period towards the emergence of religious pluralism and the neutrality of the state in matters of religion.[371] Religious belief was increasingly seen as belonging to the sphere of private choice. In elementary education, the clergy could not

---

[365] Ibid., p. 124.
[366] Ibid.
[367] Parsons, "Reform, Revival and Realignment", pp. 59–62.
[368] F. Smith, *History of English Elementary Education 1760–1902*, London 1931.
[369] C. Birchenough, *History of Elementary Education in England and Wales from 1800 to the Present Day*, London 1938.
[370] See, for example, J. McLeish, *Evangelical Religion and Popular Education*, London 1969; and E. Royle, "Evangelicals and Education".
[371] G. Parsons, "Introduction", in *Religion in Victorian Britain II: Controversies*, p. 5.

comprehend how morality might be taught apart from religion. However, as far as the state was concerned, all that mattered was that children were taught to be good, and this did not require allegiance to any particular religious doctrine. The Church of England adjusted to the new reality of religious diversity, and the state (through the courts) took the same view of its role in relation to different religious traditions. However, the tradition of the clergyman-schoolmaster was maintained within the Anglo-Catholic and Evangelical wings of the Church, so that schools which were based upon sectarian principles, or were led by headmasters who belonged to a particular Church party, continued to flourish. This was particularly the case in the rapidly growing section of English society known as the middle class.

CHAPTER 2

Middle-Class Education in Nineteenth-Century England

The meaning of 'class' has been the subject of much debate by both historians[1] and sociologists[2] in the twentieth (and now the twenty-first) century. For a contemporary of the nineteenth century, however, 'middle class' was an idea which had its roots in the previous generation[3] and which grew in strength and common usage as the century progressed. The designation 'middle class' was also applied to certain kinds of schools which differed in subjects taught, in the number of years pupils spent under instruction, and in the cost to parents. What follows is an attempt to define this elusive term before a careful analysis is made of the growth of schools that specifically catered for this social grouping. The larger story of the development of Evangelical educational provision may lack cohesion unless it is seen against the background of intense and growing concern by all Anglican Churchmen for the problems, character and prospects of the middle class.

---

[1] The literature is reviewed in D. Wahrman, *Imagining the Middle Class*, Cambridge 1995, the most recent detailed survey of class history.

[2] Probably best represented by M. Savage, *et al.* in their systematic overview of the subject: *Property, Bureaucracy and Culture: Middle Class Formation in Contemporary Britain*, London 1992; and more recently, T. Butler and M. Savage (eds), *Social Change and the Middle Classes*, London 1995. See also J. Goldthorpe, *Social Mobility and Class Structure in Modern Britain*, Oxford 1980.

[3] Briggs has suggested that one of the first recorded uses of the term 'middle classes' occurs in the title of *Enquiry into the Duties of Men in the Higher Rank and Middle Classes of Society in Great Britain*, written in 1795 by Thomas Gisbourne, an Evangelical clergyman and friend of Wilberforce. Hannah More also deliberately addressed some of her tracts to 'Persons of the Middle Ranks'. A Briggs, "The Language of 'Class' in Early Nineteenth-Century England", in A. Briggs and J. Saville (eds), *Essays in Labour History*, London 1967. For a more recent discussion of the origins of this term, see J. Smail, *The Origins of Middle-Class Culture: Halifax, Yorkshire, 1680–1780*, Ithaca 1994, and M. R. Hunt, *The Middling Sort: Commerce, Gender, and the Family in England, 1660–1780*, Berkeley, Ca., 1995.

The very notion of class, as distinguished from that of caste or legally recognized estate, is imprecise. Any attempt to determine the limits of a class or stratum in society, is a frustrating project, and of all the classes the "middle" is the least definable. This difficulty has been summed up by one of the early workers in this field, G. D. H. Cole:

> Classes...are not sharply definable groups whose precise numbers can be determined by gathering in enough information about every individual. They are rather aggregations of persons round a number of central nuclei, in such a way that it can be said with confidence of those nearer each centre that they are members of a particular class, but that those further from a centre can be assigned to the class it represents only with increasing uncertainty.[4]

More recently, the historical sociologist Michael Mann has suggested: "Defining the middle class has always been contentious. The rise of 'middling groups' immediately presented conceptual problems for nineteenth-century observers. Most used the plural 'middle classes', impressed by their heterogenity...Contemporaries left definitions to us, but our historians have been no great help...[although] Sociologists supply better concepts."[5] Before turning to these contemporary definitions, and leaving aside the concepts provided by sociologists which have been adequately summarised elsewhere,[6] a brief overview, and defence, of the ideas of these 'unhelpful' historians seems appropriate. Broadly speaking, they have all been concerned with trying to answer the question of why and how the British people came to see themselves as living in a society centred around a 'middle class'.

Dror Wahrman has recently pointed out that we used to have a remarkably straightforward answer to this question. Sometime during the late eighteenth and early nineteenth centuries, an industrial revolution transformed Britain. This new and unprecedented process was accompanied by the formation of a new social group, the 'middle class'. The 'middle class' was a major cause and beneficiary of these upheavals, and soon emerged as the focus of social and economic power. Ultimately the political system recognised the power of this new 'middle class', resulting in the Reform Bill of 1832, which admitted the 'middle class' into the parliament, which became no longer the exclusive preserve of the landed élite.[7] This convenient

---

[4] G. D. H. Cole, *Studies in Class Structure*, London 1955, p. 1. See also idem., "The Conception of the Middle Classes", *British Journal of Sociology* 1, (1950): 275–290.

[5] M. Mann, *The Sources of Social Power* vol. 2: *The Rise of Classes and Nation-States, 1760–1914*, Cambridge 1993, pp. 546–7.

[6] See especially Butler and Savage, *Social Change and the Middle Classes*.

[7] Wahrman, *Imagining the Middle Class*, pp. 1–2.

account is now recognized by many historians as unsatisfactory, many of whom even question the whole concept of an identifiable industrial revolution,[8] and in particular, its ability to drive social change. Despite this, Whiggish social historians like Asa Briggs,[9] and radical labour historians like E. P. Thompson,[10] still maintain that the half-century before the Reform Bill of 1832 witnessed an emergence of an identifiable middle class in English society. Their views are supported by other research that suggests the existence of a large and vibrant "middling" class in the eighteenth century, and even before.[11] What is now clear is that the transformation of the English social structure was a very long-term process that began well before there was any recognisable emergence of a distinct 'middle class'. *Pari passu*, such a phenomenon would sit comfortably in a schema propounded by Fernand Braudel.

When examined from the other end of this time span, the difficulty of identifying a distinct 'Victorian middle class' has been addressed by a number of historians. Apart from several 'Cottonopolis' towns, historians have found it difficult to identify a distinctive nation-wide industrial 'middle class' that would fit any Marxist stereotypes.[12] This has led some historians to present mid-Victorian society as 'bourgeoisified' and dominated by 'middle-class' ideals which have given rise to the perception of a so-called mid-Victorian 'age of equipoise'.[13] As Wahrman has suggested, "such a vision is broad and vague enough to countenance the lack of any demonstrable class specificity".[14] Other historians have come to exactly the opposite

---

[8] See N. F. R. Crafts, *British Economic Growth during the Industrial Revolution*, Oxford 1985; M. Fores, "The Myth of a British Industrial Revolution", *History* 66 (1981): 181–98; P. Mathias, "The Industrial Revolution: Concept and Reality", in P. Mathias and J. A. Davis (eds), *The First Industrial Revolutions*, Oxford 1990, pp. 1–24.

[9] See A. Briggs, *A Social History of England*, London 1994.

[10] See E. P. Thompson, The Making of the English Working Class, London 1980.

[11] See especially L. Stone, "Social Mobility in England, 1500–1700", *Past and Present* 33 (1966): 16–55, and G. Holmes, *Augustan England: Professions, State and Society, 1680–1730*, London 1982.

[12] See T. Koditscheck, *Class Formation and Urban-Industrial Society: Bradford 1750–1850*, London 1990; and R. J. Morris, *Class, Sect and Party; The Making of the British Middle Class: Leeds 1820–50*, Manchester 1990.

[13] W. L. Burn, *The Age of Equipoise*, London 1964.

[14] Wahrman, *Imagining the Middle Class*, p. 5. Wahrman points out that a notable proponent of such a view is H. Perkin, in *The Origins of Modern English Society 1780–1880*, London 1969.

conclusion, suggesting that a distinct and long-lasting middle class did not exist at all in the nineteenth century, only a *perception* of one.[15]

Of those historians that are happy to accept the existence of a distinct middle class,[16] some have suggested that the middle classes were not only divided by status but by other competing forms of social identity.[17] Political parties and religious sects and denominations attracted fierce loyalties that frequently disrupted effective class action especially in educational, cultural and charitable ventures.[18] Both Perkin and Briggs have described a progression from religious to class divisions, suggesting that one acted as a 'midwife' to the other.[19] Political studies of the period have shown the power of religious and party loyalties during the 1830s and 1840s[20] and these remained important in some of the mill towns until the 1890s.[21] Cultural studies have suggested that they were recreating society in their own image[22] and some attention has been given to the influence of agencies of the state such as education[23] and the new police.[24] The use of a variety of voluntary societies enabled the middle classes to engage in public social action, and the actions and records of these societies enable the historian to identify different aspects of middle-class ideology with

---

[15] See especially W. L. Arnstein, "The Myth of the Triumphant Victorian Middle Class", *The Historian* 37 (1975): 205–21; M. J. Weiner, *English Culture and the Decline of the Industrial Spirit 1850–1980*, London 1981; and P. Anderson, "The Figures of Descent" in P. Anderson (ed.), *English Questions*, London 1992, pp. 121–92.

[16] See especially G. Stedman Jones, *Languages of Class: Studies in English Working Class History 1832–1982*, London 1983; and P. Joyce, *Visions of the People: Industrial England and the Question of Class 1848–1914*, London 1991.

[17] R. J. Morris, *Class, Sect and Party*, p. 12. Cf. P. Bailey, *Leisure and Class in Victorian England*, London 1978.

[18] G. Kitson Clark, *The Making of Victorian England*, London 1962, pp. 145–205.

[19] H. Perkin, *Origins*, pp. 196–208, and A. Briggs, *The Age of Improvement 1783–1867*, London 1959, pp. 66–74.

[20] D. Fraser, *Urban Politics in Victorian England: The Structure of Politics in Victorian Cities*, Leicester 1976; E. P. Hennock, *Fit and Proper Persons: Ideal and Reality in Nineteenth-Century Urban Government*, London 1973.

[21] P. Joyce, *Work, Society and Politics: The Culture of the Factory in later Victorian Britain*, Brighton 1980, pp. 1–49 and 134–267.

[22] J. F. C. Harrison, *Learning and Living 1790–1960*, London 1961, pp. 38–58.

[23] R. Johnson, "Educational Policy and Social Control in Early Victorian England", *Past and Present* 49 (1970): 96–119.

[24] R. D. Storch, "The Policeman as Domestic Missionary: Urban Discipline and Popular Culture in Northern England, 1850–1880", *Journal of Social History* 9, 4 (1976): 481–509.

specific social actions.[25] This is how the ideas and value of the middle classes achieved such widespread social influence.

R. S. Neale has summarised[26] the different ways in which historians have used the concept of class and showed that there are real problems of conceptualization and terminology, which in turn have led to problems and differences in interpretation between the various categories of historical studies of class. He suggests that historians ought to agree on a common terminology for class and points to the necessity of distinguishing stratum, occupation, class and class-consciousness, as well as re-emphasising differences between Marx's notion of class-consciousness and what is better thought of as class perception.[27] He recommends the use of Dahrendorf's five-class model.[28] This is based on the idea of the existence of a middling class, which is identified by a class-consciousness that arose out of "perceptions of the nature and distribution of power in society and of people's places in it."[29] Neale argues that despite criticisms that the model is too sociologically based, the idea that *perceptions* of the connections between property and power are important for class-consciousness, is one which historians could use as well. Sadly, much of Neale's carefully reasoned argument has been either dismissed[30] or ignored by other historians; and a simpler, three-class model continues to be seen as "the natural way to think about class in an industrial society".[31] R. J. Morris has pointed out that even those who wish to change from this system retain the terminology of three classes, "amalgamating and sub-dividing them according to need".[32]

While historians today continue to debate the definition and even the existence of a middle class, for a person living in the mid-nineteenth century, the reality of such a group was unquestioned. A contemporary would have understood that there were three principal determinants of "class": income, occupation and education. That is not to say that there were not other factors, for such things as standard of

---

[25] R. J. Morris, "Voluntary Societies and British Urban Elites 1780–1850: An Analysis", *Historical Journal* 26 (1983): 95–118.

[26] R. S. Neale, "Class and Class-Consciousness in Early Nineteenth-Century England: Three Classes or Five?" *Victorian Studies* 12, 4 (June 1969): 5–32; and R. S. Neale, *Class in English History*, Oxford 1981.

[27] Neale, *Class in English History*, pp. 118–9.

[28] R. Dahrendorf, *Class and Class Conflict in an Industrial Society*, London 1959.

[29] Neale, *Class in English History*, p. 153.

[30] See R. J. Morris, *Class and Class Consciousness in the Industrial Revolution 1780–1850*, Macmillan 1979, pp. 33–4.

[31] Ibid., p. 32.

[32] Ibid.

dress, number of servants, types of transportation (carriage, cart or foot)[33] also served to categorize families into a particular social class.[34] The family background of a person also outweighed any other consideration, for if the family was already moving in the 'right circles', nothing else mattered. But Victorians were acutely aware of, and interested in, individual income. It is, therefore, perhaps not surprising that economists of education have also joined sociologists and historians in the study of class.

The Victorian Middle Class

Frank Musgrove attempted to define the Victorian "middle middle class" as consisting of those whose salaries ranged between £200 and £1,000. Those in receipt of an income between £60 and £200 he called "lower middle class"; and those whose income was over £1,000 (exclusive of the nobility and landed gentry), were described as "upper middle class".[35] Despite the use of income as his main criterion, Musgrove was well aware that this could not be used in isolation from "family background, type of education and occupation"[36] and he recognized social classification according to salary as "very unreliable", especially in a small community.[37] Such a definition, although convenient, still fails to distinguish between the middle and upper classes, for "an increase of income could not promote a middle-class manufacturer into the ranks of the gentry, and a slide into poverty would not necessarily mean that a gentleman could not remain one." Another problem in applying income as a guide to class is the fact that the most common measure of income—income tax returns—is notoriously unreliable. R. Dudley Baxter first attempted to determine the levels of middle and upper class income on this basis in 1868.[38] Quite apart from inaccuracies created by tax avoidance, the income of a particular individual might have been listed under several different schedules,[39] and company and individual incomes were not

---

[33] Morris, *Class, Sect and Party*, p. 11.
[34] See J. A. Banks, *Prosperity and Parenthood*, London 1954, p. 86.
[35] F. Musgrove, "Middle-Class Education and Employment in the Nineteenth Century", *Economic History Review* 12 (August 1959): 99.
[36] Ibid., p. 100.
[37] Ibid.
[38] R. Dudley Baxter, *National Income: The United Kingdom*, London 1868.
[39] J. A. Banks, *Prosperity and Parenthood*, London 1954, pp. 103–104.

differentiated.[40] Yet despite these difficulties in applying income as a criterion, it has some utility value. One of these is the way in which it highlights the artificiality of the traditional distinctions between manual and white collar workers. For as E. J. Hobsbawm has shown, highly-paid workers in Victorian England—the so-called "aristocracy of labour"[41]—were, in fact, much closer in culture and outlook to "small shopkeepers, independent masters, foremen, managers and clerks" than they were to the lower strata of the labouring classes.[42]

If large income played a significant part in raising a man's status—despite his occupation—from "lower" to "middle" class, a similar process was at work drawing other families over the indistinct borderline between upper middle class and upper class. A large income enabled a man, despite his association with trade and manufacture, to send his son to one of the great public schools or to one of the new proprietary schools built to cope with increasing demand for upper-class education.[43] By means of such institutions, the newly enriched family could, through its junior members, better itself socially,[44] and the family might, in the next generation, move into the coveted circles of "gentlemen".[45] The reverse was also true: inability to pay for such an education could see upper-class families move down the social scale.

More useful than trying to classify social rank on the basis of income has been the effort to grade the Victorian middle classes according to occupation. A survey of contemporary newspapers, periodicals and pamphlets reveals a remarkable agreement throughout the first forty or fifty years of Victoria's reign concerning the basic or typical middle-class occupations. In 1839 the Dean of Chichester, George Chandler, spoke of the class "consisting in the country principally of farmers,—in towns of traders, clerks, and the superior

---

[40] J. C. Stamp, *British Incomes and Property: The Application of Official Statistics to Economic Problems*, London 1927, p. 432.

[41] See Thompson, *Making of the English Working Class*, p. 262. Thompson points out that this use of the term 'aristocracy' with reference to the skilled artisan was widespread in the early nineteenth century.

[42] E. J. Hobsbawm, "The Labour Aristocracy in 19th Century Britain", in J Saville (ed.), *Democracy and the Labour Movement*, London 1954, p. 202.

[43] B. Heeney, *Mission to the Middle Classes*, London 1969, pp. 5–6.

[44] F. Musgrove, "Middle-Class Families and Schools", *The Sociological Review* 7 (1959): 169–78.

[45] Cole, *Studies in Class Structure*, p. 64. The exemplar of this providing 'gentlemanly polish' was Thomas Arnold at Rugby: see T. W. Bamford, *The Rise of the Public Schools*, London 1967.

sort of mechanics."[46] In 1865, *The Guardian* referred to the middle classes as made up principally of farmers, retail dealers and clerks.[47] Twenty years later a writer in *Blackwood's Edinburgh Magazine* described the composition of the middle classes as "The vast mass of men who in this nation of shopkeepers have become more or less rich by generations of trade. The whole mercantile and commercial fraternity are included...All the professional classes are included...and the greater host of men...who are employed as managers and clerks in the conduct of the enormous trade of the country."[48]

An examination of these contemporary definitions of 'middle class' reveals two things: that nearly all such attempts included the basic trinity of farmers, tradesmen, and clerks; and that the borderlines on either side of middle-class occupations were very fuzzy. Even such a broad definition as the following; "The whole of that vast stratum of humanity which lies between those who live by manual labour on the one and those who belong to either the territorial or commercial aristocracy on the other"[49] is deficient, for it excluded the "aristocracy of labour", which formed a significant part of the lower middle classes. On the other hand, those, like Dean Chandler of Chichester, whose interest was chiefly in the less exalted occupational groups, tended to leave the professional men and wealthier capitalists out of account. The line between the upper middle class and the upper class also became less and less clear as many capitalists and merchants bought land and established themselves as country gentleman.

These ill-defined divisions did not deter R. Dudley Baxter from making an estimate of the numbers of the combined upper and middle classes in 1867. His task was not made easier by the sociological inadequacies of the census.[50] Baxter included the following occupations in the middle and upper classes: "All persons of rank and property; Officers; Agents; Learned Professions; Mercantile Men; Dealers, tradesmen, and persons who buy or sell; Owners; Masters and Mistresses; Superintendents; Collectors; Foremen; Measurers; Clerks; Shopmen; [and other] "Special Cases", [including] Farmers and

---

[46] G. Chandler, *An Address Delivered at the Opening of the Church of England Metropolitan Commercial School, Rose Street, January 28 1839*, London 1839, p. 23.

[47] *Guardian* 15 November 1865. Cited by Heeney, *Mission to the Middle Classes*, p. 6.

[48] "What has Become of the Middle Classes?", *Blackwood's Edinburgh Magazine* (August 1885): 176.

[49] T. E. Kebbel, "The Middle Classes", *National Review* 1 (1883): 688.

[50] Cole, *Studies in Class Structure*, p. 51; and D. C. Marsh, *The Changing Social Structure of England and Wales 1871–1951*, London 1958, p. 128.

Graziers, and their Sons...".[51] By using various categories,[52] he estimated the number of men and women pursuing these occupations in England and Wales, together with their families, to be 4,870,000 in 1867. Taking his estimate of the total population in the same year (21,000,0000)[53] this would mean that the middle classes comprised 23% of the population at that time.

Most of the Churchmen who entered the field of secondary or middle-class education were not shy of using the occupational criterion to delineate their field of educational endeavour. Nathaniel Woodard is a case in point. According to Brian Heeney, Woodard felt that the great range of occupations covered by the term "middle class" made necessary "different schools offering education suitable to the different categories within that class."[54] His first school was originally planned for "the sons of gentlemen of small incomes, solicitors, surgeons with limited practice, unbeneficed clergymen, naval and military officers."[55] The second school was for the central middle-class occupations of "tradesmen, farmers and clerks";[56] his third or "lower middle school" was for the "sons of tradesmen, small farmers, mechanics, and others of limited means."[57] This threefold pattern had already been worked out at Liverpool in the 1840s.[58] It was also used in the 1860s by the Taunton Commission,[59] which adopted an occupational criterion to

---

[51] Dudley Baxter, *National Income*, p. 81.
[52] Ibid., p. 13.
[53] Ibid., p. 15.
[54] Heeney, *Mission to the Middle Classes*, p. 8.
[55] N. Woodard, *A Plea for the Middle Classes*, n.p., 1848, p. 4.
[56] *The Calendar of S. Nicolas College Shoreham...*, Shoreham 1850, p. 17.
[57] *The Calendar of The College of S. Nicolas, Lancing...*, London 1859, p. 23.
[58] Liverpool College was founded in 1842, after "friends of the established Church", mostly merchants and clergymen, met in order to found a Church of England school in Liverpool, where Roman Catholic children were already provided for. The first principal was Revd W. J. Conybeare, author of "Church Parties". See J. Murphy, *The Religious Problem in English Education*, Liverpool 1959, and D. Wainwright, *Liverpool Gentlemen: A History of Liverpool College*, London 1960.
[59] The Royal Commission of 1864–67, otherwise known as the Schools Inquiry Commission (SIC) or Taunton Commission, after its chairman, Henry Labouchere (1798–1869), the first Baron Taunton. The Taunton Commission was established to examine those schools in England not already covered by two previous Royal Commissions: the Clarendon Commission (1861–64) on the nine major public schools, and the Newcastle Commission (1858–61) on elementary education.

categorize secondary schools in a way almost identical to Woodard's schema.[60]

Victorians often indicated the meaning of "middle class" by reference to education. The typical middle-class father required a certain type or types of schooling for his son. It was "an education which differed both in the quantity and quality from that provided in the great public schools as it differed too from that provided in the many elementary schools of the country."[61] This norm of middle-class education was a reality despite the presence at one extreme of many sons of the upper mercantile and professional classes at public and proprietary schools, and at the other, of many sons of small farmers and tradesmen at parochial schools. In Victorian times, a secondary education was a requirement of the middle and upper classes. It was not the continuation of an elementary education shared with the working classes. This is why the Taunton Commission found it necessary to attempt an estimate of the number of middle and upper class children, as an essential preliminary to reporting on the state of secondary schooling.[62] It was not until the twentieth century that the term "secondary education"[63] as part of a three-tiered system, achieved its modern meaning in Britain.[64]

One way of determining the make-up of the middle classes was by reference to the school-leaving age of children requiring secondary education. This was the method adopted by the Taunton Commissioners, who divided parents of secondary school schoolboys into three groups. The first consisted of those people whose sons remained at school until at least eighteen years of age. This group, which contained "Bankers, manufacturers, and others of large mercantile business",[65] sought (and could afford) an education of the sort provided for the sons of "gentlemen of independent means" and "professional gentlemen". Below this upper level was a large number of parents who wished their sons to remain at school until about the age of sixteen; this segment of society consisted of, according to the Commissioners, the "Sons of Tradesmen in considerable business,

---

[60] For Woodard's schools, see below pp. 110–15.
[61] Heeney, *Mission to the Middle Classes*, p. 8.
[62] Report of Her Majesty's Commissioners appointed to Inquire into the Education given in Schools not comprised within Her Majesty's Two Former Commissions…(SIC Report), 1868, vol. 1, Appendix 2, pp. 6–27.
[63] For a discussion of how and when the term 'secondary education' gained currency in England, see J. H. Higginson, "Evolution of 'Secondary Education'", *British Journal of Educational Studies* 10, 2 (1972): 165–77.
[64] S. J. Curtis, *History of Education in Great Britain*, London 1948, p. 319.
[65] Heeney, *Mission to the Middle Classes*, pp. 8–9.

Farmers, Agents, Managers, Upper Clerks."[66] The third and largest group of parents of secondary schoolboys was that which consisted of people who could afford to permit their sons full-time schooling only to the age of fourteen; these people were described as "tradesmen in limited business, shopmen, clerks, upper artisans."[67]

This classification corresponds with the various definitions of middle class which had been made on the basis of occupation. Indeed, D. R. Fearon, the Assistant Commissioner whose report covered the metropolitan area, made explicit the identification between the families of such boys and members of the middle classes:

> Middle-Class boys are boys whose general education ends between their 14th and their 19th years of age....It will be convenient to divide them into three grades....By the first grade is meant those boys who stay at school till they are in their $18-19^{th}$ years of age. This grade is numerically small. It touches upon and is often blended and confused with the upper scholars....By the second grade is meant those who stay at school till they are in their $16-17^{th}$ years of age. This is in every respect the most genuinely 'middle' of any part of the class. By the third grade is meant those who stay at school only until they are in their $14-15^{th}$ year of age. The boys of this grade approach nearest to and are often blended and confused with the scholars of the primary and lower schools.[68]

This common understanding of middle-class schools provides the basis for the present study, which, in using the definition above, includes mainly first- and second-grade schools. However, it will be shown that a great demand arose for schools described by the Taunton Commission as second or third grade schools. Heeney has suggested that "those who created this demand and those who filled the wide variety of institutions which sought to meet this need, formed the nucleus of the middle class."[69] These were the parents who considered parochial schools as beneath them,[70] and the first-grade schools as far too expensive. Neither would they accept what was regarded as the degenerate classical teaching of many of the endowed grammar schools. For them, a whole new generation of middle-class schools was required—the subject of the rest of this chapter.

Using the criteria of income, occupation, and education, it is possible to discover, if not quite define, the Victorian middle class.

---

[66] SIC Report, vol. 1, Appendix 2, p. 12.
[67] Ibid.
[68] SIC Report vol. 7, p. 237.
[69] Heeney, *Mission to the Middle Classes*, p. 10.
[70] See the leading article in *The Guardian* 13 December 1865, p. 1.

The conviction that such a class existed, as well as the difficulty of circumscribing it with any precision, were both also maintained by the Victorians themselves. "What do we mean by the middle classes?" asked a clergyman in 1861. He went on to supply an answer: "It is not easy to answer this question; for society in England is happily so constituted that all are blended together, and the whole nation is truly one...[But] in the society around us we see clearly an upper, a middle, and a lower class, whose broad features make it easy to keep them distinctly separate, while between each of these lie classes which cannot be so clearly distinguished."[71] This nineteenth-century description of a three-fold class system will be used in the examination of the educational provision for the middle class that follows.

Secondary Education

Just as English society was based on a hierarchy of class, education at all levels was organized also on class lines. Be they grammar school teachers at the beginning of the century,[72] or Royal Commissioners in the closing years,[73] contemporaries regarded secondary education as middle-class education. Furthermore, it was widely recognized that there was a "distinction between the educational needs of the wage-earning class and those of the mercantile or professional class."[74] The elementary schools on the one hand and the secondary schools on the other were believed to satisfy the educational needs of these two classes, with a scholarship ladder providing a link between them. "Primary and Secondary Education", it was argued, "cannot be compared respectively to the lower and upper storeys of a single tenement. They are rather to be figured as two adjacent tenements, with an easy passage from near the top of the lower to the mezzanine

---

[71] F. V. Thornton, *The Education of the Middle Classes in England. A Lecture Delivered to members of the Mechanics Institute, Romsey...*, London 1862, pp. 4–5.

[72] O. Banks, *Parity and Prestige in English Secondary Education*, London 1955, p. 17.

[73] The Royal Commission on Secondary Education 1894–5 was known after its chairman, James Bryce (1838–1922) and limited secondary education to endowed grammar schools, public schools, private and proprietary schools. See A. M. Kazamias, *Politics, Society and Secondary Education in England*, Philadelphia, Penn., 1966, pp. 26–99; and R. C. Lilley, "Attempts to Implement the Bryce Commission's Recommendations—and the consequences", *History of Education* 11, 2 (1982): 99–111.

[74] Presidential address, Annual General Meeting of the Incorporated Association of Headmasters, January 1898.

floor of the higher of the two houses."[75] For Matthew Arnold, who had been urging the British government to "organize your secondary education" for over quarter of a century,[76] this meant the provision of adequate public schools for the growing middle classes.[77] In order to survey middle-class education in the nineteenth century, it is necessary to turn to some of the more detailed studies of secondary education over this period.[78]

Until John Roach produced his comprehensive survey of English secondary education,[79] no synoptic history of English secondary education[80] had been published since that of R. L. Archer in 1921.[81] There have been other, detailed, examinations of developments within secondary education, namely Olive Banks's sociological study[82] and Brian Simon's survey of the history of politico-educational ideas from 1780–1870.[83] Specific studies of the development of middle-class schools of a semi-public or 'private foundation' (to use a term coined by Roach), had been undertaken by Heeney[84] and more recently, David Allsobrook:[85] the latter being inspired by an earlier study by Roach on the establishment of the public examination system.[86] Of related interest, but by definition mainly concerned with the upper rather than

---

[75] R. P. Scott (ed.), *What is Secondary Education?*, London 1899, p. 168.

[76] See M. Arnold, "A French Eton; or, Middle Class Education and the State", London 1864, p. 139, in G Sutherland (ed.) *Matthew Arnold on Education*, Harmondsworth 1973, pp. 115–164; W. F. Connell, *The Educational Thought and Influence of Matthew Arnold*, London 1950.

[77] W. F. Connell, *The Foundations of Secondary Education*, Melbourne, Australia 1967, p. 1.

[78] It is confined here to books and monographs. Relevant articles will be referred to in the text and listed in the bibliography. A useful overview of educational records is provided by W. B. Stephens, *Sources for English Local History*, Cambridge 1981, ch. 7.

[79] In two volumes: J. Roach, *A History of Secondary Education in England 1800–1870*, London 1986; and *Secondary Education in England 1870–1902*, London 1991.

[80] There is, of course, a long tradition of histories of secondary education *per se*, which tend to start with Greek and Roman education, and take a more global perspective. The exemplar here would be the American history of education textbook, I. L. Kandel, *History of Secondary Education*, Cambridge, Mass., 1930.

[81] R. L. Archer, *Secondary Education in the Nineteenth Century*, London 1921.

[82] Banks, *Parity and Prestige*.

[83] B. Simon, *Studies in the History of Education 1780–1870*, London 1960.

[84] Heeney, *Mission to the Middle Classes*.

[85] D. I. Allsobrook, *Schools for the Shires: The Reform of Middle-class Education in mid-Victorian England*, Manchester 1986.

[86] J. Roach, *Public Examinations in England 1850–1900*, London 1971.

the middle classes, have been works on the development of the public school system by T. W. Bamford,[87] Brian Gardner[88] and John Honey.[89] While Bamford only touches on middle-class education in his discussion of Victorian public schools,[90] Gardner develops this theme much further[91] and Honey provides the first major study of 'public schools for the middle classes'[92] since Heeney. Mention should also be made of those studies that examine the development of the English educational system as a social institution rather than as an historical phenomenon. While P. W. Musgrave,[93] and Michael Sanderson[94] emphasise the social and economic, Peter Searby and others[95] have shown that it is possible to include such considerations within a mainstream historical approach.

Any examination of secondary education in the nineteenth century is complicated by the fact it was not represented by any single institution. Until the turn of the century, the grammar schools and the private schools were seen to fulfil this role. However, as will be shown below, many grammar schools developed different functions and, despite legal[96] and other restrictions on their curricula, successfully adapted and evolved to meet a new need. Private schools are also notoriously difficult to pinpoint in terms of their educational provision during this period, partly due to their unofficial and (in many cases) ephemeral status, as well as the extreme variations in the quality and

---

[87] T. W. Bamford, *The Rise of the Public Schools*, London 1967.
[88] B. Gardner, *The Public Schools*, London 1973.
[89] J. R. de S. Honey, *Tom Brown's Universe*, London 1977. This is largely based upon idem., "The Victorian Public School, 1828–1902: The School as Community", DPhil thesis, Oxford University 1970.
[90] See Bamford, *Rise of the Public Schools*, ch. 9.
[91] See Gardner, *Public Schools*, ch. 8.
[92] See Honey, *Tom Brown's Universe*, chs 1 and 2.
[93] P. W. Musgrave, *The Sociology of Education*, London 1979, and idem., *Society and Education in England Since 1800*, London 1968.
[94] M. Sanderson, *Education, Economic Change and Society in England 1780–1870*, London 1983; idem., *Educational Opportunity and Social Change in Britain*, London 1987.
[95] See A. Digby and P. Searby, *Children, School and Society in Nineteenth-Century England*, London 1981; and P. Searby (ed.), *Educating the Victorian Middle Class: Proceedings of the 1981 Annual Conference of the History of Education Society of Great Britain*, Leicester 1982.
[96] In 1805 the Chancellor, Lord Eldon, handed down a Court of Chancery judgement that prevented the governors of Leeds Grammar School (and thereby any other grammar school) from making changes to the classical curriculum which was laid down by the founder. See A. C. Price, *A History of Leeds Grammar School*, London 1919, pp. 133–50.

type of education they provided.[97] They have also had a bad press: the cruel caricatures of Charles Dickens[98] or the devastating satire of Matthew Arnold[99] began a tradition of private school criticism which may have reduced the amount of research interest in this sector of secondary education. Only a few attempts have been made to describe private education.[100] The most recent survey by Roach groups the many different sizes and different types of private schools under the general title of 'private foundation school'.[101] He suggests that these schools were all in their different ways semi-private *and* semi-public, and that this is a convenient term to describe those schools that fell between these two extremes. Some private schools even went on to become endowed like the grammar schools.

Historians of education frequently state that grammar schools had declined by the end of the eighteenth century,[102] and there is much evidence for this. However, it has been recently suggested that it would be better to describe these schools as having become 'differentiated' rather than having 'declined': "Some of them had risen into the group of boarding schools from which the nineteenth-century public schools were to emerge. Others had become parish schools teaching elementary subjects, the three Rs of reading, writing and arithmetic."[103] This last type of grammar school straddled the two worlds of secondary and elementary education. They taught the classics to a few boys, some of whom went on to university, and they gave a more limited education—part classical, part modern—to a more numerous group of boys who left early to enter business or trade. Many grammar schools were very successful in attracting boarders and

---

[97] The parliamentary paper, *Return of the Pupils in Public and Private Secondary and Other Schools in England*, 1897, vol. 70, provides useful information on these schools. I am indebted to W. B. Stephens for this reference.

[98] In *Nicolas Nickelby*, Dickens created the archtype in Mr Squeers of Dotheboys Hall.

[99] See, for example, M. Arnold, *Friendship's Garland: Being the Conversations, Letters and Opinions of the late Arminius, Baron von Thunder-Ten-Tronckh*, London 1871.

[100] One of these is D. P. Leinster-Mackay, "The English Private School 1830–1914, with Special Reference to the Private Preparatory School", PhD thesis, Durham University 1972.

[101] Roach, *Secondary Education in England 1800–1870*, p. 7.

[102] See N. Hans, *New Trends in Education in the Eighteenth Century*, London 1951, and R. S. Tomson, *Classics or Charity? The Dilemma of the 18th Century Grammar School*, Manchester 1971.

[103] Roach, *A History of Secondary Education in England 1800–1870*, p. 3.

paying day pupils as well as having boys 'on the foundation'.[104] In this way the grammar schools tended to be private schools as well, and "those that succeeded did so because they had been able to develop the private side".[105] The reports of the first Charity Commissioners (1818–37)[106] made it clear that a successful school was one in which the master had succeeded in attracting boarders and day pupils as well as having boys on the foundation.

The leaders of the other type of endowed school, the public school, were identified by the Clarendon Commission (1861–4)[107] as consisting of nine 'great' schools: Eton, Winchester, Westminster, Harrow, Rugby, Shrewsbury, Charterhouse, plus the two London day schools, St Paul's and Merchant Taylors'.[108] In addition to these 'Clarendon schools', as they came to be known, a number of old grammar schools, like Tonbridge, Repton, and Sherborne, were slowly moving, under efficient headmasters, towards public school status.[109] This ranking was also rapidly being acquired by many of the new Victorian public schools[110] like Cheltenham, Marlborough, Rossall and Wellington: what the Clarendon Commission described as "The four Chief Modern Proprietary Schools". By the end of the century the public school community consisted of about 100 schools, made up

---

[104] B. Simon has argued that as a result of this, the middle classes came to enjoy "a subsidised system of secondary education", which was established at the expense of the working class, who were "edged out of the grammar schools where free education had hitherto been available." B. Simon, *History of Education*, p. 335.

[105] Roach, *A History of Secondary Education in England 1800–1870*, p. 8.

[106] In 1816 Henry Brougham (1778–1868) chaired a select committee into the education of the poor in London. Under his initiative, Parliament set up the Charity Commission in 1818, a national inquiry into educational charities which came to be known as the Brougham Inquiry. See D. Owen, *English Philanthropy 1660–1960*, Cambridge, Mass., 1965, ch. 7.

[107] See the Report of Her Majesty's Commissioners on Revenues and Management of Certain Colleges and Schools…(Clarendon Report), and C. Shrosbee, *Public Schools and Private Education: The Clarendon Commission 1861–64 and the Public Schools Acts*, Manchester 1988.

[108] Though only the first seven were covered by the *Public Schools Act* of 1868. These nine "great" schools are sometimes referred to as the 'Clarendon Schools', after the Chairman of the Royal Commission, G. W. F. V. Hyde (1800–1870), the fourth Earl of Clarendon.

[109] A. F. Leach has suggested that historically there was no difference between a 'public' and a 'grammar' school, and that the cleavage had grown up in the nineteenth century as better communications made it easier to concentrate the boys of the upper classes into a few schools. A. F. Leach, *Early Yorkshire Schools* vol. 2, Leeds 1903, lxxxv.

[110] See Gardner, *Public Schools*, pp. 159–208.

from these three groups, though they differed widely in status and importance among themselves.[111] Honey has attempted to identify these schools by using some nineteenth-century school lists.[112] The six schools which are the main subject of this study—Cheltenham College, Trent College, Monkton Combe School, Weymouth College, South-Eastern College and Dean Close School—all appear at different times in these lists. Certainly by the end of the century, each of these schools was being described as a 'public school'.

The history of English public schools has attracted much attention from modern scholars, and this is one part of the story of nineteenth-century secondary education that has already been treated in considerable depth.[113] Roach has pointed out that it is extremely difficult to define a public school. In 1899, A. F. Leach argued that it was a school with high fees attracting the rich classes; that it was entirely or almost entirely a boarding school; that it was under the control of a public body, and that it drew its pupils from all parts of the country.[114] Honey has suggested that another possible contemporary determinant of public school status was academic success as measured by examination results.[115] Such a definition looks not only, as Leach did, to the preconditions, but also to what Roach describes as the 'product': "A public school could be judged in terms of how long it retained its pupils, how many of them went on to university and won university awards, how many of them entered the prestigious professions like the army, the law, and government service, and how many old boys attained distinction in their chosen careers."[116] Finally,

---

[111] Roach, *Secondary Education in England 1870–1902*, p. 119. The first *Public Schools Year Book*, published in 1889, limited its coverage to thirty schools, though that number was quickly enlarged. See Honey, *Tom Brown's Universe*, p. 250.

[112] Honey, *Tom Brown's Universe*, pp. 238–95.

[113] See E. C. Mack, *Public Schools and British Opinion Since 1860*, London 1941; V. Ogilvie, *The English Public School*, London 1957; D. Newsome, *Godliness and Good Learning*, London 1961; Bamford, *Rise of the Public Schools*; Gardner, *Public Schools*; B. Simon and I. Bradley, *The Victorian Public School*, London 1975; Honey, *Tom Brown's Universe*; J. A. Mangan, *Athleticism in the Victorian and Edwardian Public School*, London 1981; J. Chandos, *Boys Together*, London 1984; Roach, *Secondary Education in England 1800–1870*; Shrosbee, *Public Schools and Private Education*, and Roach, *Secondary Education in England 1870–1902*.

[114] A. F. Leach, *A History of Winchester College*, London 1899, p. 7. For further details on the regions that public school students were drawn from, see ch. 3 below, especially p. 133, fn. 35.

[115] Honey, *Tom Brown's Universe*, p. 244.

[116] Roach, *Secondary Education in England 1870–1902*, p. 119.

a school could be ranked as a public school simply because the public opinion of the day considered it to be such. This is why Honey's lists are historically, if not sociologially, valid. The same could be said for an institution that was often the precursor of a public school—the private foundation or private school.

During the eighteenth century, private schools had grown up in increasing numbers to serve the divergent needs of many different clientèle. Some of them offered a more modern curriculum than that provided by the grammar schools. They taught subjects like modern languages, surveying, and sometimes the natural sciences.[117] Many of the private schools taught the classics, just as many grammar schools offered modern subjects. Although attempts have been made to provide some statistics for the number of grammar school pupils at this time (based on the Charity Commissioners' Reports of 1819–37),[118] this has proved difficult in the case of private schools. One approach has been to use J. G. Fitch's report on the schools of West Riding for the Taunton Commission, and to make some generalizations based on this for the whole country. Fitch estimated that more than three-quarters of middle-class boys were educated in private schools in that area.[119] It has already been suggested that both contemporary and later historians have tended to undervalue the contribution made by private schools to the education of the Victorian middle class. What is clear is that between the beginning of the century and the 1860s, private schools grew in importance, just as many of the grammar schools declined.[120] It is also true to say that as the public schools grew in prestige after 1850, the private schools, "which had reached their heyday in the first half of the century",[121] began to decline.

The private schools were of many different sizes and of different types. The most common type was that owned by an individual or two or three partners, which was conducted for private profit. According to Roach, other schools were "at once semi-private or semi-public. They were public because they were owned and managed by groups of people sharing common and enduring interests. They were private because they lacked either the charters or the endowments of the old grammar schools and, like the schools owned by individuals, they had to pay their way in order to survive."[122] Because they possessed

---

[117] Some non-conformist academies were also teaching this wide range of subjects. See H. McLachlan, *English Education under the Test Acts,* Manchester 1933.
[118] See Roach, *Secondary Education in England 1800–1870*, pp. 56–7.
[119] SIC Report vol. 9, p. 255.
[120] Roach, *Secondary Education in England 1800–1870*, p. 4.
[121] Roach, *Secondary Education in England 1870–1902*, p. 157.
[122] Ibid., p. 157.

features of both private and public schools, Roach has suggested that the different schools within this class can be grouped together into a new category, which he has termed the 'private foundation school'.[123] Marlborough, Rossall and Bradfield are examples of schools which, in one generation, crossed the line from private foundation to public school. The same course was taken, though more slowly, by the schools founded by Woodard and by Evangelicals, as will be shown below. A substantial sub-group of these schools of private foundation are the proprietary schools, established by proprietors or shareholders, generally along the lines of the old classical grammar schools.

Although forming a prominent feature of the Taunton Commission Report, the unique nineteenth-century phenomenon of the proprietary school was, until recently, largely neglected by historians of education.[124] This paucity of research was first addressed by Donald Leinster-Mackay, who identified the commercial as well as the historical origins of these schools.[125] John Roach has also recently added to our understanding of this topic.[126] Both boarding and day schools were often set up under the joint stock principle[127] in the early 1800s. The first proprietary schools were all associated with religious groups: Mill Hill was set up in Middlesex by Congregationalists in 1808;[128] the Collegiate School at Leicester was founded by local Anglicans in 1836;[129] and a rival proprietary school was set up by Leicester Methodists in 1837.[130] Although there has always been some confusion about what characterises a proprietary school,[131] as a result of the *Joint Stock Companies Act* of 1856 and the *Limited Liability Companies Act* of 1862, most of these schools were recognizable by

---

[123] Roach, *Secondary Education in England 1800–1870*, p. 7.

[124] The first brief treatment is in Simon, *History of Education*, pp. 115–7.

[125] D. P. Leinster-Mackay, "English Proprietary Schools", *Educational Research* 8, 1 (1981): 44–56.

[126] Roach, *Secondary Education in England 1800–1870*, pp. 184–193 and idem., *Secondary Education in England 1870–1902*, pp. 215–227.

[127] For an explanation and historiography of the joint stock principle, see Leinster-Mackay, "English Proprietary Schools", pp. 45–6.

[128] See N. G. Brett James, *A History of Mill Hill School*, London, n.d.

[129] Known as the 'Leicester and Leicestershire Collegiate School', it closed in 1866 because of financial difficulties. See Z. Crook and B. Simon, "Private Schools in Leicester and the County 1780–1840", in *Education in Leicestershire 1540–1940*, edited by B. Simon, Leicester 1968, pp. 122–29. For a list of all of the middle-class schools mentioned in this work, together with their foundation dates, see Appendix 3.

[130] Known as 'The Proprietary School for the Town and County of Leicester'. See Crook and Simon, "Private Schools in Leicester and the County", pp. 122–29.

[131] Ibid., p. 45.

the consistent format of their constitutions.[132] The Taunton Commission included proprietary schools in its terms of reference for public schools together with endowed grammar schools, and listed some 123 proprietary schools altogether. It categorized them into three grades. The first grade included schools such as Liverpool, Cheltenham,[133] Marlborough,[134] Rossall,[135] Clifton,[136] Wellington[137] and Malvern.[138] Proprietary schools of the second grade included the County Schools[139] and Framlingham College in East Suffolk.[140] The Birkbeck schools in London were seen as examples of proprietary schools of the third grade.[141] The Taunton Commissioners noted, when categorizing examples of the 123 schools listed in their report, that many proprietary schools had moved away from the proprietary principle by becoming endowed. This included Marlborough, Bradfield,[142] and three of the schools founded by Woodard.[143]

---

[132] See Leinster-Mackay, "English Proprietary Schools", p. 47.

[133] Cheltenham College opened in 1841 with 146 boys. See below, pp. 132–43.

[134] Marlborough College was founded in 1843 for the sons of the "poorer professional classes and clergy." See A. G. Bradley, *A History of Marlborough College*, London 1893.

[135] Rossall School was founded as a proprietary school in 1844. It was started for similar reasons to Marlborough, *viz.* for the "sons of clergy and laymen of modest mans who sought a modern as well as a classical education". See St V. Beechey, *The Rise and Progress of Rossall School: A Jubilee Sketch*, London 1894, and W. Furness (ed.), *The Centenary History of Rossall School*, Aldershot 1945.

[136] Clifton College was founded in Bristol in 1861. See O. F. Christie, *A History of Clifton College 1860–1934*, Bristol 1935.

[137] Wellington College was opened in 1859 as a result of a public subscription in memory of the Duke of Wellington. It was aimed particularly at helping the sons of deceased army officers. See R. St C. Talboys, *A Victorian School: Being the Story of Wellington College*, Oxford 1943, and D. Newsome, *A History of Wellington College 1859–1959*, London 1959.

[138] Malvern College was founded in 1865 through the efforts of two brothers named Burrow, who bottled the famous Malvern Waters. See R. Blumenau, *A History of Malvern College 1865 to 1965*, London 1965.

[139] See below, pp. 117–24.

[140] See below, pp. 122–23.

[141] William Ellis, the promoter of civic studies in Victorian England, established these in different parts of London between 1848 and 1862. The Birkbeck Schools were regarded as "on the extreme fringe of secondary education", and might be better described as having offered superior elementary education to the upper-working class. See T. D. Wickenden, *William Ellis School 1862–1962*, London 1962, and W. A. C. Stewart and W. P. McCann, *The Educational Innovators 1750–1880*, London 1967, pp. 326–41.

[142] See below, pp. 106–7.

Proprietary schools such as these, which chose to strengthen their financial arrangements and the power of the headmaster, were more likely to survive and flourish.

The Taunton Commissioners reported that the fortunes of the proprietary schools had varied during the first thirty or forty years of their history. Depending largely upon the support of individuals for their capital outlay, it was only to be expected that some would be short-lived. For example, seven in London and eleven outside the capital, had either ceased entirely or had become private schools whose headmasters were also their proprietors. Despite this, the Taunton Commissioners reported: "the history of these schools is in a great degree the history of the recent struggles for the improvement of secondary schools".[144] Commercially they were not successful. In the majority of cases, dividends were neither paid nor expected; where they were looked for, the percentage was limited by by-law or by custom. Capital or dividends, where they were earned, were surrendered for the good of the cause.[145] Yet the Commissioners stated: "the educational character of proprietary schools stands very high...and they gain and deserve the favour of the public almost as soon as they are formed".[146] There was another reason why they were so successful, and this was because they catered for a clientèle which was increasingly class conscious.

In the nineteenth century there was a growing reluctance by parents and masters to countenance the education of children of different social ranks in the same school. One advantage of a proprietary school was that entry was restricted to shareholders. Directors could veto the transfer of shares to parents who were seen to be from the 'wrong' social grouping, and in this way they controlled pupil admission. The Taunton Commission reported on this tendency: "At Cheltenham College, and some other schools of this class, it is understood that the sons of the shopkeepers would not be admitted. 'At Clifton College and at Sydney College, Bath', says Mr Stanton, 'the governing body retain in their hands the power of rejecting any boy whom they do not consider qualified socially for the school; and as a fact would not admit the son of any resident tradesman.'"[147] Because boys of different social classes had different educational requirements, it was common to think in terms of separate schools for boys who intended to leave at

---

[143] Lancing, Hurstpierpoint and Ardingly, all in Sussex. See below, pp. 110–14.
[144] SIC Report, vol. 1, p. 314.
[145] In the case of Clifton College, the shareholders surrendered their rights when a royal charter was granted in 1877. Christie, *Clifton College*, pp. 91–2.
[146] SIC Report, vol. 1, p. 318.
[147] Ibid., p. 317.

different ages. The Taunton Commission recommended that middle-class schools be re-organized into three grades using the same categories that Woodard had put forward twenty years earlier.[148] The first grade of school with a classical curriculum would prepare boys for the universities. The second would train boys up to the age of sixteen or seventeen with a view to professional and managerial careers, while the third would carry them up to fifteen or sixteen years only.[149] The Commission also investigated girls' private schools, examining witnesses such as Miss Emily Davies, Miss Frances M. Buss, and Miss Dorothea Beale. They reported that the existing girls' schools were unsatisfactory and this new concern for the education of girls led to the founding of the Girls' Public Day School Company (later Trust) in 1872,[150] and the Church Schools Company in 1883—a subject which will be discussed later.[151]

The Taunton Commission's other recommendations amounted to no less than a complete overhaul of English secondary education, or what has been described as "the most extensive exercise in state intervention in secondary education since the days of the Tudors and Stuarts."[152] The primary need was seen as a thorough revision of the constitutions and the governing bodies of the endowed schools. Where necessary, newly endowed schools would be established and all the schools would be placed under permanent supervision by an enlarged and reconstituted Charity Commission, presided over by a Minister of Education. The *Endowed Schools Act* of 1869[153] gave commissioners powers to impose these schemes of reorganization. Within four years they had published 317 schemes. Controversy surrounding this review led to the appointment of a select committee in 1873, which ultimately praised the commissioners for their good work but admonished them for being over-zealous and too outspoken.[154] Leinster-Mackay has reviewed some twentieth-century judgements of the Act[155] and describes them as ranging from being relatively non-accusatory and

---

[148] See below, pp. 111–12.

[149] SIC Report, vol. 1, pp. 310–11.

[150] See p. 100 fn. 261.

[151] See below, pp. 100–2.

[152] Roach, *A History of Secondary Education in England 1800–1870*, p. 305.

[153] 32 and 33 Vict. 1869: 197–208. Cap. 56.

[154] *Report of Select Committee on the Operation of the Endowed Schools Act 1869*, 1873, p. iii.

[155] D. P. Leinster-Mackay, "The Endowed Schools Legislation, 1869–1874: Some Differences of Interpretation", *Educational Studies* 13, 3 (1987): 223.

balanced,[156] to the Act being seen as "a piece of 'class legislation'",[157] or a full-blown "middle-class conspiracy".[158] Many nineteenth-century headmasters and educationalists reacted "in haste and alarm"[159] to this new legislation.

Headmasters and governors of both the old grammar schools and the new foundations felt very apprehensive about their position under the 1869 *Endowed Schools Act*, fearing that their work would be damaged by outside interference. Particular fears were expressed about the initial proposals for inspection and examination, though these were dropped before the Act was passed.[160] The Headmasters[161] responded by creating a 'defence association' which developed into the Headmasters Conference.[162] Some Evangelicals saw the *Endowed Schools Act* as the 'wedge' that would lead to the "undenomination-alizing and secularizing of our middle-class grammar schools".[163] The editor of the Evangelical *Record* urged the foundation of new Church of England public schools, because "the Endowed Schools Act practically severed the connection which up to that time had more or less directly existed between the grammar schools throughout the country and the Church of England."[164] Other Churchmen delayed any plans that were already under way for new schools, until the effects of

---

[156] See Archer, *Secondary Education*, pp. 167–76, and J. W. Adamson, *English Education 1789–1902*, pp. 258–94.

[157] See P. Gordon, *Selection for Secondary Education*, London 1980, pp. 1–143; F. E. Balls, "The Endowed Schools Act 1869 and the Development of the English Grammar Schools in the Nineteenth Century", *The Durham Research Review* 5, 19 (1967): 207–16 & 20 (1968): 219–29; G. Gomez, "The Endowed Schools Act, 1869—A Middle-Class Conspiracy?", *Journal of Educational Administration and History* 6, 1 (1974): 9–18; G. Cannell, "Resistance to the Charity Commissioners: the Case of St. Paul's Schools, 1860–1904", *History of Education* 10, 4 (1981): 245–62.

[158] See especially Simon, *History of Education*, pp. 318–36; and idem., *Education and the Labour Movement 1870–1920*, London 1965, pp. 97–120.

[159] Leinster-Mackay, "The Endowed Schools Legislation, 1869–1874", p. 223.

[160] The *Endowed Schools Act* of 1869 stated that no scheme was to be made for an endowment set up less than fifty years before the passing of the Act without the consent of the governing body. However, before the Endowed Schools Bill became law, the clauses providing for examination and inspection were removed. P. Gordon, *Selection for Secondary Education*, p. 36.

[161] Particularly Edward Thring of Uppingham School. See D. P. Leinster-Mackay, *The Educational World of Edward Thring*, London 1987, pp. 97–105.

[162] See G. Baron, "The Origins and Early History of the Headmasters' Conference, 1869–1914", *Educational Review* 7 (1954–5): 223–34; and A. C. Percival, *The Origins of the Headmasters Conference*, London 1969.

[163] *Record*, 1 March 1882, p. 2.

[164] Ibid.

the legislation became clearer. By the mid-1870s the threat of government intervention had faded after the supersession of the Endowed Schools Commission. Many of the endowed schools had been given their new schemes and found the arrangements tolerable. Some Churchmen decided that the way was open for new schools to be founded along denominational lines.

This type of 'private foundation' school with denominational affiliations was to make an important contribution to English education. All the major churches played a part. Some of these were simply the private ventures of individual ministers,[165] while others provided for the education of a Nonconformist community, which "still laboured under a social and legal stigma". Dissenters like the Methodists,[166] the Congregationalists,[167] and the Quakers[168] were all involved in secondary education.[169] The Roman Catholics ran both day grammar schools and boarding schools, which in the twentieth century would become leading public schools.[170] Within the Church of England, new 'private foundation' schools were founded by representatives of each of the High Church (including Tractarian and Anglo-Catholic), Broad Church and Evangelical traditions. It is to these new Church of England middle-class schools this chapter now turns.

---

[165] Many a country clergyman depended on his private pupils to supplement an inadequate stipend, and it was perhaps to accommodate these pupils that some of the spacious Victorian rectories were built. The dependence of many Dissenting ministers on their private schools was even greater.

[166] Wesley himself founded Kingswood in 1748, and Woodhouse Grove was established at Apperley Bridge in Yorkshire in 1812. See F. C. Pritchard, *Methodist Secondary Education*.

[167] As well as Mill Hill School (see fn. 128 above), the Congregationalists founded Lewisham in Surrey (1811) and Silcoates near Wakefield (1831) for the sons of their ministers.

[168] The Society of Friends set up their first higher-grade school at Ackworth in 1779, and others were founded at Quaker centres including Wigton in Cumberland (1815), and at York: Bootham (1823) and The Mount (1831). See W. A. C. Stewart, *Quakers and Education*, London 1953. Later foundations included Leighton Park (1890) and Gresham's (1900). Honey, *Tom Brown's Universe*, pp. 292–3.

[169] For a recent overview of Nonconformist secondary education, see Roach, *Secondary Education in England 1800–1870*, pp. 174–9. Other religious groups included the Moravians who founded a school at Fulneck, and the Jews who set up two schools at Finsbury and Palestine Place.

[170] For example, Stonyhurst (1794), Downside (1606/1814), Ampleforth (1608/1802), and John Henry Newman's Oratory School in London (1859). See H. O. Evennett, *The Catholic Schools of England and Wales*, London 1944.

High Church Schools

The first major undertaking to improve middle-class education was in the 1830s through the initiative of the National Society, "the educational shock-troops of the Church".[171] Members of the Church of England saw middle-class education as an important extension of the work which the National Society was already doing among the poor. It was rapidly becoming clear that the government would start "a more active interference" in the field of education, "particularly in that of training teachers".[172] In 1838 a group of High Churchmen[173] met with the National Society Committee in order to forestall this state action.[174] They included T. D. Acland;[175] the future Prime Minister, W. E. Gladstone;[176] the eminent Vicar of Leeds, W. F. Hook;[177] and the Member of Parliament, G. F. Mathison.[178] The instigator of the scheme seems to have been Mathison, who was to outline his ideas in a pamphlet, published in 1844.[179] He made the same point that Woodard

---

[171] Allsobrook, *Schools for the Shires*, p. 58.

[172] C. Birchenough, *History of Elementary Education*, London 1938, p. 270. For a history of teacher education, see R. W. Rich, *The Training of Teachers in England and Wales during the Nineteenth Century*, Cambridge 1933; A. Tropp, *The School Teachers*, London 1957; and H. C. Dent *The Training of Teachers in England and Wales 1800–1975*, London 1977.

[173] The National Society was regarded as a High Church enclave. It was founded in 1811 by three laymen—Joshua Watson, Henry Norris, and John Bowles—all of whom were described as "Tories and High Churchmen", and two of whom were closely associated with the SPCK. H. J. Burgess, *Enterprise in Education*, London 1958, p. 21.

[174] For the only in-depth description of the National Society's campaign of 1838–9, see J. Roach, *Public Examinations in England*, Cambridge 1971, pp. 45–8.

[175] Later, to be one of the founders of the Oxford Local Examinations. See A. H. D. Acland, *Memoir and Letters of the Rt. Hon. Sir Thomas Dyke Acland*, London 1902, and W. Tuckwell, *Reminiscences of Oxford*, London 1900, pp. 88–93.

[176] Gladstone and Acland had been friends at Oxford.

[177] Walter Farquhar Hook (1798–1875) was Vicar of Leeds 1837–59, during which time he became a prominent and controversial national figure. He supported a system of national elementary education financed by rates, and was responsible for founding up to 30 elementary schools in Leeds. In 1859 he was made Dean of Chichester.

[178] See Acland, *Memoir*, pp. 87–9.

[179] G. F. Mathison, *How Can the Church Educate the People? The Question Considered with Reference to the Incorporation and Endowment of Colleges for the Middle and Lower Classes of Society...*, London 1844. In later life T. D. Acland protested that Mathison's work "had seldom been adequately recognized". He was particularly distressed upon the publication of Dean

was to make a few years later: that the Church needed to extend its influence to "farmers, tradesmen, and mechanics". Like Woodard and Sewell,[180] Mathison wanted these new foundations to be corporate in character, where collegial bodies would be established to run both middle-class boarding schools and teacher training institutions.

The suggestions of the Mathison-Acland group were taken up at once by the National Society, which formed a new committee to carry out these plans. S. F. Wood, H. E. Manning, W. E. Gladstone, and other High Churchmen met in the spring of 1838 as 'The Committee of Inquiry and Correspondence' to set about the task of creating a national system of middle-class education. Among its proposals were the formation of diocesan boards of education and the establishment of teacher training colleges. 'Middle Schools' in the towns that already provided post-elementary education for the lower-middle classes were to be taken into union with the Society and a similar type of education was to be provided in the country districts.

The idea that clergy should form themselves into local boards, and through them keep in touch with the National Society, was first put forward by Francis Close early in 1839 at a great meeting in London, with Lord Ashley[181] in the chair.[182] During that year, no less than "15 new Diocesan Boards and many subordinate boards"[183] sprang up. The Gloucester and Bristol Diocesan Board of Education was one of these, and its Cheltenham branch was chaired by Francis Close. It provides the researcher with an interesting example of one of the earliest of these new diocesan board schools. The Cheltenham committee placed a notice in the *Cheltenham Journal* on 1 May 1839 to advertise the opening of "A Commercial School, for Boys".[184] In it, they stated that "Their object [was] to afford the Children of the Middle Classes a superior Education, on moderate terms, upon the principles of the Established Church."[185] The Cheltenham Diocesan Boys' School, as it came to be known, was intended to provide "a sound moral and Christian education, in connection with the Established Church."[186] In November 1839, it was decided to increase the number of pupils at the

---

Gregory's *Elementary Education*, to find "no mention of Mr. Mathison's name in it from beginning to end." Acland, *Memoir*, p. 88.
[180] William Sewell, founder and later Headmaster of Radley College, Oxfordshire. See below, pp. 104–6.
[181] Later, Lord Shaftesbury. See Appendix 1.
[182] *Cheltenham Journal*, 18 February 1839, p. 13.
[183] Cited by Burgess, *Enterprise in Education*, p. 73.
[184] *Cheltenham Journal* 6 May 1839, p. 2.
[185] Ibid.
[186] Ibid., 15 July 1839, p. 2.

Boys' School from 40 to 100 using new premises that would include a schoolroom and accommodation for the Headmaster.[187] By the summer of 1841, this school had been transferred to "the Music Hall, Regent Street"[188] and a new school was begun in Vittoria Cottage. On 2 August 1841, the Cheltenham Diocesan Board of Education also opened a "SCHOOL FOR GIRLS...upon the same PRINCIPLES and TERMS as that which they have already established for BOYS."[189] A Mrs Joy was appointed as the "Conductress of their Establishment" and an advertisement for the girls' school stated that "The children will be well instructed in all the Branches of a good English Education, based upon the Word of God."[190]

The 1839 report of the National Society included this new part of its educational programme. The National Society wished to extend its work "so as to comprehend the middle schools, and...elevate the character of the instruction given to the children of all classes", especially those "who are immediately above the labouring classes".[191] These Middle Schools were to be given no building grants and were expected to support themselves from pupils' fees. This new direction in the Society's charter was formally established at a meeting on 21 May 1839. W. F. Hook proposed "that this meeting contemplates with satisfaction the establishment of Diocesan and Local Boards of Education in connection with the National Society, having for their object the extension of the benefits of education...as well as the establishment and encouragement of schools for the education of the middle classes, upon principles conformable to those which are embodied in the Society's charter."[192] This proposal, which was endorsed by the members of the National Society, marked the beginning of concentrated local efforts by the Church of England in connection with middle-class education. As Burgess first suggested in 1958,[193] it also marked the start of more active interference by the government in the educational field. It was this activity within the Church that precipitated the formation in 1839 of the Committee of

---

[187] Ibid., 25 December 1839, p. 2.
[188] Ibid., 2 August 1841, p. 3.
[189] Ibid.
[190] Ibid.
[191] National Society Annual Report 1839, p. 9. National Society Archives, Church of England Record Centre, London.
[192] Ibid.
[193] Criticising J. W. Adamson and S. J. Curtis for their incorrect judgements. See Burgess, *Enterprise in Education*, p. 70; Adamson, *English Education 1789–1902*, p. 123; and Curtis, *Education in Great Britain*, p. 230.

Council on Education[194] and the establishment of a National Training College.[195]

The work of the committee had wide-ranging and long-lasting results, despite the verdict of some historians, who have either described the middle-school movement as having "failed to gain momentum",[196] or stated that it "gradually died away".[197] In 1839 seven diocesan training colleges were open or in the process of being established. By this time there were school boards in eight dioceses and three in the process of being formed; for example, Bishop Blomfield founded the London Diocesan Board of Education in this year.[198] These new or re-vamped[199] diocesan boards of education under the National Society began to sponsor and encourage local efforts in middle-class schooling.[200] According to the Newcastle Report, by 1858 there were 23 of them, and their income was between £13,000 and £14,000.[201] St Mark's Chelsea was founded in 1841 as the central training institution, and a number of diocesan colleges were also set up. Gladstone addressed the National Society's annual meeting in 1847 and claimed that the Society had instigated a system of teacher training before the state had shown an interest in the subject.[202] These training colleges had come to stay, and were to make an important contribution to English education.[203]

---

[194] The Committee of the Privy Council on Education, usually known as the Committee of Council on Education, was appointed in 1839 "to superintend the Application of any sums voted by Parliament for the purpose of promoting public education". For sixty years until superseded by the *Board of Education Act*, 1899, it was the only semblance of a modern-day Ministry of Education.

[195] This proposal by Dr Phillip Kay (Kay-Shuttleworth from 1841) was later defeated due to sectarian opposition. A. Tropp, *The School Teachers*, p. 14.

[196] Welsby, *History of the National Society*, p. 12.

[197] Roach, *Public Examinations*, p. 47. Fifteen years later, Roach was not nearly as dismissive of the middle school movement, assigning it a whole chapter in his second book. See Roach, *Secondary Education in England 1800–1870*, pp. 194–207.

[198] G. E. Biber, *Bishop Blomfield and his Times*, London 1857, p. 267.

[199] The first diocesan school board, Durham, was set up as early as 1811. Francis Brown, *The Church's Part in Education*, p. 129.

[200] One such school, the Cheltenham Diocesan Boys' School, was founded in 1839 by Francis Close, whose educational work is the subject of a later chapter.

[201] See the Report of Her Majesty's Commissioners appointed to Inquire into the State of Popular Education in England (Newcastle Report), 1861, vol. 1, pp. 57–8 for a "Table of Expenditure" of the diocesan boards.

[202] National Society Annual Report 1847, pp. 68ff. National Society Archives.

[203] Roach, *Public Examinations in England 1850–1900*, p. 47.

Despite this, the National Society and its associated diocesan school boards "never quite freed themselves from the fear that a successful middle-school movement would divert funds" from the main work of the Society of providing schools for the poor.[204] Consequently, for the next twenty years, progress was slow. With no building grants to assist promoters and no guaranteed source of teachers, the obstacles were considerable. Building grants for these schools were normally refused, but, even so, there was a slight increase in their numbers. Both St Mark's and Whitelands training colleges established middle schools in 1845. In the same year the Exeter Diocesan Board founded its Commercial School, and a little later the Canterbury Diocesan Board's Commercial and Agricultural School at Aylesham obtained an excellent report from the Norwich Board's inspector.[205]

In 1861, the Jubilee of the National Society, a new effort was made to promote "a sound and religious education amongst the children of the upper division of the labouring classes and the lower division of the middle classes". The Society had drawn attention "to the small number of children belonging to the upper division of the labouring classes who receive their education in Church Schools"[206] and in 1865, two months before the first meeting of the Taunton Commission, a Middle-Class Schools Committee was appointed to "consider and report whether the Society can assist, and if so, how best, in promoting the education of the Children of the class of the poor just above those who usually attend National Schools".[207] According to Burgess, of the 800,000 children in Church day schools which were receiving State grants in 1864, it was calculated that only 14,000 belonged to this stratum of society,[208] and estimated that middle-class children occupied only 4,600 of the 430,000 places added to State-assisted Church schools during the previous nine years.[209] This time, the push to establish middle schools was more successful. The aim was to help

---

[204] Burgess, *Enterprise in Education*, p. 134.

[205] See the 8th Annual Report of the Exeter Diocesan Board, and the 35th Annual Report of the Norwich Diocesan Society. Cited by Burgess, *Enterprise in Education*, p. 134.

[206] National Society General Committee Minute Book 6, pp. 319, 327–8. National Society Archives.

[207] National Society Middle Class Schools Committee Minutes, 1 November 1865. National Society Archives.

[208] According to the first "National Society Middle Class Schools Committee Report", these were "the foremen and small employers, clerks, farmers, and superior artisans." National Society Annual Report 1869, Appendix 17, p. 78. National Society Archives.

[209] National Society Annual Report 1866, p. 12. National Society Archives.

to start schools that would support themselves from fees[210], and to this end the Society offered building grants and a system of annual inspection. Considerable progress was being made when the Endowed Schools Commission of 1869 presented a new obstacle. In 1871 the committee of the National Society declared that, until it was known what was to happen to the existing schools,[211] no more new middle schools would be founded. This ban was to be short-lived, for within a few years the Disraeli ministry, as one of its first measures, amended the *Endowed Schools Act* and transferred its work to the less controversial Charity Commissioners

The National Society both founded new middle schools and joined existing schools to their Middle-Class Schools Committee. At York there was a middle school, chiefly for the sons of farmers, called the Yeoman's School which was run in connection with the York Training College for teachers.[212] It was later merged with the Archbishop Holgate Grammar School foundation, after parents had complained about what was described as "very high church teaching."[213] In being connected with a training institution it resembled St Mark's College Upper School, established in 1841, which fifty years later had 346 pupils between 7 and 15 years of age.[214] At Lichfield there was a diocesan commercial school,[215] and National Society middle schools existed at Canterbury,[216] Bristol,[217] Lincoln,[218] Chester[219] and

---

[210] Schools with fees exceeding 25s. a quarter were to be excluded from the fund. See the National Society Annual Report 1869, p. 17. National Society Archives.

[211] For an indication of what the National Society's committee had accomplished by 1871, see the National Society Middle Class Schools Committee Report, 'Class Lists, and Examination Papers for 1871'. Francis Brown also lists "an extraordinary assortment" of ten schools from this report. Francis Brown, *The Church's Part in Education*, p. 149.

[212] Minutes of the Committee of Council on Education, 1847–8, vol. 2, p. 583. See also S. B. James, Appendix on "Middle Class Education" in *The Church and Society*, London 1869, p. 90.

[213] SIC Report, vol. 4, p. 602, and vol. 5, pp. 268–71.

[214] See A. H. D. Acland and H. Llewellyn Smith (eds.), *Studies in Secondary Education*, London 1892, p. 193.

[215] See Francis Brown, *The Church's Part in Education*, p. 22.

[216] In 1842 there were 43 pupils at the Canterbury commercial school and in 1845 when the diocese was enlarged, another middle school was set up at Maidstone. However, in 1849 the Canterbury Diocesan Board closed its training institution, and it is not clear what happened to the middle schools thereafter. See M. H. A. Berry, "The Canterbury Diocesan Training School 1840–49, in M. H. A. Berry and J. H. Higginson (eds), *Canterbury Chapters: a Kentish Heritage for Tomorrow*, Liverpool 1976, pp. 123–31.

elsewhere.[220] The report of the Committee of Council on Education provides other examples of these schools. At Liverpool, St Martin's Commercial School was an upper school for the middle classes,[221] and when the Granby Row School in Manchester was visited by Her Majesty's Inspector, he was accompanied by the inspector of the Manchester Church Education Society,[222] whose care the school was under.[223] The Society had made a recommendation in 1845 to establish "Four Commercial Middle Schools...for one portion of the population—namely, the middle class, for which scarcely any public education is provided in the parish",[224] and its members were quick to act upon it.

The reports of the Taunton Commission of 1867–8 and the Cross Commission of 1888[225] provide further information on the work of the National Society in middle-class education. According to the former report, the parochial clergy of St Pancras founded and conducted the North London Collegiate School for Boys[226] to educate the

---

[217] At Bristol the cathedral school had been united with a training and middle school. In 1845 the Diocesan and Cathedral Training and Middle Schools had 76 pupils. The training school was closed in the early 1850s when the Diocese of Bristol combined with Oxford for educational purposes.

[218] See Roach, *Secondary Education in England 1800–1870*, pp. 195–8 for a brief history of the middle school founded by the Lincoln Diocesan Board. It closed in 1853, and in 1862 the building was taken over by a women's training college.

[219] The Training College and Science School at Chester opened in 1843 and the middle school continued until 1883. See J. L. Bradbury, *Chester College and the Training of Teachers 1839–1975*, Chester 1975.

[220] For an extensive but incomplete list of these schools, see the 'Middle Class Schools' section of the *Official Yearbook of the Church of England* from 1883.

[221] Minutes of the Committee of Council on Education, 1846, p. 370.

[222] For an account of the Manchester Church Education Society, see the Minutes of the Committee of Council on Education, 1847–8, vol. 2, pp. 33–4; and M. A. Cruickshank, "The Anglican Revival and Education: A Study of School Expansion in the Cotton Manufacturing Areas of North-West England, 1840–1850", *Northern History* 15 (1981): 187–8.

[223] Minutes of the Committee of Council on Education, 1846, p. 374.

[224] S. E. Maltby, *Manchester and the Movement for National Elementary Education 1800–1870*, London 1918, p. 65.

[225] The Royal Commission on Elementary Education was named after its chairman, Richard Assheton Cross (1823–1914). See J. T. Roberts, "The Genesis of the Cross Commission", *Journal of Educational Administration and History* 17, 2 (1985): 30–8.

[226] Founded in 1850 with 40 boys, this school had 420 day boys in 1865. SIC Report, vol. 4, p. 489. It should not be confused, as Francis Brown has, with the 'North London Collegiate School', founded as a girls' school in the same year

"respectable middle classes", and it had a very good academic record.[227] It appears that some National Schools became in fact middle or higher grade schools,[228] although not classed as such by official nomenclature: the National School in the small parish of Abbott's Ann may be cited as an example.[229] Evidence to the Cross Commissioners by the Headmaster of a school attached to St Thomas', Charterhouse, explicitly stated that he had been specially allowed to run his Upper School in conjunction with the National Schools.[230] The middle schools which were set up by Revd William Rogers after he left St Botolph's (which will be examined later as examples of 'Broad Church' initiative)[231] were also reported on by the Cross Commissioners.[232] These are all examples of schools that were connected with the National Society, where the Church's teaching was an essential part of the school's curriculum.

The Bryce Commission of 1894–5[233] affords an examination of the work of the Church of England in secondary education toward the end of the nineteenth century. According to its Report, the Church Extension Association, founded in 1865 and incorporating the Education Union,[234] set up a large middle-class school in 1899 at Croydon, known as the Old Palace School.[235] In 1894 it established Sefton Park High School for Girls in Liverpool.[236] A middle-class school in Leeds is described by the Bryce Report,[237] and the Taunton

---

by Francis M. Buss. See R. M. Scrimgeour, *The North London Collegiate School 1850–1950*, London 1950. It is claimed that the Girls' Public Day Schools Company took its idea from this school.

[227] SIC Report, vol. 10, p. 209.

[228] See M. Vlaeminke, *The English Higher Grade Schools*, London 2000.

[229] See the SIC Report, vol. 1, p. 196. Here there were 89 pupils, most of whom paid only 2d a week; however "the offspring of farmers and small shopkeepers" paid as much as one shilling per week.

[230] Report of Royal Commission on Elementary Education Acts (Cross Commission), Second Report, 1887, p. 94.

[231] See below, pp. 115–17.

[232] Cross Commission Second Report, 1887, p. 157ff.

[233] In March 1894, during Lord Rosebery's ministry, a Royal Commission was issued to Mr James Bryce MP and his colleagues "to consider what are the best means of establishing a well-organized system of secondary education in England..." The Royal Commission on Secondary Education was thereafter generally known, after its chairman, as the Bryce Commission.

[234] See Francis Brown, *The Church's Part in Education*, p. 117.

[235] Report of Royal Commission on Secondary Education (Bryce Commission), 1895, vol. 9, p. 392ff.

[236] Ibid., vol. 9, pp. 282ff.

[237] Ibid., vol. 7, pp. 154–8.

Report also lists a superior grade school for about 100 boys which was run by Revd Robert Gregory, Incumbent of St Mary's, Lambeth.[238] Gregory was convinced that the "sons of mechanics and small tradesmen" in Lambeth were badly served by the private schools and neglected by the Church.[239] He started a parochial school in 1854 specifically for that social group, and such was its success that in 1860 he erected new buildings for this middle-class National School.[240] He was also successful in gaining a government grant for the school's maintenance.[241] Gregory was a great supporter of the scheme for a national system of middle-class Church schools which was being developed by Woodard.[242] In 1865, when Woodard formed a Central Committee for his schools in London, mainly for fundraising,[243] Gregory was appointed Honorary Secretary. He was also Treasurer of the National Society,[244] where he was an active promoter of the work of the Middle Class Schools Committee.[245] Gregory was a canon and later Dean of St Paul's Cathedral; he was a well-known Anglo-Catholic. His High-Churchmanship exemplifies the fact that although the work of the National Society received the support of Churchmen of all persuasions, the Society was the conception, and remained largely the preserve, of the High Church party.[246]

---

[238] SIC Report, vol. 5, pp. 605ff.

[239] See R. Gregory, *Do Our National Schools Provide Education for All Whom they Ought to Train?*, London 1865.

[240] A good four years before the Taunton Commission began, which does not support David Allsobrook's contention that "The efforts of Gregory and Rogers...were independent responses to the Government's setting up the SIC". D. I. Allsobrook, *Schools for the Shires*, p. 196. On the other hand, this was probably true for William Rogers, who set up his first middle-class school in St Botolph's in 1866, i.e. while the Commission was still meeting. See below, pp. 115–17.

[241] SIC Report, vol. 5, p. 613.

[242] In 1857, Gregory put his parish temporarily in the hands of others, and for several months became a full-time travelling secretary for the Corporation. B Heeney, *Mission to the Middle Classes*, p. 43.

[243] By 1875, it had been responsible for raising £24,950. B. Heeney, *Mission to the Middle Classes*, p. 44.

[244] Gregory "used to attribute his financial ability to the fact that he had been engaged in business, in a Liverpool shipping firm, before ordination." M. Donovan, *After the Tractarians*, Glasgow 1933, p. 92.

[245] See the National Society General Committee Minutes, 10 November 1865. National Society Archives.

[246] Soloway, *Prelates and People*, p. 374.

This was especially the case after June 1852,[247] when the Evangelical incumbent of Cheltenham, Francis Close (1797–1882),[248] "set his face against the National Society"[249] and, together with two or three hundred Evangelical clergy,[250] "marched out of the National Society's Annual Meeting".[251] Adjourning to a nearby coffee house they set up their own Society, calling it 'The Church of England Education Society'. *The Record* announced, "We bless God that at length we see instituted a Society which will prevent the education of the youth of this country from being committed into the hands of the National Education Society, with its Romanizing training schools at St Mark's, Chelsea, and its continued efforts to reduce our country parishes under the influence of Tractarianism."[252] The new Society formed a committee, which under the chairmanship of J. C. Colquhoun (1803–1870),[253] included a number of Evangelical leaders and several Members of Parliament.[254] Close was concerned about the Tractarian teaching and theology which he felt had crept into the National Society's schools and diocesan training colleges. By this time there were already a number of National Society training colleges in existence: at Battersea, Chelsea, Whitelands, Chester, York, Ripon and Durham. He accused St Mark's, Chelsea, of using "medieval ritual" in

---

[247] The date of this event has been the centre of some confusion, stemming from what appears to be an incorrect date used by G. T. Berwick in 1939, which was then copied by Henry Burgess. See G. T. Berwick, "Close of Cheltenham: Parish Pope" *Theology* 39 (1939): 13–4, and Burgess, *Enterprise in Education*, p. 142. The error was corrected by Richard Aldridge in 1976, who identified the correct date from a report of the proceedings of the annual meeting held on 10 June 1852 in the National Society's *Monthly Paper* July 1852, p. 197. See R. Aldridge, "Uncertain Vintage: the Origins of the Church of England Education Society", *History of Education Society Bulletin* 18 (1976): 42–3. Unfortunately, the correct timing of this event has been recently confused by Nigel Scotland, who suggests that this meeting took place in November 1845. See N. A. D. Scotland, "The College of St. Paul and St. Mary, Cheltenham: A Unique Evangelical Enterprise in Anglican Higher Education", *History of Education Society Bulletin* 44 (1989): 26.

[248] See Appendix 1.

[249] Scotland, "The College of St Paul and St Mary, Cheltenham", p. 26.

[250] Also the laity. See H. J. Burgess, "The Work of the Established Church in the Education of the People 1833–1870", PhD thesis, London University 1954, p. 332.

[251] Burgess, *Enterprise in Education*, p. 142.

[252] *Record,* 26 May 1853, p. 13.

[253] See Appendix 1.

[254] The Society's Vice-Presidents included the Earls of Effingham, Shaftesbury, and Cavan; Lord Charles Russell; and the Bishops of Manchester, Sydney and Mauritius.

its chapel services, and commented "I would just as well send a youth to be instructed at the Vatican at once, as to one of the National Society's training schools, to be instructed in the doctrine of the Church of England."[255]

Plans had been under way for an Evangelical training college in Cheltenham since 1845, when Samuel Codner[256] convened a meeting of local clergy and laymen, chaired by Francis Close, to found an Evangelical training school for teachers. In 1847 this committee opened The 'Church of England Training School at Cheltenham'.[257] Religious education at the College was spelled out by the tightly-worded foundation deed as being always *"strictly Scriptural, Evangelical and Protestant* and in *strict* accordance with the *Articles and Liturgy* of the Church of England, *as now by law established*, in their literal and grammatical sense; and that these principles should *for ever* be preserved as a most sacred trust at any sacrifice of pecuniary loss or temporal interest".[258] The Evangelical perspective contained within this trust document remained legally binding on the College well into the twentieth century. As will be seen later, this was something which Francis Close was unable to achieve for his other great educational interest, the Cheltenham Proprietary College.[259]

The Bryce Commissioners studied the existing provision for secondary education from the public schools downwards, and took into account the findings of their Taunton Commission predecessors. Like the Taunton Commission, they also included girls' schools and girls' education within their survey. However, the Bryce Commission took this one step further: instead of simply calling women before the Royal Commission, they included three women in its membership.[260] The

---

[255] Speech of the Revd F. Close, at a public meeting held in Ipswich on Monday 25 October 1847; Cheltenham 1863, p. 16. Cited by Munden, *A Cheltenham Gamaliel*, p. 41.

[256] Codner was a Dartmouth merchant and philanthropist who was already involved in education in Canada. In 1823 he had founded the Society for the Education of the Poor in Newfoundland, which by 1836 had 43 schools in the province which catered for 12,000 pupils. Munden, *A Cheltenham Gamaliel*, pp. 41–2.

[257] In 1921 this became the separate colleges of St Paul and St Mary. These merged in 1979 to form the single College of St Paul and St Mary, which then merged with the Gloucestershire College of Art and Technology in 1990 to create Cheltenham and Gloucester College of Higher Education, which in 2001 became the University of Gloucester.

[258] *The Trust Deed of the Church of England Training Schools at Cheltenham*, Cheltenham 1861, pp. 7–8. Cited by Munden, *A Cheltenham Gamaliel*, p. 43.

[259] See ch. 3 below.

[260] Mrs H. Sidgwick, Mrs S. Bryant and Lady F. Cavendish.

Commission identified the educational success of the Girls' Public Day Schools Company, Ltd.,[261] with its 7,111 pupils in 36 schools, and the effect this had had on other educational innovators. The Boys' Public Day School Company and the Church Schools Company,[262] both founded in 1883, proposed to educate children "above the elementary class", and "of all classes above those usually attending public elementary schools". The first-named company aimed at providing "a sound and useful education", including "moral and religious training on a Christian basis".[263] The Church Schools Company's object was to combine "a thoroughly efficient secular education" with definite religious teaching "in accordance with the belief and practice of the Church of England". As another High-Church initiative,[264] it warrants closer examination.

The suggestion of a company for Church day schools was first put forward at the Central Committee of the Diocesan Conferences and a preliminary meeting was held in the Westminster offices of the National Society on 17 April 1883. The Chairman was the Archdeacon of Ely, William Emery (1825–1910)[265] and others present included H. C. Raikes and G. Cubitt (both MPs), and Robert Gregory.[266] A large provisional committee was appointed whose members included "the Archdeacon of Canterbury,[267] sixteen bishops and four heads of

---

[261] Founded in 1872 by Mrs William Grey (*nee* Maria Shirreff) in association with the Society of Arts "to supply for girls the best possible education corresponding with the education given to boys in the great public schools of the country." The Company's first 'High Schools' were established in Chelsea (1873), Notting Hill and Croydon (1874). See L. Magnus, *The Jubilee Book of the Girls' Public Day School Trust 1873–1923*, London 1923; and J. Kamm, *Indicative Past: A Hundred Years of the Girls' Public Day School Trust*, London 1971.

[262] See the *Church Schools Company, 1883–1933*, London 1934.

[263] Cited by Adamson, *English Education 1789–1902*, p. 453. Although it managed three schools with total accommodation for 680 pupils in 1894, the Boys' Public Day School Company did not last the decade.

[264] Despite its chairman being a well-known Evangelical: William Emery, Archdeacon of Ely (see Appendix 1). He was said to possess, " not only...great determination, but also...tact". E. Moberley Bell, *A History of the Church Schools Company 1883–1958*, London 1958, p. 11. It was certainly rare to find Evangelicals working so closely with High Church Anglicans during this period.

[265] See Appendix 1.

[266] V. Hope, *The First Hundred Years of the Church Schools Company*, n.p. 1984, p. 11.

[267] Canon Francis Holland.

Cambridge colleges as well as several distinguished laymen".[268] It drew up a manifesto which stated that the purpose of the company was to found "Church Schools for Boys and Girls of the classes above that attending elementary schools..., and it is now proposed to establish such schools in different parts of the country, in which superior education in accordance with the principles of the Church of England...will be provided."[269] A public meeting presided over by the Archbishop of Canterbury[270] appealed for capital of £100,000, and a Council was appointed. On 12 July 1883, legal formalities having been completed,[271] the Church Schools Company came into being. A Prospectus was published in February 1884 and by June the company had 570 shareholders.[272] By 1885 the Company managed ten schools, although they were all small and the total number of pupils under instruction was only 378.[273] However, by 1897, another 23 schools had been founded and the Company was responsible for 2,445 children.[274] As will be shown below, its success provided both the encouragement and a spur for other sections of the Church of England which were concerned for middle-class education, for later in 1883 the *Evangelical Church Schools Company* was formed.[275] However, well before

---

[268] Hope, *Church Schools Company*, p. 11.

[269] Cited by Bell, *Church Schools Company*, p. 9.

[270] Edward White Benson (1829–1896), Archbishop of Canterbury 1882–96. He later showed his personal support for the scheme by purchasing £1,000 worth of shares in the Company. See the *Prospectus and List of Shareholders of the Church Schools Company, Limited, for Boys and Girls*, 1 February 1884, p. 2. Lancing College Archives.

[271] This included a motion before the Lower House of Convocation of Canterbury by George Anthony Denison (1805–1896), Archdeacon of Taunton and a notorious High Church agitator. See his letter to the editor of the *Morning Post* in December 1883, reprinted as 'The School of 'The Church Schools Company'", in Lancing College Archives. Burgess describes how Denison led the "High Church-Tractarian coalition" in the violent debates that racked the National Society annual meetings in the late 40s, which centred on opposition to the so-called "management" and "conscience" clauses. Burgess, *Enterprise in Education*, p. 150. Arthur Burns stated of Denison that "No-one was a greater thorn in the flesh of the Evangelical archbishop J. B. Sumner". A. Burns, "W. J. Conybeare", p. 323. See also references to "the pugnacious Archdeacon" in *The Record* 9 June 1851 and 7 June 1852.

[272] *Prospectus and List of Shareholders of the Church Schools Company*, pp. 2–4.

[273] Bell, *Church Schools Company*, p. 23.

[274] Ibid., p. 39. These were mostly girls, for in 1892 the Company had decided that there was "no demand" for boys.

[275] Although there is no evidence that this was founded as a rival organization, the choice of name suggests that the Evangelicals saw themselves as providing an Evangelical alternative.

Evangelicals began showing an interest in middle-class education, Tractarian and Anglo-Catholic members of the High Church party were busy founding new middle-class schools. This alternative Church of England initiative is the focus of what follows.

Tractarian and Anglo-Catholic Schools

Brian Heeney was at pains, in 1961, to point out that although Woodard "was the chief apostle of Tractarianism to secondary education, he was not the only one. Nor, indeed, was he the first."[276] This was despite the fact that Woodard was the main subject of his thesis. Mention has already been made of the role played by High Church laymen[277] and High Church and Tractarian clergymen[278] in the effort to extend the work of the National Society amongst the children of the middle classes. In the great expansion of the public school system which followed "the coming of the railways"[279] and Arnold's reforms at Rugby,[280] a number of other public and private foundation schools arose out of the Anglo-Catholic impulse that came to be known as the Oxford Movement.

The first of these was due to the work of Revd William Sewell (1804–1874), "one of the great public school founders of the Victorian era".[281] Sewell was a Greek scholar and Professor of Moral Philosophy at Oxford 1836–41. During this time he was exposed to the teachings of John Keble and John Henry Newman, the co-founders of the Oxford Movement. C. H. Pearson, a contemporary of Sewell, wrote in his *Memorials* that "[Sewell's] first ambition had been to lead a party of Moderates in the Oxford Movement, and there was a moment when he

---

[276] B. Heeney, "The Established Church and the Education of the Victorian Middle Classes: A Study of the Woodard Schools, 1847–1891", DPhil thesis, Oxford University 1961, p. 28.

[277] Exemplified by S. F. Wood and W. E. Gladstone. Gladstone was a very active supporter of new Church of England schools, especially the Woodard schools. He was also largely responsible for the foundation Glenalmond School in Scotland in 1847.

[278] Exemplified by Archdeacon (later Cardinal) H. E. Manning, Canon (later Dean) R. Gregory and Archdeacon G. A. Denison.

[279] M. L. Clarke, *Classical Education in Britain, 1500–1900*, London 1959, p. 88. Cf. Bamford, *Public Schools*, p. 60.

[280] See Bamford, ibid.

[281] Gardner, *Public Schools*, p. 163. Curiously, Gardner here also describes Sewell as "very much part of the Evangelical Movement", perhaps mistaking Sewell's Tractarian 'enthusiasm' for another brand of churchmanship.

was actually regarded as a possible rival to Newman".[282] Despite being accused throughout his life of being a 'Papist',[283] and even a Jesuit,[284] Sewell "believed in the Church of England", and his "attachment to the Prayer Book was sincere and even passionate".[285] In 1840, Sewell spent the long vacation in Ireland, during which he became "distressed beyond measure" at the decay in the Irish Church. He returned to Oxford "deeply convinced that the troubles of Ireland arose from the mischievous and secret scheming of Roman agents"[286] and decided that what Ireland needed was a major public school, in order "to guide the Irish through their natural leaders"[287][sic]. In 1843 with a group of Irish friends,[288] Sewell founded the College of St Columba at Rathfarnham near Dublin; what was still described in 1956 as "the only Public School in the Republic."[289] Sewell laid great stress on "religious training, carried out…in full accordance with the principles of the Prayer Book"[290] as the focus of the school. The whole life of the College was to revolve around its Chapel, where the full choral services of Matins and Evensong were to be celebrated daily. The feasts of the Church, in accordance with the Book of Common Prayer, were also to be observed by the whole school, as were fasts by the

---

[282] Cited by C. Hibbert, *No Ordinary Place*, London 1997, p. 37.

[283] Before the first term started in 1847, it was reported that four Irish harvesters came to the Warden's house one Sunday, "asking if Mass was to be celebrated that day." A. K. Boyd, *The History of Radley College*, Oxford 1948, pp. 33–4.

[284] Ibid., pp. 31–2. This was not based on fact, for Sewell had "an obsessive mistrust of Jesuits", and at one point in his life made a large collection of their works, and "lost no opportunity of making [him]self acquainted with the secret machinery and working of the Society." Hibbert, *No Ordinary Place*, p. 17. See also "The Reminiscences of Dr William Sewell", vol. 1, pp. 264–6, cited by L. James, *A Forgotten Genius*, London 1908, p. 84.

[285] James, *A Forgotten Genius*, p. 39.

[286] Ibid., p. 79.

[287] Ibid. Ironically, two of the founders of the school, Lord Adare and William Monsell, were later received into the Roman Catholic Church.

[288] The three other 'Founders' were: E. R. W. W. Quin, the third Earl of Dunraven; William Monsell, MP for County Limerick 1847–73 (later Lord Emly), and Revd J. H. Todd, Senior Fellow of Trinity College, Dublin. See James, *A Forgotten Genius*, pp. 86–94. Archbishop J. G. Beresford, Primate of Ireland, was also one of the early supporters, and he was to later become a governor of the school.

[289] M. C. O'Neill, "St Columba's College", *The Irish Tatler and Sketch* 65 (April 1956), p. 49. This is not true, as by this time there were a number of other public schools in the Republic of Ireland, including The Royal Belfast Academic Institution, Belfast (founded 1810); Coleraine Academic Institution, Coleraine (1857); and Campbell College, Belfast (1894).

[290] Boyd, *Radley College*, p. 4.

Warden and Fellows (as the headmaster and masters were known). Irreconcilable differences of opinion over these strict rules of fasting eventually led to the resignation of Sewell and the Warden of St Columba's. However, this did not discourage both men from jointly founding, within months of abandoning the Irish venture, a new school just outside of Oxford.

Convinced of the success of his experiment in Ireland, Sewell and the previous Warden of St Columba's, Revd R. C. Singleton, now determined to establish a similar public school in England that was to be based on the ideas of the Oxford Movement. "Fasts and Feasts were to be visibly observed", wrote Singleton in his Journal, and the new school was to have "a Chapel, an Organ, a Bell, a Library, a Common Room, a Warden, and six or seven Fellows".[291] A lease was taken on Radley Hall, five miles from Oxford, near Abingdon,[292] and St Peter's College, Radley (as it was first known) opened with three boys in 1847.[293] At the ends of the next three years the roll was 36,[294] 72 and 84 respectively. Thus Radley gradually expanded. The school gained an unwanted notoriety for the poverty of its food:[295] Sewell seems to have seen to it that the boys were always under-fed and hungry[296]— one account tells of how "bulbs, flowers, acorns, were taken from the park and eagerly devoured"[297] by the boys. Despite this and other criticisms, Radley quickly became a model for other supporters of the Oxford Movement who were interested in middle-class schools. One of these was Nathaniel Woodard, who visited Radley in 1848, soon

---

[291] "Journal of Revd Robert Corbet Singleton", cited by James, *A Forgotten Genius*, p. 155.

[292] Hibbert, *No Ordinary Place*, p. 23.

[293] Two of these boys won scholarships to Oxford and obtained first-class honours. See E. Bryans, *A History of St. Peter's College, Radley, 1847–1924*, Oxford 1926.

[294] This number included two of the sons of the Bishop of Oxford, Samuel Wilberforce. He was to later withdraw his children from the school after he became unhappy with their progress.

[295] Contemporaries of Alexander J. G. Downer, a pupil at Radley 1964–70 and the Foreign Minister of Australia (1996–), are quoted as describing the food as "foul". *Sun-Herald*, 3 July 1994, p. 30.

[296] Other accounts talk of "gross neglect" of the boys. The son of Henry Wilberforce died at the College and the grieving parents, upon arriving at Radley, were "soundly rated by Sewell for sending so delicate a child there, and injuring, by his inevitable death, the good name of the college". T. Mozley, *Reminiscences Chiefly of Oriel College and the Oxford Movement* vol. 2, London 1882, pp. 27–8.

[297] Gardner, *Public* Schools, p. 171.

after he had started his 'Grammar School and Collegiate Institution' in Shoreham, Sussex.

Singleton described his visitor somewhat patronisingly as "a Mr Woodard who is trying to establish a school for the middle classes on the Church System at New Shoreham. He seems to have a good deal of energy and boldness...I dare say he is just the man for the work."[298] Sewell told Woodard about his plans to found free or inexpensive schools for the poor on the expected profits of Radley. Sewell believed "that it was an important thing to make the rich pay for the poor"[299] and had originally planned to "educate and support every tenth boy for nothing"[300] at Radley. Although this idea was never implemented at Radley, the concept of using the profits of a first-grade middle-class school to support the work of a second- or third-grade middle-class school was one that Woodard took up. He returned to Sussex and split his Shoreham School into St Mary's Grammar School, a day school for the lower middle class, and St Nicolas's Grammar School, a boarding school for upper middle class.[301] In 1849 Woodard began another boarding school at Shoreham, which he named St John's. This school was for the sons of "tradesmen, farmers and clerks"[302]—the so-called 'middle middle classes'. It moved to Hurstpierpoint, after which the school came to be known, in 1850. Sewell had first outlined an idea of a central school from which other schools might be sent out, like colonies into the "waste places", in a letter to Lord Adare in 1840. This idea of setting up a first-grade "mother" school from which others would grow was later to find its fulfilment in the system of Woodard schools, which in this and other ways owed much to Sewell's inspiration. The lack of recognition by recent historians[303] of Sewell's pioneering work in middle-class education, justifies the title that Lionel James chose for his biography of Sewell: *A Forgotten Genius*.

Financial difficulties led to Sewell taking over the Wardenship of Radley in 1853, which meant relinquishing his comfortable and lucrative Oxford fellowship. During this time, Radley became the target for Evangelical concern about the rise of 'Tractarian' schools. In 1855, Francis Close reviewed a book of sermons which Sewell had published for his pupils. His review was entitled *High-Church Education Delusive and Dangerous: being an exposition of the system adopted by the Rev. W. Sewell BD, Warden of St Peter's College,*

---

[298] Cited by Hibbert, *No Ordinary Place*, p. 45.
[299] Singleton's Journal; cited by James, *A Forgotten Genius*, p. 155.
[300] James, ibid., p. 155.
[301] Known collectively as SS Mary and Nicolas Grammar School.
[302] Cited by Heeney, *Mission to the Middle Classes*, p. 32.
[303] The exception being Brian Gardner.

Radley..., and it included criticisms of Woodard's scheme. Close, who described himself as "a Christian educationalist", admired Sewell's attempt to "interweave the highest feelings and principles of religion into the entire system of education".[304] However, he went on to criticise his 'Roman' interpretation of the Bible and Prayer Book, and referred to the "the secret plague of Romanism which lurks in his system".[305] Although Sewell was regarded by many as an inspiring teacher and preacher, he was not a good financial manager. In 1861, after a meeting of creditors, he resigned as Warden. The school was taken over by "a pious business-man and politician",[306] J. G. Hubbard (1805–1889).[307] Within a short space of time, Radley passed from Hubbard into the hands of its trustees,[308] thus becoming a truly 'public' school.[309] However, it still did not own the buildings or land that it used. In 1899 Radley estate was put up for sale and the trustees were able to buy the freehold of Radley Hall and 136 acres of surrounding land for £13,000. Today, Radley has over 600 pupils and is regarded as one of the more successful public schools in England. Since providing the location of the 1980 television series, *Public School*, it has also become one of the best known.

St Andrew's College, Bradfield, was also known as having a "character for High Churchism".[310] It was founded in 1850 by Revd Thomas Stevens, Rector of Bradfield and lord of the manor. The living had been in the hands of Stevens' family for some generations, and on his father's death Thomas restored the parish church in considerable style. The reasons for the school's foundation are not clear. Some have said that Stevens opened the school in 1850 in order to provide a choir suitable for his grand new church.[311] Others suggest that his motive

---

[304] F. Close, "High-Church Education Delusive and Dangerous: being an exposition of the system adopted by the Revd. W. Sewell BD, Warden of St Peter's College, Radley; and advocated in a volume of sermons addressed by him to the students", in idem., *Footsteps of Error*, London 1863, p. 362.

[305] Ibid., p. 390.

[306] Gardner, *Public Schools*, p. 171.

[307] Later the first Baron Addington.

[308] Or 'Council' as they became under a Royal Charter of Incorporation soon after the death of Addington.

[309] The SIC Report, vol. 11, listed it as a proprietary school, although Leinster-Mackay has pointed out that it was also regarded as a 'Collegiate' school. Thus it would seem that Radley was a private, a collegiate, a proprietary, *and* a public school at different stages. Leinster-Mackay "English Proprietary Schools", p. 46.

[310] A. F. Leach, *A History of Bradfield College*, London 1900, p. 42.

[311] Gardner, *Public Schools*, p. 176.

was financial.[312] Whatever the case, he started with six boys, and by 1852 there were 32. Stevens modelled the school on Winchester, and like Radley it seemed to set a high social and educational standard from the start, with fees in 1852 set at £100. It was very much a Church school, and was designed "for the encouragement of religious and useful learning and for the careful education of boys as loving children of the Church of England".[313] Like Radley, the Tractarian label it soon acquired was somewhat of a liability, and "militated against the increase of the school".[314] Bradfield's first historian notes that Stevens "was always trying to tear off the label of Ritualism which people were always trying to fasten on the school".[315] In the 1870s the financial situation of the school became very serious, and at the end of 1879 the Headmaster and some of the staff resigned. Two years later the founder himself went bankrupt, with debts of £160,000. Stevens resigned from the school, the rectory was sequestered, and the manor and its lands sold.[316] However, the 13 acres of the college had been placed in a trust, so like Radley, the foundation survived. By 1886 the school had recovered, and from that date it made steady progress.

Another Anglican clergyman who was involved in a similar foundation was Revd P. R. Egerton,[317] who in 1859 purchased an empty building at Bloxham, near Banbury in Oxfordshire. The building had been opened as All Saints' School in 1855 by one of Woodard's former masters,[318] but it was closed within a short time.[319] Egerton bought it on an impulse,[320] and after offering the school again to Woodard (without success), he decided in 1860 to open his own school "for the education of the Sons of Tradesmen, Farmers, Clerks,

---

[312] The church restoration had cost Stevens £30,000 and he may have hoped eventually to recover some of this through the school. J Blackie, *Bradfield 1850–1975*, Bradfield 1976, p. 6.
[313] Cited by Gardner, *Public Schools*, p. 176.
[314] Leach, *A History of Bradfield College*, p. 42.
[315] Ibid. This was despite the fact that Stevens himself was "quite unsympathetic towards the various Catholic practices that grew up as a result of the movement. He had no use for vestments, for candles or incense". Blackie, *Bradfield*, p. 2.
[316] Gardner, *Public Schools*, p. 176.
[317] Fellow of New College, Oxford, and Curate of Deddington.
[318] Revd J. W. Hewitt.
[319] Hewitt offered it to Woodard in 1857 for £5,000. Heeney, *Mission to the Middle Classes*, p. 156; and K. E. Kirk, *The Story of the Woodard Schools*, Abingdon 1952, pp. 107–8.
[320] Some unexplained fancy caused him to buy the school after just one passing glimpse of it. Kirk, *The Story of the Woodard Schools*, p. 108. Perhaps the discount price of £1,550 was 'an offer too good to refuse'.

and others of the Middle Classes".[321] It was said that he wanted to inculcate in his pupils "the clear, distinct, systematic teaching and practice of the Church".[322] Like Radley, Bloxham was characterised by frequent chapel services. Confession was also encouraged. The Chaplain was "strong on the point that the blessing of sacramental confession was part of the Catholic heritage of the Church of England".[323] Egerton's links with Woodard were always close. As mentioned above, he had tried unsuccessfully to transfer the school to St Nicolas College soon after he purchased it in 1859. In 1880 he made another attempt to give the school to Woodard, and the Provost "seriously considered making it the central school of the new Midlands Division."[324] But Woodard's fear of over-expansion and his insistence of sound financial policy led to its rejection for a third time.[325] Nevertheless Egerton became a non-resident Fellow of the Midlands Division in 1882, in 1884 he handed the school over to trustees. In 1896, five years after Woodard's death, the school was taken over by the Woodard Corporation.[326]

According to C. P. S. Clark, there was another school which was closely associated with the Tractarians and which was founded in the home of the movement itself.[327] St Edward's School was founded by Revd Thomas Chamberlain in 1863 at New Inn Hall Street, Oxford. It was opened "to place within the reach of parents of inadequate means a school where their children could be brought up in the true principles of the Church".[328] Chamberlain, a don at Christ Church College, and a follower of Keble and Newman, took little interest in the school after its foundation, although the school had expanded to 49 boys by 1866. Under Revd A. B. Simeon, St Edward's moved to its present site in North Oxford in 1869, where it continued to flourish, despite accusations of 'Romanism' which were similar to those also being levelled at Radley and the Woodard schools. The *Oxford Guardian* set the tone for popular public feeling towards such 'Tractarian' initiatives: "It would seem but fair that parents should fully comprehend the religious proclivities of teachers, who at the recent laying of the foundation stone of the School Chapel by the Bishop, in

---

[321] First School Prospectus, reprinted in *All Saints' School, Bloxham 1860–1960*, n.p. 1960, p. 8.
[322] *History of All Saints' School, Bloxham 1860–1910*, Bloxham 1925, p. 49.
[323] Ibid., p. 36.
[324] Heeney, *Mission to the Middle Classes*, p. 157.
[325] Or, a fourth time if Hewitt's first offer to Woodard is included in the count.
[326] See *History of All Saints' School, Bloxham 1860–1910*.
[327] C. P. S. Clarke, *The Oxford Movement and After*, London 1932, p. 157.
[328] Heeney, *Mission to the Middle Classes*, p. 157.

their ceremonial appointments simply plagiarised Rome...The whole ceremony...seemed to the outsider nothing if not Roman...[we] have little sympathy for such partisans as those who have created St. Edwards's School."[329] Simeon overcame these, as well as the everpresent financial problems, and managed to keep the school going until his resignation in 1892. During this time, the school was offered to Woodard in 1872, and again in 1882, when it was declined because of a heavy mortgage.[330] In 1919 the school was finally taken over by the Woodard Corporation, although eight years later it left the group. St Edward's is now an independent school of over 600 pupils.[331]

A number of other new schools were founded as a result of the religious revivalism of the Oxford Movement. In 1846, Revd Edward Monro founded St Andrew's College at Harrow Weald "for the transmutation of raw ploughboys into sweet choristers and good scholars".[332] It attracted much attention in Tractarian circles. John Keble and Henry Manning preached at the opening ceremony, and W. E. Gladstone, A. Beresford Hope[333] and Keble donated annual prizes. The type of education provided was the subject of an enthusiastic lead article in *The Guardian* in 1851.[334] However, the school collapsed when Monro left for a parish at Leeds in 1860.[335] In 1851, a small public school at Harlow, called St Mary' College, was founded by Revd Charles Goulden. Ten years later it was described as "one of those institutions which have sprung from the recent revival in the Church of England".[336] In these and various other ways, attempts were made to instil Anglo-Catholicism into the arena of middle-class

---

[329] Cited by Gardner, *Public Schools*, p. 189.

[330] Heeney, *Mission to the Middle Classes*, p. 157.

[331] See the school's website, http://www.stedward.oxon.sch.uk/stedwards/master_registrar.html (link to St Edward's ISC entry; accessed March 2004).

[332] Mozley, *Reminiscences* vol. 2, p. 22.

[333] Alexander Beresford Hope (1820–1887), the conservative MP for Maidstone (later Stoke-on-Trent, and then Cambridge University), was a well-known Anglo-Catholic spokesman and philanthropist. He built All Saints Church, Margaret Street, London, at his own expense, and purchased the site of St Augustine's College, Canterbury.

[334] *Guardian* 5 November 1851, p. 13. *The Guardian* was founded in 1846 by "a combination of young Oxford men" and quickly developed into the organ of High-Church Tractarians. See Altholz, *The Religious Press* pp. 27–8.

[335] See B. Heeney, "Tractarian Pastor: Edward Monro of Harrow Weald I. The Practice of the Parish Ministry", *Canadian Journal of Theology* 13, 4 (1967): 241–53.

[336] J. Skinner, *The Church in the Public School*, London 1861, p. 13. Cited by Heeney, *Mission to the Middle Classes*, p. 50.

education. Some ventures, like St Mary's, Harlow, or St Andrew's, Harrow Weald, were relatively small and short-lived. Others, like the two schools founded by William Sewell, and the schools which were founded in or around Oxford, were permanent. All of these schools owed their origin to Tractarian or Anglo-Catholic sympathisers, and this became a small but very active sector within the Victorian secondary school scene. However, none of them could compare in size or success with the scheme which Woodard began at Shoreham. Nor did they exhibit the same rigour in the application of Anglo-Catholic principles to every part of school life which was to characterise Woodard's schools: "The theology and piety of the Anglo-Catholic Revival, to which Woodard himself was firmly attached, permeated his Society, produced a novel type of public school religion, and carried the message of the Oxford Movement to thousands of Victorian boys and girls most of whom were sons and daughters of middle-class parents."[337] It was for this reason that, as will be seen later, Evangelical concern was mainly centred on the Woodard schools.

The story of the Woodard schools has already been told.[338] The most comprehensive treatment has been by Brian Heeney,[339] now the recognised authority on the movement. In undertaking research for an Oxford DPhil,[340] Heeney read all 9,000 of Woodard's letters, most of which are preserved in the archives of Lancing College. Virtually all of this correspondence is directly connected with the organization and development of SS. Mary and Nicolas College, "the Corporation which he established as an Anglo-Catholic mission to middle-class England and as the national agent of middle-class schooling."[341] Heeney points out that Woodard's biographer, Sir John Otter,[342] devoted only nine pages in his *Memoir* to Woodard's first thirty years, because after that

---

[337] Heeney, *Mission to the Middle Classes*, p. 52.

[338] First by the Headmaster of Hurstpierpoint and Provost of Denstone, E. C. Lowe, in *S. Nicolas College and its Schools*, London 1878. This was followed by K. E. Kirk, *The Woodard Schools*; a scholarly although understandably biased account, for Bishop Kirk was Provost of Lancing 1937–44 and President of the Woodard Corporation 1946–54. The most recent history is not much more than a list of schools with brief descriptions; see L. and E. Cowie, *That One Idea: Nathaniel Woodard and his Schools,* Ellesmere 1991.

[339] Heeney, *Mission to the Middle Classes: The Woodard Schools 1848–1891*.

[340] B. Heeney, "The Established Church and the Education of the Victorian Middle Classes. A Study of the Woodard Schools, 1847–1891", DPhil thesis, Oxford University 1961.

[341] Heeney, *Mission to the Middle Classes*, p. 1.

[342] J. Otter, *Nathaniel Woodard: A Memoir of His Life,* London 1925. See also B. Handford, *Nathaniel Woodard*, printed notes of a lecture delivered at Hurstpierpoint College 5 November 1974. Lancing College Archives.

time his life was almost wholly identified with his accomplishments as 'Founder' of the Corporation. Histories of the individual schools also abound,[343] however they do not contribute anything more to Heeney's scholarly account.

Woodard was a great student of the classes. He particularly liked to sub-divide the middle-class, and his schools were all class-designated with finely drawn distinctions. He first expounded his ideas in the pamphlet, *A Plea for the Middle Classes* (1848), in which he talked of schools of two classes: "the first would be suitable for the sons of the higher kind of tradesmen, professional men, and gentlemen of limited means; the second for the children of quite small tradesmen or even hucksters. These latter are a very important class, perhaps the most important; and with a little diligence and management *might be picked up by thousands.*"[344] Soon the original two classes he outlined in 1848 had become three with the division of the higher group into a school for the "sons of gentlemen of limited means" and another for the "sons of tradesmen and farmers". As already mentioned, Woodard's first school, which he later subdivided into two schools, was at Shoreham in Sussex. In 1848 he founded Lancing as one of his "upper schools" for the "sons of clergymen and gentlemen of limited means."[345] Lancing was taught and administered on the assumption that a fair proportion of its boys would go on to Oxford or Cambridge. In the following year, Woodard supervised the foundation of Hurstpierpoint,[346] a "middle school" which was located just outside of Shoreham.[347] Soon after the boys at St Nicolas's Grammar School moved to Lancing in 1857, a "lower school" was opened in temporary premises[348] in Shoreham in 1858. It was known as St Saviour's, Shoreham (later, Ardingly),[349] and within a year it had 200 pupils. This third-grade school was for a class of people who, Woodard wrote, were trying to maintain their families

---

[343] See below, *passim*.

[344] N. Woodard, *A Plea for the Middle Classes*, n.p. [his italics]. Despite being widely circulated, this poorly printed pamphlet was never published. His other works included *Public Schools for the Middle Classes: A Letter to the Clergy of the Diocese of Chichester,* London 1851; and *The Society and Schools of St Mary and St Nicolas College,* London 1878.

[345] See B. Handford, *Lancing College*, Chichester 1986. In 1857 St Nicolas Grammar School was removed from Shoreham to Lancing, which henceforth became the headquarters of "The Society of SS. Mary and Nicolas, Lancing".

[346] The full name of Woodard's schools included the name of a patron saint. For convenience, this will be discarded.

[347] See M. A. McAdam and H. R. Holloway, *Hurstpierpoint College, 1865–1965*, New Shoreham 1965.

[348] In 1870 the school was housed in permanent accommodation at Ardingly.

[349] See R. Perry, *Ardingly, 1858–1946*, London 1951.

in a "respectable" way on £150 to £200 a year. These were the families, he argued, which would produce missionaries and schoolmasters, men who were not likely to be produced by richer families. "It is not fair to expect that Public boarding Schools for the Lower Middle Classes would furnish a good quota of such men as could do good services in each of these capacities, both at home and abroad."[350]

In 1878 the annual payments at the three Sussex schools were as follows: Lancing from £60 to £100 a year, Hurstpierpoint £30 to £35, Ardingly only 15 guineas. Before Woodard died in 1891, eight other boys' schools had been opened, including three new schools in the Midlands: Denstone in Staffordshire (1873),[351] Ellesmere in Shropshire (1884), and Worksop in Nottinghamshire (1885). Woodard refused to make the education of girls a part of his scheme, although circumstances "forced upon him a kind of morganatic alliance with a number of new girls' schools,"[352] to which he lent a lukewarm support.[353] In 1880 he wrote, "Public Schools for girls are of very doubtful merit. Religious homes or convents are more in harmony with my ideas".[354] Despite this, today there are 45 schools[355] in the Corporation, of which 17 are for girls. In keeping with Woodard's 'missionary' vision, there are also three overseas schools, including one in Queensland, Australia.[356]

Woodard's experience as a parish clergyman in Bethnal Green and Shoreham had convinced him that the middle classes were estranged from the Church, and that schools for the labouring poor would never be completely successful so long as the employers remained ill-educated and opposed to the Church. In forming his Corporation, Woodard grasped the concept of a national system of secondary education administered by the Church of England. At its heart, this was not an innovation but rather a return to an older concept of public

---

[350] N. Woodard, *St Nicolas College: St Saviour's Lower Middle Class School*, Brighton 1859, pp. 9–10.
[351] See D. J. Hudson and M. K. Swales, *Discovering Denstone*, Denstone 1979.
[352] Adamson, *English Education*, p. 277.
[353] However, his friend and co-worker, Robert Lowe, supported and oversaw the inclusion of girls' schools in the Society from 1872. See Heeney, *Mission to the Middle Classes*, p. 37.
[354] Otter, *Nathaniel Woodard*, p. 274.
[355] See http://www.woodard.co.uk/woodardframes.html (accessed March 2004), for a complete listing.
[356] St Margaret's Anglican Girls' School, Ascot, Queensland. Woodard frequently received requests to set up new schools in the British colonies. He first received a communication from Sydney, Australia, c.1865. B Heeney, *Mission to the Middle Classes*, p. 154.

education in which the Church was "restored to its ancient office of national educator".[357] In a published letter to the Marquis of Salisbury,[358] Woodard set forth his full scheme as it was in 1869. The country was to be arranged into five divisions—"one for the east, one for the west, one for the north and one for the south, and one (the most important of all) for the Midland counties".[359] Each division would maintain a boarding school for three grades, respectively for the rich, for persons of good incomes, and for small tradesmen, farmers, artisans and persons who were likely to become employers. The schools of each division would be directed by a body such as the Lancing Society, each having its provost and twenty-four fellows: half of them resident clerics, half non-resident laymen. Professional schoolmasters would be trained in the schools of the second grade.[360] The five provosts and one hundred and twenty fellows would be empowered to make by-laws for all the schools, and each bishop would be the official visitor of the schools within his diocese.[361] There would be no intervention by the state in this system of secondary education; Woodard wrote "state activity had gone far enough within the limits of elementary education". He estimated that about quarter of a million pounds had been expended on the Woodard schools since 1849, and that "two and a half millions" would be required for full implementation of the scheme he proposed.[362]

Woodard was very successful in gaining support for his scheme, and his skill in extracting money from the rich and famous was legendary.[363] Lord Halifax[364] once told him, "it is a privilege to receive

---

[357] Adamson, *English Education*, p. 278.

[358] The future Prime Minister was one of the Society's trustees.

[359] N. Woodard, *The Scheme of Education of St Nicolas...*, London 1869, p. 16.

[360] Expenses for a three- or four-year university course in the 1860s might have come to £600–800, which was beyond the reach of many in Woodard's first-level schools and of nearly everyone in the rest of his schools. For this reason, Woodard himself undertook the training of teachers for his schools. A training department, which awarded the "Associateship of St Nicolas' College", or ASNC, was attached to Hurstpierpoint. Honey, *Tom Brown's Universe*, p. 57.

[361] N. Woodard, *The Scheme of Education of St Nicolas...*, London 1869, pp. 15–6.

[362] Ibid.

[363] At a luncheon and garden party held to celebrate the opening of Denstone, Woodard came away with gifts to the value of over £5,000. At another luncheon, given in Manchester for 200 people, he raised £20,000. At yet another luncheon he informed the wealthy guests that that they would not be allowed to leave the room until they had subscribed £10,000 between them. Hibbert, *No Ordinary Place*, p. 28.

a begging letter from you."[365] He was also the master of what is today known as public relations: "From 1848 on there issued from Woodard's pen a stream of pamphlets, circulars, subscription lists, invitations to fêtes and meetings, reports, appeals and sermons".[366] However, there were those who, while supportive of his aim to provide "good, cheap, Church education for the middle classes",[367] were also highly critical of the Anglo-Catholic flavour of his schools. Woodard was a convinced disciple of Keble, Pusey and Newman,[368] and these were times of fierce Church party wrangling, when "prejudice was easily awakened at the least suspicion of anything which could be stigmatised as 'Popery'".[369] The first controversy arose out of Woodard's approach to confession, an issue which had dogged him since the start of his career.[370] Many Anglo-Catholics took the view that the command in the Prayer Book that priests could hear confessions from only either the sick or those preparing to receive Holy Communion, "cannot be construed into a command not to receive confessions on any other occasions".[371] In Woodard's 1848 *Directions to Chaplains*,[372] there was a section on the hearing of pupil confessions, and no mention was made about restricting the administration of this rite to the sick or to communicants. This was regarded by Evangelicals (as well as many 'moderate' Anglicans) as an outrage, and a clear contravention of the spirit of a Reformed Prayer Book. As will be seen below, in frequent and vociferous ways they expressed their disgust at this and other examples of "Romanist"

---

[364] Sir Charles Lindley Wood, second Viscount Halifax (1839–1934), was president of the English Church Union, 1868–1919 and 1927–34, and a leading lay Anglo-Catholic.

[365] Cited by Hibbert, *No Ordinary Place*, p. 28.

[366] Heeney, *Mission to the Middle Classes*, p. 41. He was also successful in getting articles published in academic and educational journals: Lord Brougham's speech in support of the Woodard Schools was reprinted in full as "Middle-Class Education", *English Journal of Education* (1 July 1861): 228–236.

[367] Ibid., p. 25.

[368] He went up to Oxford soon after Keble's assize sermon and the publication of Newman's first Tract.

[369] Adamson, *English Education*, p. 278.

[370] In 1843, soon after he was made Deacon, Woodard preached a sermon on confession, which, despite his own earnest pleadings and those of parishioners, resulted in his removal from St Bartholomew's, Bethnal Green, by the diocesan, Bishop Blomfield.

[371] F. W. Cornish, *The English Church in the Nineteenth Century*, London 1910, p. 85.

[372] N. Woodard, *St Nicolas College: Directions to Chaplains*, New Shoreham 1848. Reprinted in Heeney, *Mission to the Middle Classes*, Appendix A.

practices in the Woodard schools. It was also one of the motivations for a rival movement of Evangelical middle-class schools.

Broad Church Schools

Apart from the influence of Evangelicals on middle-class education, which is the subject of the rest of this book, there was another initiative in nineteenth-century secondary education, the waters of which rose from a very different spring. This was the work of so-called 'Broad Churchmen'. Over the last twenty years, there has been a renewed interest in the influence of this group in shaping the function of today's system of secondary education, especially their significance in the formation of middle-class day schools, and the system of Oxford and Cambridge "locals".[373] Broad Church involvement in middle-class education centres on two Anglican clergymen: William Rogers and J. L. Brereton. The County School movement initiated by Brereton has generally been regarded as the most significant and wide-reaching of the two—some even comparing it with the impact of Woodard.[374] However, at least one historian has pointed to the work of Revd William Rogers (1819–1896) as having an even greater impact.

David Allsobrook has boldly suggested that William Rogers was "the single most active promoter of new middle-class schools in the mid-Victorian era".[375] Like Woodard, he became famous as both a fundraiser and founder of middle-class schools. Unlike Woodard, however, he was a Broad Churchman whose liberal views earned him the soubriquet, 'Hang Theology Rogers'. Rogers was regarded as an expert on the subject of education. As Incumbent of St Thomas's, Charterhouse, from 1845, he opened day schools for the children of the street traders of his educationally neglected parish, and in 1862 he also opened a 'middle-class' school for a higher class of pupil. In the 1850s Rogers was a trustee of one of the country's richest foundations, Alleyn's Charity,[376] and he also served on the Newcastle Commission. William Rogers was a well-connected Etonian: he counted people like

---

[373] See especially Allsobrook, *Schools for the Shires*.
[374] See Honey, *Tom Brown's Universe*, pp. 47–103.
[375] Allsobrook, *Schools for the Shires*, p. 195.
[376] Rogers was involved in the re-organization of Alleyn's charity from 1857. The Alleyn's estate became even richer when the governors sold part of it for a new railway line in the 1860s for £100,000. This eventually led to the formation of two schools in 1882: Dulwich College (originally founded in 1619), and Alleyn's (the Lower School). See A. R. Chandler, *Alleyn's*, Henley on Thames 1998.

Jowett, Stanley, Northcote, Hobhouse, Gladstone and Pakington among his wide group of friends.[377] In 1863 Rogers became Rector of St Botolph's, Bishopsgate, and it was here that he launched his greatest educational project.

Soon after his arrival in the City, Rogers became convinced that for the children of "clerks...and tradesmen with moderate resources"[378] in his parish, no educational provision had been made. Spurred on by the Taunton Commission, he proposed in early 1865 that the "City parishes should combine in the establishment of a day school for the children of parents who could not afford to pay more than, say, £1 per quarter for their education."[379] With the Lord Mayor of London[380] as his greatest supporter, and the Bishop of London[381] as Visitor, Rogers initiated the 'Corporation for Middle Class Education'. In November 1865 he held a great public meeting of bankers, merchants and businessmen in the City of London, "for the purpose of establishing a middle-class school which would produce candidates fit to be clerks in the great metropolitan houses".[382] The promoters sought sponsorship for as much as £100,000 for the establishment of a 'central school' and smaller affiliated schools.[383] Within a month of the meeting they had raised half of this amount.[384] A year later, a school was opened in temporary buildings in Bath Street, and by the end of the first term it contained 518 pupils. It was at the opening of this school that Rogers made the fateful remark, "Hang economy, hang theology, let us begin...".[385] The foundation stone of a new school building on Cowper Street was laid in December 1868, and from the time it opened the numbers "stood steadily at 1,000".[386] No other affiliated schools were established.

Rogers' views on the place of religion in education (or lack of it) were not fully evident at first. The Bishop of London initially

---

[377] Heeney, *Mission to the Middle Classes*, p. 165.

[378] R. H. Hadden (ed.), *Reminiscences of William Rogers, Rector of St Botolph's, Bishopsgate*, London 1888, p. 157.

[379] Ibid., p. 158.

[380] Alderman W. S. Hale (1791–1872), Mayor of London 1864–5.

[381] Archibald Campbell Tait (1811–1882) was Bishop of London 1856–68 and Archbishop of Canterbury 1868–82.

[382] *Times* 8 November 1865, p. 8.

[383] *Guardian* 17 January 1866, p. 13.

[384] Allsobrook has suggested that when Rogers asked for financial support for the proposed school, he used blackmail by playing on the fears of the Livery Companies about possible Government intervention in their lucrative charities. Allsobrook, *Schools for the Shires*, p. 195.

[385] Hadden, *Reminiscences*, p. 167.

[386] *Guardian* 3 July 1867, p. 13.

supported the scheme because he was under the impression that "undenominational" religious instruction would form part of the school curriculum. But by mid-1867 the purely secular nature of the school's instruction had been exposed and episcopal approval was withdrawn.[387] Rogers said that he sought donations from "Portugese, Greeks, Parsees and members of all denominations",[388] and promised the Jewish Lord Mayor that the school would be "free, unfettered, and unsectarian."[389] Unlike his High Church and Evangelical colleagues, Rogers believed that the middle class was a "religious class", and that no definite religious instruction was necessary for them in his day schools. Rogers hoped that pupils would distil "a religion common to all citizens" from the regular secular classroom instruction.[390]

The other liberal-minded Churchman to enter the realm of secondary education was Revd J. L. Brereton (1822–1901), Rector of West Buckland in Devon. John Honey suggested in 1977 that Brereton and his "County Education" movement of the nineteenth century had been "almost totally neglected" by historians.[391] Perhaps as a result of this, Peter Searby produced his study of Brereton[392] within two years of Honey's book, and soon after, John Roach included a short but pithy comparison of Woodard and Brereton in his 1986 survey of secondary education. Both of these were heavily indebted to Honey's prior work, although Searby sheds some interesting new light on the influence of Brereton's quixotic personality[393] and also on the formation of the Graduated County Schools Association.[394] Searby, who was until recently a lecturer in Education at Cambridge University, was also interested in the history of Cavendish College at Cambridge.[395] Finally, Honey's suggestion of neglect has now been more than remedied by David Allsobrook's *Schools for the Shires*, which places Brereton and

---

[387] Ibid. Letter from the Bishop of London, and the leading article.
[388] SIC Report, vol. 5, p. 484.
[389] Hadden, *Reminiscences*, p. 162.
[390] SIC Report, vol. 5, p. 476.
[391] Honey, *Tom Brown's Universe*, p. 58.
[392] P. Searby, "Joseph Lloyd Brereton and the Education of the Victorian Middle Class", *Journal of Educational Administration and History*, 11, 1 (1979), pp. 4–14.
[393] Searby states at the outset of his essay that it "attempts to stress the importance of the individual personality to the historian." Ibid., p. 4.
[394] Ibid., pp. 11–12.
[395] Searby's proposed book, *A College That Failed*, which according his own footnote in 1979 was to be a "fuller account of Cavendish, with complete references", was never published. In 1982 he wrote *The Training of Teachers in Cambridge University: The First Sixty years 1879–1939*; however, it does not mention Cavendish College.

his aristocratic sponsor, Lord Fortescue, centrally within this development in secondary education. Some of Allsobrook's research is also based on material which Roach presented in his *Public Examinations in England 1850–1900*, another nineteenth-century development which became a central component to Brereton's new system.[396] What follows draws upon Heeney's pioneering introduction of Brereton, Honey's comprehensive survey of his life and work, and Allsobrook's contextualization within the wider history of nineteenth-century middle-class education.

J. L. Brereton was educated at Rugby under Thomas Arnold (1795–1842), and he came away from the school with a deep respect for the work of the famous schoolmaster.[397] He also took on Arnold's Broad Church beliefs, particularly his ideas of a Protestant unity, which Arnold expressed in his *Principles of Church Reform*.[398] Unlike Woodard, Brereton put little emphasis on strict Churchmanship and later encouraged the sons of Dissenters to enter his schools, where religious education and chapel services were always of an "undenomational" kind. He wanted Anglicans and Nonconformists to co-operate and he was anxious to create an atmosphere in his schools which would make this possible. Soon after arriving at West Buckland, Brereton formed a close friendship with Viscount Ebrington (later, the third Earl Fortescue), a local magnate and MP.[399] Brereton formed his views on education through long talks with the Fortescues, father and son, both of whom also had an interest in middle-class education.[400]

Brereton first outlined his ideas in 1858 in *Principles and Plan of a County School* which, as Allsobrook has pointed out, "owed its inspiration, if not its specific proposals, to Thomas Arnold".[401] Brereton himself acknowledged his debt to Arnold.[402] However, as Allsobrook has also suggested, while Thomas Arnold was the first

---

[396] See also J. Roach, "Middle-Class Education and Examinations: Some Early Victorian Problems." *British Journal of Educational Studies* 10, 2 (May 1962): 176–193.

[397] Honey, *Tom Brown's Universe,* pp. 59–60.

[398] T. Arnold, "Essays on Educational Topics", *Miscellaneous Works of Thomas Arnold*, London 1845, pp. 257–320.

[399] Lord Hugh, the third Earl Fortescue (1818–1905), sat in the House of Commons as a Whig MP for Plymouth 1841–52 and for Marylebone 1854–59, and was a Junior Minister in the 1840s. In 1961 he succeeded his father, the second Earl.

[400] Fortescue's own books included *The Devon County School: Its Objects, Costs and Studies*, Exeter 1862, and *Public Schools for the Middle Classes*, London 1864.

[401] Allsobrook, *Schools for the Shires*, p. 43.

[402] See the *Lynn Advertiser* 9 November 1895. Cited by P. Searby, "Joseph Lloyd Brereton", p. 4.

Englishman to put forward the idea of a 'county' university, the concept of a county college had been suggested for Ireland some time before Arnold took it up.[403] Roach has pointed out that B. F. Duppa, a secretary to the Central Society of Education 1836–40, also put forward a scheme in 1839[404] which was "remarkably similar to Brereton's later County Schools."[405] Heeney also noted that Woodard had publicised his ideas for middle-class education in his *Plea* in 1848. Brereton's plan was outlined in 1861 and 1864;[406] and in 1874 he set forth his mature ideas, adjusted to take account of the Taunton Commission's work, in his book *County Education: A Contribution of Experiments, Estimates, and Suggestions*.[407] His plans for a school at West Buckland, described as a "Farm and County School", were to be modelled on the public school pattern with three notable variations: it was to combine study with practical apprenticeship on an attached school farm; its curriculum was to be basically non-classical; and the capital for its foundation was to be raised by selling shares upon which a dividend of 5% was to be paid—the proprietary principle in fact. The fees were expected to range from £10 to £45 per year, depending on how much time each boy spent on farm work and study respectively.[408]

Like Woodard and the Taunton Commission Report, Brereton talked about schools of three grades. The farmer who worked 200–300 acres was, he argued, "the midmost man in England", and on an average income of £200 he could not afford to pay a boarding fee of more than about 30 guineas.[409] This was the charge at the Devon County School, West Buckland, which Brereton and Fortescue opened in 1858. Below this in the hierarchy, a school for the sons of "smaller farmers, tradesmen and artisans" could be provided at around £15 per annum "if the boys also did some agricultural work".[410] In Brereton's structure such a school represented a third grade; West Buckland the second grade; and a first grade school could be provided at fees of

---

[403] Allsobrook, *Schools for the Shires*, p. 43. For middle-class education in Ireland, see ch. 4 pp. 97–101.

[404] B. F. Duppa, *County Colleges of Agriculture*, London 1839, pp. 59–86.

[405] Roach, *Secondary Education in England 1800–1870*, p. 169.

[406] See J. L. Brereton, *County Education: A Letter Addressed to the Right Honourable the Earl of Devon*, London 1861; and Fortescue, *Public Schools for the Middle Classes*.

[407] J. L. Brereton, *County Education. A Contribution of Experiments, Estimates and Suggestions*, London 1874.

[408] J. L. Brereton, "Principles and Plan of a Farm and County School" in Fortescue, *Public Schools for the Middle Classes*.

[409] Brereton, *County Education*, 1874, pp. 8 and 122.

[410] Ibid., pp. 31 and 121.

about £50 per annum.[411] The proposed fees for second- and third-grade schools were similar to what Woodard charged at Hurstpierpoint and Ardingly, though Lancing was considerably more expensive than Brereton's projected first-grade school. Brereton also had plans for a national organization, but unlike Woodard and the National Society's Middle Class Schools Committee, his local unit was to be the county, rather than the parish or the diocese.

The whole country would be divided into four administrative "provinces", each with its centre at a university (Oxford, Cambridge, London and one in the North), and each comprising a single educative unit.[412] At every one of these four university centres, a "County College" was to be established with three principal purposes: to connect the University Local Examinations with university residence;[413] to enable the graduates of county schools to obtain a cheap degree at a relatively early age; and to train a supply of masters for the local schools. In 1876 Cavendish College[414] was opened at Cambridge.[415] It was recognized as a "public hostel" by the University in 1882, and by 1883 it had 96 students. Despite a reorganization in 1888, and continued support from a wide cross-section of Anglicans,[416] the College collapsed in 1892.[417]

Although Brereton was responsible for founding a number of other institutions, his reckless and over-ambitious approach to money meant that none of his schools ever established a firm financial footing.

---

[411] Brereton, *County Education*, pp. 123 and 21.

[412] Ibid., p. 124. See also J. L. Brereton, *The County College: an Educational Proposal Addressed to the University of Cambridge*, Cambridge 1872.

[413] Roach has pointed out that Brereton and Fortescue were among the first people to suggest the idea of external examinations as "a gauge of scholastic efficiency and a stimulus to effort" in the 1850s. The concept was taken up by Acland and Temple, who initiated the Oxford Locals in 1857, followed by the Cambridge Locals in the next year. See T. D. Acland, *Middle-Class Education. Schemes of the West of England Examination and Prizes...*, London 1857, and Roach, *Public Examinations*, pp. 65–9.

[414] Named after the largest shareholder, William Cavendish, the seventh Duke of Devonshire.

[415] For Cavendish College, see W. M. Saunders, "Cavendish College, Cambridge", *Cassell's Family Magazine* (1885), pp. 300–2; B. Little, *The Colleges of Cambridge 1286–1973*, Bath 1973, pp. 133–7; and T. H. Simms, *Homerton College 1695–1978*, London 1979, pp. 35–45.

[416] In 1884 two boys from Lancing and one from Hurstpierpoint were at Cavendish.

[417] The empty buildings were bought by the Congregational Board of Education for its training college, Homerton College, in 1894. For Homerton College, see T. H. Simms, *Homerton College 1695–1978*.

Brereton regarded himself as something of a practical economist, and his books and pamphlets were full of formulae on raising capital and calculations on how the schools could be managed 'on a shoestring'.[418] In reality he was financially inept and the foundation money he raised and the fees he set were always hopelessly inadequate. His grand plans for the education of girls, through the Graduated County Schools Association formed in 1884, had to be abandoned—but only after the bank forced it into liquidation in 1887.[419] His Norfolk County School at Elmham near East Dereham initially showed great promise,[420] but it soon fell on hard times and went into liquidation in 1893.[421] He was accused of financial mismanagement on more than one occasion,[422] and his fellow directors at Cavendish even accused him of being a "swindler".[423]

Brereton's ideas on middle-class education were more lasting than his practical achievements. Despite their financial problems, Brereton's schools were the inspiration for many other initiatives in county education and he spawned many imitators. Brereton was well aware of this, and even encouraged it. In 1875 he wrote: "Though West Buckland claims to be the first County School established...it is by no means the only one, and...many others with equal success, and some with greater advantages to offer, are spread over the country, most of which in name, and all to a great degree in plan, acknowledge that they started from one source."[424] The Taunton Commission, to which both Fortescue and Brereton had given evidence, gave details of a number of these other middle-class boarding schools in the counties. Some of them went on to become major public schools in the next century.

---

[418] Honey, *Tom Brown's Universe*, p. 64.

[419] See Searby, "Joseph Lloyd Brereton", pp. 11–12.

[420] Founded in 1874 with 68 boarders. See J L Brereton, *County Education: The Reports of the Devon and Norfolk County School Associations...*, London 1875, p. 13; and Honey, *Tom Brown's Universe*, pp. 69–72. The Norfolk County School at Elmham was unusual in that it was the only county school which built a chapel.

[421] In 1957 the main building was demolished. The outbuildings were converted into a broiler farm and the chapel into a centrally-heated piggery. Honey, *Tom Brown's Universe*, p. 103.

[422] His friend and financier, Lord Fortescue, frequently expressed his concerns. His letters to Brereton on financial matters are notable by their special concern for the welfare of Brereton's wife and 11 children.

[423] Honey, *Tom Brown's Universe*, p. 87.

[424] J. L. Brereton, *County Education: Accounts of the Devon and Norfolk County School Associations...*, London 1876, p. 6.

All of Brereton's imitators seemed to have aimed for the same clientèle as the West Buckland School and charged similar fees. The East Devon County School was founded in 1860 by Revd C. S. Bere[425] at Sampford Peverell in Devon, where he established a school for "the instruction of the sons of the middle classes, especially of the agricultural classes".[426] Fees were set at around £30 per year and the Taunton Report listed it as having 35 boarders and 15 day boys in 1868.[427] Pupil numbers increased to 80 boarders in 1873, but by 1882 it had only 32 boarders.[428] It closed in 1886 with debts of over £2,000.[429] Another similar institution was Dorset County School, founded in 1864 for the "sons of yeomen, tradesmen, merchants and professional men". In 1868 it had 75 boarders paying between £30 and £34 each per year.[430] At Wellington in Somerset, a former private school begun in 1842, the West Somerset County School, offered a non-classical education "with an emphasis on agricultural science and handicrafts." In the twentieth century this school became a direct grant school, known as Wellington School, Somerset.[431] In 1866 a group of landowners[432] and ironmasters[433] established a limited company to found Bedford County School, which opened in 1868 with 70 pupils. According to Honey, the school "flourished under a succession of able headmasters" and it was helped by the favourable educational environment of the town of Bedford.[434] One later foundation in 1882 was the North-Eastern County School at Barnard Castle, where existing endowments[435] were used to provide a school for local middle-class boys. The first Headmaster was Brereton's son, Frank, a graduate of Cavendish College.

The best known and arguably most successful of the County Schools were both founded in 1865. The Suffolk County School at Framlingham (later, 'Framlingham College') was established as the Albert Middle Class College, in memory of the Prince Consort, "for

---

[425] Rector of Uplowman, near Tiverton, 1858–85. Prior to this, Bere was one of Cotton's early appointments at Marlborough.
[426] SIC Report, vol. 14, p. 516.
[427] Ibid. See also C. Bere, "Account of Sampford Peverall Proprietary School" in the SIC Report vol. 22 p. 95–8.
[428] Heeney, *Mission to the Middle Classes*, p. 320.
[429] Honey, *Tom Brown's Universe*, p. 68.
[430] SIC Report, vol. 14, p. 471.
[431] See Honey, *Tom Brown's Universe*, p. 68.
[432] W. H. Whitbread and Lord Charles Russell.
[433] James and Charles Howard.
[434] Honey, *Tom Brown's Universe*, p. 68.
[435] St John's Hospital, Barnard Castle. Honey, *Tom Brown's Universe*, p. 85.

the better education of the middle classes of the county of Suffolk".[436] It was the initiative of Fortescue's friend, Sir Edward Kerrison,[437] and by the end of its first term, the College had 268 boarders. The school received valuable land from Pembroke College, Cambridge, after the reorganization of the Hitcham Bequest (1636) by the Charity Commissioners.[438] By the time the Taunton Commissioners made their report, the school numbers had increased to 309.[439] The Surrey County School at Cranleigh[440] was founded in 1862 by the local rector, Canon J. H. Sapte,[441] and the local MP, Mr George Cubitt.[442] The school was built on donations (there were no shareholders), and its object was "to provide a sound and thorough public school education, on the principles of the Church of England, for the sons of farmers and others throughout the agricultural districts of Surrey".[443] It opened in 1865 with only 22 boarders and four day boys, but within six months it was full. According to the Taunton Report, by 1868 it had 177 boarders and the buildings had been expanded to accommodate up to 300 pupils.[444] Today the school accommodates 550 pupils.

The County School movement was a significant effort by Broad Churchmen to enter the realm of secondary education. It was not a unified movement, although Brereton's plans provided a basis for other independent promoters. Despite the "Anglican correctness" of

---

[436] Charity Commissioners Annual Report, 1863. Cited by J. Booth, *Framlingham College: The First Sixty Years*, Ipswich 1925, p. 15.

[437] Sir Edward Clarence Kerrison (1821–1886) was the MP for East Suffolk 1866–77. Honey, who was the first person to identify Kerrison as a close colleague of Fortescue, incorrectly records his name as 'Kerrigan'. Honey, *Tom Brown's Universe*, p.65.

[438] See Booth, *Framlingham College*, pp. 14–5.

[439] SIC Report, vol. 21, pp. 100–1.

[440] 'Cranley' became 'Cranleigh' in 1867 to avoid postal confusion with Crawley. The new spelling will be used here.

[441] John Henry Sapte was one of Samuel Wilberforce's first ordinands and was Rector of Cranleigh for 56 years, 1847–1903.

[442] George Cubitt (Lord Ashcombe from 1892) belonged to the immensely successful London building family that developed the Duke of Westminster's estate in Belgravia and the Duke of Bedford's estates in Tavistock Square and Gordon Square. He was MP for West Surrey 1860–85. The firm is today part of the large British building company, Holland, Hannan & Cubitts.

[443] 1863 Prospectus, cited by A. J. Megahey, *A History of Cranleigh School*, London 1983, p. 12.

[444] SIC vol. 11, p. 157.

Cranleigh[445] and the "Churchiness" of Framlingham—where the religious education was always "in accordance with the doctrines and practice of the Church of England"[446]—the County Schools were characterised by a "liberal" approach to the role of religion in the life of the school. This contrasted starkly with Woodard's schools, where "The inculcation of religious truth, the preservation of Church dominance in secondary education, the maintenance of the unity of secular and sacred knowledge by resistance to the conscience clause principle...were all fundamental to Woodard's purpose."[447] Brereton himself recognized and welcomed the influence of dissent on the middle classes, expecting his schools and colleges to be comprised of up to one-third Nonconformists. He was even willing for other religions to be taught, stating in 1861 that "a free opening...should be given to the special religious instruction of such public representatives of religious bodies as the directors of the school would sanction".[448] Both Brereton and Rogers were willing, and even eager, to sacrifice "Church principles" for the sake of their educational aims. This abandonment of Church—and possibly even Christian—teaching was anathema to members of both the High Church and Evangelical parties, and this is one of the reasons why Evangelicals were keen to set up their own middle-class schools. A number of individual Evangelicals interested in education founded middle-class schools from 1862–1868, a period which was contemporaneous with the early work of Woodard and Brereton. However, well before any other individuals—Broad Church, Anglo-Catholic or otherwise—had taken the initiative, an Evangelical who had achieved a national profile for his pioneering efforts in infant and elementary education, burst upon the scene. This person was Revd Francis Close of Cheltenham.

---

[445] See Heeney, *Mission to the Middle Classes*, p. 164 for a public response by the Headmaster in 1867 to accusations of a lack of Church of England character at Cranleigh.
[446] Cited by Heeney, *Mission to the Middle* Classes, p. 164.
[447] Ibid., p. 164.
[448] See Brereton, *County Education* 1861, p. 18.

PART II

INDIVIDUAL EVANGELICAL INITIATIVE

CHAPTER 3

Francis Close at Cheltenham

When Queen Victoria ascended the throne in 1837, the town of Cheltenham had already become synonymous with the name of its principal clergyman; Francis Close (1797–1882).[1] Lord Alfred Tennyson, who lived in St James' Square, Cheltenham, referred to his home-town as "a polka, parson-worshipping place, of which Francis Close is Pope".[2] Close was often the subject of contemporary ridicule,[3] but also of respect, for "through his preaching, his personality and his pamphlets",[4] the Perpetual Curate of St Mary's wielded great influence on the town of Cheltenham during the thirty years he was in charge of the parish.[5] He was a popular preacher, attracting a huge congregation at the parish church each Sunday. He published over seventy tracts and pamphlets on religious and educational topics, and was responsible for helping to found a large public school, three middle-class schools and a college for training teachers. He built four churches[6] in Cheltenham, each with its own Infant and National School[7] and he also revived the

---

[1] See entry in Appendix 1 for a description of Close's pre-Cheltenham period, and Munden, *A Cheltenham Gamaliel*, pp. 3–17.

[2] W. E. Adams, *Memoirs of a Social Atom*, London 1903, vol. 1 p. 23 fn. 1. Tennyson's description of Close as 'Pope' was first reported in the *Morning Post* in 1858. See A. F. Munden, "The Anglican Evangelical Party in the Diocese of Carlisle in the Nineteenth Century with particular reference to the ministries of Bishop Samuel Waldegrave and Dean Francis Close", PhD thesis, Durham University 1987, p. 211 fn. 10.

[3] The Hon. Grantley Berkeley, Earl Fitzhardinge, stated that "...fifty pairs of slippers were worked for the parson, and presented to him, as if he had been a centipede...". Recollections of the Hon. Grantley Berkeley, cited in "Notes on Francis Close", ff 27 p. 2. Dean Close School Archives.

[4] Hennell, *Sons of the Prophets*, p. 105.

[5] See Contem Ignotas [R. Glover], *The Golden Decade of a Favoured Town*, London 1884, *passim*.

[6] St Paul's (consecrated 1831), Christ Church (1840), St Peter's (1849) and St Luke's (1854). S. T. Blake, *Cheltenham's Churches and Chapels AD 773–1883*, Cheltenham 1979.

[7] See R. R. Rusk, *A History of Infant Education*, London 1933; and P. McCann and F. Young, *Samuel Wilderspin and the Infant School Movement*, London 1982.

town's ancient grammar school. By the time he was made Dean of Carlisle in 1856, Francis Close had become "a leading spokesman and apologist for education",[8] and Cheltenham was regarded as a national centre for education as well as a "stronghold of provincial Evangelicalism".[9] One contemporary observed that for the first half of the nineteenth century, "the history of the town for all that period was the history of a single clergyman".[10] Tennyson's title for Close—"Protestant Pope"—may have been an exaggeration, but it was not an undeserved one in terms of the influence yielded on one town by just one man.

Francis Close was the Perpetual Curate[11] of Cheltenham parish church between 1826 and 1856. During this time, he was also Chairman of the Vestry Committee in an era when many of the tasks that later became the business of the town council were carried out by the parish vestry.[12] Part of the reason for Close's influence was that he was incumbent of the whole town during a significant period in its development as a fashionable spa. From 1821 to 1851 the population of Cheltenham grew from 13,396 to 35,051. To this could be added at least 10,000 visitors during the height of the 'season' each year. Each week the local newspapers carried the names of members of the royal family, aristocracy and gentry who had arrived or departed.[13] They also reported on the entertainments and social activities. Summer balls were held in the Montpellier Rotunda from July to October, and winter balls at the Assembly Rooms from December to April. Besides these, there were concerts, recitals and readings;[14] the theatre, hunts and

---

[8] Munden, *A Cheltenham Gamaliel*, p. 35.

[9] Ibid., p. 19.

[10] Adams, *Social Atom*, vol. 1 p. 11.

[11] A perpetual curate was a person who carried out the duties of a priest in a parish, but who was not a vicar or rector. The position was a permanent one (hence 'perpetual'), but it had a different legal standing to the other two positions, including the fact that the person did not have to be formally instituted. In 1863, the title was changed and Close's successor became the first Rector of Cheltenham. Perpetual curacies were abolished in England in 1968.

[12] Vestries, of which Nonconformist and irreligious parishioners could be members, were often the scene of fierce controversies over such issues as the levying of church rates.

[13] In 1823, the visitors included "4 Dukes, 3 Duchesses, 6 Marquises, 5 Marchionesses, 4 Bishops, 10 earls, 8 Countesses, 53 Lords, 70 Ladies besides a host of Honourables, Baronets, foreigners of title and other persons of distinction." J. Goding, *Norman's History of Cheltenham*, Cheltenham 1863, p. 45.

[14] Cheltenham soon became a literary centre, a tradition that continues today with the Cheltenham Literary Festival being held in October each year.

horse-racing. The number of visitors and the development of new spas, particularly those at Montpellier and Pittville, encouraged a great deal of speculative building. Joseph Pitt, from whom Charles Simeon had purchased the right of selecting the incumbent of the parish in 1816, was the greatest of all the speculative builders and financed the Pittville estate, a huge residential housing development centred on the Pittville Pump Room.[15] In 1823 it was reported that contracts for new houses in the town amounted to £450,000, and that between 400 and 500 men were employed in the building trades.[16]

By that time Cheltenham was one of the fastest growing centres in Britain, and Francis Close its new incumbent. Thus the stage was set for a thirty year ministry in which the Perpetual Curate of the town became not only the town's single most influential figure, but also gained something of a national reputation. His reputation was achieved for a number of reasons including his denunciation of Cheltenham's race[17] and theatre goers,[18] his tirades against the Chartists[19] and Owenite radicals including Holyoake,[20] and his constant criticism of the growing ritualist trends in the Church of England.[21] However, "it was without doubt for his contribution to education both in a local and a national context that Close deserves to be considered a minor

---

Distinguished literary figures who 'took the waters' in the nineteenth century included Lord Byron, Jane Austen and Charles Dickens. The latter wrote of Cheltenham; "Rarely have I seen such a place, that so attracted my fancy".

[15] The Pittville Pump Room was opened in 1830 at a cost of £60,000—a huge sum in those days. Goding, *History of Cheltenham*, p. 549. It is today regarded as one of the finest Regency buildings in Cheltenham.

[16] Ibid., p. 547.

[17] See F. Close, *A Letter addressed to the Inhabitants of Cheltenham on the subject of the Races*, London 1830.

[18] See, for example, F. Close, *The Stage Ancient and Modern its tendencies on Morals and Religion. A Lecture by Francis Close D.D*, London 1877.

[19] F. Close, *Sermon on the Occasion of the Visit of the Chartists to Cheltenham Parish Church*, London 1840.

[20] See O. Ashton, "Clerical Control and Radical Responses in Cheltenham." *Midland History* 8, 1983, p. 137.

[21] See, for example, F. Close, *Semper Idem or Popery Everywhere and Always the same*, London 1851; *The Restoration of Churches is the Restoration of Popery*, London 1844; *The Roman Antichrist and Lying Spirit*, London 1846; *The Catholic Revival or Ritualism in the Church of England*, London 1866. His caustic comment on Newman's *Tract 90* was: "I would not trust the writer of that Tract with my purse."

Francis Close (1797–1882)

national figure."[22] It is for this reason that Francis Close provides an early focal point of this study.

As the town expanded, Close extended his ministry by founding schools and churches to meet the needs of all social classes. His interest in education, first during his curacy at Kingsbury and later—and more significantly—at Cheltenham, resulted in his becoming a leading national spokesman on education, a position which was unrivalled among Evangelical clergy of the time.[23] When he left Cheltenham in 1856, it was suggested at a public meeting that "the Francis Close institution"[24] should be erected to mark his achievements. Four years after his death, the Dean Close Memorial School was opened with that object in mind.[25] At the dedication ceremony, Revd Canon Brooke, Rector of Bath, articulated Close's contribution to education as follows:

> Dean Close was both a good and a great man. He was a man of very great power...one could not long be in his presence...without feeling that he was a man of cultivated and powerful intellect...and perhaps one of the best organizers that ever lived. He did not think that any way of perpetuating the memory of Dean Close could have been found more congenial to his life work than that which had been followed [sic]. Education—the education of the upper middle-classes, the education of the poor, the training of teachers, the whole was dear to his heart...[26]

The first of these three areas of educational endeavour—the education of the middle-classes—is the subject of the rest of this chapter. For Francis Close was largely responsible for the re-invigoration of the town's ancient grammar school and the foundation of a new public school, Cheltenham College. As will be shown later, Close regarded these two institutions "as his right hand and his left hand".[27]

---

[22] N. A. D. Scotland, "The Centenary of Dean Close School and the Contribution of Francis Close to Education", *History of Education Society Bulletin* 40 (Autumn 1987): 31.
[23] Munden, *A Cheltenham Gamaliel*, p. 35.
[24] *Cheltenham Journal*, 8 November 1856, p. 1, "Testimonial to Francis Close".
[25] See ch. 9 below.
[26] *Cheltenham Examiner*, 19 May 1886, p. 3.
[27] *Cheltenham Free Press and Gloucestershire Herald,* 25 December 1852, p. 4.

Cheltenham College

Throughout the first half of the nineteenth century, Cheltenham's population continued to swell with fashionable new residents, many of whom were connected with the Army and the East India Company.[28] Cheltenham spa became a fashionable place to which "the old Indians, civil and military" would retire; "the fleeting remnants of whose livers sent them to drink the Cheltenham waters".[29] Before long these men began to realise the need for adequate schooling for their sons, and later—their daughters.[30] On 9 November 1840, a small group met in Major General George Swiney's drawing room to discuss the setting up of a new school. Five resolutions were unanimously agreed:

1. That it is the opinion of this meeting that a Proprietary Grammar School, on the plan of those so successfully established in other parts of the country, is highly desirable in the town of Cheltenham.
2. That means be adopted for the establishment of such a school.
3. That the school be conducted strictly in conformity with the principles of the Church of England.
4. That the price of each share be £10 and the annual charge for each pupil £12.
5. That the following gentlemen be appointed a Provisional Committee to devise the best means of carrying the foregoing resolutions into effect and to report the result at a General Meeting of the Proprietors to be hereafter called:

Provisional Committee
Revd. S. Middleton,   Capt J. S. Iredell,
G. S. Harcourt, Esq.,   Fenton Hort, Esq.,
Capt. Robertson [31]

---

[28] See M. C. Morgan, *Cheltenham College: The First Hundred Years*, London 1968, pp. 7–8 and also G. Hart, *A History of Cheltenham*, Leicester 1965, p. 214.
[29] A. F. Leach (ed.), *A History of Bradfield College*, Oxford 1900, p. 3.
[30] Cheltenham Ladies' College was founded in 1853 as a new proprietary college for girls, initially with strong links to the boys' college. See D. Beale, *History of the Cheltenham Ladies' College,* Cheltenham 1904 and A. K. Clarke, *A History of the Cheltenham Ladies' College 1853–1953*, London 1953.
[31] C. H. Pigg (ed.), *Cheltenham College Register 1841–1919 Additions and Corrections 1919–1951*, Cheltenham 1953, xi.

George Simon Harcourt (1797–1868) and James Shrubb Iredell (1793–1872) were co-founders of the new school[32] and they were both military men.[33] The other members of the provisional committee reflected the social background from which the college gained much of its support.

The first meeting of the Board of Directors resolved that shareholders had to be from the middle and upper classes, and the sons of tradesmen were strictly excluded. "No person should be considered as eligible who shall not be moving in the circle of a gentleman. No retail trader being under any circumstances to be so considered."[34] Unlike other public schools that relied largely on boarders, nearly two-thirds of the boys who entered the college in its first year lived locally.[35] As a result of this, within seven years many of the local private boys' schools in Cheltenham were forced to close.[36] By 1854, there were nearly 600 boys at the College; of whom 400 lived in twelve boarding houses and eight private houses. Cheltenham Proprietary College had become one of the largest public schools in the country, and no other Cheltenham school could rival it—although, as will be shown below, some would try.

In the opinion of T. W. Bamford, the public schools' historian, Cheltenham College was a landmark in nineteenth-century education, not just because it was the first of the major Victorian schools,[37] but because "it combined great success with undoubted reputation, both for the classics and the accepted career of government service."[38] From the beginning it was intended that there should be two departments—one for boys destined for university, and the other for those who

---

[32] Morgan, *Cheltenham College*, p. 3.
[33] Harcourt had fought at Waterloo and Iredell had served in the East India Company. Pigg, *Cheltenham College Register 1841–1919*, xii.
[34] Minutes of the Board of Directors of the Proprietary College (hereafter "Minutes of the Directors"), 10 November 1840. Cheltenham College Archives. As shall be shown later, retailers and other members of the same class were expected to send their sons to the Grammar School.
[35] Bamford, *Public Schools*, p. 26; and idem., "Public School Towns in the Nineteenth Century", *British Journal of Educational Studies* 6, 1 (November 1957): 25. Rugby is a case in point, where "migrant" parents moved into the town for the education of their sons. With the advent of railways, however, this became less and less necessary and public schools became truly 'public', with pupils being drawn from all over the nation.
[36] *Cheltenham Free Press*, 25 December 1847, p. 408.
[37] Others included Marlborough (founded 1843), Wellington (1859), Clifton (1860), and Malvern (1865). See especially Gardner, *Public Schools*, pp. 159–208, and ch. 2 above.
[38] Bamford, *Public Schools*, p. 26.

intended to enrol in the Army.[39] In the Classical Department, traditional subjects such as classics and mathematics were taught as well as modern history, French and German. Examinations were carried out each year by examiners from Oxford and Cambridge. The Military and Civil Department[40] was modelled on similar departments at Woolwich[41] and particularly Addiscombe,[42] so that the 'Addiscombe class' prepared boys for that school in Latin, mathematics, French and German, fortification,[43] surveying,[44] military drawing, experimental science,[45] Sanskrit and Hindustani. The last subject was taught by a Professor of Oriental Languages, a position which was created in 1845[46] because it was said that "no officer can be appointed on the staff in India without it."[47]

Although Close was not one of the founders of the college, it was a venture which he was intimately involved in, from the beginning. At a second meeting of the Provisional Committee in November 1840, it was resolved "That in order to obtain the greatest amount of practical information, respecting the best mode of organizing a Proprietary Grammar School, it is desirable that the parochial clergy of Cheltenham and its immediate vicinity, being share-holders, be invited to favour this committee with their attendance."[48] Close and the

---

[39] See T. Hearl, "Military Education and the School Curriculum 1800–1870", *History of Education* 5, 3 (1976): 251–64.

[40] Before this it was called the 'Modern Department'. *Cheltenham College Fourth Annual Report*, 1845.

[41] The Royal Military Academy, Woolwich (1741–1939) trained artillery and engineer cadets. See F. G. Guggisberg, *The Shop: The Story of the Royal Military Academy, 1741–1900*, London 1910.

[42] The East India Company's "military seminary" at Addiscombe, Croydon (1809–1861) was regarded as being very "up-to-date in curriculum and method". T. Hearl, "Military Academies and English Education", *History of Education Society Bulletin* 2 (1968): 17. For a history of the school, see H. M. Vibart, *Addiscombe: Its Heroes and Men of Note*, Westminster 1894.

[43] Fortification was taught at the college by means of a sand model, based on the Addiscombe pattern, in a specially built room erected in 1845.

[44] In 1854 an observatory was erected on the tower roof.

[45] Drawing was mainly for the Army candidates and experimental science for the candidates for the Royal Engineers.

[46] The first professor was Captain A. D. Gordon, father of Adam Lindsay Gordon, the Australian poet. A. L. Gordon was one of the first boys to attend the College in 1841. See E. Humphris, *The Life of Adam Lindsay Gordon*, London 1912, pp. 14–15.

[47] Minutes of the Directors, 8 July 1845.

[48] Ibid.

minister of Holy Trinity church, Revd John Browne (1795–1857),[49] were the two clergy whom the committee approached, and both were appointed clerical vice-presidents of the college. Close wrote that they were asked "to assist in the creation of a school in which our sons might have a first-rate education on reasonable terms, [and] our answer was in effect, that if those religious principles which we valued above all things, were secured to the College, and were inwrought in its constitution, we would cordially work with them."[50]

These 'religious principles' were vaguely outlined in the college's *Rules and Regulations*, which stated: "This Institution is established to provide for the Sons of Gentlemen a sound Religious, Classical, Mathematical, and General Education of the highest order, on moderate terms, and in strict conformity with the principles and doctrines of the United Church of England and Ireland."[51] Although the 'principles and doctrines' were not defined, it was clear that the college was to be based on Evangelical beliefs and that no Tractarians or Roman Catholics would be employed by the College. However, by not stating this explicitly in the Regulations, the college could not ensure its Evangelical character for future generations. It was certainly much more open than the foundation trust of the teacher training college that Francis Close founded in 1847 as a means of training schoolteachers with Evangelical convictions.[52] This emphasised the importance of the Scriptures, the Thirty-nine Articles and the Liturgy of the Church of England, and stated that these principles must be preserved *for ever*.[53]

On 26 November 1840, the first meeting of the proposed 'Cheltenham Proprietary School' was held with Francis Close as chairman. The administration of the College was vested in a board of twelve directors. They had extensive powers that included the management of all property, control of finance, appointment of the

---

[49] Browne was the Curate of Holy Trinity between 1828–57. He was "an outstanding preacher, and second to Close in the ministerial hierarchy in town." Munden, *A Cheltenham Gamaliel*, p. 34.

[50] F. Close, *A Letter to the Proprietors of Cheltenham College and to those Parents who have Sons in the School*, Carlisle 1862, p. 4.

[51] *Rules and Regulations of Cheltenham College, Instituted 1840*, Cheltenham 1859, p. 9.

[52] The Church of England Training Schools at Cheltenham. See above, p. 99.

[53] Cheltenham Training College Foundation Trust Deed, 1848. Cited by C. More, *Training of Teachers, 1847–1947: History of Church Colleges at Cheltenham*, London 1992, p. 13. The emphasis is in the original. See also C. More, *A Splendid College: An Illustrated History of Teacher Training in Cheltenham 1847–1990*, London 1992, ch. 7.

principal[54] and theological tutor, payment of salaries, regulation of the boarding houses and control of discipline with powers to suspend or expel pupils. The principal, who had to be a clergyman, was responsible for "The internal regulation of the School"[55] which included the appointment and dismissal of staff (with the exception of the theological tutor). He was completely accountable to the directors, to whom he had to "confer and consult with...on all matters tending to the advantage of the institution."[56] He was not permitted to attend their meetings. It was this over-accountability of the principal to the board that led to the resignation of the school's first principal, Dr Alfred Phillips. In his opinion, "this hitherto flourishing college is in the same vortex of trouble, jealousy, misunderstanding and disunion which has proved destructive to others before it."[57]

The Board of Directors, as the Governing Body was first called, bore that name till 1862, when its title was changed to Council. The Council thereafter consisted partly of Life Members, not necessarily shareholders of the College, and partly of Triennial Members who retired by rotation, elected by the shareholders from their own body. The proprietary system remained in force till 1894, when the College was incorporated by an Act of Parliament, with perpetual succession and a common seal and the right to hold lands in perpetuity, the rights of the existing proprietors being bought out and extinguished.[58] Although all authority was vested in the Board of Directors, as vice-president, Close had a great deal of control. He chaired the meetings of the board and invariably prepared the annual report. His speech at the annual speech day and prize giving was certainly as important as the principal's speech. From 1841, Close was a trustee shareholder in the college and he chaired the proprietors' annual meeting. After 1845, he and Revd John Browne were given responsibility by the board for the selection of the theological tutor. This guaranteed that the first three successive theological tutors would all be convinced Evangelicals. From 1854–56 he was also chairman of the discipline committee. The members of this committee paid regular visits to the boarding houses to deal with "immorality, wilful breach of discipline, or flagrant misconduct".[59] In the early days of the college, before the permanent building was available, Close was also one of the four members of the

---

[54] Cheltenham College was unusual for the time in using this title for the school's headmaster.
[55] *Rules and Regulations*, p. 20.
[56] Ibid., pp. 22–3.
[57] Minutes of the Directors, 27 August 1844.
[58] Pigg, *College Register 1841–1919*, xiii.
[59] *Rules and Regulations*, p. 20.

'house' committee. At first, this committee negotiated to rent Rodney Villa until Close suggested that two large houses in Bayshill Terrace, "in a Central part of the Town",[60] could be adapted as a school and would provide more space. There was also a field opposite, which could be used as playing grounds. By February 1841, the property had been rented[61] and the necessary conversions were carried out before the opening of the school in July.

The opening ceremony took place in the Cheltenham Assembly Rooms on Thursday 29 July 1841. On the platform were the directors and their families. The floor was filled "by the most influential ladies and gentlemen of the town and neighbourhood"[62] and in all, 800 people were admitted by ticket. One observer described the scene thus:

> About ten minutes past twelve, the Rev. Dr. Phillips, the Principal of the new College, the other Masters, the Rev. F. Close, Incumbent of Cheltenham, and the Rev. John Browne, of Trinity Church, entered in full canonicals...amid the cordial plaudits of the meeting...Immediately opposite the reverend gentlemen, the boys, who have already been examined and classed, to the number of 108, were ranged, each with his academic cap in his hand, and formed objects of great interest with the meeting.[63]

The acting president, Thomas Kingscote, opened the proceedings with a short speech that contrasted the perils of a purely secular education and the merits of a religious one and made clear that the college was intended to be a religious foundation. Close followed with another speech in which he explained how the Proprietary College "from first to last would be a Religious and Christian Institution".[64] Its religion was to be

> ...the written religion of the word of God. He meant the Bible in all its holiness and its fullness; the Bible with freedom of access to all, taught in the spirit of lowliness and in the spirit of prayer...he meant the religion of the creeds, homilies, liturgies, and *written* divinity of the Church of England. By religion he meant the religion of the martyred reformers—the religion of the thirty-nine articles...This was the religion which he would interweave in the daily instruction and practice of the Cheltenham Proprietary College.[65]

---

[60] Pigg, *College Register 1841–1919*, xiii.
[61] Ibid. Pigg incorrectly states that these buildings were purchased outright. This was corrected in the next edition of the *Register*.
[62] *Cheltenham Journal*, 2 August 1841, p. 2.
[63] Ibid.
[64] Ibid.
[65] Ibid.

A few months after the official opening of the school in July 1841, advertisements were placed in local newspapers for a suitable site for the erection of a permanent building for 300 pupils. Several locations were investigated by the board, and eventually Sandford Field, with a frontage of 300 feet to the Bath Road, was obtained. The land was conveyed for a sum of £4,009 to nine trustee shareholders, one of whom was Close. A further advertisement sought plans and estimates for a new building, and as a result of this, a design described as being in 'Tudor or Perpendicular English' style was accepted. It consisted of a central tower with wings on either side that comprised the school room, gymnasium, a central lecture room together with smaller classrooms and offices. The total cost, including land and fittings, was £14,594.[66] Work began in September 1842, and the new premises were opened on 22 June 1843.

In his report of the public opening of the new building in June 1843, the editor of the *Cheltenham Journal* wrote in his introduction of the "more extended effects to be expected from the Christian and scriptural education" of the boys at Cheltenham College. In a very clear reference to the individuals associated with what came to be known as the Oxford Movement, he said:

> We live in times of tribulation for the Church; we see some of her most learned professors at one University questioning the right of private judgement—palliating the abominations of Popery—and hurrying us on towards Rome; we hear of numbers of the country clergy aping the fantastic tricks of the Professors, and turning their Protestant Churches into Romish mass-houses...we thought it not impossible that an antidote to this theological bane might be supplied from our infant College at Cheltenham...[67]

Close's address at the official opening was also reported by the *Cheltenham Journal*. In it, he commented on the type of 'religion' to be taught in the school:

> In our primary meeting we not only spoke of religion generally but we defined the special kind of religion we would have taught in this School; we called it the *plain, honest, Protestant evangelical religion of the written Church of England*. We pledged our integrity, that as far as any human wisdom may go, we never would have any master or teacher belonging to this school but such as embraced the religion of the Liturgy, the religion of the Homilies, the creed of the Martyred Reformers in the true literal sense of the terms.[68]

---

[66] Minutes of the Directors, 20 June 1844.
[67] *Cheltenham Journal*, 26 June 1843, p. 2.
[68] Ibid.

Cheltenham Proprietary College, 1843

Although the college was not founded to provide direct opposition to Tractarianism, it is clear that this became a driving force for some of the people associated with its early development, especially the Chairman of the Board.

Close made the theological position of the Board perfectly clear when offering the principalship to Revd William Dobson (1809–1867) in 1845. He wrote, "you are probably aware that the principles upon which this college is founded are directly opposed to Tractarianism, in all its forms and modifications."[69] Dobson replied by outlining his own theological position in which he stated: "If, by opposition to Tractarianism, is meant opposition to a system involving doctrines and practices more or less closely allied to Romanism, a system which would introduce practices unknown to or at variance with the spirit of the Reformation, such for instance as bowings to the altar, the use of the cross and other details of the same kind then I should join in such opposition, should circumstances appear to call for it, with perfect readiness."[70] This reply satisfied the directors, and on this "strong disclaimer of Tractarian principles",[71] Dobson was appointed principal.

At this time, few Tractarians were applying their theology to public school education[72] and the "Romanist threat" was seen to be mainly

---

[69] Minutes of the Directors, 18 January 1845.
[70] Ibid.
[71] Minutes of the Directors, 22 January 1845.
[72] As discussed above, Revd Edward Monro had founded St Andrew's College at Harrow Weald in 1846, and William Sewell had founded Radley College near Oxford in 1847.

against Church liturgy and worship. However, by 1848, Nathaniel Woodard had founded Shoreham Grammar School and Collegiate Institute (later to become Lancing College), and this was followed by Hurstpierpoint in 1849 and St Saviour's School (later Ardingly) in 1870. Francis Close was aware of the growing influence of Tractarians and Anglo-Catholics in educating the middle classes, and in 1861 he vigorously attacked them in his pamphlet, *High-Church Education Delusive and Dangerous.* The essay was mainly aimed at William Sewell of Radley College,[73] but Close took the opportunity to criticise what he described as Woodard's opposition to scripture, and his "Romeward direction". In June 1858 the second Principal of Cheltenham College, William Dobson, resigned under a cloud of "vexations, annoyances and turmoil"[74] which included the accusation that he had introduced the practice of 'intoning' into the college services at St Luke's church. Some of the proprietors "feared it was the thin end of a Tractarian, or even Popish, wedge"[75] and they were keen to rid the college of any such tendencies.

St Luke's church was opened in 1854 on a site donated by Francis Close and his wife, which was next to Cheltenham Hospital (hence the name) and near to Cheltenham College. It was convenient for the congregation in the National School on Bath Road and was in close proximity to Cheltenham College which, it was hoped, could use it "as a quasi-chapel".[76] Since Cheltenham College opened in 1841, the teaching staff and pupils had attended various churches in the town. The new church was built to accommodate the College community, and the proprietors gave £200 towards the building costs, as well as inviting individuals associated with the school to contribute. When it was opened, 300 boarding pupils attended the morning service (and a further 100 went to other churches) and everyone in the afternoon—the 400 boarders, the 200 day pupils, the staff and their wives.[77] In 1855, the Incumbent[78] of St Luke's, W. F. Handcock,[79] attended the

---

[73] It was a review of a book of sermons which William Sewell had recently published. See above, p. 105.
[74] Morgan, *Cheltenham College*, p. 31.
[75] Ibid., pp. 31–2.
[76] *Cheltenham Journal*, 23 December 1854, p. 13.
[77] A. F. Munden, *A History of St Luke's Church, Cheltenham 1854–2004*, Cheltenham 2004, pp. 12–13.
[78] The early incumbents were known as Perpetual Curates and later as Vicars or Priests in Charge of St Luke's.
[79] William Fraser Handcock (1822–1907) was a curate to Francis Close at Cheltenham 1851–54; Vicar of St Luke's, Cheltenham 1854–74; and Vicar of St Luke's, Redcliffe Square, South Kensington 1874–93.

afternoon College service and was "disturbed to find that some of the congregational responses were being intoned and not said." The principal of the college, William Dobson, considered that his complaints were unjustified; however, "the controversy entered the public domain"[80] and was reported as far away as London. This estrangement between St Luke's and the college resulted in the Directors' deciding to build a separate college chapel, which was opened three years later.

The presence of Francis Close on the Board of Directors from 1840–1856, as well as other Evangelical board members, both clerical and lay, ensured that Cheltenham College retained its Evangelical ethos for at least twenty years. Many members of staff and parents were anxious that their sons received a "first-rate education on reasonable terms"[81] under Evangelical principles. These parents included Francis Close himself, who expressed his confidence in the school by having all four of his sons educated at the College.[82] Close also believed that the provision of a theological tutor at the college, whom he and Brown had appointed, guaranteed Evangelical teaching. A proposal to abolish the post of theological tutor in 1861 was a matter of great concern to him, as was the suggestion that came from a disgruntled group of proprietors that the college change its *Rules and Regulations*.

After the prize distribution of 18 June 1861, a meeting of the proprietors of Cheltenham College was held where "a discussion took place, and complaints were made which ultimately resulted in…a radical change in the constitution of the governing body of the college."[83] A special general meeting of the proprietors was called for 13 November 1861, at which a committee was appointed "to revise the rules and regulations of the college, and to suggest any further improvements which may be necessary in the constitution of the college."[84] The resolutions passed were "considered adverse to the Directors, and on the following day the board met and resolved to resign."[85] By this time, Close had left Cheltenham to be Dean of

---

[80] Munden, *A History of St Luke's*, p. 13.
[81] Close, *A Letter to the Proprietors*, p. 4.
[82] The youngest, Charles Samuel (1831–1865) entered the school as it was opened in July 1841. His three elder brothers entered the school in January 1842 and all subsequently entered the Army and the Navy.
[83] Goding, *History of Cheltenham*, p. 641.
[84] *Report of the Committee Appointed at a Special General Meeting of the Proprietors of Cheltenham College, on 13 November 1861*, Cheltenham 1861, p. 3.
[85] Goding, *History of Cheltenham*, p. 642.

Carlisle, and Revd Edward Walker was Rector of Cheltenham. Like his predecessor, Walker was also vice-president and chairman of the Cheltenham College Board of Directors.[86]

The committee of nine members published their report on 18 December 1861, and their recommendations were adopted at an Adjourned Special Meeting of proprietors on 5 February, 1862. The revised rules and regulations brought about a storm of protest from a number of individuals including Close. One outcome was the resignation of the third principal, Henry Highton[87] and the appointment of Revd Alfred Barry[88] as his successor. One of the founding proprietors, Captain J. S. Iredell, also withdrew his support. The changes in the constitution, especially the abolition of clerical vice-principals and their power to appoint theological tutors, led to a progressive weakening of the school's Evangelical ethos. The departure of Thomas Boultbee (1818–1884)[89] in 1863 and Edward Wawn (1825–1866)[90] in 1864 eventually saw the end of the office of theological tutor,[91] a post which had been the brainchild of Francis Close and an important means of maintaining Evangelical character.[92]

---

[86] Edward Walker was Perpetual Curate of Cheltenham 1857–61 and Rector from 1861–72. His involvement with Cheltenham Proprietary School (for boys aged 6 to 12 years) was more significant than with Cheltenham College—particularly after 1862. Walker also preached the annual sermon at Cheltenham Grammar School, a tradition initiated by Close. See A. M. Munden *Wearing the Giant's Armour: Edward Walker (1823–1872) The First Rector of Cheltenham*, Cheltenham 2003.

[87] Henry Highton (1816–1874) was Principal of Cheltenham College 1859–62.

[88] Alfred Barry (1826–1910) was Principal of Cheltenham College 1862–68; Principal of King's College London 1868–83; and Bishop of Sydney, Metropolitan of New South Wales and Primate of Australia 1884–89. The *DNB* records that he lost his entire library at sea—presumably one of the hazards in those days of accepting a colonial bishopric!

[89] See Appendix 1.

[90] Edward Bickersteth Wawn was assistant theological tutor 1853–64.

[91] In the history of the school, there were three theological tutors; W. F. Wilkinson 1844–47, J. W. A. Taylor 1848–52 and T. P. Boultbee 1853–63, together with two assistant theological tutors; W Guilder 1851–53 and E. B. Wawn 1853–64.

[92] This decline in Evangelical persuasion was exemplified in 1876 when a master at the College distributed the Tractarian *Altar Manual* among the pupils. This action prompted a flurry of correspondence including a letter to the College authorities from the Church Association "to ask whether they had repudiated or endorsed the action of the master". (Minutes of the Church Association General Purposes Committee, Church Society Archives.) Tellingly, the school decided to take no action.

This was a matter of deep concern to Close, who "from the ignorance of the Deanery of Carlisle",[93] wrote a response to the proposed changes entitled *A Letter to the Proprietors of Cheltenham College, and those Parents who have Sons in that School* (1862). In his opinion, "Parents have been induced to send their boys to the School in the confidence that, whatever else they were taught, they would learn sound doctrine, high principle, and generous sentiments, from the lips of their special religious instructor!"[94] Parents from home and overseas "send their sons to that which they believed to be a safe shelter alike from the fopperies of Tractarianism and the seductive sophistry of Latitudinarianism. Break up this character of your College, introduce the High Church or Broad Church principles in their full development, and the consequences will be easily predicted."[95] For Close, the strength of the college was expressed in its theological teaching. To remove this would mean that the college would pass "into totally different hands, under totally different Theological colours, and as I think, most probably, into inefficiency and decay".[96] His letter was a classic case of 'too little, too late', for the resolutions had been passed fifteen days earlier. His prediction that the Evangelical outlook would be lost was correct, even if his suggestion that the college would decline in numbers was not. However, the opening of Dean Close Memorial School in Cheltenham twenty-five years later would ensure that Evangelical education in Cheltenham might have been temporarily 'down', but not altogether 'out'.

Cheltenham Grammar School

The Cheltenham Free Grammar School was endowed and established in 1574 by Richard Pate of Minsterworth (1516–1588), a wealthy Elizabethan lawyer and politician. Pate was the Member for Parliament for Gloucester, where he also held the position of Recorder, or chief magistrate. His duties included overseeing the confiscation of the properties of the chantries, ordered by Edward VI in 1547. Queen Elizabeth I later added to Pate's Foundation by granting lands for a school and a hospital, and under an indenture dated 6 October 1586, she was made 'Foundress' of the school. The nomination of the Headmaster was vested in the President and seven Fellows of Corpus Christi College, Oxford, who became known as the patrons or trustees

---

[93] Morgan, *Cheltenham College*, p. 37.
[94] Close, *Letter to the Proprietors*, p. 5.
[95] Ibid., p. 5.
[96] Ibid., p. 11.

of the school. Richard Pate was a pious man and he included in the school's statutes that "all boys admitted to the School must be required to accept instruction in religious as well as in general knowledge". This religious requirement fitted in well with Francis Close's ideals for a good school, and it was to later provide him with an opportunity to reform the school along Evangelical lines.

By the nineteenth century, Cheltenham's Grammar School, along with many other endowed grammar schools,[97] had declined considerably. In 1800 the Headmaster, Revd Henry Fowler, wrote to the President of Corpus Christi[98] that the number of scholars at the school was only three: "one of them is a boy of some Promise, and the other two of none at all".[99] He did not say how many private pupils there were. In another letter to the president in 1802, he said that there were now only five boys in all, of which only one could be said to be on the Foundation. This meant that only one complied with the conditions laid down in Pate's original statutes, and the other four were effectively private pupils. One contemporary account describes how the school "had fallen in reputation and usefulness" and only a few boys were on the Foundation. "The funds were mismanaged, the property neglected, and the school was of little advantage to the neighbourhood."[100] Proposals were even entertained for the school to be sold to make way for a railway station. For generations, it seemed, the school had been run by a local clergyman who had it as an additional source of income over and above his country parish. In this way it was like many of the other old grammar schools of the time, which "in their struggle for existence were taught by the nearest vicar or curate".[101] The problem demanded an investigation of the way the ancient charity was being managed by its trustees, the President and Fellows of Corpus Christi College. All over England investigations of a similar kind[102] were going on, prompted by the moribund condition of the endowed grammar schools.

---

[97] See N. Carlisle, *A Concise Description of the Endowed Grammar Schools in England and Wales* vol. 1, London 1818, p. 446.

[98] Dr John Cooke. The President and seven Fellows of Corpus Christi College were, under the deed of foundation, the trustees of Pate's charity.

[99] Letter to Dr John Cooke from the Revd Henry Bond Fowler. Cited by A. Bell, *Tudor Foundation: A Sketch of the History of Richard Pate's Foundation in Cheltenham*, Chalfont St Giles 1974, p. 92.

[100] Alfred Harper (ed.), *History of the Cheltenham Grammar School; from its Remodelling under the Chancery Deed of 1851, as Collected from the Newspaper Reports*, Cheltenham 1856, p. 4.

[101] R. F. McNeile, *A History of Dean Close School*, Shrewsbury 1966, p. 1.

[102] Resulting from the Brougham Inquiry or Charity Commission, 1818–37.

In 1818, the management of the grammar school was formally investigated by the Cheltenham Vestry, but the case against the Pate Foundation which they brought before the Court of Chancery met with no success. Nicholas Carlisle's survey of 475 endowed grammar schools published in 1818, reported of Cheltenham "that the Parishioners of this Place are much dissatisfied with the management of their School".[103] When Francis Close was appointed Perpetual Curate in 1826, he became chairman of the parish Vestry and took up the grammar school cause with renewed vigour. Close had several meetings with the President and Fellows of Corpus Christi College over the next 20 years, but to no avail. During this time, frequent attempts were made by Corpus Christi to wind up the case on the grounds that such an august body as the fellows of an Oxford college could not be accused of mismanagement. In 1831, the Vestry published a Report on the "suit in Chancery now pending between the Parish of Cheltenham and the College, with a view to the closing or compromise of the said suit."[104] In 1843, the "First Report of the Charity Committee Appointed last June" was published in the *Cheltenham Journal*. It was reported that one of the authors, a Mr Hollis, "was afraid almost to speak of the management of Pate's charity; to his mind it presented something in the shape of peculation; the funds of the charity had been widely misapplied; in plain English; a robbery had been committed".[105] It took the combination of the passing of an Act of Parliament in 1848 and the death of the Headmaster in 1849 to provide Close and his Vestry with the opportunity they needed to bring about change.

On Easter Tuesday 1848, a new committee was appointed by the Vestry to "consider if any, and what steps ought to be taken by the Inhabitants of Cheltenham for improving the condition of the Cheltenham Free Grammar School".[106] Earlier that year, Parliament had passed *An Act for Improving the Condition and Extending the Benefits of Grammar Schools*,[107] and it was hoped that this would provide the Vestry with the legal means to reform the school. A survey was made of the Foundation's property by a sub-committee of three

---

[103] N. Carlisle, *A Concise Description of the Endowed Grammar Schools in England and Wales* vol. 1, London 1818, p. 446.

[104] *Report of a Committee appointed at a Vestry Meeting held on the 6th Nov. 1828, to meet a Deputation from the College of Corpus Christi*, published in *The Grant of Richard Pate, Esq. by which he founded The Free Grammar School and Hospital, in the Town of Cheltenham, in the Year 1578*, Cheltenham 1833.

[105] *Cheltenham Journal*, 25 December 1843, p. 2.

[106] Harper, *Cheltenham Grammar School*, p. 5

[107] 3 and 4 Vict. 1847: 113–119. Cap. 77.

members[108] and the total value of the property was estimated to be £38,093 with an estimated annual income, £2,933.[109] This was considerably more than what the school was receiving from the Foundation. However, any further review of the school was "met by a difficulty which could not be removed during the life of the Head Master".[110] The Corpus Christi trustees and their employees, including the Headmaster, Henry Hawkins, had once again closed ranks.

The Vestry did not have to wait long: Henry Hawkins died on 26 January 1849 and the school immediately came under the provisions of the new Act. The Vestry "felt it to be their duty at once to communicate with the President and Scholars of Corpus Christi College".[111] On the day of Hawkins' death, Close dispatched a letter to the President of Corpus Christi College, stating:

> We do not desire in the least to interfere with your appointment of a successor but we feel it to be our duty to call your attention to the important opportunity thus afforded for the improvement of the regulations of this School in many particulars and for the introduction of a Teacher of talents and character calculated to raise the School to a level with any other endowed school in the kingdom.[112]

Ten days later, Close led a deputation of the vestry committee to Corpus Christi College and they met with the school's Trustees. This was followed by a letter from the President of Corpus Christi to Francis Close in which he stated "that there is no very serious ground of difference between us".[113] It seemed that the differences between the Trustees and the inhabitants of Cheltenham had been finally resolved. In November 1851, the Corpus Christi patrons of the grammar school acknowledged the failure of their defence in the Chancery Court case, which had lasted altogether thirty-three years, and a new trust deed was drawn up and entitled: "The scheme of the President and Scholars of Corpus Christi College, Oxford, for the

---

[108] Daniel Humphris, Edward Newman and John Goding. Goding was author of *Norman's History of Cheltenham*, 1863.

[109] *Pate's Grammar School, Cheltenham: Detailed Report of the Committee Appointed, by the Parish, in Vestry assembled, on Easter Tuesday 1848.* Cheltenham 1849, p. 9.

[110] Ibid., p. 3.

[111] Ibid., p. 11.

[112] Cited by Bell, *Tudor Foundation*, p. 135. The letter was signed by Francis Close, as well as William Hassell and George Engall, churchwardens.

[113] *Pate's Grammar School, Cheltenham: Detailed Report*, p. 11. The letter from the President of Corpus Christi College was published as a poster on 13 February, 1849.

future management of the Cheltenham Grammar School, as allowed by the Master in Chancery, and confirmed by order of 11 November 1851".[114]

Close was appointed vice-chairman of the new Board of Governors of the grammar school and he took the chair at the anniversary meeting and prize-giving of 1850. The *Cheltenham Chronicle* gave over a whole page to reporting this event. From the list of prizes in the article, we can obtain a good idea of the school's curriculum, which had undergone some major revisions. Like Cheltenham College, the school was divided into Classical, Civil and Military Departments and one of the languages taught was Hindustani. Other subjects included Classics, Divinity, French, German, Mathematics and Drawing. The similarity of the new curriculum of the Grammar School to that of the College may have been a result of Francis Close being a vice-chairman of both institutions—thus putting into practice his statement about the two schools being his 'left and right hands'. However, it is clear that any secondary school which hoped to cater for the sons of Cheltenham residents would need a curriculum designed for boys who were destined for the military or civil services, as so many of the parents came from these professions.

In 1851, the governors announced their intention of providing accommodation for boarding. Yearsley's Hotel, next door to the Elizabethan school house, was leased for this purpose. The school was briefly closed during minor alterations, and in May 1852 it re-opened with about 100 boys under a new headmaster, Edward R. Humphreys.[115] At a ceremony to mark the occasion of the re-opening of the school, Close spoke about his efforts to resuscitate the school: "I have acted upon every committee which has been formed, and I have been concerned in all the negotiations which have taken place with the President and Fellows of Corpus Christi College to the present time...".[116] Although he had, by then, relinquished his position of vice president, it was clear that as incumbent of Cheltenham, he would continue to maintain his connection with the school. He went on to say that "As the boys in this school have an ancient seat in my Church—and as the Headmaster is not at present in holy orders—I shall be happy in any respect and in every respect to afford them any religious

---

[114] Harper, *Cheltenham Grammar School*, pp. 12–18. This was amended in October 1888 and again in November 1900, when a new trust deed was printed entitled: *Scheme for the Administration of the Charity School known as Pate's Grammar School and Hospital Charity, Cheltenham*, Cheltenham 1900.

[115] From 1849 until Humphreys' appointment in 1852, Henry Hawkins' son, William, kept the school running,

[116] *Cheltenham Free Press and Gloucestershire Herald*, 8 May 1852, p. 2.

instruction or religious advantages that my Church or time will allow."[117] Like so many of Close's other educational activities, this was one in which he intended to retain his influence.

A timetable shows the school curriculum very shortly after it was re-opened. There were six classes and the programme of work covered only a limited range of subjects: Latin, Greek, Ancient History, and Mathematics were taught during the week. French, Drawing and German were taken separately: French two days a week, and Drawing (landscape, mechanical, military and architectural) on two days per week. Drilling and Fencing took place during the lunch hour each day, and on Wednesdays and Saturdays there were classes in Dancing and Callisthenics.[118] From 1853, Science was made part of the curriculum in both the Classical and Commercial departments—a very innovative provision for this time. By 1854, Divinity was included in the curriculum. The Evangelical views of the school's governors, including Close, can be seen in the following statement from the examiners' report of that year:

> Divinity, we are happy to say…has not been taught as a mere bye concern, but as vindicating to itself the place of chief importance amongst the varied subjects of instruction. Many boys, in all classes, evinced a remarkable knowledge of the facts and doctrines of Scripture…and some of the boys in the first class superadded to this knowledge of Scripture an acquaintance with Liturgical subjects, not only highly creditable, but showing that they had entered into the subject with no common interest.[119]

This was in keeping with the will of the Founder of the school. In his trust deed, John Pate stated that the scholars of the school should be "perfect in Christian knowledge and virtuous living", and that they should be carefully taught "notable sentences out of the Holy Scriptures."[120] John Pate's Puritan convictions were entirely consistent with the views of his nineteenth-century Evangelical successors.

Humphreys achieved a great deal during his seven years as Headmaster, although the appointment was not without its problems.[121] The most serious of these was his propensity to spend money which had been loaned to the school by wealthy parents, without any

---

[117] Ibid.

[118] Bell, *Tudor Foundation*, p. 26. I was unable to locate the original timetable, which Arthur Bell lists as being located in the archives of Corpus Christi College.

[119] Cited by Harper, *Cheltenham Grammar School*, p. 9.

[120] Cited in *Pate's Grammar School, Cheltenham: Detailed Report*, p. 12.

[121] See Bell, *Tudor Foundation*, pp. 136–155.

consideration to the means of repayment. Despite the competition from the College, the new Headmaster attracted a large number of pupils to the school. In 1851 there were 150 pupils and by 1855 there were 300—a substantial increase. By this time the school façade incorporated an 'additional building'. Until it was purchased by the school, the adjoining premises had been operating as Yearsley's Hotel.[122]

As already mentioned, one of the changes to the curriculum which Humphreys instituted was the introduction of Science as a subject. In April 1853 it was reported that the Grammar School had started classes in Practical Science. These were "backed by some of the most wealthy and spirited of the inhabitants", according to the *Cheltenham Free Press*. On 21 May 1853, the paper printed a report of the visit to the school by the eminent scientist, and advocate of science and technical education, Dr Lyon Playfair.[123]

> The Cheltenham Grammar school was honoured with a visit on Thursday, from Dr. Lyon Playfair, who was present at one of the usual Lectures in Practical Science, given by T. Wright, Esq. M.D. The audience, besides the recently organized Classes of Pupils, consisted of a large, yet select assemblage of the respectable inhabitants, who seemed much interested with the Scientific definitions and illustrations, pertaining to the structure of Fossils and Shells. Those of the Star-fish occupied a prominent place, and one illustration of its formation called forth especial tokens of approbation.[124]

The attention of Prince Albert was drawn to the innovations at Cheltenham Grammar School in science teaching, and in 1856 the Prince was "graciously pleased" to make a gift to the school of a book on the natural history of Dee Side.[125]

Close continued to take an active interest in the affairs of the school. Although he regarded Cheltenham College and Cheltenham Grammar School "as his right hand and his left hand",[126] he believed that "had the Grammar School taken its start only a few years sooner", there

---

[122] Also known as 'Yearsley's Boarding House'.
[123] Lyon Playfair (1818–98) was a distinguished chemist who assisted in organizing the two London Exhibitions of 1851 and 1862. See J. W. Adamson, *English Education*, London 1964, p. 292 and W. Reid, *Memoirs and Correspondence of Lyon Playfair*, London 1899.
[124] *Cheltenham Free Press and Gloucestershire Herald*, 25 December 1852, p. 4.
[125] The book was E. Lankester (ed.), *The Natural History of Dee Side and Braemar*, London 1855.
[126] *Cheltenham Free Press and Gloucestershire Herald*, 25 December 1852, p. 4.

would have been no need to found Cheltenham College.[127] Close deplored Humphreys' attitude of "petty rivalry" towards the College, for in his opinion there was ample room in Cheltenham for both institutions. At the 1852 Christmas distribution of prizes he was reported as saying that "as he should be very sorry to part with either of his hands, he should be sorry to see either of these institutions decline or fall."[128] On the other hand, the Headmaster's competitive attitude towards Cheltenham College was reflected in his 1853 decision that the Grammar School boys should wear a 'cap' which was identical, at least in style,[129] with that already worn by the boys of Cheltenham College. As soon as Close became aware of this decision, he wrote to Dr Norris, the President of Corpus Christi College, Oxford. Close said that he "sought to avert the untold mischief which will arise by the adoption of the College cap by the boys of the Grammar School." He confessed that he did not know how this had come about. He went on, "I am very sorry to say, in confidence to you, that in my interview with Dr. H., I detected much in his *spirit* that augurs ill for the School—an acid feeling, and a petty rivalry towards the College was too obvious..." He then went on further:

> any attempt to place the lowest tradesman's son, on a par, with so powerful and flourishing an establishment, as the College, which is (whether right or wrong) so *exclusive* in its character, will only recoil on the older Foundation and press it lower in the scale...it may be foolish pride, but there is no doubt that our aristocrats here would not endure that their butcher's boy, and their own boy, should be wearing the same cap...[130]

By 1855, the relations between the Grammar School and the College seemed to have improved to the point that the Headmaster, Dr Humphreys, wrote to the *Cheltenham Examiner* of "the very friendly feeling which has grown up between the scholars and masters of our two leading educational establishments".[131] Close referred to the "frequent cricket matches" which took place between the boys, and the use of textbooks in each school which were written by masters in the other. This included "the works of Dr. Humphreys, the Head Master [which were] also introduced into the College with the express

---

[127] Harper, *Cheltenham Grammar School*, p. 124.
[128] *Cheltenham Free Press and Gloucestershire Herald*, 25 December 1852, p. 4.
[129] A picture in the *Illustrated London News* for 1851 shows Cheltenham College boys wearing what is commonly known as a 'mortar board' academic cap.
[130] Letter from Francis Close to Dr Norris, 5 July 1853. Corpus Christi College Archives.
[131] The *Cheltenham Examiner*, 12 September 1855, p. 4.

sanction and commendation of Revd. J. Dobson, the Principal of that establishment."[132] Whether this *entente cordiale* was genuine or not, Close was clearly anxious to promote harmonious relations between two institutions with which he was intimately involved.

The new Headmaster was not a supporter of Francis Close, despite their amicable professional relationship. This may account for his appointment by governors who had suffered defeat at the hands of the parish Vestry in the Chancery Court. What is more, he was a layman, and the appointment of a school master who was not a clergyman was unusual for the time, and a particularly difficult concept for Close. The appellation 'E. R. Humphreys, M.A., LL.D.'; that is, a Doctor of Law rather than a Doctor of Divinity, was an anomaly in his whole view of the position of schools in relation to the Established Church. As soon as he could, he suggested to the Corpus Christi patrons that the new Headmaster should be encouraged to consider becoming a candidate for Holy Orders. He even mentioned the Headmaster's lack of religious qualifications at the school's re-opening ceremony (after renovations) in May 1852.[133] Humphreys was anxious to deflect attention from this perceived inadequacy for he had no desire to be in orders, and in fact he had no Oxford degree[134]—a deficiency he had succeeded in concealing from the Oxford patrons. It was fortunate for Humphreys that Close was near the end of his time in Cheltenham, departing in 1856 "amidst showers of congratulations and gifts" to become Dean of Carlisle. Had Close remained in Cheltenham, it is possible that Humphreys would have been exposed earlier as the fraud that he was later shown to be,[135] both in terms of his qualifications and his conduct.

Humphreys allowed Francis Close and Archibald Boyd (1803–1883),[136] minister of Christ Church, Cheltenham, to assist in the religious instruction of the grammar school pupils. Close was anxious to strengthen the links with the school which was situated so near to

---

[132] Ibid., p.4. These books were later found to have been 'ghosted' by a Mr H. Owgan of Clifton, who charged Humphreys a substantial fee. See the *Cheltenham Chronicle*, 5 August 1859, p. 5 and *Cheltenham Chronicle*, 16 August 1859, p. 5.

[133] Harper, *Cheltenham Grammar School*, p. 31.

[134] Humphreys entered Magdalene College, Cambridge, on 24 March 1836 but he did not take his degree. In 1844 he was appointed Headmaster of a small three-teacher school at Prince Edward Island, off the east coast of Canada. His MA and LLD were honorary degrees, conferred on him by Edinburgh and Aberdeen universities respectively. Bell, *Tudor Foundation*, pp. 136–9.

[135] He was "bogus as a scholar, incompetent as an administrator, and financially dishonest", according to A. Bell, *Pleasure Town*, p. 21.

[136] See Appendix 1.

the parish church, and to provide the "religious instruction or religious advantages"[137] he had promised in his speech of May 1853. Humphreys accepted Close's offer to hold an annual service for his school at the nearby Parish Church, although it is possible that Close had drawn the Headmaster's attention to Pate's 1586 Indenture, which stated that the boys should attend an annual service at the parish church.[138] The first of these was on 23 June 1853, and the sermon was published in the school's Report for that year.[139] After the second service, which followed a court case brought by the parents of a boy who had been flogged by the drill master Sergeant Livingstone,[140] Close set the pupils an essay, 'Obedience and Disobedience, their Causes and Consequences.' He also made his own attitude clear: "no one was more opposed to corporal punishment than himself, indeed he believed it would be generally found that the character of a school was good or bad, exactly in inverse ratio to the amount of its punishments...but he believed that there were some instances wherein it was necessary".[141]

The case against the drill master was dismissed[142] and Humphreys and the Grammar School remained very popular in Cheltenham. In November 1855, he held a public dinner at the school for the Prime Minister, Lord John Russell.[143] However, in 1859 his debts, which amounted to £26,000—a vast sum in those days—were made public when bankruptcy proceedings were started against him. He fled to the United States, taking with him the wife of Dr. Stephen Comyn, one of his own governors, and was later arrested as an undischarged bankrupt in Boston. As was observed by the first historian of the school, "No scandal caused a greater frisson, not merely in Cheltenham but throughout the land."[144]

While Humphrey's association with the school was to be forever associated with a scandal, Close's contribution to the school was recognised for perpetuity through the Gwinnett-Close scholarship that

---

[137] Harper, *Cheltenham Grammar School*, p. 31.

[138] Bell, *Tudor Foundation*, p. 39.

[139] *Report of the First Annual Examination and Distribution of Prizes; Also the Substance of a "Familiar Discourse" Delivered to the Scholars, in Accordance with the Will of the Founder, by the Revd F. Close A.M. on June 23, 1853.* Cheltenham 1853.

[140] Bell, *Tudor Foundation*, pp. 148–9.

[141] Harper, *Cheltenham Grammar School*, pp. 84–6.

[142] Ibid., p. 112. The judge ruled that the schoolmaster was acting in *loco parentis*.

[143] Ibid., pp. 162–3. Close, as well as seven other Cheltenham senior clergy, was present at the dinner.

[144] Bell, *A Tudor Foundation*, p. 154.

was established in 1883.[145] Mr W. H. Gwinnett was a former pupil and Chairman of Governors from 1881–1891.[146] Meanwhile, the school buildings were demolished in 1887 and a new building was opened in 1889 on the same site in the High Street. In 1905, a school for girls was begun in buildings nearby that were formerly known as Livorno Lodge. It was first called the County High School for Girls, then Pate's Grammar School for Girls. The first Headmistress, who started with 107 girls, was Miss Helen D. Heatley. In 1939, new buildings for the Girls' School were opened at a site on the edge of Cheltenham and in 1946, because of changes in government funding arrangements, a junior school was established in Livorno Lodge. The 150 pupils who began at Pate's Junior School were initially drawn from the two older schools who had to relinquish their junior departments. By now, this collection of three schools under the Pate Foundation were commonly known as the 'Pate Schools'. In 1965, the boys' Grammar School moved to new buildings[147] on Princess Elizabeth Way at the edge of town. What remained of the late Victorian school buildings on High Street was demolished. In 1986, the Girls' Grammar School and the Boys' Grammar School were combined to form a new co-educational school known as Pate's Grammar School, which today has over 900 pupils.[148]

---

[145] *Looker On*, 23 October 1886, p. 682. W. H. Gwinnett donated £100 in 1883 to fund a prize in the memory of Francis Close, and three years later the school made an appeal for more funds. The scholarship has since been amalgamated into other prize funds.

[146] W. H. Gwinnet (1809–1891) was a very active member of the Cheltenham parish vestry and a descendant of Mr Theodore Gwinnett, a local solicitor who "played a most active part in the legal affairs of the town". The younger Gwinnet was instructed by the Vestry in 1819 to begin proceedings against 'the Principals of Corpus Christi College'. G. Hart, *A History of Cheltenham*, pp. 155, 318.

[147] The new school buildings were designed by the same firm of architects who built the Barbican centre in London, and it was commented at the time that "the new Grammar School might prove to be a major influence on the design of grammar schools." This was not to be, for by the 1980s these buildings had been diagnosed with 'concrete cancer'. In what is a very poor commentary on twentieth-century engineering compared with that of the sixteenth century—for the original school buildings on High Street had lasted for over 300 years—these new buildings were demolished in 1995.

[148] Since 1999, it has been a voluntary aided school, supported by the Pate's Foundation. *1999 OFSTED Report on Pate's Grammar School, Cheltenham*, London 1999. See http://www.pates.gloucs.sch.uk/the_school.html (accessed March 2004). Despite its Foundation, the school today has no connection with the Church of England.

Francis Close was involved in the founding of two other middle-class schools in Cheltenham. On 27 January 1845, the Cheltenham Commercial and Classical Proprietary School on Church of England Principles was opened in North Parade House, Winchcombe Street. This school was not considered a rival to Cheltenham College, as it catered for a lower social group: "the sons of professional men, tradesmen, farmers and others, upon the most moderate terms".[149] The idea of a new proprietary school was first raised at a meeting on Wednesday 20 December, 1843, at which "the parties projecting this measure, disclaim the imputation of rivalry and opposition to the Proprietary College, Bath Road, and ground their justification upon the necessity that exists, in order to supply the means of education commensurate with the wants of the town and neighbourhood."[150] Close's evangelical influence could be seen in the name for the school, and in its foundation documents, which stated that the school was "to be conducted strictly upon the principles of the reformation". [151] A total of thirty-four £10 shares were issued; however, in 1850 the entire management of the school was transferred to the Headmaster, a Mr T. Bowman. It is not known how long this school survived, but it probably closed as a result of the revival of the Cheltenham Grammar School in May 1852.

On 30 September 1853, a small group of citizens held the first of a series of meetings in order to found a school for girls on the same pattern as Cheltenham College. They included Revd C. H. Bromby (1814–1907), Vicar of St Paul's Church, Cheltenham and first principal of the teacher training school which Francis Close founded eight years earlier,[152] and Revd H. Walford Bellairs, who was at that time H. M. Inspector of Schools for Gloucestershire.[153] It was resolved at this and the following meeting

> That an Institution for the daughters and young children of Noblemen and Gentlemen be established in Cheltenham and be entitled The Cheltenham College for the Education of Young Ladies and Children. The College to be established by means of one hundred shares of £10 each; the possessor of each share to have the

---

[149] *Cheltenham Journal*, 25 December 1843, p. 2.
[150] Ibid.
[151] Ibid., 4 March 1844, p. 2.
[152] C. H. Bromby was Principal of the Cheltenham Training College from 1847–1864. C. More, *The Training of Teachers, 1847–1947*, p. 9 and chs 2–3. He later became the first first Bishop of Tasmania in 1864.
[153] He was a high churchman who was subsequently Vicar of Nuneaton and an Honorary Canon of Worcester.

right to nominate a Pupil and a vote at annual and special meetings.[154]

The six founders formed a governing council and Revd H. A. Holden, Vice-Principal of Cheltenham College, was appointed secretary. Thus the link with the boys' college, "that elder brother, under whose protection alone our College could not have grown up",[155] was further enhanced.[156] The council was "anxious not to associate the College exclusively with a [Church] party" at a time "when cleavage within the Church was deep and wide". So they initially avoided asking Francis Close to be president of the college council, as he was regarded as holding "extreme Low Church views".[157] However, Close and five other Cheltenham residents who were also approached, refused to become vice-presidents, and the council realised that "without his name the enterprise was fore-doomed to failure".[158] Eventually the presidency of the council was offered to Francis Close and he accepted, although he does not appear to have played a very active role in the school.[159]

The first prospectus was issued in October 1853 and in November a Mrs Proctor was appointed to the title of principal, although it was her daughter, Miss Annie Proctor, who was the real head of the college. Miss Proctor was officially named the vice-principal, but as she was given the responsibility of the "management of the educational working of the College"[160] she came to be regarded as the first principal of the school. The school opened on 13 February 1854 at Cambray House, "a fine Georgian house with a lovely garden"[161] with eighty-two pupils. The school remained there until it moved to new premises on Montpellier Street in 1873, by which time it had over 600 pupils. In 1858, Miss Dorothea Beale succeeded as principal, and her long and very succesful reign was to last for nearly fifty years. During this time she "raised the standards to supreme heights of excellence".[162] Her views were not regarded as Evangelical. Like the

---

[154] Clarke, *Cheltenham Ladies' College*, p. 26.

[155] Dorothea Beale, replying to the Mayor's Address, 1901. Cited by Clarke, *Cheltenham Ladies' College*, p. 28.

[156] Later, the Chairman of the Ladies' College Council was frequently also the Principal of Cheltenham College.

[157] Clarke, *Cheltenham Ladies' College, 1853–1953*, p. 30.

[158] Ibid.

[159] G. Hart, *A History of Cheltenham*, p. 216.

[160] Clarke, *Cheltenham Ladies' College*, p. 31.

[161] Ibid., p. 29. It was well known locally as the house where the Duke of Wellington had stayed for six weeks in 1823.

[162] E. R. Raikes, *Dorothea Beale of Cheltenham*, London 1908, p. 13.

changes to the constitution at the boys' college in 1862, her appointment had occurred after Close had left Cheltenham. Cheltenham Ladies' College and other, later, foundations were examples of a new period in Cheltenham, when the long and powerful reign of Cheltenham's Evangelical educationalist had come to an end. However, his educating spirit lived on, although not initially in Cheltenham. Close's work at Cheltenham received national attention and inspired other Evangelicals to become involved in education, so that by the 1860s a number of other clerical and lay Evangelicals had taken on the challenge of founding middle-class schools. The first of these men had a direct personal connection with Francis Close, for Talbot Greaves had been the great man's curate at Cheltenham before moving to the seaside town of Weymouth.

CHAPTER 4

Talbot Greaves and the Founding of Weymouth College

Although Melcombe Regis was officially joined to the adjacent town of Weymouth in the fifteenth century, four centuries later the two names were still being used to distinguish between different parts of what was, and is, essentially the same urban area. Weymouth, an ancient port town, was first made famous by King Henry VIII who built a castle on the peninsula near to the naval station of Portland Roads. This later became "one of the strongest naval stations in England". Then in the early part of the nineteenth century, King George III held court at Weymouth. Monuments to the farmer-king abound in the town and in the surrounding countryside, where he "delighted the peasantry of Dorset by his freedom and affability". The little statue of the king which stands today at the centre of the main roundabout is a reminder of the effect of a sovereign's choice of holiday-location on the status and prosperity of a provincial town: similar statues can be found in Queen Victoria's favourite seaside resorts of Ramsgate and Brighton. However, the figure of a rider superimposed "in futile compliment" to His Majesty King George III on one of the ancient chalk White Horses located just outside the town, was neither subtle nor complimentary. Anyone making a similar gesture of fealty to the Queen today would discover a very different meaning of being at Her Majesty's pleasure, for this is now a protected site. It was on these rolling chalk downs that Weymouth's first public boarding school was built to cater for the sons of middle-class Evangelicals.

Weymouth College was opened by "a small but select body of churchmen"[1] under the leadership of Talbot A. L. Greaves (1826–1899), the Rector of Melcombe Regis.[2] Greaves was curate to Francis Close at Cheltenham from 1854 to 1855, before moving to Dorset where he was appointed Rector of Melcombe Regis with Christchurch

---

[1] "A Great Proprietary School. The Story of Weymouth College", *St James's Budget*, 18 May 1894, p. 21.
[2] See Appendix 1.

and Radipole, 1856–81.³ A protégé of Francis Close and the Simeonites,⁴ Greaves was described in his *Times* obituary as a "staunch advocate of Evangelical principles".⁵ He was also said to be one of "the most eloquent of the preachers of the nineteenth century", and loquacious he must have been because several witnesses describe how "though he preached for one hour in the morning and for three-quarters of an hour in the evening, his flow of language was such that none of us recollect being bored."⁶ Visitors flocked to Weymouth to 'sit under' his teaching, and one resident wrote, "the Gospel has come to town." The church was frequently "full to overflowing, and many stood in the aisles."⁷ Talbot Greaves was responsible for enlarging and putting new pews in St Mary's church⁸ at an estimated cost of £3000.⁹ He also built himself a new rectory, laying out the extensive grounds of what was until recently,¹⁰ Connaught House at Portmore Gardens in Rodwell.

In 1859 Greaves and five other "like-minded gentlemen" formed a board of Trustees to enlarge and improve an already existing school in the parish of St Mary. It was to cater for the lower middle classes and was initially known as the Middle School.¹¹ As well as the rector, the board included Mr (later Sir) John Coode, Mr William Eliot, Mr George Andrews, Mr J. A. Curme and Mr Richard Eliot, who acted as

---

3   The Greaves family were well-known Evangelicals. See T. C. F. Stunt, "The Greaves Family." *Notes and Queries* (October 1981): 405–8.
4   This was the name coined in the nineteenth century for those Evangelicals who had studied under, or been influenced by, Charles Simeon at Cambridge. They were also known as 'Sims'.
5   *Times*, 21 February 1899, p. 7. See also C. G. Falkner, *History of Weymouth College to 1901*, London 1937, p. 45. Greaves was President of the local auxillary of the Church Association, and wrote the Church Association tract, *The Best Means for the Advancement of Spiritual and Evangelical Religion in the Church of England*, London, n.d.
6   Falkner, *Weymouth College*, p. 45.
7   Not all of these visitors appreciated long sermons, however, for it is recorded that as the result of a visitor's complaint, the churchwarden of the time, "being somewhat officious", purchased a large-faced clock and fixed it to the gallery where it could be clearly seen by the preacher. Apparently "the Rector noticed this diabolical engine when he next preached, and in future never opened his eyes from the beginning of his discourse until the end." Falkner, *Weymouth College*, p. 45 fn. 3.
8   *Alumni Cantabrigienses* exaggeratingly states that he "built a new church".
9   "Proposed Enlargement and Re-Pewing of Melcombe Regis Parish Church, Weymouth" pasted in J. B. Kerridge, "Weymouth and Melcombe Regis Local Rakings", 1866. Weymouth College Archives.
10 It burnt down in 1998 while builders were doing renovations.
11 For National Society Middle Schools, see above, pp. 95–99.

Talbot Greaves (1826–1899)

the Honorary Secretary.[12] Talbot Greaves would have gained considerable experience in the setting up and running of schools while he assisted Francis Close at Cheltenham, and preparations for the new school were quickly under way. Mr E. Thurman was appointed Headmaster and began receiving a "select number of boarders" at his residence. A site near the Westham Bridge and facing the Backwater[13] was bought for £500, and new school premises consisting of a large schoolroom, classrooms and offices were completed[14] and opened on 12 December 1860. In numbers, the school flourished: by May 1861, the Headmaster reported that there were 80 pupils. Financially, however, the zeal of the Trustees was "not according to knowledge": the cost of building and furnishing exceeded estimations by over 50 per cent. Unable to cheapen their rate of borrowing, they resolved on 15 August 1862, to institute in these new premises, after Easter 1863, a school of a quite different character—a "first-class Grammar School", under a clerical headmaster. Other premises were found for the Middle School and its Headmaster, and on 14 April 1863 Weymouth Grammar School was opened at the recently-vacated buildings on Commercial Road.

The incentive for a new public school was explained at the school's jubilee celebrations as arising mainly "from a religious impulse". Reference was made to the Woodard schools and the need for an

---

[12] *St James's Budget*, 18 May 1884, p. 21. Eliot was later the Deputy Chairman of the College Council.

[13] A tidal stream which encircles the old town of Weymouth and is now known as the "Inner Harbour".

[14] The architect was a Mr Crickmay and the builder was Mr E. C. Seaman.

Evangelical equivalent: "There was another set of schools which had been singularly successful and which arose under a different kind of religious influence. But the Evangelical school in the Church of England felt it essential at that time that the great principles of religious education should be adequately represented in the public school life of this country, and for that reason they founded Weymouth College, among other schools."[15] The Trustees of Weymouth Grammar School, as the new school was first called, stipulated that the boys should be "well-born", that they should "cheerfully submit to be instructed on all branches of education that are of general and acknowledged utility", and that they should "read their Bibles by the light of the Established Church".[16] A later prospectus stated that the school was founded to "provide for the Sons of Gentlemen a Classical, Mathematical, and General Education of the Highest class". The "religious teaching" was described as being based "on sound Church of England principles".

On 26 November 1862, the first Headmaster of Weymouth Grammar School was appointed: 34-year-old Revd John Ellis, MA. Ellis had been a scholar of St John's College, Cambridge, and took his degree and was ordained in 1852. Later he served as Assistant Master at Marlborough College until 1856,[17] and then as Master of the Cathedral School at Salisbury. Ellis was an Evangelical "in the sense understood in those days",[18] and this would have been an important prerequisite for a school whose board was chaired by "that great protagonist of Protestantism",[19] Talbot Greaves. The founding Headmaster led school prayers night and morning, with readings of passages from the Bible. An ex-pupil recalled that they had "very much more of the Bible than nowadays...and it sank into our subconscious memories. But Ellis put into our heads wider visions by referring to Commentaries—the *Speaker's Commentary* in particular."[20] The Headmaster took the pupils to divine service at St Mary's on Sundays and on Holy Days, and monthly communion at St John's. He prepared all candidates for Confirmation, and "thoroughly grounded them in the Church Catechism". This was the sort of

---

[15] "Fifty Years On: The Weymouth College Jubilee", *Southern Times*, 19 July 1913.
[16] School Prospectus, cited in *The Dorset Yearbook* 1923, p. 34.
[17] Under the headmastership of G. E. L. Cotton, later Bishop of Calcutta, 1858–66. Honey, *Tom Brown's Universe*, London 1977, pp. 109–110.
[18] Falkner, *Weymouth College*, p. 46.
[19] *The Dorset Yearbook* 1923, p. 34.
[20] Cited by Falkner, *Weymouth College*, p. 47.

religious grounding that Evangelical parents would have been looking for in such a school.

Ellis started with 35 boys in 1863. At the end of the first term an examination was held, followed by the first Speech Day. Number 13 Belvedere Road, not far from the Burdon Hotel, had been rented as temporary accommodation for the Grammar School Headmaster and his boarders. These arrangements, however, were satisfactory to neither the Middle nor the Grammar school. Ellis, who started work in April 1863 with the temporary assistance of A. C. Pearson, was a month later demanding more accommodation for boarders, as well as for himself and for his permanent Second Master, Revd E. Sanderson. Meanwhile the Middle School was suffering in its new premises, and on 11 July 1863, Ellis was appointed to inspect it, and to assist and direct Thurman in its management. The Trustees quickly agreed to Ellis's solution for the congestion: to find "ampler and expansible" accommodation for the Grammar School, and let the Middle School revert to its old quarters.

A site on Melcombe Common abutting Dorchester Road was leased to two of the Trustees by Sir Frederick J. W. Johnstone for ninety-nine years from 24 June 1864.[21] Mr G. R. Crickmay was appointed again as architect,[22] and plans were submitted and approved. The builder was a Mr Reynolds. The first sod for the foundation of the new buildings was cut in February 1864, although building did not begin until 7 March.[23] At the end of the Christmas term the boys received notice to re-assemble on 19 January 1865, at the new buildings on Dorchester Road. Work on the buildings had been completed over the winter and the fitting-out process had begun. However, when this day arrived, the new school was still not ready for use, and it was to be another two weeks before the change-over was completed. The pupils' return to school had to be postponed until the next month. As well as time expirations, there were also cost excesses, for as with the Middle School, the builder's calculations had fallen well short of the final costings. Reynold's estimate was £4,400; the actual cost was listed in

---

[21] On 25 March 1871, when the building was enlarged, a further strip 20 feet wide on the south-east side was let for the remainder of the same period. The site was conveyed for that period by the lessees to the general body of the Trustees (who formed the governing body of the School) in a deed of 12 August 1864.

[22] He had designed the buildings on Commercial Road.

[23] See the 1873 Weymouth College Prospectus.

the 1873 Prospectus as totalling £5,600.[24] On 8 February 1865, the term was opened by prayer in the new 'Big Schoolroom'.

While the new buildings were being completed, the School continued to grow in numbers and more accommodation was required. In the autumn term of 1864, the Second Master, Revd Edgar Sanderson,[25] opened a Boarding House at 2 Wellington Terrace[26] on the main road, just south of the what is now Fernhill Avenue. Sanderson was replaced by Revd Richard Lee, who left in 1870 to become Assistant Master, and then (in 1876) Headmaster of Christ's Hospital[27]—a sign perhaps that Weymouth School had 'come of age' as a Public School. In the year that he left, a Members' Exhibition of £30 was jointly founded by the two members of Parliament for the borough: Sir Henry Edwards and Sir Frederick Johnstone. As Lord of the Manor, Sir Frederick founded another prize of £20. Perhaps the most important event of 1865—at least for the boys—was the first school cricket match, which was played in the autumn of that year.[28] Before long, the school governors began to think that the progress of the school had outstripped the meaning of its name, and from 1 August 1867, it was changed to "Weymouth Collegiate School" with an appropriate Latin motto, *Timor Domini sapientiæ principium*.[29] The old name "Grammar School" lingered on in the Trustees minute book until September 1870, after which "Collegiate School" became regular. However, it was not until 27 March 1875 that the following resolution was passed: "The name of the School shall be changed to the Weymouth Collegiate School". This probably represents a belated decision to incorporate the altered title into the Trust Deed.

The board then turned its attention to the old Middle School, which had all but closed. In 1865, proposals had been made for the sale of the school buildings at Commercial Road; however, their disposal seems to have caused the Trustees some anxiety and the sale did not go

---

[24] The workmanship was also defective, for within five years the Headmaster had to present the Trustees with a bill of £247 for repairs to gables and other building defects.

[25] Sanderson was formerly a scholar of Clare College, Cambridge, and was appointed Second Master in 1863. At the same time he held curacies: first at Melcombe Regis 1863–4 and then at Bincombe 1864–5. After leaving the School in 1865, he became a voluminous and popular writer of educational books, some of which were reprinted several times.

[26] Not Wellington Place as stated in Falkner, *The Book of Records of Weymouth College*, London 1897, p. 1.

[27] Still then located in London.

[28] This was at the grounds of the Weymouth Cricket Club at Chaphay's Lake. Weymouth College lost.

[29] "The fear of the Lord is the beginning of wisdom."

ahead. Other changes followed: a restart under a Mr Kirk in 1867; its conversion into an Infirmary in 1868; then finally on 4 March 1869, Revd John Ellis, the Headmaster of the Collegiate School, was appointed by its four trustees[30] to develop it as a school for the commercial classes in the town. It was suggested that its old name, the "Middle School", be used. This name survived until April 1876, when the new name "Melcombe Regis School" superseded it. An advertisement, which lists a Mr J. A. Curme as a fifth Trustee, described the purpose of the school as: "to provide for the sons of tradesmen, occupiers of Land and others (constituting that large and influential section termed the Middle-classes), a most liberal, comprehensive, and Scriptural Education, on the lowest possible terms".[31] Ellis remained in control of the school for some four years, appointing as his Assistant someone who was to make his mark later as a Headmaster of the Collegiate School: Revd J. A. Miller. But he failed to make it a financial success, and on 30 June 1873, Ellis withdrew his efforts and concentrated on the senior school. The management of the two schools was once more divided. Ellis confined himself to the Collegiate School, while Miller was appointed by the five Trustees as Headmaster of the Middle School. It flourished greatly under him: the number of boys at the Melcombe Regis School rose from four at the restart in 1869 to 40 in 1874 and 120 in 1879. For most of this time Miller was also curate of the parish of Melcombe Regis 1871–89.

The year 1870 was a memorable one for the Collegiate School, for Speech Day on 22 July was the first time visitors were invited to a prize-giving. The *Dorset County Chronicle* notes it as "the first public demonstration of the kind in connection with the School."[32] At the prize distribution there was great rejoicing, for everything was flourishing "like a green bay tree",[33] and the Headmaster was already beginning to ask for more accommodation. New buildings were begun, and a lecture room, two new dormitories and two rows of studies "arose upon the scene". These rooms were erected against the original north-east face of the school, and this accounts for the wood-cased down-pipes in the inner corners and the occasional floods recorded in dormitories 4 and 5.[34] In the next year, French was added to the

---

[30] T. A. L. Greaves, R. Eliot, G. Andrews and W. Eliot.
[31] Advertisement pasted in Kerridge, "Weymouth and Melcombe Regis Local Rakings".
[32] *Dorset County Chronicle*, 28 July 1870.
[33] "Fifty Years On", *Southern Times*, 19 July 1913.
[34] Falkner, *The Book of Records of Weymouth College*, p. 2.

curriculum and a Frenchman to the staff,[35] and the following year, Science and German.[36] The year 1872 was also notable for the acquisition of the cricket field behind the buildings for the princely sum of £5,000. The Headmaster was so pleased with this great achievement that, in lieu of Latin prose one morning, "he and the First Class solemnly proceeded to measure the acreage and beat the bounds of the new domain."[37] One distinguished Old Weymouthian described the cricket field as

> ...probably the finest in the south of England. It stands high and looks towards the Down and the famous White Horse and Rider (King George III) carved out of the chalk. To the East is Weymouth Bay, with the long line of St Aldhelm's Head in the distance. There was room on this great grass expanse for three or four games of cricket to go on at the same time, and during the school summer holidays the ground was used for county matches.[38]

A period then followed in which the school's fortunes declined. From 1870 to 1885 there was dissension amongst the members of the School Council, and "the fair name of the School began to tarnish". The nature of the difference of opinion is not documented, and without the School Council Minute Books, which were lost long ago, it can only be surmised that it was of sufficient importance to become a public matter. School numbers ran down from nearly a hundred in 1876 to less than half that number three years later. It is perhaps significant that Talbot Greaves resigned as Chairman of the Council in 1876, and that numbers declined from around this time. In 1879 a new Headmaster was appointed: Revd Charles R. Gilbert, MA. Gilbert was formerly Assistant Master at Derby School, and was a scholar of Christ's College, Cambridge.[39] When he arrived in the autumn of 1879, he "found but half-a-dozen boys to meet him in the schoolroom." A fresh start was made and the name of the school changed to "Weymouth College", with the new motto *Ora et Labora*. Numbers rose to 50 as the schools fortunes began to improve. However, within a few years dissension rose again between the Board

---

[35] An Alsation refugee from the Franco-German war, who, according to one Old Boy, "could easily be beguiled into telling of Père la Victoire, and how he himself came to be wounded in a glorious assault."

[36] The German master, Professor Hermann Hoffert from Tübingen, Germany, was the object of much ridicule by the boys for his insistence of asking 'one and all', "*Sprechen Sie Deutsch?*"

[37] Falkner, *Book of Records* College, p. 2.

[38] B. Sewell, *My Dear Time's Waste*, London 1966, p. 10.

[39] He later went on to become Headmaster of St Peter's School in York 1885–90 and Headmaster of King Henry VIII School in Coventry 1890–1905.

and the Headmaster, and Gilbert resigned in the autumn term of 1884. While the chroniclers of the school devote very little space to the achievements of the second Headmaster, it is significant that Weymouth College boys began sitting Oxford and Cambridge examinations in his final year—an important milestone in the history of an English public school.

The Trustees now turned to the Headmaster of Melcombe Regis School, Revd John A. Miller, for help. In January 1885, Mr Miller was appointed the third Headmaster of Weymouth College, and he transferred to the College together with fifty of his most senior boys. There is no record of what became of the Middle School, although it can be assumed that it closed at this point because its Trustees, who were the same Trustees as the College, wished to concentrate their energies on the newer school. The next ten years were a period of steady growth for Weymouth College, both in numbers and in school infrastructure. In 1888, the school reached the coveted "century",[40] and in that year, alterations to the existing buildings included an extension to the dining room, a new matron's room, and 'Sick Quarters'. In 1890 these new building extensions, which included several class rooms, masters' rooms and a gymnasium, were ready for use. An academic high-point was also achieved when two Balliol scholarships were awarded in this year.

As the enrolments grew, there was a need for more accommodation. Some years earlier, a new Boarding House named Boscobel was opened by Revd H. P. Price on the Dorchester Road close to the main buildings. In 1903 this became the Junior or Preparatory School. Until then, a private school known as Cleveland House acted as a kind of unofficial preparatory school for the College. This was run by Revd Arthur Sewell and was close to the College.[41] The headmastership of the school eventually became associated with the Moules, who were both a distinguished Dorset family[42] and well-known Evangelicals. Revd Henry Moule (1801–1880) was Vicar of Fordington, Dorset from 1829 to 1880,[43] and during this time he was very active in the Dorset Clerical Meeting,[44] one of many such Evangelical societies across the

---

[40] See the *Clavinian*, June 1888, p. 13. Weymouth College Archives.

[41] See Sewell, *My Dear Time's Waste*, p. 10. Brocard Sewell was Arthur Sewell's grandson.

[42] Horace Moule the elder was a close friend of William Barnes and Thomas Hardy, the Dorset poets.

[43] During this time he ran a rectory school for "some fifteen or sixteen boys…" D. P. Leinster-Mackay, *The Rise of the English Prep School*, Lewes 1984, p. 79.

[44] In 1833 he was instrumental in putting an end to the Dorchester races.

country.⁴⁵ He had six sons, of which the youngest, Handley C. G. Moule (1841–1920),⁴⁶ became the first Principal of Ridley Hall, Cambridge in 1881 and then Bishop of Durham in 1901.⁴⁷ Bishop H. C. G. Moule later described the Dorset Clerical Meeting as "rare and memorable for lofty character, calm and unworldly Christian courage, noble piety, a high average of culture, and untiring fidelity to their sacred charge."⁴⁸ The Moule family connection with Weymouth College was first provided by Ernest C. H. Moule, who was appointed Headmaster of the Junior School in 1910, and then later by E. C. Moule who was the last Headmaster of Weymouth College. Ernest C. H. Moule, known affectionately by the boys as 'Uncle Ernest', was an extraordinary personality. When on duty he always wore a Cambridge MA gown and carried a mortar board, despite the fact that he had never taken a degree. As one Old Weymouthian describes it, "To see him sweep into the chapel and up the aisle thus attired was to receive a lesson in deportment worthy of Mr Turveydrop in *Bleak House*."⁴⁹

The school chapel mentioned in the account above was opened in October, 1896. Until then, the boys had been compelled to attend the ordinary public services at the parish church of St Mary in Melcombe Regis.⁵⁰ "Weymouth College", said the *Southern Times* at the time, "has grown so rapidly of late years that it was felt that this arrangement could not much longer continue, and, stimulated by the energetic spirit of their headmaster, the boys threw themselves into the scheme of erecting their own place of worship with wonderful enthusiasm and sacrifice."⁵¹ Old Weymouthians from all parts of the world "rallied round" the Headmaster in the project, and from 1890 when the chapel fund opened, to 1895 when the foundation stone was laid by the

---

[45] See ch. 1. It is not known if Talbot Greaves was a member of the Dorset Clerical Society, but it can be safely assumed that most Evangelical clergy in the region would have been connected to such a group. He was later the chairman of the Clerical and Lay Association (Western District) which was based in Bristol (see ch. 9).

[46] See Appendix 1.

[47] Other sons of note were George E. Moule (1829–1912), Bishop of Mid-China 1880–1907; Arthur Moule, Archdeacon of Mid-China from 1881; and Horace Moule, who may have provided some traits for Thomas Hardy's character, Angel Clare, in *Tess of the D'Urbervilles*, as did other members of the Moule family for Clare's relatives. See A. Pollard's entry for Henry Moule in *Blackwell's Dictionary of Evangelical Biography*.

[48] H. C. G. Moule, *Memories of a Vicarage*, London 1914, pp. 43–4.

[49] Sewell, *My Dear Time's Waste*, p. 11.

[50] Talbot Greaves was by then Vicar of Christ Church, Clifton, Bristol (1881–91), where he was involved in the foundation of Dean Close School (see ch. 9).

[51] "Fifty Years On", *Southern Times*, 19 July 1913.

Bishop of Salisbury in April, sufficient funds were raised so that the building was erected almost entirely out of freewill offerings—"an eloquent tribute to the love which they bore for their school." The Bishop returned in the following autumn to open the chapel and dedicate it to Saint Michael and All Angels.

Weymouth College, 1894

At the end of 1901, Revd John Miller retired, having led the Middle School for eleven years and the College for another sixteen years. Despite being honoured in 1895 by being made an Honorary Freeman of the borough "for the eminent services he has rendered...in the advancement under his headmastership of Weymouth College into the front rank of the public schools of England", he left at the end of 1901 with some ill-feeling between himself and the Council, and with the school in considerable debt. By this time, the School Council had formed the Weymouth College Company Limited to administer the school, and Colonel (later Sir) Robert Williams MP,[52] was its third chairman. As his contract required, Mr Miller had given six months' notice of his resignation, so the Council had known about his imminent departure from July. In August 1901, H. C. Barnes-Lawrence, then Headmaster of the Perse School, Cambridge, received a letter from Colonel Williams, inviting him to "come to Town and see him at the House of Commons".[53] Barnes-Lawrence went, and was "much to his astonishment", offered the Headmastership of Weymouth College. He took very little time to accept the offer, observing that "he had been at Perse for seventeen years and was, to use a favourite expression 'abiturient'...and...was not adept in those banauscic [sic] arts which were then, as they are now in a less degree, essential to the successful conduct of such a School..."[54] He commenced duties at Weymouth in January, 1902.

The start was not auspicious, for immediately upon his arrival he received an invitation from his new chairman to visit him at once. He met the Colonel at his home at Bridehead, Dorset, and was confronted with the news that the School was bankrupt. This was hardly encouraging, but Barnes-Lawrence was a Yorkshireman and stuck to his County's motto, "it's dogged as does it", agreeing to remain as Headmaster despite having come on board what appeared to be a sinking ship. The Headmaster of the Junior School was at that time Mr W. T. Keeling, a near relative of Mr Sydney Gedge (1829–1923) MP, a leading London solicitor and well-known Evangelical Churchman.[55] Gedge was Chairman of the Church of England Evangelical College and Schools Company, the body that administered Trent College at Long Eaton, Nottinghamshire.[56] Keeling had invited him down to Weymouth to advise him on his own position in the crisis, and had asked his Headmaster if he would like to meet him, which he did. It was at this meeting that either Keeling or Barnes-Lawrence (the records are not clear here) presented Mr Gedge with the following extraordinary proposal: "Why should not your Board take over our school?". To their surprise, Mr Gedge offered to present the suggestion to the Board, and the minute books of the Evangelical Schools Company record a copy of a letter from Gedge to Williams dated 12 February 1902, in which he wrote that, provided certain conditions

---

[52] Robert Williams was head of the London banking firm of Williams, Deacon and Co. His business partner, John Deacon, was one of the founders of South-Eastern College at Ramsgate in 1879.
[53] R. R. Conway, *Weymouth College 1901–1927*, Weymouth 1947, p. 5.
[54] Ibid., p. 5.
[55] See Appendix 1.
[56] See below, ch. 10.

regarding its current finances were met, "The Directors of the Church of England Evangelical College & School Co. are not indisposed to take over Weymouth College".[57]

A General Meeting of the Weymouth College Company was held the following month, and a resolution was adopted that the company go into liquidation. A liquidator was appointed and the board of the Evangelical Schools Company then called a special meeting on 15 April 1902, in order to discuss the purchase of Weymouth College. In the absence of communication from the liquidator of Weymouth, another meeting was called for the following Monday. At this special meeting an offer was presented from the liquidator, but it was rejected by the board because it did not meet the strict financial arrangements which Mr Gedge had put forward. Colonel Williams, the out-going chairman of Weymouth College Company, immediately amended this offer, giving a personal guarantee of £500. This was accepted at a further meeting of the Board the following day, which resolved that "the Weymouth School be taken over by this Company at once on the terms of the Liquidators letter of April 21st 1902."[58] By 13 May the Headmaster of Weymouth College was reporting to his new employers[59] in London, who amongst other things resolved that the cross on the Communion table in the Chapel be removed "if it could be legally done".[60] Clearly the Board intended to live up to the 'Evangelical' part of its name, and was keen to take control of its third school. The Company's second school had been purchased ten years earlier: Trent College had been founded along similar lines by a prominent Evangelical, Francis Wright—the subject of the next chapter.

Postscript

Weymouth College closed at the end of Lent term in 1940. Beset by financial difficulties which were exacerbated by World War II, the Evangelical Church Schools Company (as it was known from 1919) decided that it could no longer support both Weymouth College and

---

[57] Meeting of the Board of the Church of England Evangelical College and Schools Company, 21 March 1902. Minute Book B, Trent College Archives.
[58] Meeting of the Board on 23 April 1902. Minute Book B, Trent College Archives.
[59] The Church of England Evangelical College and Schools Company. See below, ch. 10.
[60] Meeting of the Board on 13 May 1902. Minute Book B, Trent College Archives.

Trent College during such trying times. The Headmaster of Dean Close School offered to set up a 'Weymouth House' with the surviving boys,[61] however the Governors of Weymouth did not think that Dean Close School was itself viable, and they declined the offer.[62] In the end, the forty boys who remained went to Wellingborough School, where a Weymouth House was set up under Mr T. S. Nevill, who had been Second Master at Weymouth.[63] The Headmaster, Mr E. C. Moule, went to Sherborne School as a classical master. The *Southern Times* reported the closure of the school as follows: "It is the first English public school to be a victim of the economic difficulties caused by the war, and the Bishop of Salisbury, who preached at the final school service in the College Chapel on Sunday, ominously predicted a similar fate for other English public schools; 'The whole system is changing' he said."[64]

In July 1940, Weymouth suffered its first air raids. Almost four years later, as the Allied forces were gathering in the neighbourhood for the invasion of Normandy, there was another major air raid which severely damaged the Weymouth and District Hospital. Patients were evacuated to the adjoining buildings of Weymouth College while repairs were effected.[65] During this time the main buildings of the school were converted into a hospital under the Ministry of Health. The Conway Memorial Window was removed to Preston church, and the organ and School War Memorial were transferred to the church at Radipole. In 1949, what were Weymouth College buildings became Weymouth Training College, a teacher training college for women. Later, its name was changed to the Weymouth College of Education, then the Dorset Institute of Higher Education. Today it is part of the Weymouth College of Further Education,[66] and the original buildings lie derelict and boarded up.

---

[61] The first of these amalgamation discussions had begun in November 1939. Another meeting was held between the two Headmasters in December 1939. However, the idea was abandoned in January 1940. Governors' Executive Committee Minutes, Dean Close School Archives.

[62] "H. Elders Memoirs", p. 17. Dean Close School Archives.

[63] There was also a historical, personal connection between the Headmasters of Weymouth and Dean Close, since the marriage in 1911 of Claire Flecker, daughter of the Headmaster of Dean Close School, and Revd Edward Sherwood, Headmaster of St Lawrence College.

[64] *Southern Times*, 29 March 1940.

[65] M. Boddy and J. West, *Weymouth: An Illustrated History*, Stanbridge 1983, p. 145.

[66] The College website states that it has approximately 3,000 pupils and "specializes in stone masonry courses and has developed a flourishing arts division."

However, like all institutions, it is the people associated with Weymouth who provide the most important memorial to the school. In the course of its existence, the school produced a number of distinguished men. It tended to specialize in clergy, missionary bishops, army and naval officers, and settlers and administrators in all parts of the colonies. This is perhaps not surprising considering the influence of Evangelical missionary organizations such as the Church Missionary Society (CMS),[67] which would have found fertile ground in the boys at Weymouth. Probably its best known alumnus was Henry Moseley, the brilliant chemist who worked with Lord Rutherford at Cambridge.[68] There were many others,[69] and there is no doubt that they would all be saddened by the state of their old school today, with its broken windows looking across a deserted cricket ground to the rider who watches in perpetuity from his chalk mount.

---

[67] Founded in 1799 as the Society for Missions to Africa and the East, it changed its name in 1812. By the time of its jubilee year in 1848, the CMS had sent out 350 missionaries and established 102 mission stations. See Stock, *History of the CMS*, 4 vols; and J. Murray, *Proclaim the Good News: A Short History of the Church Missionary Society*, London 1985.

[68] Henry G. J. Moseley (1887–1915), was a pupil at Weymouth College from 1899–1904. He worked with Lord Ernest Rutherford, the pioneer of atomic science, at Manchester and Oxford and developed the application of X-ray spectra to study atomic structure. His discoveries resulted in a more accurate positioning of elements in the Periodic Table by closer determination of atomic numbers.

[69] For example, Henry Sturmey, of Sturmey Archer bicycles; C. F. G. Masterman, the Liberal politician and Cabinet Minister; Stuart Hibberd, the BBC announcer; and Flight-Lieutenant Stainforth, the Schneider Trophy winner. To commemorate this last achievement, a weather vane was presented to the school in 1935. J. T. Inskip, *A Man's Job*, London 1948, p. 109.

CHAPTER 5

Francis Wright and the Founding of Trent College

The connection between the magnificent gothic-revival façade of St Pancras Station, London, and a Midlands middle-class boys' school is not obvious today, but it will be seen that the early years of Trent College were inextricably linked with the fortunes of the Midland Railway company for which St Pancras Station was its London terminus. One of the principal shareholders of the company, Francis Wright, was also the founder and principal benefactor of Trent College at Long Eaton, Nottinghamshire. The Wright family's connection with the school continued through the nineteenth century and well into the twentieth.

Francis Wright (1806–1873) of Osmaston Manor in Ashbourne, Derbyshire, was from an old Midlands family.[1] His ties with the district could be traced back to the seventeenth century when John Wright, the captain of a roundhead calvary regiment in the Civil War, settled in Nottingham at Lenton Hall. From that time, the Wrights are found connected by marriage with many well-known names in the surrounding three counties, including the Rotherham, Sherbrook, Moseley, Beresford,[2] Byng, Cunliffe and Fitzherbert[3] families. Francis's father, John Wright (1758–1840) was one of the founders of the Butterley Iron Works in 1790.[4] By 1830, the year that Francis Wright was made an equal partner, the Wright family firm had become a huge conglomeration of iron and coal mines, iron-works and engineering construction.

Osmaston Manor itself was a Butterley project,[5] built in 1846–9[6] on land just outside the village of Osmaston, near Ashbourne, Derbyshire.

---

[1] See G. Smith (ed.), *Recollections of the Late Francis Wright*, London 1873.
[2] John Wright married Elizabeth Beresford in 1791.
[3] Francis Wright married Selina Fitzherbert in 1830.
[4] The others being Benjamin Outram, William Jessop and Francis Beresford. See R. H. Mottram and C. Coote, *Through Five Generations: The History of the Butterley Company*, London, n.d., and R. Christian, *Butterley Brick: 200 Years in the Making*, London 1990.
[5] 350 tons of cast iron were used in the construction of the building, and "the principal part of the works was carried on by mechanics in the employ of Mr.

The house had a magnificent frontage which was "over one hundred yards long", and it had "stabling for seventeen horses, its own brewhouses, bakery and provision for forty indoor domestic staff."[7] It was remarkable for its use of new engineering techniques, which attempted to remove the need for chimneys,[8] and its unusual design and special features, which made it a (somewhat dubious) Christian landmark. John Barton,[9] a close friend of two of Francis's sons, Henry and Frank, was a regular guest at Osmaston Manor in his youth. Upon his first visit in 1854, he remarked that the house "seemed to bear the motto 'Holiness to the Lord': for the balustrade was itself composed of stone letters three or four feet high, and visible half a mile off, forming words adapted from a verse in Ecclesiastes: 'The works of our hands are vanity, but whatsoever God doeth it shall be for ever.'"[10] Less than thirty years after it was built, Osmaston Manor was abandoned by Wright's eldest son and heir, John Wright,[11] and it soon fell into rack and ruin.[12]

Francis Wright had been in control of the Butterley Company for thirty-five years when he decided to finance the establishment of a school "dedicated to the cause of the broad Evangelical principles of the Church of England in the face of the threat of popish practices creeping in".[13] According to G. R. Balleine, the impetus for his decision was a paper on middle-class education which was read before the Midlands branch of the Clerical and Lay Association.

Wright." The house included an indoor swimming pool, a two-storey orangery and a racket court, all of which were roofed with "wrought iron principles and a covering of slate and glass". *Derbyshire Advertiser*, 20 July 1849.

[6] For an account of the building of Osmaston Manor, see the *Derbyshire Advertiser*, 20 July 1849. Francis Wright arranged for the Vicar of Osmaston, Revd W. B. Hayne, to hold a service for the workmen every Wednesday morning during the three years of construction.

[7] J. Loder, *Trent 1868–1978*, n.p. 1968, p. 2.

[8] The smoke from fireplaces was channelled into the cellars and piped beneath the kitchen gardens to emerge from a tall ornamental tower behind the house. The experiment failed, and chimneys were later added to the building.

[9] John Barton (1836–1908) was a CMS Missionary in India 1860–76; Vicar of Holy Trinity, Cambridge 1877–93; Secretary of the CPAS 1893–99; and Secretary of the CMS 1900–02. He was Bishop H. C. G. Moule's brother-in-law.

[10] C. E. Barton, *John Barton: A Memoir*, London 1910, p. 5.

[11] This was despite changing his name from 'Wright', to 'Osmaston'.

[12] Nat Gould, the racing novelist, visited the house in 1883 and described it as "a scene of desolation, a wilderness of weeds and decay..." Cited by Loder, *Trent*, p. 3. The house was demolished in 1934.

[13] Loder, *Trent*, p. 1.

Francis Wright (1806–1873)

This organization had been formed soon after the Western District Clerical and Lay Association was founded in Bristol in 1858.[14] Francis Wright and Sir Matthew Blakistone[15] were admitted as members of the parent organization at a meeting of the committee on 27 April 1858.[16] Very soon, these two men had formed the Clerical and Lay Association for the Midland District and Blakistone was appointed the first president. The Association grew quickly so that within a year it had 105 members.[17] They were drawn mostly from Derbyshire, but they also came from Leicestershire and Nottinghamshire. The Rules of Association were the same as for the Western District, with some minor changes. The first Committee had 23 members which included Francis Wright's eldest son, John Wright; and Revd E. W. Foley[18] and Revd Henry Cheetham[19] as Secretaries. The Association held its first

---

[14] See ch. 9.
[15] Of Sandbroke Hall, Ashbourne, Derbyshire.
[16] First Minute Book of the Church of England Clerical and Lay Association (Western District).
[17] *Report of the Proceedings at the First Annual Conference, held at Derby, on 19th and 20th June, 1860...*, Church of England Clerical and Lay Association for the Maintenance of Evangelical Principles (Midland District), Derby 1860.
[18] Later, a Trent College governor 1866–93. See below, p. 180.
[19] Henry Cheetham (1827–1899) was Perpetual Curate of Quordin, Leicestershire 1858–70, and later Bishop of Sierra Leone 1870–82.

conference at Derby on 19 and 20 June 1860. At this time, it included nine branches: Derbyshire, which was the largest, followed in size by Nottinghamshire, Leicestershire, Warwickshire and Lincolnshire. Kent, Surrey, Staffordshire and Cumberland were also listed in the first Annual Report, but each of these districts had only one member.[20] The third conference took place on 30 June and 1 July 1862 and was chaired by the second president, Robert Hanbury MP.[21] By 1863, two new branches were added: Chesterfield and Ashbourne. At this time there were 233 members: 139 clergymen and 94 laymen,[22] and Francis Wright had been appointed the Association's third president.

It was at a meeting of the Midland Branch of the Clerical and Lay Association in 1865 that the president, Francis Wright, first proposed the idea of Trent College. Soon afterwards, he chaired another meeting in Derby which was attended by "notable citizens of three counties—Derbyshire, Nottinghamshire and Staffordshire", seeking "to establish a school where teaching would be based upon the Scriptures in accordance with the principles of the English Reformation."[23] About £25,000 was subscribed with the intention of making grants of £4,000 to £5,000 to each of the colleges like Trent College which were to be established in the Midlands. In the end, Trent College was the only school of this type founded in the district, and the subscribers to the scheme had "the greater part of the money returned". This was obviously of some regret to Francis Wright, so that at the Trent College Speech Day eleven years later, he championed the work of Trent College but alluded to the potential of the original, much grander vision:

> The work was very much a single work; he was grieved to say that very few such colleges had been instituted, though the promoters of Trent College had desired and hoped that their example would be followed in other parts of the country. The failure of the scheme was a striking manifestation of the state of feeling in the country. They should be thankful, therefore, that the college had been so

---

[20] *Report of the Proceedings at the First Annual Conference.*

[21] Robert Culling Hanbury (1823–1867) was MP for Preston and lived at Ashbourne, Derbyshire. His son, Edmund Hanbury, later became Chairman of the Evangelical College and School Company 1895–1913 (see below, p. 189).

[22] *Report of the Proceedings of the Fourth Annual Conference, held at Nottingham, on June 2nd and 3rd, 1863, with a list of Members.* London 1863.

[23] *Long Eaton Advertiser*, 19 July 1968, p. 7.

Francis Wright and the Founding of Trent College

successfully established, and they ought to try to make its success continue.[24]

From this list of subscribers who met in Derby, came the founding directors of Trent College. These "notable citizens" were listed by the school's first historian, M. A. J. Tarver, as:

DERBYSHIRE:

Francis Wright, of Osmaston Manor.
William Thomas Cox, of Spondon Hall.
Thomas William Evans, of Allestrie
Clement Broughton Kingdon, of Hulland Hall.
Rowland Smith, MP, of Duffield.
Richard Sale, of Barrow-on-Trent.
Lord Vernon, of Sudbury.
Francis Beresford Wright, of Aldecar.
Henry Wardle, of Burton.

STAFFORDSHIRE:

Michael Arthur Bass,[25] MP, of Burton.
Charles Walter Lyon, of Silver Hill.
Robert Sherratt Tomlinson, of the Woodlands.

NOTTINGHAMSHIRE:

Robert Holden, of Nuttall Temple.
William Sanday, of Ratcliffe-on-Trent.
William Windley, of Nottingham.[26]

In the early days of Trent College, "these were far more than mere names."[27] Every month they met at the college, where there was always a luncheon in the Hall, speeches, and a request (always granted) for an extra half-holiday. In these very early days, Trent College was immensely aided by its Directors, who "took a keen personal interest in the school and did much to keep it full." These

---

[24] Pasted copy of newspaper report of the Trent College Speech Day, June 1871. F. Lott, "Early Records. Trent College", 1869–73, p. 3 [my pagination]. Trent College Archives. Lott was a pupil of the school from 1869–72.

[25] Of the well-known brewing family, Bass & Co.

[26] M. A. J. Tarver, *Trent College 1868–1927: A Rough Sketch*, London 1929, pp. 4–5.

[27] Tarver, *Trent College*, p. 5.

"prominent laymen in the Midland Counties"[28] formed themselves into a limited liability company, known as Trent College Company.

As well as having Directors to govern the school, another group of distinguished men known as 'Patrons', also took an active share in the development of Trent College. In the 1880s they included the Duke of Devonshire; the Bishops of Lichfield and Lincoln; Earls Howe, Manvers, Spencer, Lichfield, and Harrowby; and Sir Tonman Mosley.[29] The patrons nominated new pupils and presided at Speech Days. Through their influence they helped to promote the school. There was also a Council of Reference, in which the most prominent person seems to have been Dr S. A. Pears,[30] Headmaster of Repton School, who was described rightfully as having "made Repton what it is."[31] Pears was a frequent visitor to the school, where "He had more to do than any other with the institutions, the working order, and everyday life of early Trent; a better guide and friend nowhere could have been found, and many a time has Mr Fenn [the first Headmaster] looked to him for advice."[32] Repton was regarded by the directors as a leading public school whose Headmaster upheld the Reformed Anglican faith, and therefore a school upon which Trent could model itself. Not so the new Woodard schools such as at nearby Denstone, which was looked upon with great concern by these later supporters of Trent. Tarver wrote:

> The enemy was the Oxford movement as embodied in Dr. Woodard, and the schools which his influence created. Worthy men of Derbyshire, Staffordshire, and Nottinghamshire were alarmed for the future of the race. They accepted Repton as a seat of godly learning, but they saw quite clearly that the dreaded new schools would penetrate more deeply into the vitals of England than Repton could

---

[28] "Report of the Inspection of Trent College, Long Eaton, Derbyshire." Board of Education, London 1929, p. 3.

[29] Great-grandfather of the future politician and Fascist leader, Sir Oswald Mosley (1896–1980). Tarver incorrectly lists Sir Tonman's son, Sir Oswald Mosley (1848–1915), as one of the College founders. I am indebted to Mr Toby Leadbetter for drawing my attention to this error.

[30] Steuart Adolphos Pears (1815–1875) was Headmaster of Repton School 1854–74, during which time he raised the numbers from 50 to 250 boys. He was a "strict Evangelical", travelling in 1843 to Zürich on behalf of the Parker Society "to search for letters relating to the English Reformation." A. Macdonald, *A Short History of Repton*, London 1929, pp. 168 and 170. See also C. S. C. Bowen, "The English Evangelical Clergy", *Macmillan's Magazine* 3 (1860): 113.

[31] Tarver, *Trent College*, p. 5.

[32] Cited by Tarver, ibid.

Francis Wright and the Founding of Trent College

do, because they were cheaper. The only practical reply to the invasion was a school with low fees which could teach the faith as they held it; and at the same time should offer a good general education capable of attracting pupils.[33]

So it was that "On a sultry day in the summer of 1866 four gentlemen got out of the train at Trent and lunched."[34] This was the advance party that was to select a site for the new school. With Francis Wright present, it is perhaps not surprising that they not only chose to travel on the main line of the Midlands Railway Company to perform this task, but also they alighted at one of its new junctions, named after the nearby river Trent.[35] As a result of the decisions made that day (helped again no doubt by the Wright connection with the railway company), the platform notice at the station was to change from reading just "Trent" to "Trent (for Trent College)". This sign remained until the nearby village of Long Eaton grew into a community of sufficient size to make the town, rather than the river, or even the school, the major landmark of the area.

The men walked across the fields to "the little village of Long Eaton, which then consisted of a few thatched cottages and a farm or two".[36] It is known from "a report by Mr F. W. B. Smith,"[37] that one of the buildings, not mentioned in this account, which also made up the village, was a National School, opened only a few years before to replace the old village school in the Market Place. In fact, Long Eaton was to become something of an educational centre with the local School Board erecting first High Street School in 1876, then Derby Road School in 1886, then Tamworth Road School in 1893 and Derby Road Boys' School in 1901. Trent College may have become the premier school in the district, but it was not the only one. There is no doubt, however, that these other schools catered for a very different clientéle.

The party "crossed the narrow canal[38] bridge, pushed on further along the country lane, and finally came to a gate in a hedge on the

---

[33] Tarver, ibid., p. 4.
[34] Ibid., p. 3.
[35] What is today Long Eaton station was originally called Trent Station. C. E. Stretton, *The History of the Midland Railway,* London 1901, p. 90.
[36] Five years later, not much had changed: Abraham Shuker, on his way to an interview with the first Headmaster, described the town as "a straggling village with four farmhouses and fold yards, corn and hay stacks and black pigs wallowing in the mud." J. Loder, *Trent 1868–1978*, p. 5.
[37] A. Hooper, *Sketches of Long Eaton and District,* n.p. 1954, p. 71.
[38] Erewash Canal, which also marks the border between Derbyshire and Nottinghamshire.

left." Revd E. W. Foley[39] was one of those pioneers. He was also one of the early governors, and there is a plaque to his memory in the school chapel today. "He leaned on the gate and saw a magnificent view of the Red Hills and of the Soar Valley stretching away to Charnwood. Some two hundred and fifty yards beyond the gate the ground fell away, leaving a bank." It is likely, according to M. A. J. Tarver, that he could not see this bank from the gate, despite the fact that it would, in the future, provide the school building with a commanding view over the playing fields below, and across to the Charnwood Hills. Nevertheless, Foley "uttered four memorable words, 'This is the spot,' and it was."[40]

The site was purchased and on 3 December 1866, less than four months since the party of four had set out from Trent Station, the foundation stone was laid by Sir William Cavendish (1808–1891), the seventh Duke of Devonshire.[41] Frederick Peck of Furnival's Inn, London[42] was appointed as the architect, and work began almost immediately. Francis Wright was closely involved with the project from the start: "He laid out the grounds and terrace [of Trent College] in a large, handsome, open style, planting the turfy ground with choice trees; and when the avenue to the college was completed he said, 'Think what it will be in thirty years hence!'"[43] The relative speed at which a school board had been formed, the site chosen and building work had begun—all within the space of six months, was due not just to the energy and influence of the founder, as significant as this was. There was another, perhaps more urgent, motive for founding a new middle-class school along Evangelical lines. For Nathaniel Woodard, whose work at Hurstpierpoint and Lancing in the south was now well known, had recently launched an appeal for a middle-class boarding school in the Midland counties. As early as 1851 Woodard had "turned his eyes northward, and had seen the need for middle-class Church

---

[39] Edward Walwyn Foley (1866–1893) was Vicar of All Saints, Derby 1849–72 and then Rector of Jevington, Sussex 1872–93.
[40] Tarver, *Trent College*, p. 3.
[41] The seventh duke had enjoyed a brilliant academic career at Cambridge and "was not impressed by Newman's followers". The Dukes of Devonshire have retained their connection with the school, the present duke being President of the governors.
[42] *Derbyshire Advertiser*, 8 May 1868.
[43] Smith, *Recollections*, p. 7. The school's tradition of tree planting was to continue into the next century, particularly following the appointment as Chaplain in 1901 of Revd G. J. S. Warner, previously a master at South-Eastern College, Ramsgate (see ch. 8 below), who planted thousands of trees in the school grounds, with as many as six hundred different species.

schools in the Midlands".[44] By 1864 he was in correspondence with several Midlands clergy,[45] and late in 1866 Sir Percival Heywood[46] of Doveleys, Staffordshire, offered him a site and £1,000 for the construction of a "second Hurst"[47] at Denstone near Uttoxeter.[48] The Denstone Middle School Committee was formed in 1868, with Revd G. R. Mackarness[49] at its helm.[50] There was a great deal of resistance by local Evangelicals to the scheme, of which the paper on middle-class education read at the Midlands Clerical and Lay Association meeting was just one example.[51] In 1867 a local newspaper had condemned the "Denstone College scheme for turning out a hundred Puseyite children every year"[52] and another pamphlet warned against "a great Jesuit plot to contaminate the backbone of England."[53] Despite this opposition, early in 1868 St Chad's School at Denstone was founded as "a Public Boarding School for the commercial and agricultural classes of the Midland Counties".[54] In June of that year, the chairman of the Denstone Middle School Committee wrote to Nathaniel Woodard to tell him that work had begun on the building. "The ridge of the hill at Denstone shows a very busy scene just now. From 60 to 100 men are at work, and the foundations are being rapidly cut out, and prepared. The hot, dry weather is very much against the contractor. Sir Percival Heywood returns tomorrow, and will no doubt

---

[44] Letter from Nathaniel Woodard to Julius Hare, 9 December 1851. Lancing College Archives.

[45] Including Ernest Tower, Vicar of Earl's Shilton in Leicestershire, who was "a very energetic and enthusiastic agent". A number of small meetings were held in Leicester, Burton and other places "to prepare the way." J. Otter, *Nathaniel Woodard*, London 1925, p. 175.

[46] Sir Percival was the son of a prosperous Manchester banker.

[47] Letter from Nathaniel Woodard to Lord Cranborne, 21 November 1866. Lancing College Archives. Hurstpierpoint is often referred to as 'Hurst'.

[48] The site was Moss Moor, a fifty-acre farm situated near the village of Denstone in the Churnet and Dove valleys. It was located in a remote part of Staffordshire, which had been "long a centre for cock-fighting". Cowie, *That One Idea*, 1991, p. 61.

[49] George Richard Mackarness (1823–1883) was Vicar of Ilam, Staffordshire 1854–74 and Bishop of Argyll and the Isles 1874–83.

[50] Lancing College Archives contain correspondence from June 1868, in which the name of the committee and the secretary's address is printed as part of the letterhead.

[51] See above, pp. 174–6.

[52] Cited by Cowie, *That One Idea*, p. 61.

[53] Cited by Hudson and Swales, *Discovering Denstone*, p. 8.

[54] Cowie, ibid., p. 61.

double himself to the work."⁵⁵ In 1873 Lord Shrewsbury⁵⁶ held a huge garden-party at his home, Alton Towers. This raised £5,000 for the school and was used to build its Big Schoolroom. 'St Chad's College at Denstone' opened in July of that year with accommodation for 200 boys,⁵⁷ although the buildings were not completed until 1878.

Nathaniel Woodard and the Denstone Middle School Committee were anxious from the start to appoint a bishop as Visitor to the new school, in order to give the scheme some measure of respectability and to remove the extremist label which the Evangelicals had so vigorously applied to the whole Woodard movement. The Bishop of Lichfield, John Lonsdale,⁵⁸ had presided over "an important meeting…at Burton-on-Trent, in January, 1867…for the purpose of taking the scheme into consideration."⁵⁹ Later that year, he received a petition signed by over a thousand citizens, asking him to withdraw his support for the new project. His answer was to take the chair at the "stormy" public meeting at Stafford on 19 October 1867, where he spoke warmly in support of the Woodard Schools and said that their Churchmanship "was identical with his own".⁶⁰ The support which Bishop Lonsdale gave the College that day was his last action on earth, for he returned to his home, Eccleshall Castle, and died the same evening.⁶¹ The next Bishop of Lichfield, G. A. Selwyn,⁶² was then approached by the school committee, and his reply on 23 January 1868, was encouraging, even if it did contain a scarcely concealed episcopal grab for power:

---

[55] Letter to Nathaniel Woodard from the Revd G. R. Mackarness, 20 June 1868. Lancing College Archives.

[56] Charles John, the nineteenth Earl of Shrewsbury.

[57] J. Otter, *Nathaniel Woodard: A Memoir of His Life*, London 1925, p. 254.

[58] John Lonsdale (1788–1867) was Bishop of Lichfield 1843–67 where he "proved himself to be a very able bishop with a wide knowledge of ecclesiastical law." N. A. D. Scotland, *Good and Proper Men: Lord Palmerston and the Episcopal Bench*, Cambridge 2000, p. 207. See also E. B. Denison (ed.), *The Life of John Lonsdale, Bishop of Lichfield*, London 1868.

[59] *Monthly Intelligencer* 2, 1 (March 1868): 14.

[60] Hudson and Swales, *Discovering Denstone*, p. 9.

[61] See R. M. Grier, *John Allen Vicar of Prees and Archdeacon of Salop: A Memoir*, p. 124; and W. Beresford, *Diocesan Histories: Lichfield*, London, n.d., p. 288.

[62] George Augustus Selwyn (1809–1878) was Bishop of New Zealand 1841–67 and Bishop of Lichfield 1867–1878. See G. H. Curteis, *Bishop Selwyn of New Zealand, and of Lichfield*, London 1889; L. Creighton, *G. A. Selwyn, D.D., Bishop of New Zealand and Lichfield...*, London 1923; and T. E. Yates, *Venn and Victorian Bishops Abroad*, London 1978, pp. 44–75.

Before I accept the office of Visitor, I think that I ought to know what is understood of the name. If... it means that the managers as the leaders of the Church work [*sic*], will submit [to] "the godly admonitions" of the Bishop, and do or leave undone such things as he may suggest, then I would most gladly accept the office, and I think that I may then be able to stem the opposition, a specimen of which has already reached me.[63]

The chairmanship of the committee had been a much more difficult post to fill, having first been declined by Mr Webb of Newstead, before Revd G. R. Mackarness of Ilam parish near Ashbourne in Derbyshire accepted the position. He was to be succeeded by his brother-in-law the Vicar of Denstone, Revd Henry Meynell.[64] The idea of a school at Denstone had been suggested by Sir Percival Heywood in mid-1866 as a memorial to his recently departed son, Graham Percival Heywood. This was the same year that Francis Wright suggested a similar foundation at Long Eaton.

Thus the later supporters of the scheme at Long Eaton became the detractors of the scheme at Denstone. The battle lines of each camp were drawn, and each was anxious about the effect the other would have on the huge task of fundraising. The chairman of the Denstone Middle School Committee sent Woodard a copy of a letter which the Vicar of St George's at Wellington, Shropshire, had written, in which he stated, "I very much wish that the promoters of the scheme w[oul]d do all they can to remove the suspicion which attaches to it: I think this might be done by their publishing the Trust Deed."[65] Indeed the suspicion was so great that invitations to attend the school's Foundation Day ceremony were refused by the Bishops of Oxford, Chester, Hereford, Worcester, Lichfield[66] and Rochester. The Denstone Committee had to make do with an Archdeacon—albeit a distinguished one—Revd John Allen, Vicar of St George's, Prees and Archdeacon of Salop 1847–86.[67]

---

[63] Copy of letter from the Bishop of Lichfield and New Zealand to the Revd G. R. Mackarness, 23 January 1868. Lancing College Archives.

[64] Henry Meynell, "of the well-known Staffordshire family" was Curate-in-Charge of Denstone parish, Uttoxeter. He was later appointed Provost of the Woodard Corporation 'Midlands district'; and in 1897, Provost of the Western district.

[65] Copy of letter to Mr Bird from the Revd William Allen, 12 October 1868. Lancing College Archives.

[66] This was despite his previous support of the school.

[67] See R. M. Grier, *John Allen Vicar of Prees and Archdeacon of Salop: A Memoir,* London: Rivingtons 1889. Allen was the first HMI appointed to inspect church schools by (Sir) James Kay (later) Shuttleworth in 1839.

Woodard and his supporters were anxious to allay the fears of those who were opponents of the Oxford Movement, but felt that public meetings and the publication of trust deeds did not serve this purpose. It was this perceived hypocrisy which James Bateman, a well-known Evangelical[68] and vocal critic of the Woodard scheme, sought to expose. First of all he pointed out to Woodard, in a letter dated 30 October 1868, that most of the people who attended the Denstone opening ceremony were well-known High Churchmen: "Allow me to remark that among the company assembled at Denstone the other day—with the exception of Archdeacon Allen & my kind-hearted friend Lord Shrewsbury who support everything—I only noticed two names (one clerical & one lay) not connected with the high or "ultra-high Church party!"[69] Bateman then wrote to the *Staffordshire Advertiser*[70] calling for Woodard and his supporters to make public their convictions, or lack of them, by "providing some kind of legal security that [their] Society shall stick to the Church of the Reformation as by law established in these realms."[71] In due course he was able to do this himself, as the Church Association in London obtained, from the Court of Chancery, a copy of the Trust Deed. He refused Woodard's request for a 'private' meeting as he though that "the public mind is now distrustful of your scheme",[72] and whatever they discussed should be done in public.

By this time, the buildings at Long Eaton had been completed and Trent College opened in April 1868 with 53 boys. Revd Thomas Ford Fenn, MA, of Trinity College, Cambridge, was appointed the first Headmaster.[73] Early accounts of Trent College and its life in those first

---

[68] James Bateman (1811–1897) was on the Council of the Church Association 1870–80, and sometime editor of *The Rock* and the *English Churchman*. He was also on the committee of the London Society for Promoting Christianity amongst the Jews, and a Fellow of the Royal Society.

[69] Letter from James Bateman to Nathaniel Woodard, 30 October 1868 [his emphasis]. Lancing College Archives.

[70] A newspaper that was later described by the Editor of *The Rock* as having "an unaccountable weakness for these schools". *Rock,* 26 June 1874, p. 437.

[71] Letter to Nathaniel Woodard from James Bateman, n.d. ['Tuesday']. Lancing College Archives.

[72] Ibid.

[73] Son of Revd Joseph Fenn of Blackheath. He and his five brothers were all at Trinity College, Cambridge; two were Wranglers (the highest-ranked first-class candidates in the mathematical tripos), one a First Class classic, and the other three took Double Honours. The eldest of the Fenn brothers, Canon J. F. Fenn (1820–1884) had a distinguished clerical career as Vicar of Christ Church, Cheltenham 1860–84 and chaplain to the Bishop of Gloucester and Bristol. He

years are few, although one early work, "Some Old School Lists 1870–89",[74] which announced itself as the first published report on the school, noted that it was "designed as a boarding school for the boys of the middle-class; that is for the sons of farmers and men of business and of such professional men as are not able to meet the expenses of the great public schools".[75]

An Early Picture of Trent College

Another writer suggested that the new school was "especially intended for the upper middle classes…[such as] clergymen and members of the legal and medical professions….upper-class farmers and first-class tradesmen to whom such a school will be a great boon".[76] With a view to keeping the expenditure on board and salaries at a modest figure, the Directors resolved that the boys should be admitted at eight years old and not be allowed to remain after seventeen. The inclusive fee was fixed at £40 per annum, terms which were "so much higher" than Denstone, that one local Evangelical clergyman, Revd Warden Stubbs,[77] "feared that the Woodard schools would beat them".[78] But

---

was a great supporter of the College, and as sponsor of the annual Monitors Prize was frequently a guest of honour at school speech days.

[74] *Long Eaton Advertiser*, 19 July 1968 refers to this document; however, I have been unable to locate it in the school archives.

[75] *Long Eaton Advertiser*, 19 July 1968.

[76] Letter from 'A Shareholder' to the *Derbyshire Advertiser* and reprinted in Smith, *Recollections*, p. 45. Despite these comments, with fees fixed at £40 per annum, it is likely that the school would have attracted the 'middle' middle class parent. Upper middle-class schools at this time were charging around £100 per annum.

[77] Warden Flood Stubbs was Vicar of Rocester, Staffordshire 1857–69 and one of the authors of the booklet, *The Woodard Schools*, published by the Church Association.

not if God was on their side: at the school's opening ceremony, the chairman of the Board, Francis Wright, stated that he "hoped that the Lord's blessing would rest upon the first scholars, thoroughly imbued with every necessary attainment, and impressed with a desire to stand up for the Gospel of Christ".[79]

By 1870 the number of boys had risen to 250 and at the Prize Day, in the Michaelmas Term of that year, Francis Wright presented the prizes and Revd Thomas Stephens of Magdalen College, Cambridge, gave his examiner's report on the school. It gives a picture of how rapidly the school had grown, both in numbers of pupils and in numbers of teaching staff in just two years:

> The school consists of 250 boys, all boarders, and for the most part sons of men of business. In the course of instruction, Arithmetic, French, and the ordinary English subjects, receive the greatest amount of attention; Latin is taught throughout the school, and Euclid, Algebra, Greek or German in the higher forms. The teaching power...being, besides the Head Master, for the Upper School, five assistant masters, a French and an English master—and for the Lower, four assistant masters, all resident. There are also special masters for German and part-singing, and regular instruction is given in gymnastics, swimming, field-drill, &c., by a resident sergeant.[80]

In 1871 the Church Congress was held at Nottingham and during the week "some of the eminent persons who read papers at Nottingham visited Trent College and expressed their warm interest in the work being done there."[81] Dr Alfred Barry, Principal of King's College, London,[82] preached a sermon in the school chapel on "the temptations, difficulties, and advantages, of a public school", and Revd E. H. Bickersteth (1825–1906),[83] Vicar of Christ Church, Hampstead, gave an address to the boys on the subject of ambition. The pupils were constantly reminded particularly of the Protestant nature of their Anglican school, reflecting, no doubt, the bitter debates that were raging between the Anglo-Catholic and the Evangelical parties of the

---

[78] *Monthly Intelligencer* 2, 4 (June 1858): 71.
[79] Tarver, *Trent College*, p. 10.
[80] Lott, "Early Records", p. 3.
[81] Untitled newspaper clipping dated by hand October 1891. Lott, "Early Records", p. 6.
[82] Later, Principal of Cheltenham College 1862–68 and Bishop of Sydney, Australia 1884–89. See above, p. 142, fn. 88.
[83] See Appendix 1.

Church of England. Lord Harrowby[84] outlined the religious virtues of the school at the annual prize-giving ceremony for that year:

> It is a great comfort that there is such a college as this, where, without hindrance, and without intolerance, a religious Church of England education can be given to the children of those parents who desire such an education to be given to their sons. I am not an intolerant churchman, but I do think that our Church represents the best model for an education... I hope we are doing a good work here and are embuing the middle-class with a sound religious education, without any animosity towards our Nonconformist brethren, and without enforcing our opinions upon those who object to the principles of the Church of England. When I say the Church of England I mean the old Church of England, not the new Church of England—such religion as is contained in our Prayer-Book, not such as is developed outside it.[85]

In stark contrast to the Woodard schools, whose school chapels were from the start a central part of the school building, the chapel at Trent was for the first seven years of Trent's existence, a temporary, galvanised iron structure "alongside the Gymnasium, distant about a yard."[86] Although the founders had always planned that the chapel should be a "prominent part of the School buildings...there was a feeling on the part of many that a separate subscription should be raised for this purpose, so that the Chapel intended solely for the worship of God should be built as a labour of love and a free-will offering, and not as a business arrangement."[87] However, the chapel subscription fund was to receive an unexpected boost in 1873, for reasons no-one could have wished for: "The subscription list remained open, and year after year contributions were added, large or small, until some hundreds of pounds were promised. Still the desired end seemed far off, when it pleased God to take from us, after a very short illness, our friend and founder, the Chairman of Directors, Mr Francis Wright."[88]

---

[84] The third Earl of Harrowby, D. F. S. Ryder (1797–1882), was a well-known Evangelical. He was a Conservative MP and a friend of Shaftesbury, sharing his concern for philanthropic and social justice causes.
[85] "Trent College Speech Day June 1871", Lott, "Early Records", pp. 11–12.
[86] Abraham Shuker, on describing his first impressions of the school. Loder, *Trent*, p. 5. South-Eastern College in Ramsgate had a similar arrangement, with chapel services being held in the so-called 'tin tabernacle' from 1884–1927. Prior to this, the pupils attended services at the local parish church.
[87] Cited by Loder, *Trent*, p. 2.
[88] Ibid.

Around the time of Francis Wright's death "A desire then sprung up in many minds at once to make the Chapel of our College a memorial to the memory of one whom, we believe, as much as to any one in the world, we owe the existence of Trent College."[89] A sum of £3,000 was immediately raised, nearly half coming from Wright's sons and relatives, and the work was begun immediately. The architect was a Mr Robinson, who had designed St Luke's Church in Derby. By Speech Day of the following year, enough donations had been received for a foundation stone to be laid, which was performed by a friend and neighbour, Lord Vernon of Sudbury. The Chapel was opened in 1875.

On-going support for the school by Francis Wright's successors—specifically, his three sons—was variable. The eldest son of the founder, John Wright, inherited a legacy of £125,000 and promptly severed his connection with the family firm. His second son was the well-known Evangelical clergyman, Henry Wright.[90] Henry Wright became a major benefactor of Monkton Combe School, near Bath, which was later associated with Trent College. The third son, Francis Beresford Wright,[91] succeeded his father as head of the Butterley Company and following his father as Chairman of Governors. It was he who continued the family's direct connection with Trent College. An early, undated, school prospectus lists an annual Divinity Prize of £5 given by Francis Beresford Wright and the 1887 Prospectus lists Arthur Fitzherbert Wright[92] and Frederick Wright as directors during this period. The close connection between Trent College and the Wrights of the Butterley Company continued into the next generation: as late as 1943 the Company, under the chairmanship of Edward Fitzwalter Wright, decided to endow six annual scholarships for the sons of Butterley employees. In 1946, however, the coal industry was nationalised and the Butterley Company was sold—together with Butterley Hall in Derby, the eighteenth-century manor house that had been the original headquarters of the company. The Butterley Scholarships were not renewed and so the connection between Trent College and this famous Midlands company which had grown out of the Industrial Revolution, ceased.

---

[89] Ibid.
[90] See Appendix 1.
[91] Francis Beresford Wright (1873–1911) became a JP for Derbyshire and Warwickshire and lived first at Aldecar Hall, Langley Mill, Derbyshire and later at Wootton Court, Warwickshire. He was one of the four original Trustees of Ridley Hall, Cambridge and Wycliffe Hall, Oxford.
[92] Arthur Fitzherbert Wright was the eldest son of Francis Beresford Wright and a director of the Butterley Company, 1891–1937.

Trent College was to be associated with another company in its early years. In February 1893, the College was taken over by a new Board of Governors, which had been formed to buy Trent from the original directorate, seeing that "most of the original directors [had] died".[93] The Church of England Evangelical College and School Company Limited[94] was formed by the Union of Clerical and Lay Associations on 12 February 1891. They continued the Evangelical vision of its founder and first directors, but the school faced some very serious financial problems during this time. In October 1893, the directors resolved that it was necessary to appoint a new Bursar to Trent College, and an undermaster at the school, Revd I. A. Smith, took up this position. By November, Smith had resigned[95] to take up the post of vice-principal of the Training College at Cheltenham.[96] The school's financial woes continued—Tarver describes this period as "The Sinking Ship"[97]—and in 1895 the then Headmaster, Revd W. H. Isaacs, left to become a classics master at Dean Close School in Cheltenham.[98] At the same time, Edmund Hanbury[99] joined the board and in 1895 he succeeded Sydney Gedge as chairman, a position which "he filled until the day of his death".[100] Hanbury was assisted by W. D. Cruddas MP[101] and his two daughters who were "noble supporters" of

---

[93] *Illustrated Sporting and Dramatic News*, 12 November 1937, p. 359.

[94] See ch. 10 below.

[95] He did so under a cloud—the school auditors later refused to sign off his balance sheet because of the "manner in which Mr Smith had kept the books", particularly with regards an "item of £2375.2.1 for petty cash of which no explanation was given!" Minute Book A, October 1893, p. 115.

[96] Founded in 1847 by a committee chaired by Francis Close. Smith was Vice-Principal 1893–1908, when he left to become Principal of Ripon College.

[97] Tarver, *Trent College*, passim.

[98] See ch. 9 below.

[99] Edmund Smith Hanbury (1850–1913) was the eldest son of Robert Hanbury, MP for Preston, who died in 1867. As eldest grandchild of Robert Hanbury the elder (1847–1884), he became heir to the family's interest in the large London brewing firm: Truman, Hanbury and Buxton. The Hanbury family was, according to the *DNB*, "largely responsible for the birth of Haileybury from the ashes of the old East India Company's College." Edmund Hanbury was also a member of the Haileybury College Council 1884–1913 and Treasurer 1892–1913.

[100] A house in the school is named after him and there is a two lancet stained glass window in the school chapel in his memory.

[101] W. D. Cruddas was President of the School Council 1905–1912, during which time he was also President of the National Church League (1906–12). He was a partner in Armstrong Vickers and a leading benefactor of Evangelical causes. The Cruddas family were the major financiers of Trent College's first purpose-built science laboratory, known as the Kelvin School.

the scheme, helping to finance the building of Trent College and also Weymouth School.[102] Hanbury was succeeded as chairman in 1913 by the Evangelical Dean of Canterbury, Henry Wace (1836–1924).[103]

The school prospectus for 1895–96 lists a Special Entrance Scholarship, in addition to those given by the College, of £15 for two years, given by the Clerical and Lay Association (Midland District). In 1898, the Headmaster of Trent College, Revd J. S. Tucker,[104] told the Clerical and Lay Association (Western District) meeting that "the High Church Woodard Schools had already educated 20,000 boys, and were quietly and unobtrusively training a body of laity and clergy who would undo the work of the Reformation."[105] Tucker admitted that the Evangelical schools could not keep pace with this, they were in any case fewer in numbers, but they did (he said) "teach definite doctrines to boys who were ripe for it." While the Evangelical founders of the school were not necessarily motivated by such party feeling, later staff and supporters clearly were. Like the fourth Headmaster, they saw the Woodard schools as the enemy, and they were not afraid of saying so.

This was particularly the case for the school's first historian, M. A. J. Tarver, who attempted to superimpose the strong party feeling which existed among Anglican Evangelicals during the Prayer Book revision controversy of 1922–8,[106] onto a period 50 years earlier when the school was founded. His bold statement in the opening pages of *Trent College 1868–1927*, that "The enemy was the Oxford movement as embodied in Dr. Woodard",[107] was not a sentiment that the school's founder, Francis Wright, ever expressed. Nevertheless, it has been

---

[102] The Cruddas family also gave generously towards the building of St John's Hall, an Evangelical college at Durham University. One of St John's buildings is named Cruddas House. See "St. John's Hall, Durham" in *The Record*, 4 April 1913, pp. 317–320.

[103] See Appendix 1. Wace joined the Council in 1901 when he was Rector of Exeter College, Oxford.

[104] Tucker was a well-known Evangelical, and an examining chaplain to F. J. Chavasse, the Bishop of Liverpool.

[105] *Report of the Proceedings of the 41st Annual Meeting, held at Bath, 24 and 25 May 1898*. Bath 1898, p. 17.

[106] In October 1922 the Church Assembly's House of Bishops introduced the Revised Prayer Book (Permissive Use) Measure. This resulted not only in three years of debates in the assembly, but produced a torrent of rival proposals, criticism, comment and protest, particularly from Evangelicals who were generally opposed to any revision which would entail a disturbance of the balance of doctrine contained in the existing Prayer Book. Despite not being approved by the House of Commons, a revised Prayer Book was published at the end of 1928.

[107] Tarver, *Trent College*, p. 4.

slavishly repeated in newspaper articles and histories of the school;[108] to the point that Trent College has frequently been described by modern scholars as having been founded in direct opposition to Woodard's school at Denstone.[109] As has been suggested above, there is no evidence for this interpretation. If there were any reaction to Woodard by its founding fathers, it was one of respect and encouragement. Their concern was for the education of their children rather than the extension of their religious views. This was also the case for the clerical founder of a school in a village just outside of Bath, Somerset. Neither Francis Pocock, nor the three owners who followed him, described Woodard as a threat. It was a pastoral rather than party concern that resulted in the foundation of another Evangelical middle-class school.

---

[108] The most recent being, *A Celebration of Trent College*, by F. W. B. Leadbetter, Nottingham 2002.

[109] See, for example, Gardner, *Public Schools*, pp. 192–3; Honey, *Tom Brown's Universe*, p. 96; Evans, "Town, Gown and Cloth", p. 8; Wellings, "Aspects of Late Nineteenth-Century Evangelicalism", p. 144–5; and Royle, "Evangelicals and Education", p. 126.

CHAPTER 6

Francis Pocock and the Founding of Monkton Combe School

For a school that was to become famous for the number of its pupils who went to the mission field—even going so far as listing them on an Honour Board in the Dining Hall[1]—it is of some significance that the early history of Monkton Combe School can be traced back to the great nineteenth-century missionary-explorer, David Livingstone (1813–1873). In 1858, Palmerston's ministry granted £5,000 to Dr Livingstone for the exploration of the Zambezi. Livingstone was 45 and had already spent his early years in Bechuanaland, where he had begun opening up Central Africa for 'Christianity and commerce'. After a triumphal tour of England, which included the founding of the Universities Mission to Central Africa (UMCA)[2] at Cambridge University, Livingstone left in March of that same year for 'the dark continent'.[3] On his way to the Cape of Good Hope, he called in at Freetown, Sierra Leone, where he stayed for six days. On one of these days he breakfasted with Revd Francis Pocock, chaplain to the bishop, and at some point during this meeting Livingstone showed Pocock his badly-scarred shoulder, the result of a mauling by a lion fourteen years

---

[1] This is still hanging in what today is called the Old Hall. Altogether the 'missionary board' lists 152 Old Monktonians who went to the mission field over a period of 108 years. The first missionary was A. Morgan, who went to South India with CMS in 1872, and the last one listed is M. A. Currie, who went to Pakistan with CMS in 1980. The list was closed in that year with the following explanation: "In recent years the definition of Missionary work has been broadened and the opportunities for Christian Service have increased [so that] the term 'Missionary' has therefore become difficult to apply". *Monkton Combe School Register,* 37th edn., 1994.

[2] Now known as the United Society for the Propagation of the Gospel, which was formed by its merger in 1965 with the Society for the Propagation of the Gospel in Foreign Parts.

[3] Although the expedition of 1858 to 1863 mapped a vast area of Africa hitherto hardly known at all to Europeans, in human terms it was a disaster as many of the white members of the expedition died, including Livingstone's wife, Mary. This led to the UMCA withdrawing its support for the expedition. See J. P. R. Wallis (ed.), *The Zambezi Expedition of David Livingstone 1858–63,* 2 vols, London 1956.

before. The connection between Livingstone (including his scarred shoulder), Africa, and Francis Pocock was to eventually become part of the history of Monkton Combe School, as will be shown below.

Francis Pocock (1829–1919) had as a young man felt the 'missionary call'. He attended St Aidan's Theological College at Birkenhead[4] and from there went straight to Sierra Leone with his wife. He was ordained soon after he arrived and, from 1855 to 1858, worked among Africans as Chaplain to the Bishop, John Weeks (c.1800–1857).[5] Like so many of his contemporaries, Pocock and his wife were ill-prepared for the environmental conditions of the tropics, so that in 1858 while Livingstone was on his way to a second missionary expedition, Pocock was already preparing to return to England because of ill-health. Mr and Mrs Pocock left Freetown two months later on the Royal Mail steamship, *Candace,* bound for Plymouth. The journey was a disaster. On 4 May the *Candace* and the Dutch-registered ship, *Ida Elizabeth,* collided. The *Candace* sank almost immediately, and the ship's master, two passengers and four seamen were drowned.[6] However, the rest of the crew and passengers, including Pocock and his wife, were picked up by the Dutch ship and transferred to Cadiz four days later, from whence they made their way back to England on a P & O ship.[7] Soon after, Pocock took up a curacy at Little Faringdon, Oxfordshire, but continued ill-health led him eventually to Bath where he was able to 'take the waters' while serving as a curate; first at St James's, Southgate in the city and later at Widcombe on the outskirts. While he was curate of Widcombe, he was offered the living of Monkton Combe in the Midford valley three miles to the south of Bath. The patron at that time was Henry Calverley (1794–1874), Vicar of South Stoke with Monkton Combe,[8] who later

---

[4] See above, p. 42, fn. 223.
[5] See Appendix 1 for a short biography of Weeks; also D. T. Barry, *CMS Register of Missionaries and Native Clergy from 1804 to 1904*, London 1906; C. Fyfe, *A History of Sierra Leone*, London 1962; and Stock, *History of the CMS.*
[6] "Wreck of the R.M.S. *Candace*", *Lloyd's Register*, 1858.
[7] Details of this incident were first recorded in a printed copy of Revd D. L. Pitcairn's "Memorial Sermon on the Revd. Francis Pocock", 23 March 1919, p. 2, located in the Monkton Combe School archives. Pitcairn was Vicar of Monkton Combe 1883–1918.
[8] From medieval times, Monkton Combe (then known as Cume) had been a Chapelry of South Stoke. It was serviced by a small church in the village of Monkton Combe, which seated about 100 people. In 1832 a new church was built in the village of Combe Down largely to service the quarry workers living on high ground between Monkton Combe and Bath. The union of Monkton Combe and South Stoke continued until 1844, when Monkton Combe became a separate parish—still including, as it always had done, Combe Down. Finally in

also provided the land for a vicarage and £500 towards building it. In 1863 Francis Pocock was appointed Vicar of Monkton Combe on the very modest stipend of £45 a year.

Pocock was now 34 years old and, despite the ill-health which had brought him to Bath, must have been a man of some vigour and drive. For within the next five years he had the small church which serviced the village of Monkton Combe demolished and, with the support of his patron and parishioners, built a new one more than three times the size.[9] During this time he was also responsible for building a new vicarage, a new village water-supply[10] and two new parish schools.[11] His energy did not stop at public works, for in September 1867, Pocock privately purchased two large houses in the village[12] as well as three nearby fields. Although these properties were later to become the nucleus of his new school, it appears that Pocock's motivation for this purchase was at the time purely financial—they were a good investment. The school's historian, A. T. Wicks, records that it was an estate which "had to be sold,"[13] and from this and other sources it can be assumed that the buildings and attached estate were being sold at a bargain price. Francis Pocock was not a wealthy man, and in order to purchase them he had to take out a mortgage. The property belonged to a Mr Jones and the purchase price was about £1,000. The farm, which was occupied by a man called Bodman,[14] was bought by Pocock later.

The idea of turning these buildings and the associated land into a school did not seem to occur to Pocock until some time later, for in the following year Pocock began taking pupils into his own house for

---

1863 the parishes of Monkton Combe and Combe Down were separated and Mr Pocock arrived to be the first Vicar of Monkton Combe for that village alone.

[9] The new church, completed in 1865, seated around 300.

[10] He obtained permission from Major Vaughan-Jenkins to lay down pipes from the spring in the grove to the village. D. L. Pitcairn, "Memorial Sermon on the Revd. Francis Pocock", p. 6.

[11] His establishment of the 'Church of England Day School' is recorded on a memorial tablet in the village church. An article in the *Bath Evening Chronicle* records the ceremony at which the Bishop of Bath and Wells dedicated eight 'Pocock Memorial bells'. *Bath Evening Chronicle*, 4 July 1927, p. 13.

[12] One of the buildings Pocock purchased was the local public-house, the *King William IV*; the other was a house built in the previous century which had formerly been occupied by a bacon-merchant. The *King William* continued to be used as an inn until, a few years later, the local wheelwright opened his house for the same business.

[13] A. T. Wicks, "Notebook 1", p. 1. Monkton Combe School Archives.

[14] The names of the two owners were not known until Pocock mentioned this some 30 years later. See the anonymous MSS, "Brief notes taken down from Mr. Pocock", in the Monkton Combe School Archives.

instruction. His motivation appears not to be that which was so common for this period: a means of supplementing his income, but rather he saw it as an opportunity to "train them as missionaries".[15] The first of these was a boy called Edwin Woodley, who moved into the parsonage in January 1868. Unfortunately Edwin died at the end of his first term—not an auspicious start to this new venture! It is possible that the idea of taking in pupils for religious as well as limited secular instruction may have been suggested in the previous year by some friends, for when he attended the school prize-giving ceremony in 1899, he said that he "first conceived the idea [of starting a school] when some missionary friends came to him asking him to take a few pupils".[16] According to Pocock's later recollections, this was done "very much against his will".[17] His initial reluctance may have been because he felt that his theological college training and missionary experience were not the stuff of a clerical schoolmaster, who was typically a university scholar as well as a clergymen.[18]

The next enrolment of pupils came about by a chance meeting with Miss Maria Charlesworth, the best-selling Evangelical children's writer[19] who also had a well-known interest in helping the poor. She came to Monkton Combe in search of a retired blind shepherd about whom she had written in one of her books. In due course she met Francis Pocock, and, as their interests were similar, a friendship developed which was later described as "something like that of Wilberforce and Hannah More previously in the same century".[20] Miss Charlesworth "was very much interested in education and did a great deal for poor schools in South London".[21] It is likely that she encouraged Pocock to start a school, something which he had already begun in a small way with the enrolment of Edwin Woodley. Maria must have been impressed by Pocock's ability, for by the summer of

---

[15] "Brief notes taken down from Mr Pocock."
[16] *The Monktonian*, December 1899, pp. 6–7.
[17] "Brief notes taken down from Mr. Pocock."
[18] See Leinster-Mackay, *The Rise of the English Prep School;* especially ch. 6 on clerical headmasters.
[19] Maria Louisa Charlesworth (1819–1880) wrote over 32 different books of which *Ministering to Children* went to eight editions, and was last published in 1928. See A. G. Newell, "Studies in Evangelical Popular Prose Literature: its Rise and Decline", PhD thesis, Liverpool University 1976, pp. 539–5.
[20] Wicks, "Notebook 1", p. 2.
[21] Letter from M. E. Relton to H. J. Powell, daughter of Frederick Charlesworth, who was Maria's nephew. Monkton Combe School Archives.

1868, there were five boys receiving instruction from Mr Pocock, of which three were her nephews.[22]

Some time in 1868 the Pococks moved with their tiny school to the old bacon-merchant's house,[23] which was also known as the 'Portico House'. Pocock stated in his memoirs that the school was held "in the block where the [existing] prefects' room is including the boot room, and the room over it, and also a small room on the other side of the building from the boot room."[24] Space was at a premium but although he owned the adjacent King William IV Inn, the school did not move into this building until after 1872. Perhaps the inn-keeper provided a good income from which Pocock could finance further expansion of the school. In March 1869, Pocock bought, for £235, five further pieces of land, some of which had cottages on them. These lay in what is now the school garden. This purchase suggests that Pocock was aiming to consolidate his property, presumably with the intention of enlarging his school. But none of this new property gave him any classroom space.

By now the Portico House began being known by the locals as the 'Vicarage', and the building which Pocock had built as the vicar's house continued to be called the 'Parsonage'. Nevertheless, the *Bath Directory* continued to list the vicar's residence as 'The Parsonage' right up to the time Pocock and his family left the village in 1875, not distinguishing between the old one and the new. George R. F. Prowse (1860–1946), a pupil at Monkton Combe from 1871 to 1874,[25] drew a rough map in 1919 of the school he knew as a boy. On it he shows the Portico House as "School the only new building in my time [sic]",[26] which is surprising since the old parsonage was newly-built and the new 'Vicarage' at least a century old. What Prowse may have been referring to here was a totally new structure which had been built adjacent to the schoolhouse. Sometime around 1871, Pocock had a building adjacent to the Portico House pulled down, and erected a new two-storey building comprising a downstairs classroom and a dormitory upstairs. This building still stands today, and is part of the staff room.

---

[22] These were the twins Edward Charlesworth (1853–1901) and John Charlesworth (1853–1941), and their younger brother, Frederick Charlesworth (1855–1935).
[23] See above, p. 195, fn. 12.
[24] "Brief notes taken down from Mr. Pocock."
[25] He was later appointed Principal of Oakville School, Manitoba, Canada.
[26] G. R. F. Prowse, "Letters from Various Old Monktonians", in A. F. Lace, *A Goodly Heritage*, Bath 1968, p. 12.

Pocock ran the school single-handedly from May 1868 until April 1869, assisted only by his wife and servants. Mrs Pocock was greatly loved by the boys, and was described by one as "a godly loving mother to us all".[27] The four upstairs rooms were probably used by the Pococks as their living and bed rooms, with the ones downstairs comprising the schoolroom,[28] boys' dormitory, as well as kitchen and dining room. The servants would have came in from the village or occupied one of the upstairs rooms. There was clearly a need for more teaching staff, for although Pocock was regarded as a great Bible teacher, he was not a 'university man'.[29] George Prowse wrote that "Francis Pocock was a divinity trained man not at any university but, as was more common then than now, he was an expert Hebrew scholar. He only took us in Scripture—the old strict Evangelical exegesis...".[30] Even if it was hoped by the parents and relatives of the boys that they would enter the Church or the mission-field,[31] clearly a much wider curriculum was required for those who wished to do this via university.

In the next year Mr Pocock obtained two assistants: Revd Francis Bishop and Mr Henry Carpenter. The former came *circa* May 1869, having previously been ordained deacon after attending two theological colleges. He became Mr Pocock's curate and Assistant Master.[32] Carpenter came from Trinity College, Dublin, at about the same time. He lived at Midford, some 1 ½ miles away, where he also ran a mission church in a barn.[33] Carpenter served as an Assistant Master to Pocock during three discrete periods between 1869 and 1888. All three school masters had parish duties, so it is perhaps just as well that the school numbers rose only very slowly. A. F. Lace[34] has

---

[27] Ibid.

[28] Henry Carpenter, the Assistant Master wrote that, when he came, "the old Counting House which stood next to the dwelling house on the side nearest the present dining room was used as the school room".

[29] St Aidan's Theological College catered mainly for non-graduates.

[30] Letter from Prowse to Wicks, August 28, 1937. Monkton Combe School Archives.

[31] It is recorded that Miss Charlesworth was very disappointed that not one of her nephews had been ordained.

[32] Francis Bishop later went on to become chaplain to the Central London District Schools.

[33] His wife assisted in the services there. In 1882 Carpenter was made a curate of South Stoke for the purpose of the 'ministry at Midford', and masters and boys from the School assisted him.

[34] Captain A. F. Lace, author of the first published school history, joined the Junior School staff in 1920, and was Assistant Master of the Senior School from 1927 to 1958, except from 1939–45 when he was with the King's African

traced, by various means, the names of 54 boys present during Pocock's years, so if it is assumed that each boy stayed for about two years, at this time the average number of boys in the school each year would have been approximately 15 pupils. In the first few years we know that there were fewer—a school photograph taken in 1869[35] shows only six boys—but by 1874 there were at least 19, and possibly 22 boys.

Francis Pocock (1829–1919)

The boys attended the village church, of which Revd F. Pocock was the incumbent. It was here that Pocock was seen at his best. He was described by one the boys as "an incomparable expounder of the Bible. After all the wear and tear of a very busy and changeable life his lessons stand out to-day as clear in my mind as the day they were uttered. As a preacher he was in direct descent from Simeon and the great Evangelicals."[36] George Prowse also refers to Pocock's voice which "in its bell-like resonance was in a small way like

---

Rifles and at Arusha College, Tanzania.

[35] A rare picture, considering that photographic negatives were invented only in 1839. Unfortunately the original has been lost, and the only copy is that printed in Lace, *A Goodly Heritage*, p. 19.

[36] Cited by Lace, *A Goodly Heritage*, pp. 20–21.

Gladstone's".[37] Although Pocock was not as educated as the other masters, and taught only the Scripture classes, he clearly had a lasting influence on the boys. From the list of nineteen competitors who were listed in the printed programme for the 'Monkton Combe Collegiate School Athletic Sports Day' for June 1894, six went on to be ordained and three became missionaries. The interest in mission would no doubt have been encouraged by Pocock's own missionary stories from Sierra Leone, especially his breakfast meeting with David Livingstone. This chance meeting was to have its conclusion in another unusual event which occurred early in 1874 when Pocock set off for London to identify Livingstone's body, which had been transported to England from Zanzibar.[38] One of the boys later wrote, "Nothing affects me so closely as the Monktonian connection with Livingstone."[39] Of those who became missionaries, A. Burtchael went to West Africa in 1877— "the first School martyr. He went cheerfully and knowingly to his death in the mission field"[40]—dying in 1880 in Sierra Leone. Revd A. Morgan, like Burtchael, was trained at the Church Missionary College at Islington[41] and then served for seven years in South India. Another with a missionary connection was Revd A. J. P. Shepherd who, after holding a chaplaincy at Lahore under Bishop T. Valpy French[42] and a

---

[37] Letter from Prowse to Mr Powell of 11 February 1928. Monkton Combe School Archives.

[38] The body had arrived here after being carried well over a thousand miles by his faithful African servants. Although at this point it had been easy to identify the body as the mark of the old lion-wound was plainly visible, by the time it arrived in London two months later and almost a year after death, it was so decomposed that questions were raised as to whether this was indeed Livingstone's corpse. So the authorities of the day asked anyone who could identify the body to come to London for that purpose. Mr Pocock was able to do this by pointing out the traces of a fracture, which were consistent with Livingtone's shoulder wound.

[39] Lace, *A Goodly Heritage*, p. 19.

[40] Prowse, cited in *The Old Monktonian Gazette*, March 1959, p. 79.

[41] Founded in 1825, the CMS Training College was later caricatured by Anthony Trollope in his novel *Rachel Ray*, where Revd Samuel Prong was described as being deficient because "he was not a gentleman", having "been educated at Islington" and that sometimes he "misplaced his 'h's'". A. Trollope, *Rachel Ray*, Oxford 1988 (1863), p. 52. I am indebted to Arthur Pollard for this reference.

[42] T. Valpy French was an incumbent at Cheltenham (St John's 1864, and St Paul's 1864–68). Stock called him "the most distinguished of all CMS missionaries." *History of the CMS*, vol. 2, p. 65.

lectureship at Oxford, became Director of the Church Missionaries' Children's Home at Highbury[43] 1881–86.

Many of the boys in these early years did not stay with Pocock for all of their schooling. Charles Cowan went to Shrewsbury, Blandy to Sherborne, Prowse to Haileybury, and the Charlesworth brothers went from Monkton Combe to Marlborough. Clearly in its early years, many parents saw the school as a prep school rather than a place that could prepare their children for direct entry to University.[44] In this sense, Monkton Combe did not really 'come of age' until the next Headmaster when, instead of boys progressing from Monkton Combe to one of the great public schools, there were examples of the children of devout parents being transferred from schools like Marlborough to Monkton Combe.[45] For the first 23 years of its life, Monkton Combe School was privately owned, with Mr Pocock the first of four landlords. In 1874 Mr Pocock was again considering closing the school, but another chance meeting early in the following year prevented this from happening.

One Sunday in February or March 1875, Revd J. A. Jamieson, then of St Stephen's, Lansdown, Bath, preached for Mr Pocock on behalf of the Church Pastoral Aid Society.[46] In the course of conversation he learnt that Mr Pocock was considering closing the school. One account says this was because of ill-health; another because he was having problems getting good staff. However, it was no secret that Pocock was always a reluctant Head, being trained as a missionary-pastor rather than a schoolmaster. As it happened, on the next Sunday Mr Jamieson was to preach on behalf of the same society at the village church at Fosbury in Wiltshire, where Revd R. G. Bryan was Vicar. Mr Bryan had been there twenty years and had a few boys living with him whom he taught.[47] Jamieson learnt that Mr Bryan was keen to expand his teaching activities[48] and so, armed with his intelligence

---

[43] This was opened by the CMS in some rented houses in Milner Square, Islington in 1850 and transferred to new buildings at Highbury Grove in 1853. Stock, *History of the CMS*, pp. 48–9.

[44] See Leinster-Mackay, *The Rise of the English Prep School*. This situation was to change, for by 1888 one of the masters of Monkton Combe School and R. G. Bryan's son-in-law, Charles Howard, opened a Preparatory School, Monkton Combe Junior School, on Combe Down (about one mile from Monkton Combe) where "Boys [are] prepared for Entrance Examinations at Monkton Combe or other Schools". *Rock*, 9 March 1888, p. 16.

[45] See below, p. 208.

[46] For the Church Pastoral Aid Society, see below, pp. 250–56.

[47] As well as this, he was teaching some of his own children.

[48] It is known that as early as 1864 he was thinking of a move back into teaching; for in that year he asked for and obtained a letter of recommendation from

about Mr Pocock's wish do just the opposite, he put these two men into communication with one another. The result of this was that Mr Bryan was offered the headmastership of Monkton Combe Proprietary School, as it was then known, and Mr Pocock sought and obtained the living of St Paul's in Poole,[49] in the diocese of Salisbury. The only other matter that needed to be resolved was the lease of the school buildings and property.

The business negotiations between Mr Pocock and Mr Bryan must have been carried out in a considerable hurry. Bryan and Pocock met for the first time in March; there are records showing that a lease on the *King William* was signed in April; and Bryan and his family and pupils moved to Monkton Combe in May. Perhaps because of the lack of time, poor records were made, so that now there are conflicting accounts as to who exactly was the leaseholder of the school over this period, and when the documents were signed. An article in the *Old Monktonian Gazette* states that Mr Pocock leased to Mr Bryan "the *King William* and the Old Vicarage".[50] However, the actual title deed shows that the Old Vicarage and its grounds were not leased to Bryan at this time.

Although there is very little appreciation of this in A. F. Lace's school history,[51] it appears that another interested party had recently come onto the scene: a wealthy evangelical clergyman by the name of Alfred Peache. Revd Alfred Peache (1818–1900), Perpetual Curate of Mangotsfield with Downend, Bristol, was the son of James Courthope Peache (1782–1858), an extremely wealthy London businessman with a yearly income estimated at £50,000—a huge sum in those days.[52]

Malta Protestant College, where he had been Vice-Principal from 1846–1854. He also had in his possession a testimonial by Lord Shaftesbury, which he had obtained on leaving the College at Malta. According to his daughter, there had also been talk of his going to teach at Cheam School. "Reminiscences", in *The Old Monktonian Gazette*, May 1959, p. 106.

[49] This is now contiguous with the town of Bournemouth in Dorset. Pocock later came back to Bath and was for 14 years the Minister of Portland Episcopal Chapel and "also took a great interest in the work of the Young Men's Christian Association." Pitcairn, "Memorial Sermon on the Revd. Francis Pocock", p. 3.

[50] *The Old Monktonian Gazette*, March 1959, cited by Lace, *A Goodly Heritage*, p. 25.

[51] Apart from brief references on pp. 28 and 46 of Lace, *A Goodly Heritage*.

[52] See Appendix 1.

Alfred Peache (1818–1900)

In 1857, James Peache and his eldest son and heir died six weeks apart, and Alfred and his sister Kezia (1820–1899) inherited the family fortune. Both Alfred and Kezia generously supported Evangelical causes such as the Church Missionary Society and the London College of Divinity.[53] Kezia was also a great supporter of local charities in Wimbledon, the home of her parents. During ministries at Heckfield cum Mattingley, Hampshire (1854–1859)[54] and the Perpetual Curacy of St James Church, Mangotsfield (1850) with Christ Church, Downend (1859–1878), Peache donated most of his fortune 'to educational purposes'.[55] While at Bristol, Peache was a member of the Church of England Clerical and Lay Association (Western District) which co-founded Dean Close Memorial School in Cheltenham.[56] In April 1875, he bought the leasehold of Monkton Combe School from Francis Pocock, which then comprised the Portico House, the old King William Inn, and the adjacent ground and buildings.[57]

The tenancy had already been arranged: on 7 April 1875, Mr Pocock had signed over his successor, Mr Bryan, as tenant for a period of twenty-one years at a rent of £116 per annum.[58] The tenancy lease included an option to purchase at any time within the next twelve years, but before this could be exercised, and within a month of Bryan signing the tenancy agreement, Alfred Peache had became the new owner of the School. It is not clear when the lease for the Portico House was signed, as this document is not among the School deeds. It is known, however, that a new Vicar of Monkton Combe was appointed in a very short period of time, so that as soon as Mr Pocock moved to Poole, Revd A. G. Gristock moved into the Portico House to take up his combined parish and school duties. Mr Gristock was a scholar of Magdalen College, Oxford, and over the next eight years was regarded as the 'right-hand man' of the new principal, Mr R. G. Bryan.

Reginald Guy Bryan (1819–1912) was a pupil at Rugby of Dr Arnold, from where he went as a mathematical scholar to Trinity

---

[53] See Munden, *History of St John's College*. Peache and his sister gave upwards of £120,000 to the College.
[54] Peache and his wife lived at Danmore Cottage and were neighbours of Charles Kingsley at Eversley.
[55] Peache supported the schools in his parish and was a generous benefactor to the Clergy Daughters' School, which was founded in Gloucester in 1831 and moved to Bristol in 1836. See Munden, *History of St John's College*, p. 16.
[56] See ch. 9 below.
[57] See D. A. Peache, "Notes on the Peache family", cited by Munden, *History of St John's College,* p. 30.
[58] Lace, *A Goodly Heritage*, p. 26.

College, Cambridge, around 1838. While there he was converted, apparently through the shock occasioned by the mysterious death of his brother who disappeared while with an exploring party in Australia. This event and the influence of another brother led to a complete change of heart. So it was that having taken his degree in 1842, he was ordained the same year. After a curacy in Sheffield, where he was responsible for planting a church in a new parochial district, he moved to Malta in 1846 where he became Vice-Principal of the Malta Protestant College.[59] In 1854, Bryan returned to England[60] where he accepted a country living in Wiltshire[61] and there he remained for twenty years. When he moved to Monkton Combe and took over from Mr Pocock, he brought with him 13 boys including two of his own sons. Adding this to Mr Pocock's five boys made a total of 18 boys who started with Mr Bryan at Monkton Combe in April 1875.

During Bryan's first term as Principal, as he preferred to be known, an incident occurred which further reinforced the connection of the school with mission to the continent of Africa. Bryan received a visit from the Principal of the CMS Training College, Revd W. H. Barlow,[62] who came to find out whether he would be willing to accept into his school two African boys from Sierra Leone. Barlow was a great supporter of Evangelical schools, "doing all he could to promote the success of schools such as Dean Close School at Cheltenham, St Laurence College [sic], Ramsgate...Trent and Weymouth Colleges".[63] The reason why Monkton Combe School had been selected was

---

[59] Established after CMS withdrew from Malta in 1846 "as a centre and rallying-point for evangelical work of all kinds in the Mediterranean." Stock, *History of the CMS*, vol. 2, p. 141. It was supported by Francis Close and other leading Evangelical clergy, but closed in 1865. See S. Mallia, "The Malta Protestant College", *Melita Historica* 10 No. 3 (1990): 257–282, and A. F. Munden "The Munificient Friend of Israel—Jane Cook of Cheltenham (1775–1851)", *Cheltenham Local History Journal* 17 (2001): 38.

[60] This was *not* because "the School had to be closed during the Crimean War", as stated by Lace in *A Goodly Heritage*, p. 25. Malta Protestant College closed down some time "after July 1865". The last Principal, Revd C. H. Miles, left Malta with his wife on board the *S.S. Kedar* on 14 August 1865. See S. Mallia, "The Malta Protestant College", p.282. It is likely that Bryan returned to England for health reasons. His wife had also been seriously ill in Malta in 1851, during which time they returned briefly to England.

[61] E. R. Bevan, *Wilmot Eardley Bryan: A Memoir*, Bath 1935, p. 7.

[62] See Appendix 1. Lace incorrectly records the visitor as "R. G. Barlow", seemingly conflating Barlow's and Bryans's initials. Lace, *A Goodly Heritage*, p. 27.

[63] Ibid., p. 137. He was also a member of the Council of the Evangelical Church Schools Company (see ch. 10 below).

because Barlow had known of Bryan's work in Malta and, hearing that he was starting a school, had suggested it to the boys' guardian. This person was none other than Revd Henry Wright (1833–1880),[64] Secretary of the Church Missionary Society and a member of the well-known Wright family of Osmaston, Derbyshire.[65]

The story he told Mr Bryan was intriguing: after a visit to the headquarters of the Church Missionary Society in London he found upon leaving the building that he had forgotten something. Turning back, he met at the entrance the Honorary Secretary, who was standing there with two African boys. "Ah, Barlow," said Mr Wright, "I wonder if you can help me. I want to find somewhere where these two boys can continue their education before they go back to West Africa." Barlow thought of Bryan and his new school, and as he knew that he was going to Bristol in the next few days, offered to speak to Mr Bryan on the Honorary Secretary's behalf. This was how Obadiah Moore and Samuel Spain—the two boys—came to be enrolled at Monkton Combe around July 1875. They joined George Nicol, the son of the first Bishop of Sierra Leone, who had already made a name for himself as a star sprinter. Like many other schools of the period, there was no colour bar at Monkton Combe, and the 1881 census return shows that as many as six African pupils were enrolled at the school.

This chance meeting not only provided two more boys for the school, but it also brought its activities to the attention of the wealthy and indefatigable Secretary of the CMS. Henry Wright's father, Francis Wright, had recently died, and part of his inheritance was an interest in the Butterley Company, which was by now a huge conglomerate of coal, steel and railways.[66] Soon Mr Wright was taking a lively interest in the school, not only investing money in it, but also, in due course, putting four of his own sons under Mr Bryan's care. His first purchase for the school was Combe Farm, the 66 acre property which surrounded the school, and Combe Farm House, which the school had rented to house masters and boys since Pocock's day. Wright instructed Bryan to "Buy the lot" in 1877 for £4620.[67] He then leased it to Mr Bryan for £140 per annum.[68]

---

[64] See Appendix 1.
[65] See above, pp. 173–4.
[66] It is recorded that part of the CMS income for 1873 included an anonymous "thank-offering" of £5,000, and a contribution of £8,000 "in memory of Francis Wright" from his family. Stock, *History of the CMS,* vol. 3, p. 51.
[67] *The Old Monktonian Gazette,* November 1959, p. 109.
[68] The lease documents show that it was actually held in the name of R. B. Bryan, R. G. Bryan's son.

Henry Wright (1833–1880)

In the same year he bought from Mr Peache the rest of the school property, namely the *King William*, the Portico House and the land to the south of them. The purchase price was £3,000, which was £1,275 more than Pocock had paid for it, but no doubt some value would have been attached to the goodwill.

Having purchased all of the school buildings and most of the surrounding land for the school, Mr Wright set about making major improvements to his new acquisitions. In 1877 he financed the building of a new dining hall block complete with dormitories above, and the raising of the roof of Mr Pocock's old schoolroom in the Portico House, which enabled another new dormitory to be built. Mr Wright also took an interest in the spiritual life of Monkton Combe village. First, he bought the advowson[69] of the living of Monkton Combe and put it into an Evangelical Trust.[70] Then he built an aisle for the use of the school in the village church. The living has been held by Evangelicals ever since, with perhaps the most famous incumbent from 1918–61 being Revd Percy Warrington (1889–1961). As secretary of the Church Trust Society and the Martyrs' Memorial, "Warrington's vicarage [became] the administrative centre of some thirteen public

---

[69] An advowson is the legal right to appoint the incumbent (rector or vicar) of a parish. It was also known as the right of patronage.
[70] See W. A. Evershed, "Party and Patronage in the Church of England 1800–1945: A Study of Patronage Trusts and Patronage Reform", DPhil thesis, Oxford University 1985.

schools" which were acquired or founded by the Trust between 1921 and 1930.[71]

Henry Wright was so impressed with Mr Bryan's school that in 1879 he moved his eldest son, Leslie, from Marlborough to Monkton Combe. Leslie was later to be joined by his three younger brothers, Alfred, Harry and David. It appears that Leslie missed the ball games he played at Marlborough—racquets and fives[72]—and he persuaded his father to build courts for this sport at Monkton Combe. It is likely that some of Leslie's other schoolfellows would have been familiar with the game, for two pupils who later "sat in the House of Lords by hereditary right"[73] had been recently transferred by their parents from Eton. The courts were completed in 1882 but after Leslie left they became something of a white elephant until they were converted into a gymnasium in 1895. However, any other new building projects that he had planned would soon have to be put on indefinite hold, for on Friday 13 August 1880, Henry Wright drowned in Lake Coniston.[74]

News of his death reached the headquarters of the Church Missionary Society that same day, via a telegram which his brother-in-law, Mr (later Sir) Douglas Fox sent: "Our dear brother Henry Wright was drowned this morning while bathing." Wright's death had far-reaching ramifications for at least three groups of people. For the Wright family, they had lost a husband and father at the relatively young age of 47; for the CMS, its highly respected Honorary Secretary was no longer available to provide the leadership and personal financial support which Wright had lent to so much of its work; and for the fledgling Monkton Combe School, its most significant and generous supporter had been lost at a critical time in its development. When the news of Henry Wright's death reached Monkton Combe

---

[71] Schools which were founded or acquired and re-founded by Warrington and the Martyrs' Memorial and Church of England Trust include Wrekin 1921, Stowe and Canford 1923, Westonbirt 1928, Felixstowe 1929, Harrogate 1924, Lowther 1927, and Jersey 1928. For information on Warrington, see the *DNB* and ch. 5, "Roxburgh and Warrington", in N. Annan, *Roxburgh of Stowe*, London 1965, pp. 79–92.

[72] "Fives" was developed principally at three English public schools, producing three different games: Winchester fives, Eton fives and Rugby fives.

[73] A. F. Lace, "Notes", Monkton Combe School Archives. Lace was referring to Montague Waldegrave (1867–1953), the fifth Baron Radstock 1937; and Archibald Kennedy Cassilis (1872–1943), the fourth Marquis of Ailsa 1938.

[74] The Wright family had gone to the Lake District for a holiday on 29 July 1880. On the morning of Friday 13 July he and his two elder sons, Leslie and Alfred, went for a swim in Lake Coniston, where Henry Wright "sank, to rise no more." Stock, *History of the CMS*, vol. 3, p. 259.

later that day, many would have held grave fears for the future of the School.

Fortunately, Henry Wright's generous financial support of Monkton Combe School had placed it on an excellent footing. Over the preceding few years the school had also grown substantially in the number of pupils and staff, as well as in buildings. Student numbers had risen from eighteen in 1875 to sixty in 1880. In 1877 there were only five staff, whereas by 1880 there were ten on the payroll. These were "mainly Oxford and Cambridge men", several of them being Scholars of their Colleges and a large proportion of them later taking Holy Orders. The aim of most of the boys was to go to Oxford or Cambridge, and by 1882 there were twelve Monktonians in residence at Cambridge and ten at Oxford. For a long time the first name in the School Register as the winner of an Open University award was E. N. Coulthard, who won an exhibition to St John's College, Cambridge.[75] Another who went on to Cambridge was W. S. Moule (1864–1949),[76] who became a well-known Evangelical clergyman and a distinguished author. Moule left a more complete written record of those days than any other pupil, and one of these recollections provides an insight into the rural setting of the school:

> Immediately outside the dormitory windows on one side were meadows sloping upwards from the road, with cows almost level with our windows; on the opposite side they looked across the valley to the wooded hills. We were embosomed in the purest unspoilt country...In our dormitories the country looked at us, we smelt it as soon as the window opened, the doors leading to it stood open, nothing hindered picking wild roses or sweet violets in their seasons in a few odd minutes.[77]

The school magazine, *The Monktonian*, first appeared in the Lent Term of 1879. The editorial included four texts of Scripture, thus illustrating the Evangelical stamp of the School. One of them, "Whether ye eat or drink, or whatsoever ye do, do all to the glory of God", was often used by a later headmaster as a grace before meals. The third article is a learned one, unsigned, on the Inspiration of Scripture. The writer's object was to show that the Authorised Version's translation of 2 Timothy 3:16, "All scripture is given by inspiration of God, and is profitable...", was correct and that some

---

[75] Coulthard later went on to become the Vicar of St James, Bermondsey 1893–1908. See below, p. 321, fn. 83.

[76] See Appendix 1. W. S. Moule was at Monkton Combe School from 1877 to 1881.

[77] Letter to Lace from W. S. Moule, cited by Lace, *A Goodly Heritage*, p. 31.

alternative wording which was being suggested at the time; "Every scripture God inspired is profitable", was not acceptable. Whatever the reading of this passage, the verse was to become an important one for many pupils who passed through the School, for it was later included in the Basis of Faith of the Monkton Christian Union. In 1877 Bryan started a system of prefects, in the manner of his old Headmaster, Thomas Arnold of Rugby. One of the rules laid down for these boys to enforce was that "there should be no reading of books in the dormitory other than the Bible or devotional books."[78] Arnold had also condemned "the great number of exciting books of amusement, like Pickwick and Nickleby etc." and Bryan probably also had in his mind the 2 Timothy 3 passage that placed such great store on the importance of the Bible. The principal of Monkton Combe School was the sort of man who practised what he preached.

R. G. Bryan was a student of education, and wrote a long treatise on it which he called, *Advice to Parents on the Early Preparation of their Boys for School*. After emphasising the need for good preparation at home before coming to school, he discusses the value of various subjects taught at school. He then outlines how to reduce the difficulties and increase the pleasures of learning: "Help kindly, but examine strictly" is a recurring theme. He goes into some detail about how best to teach the early stages of Latin, which should be preceded by English learnt from St John's Gospel. He then goes on to explain the best methods for teaching Mathematics, mentioning a book called *Tangible Arithmetic*, which required the use of a large number of small wooden cubes, and also advocating the use of paper circles. Bryan concluded by saying, "the learner will be inspired by the realisation that the teacher (namely at first the mother) is guided by principles whose source is in Heaven and which lead to a life of patient service on earth."[79] Like other clerical headmasters, R. G. Bryan saw teaching as a practical expression of one's faith.

The second issue of the school magazine[80] included a missionary article by an Old Monktonian, A. Burtchael, writing from Sierra Leone. This was to become a regular feature of these early magazines. H. P. Napier, a young master who spent his first seven years of teaching at Monkton Combe and who was curate of the parish for four

---

[78] Devotional books which were deemed appropriate for Sunday reading were sometimes chosen for the pupils. In the 1950s, The Leys School Library included in their collection, books with a gold 'S' on the spine, signifying "authorised for Sunday reading". Patrick Armstrong, pers. comm., January 2002.

[79] Lace, *A Goodly Heritage*, p. 45.

[80] *The Monktonian*, August 1879.

of those years, left in 1889 to become a missionary headmaster in Ceylon.[81] The first edition of the school *Register* shows that of the 400 boys who had passed through the school, seventy had been ordained, and of these twenty-five had gone on to the mission field. That so many Old Monktonians went into the Church was undoubtably due to the influence of the first two Headmasters, Mr Pocock and Mr Bryan, both devout and missionary-minded clergymen. The staff that they appointed would also have exerted a great influence on the boys, for they were chosen to be "in sympathy with the aims of the School" and a number of them were ordained after leaving. A paper of an unknown date survives, which shows what qualifications the principal wanted in his staff. Essentials were: (1) Protestant and Evangelical views on the principles and basis of the Evangelical Alliance,[82] (2) evangelistic and pastoral aims, as well as scholastic, (3) First or Second Class Honours degree, (4) powers as a teacher and as a disciplinarian. Non-essentials included games and book-keeping. In another undated manifesto on the sort of schoolmaster the principal was seeking to employ, he stated that a necessary spiritual qualification was "Believing all the promises made by God in His Word, he will aim to live accordingly, and to persuade his pupils to do likewise."[83] Bryan defined the aim of the school in an early prospectus with the words, "Its main object has been the *spiritual* welfare of the boys. Great care is exercised in the choice of Masters, to obtain only those who will assist in the above object. The religious teaching is Protestant and Evangelical."[84] Another factor which explained the large number of boys who went on to become missionaries, was the families from which the boys were drawn, for before 1900, forty-one of the boys were known to be the sons of missionaries.

Some of the older boys would have gained "a further outlet for testimony" when on Sundays they went up to a hamlet called Mount Pleasant on Combe Down, where they "used to conduct mission services" in a small Mission Room. As one boy recalled, "It never occurred to us that we should be silent about the centre of all living, as the knowledge of God and of Jesus Christ was assumed to be in the life

---

[81] Principal of Trinity College, Kandy, Ceylon 1890–1900.

[82] An interdenominational association for Evangelical union founded in 1845 as a defence against "Infidelity, Popery, Puseyism and Plymouth Brethrenism". Wolffe, *The Protestant Crusade*, p. 137. See J. R. Wolffe, "The Evangelical Alliance in the 1840s", *Studies in Church History*, 23 (1986): 333–46; and I. Randall and D. Hilborn, *One Body in Christ,* Carlisle 2001.

[83] "A Call for Consecrated Educational Talents", Monkton Combe School Archives.

[84] Monkton Combe School *Prospectus*, Summer 1895.

of the School and the example of our Headmaster."[85] Another boy wrote about the School's connection with a mission-hall in the village of Conkwell. "On Sunday afternoons, we all went up to Conkwell, where Mr Howard[86] took the service."[87] It appears that as early as May 1889, the school had started running services at the village in a building that had originally been built as a Nonconformist Chapel. "Many Monktonians, both ordained and lay, served part of their apprenticeship in the service of Christ by conducting services at Conkwell."[88] During this period a "steady stream continued to take holy orders", with "fifteen Old Monktonians going into the Mission Field". An advertisement for Monkton Combe School in *The Rock* newspaper emphasised the school's proud record in this area: "During the last 18 years, 66 past members of the school have been ordained Clergymen of the Church of England, and 21 have been sent to the Foreign Mission field…"[89] The large number of ex-Monktonians who went into the Church[90] or the mission field was being used to 'market' the school to potential parents.

In 1893 the Gleaners' Union was started in the school "to promote interest in Missions", and this was run in conjunction with the CMS. The meetings consisted of talks on missionary topics, followed by prayer. On 21 May 1897, the first of these, entitled a 'Magic Lantern Lecture', "for Gleaners only", was held in the Science Room.[91] The Old Monktonians were also active in missionary causes, forming the Old Monktonian Prayer Union in 1882. This continued to meet until 1918, when the Old Monktonian Missionary Union was formed. Although the connection between the School and Mission was never to be as direct as in the days of Henry Wright—when it could be said that the Secretary of the Church Missionary Society was also the school's landlord—the missionary tradition at Monkton Combe School was to

---

[85] W. S. Moule, cited by Lace, *A Goodly Heritage,* p. 56.

[86] Mr Charles Howard was the founder and first Headmaster of Monkton Combe Junior School, 1888–93.

[87] L. H. Gamlen, "O.M. Reminiscences", 1940. Gamlen was at Monkton Combe Junior School from the Summer Term of 1889 and started at Monkton Combe School in the Lent Term of 1891.

[88] Lace, *A Goodly Heritage*, p. 122.

[89] *Rock,*, 5 May 1893, p. 1.

[90] Perhaps the most famous was Graham Leonard (1921–), Bishop of Truro 1973–81 and Bishop of London 1981–1991. Despite his association with Evangelicalism at school and in his first term at University, Leonard became a well-known, and often controversial, Anglo-Catholic spokesperson.

[91] Lace, *A Goodly Heritage*, p. 166.

continue until well into the next century, and beyond, for Monkton Combe school remains a favourite amongst missionary parents today.

When Henry Wright died, his estate passed to the eldest son, A. Leslie Wright (1862–1938), who was still a pupil at Monkton Combe School. From 1880, the extraordinary situation existed whereby the landlord of Monkton Combe was also one of its pupils. A. Leslie Wright remained in the school until summer 1882, when he went up to Christ Church, Oxford.[92] A few years later negotiations were started to hand the School over to an Evangelical organization, as this was seen as more appropriate than ownership by one individual. Henry Wright may have had something like this in mind before he died, for an undated circular from around this time stated that "Before his death, Mr WRIGHT had expressed his earnest desire that the school should be placed in the hands of Evangelical trustees, but his sudden death prevented the accomplishment of his purpose. His son, Mr. LESLIE WRIGHT, with Mr. BRYAN'S concurrence, [was] desirous of giving effect to the wishes of his father..."[93] In due course negotiations were started to hand the School over to such a body.

In 1886, or earlier, the Union of Clerical and Lay Associations[94] was offered the opportunity of purchasing "the premises and the school" from Leslie Wright. The exact date is not clear because, as mentioned above, the circular put out by this body is undated. The earliest letter written by Mr Bryan on this subject is one of December 1886, so it can be assumed that these negotiations began around the middle of the decade, when the Principal of Monkton Combe School first suggested to the Clerical and Lay Union that they should "purchase [the] Monkton Combe property, in order to secure that the existing School should be carried on there permanently upon Evangelical principles".[95] Not surprisingly, he was also anxious to negotiate with the new landlords "that power which usually belongs to the Governing body of a Public School, especially the power to appoint and remove the Head Master, or Principal."[96] Correspondence on this matter continued over the four year period during which time the Clerical and Lay Union continued in their efforts to raise funds for

---

[92] J. Foster, *Oxford Men and Their Colleges*, p. 427. Foster has Wright listed in the 1881 'class of commoners'.

[93] "Monkton Combe School" An undated, printed appeal to buy the school from Mr Wright by the Clerical and Lay Union, p. 1. Monkton Combe School Archives.

[94] See below, pp. 238–50.

[95] Printed letter from R. G. Bryan to S. Gedge, 21 February 1894, p. 1. Monkton Combe School Archives.

[96] Ibid.

the purchase of Monkton Combe School. When Bryan was satisfied that the members of Union Sub-Committee were not going to replace him, he joined the fundraising effort in 1890 by issuing 100 circulars on behalf of the Clerical and Lay Union to "Donors and Shareholders" of the School.[97] This resulted in some parents of boys in the school coming forward with donations—one of them, Mr R. C. L. Bevan,[98] donating £500 to the scheme.

The Evangelical press was recruited to help raise funds. An article in *The Rock* played on party feeling. "Evangelicals will be the laughing stock, and justly so, of our Ritualistic friends if we cannot raise 3000*l*, to secure, under an Evangelical trust, this place for middle-class and higher education."[99] The trustees chosen for the scheme were Canon Brooke, Revd F. E. Wigram, and Messrs Claude Bosanquet and Leslie-Melville. The money required was 6,000*l*, an amount which, it was said, "Canon Woodard would have no trouble in raising". It was also suggested that "a central authority, and permanent resources"[100] would reduce the need for such repeated, separate appeals. Within twelve months such a body had been formed.

In April 1891 the land and buildings of Monkton Combe School were bought by the Church of England Evangelical College and School Company Limited, a body which had been formed by the central committee of the Union of Clerical and Lay Associations for this specific purpose.[101] The matter of who should run the School—the principal or the new directors—then became a focus of discussions between Bryan and the new owners. By 1894 it had degenerated into a conflict, "one party striving to obtain, the other to retain, the management of the School".[102] Complete resolution of this matter would not occur until the next century, when there was a further change of both principal and owner. In 1898 *The Rock* newspaper recorded the occasion of the opening of the new school hall and gymnasium at this "seminary of sound learning" by the Bishop of Bath

---

[97] Ibid, p. 2.
[98] Bevan was a merchant banker. His son, Edwyn R. Bevan, was one of the school's best scholars. In 1888 he won the Senior Classical Scholarship to New College, Oxford, where he became an Honorary Fellow 1914–43. He was a lecturer in Hellenistic history and literature at King's College, London, 1922–33.
[99] *Rock*, 23 May 1890, p. 3.
[100] Ibid.
[101] This was the same organization which took over Trent College in 1893 and Weymouth College in 1901. See ch. 10 below.
[102] Letter from Bryan to Gedge, 21 February 1894, p. 4.

and Wells, A. G. Hervey.[103] In his sermon, he "gave cordial recognition of the Protestant basis of the education given at the school", and he told the pupils that "They must be obedient to the Rubrics of the Prayer Book". He said it was important that the boys of the school "held firm to that Evangelical teaching, to that faith in Jesus Christ".[104] Under the directorship of the Evangelical College and School Company, the school would continue in perpetuity to be "a place of Evangelical Education".[105]

In 1901 a new, locally based body known as 'The Monkton Combe School Company Limited' was formed to take over the lease of the school. The Articles of Association of the Company stated that one of its objects was to carry on the school "as an Evangelical School...on Protestant and Evangelical principles" such "as will be approved by the Church of England Evangelical College and School Company, Limited, who are Landlords of part of the School property...".[106] On 23 October 1907 the land and buildings were purchased back from the Evangelical Church Schools Company (as it had come to be called) by the Monkton Combe School Company, so that the local school board became both owner and operator of the School for a sum of £5796. Despite this change of ownership, and the conflict that preceded it, the connection between Monkton Combe and the Evangelical Church Schools Company was to continue in the person of Revd D. L. Pitcairn, Vicar of Monkton Combe from 1883. Mr Pitcairn was a Director of the Evangelical Schools Company for thirty-two years and Chairman of it for sixteen, and at the same time he served on the board of Monkton Combe School Company.

The Evangelical Church Schools Company is one of four Evangelical organizations which were associated with middle-class schools in the nineteenth century. These organizations, and the schools which they founded, are the subject of the next part of this study. Not until 1921, when a new Vicar of Monkton Combe, Revd Percy

---

[103] Arthur Charles Hervey (1808–1894), Bishop of Bath and Wells 1869–94, was regarded as being supportive of Evangelicals, having "been driven by ritualistic action to entrench himself firmly within the lines of the Reformation." F. Arnold, *Our Bishops and Deans*, London 1875, vol. 2, p. 62.

[104] *Rock,*, 2 December 1898, p. 786.

[105] *Monktonian* 7, 5 (February 1892): 22.

[106] In 1935 the School Company was reconstituted and its Memorandum of Association dropped the words "Church of England" and stated its object as "to provide first-class education combined with sound religious training on Protestant and Evangelical principles." However, in 1945 the words "Church of England" were restored to the school prospectus, which ever since then has printed the following: "The services are in the Evangelical tradition of the Church of England with which the school has always been associated."

Warrington, made the Monkton Combe Vicarage the administrative centre for his Martyrs' Memorial and Church of England Trust schools, would a single clergyman have so much involvement in the founding of an Evangelical school. For the period 1868–1902, it was the collective effort of Evangelicals which had the greatest impact on the education of the middle classes.

PART III

CORPORATE EVANGELICAL INITIATIVE

CHAPTER 7

Evangelical Societies and Middle-Class Education

The Church Association

Evangelical concern over the growth of Ritualism and the formation of the English Church Union in 1859[1] led to the foundation of a society in 1865 that would, it was hoped, provide a means by which "loyal members of the Church should combine for the defence of its Protestant character".[2] The Church Association was established "To uphold the Doctrines, Principles, and Order of the United Church of England and Ireland, and to counteract the efforts now being made to pervert her teaching on essential points of the Christian faith, or assimilate her Services to those of the Church of Rome; and to effect these objects by publicity through lectures, meetings, and the use of the press, by appeals to the Courts of Law to ascertain what the law is, and by appeals to parliament."[3] The first Chairman was the retired MP, John Campbell Colquhoun,[4] who had taken a prominent part in opposing the Maynooth Grant of 1845.[5] Other founding members included well-known Churchmen such as Revs Edward Auriol (1805–1880), Joseph Hoare (1851–1906), Daniel Wilson (1778–1858), and Canon W. W. Champneys (1807–1875).[6] The first report of the Church Association in 1866 listed four districts—London, Midland, Northern and Southern—and 16 auxiliary or branch associations, each with a

---

[1] See above, p. 35, fn. 175. During the early 1850s the regional branches of the English Church Union were important avenues for High Church and Tractarian activity.
[2] [C. A. Bury], *The Church Association*, London 1873. See also J. Bateman, *The Church Association: Its Policy and Prospects Considered in a Letter to the Chairman*, London 1880.
[3] *Church Association Tracts*, vol. 1, p. 1. Church Society Archives, Lambeth Palace Library.
[4] See Appendix 1.
[5] See above, p. 35, fn. 170.
[6] Appendix 1 contains brief biographical details for each of these four men.

local secretary.[7] By 1869, there were 138 branch Associations and the Church Association had over 8,000 members.[8] Part of its work was polemical; tracts and pamphlets were published against Ritualism, lectures and other meetings were arranged. However, its other main purpose was litigation against 'Ritualist practices', and at the conference of November 1867, a Guarantee Fund of £50,000 was launched, to assist parishioners in appeals to law courts. During this period the Church Association developed a number of affiliates, creating the National Protestant League for electoral work, especially among the lower classes, in 1890, co-ordinating political campaigning with Austin Taylor's Lancashire Laymen's league from 1902 onwards,[9] and absorbing the Evangelical Protestant Union, another ultra-Protestant group, in 1911.[10] Today's successor to the Church Association is the Church Society, which was formed by an amalgamation of the Church Association and the National Church League[11] in 1950.

In the Spring of 1868—the year that Francis Pocock moved his newly founded school into the old bacon-merchant's house in Monkton Combe—the Church Association held its inaugural 'Conference of Protestant Clergy and Laity' at Willis's Rooms in London.[12] The Council of the Church Association convened two conferences in 1868: the first on 13 May in London, and the second at Manchester on the 6 and 7 October. It was hoped that these two events would become an annual fixture on the Evangelical calendar, with the May conference being held each year in the capital,[13] and the Autumn conference, "in

---

[7] Birkenhead, Brighton, Carlisle, Devonport, Folkestone, Hulme, Leamington, Liverpool, Ryde, Shrewsbury, Southport, Taunton, Tiverton, Tunbridge Wells, Weston-Super-Mare, Wolverhampton. See *The First Annual Report of the Church Association*, London 1866, p. 2.

[8] *The Fourth Annual Report of the Church Association,* London 1869, p. 13.

[9] *Record*, 10 October 1902, p. 941.

[10] *Record*, 17 March 1911, p. 250.

[11] Founded in 1906 from an amalgamation of the Church of England League (a successor of the Ladies' League) and the National Protestant Church Union—see the "Stemma of the Church Society" on p. 223.

[12] Located at King Street, St James's, London.

[13] Early in the nineteenth century the main Evangelical societies established the practice of holding their annual meetings between April and June. This became an annual "Evangelical jamboree" in the capital with meetings and other activities from early morning to late at night during the week. See Bradley, *The Call to Seriousness*, p. 139. Most of the 'May Meetings' were later held in Exeter Hall on the Strand. At first there were about thirty of these meetings; they numbered 97 in 1881 and later rose to 415. L. W. Cowie, "Exeter Hall", *History Today* 18 (1968): 392.

some important centre in the country".[14] Seven subjects were discussed at the May conference of 1868, of which the second one listed in the Annual Report was "Middle Class Education".[15] The issue had first been raised in a November 1867 *Monthly Intelligencer* article[16] entitled "Middle Class Education in Staffordshire", which reported on the proposed "School for the Commercial and Agricultural Classes of the Middle Counties, in connexion with the St. Nicholas College, Lancing, Sussex"[17] at Denstone, Staffordshire.[18] It was also raised in a "Pamphlet on Schools" by Mr Henry Wardle, which the Council of the Church Association had discussed at its meeting on 6 February, 1868.[19] A list of the topics "selected for discussion at the Conference" was circulated to all members of the Association, and one of these read as follows, "The objectionable character of the Woodard schools, and what steps should be taken to meet the case."[20] Until then, the Church Association had been primarily concerned about 'ritualistic' practices amongst the clergy of England. It had now turned its attention to the so-called ritualistic schools of the realm, namely those which were under 'Mr. Woodard's scheme'.

The topic of the Woodard schools was opened at the May Conference by James Bateman. He gave a brief outline of the "origin, progress, and present position" of the Woodard schools, "in order that [one] may be the better able to appreciate the gravity of a movement that is, I am convinced, fraught with the utmost danger to the future welfare and integrity of our Protestant Church."[21] He then proceeded to give an account of the history of the foundation of the College of St Nicholas, Lancing; St John's, Hurstpierpoint; St Saviour's School, at New Shoreham; and "In an evil hour for the peace of the diocese to which I myself belong [Lichfield]…the establishment of schools at Denstone near Uttoxeter".[22] Bateman then discussed the "discipline and theological bias of the Sussex schools". He said that it was difficult to gain an accurate impression of this because the Masters of

---

[14] Church Association *Annual Report* 1868, p. 45.
[15] Ibid.
[16] The official organ of the Church Association, the *Monthly Intelligencer* (1867–84) later changed its name to the *Church Intelligencer* (1884–1938).
[17] *Monthly Intelligencer*, 9 (November 1867): 114.
[18] St Chad's College, Denstone. See ch. 5 above.
[19] Church Association General Committee Minute Book 1, p. 85. Church Society Archives.
[20] *The Woodard Schools*, London 1868, p. 1. Church Society Archives.
[21] *The Woodard Schools*, p. 2. A shorter version of this speech was also reported in the *Monthly Intelligencer* 2, 4 (June 1868): 70–71.
[22] *The Woodard Schools*, p. 7.

the schools "*are all bound to secrecy!*"[23] However, he concluded that "the uniform support that Mr. Woodard receives from the Tractarian and Ritualistic party", spoke for itself, "for they evidently regard him as *doing their work.*"[24] Finally, Bateman compared the work of Woodard with that of the Ignatius Loyola, and he closed with the remark that "unless some method be found of arresting its progress, this Lancing confederacy will ere long inject the subtle poison of priestcraft into the veins of the very life-blood of English Society."[25] Thus began the conference's 'Middle Class Schools' debate, and the rest of the day was taken up with discussion of this one subject.

The second speaker, Revd Edward Hathaway (1818–1897),[26] Rector of St. Ebbe's, Oxford, attempted to address "The question as to how the danger may best be met or neutralised".[27] It was not all negative. He pointed out that "Mr. Woodard had the foresight to discern, earlier than others, that the great want of the day was a solid Education for the Middle Classes of England on a religious basis";[28] however, he said that although Woodard was "not a conscious Romaniser", he was nevertheless "a *very high* Patristic churchman".

He attributed Woodard's success to "his admirable sagacity and unflinching perseverance" and suggested that "with the noble exception of the Trent College and one or two other institutions in which the teaching is Scriptural", that the "Education of the Middle Classes of this country is in danger of being monopolised by the Tractarian party".[29] He suggested that "Evangelical Churchmen" could "step forward and take it out of those hands" by setting up a "Provisional Committee, whose duty it shall be to draw the attention of the country to the importance and pressing need of Education for the Middle Classes on Evangelical principles". In this way, Evangelicals could "counterwork, on a pure Protestant and Scriptural basis, the whole of Mr. Woodard's sagacious and well-compacted [*sic*] but most mischievous enterprise".[30]

---

[23] Ibid., p. 9. The italics are his.
[24] Ibid.
[25] Ibid., pp. 13–14.
[26] See Appendix 1.
[27] *The Woodard Schools,* p. 13. All of the quotations in the rest of this paragraph are from this booklet published by the Church Association.
[28] Ibid., p. 14.
[29] Ibid., p. 15.
[30] Ibid., p. 16.

Evangelical Societies and Middle-Class Education

Stemma of the Church Society

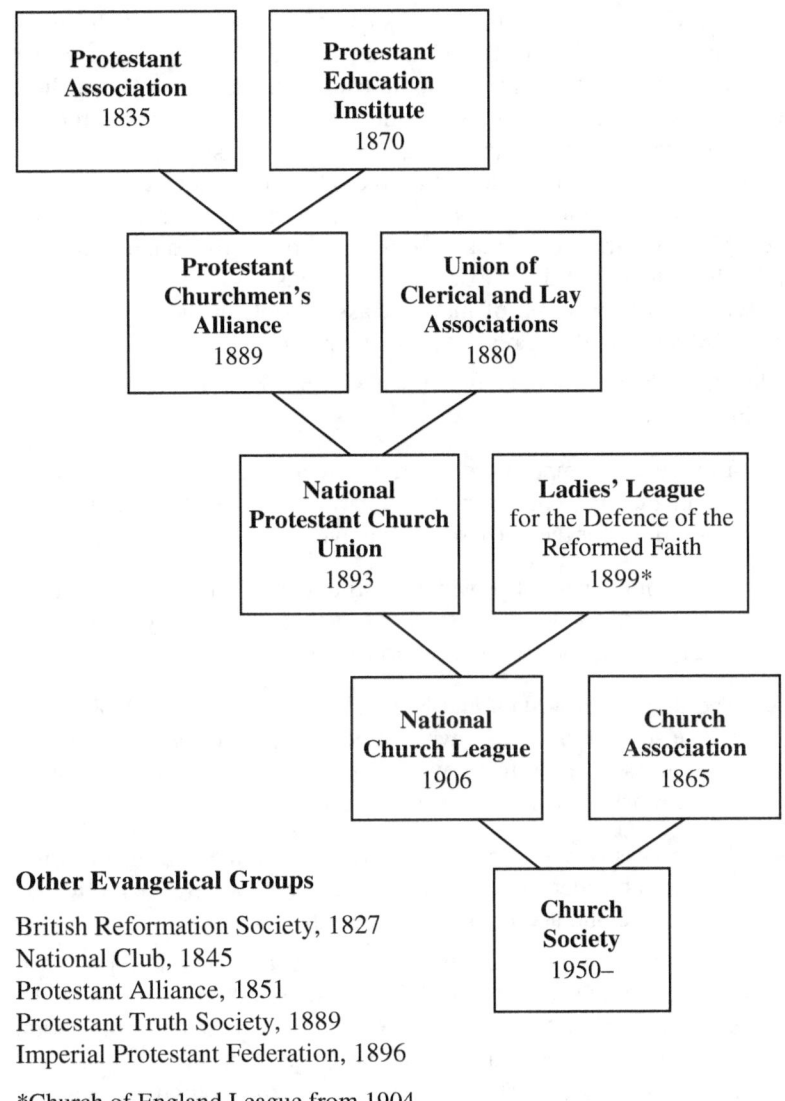

Other Evangelical Groups

British Reformation Society, 1827
National Club, 1845
Protestant Alliance, 1851
Protestant Truth Society, 1889
Imperial Protestant Federation, 1896

*Church of England League from 1904

The *Monthly Intelligencer* reported that the members attending the May Conference had agreed that "It was not within the province of the Church Association to form schools to counterwork those of Mr. Woodard, but it was within its province to awaken the consciences of Protestant Churchmen to the necessity of taking some such step." Hathaway suggested that the Council "might put forward a paper distinctly showing the want of middle-class schools on an Evangelical religious basis, and the dangers to which parents and their children are subjecting themselves by accepting the bait of a small payment for education". It was suggested that the Church Association form a central committee in London "to ascertain what localities are unoccupied by Mr. Woodard's schools, and to try, by counterworking, to take the sting out of those existing Institutions".[31]

Discussion of the topic of middle-class schools at the May Conference of 1868 resulted in a resolution being passed

> That the Church Association...issue a paper embodying the following points:—
>
> 1. The general importance of middle-class education, and the unsatisfactory character of some of the largest existing institutions for the purposes of supplying it.
>
> 2. The desirableness of providing Institutions suitable to the wants of the middle classes, in which a sound education may be given on Protestant and Evangelical principles.
>
> 3. The duty of Protestant and Evangelical Churchmen to look the whole subject in the face without delay, and to endeavour to set foot an Association for providing such a middle-class education as the times demand.
>
> 4. The necessity of forming a Central Committee in London, in order to consider the best mode of carrying into practical effect the views embodied in the proposed paper.[32]

A provisional committee of the Church Association was formed "to consider whether any and what steps could be taken to promote the Establishment of five Schools for the Middle Classes in connection with the Church of England on thoroughly sound Protestant and scriptural principles".[33] The experience of the Woodard schools suggested that middle-class schools, once started, could be made self-

---

[31] *Monthly Intelligencer* 2, 4 (June 1868): 72.
[32] *The Woodard Schools*, p. 1; and *Monthly Intelligencer* 2, 4 (June 1868): 72–3.
[33] Church Association *Annual Report* 1868, p. 46.

supporting, providing there was "a self-denying zeal in those who carry them on."[34] However, it was realised that they would need "to appeal to the liberality of Christian givers"[35] in order to fund such a project. Sites would need to be purchased, buildings built and money expended in order to get the scheme off the ground.

The first meeting of the Provisional Committee was chaired by the President of the Church Association, Revd E. Auriol (1805–1880), Rector of St Dunstan's-in-the-West, Fleet Street.[36] Other committee members included Revd J. C. Ryle of Stradbroke, Suffolk; and Canon Edward Hoare, of Tunbridge Wells. Ryle was later to become the first Bishop of Liverpool, where he was remembered for the number of new churches and schools he built, as well as his tract writing.[37] Edward Hoare was to be one of the key people behind the founding of the South-Eastern College in Ramsgate.[38] The Honorary Secretary was Revd Edward Hathaway, who wrote a pamphlet on "Middle Class Education" which was sent to each member of the Provisional Committee and to the Association's Editorial Committee in June 1868. It was hoped that "if promises of pecuniary and personal support [were] received..., a permanent Association [would]...be organized, charged with the duty of establishing a School, in some favourable locality, by way of experiment and model."[39] The annual report of the Church Association for that year stated:

> The Council trust that this new Association will meet with support from all who desire that the youth of the Middle Classes in this new country should be saved from the pernicious practices of auricular confession, priestly absolution, the celebration of masses for the dead, and Romanising principles inculcated at the schools established by some of the Ritualistic party in the Church of England.[40]

The Woodard schools were clearly in their sights.

The Minutes of the Church Association's General Purposes Committee record that at a meeting on 1 June 1868, it was resolved "that the Secretary be instructed to write to Mr Chambers and request him to favour the Committee with a report of his observations on the

---

[34] *Appeal for Protestant Middle Class Schools*, London: The Church Association, n.d. [1868], p. 3.
[35] Ibid., p. 4.
[36] See Appendix 1.
[37] He composed upwards of 200 tracts; see Appendix 1.
[38] See ch. 8 below.
[39] *Appeal for Protestant Middle Class Schools*, p. 4.
[40] Church Association *Annual Report*, 1868, p. 46.

Woodard schools...as well as his quotations which are very valuable, with a view to their being printed by the Assocn".[41] Three days later, on the 4 June 1868, it was resolved at a Council meeting "that the four papers on the Woodard Schools to be written by the Messrs Bateman, Chambers, Hathaway & Kent, be put up in type in communication with Mr Hathaway, and sent to the Editorial Committee". This was duly done and the Church Society archives contain the "last proof received 19 September from the Printer"[42] of what was to be part of the series, "Church Association Papers". Entitled *The Woodard Schools*, it provides a comprehensive and insightful overview of the Evangelical response to Woodard's scheme, which by then had been in operation for twenty years. Running to thirty-five pages, it was published by the Manchester Conference Committee and distributed at the Autumn Conference of the Church Association on 6 October 1868.

Revd James Bardsley[43] opened this conference with "the consideration of the subject of middle-class education".[44] He said that "with respect to education, the middle classes had been neglected" and "The Woodard schools did not supply a purely Church of England education."[45] For example, "Dr. Wigram, the late Bishop of Rochester, found out that confession was practised at the school at Lancing."[46] He proposed that a chain of schools, "like those in Sussex", be established throughout the country. Trent College was held up as an example of "what was to be done", and he suggested that what was wanted in "this and the neighbouring dioceses was a large school for middle-class education, say with a hall, chapel, dormitories, and accommodation for 600 or 700 boys".[47] A Dr Jardine said that "he was of the opinion that, in some points, the scheme of Mr. Woodard was worthy of their imitation, although that plan as a whole was a deep scheme to undermine the Protestantism of England."[48] Revd J. C. Ryle then spoke.

---

[41] Church Association General Purposes Committee Minute Book 1, p. 45. Church Society Archives.

[42] Handwritten note on the cover page of *The Woodard Schools*. Church Society Archives.

[43] Rector of St Ann's, Manchester 1857–79 and Honorary Canon of Manchester Cathedral from 1871. Bardsley had seven sons, all of whom became clergymen. One of them, J. W. Bardsley, became Bishop of Sodor and Man 1887–92, then Bishop of Carlisle 1892–1904.

[44] *Monthly Intelligencer* 2, 9 (November 1868): 202.

[45] Ibid.

[46] See Appendix 1 for further information on J. C. Wigram, including an explanation of this reference.

[47] Ibid, p. 203.

[48] *Monthly Intelligencer* 2, 9 (November 1868): 203.

He said:

> Whilst they had slept, the enemy had come in. There was a great mischief in the Woodard system: these were the very schools that fed the Ritualistic congregations. He appealed to any one who had been to a Ritualistic church whether the vast proportion of the congregation did not consist of those young men and women of the middle classes whom they had so long neglected, and not supplied with a downright Protestant education. Something was needed to be done...[49]

Ryle had in fact already done something. In his own county of Suffolk, he was influential in the founding of a middle-class school at Framlingham, as a memorial to the Prince Consort.[50] It had been built at an expense of £20,000, and was already full with 300 boys. He urged those at Manchester to establish similar "self-supporting Church of England, Protestant evangelical middle-class colleges and large schools",[51] and suggested that if they did not "they must not be surprised" if the children of the middle-classes are educated at Woodard schools.

Mr Andrews, Vice-Chairman of the London Church Association, said "the evils of the educational system, originated and carried on by Mr. Woodard, had been patent to all the members of the Church Association for some time." He pointed out that "nothing could be done without money", and that he "knew of no place where the money question could be so successfully opened as in Manchester".[52] A private appeal for funds by a Mr John Martin resulted in the "securing [of] promises of support to the amount of £19,000".[53] As a result of this, it was decided to set up a formal body or 'Association' for the purpose of raising and disbursing funds "...to establish schools in connection with the Protestant and Reformed Church of England, to be conducted in accordance with its doctrines and principles as set forth in the 39 Articles and the Book of Common Prayer."[54] One of the aims of such an organization would be "to extend to the Middle Classes as much as possible of the manly English training of mind and body, which has been one great merit of our public school system", as well

---

[49] Ibid.
[50] Framlingham College. See above, pp. 122–3.
[51] *Monthly Intelligencer* 2, 9 (November 1868): 203.
[52] Ibid., p. 204.
[53] This was later reported by W. A. Scott Robertson in "Middle Class Education", *Churchman* 36 (September 1882): 449. Canon W. A. Scott Robertson was at that time Rector of Elmley, Worcestershire, and a very active member of the Church Association.
[54] *Monthly Intelligencer* 2 (February 1869): 305.

as take advantage of the opportunities afforded "by a manly and simple system" in order to "endeavour to sow the seed of eternal life in young hearts, and to win them to Christ".[55] Statements such as this suggested that such schools would be not just Evangelical, but also evangelistic.

The Association for 'Middle-Class Schools' met for the first time on 13 January 1869. The meeting was attended "by a considerable number of clergy and laity". Edmund Hanbury chaired the meeting, and letters from the Archbishops of Canterbury and York and the Bishops of Durham, Lincoln, Norwich, Ripon, Carlisle, and Bangor, "expressing their general approval", were read. It was stated that a paper had been circulated "to ascertain whether the plan would be likely to meet with extensive support" and that offers exceeding £19,000 had already been made towards the erection of five schools. The committee produced a statement that explained the purpose of the Association, and invited further contributions. This was published in the Evangelical press. Later that year, the *Monthly Intelligencer* published an article that explained how the Association would allocate the money:

> The Association…is prepared to give grants in aid of sums from £4000 to £5000. Each to assist in founding Five Boarding Schools in different parts of the country. The applicants for these grants in aid will have to satisfy the Committee on the following points:—
>
> 1st. That the buildings will be capable of accommodating three hundred boarders.
>
> 2nd. That in a secular point of view the school will provide a thoroughly sound and efficient English education equal to any school of its class.
>
> 3rd. That such a provision will be made for the management of the school as shall secure in perpetuity that its religious teaching shall be in accordance with the doctrines and principles of the Reformed Church of England.[56]

It would seem that no such applicants came forward, and therefore no grants were made.

According to a letter to the editor of *The Record*,[57] the committee then corresponded with "friends" at Manchester, urging them to start a school. Their answer was that "trade was bad, but when there was a favourable turn they could raise 50,000*l* or more for such an object".

---

[55] "Appeal for Protestant Middle Class Schools", p. 3, Church Society Archives.
[56] *Monthly Intelligencer* 3 (September 1869): 203.
[57] *Record*, 17 February 1882, p. 2. All of the quotations in this paragraph are from this article.

Two members of the committee went to Bristol to raise support for a new school there, but it was said by more "friends of the Association" there that "they were already supplied with all varieties of schools" and so the idea was dropped. Identifying himself only with the initials, 'J. M.', the same correspondent recalled that Lord Fortescue, the Patron of the County Schools of Devon, was asked "whether he could use his influence to forward the erection of such a school". The Earl had said, "it was utterly useless to make the attempt; [as] it would obtain no support". This was especially the case if the schools were to be set up on along party (i.e. Evangelical) lines: "If the object was to establish a school, with the Bishop at the head, and without any distinctively religious principles, he thought that support might be obtained for it." The same writer also recalled that "a clergyman in Kent thought that there were influential noblemen and gentlemen in his neighbourhood who might be induced to come forward, but after a fruitless trial he gave up". The point of the letter was to remind the readers of the difficulty of such a project, and to explain how and why the scheme of 1868, ultimately failed. However, before providing his explanation for why it failed, he provided, some 14 years after the events, an account of what happened to the money which was donated to the cause.

The offers of support for the Central Fund were made on the basis that the money would be used to support the founding of five different schools, or to look at it another way, "one-fifth of the amount" donated was to be made available for the founding of one school. As these donors "were not willing to allow their promises to be held over indefinitely", after two years, "the Committee were constrained to abandon the scheme and return such contributions as had been paid."[58] Prior to this, however, the committee approached the donors to obtain their "consent to have the whole or a large part of their promised contribution concentrated on one school within twenty or thirty miles of London as a model school"; however, most of them "declined to do so".[59] An attempt was made also to set up "a Committee of London gentlemen...prepared to take the initiative"[60] to found a school with the £10,000 which had already been collected. No one was willing, all the money was returned, and the initiative to set up Evangelical Middle-Class schools which was first raised at the Church Association Conference in May 1868, was abandoned.

The Endowed Schools Commission 1864–68[61] also made the position of such schools very doubtful, and the committee was soon

---

[58] Ibid.
[59] Ibid.
[60] Ibid.
[61] See ch. 2 above.

disbanded through lack of interest. An editorial in *The Record* complained that "the undenominationalizing and securalizing [*sic*] of our middle-class grammar schools, which was effected...by the *Endowed Schools Act* of 1869",[62] had scuttled plans for new Evangelical schools. After a period of very little discussion, the Church Association decided to support the new Board Schools because, according to the Chairman of its Council, Alex W. Cobham, "religious differences amongst Established Church and dissenters, as well as the rise of Anglo-Catholicism have hampered their work"[63] in promoting other forms of middle-class education. The editor of *The Rock* criticised this decision in an article entitled "The Church Association and Church Schools", where he wrote: "We are sorry to see that the Church Association seems to be throwing the weight of its influence into the scale against Church Schools."[64] He encouraged Evangelicals to be more entrepreneurial in the raising of funds for new schools, "lest the influence of Anglo-Catholicism" caused the "undoing of the work of the Reformation".[65] However, the lack of support from such an active organization as the Church Association would severely limit Evangelical endeavour in this area.

At about this time a movement for union amongst Evangelicals was initiated by the editor of the *Christian Advocate* and Vicar of Christ Church, Surbiton, Revd Edward Garbett (1817–1886).[66] Largely on his initiative, a conference was held on the subject at Cannon Street Hotel in January 1870. Joseph Hoare took the chair, and the meeting was well attended. Canons Christopher, Cadman, Auriol, Garratt and the lawyer Sydney Gedge were among the speakers, and a provisional committee was appointed to work out a scheme of union.[67] J. C. Ryle did not give an address, although at the Islington Clerical Meeting the day before he had stressed the need for organization,[68] and advocated a warm support for the conference. Daniel Wilson, on the other hand, was sceptical, and Joseph Bardley firmly deprecated the formation of any association that would be antagonistic to the Church Association.[69] Lord Shaftesbury "grumbled in his diary at the prospect of one more

---

[62] Editorial in the *Record*, 1 March 1882, p. 2.
[63] *Rock*, 15 December 1893, p. 6.
[64] *Rock*, 1 December 1893, p. 8.
[65] Ibid.
[66] See Appendix 1.
[67] *Record*, 26 January 1870, p. 2.
[68] See J. C. Ryle, *We must Unite! Being Thoughts on the Necessity of Forming a Well Organised Union of Evangelical Churchmen*, London 1868.
[69] *Record*, 21 January 1870, p. 3.

being added to the surfeit of unions with which they were faced",[70] but the Editor of *The Rock* was loud in his praise of Garbett, and earnestly recommended the remodelling of the Church Association—mistakenly believing this to be Garbett's object.[71]

Garbett and others were anxious for a union which was wholly independent of the Church Association.[72] They were overruled, however, by the majority at the Cannon Street Conference, and the provisional committee was told to confer with the Council of the Church Association. The Church Association declared in the next annual report that they were "...unanimous in the opinion that the formation of a separate organization would be fruitful in the elements of misconception and opposition, and would tend in its results rather to create divisions in the Evangelical body, than to produce either union of sentiment or community of action."[73] The Council put forward proposals for a Clerical and Lay Union which was to be, in effect, a branch of the Association, at the annual meeting of the Church Association in March 1871. The inaugural conference of the Clerical and Lay Union was held on the morning of 11 May 1871,[74] where Mr Valpy read out the scheme submitted by the committee which included establishing "communications with clerical and lay associations...and to encourage the formation of them where they do not at present exist."[75] However, the first report of the Clerical and Lay Union of 1871 announced that the long-established Western District Clerical and Lay Association and the Carlisle Evangelical Union had both declined to join the new Union. Tension between the Council and Edward Garbett, and growing distaste amongst Evangelicals of the prosecution policy of the Association, resulted in yet another organization being formed two years later. At a conference at the Cannon Street Hotel on 2 July 1873, it was resolved that "the Clerical and Lay Associations should unite with all Protestant Churchmen in an 'Evangelical Union of the Church of England' for the promotion of Church Reform".[76] The

---

[70] Shaftesbury's MSS Diary, 25 January 1870. Cited by A. Bentley, "The Transformation of the Evangelical Party in the Church of England in the Later Nineteenth Century", PhD thesis, Durham University 1971, p. 80.
[71] *Rock*, 25 January 1870, p. 13.
[72] See E. Garbett, *Union Among Evangelical Churchmen*, London 1870; idem., *Evangelical Principles: A Series of Doctrinal Papers Explanatory of the Positive Principles of Evangelical Churchmanship*, London 1875.
[73] Church Association *Annual Report* 1870, p. 17.
[74] Chaired by Lord Shaftesbury. Minutes of the Clerical and Lay Union, Church Society Archives. See also "Clerical and Lay Union Conference", *Monthly Intelligencer* 5, 4 (1 June 1871): 157–173.
[75] *Monthly Intelligencer* 5, 4 (June 1871): 158.
[76] *Record*, 13 August 1873, p. 11.

Clerical and Lay Union held their last meeting on 26 February 1873,[77] and the new Evangelical Union was formed five months later. However, within a year of this meeting, the Evangelical Union for Church Reform faded quietly out of sight, and probably out of existence. Any further attempts at forming a union of Evangelicals would have to be made by the Clerical and Lay Associations,[78] which continued to grow in strength and influence.

The Church Association was successful in making two later forays into the field of middle-class education. The first of these was the publication of a list of schools that were regarded as having a sufficiently 'distinctive' religious ethos.[79] In 1873, Revd R. G. Bryan wrote to the Church Association to suggest "that a register should be kept by the Association, of Schools where Evangelical parents might send their children".[80] Bryan was at that time Vicar of Fosbury, where he had a few boys living with him whom he taught, as well as his own children. It was two years before his propitious meeting with Messrs Jamieson and Pocock, which resulted in his becoming the second Headmaster of Monkton Combe School.[81] His letter was read by the Church Association Council and tabled at a meeting of the Church Association General Purposes Committee on 19 May 1873. The suggestion for a keeping of a register of 'Evangelically inclined' schools was favourably received, and the committee wrote to the Association's branches for suggestions of suitable schools. On 5 January 1874, the General Purposes Committee decided to advertise also "for applications to a register of Evangelical Schools" three times per year in the newspapers, *The Record* and *The Rock*. By then, the Association had received more than one request for such a register, many from parents who were anxious to find schools which were suitably "distinctive" for their children. The Annual Report of the Church Association for 1873 included an entry on this topic under the heading, "Register of Schools"; "The applications to the Secretaries to recommend Schools where sound Protestant Doctrine is taught, have become so general, that the Council lately determined to open a

---

[77] Minutes of the Clerical and Lay Union, Church Society Archives.

[78] A further attempt at party organization was made in March 1879 when the 'Evangelical Protestant Union' was formed by Bristol MP, James Inskip, and others. By October 1884, the Union claimed 1,000 members. However, it never became more than a fringe organization and attracted none of the outstanding Evangelical leaders. See the *Record*, 24 October 1884 and 7 November 1884 and the *Salford Chronicle*, 18 October 1884.

[79] See Appendix 2.

[80] Church Association General Purposes Committee Minute Book 2, pp. 634–5.

[81] See ch. 6 above.

Register, in which such Schools could be entered. The application to their Branches for information having been well responded to, a large number of such Schools is now on their list, and in many cases parents have already found the benefit."[82] A "List of Schools...where Religious Instruction is a Special Feature and of a Strictly Evangelical Character" was published in the Association's organ of communication, the *Church Intelligencer*.[83] It gave the name and location of each school, its 'Principal', and the fees per annum. The list remained a regular feature until the last issue of the *Intelligencer* in August 1924, and this marked the end of the Church Association's involvement in secondary education.

The second initiative in education did not occur until the last decade of the century. In what was a very delayed response to the success of various Clerical and Lay Associations in establishing middle-class schools,[84] a recommendation was adopted at the Church Association's Conference on 25 October, 1892, "That increased support be given to the existing Protestant Middle Class Schools for Boys, the necessity of largely increasing their numbers being urgent; and that steps be taken for the formation of similar schools for Girls."[85] The small trickle of donations which came into the Church Association offices were not sufficient to make a substantial donation to this cause, and a girls' school along similar lines to that already in existence for boys' was never founded. However, the Church Association Council resolved in January 1893 to use the funds contributed in support of this scheme to provide "exhibitions at Middle Class Schools".[86] In the following year, "Grants for Education" were proposed by "Mr Smith and Major Hewitt" at a meeting on the 21 June, "to encourage Protestant teaching in places of Education".[87] As a result of this, two scholarships of £15 each, tenable for two years, and an exhibition to Ayerst Hall, Cambridge,[88] tenable for two years, were provided for pupils at

---

[82] Church Association *Annual Report* 1873, p. 38.
[83] The list is reproduced in Appendix 2.
[84] See chs 8 and 9 below.
[85] Church Association Council Minute Book 10, p. 13.
[86] Ibid., p. 82.
[87] Ibid., p. 229.
[88] Ayerst Hall was opened in 1884 by Revd William Ayerst (1830–1904) on 'Parker's Piece' near Queen Anne Terrace in Cambridge "to aid men of modest means in obtaining a university degree and theological training". In 1893, the Hall moved to new buildings on Mount Pleasant on the left bank of the Cam, where it remained until it closed in 1896. See Little, *The Colleges of Cambridge*, pp. 173–174; W. W. Grave, *Fitzwilliam College, Cambridge 1869–1969*, Cambridge 1983, pp. 14–15 fn. 3; and A. F. Munden and N. Pollard,

Hermosa School, Ealing.[89] Both of these new institutions were to have a very short history—Ayerst Hall closed in 1896, and Hermosa Proprietary School in 1901.[90] It would appear that like many of the Church Association's court cases, its involvement would have a negative rather than a positive effect—the so-called "kiss of death". The initiative for founding and growing Evangelical middle-class schools was to pass to the individual Clerical and Lay Associations and their London-based Union.

The Clerical and Lay Associations

Despite the revival of Convocation in 1850 after a long break,[91] and the holding of the first national Church Congress in 1861,[92] many

---

Anglican Theological, Missionary and Educational Institutions, Coventry 1988, p. 45.

[89] Church Association Council Minute Book 10 and Church Association General Committee Minute Book 4.

[90] The privately owned Hermosa School began life as the Church House School in 1820, becoming Ealing College in 1880 when it moved to new premises on Hamilton Road, Ealing. The school rapidly declined when the fourth Headmaster retired in 1886; however, in 1888 Revd Edward C. Britton purchased the school and became the fifth Headmaster. He renamed it Hermosa School, after a school he had formerly kept in Devonshire. Britton was "strongly evangelical and protestant in his principles" and he obtained the support of a number of leading Evangelicals for his new foundation, including the Rector of Cheltenham, Canon C. Bell, and the Dean of Achonry, H. Townsend; both of whom are listed as patrons of the school. Britton trained for the ministry at London College of Divinity and was at one time, editor of the Evangelical newspaper, *The Rock*. The school was frequently mentioned in *The Rock* in lists of Evangelical schools. In 1893, Britton resigned as Headmaster and in the following year the name of the school was changed to The Proprietary School, Ealing. It closed in 1901. A new school named Ealing College was founded on the same site in 1925. See H. Egan, *Ealing College 1820–1970*, Gloucester 1969; and *Victoria County History* series for Middlesex, vol. 7, p. 168.

[91] Convocation had not been allowed to transact any business since Robert Walpole prorogued it in 1717, in order to prevent it from censuring the sermons of Bishop Hoadley. See S. L. Ollard and G. Crosse, *A Dictionary of English Church History*, London 1912, pp. 278–9.

[92] Held in the hall of King's College Cambridge in November 1861 and presided over by Archdeacon William Emery, an Evangelical (see Appendix 1). Despite this, "there was a good deal of hesitation on the part of the Evangelical clergy and laity about attending the Congress." Stock, *History of the CMS*, vol. 2, p. 357.

Evangelicals preferred local conferences to diocesan and national gatherings such as these. They also valued the support and work of the laity, who were largely excluded from such events. By 1880, eighteen new Evangelical organizations were meeting in the regions to "take counsel together" and to hold annual conferences. They were known as the Clerical and Lay Associations.[93] Some of these conferences were timed to follow larger events such as the Islington Clerical Meeting in London, which now numbered some 300 attendants.[94] Others, like the Aggregate Clerical Meeting in Tunbridge Wells[95] were the result of several local clerical societies combining together.[96] The Clerical and Lay Associations were primarily for personal fellowship, and their annual conferences were largely devotional or concerned with the practical application of faith in God. However, current issues were by no means ignored, and one of these was the provision of middle-class education.

The first Clerical and Lay Association was formed in the West Country, where there had been a large concentration of Evangelicals since the eighteenth century. By the end of 1858, there were plans for the formation of other Associations in Carlisle, Derby, and Dorset. To avoid confusion, the founding Association began to add parenthetically the title 'Western District' to its name. The Dorset association did not eventuate;[97] however, branch associations formed at Derby (calling itself the Midland District) and Carlisle (known as the Carlisle Evangelical Union). The latter gained the active support of the newly appointed Dean, Francis Close. Revd J. S. Jenkinson, Vicar of Battersea, was recorded as the local secretary for a branch in London, but for the time being this had no other members. Information about the activities of these Associations is today quite scarce.[98] Sources include articles in *The Record* newspaper; conference reports; and a list which appeared in the *Church of England Year Book* from 1885

---

[93] The first published reference to individual Clerical and Lay Associations was in G. R. Balleine, *A History of the Evangelical Party*, London 1908, p. 273. Despite their size, significance and ubiquity, the only significant study of these Evangelical organizations has been: J. Kent, "Anglican Evangelicalism in the West of England, 1858–1900", in *Protestant Evangelicalism: Britain, Ireland, Germany and America c.1780–c.1950: Essays in Honour of W. R. Ward*, Oxford 1990, pp. 179–200.

[94] *Times*, 6 February 1879.

[95] See ch. 8 below.

[96] J. H. Townsend, *Edward Hoare, M.A.*, London 1897, pp. 128, 185.

[97] It was to remain part of the Western District.

[98] The most complete collection is in private hands. The Annual Reports of a number of the associations are pasted into the General Committee Minute Book for the Clerical and Lay Association (Western District).

under the heading 'Clerical and Lay Conferences'. From these and secondary sources,[99] the following list of the nineteenth-century Church of England Clerical and Lay Associations, together with their foundation dates, has been compiled:[100]

Western District (1858)[101]

Midland District (February 1859)[102]

Evangelical Union for the Diocese of Carlisle (July 1859)[103]

Devon and Cornwall (1860)[104]

Southport Clerical and Lay Evangelical Association (1861)[105]

Middlesex, Hertford, and Essex Clerical and Lay Association (1861)[106]

Northern Home Counties District (February 1862)[107]

Eastern District (1862)[108]

East Lincolnshire Clerical and Lay Association (1866)[109]

East Anglia Clerical and Lay Union[110]

Ludlow, Leominster and Tenbury Lay and Clerical Church Association[111]

---

[99] There are three: Balleine, *History of the Evangelical Party*; Bentley "The Transformation of the Evangelical Party"; and Kent, "Anglican Evangelicalism in the West of England".

[100] Some used their full title, which was 'The Church of England Clerical and Lay Association for the Maintenance of Evangelical Principles', followed by their district name.

[101] See below, ch. 9.

[102] See above, p. 174–6.

[103] Founded in August 1859 by Canon T. D. Harford-Battersby (1822–1883), Vicar of St John's, Keswick. See Battersby and Battersby, eds. *Memoir of T. D. Harford-Battersby*, London 1890, pp. 135–140.

[104] See the *Church of England Yearbook* and the *Record*, 30 June 1871, p. 13.

[105] See the *Church of England Yearbook*. This organization still exists today.

[106] See Balleine, *History of the Evangelical Party*, p. 216.

[107] See the article, "Annual Conference of the Northern Home Counties Clerical and Lay Association" in *The Rock*, 14 November 1873 p. 769; and Kent, "Anglican Evangelicalism in the West of England", p. 184, fn. 8. It held its first Conference on 30 June and 1 July 1862 under the Presidency of Robert Hanbury, MP.

[108] See Balleine, *History of the Evangelical Party*, p. 216, and Kent, ibid., p. 184, fn. 8. This Association was based in Norfolk.

[109] Also known as the "East Lincoln Association". See Balleine, *History of the Evangelical Party*, p. 216.

[110] Also known as the "Ipswich Clerical and Lay Union". *The Record* 11 June 1866, p. 6.

Evangelical Societies and Middle-Class Education 237

    South-Eastern Clerical and Lay Church Alliance (1871)[112]
    Yorkshire Evangelical Union (1878)[113]
    Craven Evangelical Union (1883)[114]
    Durham and Northumberland Clerical and Lay Society (1884)[115]
    North-Western District[116]
    Tunbridge Wells[117]
    Surrey[118]

This made a total of eighteen Clerical and Lay Associations which were founded since 1858. Each held an annual conference at which the Evangelicals of the neighbourhood "might meet and take counsel together".[119] As suggested above, many Evangelicals chose to attend these more exclusive conferences than take part in their ruridecanal, diocesan and national Church gatherings.[120] Evangelical leaders such as J. C. Ryle were very concerned about this. While Ryle attended the conferences himself, he believed that it remained a great source of weakness for the Evangelical party that most of its members attended these private, local conferences at the expense of engaging with the

---

[111] See John Cawood, *Is Revision of the Prayer-Book Desirable at the Present Time? Being the Substance of a Paper Read Before the Ludlow, Leominster, and Tenbury Lay and Clerical Church Association, at Ludlow, etc.*, London 1869.

[112] See ch. 8 below.

[113] *Church of England Yearbook*. Full name: 'The Yorkshire Evangelical Union of Clerical and Lay Members of the Church of England'. Also known as 'York Clerical and Lay Union' and 'Yorkshire Evangelical Union and Conference'.

[114] Craven was an ecclesiastical district in the diocese of Liverpool. The fourth annual meeting of this Union was held in January 1885 at Leeds; their Conference of that year was at Huddersfield. See the *Church of England Yearbook*.

[115] See the *Church of England Yearbook*.

[116] See the *Report of the United Conference of the Western, North-Western, and Midland Districts of the Church of England Clerical and Lay Association, held in Birmingham, June 4 and 5, 1878...*, London 1878.

[117] Edward Hoare's Aggregate Clerical meeting. See ch. 8 below.

[118] See Balleine, *History of the Evangelical Party*, p. 216. This is the only reference I have found to this Clerical and Lay Association, although it is listed as a branch to the Midland District in their *Report of the Proceedings at the First Annual Conference*, p. 7.

[119] Balleine, *A History of the Evangelical Party*, p. 216.

[120] Such as the annual Church Congress, which began as an unofficial national gathering for the Church's clergy in 1861.

wider Church;[121] "These things ought ye to have done", he said, "and not to have left the others undone."[122]

Three of these associations are especially important to this study as they became involved in the provision of middle-class schools. South-Eastern College in Ramsgate was the creation of its namesake, the South-Eastern Clerical and Lay Alliance. The idea of a middle-class boys school in the Midlands was first raised by the Midlands Clerical and Lay Association in 1865, although as seen above,[123] the idea became reality through the almost single-handed work of Francis Wright. Dean Close Memorial School in Cheltenham was the result of discussions between the Western District Clerical and Lay Association and the central committee of a new Union of Clerical and Lay Associations in London.

The Union of Clerical and Lay Associations

By the 1870s, there was a good deal of dissatisfaction amongst Evangelicals with the results of the Church Association's policy of litigation. The long series of victories in the Courts had "failed to check the progress of Ritualism, and the imprisonment of Mr. Green[124] and others [had] caused, however illogically, a reaction of feeling".[125] The organization came to be known by its critics as "The Persecution Society, Limited",[126] and even some Evangelicals "thought it useless to

---

[121] Ryle delivered papers at 12 church congresses. A. Munden, Pers.Comm. See also J. C. Ryle, *Our Diocesan Conference*, London 1879.

[122] Cited by Balleine, *History of the Evangelical* Party, p. 216. Another Evangelical who shared his concern was J. C. Colquhoun, who wrote *Shall Protestant Churchmen Take Part in Convocation and Diocesan Synods?*, London 1869.

[123] See ch. 5 above.

[124] Sidney Faithorne Green, Rector of St John's, Miles Platting 1869–82, was imprisoned in March 1881 under the *Public Worship Regulation Act*. He was released 19 months later. On the prosecution and its aftermath, see Yates, *Anglican Ritualism*, pp. 263–9; P. T. Marsh, *The Victorian Church in Decline: Archbishop Tait and The Church of England 1869–1882*, London 1969, pp. 275–9; and Bentley, *Ritualism and Politics*, pp. 108–12.

[125] Stock, *History of the CMS* vol. 3, p. 280. See also Yates, *Anglican Ritualism*, ch. 5; "The Attempt to Control Anglican Ritualism".

[126] A phrase allegedly used by the Bishop of Peterborough in the House of Lords, which he later corrected in a letter to *The Guardian* on 23 November 1876. He maintained that he had used the word 'prosecute', not 'persecute'. *Church Intelligencer* 10 (1876): 379, 413. I am grateful to Alan Munden for pointing

regard the Church Association as a common centre round which Evangelical men would be ready to rally in times of distress."[127] The Council of the Church Association in their annual reports complained of the growing half-heartedness, as they considered it, of "the waning love, the dubious attitude, and the declining firmness, of once-familiar friends", from which, they said, they suffered more than from "the trenchant obloquy of an unscrupulous foe."[128] This "waning of love" could be attributed to the bitterness and ill-feeling which had resulted from the Church Association's policy of persecution. Talk began afresh of a new Union of Evangelical "Conferences or Clerical and Lay Societies"[129] which would be completely independent of the Church Association. "Such a gathering of representatives", it was suggested, "might with propriety be held the day following the long-established Islington Clerical Meeting in January each year."[130]

Immediately after the Church Congress of 1880, "Bishop Perry, Canon Hoare, Dr. Boultbee, and other leading men"[131] met in private to discuss how to set up "a new rallying point for the general body of Evangelicals".[132] A resolution was passed "that a provisional central committee should be formed in London for ascertaining the wishes of the chairmen and secretaries of [the] Evangelical Conferences throughout England."[133] In May 1880 this committee, together with "representatives of several of these Conferences"[134] met in London under the presidency of Bishop Charles Perry (1807–1891)[135] and drew up the following resolution:

> Under the circumstances of the Church of England, it was desirable to establish more communication between existing Clerical and Lay Associations formed and conducted on Evangelical principles. That there be an Annual Conference of representative men from the different Clerical and Lay Associations, and also occasional

---

this out to me, as the expression has previously been widely attributed to an editor of the *Church Times*.

[127] *Record*, 17 January 1881, p. 3.

[128] Church Association *Annual Report* 1885. Cited by Stock, *History of the CMS* vol. 3, p. 280.

[129] *Record*, 17 January 1881, p. 3.

[130] Ibid.

[131] Stock, *History of the CMS* vol. 3, p. 280. The other men included Canons Garbett and Money and Revd J. C. Ryle. See Appendix 1 for biographical information on all six men.

[132] Ibid.

[133] *Record*, 17 January 1881, p. 3.

[134] Ibid.

[135] See Appendix 1.

Conferences to be called together on special occasions. That there be a Committee, with a Secretary, whose duty shall be to act as a centre of communication amongst the different Associations and to summon a Conference when thought necessary.[136]

The first meeting of the new body was held in the Cannon Street Hotel in January 1881, on the day following the Islington Clerical Meeting. The meeting was presided over by Lord Midleton,[137] President of the South-Eastern Clerical and Lay Alliance. Other members of the provisional committee included Bishop Perry, Dean Fremantle, Canons Hoare and Money,[138] and Archdeacon Bardsley.[139] Papers were read on the "Reasons for United Action" and "The Method of United Action" by Joseph Bardsley and Joseph Hoare respectively, followed by discussion. The need for such united action was highlighted by the appearance in that morning's newspapers of "the Ritualistic list of grievances signed by Dean Church and others."[140] A Central Committee of Vigilance was appointed, and it was decided to present a memorial against Ritualism to counter that on toleration by Dean Church. "Thus, without any great flourish of trumpets, there has been quietly launched an organization which, under the blessing of God, may command untold influence in the future of the Evangelical body."[141] The editor of *The Record* was clearly optimistic about the Union's prospects.

Revd J. W. Marshall of Blackheath,[142] became secretary of the central committee, together with Revd J. Solway of Broxbourne. They were largely responsible for deputations to local associations, encouraging them to join the federation, and for the formation of new societies. In 1884 it was reported that when the proposed associations of Ely, Hereford and South Wales were put into operation, the Union

---

[136] *Record*, 17 January 1881, p. 3.

[137] William Broderick (1830–1907), the eighth Viscount Midleton, was MP for mid-Surrey 1868–70; President of the National Protestant Church Union; and Lord Lieutenant of Surrey 1896–1905.

[138] Short biographies of all four of these men can be found in Appendix 1.

[139] Joseph Bardsley (1825–1896) was Perpetual Curate of St Silas, Liverpool 1857–60; Vicar of Bradford 1880–96; and Archdeacon of Craven 1894–96.

[140] *Record*, 17 January 1881, p. 3. Richard William Church was Dean of St Paul's 1871–90 and a leading Anglo-Catholic exponent and spokesman.

[141] Ibid.

[142] Joseph William Marshall was Vicar of St John the Evangelist, Blackheath 1875–1909; an honorary Canon of Rochester Cathedral in 1900; and an honorary Canon of Southwark Cathedral when it was instituted in 1905. At one point he was secretary of both the Clerical and Lay Union and the Protestant Churchmen's Alliance.

would include nineteen associations, with two kindred societies at Tunbridge Wells[143] and Carlisle,[144] and would be represented in twenty-seven dioceses out of thirty-two.[145] Revd H. W. Webb-Peploe (1837–1923)[146] gradually became a dominant influence on the representative council, which generally held its annual meeting in his Church House at St Paul, Onslow Square. The Union of Clerical and Lay Associations merged with the Protestant Churchmen's Alliance in May 1893 to form the National Protestant Church Union.[147] However, well before this happened, the Union turned its attention to the issue of education for the middle classes.

The growth and success of the Woodard schools throughout the 70s and early 80s meant that the subject of Evangelical middle-class education continued to be a topic of discussion among the Evangelical constituency. On 5 May 1881, the Central Committee of the Union of Clerical and Lay Associations accepted the Report of a Special Sub-Committee, which stated: "Schools, based on the principles of the Reformation, and conducted on the footing of Public Schools, should be established and maintained in well-selected centres, such as Trent College, near Nottingham; the South-Eastern College, Ramsgate; the Close College [sic], Cheltenham; and the Monkton Combe School, Bath..."[148] It was proposed that a fund should be opened to "promote these objects", and that "the Secretary be requested to confer with the Associations"[149] on this and other means of "promoting the cause of Evangelical Churchmanship". One of the objects of this fund was to provide grants for "The establishment of Schools...in which education shall be based on the distinctive principles of the Reformation."[150] It was also proposed that some of this money be used towards endowments for Wycliffe and Ridley Halls.

In 1882, the issue of Evangelical middle-class education was the subject of a series of letters in *The Record* which ultimately resulted in the Union of Clerical and Lay Associations' taking up the cause in earnest. The author of the first of these letters identified himself only

---

[143] Edward Hoare's Aggregate Clerical Meeting. See above, pp. 257–59.
[144] The Carlisle Evangelical Union.
[145] *Rock*, 22 February 1884, p. 127.
[146] See Appendix 1.
[147] See "Stemma of the Church Society" on p. 223.
[148] "Union of Clerical and Lay Associations"; printed report of a special sub-committee pasted into the Minute Book of the Western District Clerical and Lay Association.
[149] Ibid.
[150] Ibid.

as "F. P.", and his letter was re-printed on 16 January 1882 under the title "Scriptural Education for the Middle Classes". He wrote:

> Letters have appeared in your columns from time to time urging the importance of the establishment of schools of a distinctly Protestant and Evangelical character with a view to counteracting the "Woodard Schools" and other similar institutions, but beyond the opening of the South-Eastern College at Ramsgate...no steps appear to have been taken to supply this widely felt need.[151]

He then went on to describe the growth and development of the Woodard schools, for "scarcely a year passes without the opening of some new school by Canon Woodard" and he listed the number of pupils at each school. As if this was not bad enough, "F. P." identified other schools of a Ritualistic kind. According to him, "these figures...do not by any means show the full extent of the educational movement, which is under exclusive control of the priest party." He suggested that in the diocese of Oxford, "though no "Woodward [sic] Schools" are to be found, educational establishments of an ultra-Ritualistic character [were] numerous." These were the schools whose staff were members of the Anglo-Catholic "Society of the Holy Cross" or the "Confraternity of the Blessed Sacrament" or the English Church Union. He listed six such schools "to which Ritualistic parents can entrust the education of their sons, while in the same area there appears to be not a single first-rate institution based on sound Protestant and Evangelical Principles". But there was even more to concern the reader, for many Ritualistic clergy had founded middle-class schools in their parishes: "St. Mary Magdalen's, Paddington, St. John the Divine's, Kennington, St. John's Torquay, and St. Saviour's, Eastbourne, [were] only a few examples out of many". Furthermore, a number of schools for ladies were listed at which, "as in the Romish convent schools, "Catholic teaching" is the primary consideration". The letter was well researched and provocative, and letters of response came pouring in.

In the next issue of *The Record*, Revd G. Everard of St Mark's, Wolverhampton, wrote in support of "F. P.", and suggested that a meeting be arranged "during the first week or two of May, when a few of the friends of evangelical truth who have influence or large means might take counsel and endeavour at once to take some steps to provide a few centres of education to which a parent might safely send his children".[152] The significance of holding a meeting in early May

---

[151] *Record*, 16 January 1882, p. 2. All of the quotations in this paragraph are from this article.
[152] *Record*, 20 January 1882, p. 2.

was that this was when the Church Association's May Conference was held in London. It was, for Evangelicals, "Conference Season". Three days later, two other correspondents took up the issue.

The first, Revd James Johnson[153] of Christchurch, Macclesfield, wrote to remind readers that "The South Eastern College at Ramsgate [was] not...the only establishment intended to counteract the influence of the Woodard schools", for this was "the very purpose for which Trent College was founded".[154] The second writer, writing under the pseudonym "Clericus", suggested that one of the reasons for the success of the Woodard schools was their relatively low fees, and that there was a need to provide schools not just for the middle classes, but also "for clergymen...of limited means". He said that many curates with sons "were forced to avail themselves of Denstone and similar colleges for their sons, owing to their limited incomes".[155] The same applied to beneficed clergy who had a large number of sons, several of them having "expressed their deep anxiety in not being able to send their sons to Evangelical public schools, on terms equal to those worked by the Ritualists".[156] It is interesting to note that at around this time, Trent College offered a reduction for fees to the sons of clergymen.[157]

The next writer on this issue, an E. Latham, suggested that a committee be formed, "and a small sum raised" to set up " a good middle school".[158] He wrote, "Such an action would be an immense boon in many places" and (with a touch of naivety) suggested that "save in the starting, [it] ought to cost nothing."[159] The editor of *The Record* took up the topic in the 27 January 1882 issue, and discussed it at length: "It is very painful to be compelled from time to time to call attention to defects or abuses of institutions and plans of usefulness which are greatly wanted in England", he wrote. "The Woodard Schools...are established in the interest of the ultra-Ritualist party...and...The stealthy and steady growth of this organization is

---

[153] James Johnson was chaplain to the Home and Colonial Training College 1869–81 and Incumbent of Christ Church, Macclesfield 1881–3. The Home and Colonial Training College opened in 1836 and closed in 1928.

[154] *Record*, 23 January 1882, p. 3.

[155] This was despite the existence of two schools that were specifically set up for the sons of clergy: St Edmund's, Canterbury (1749); and St John's, Leatherhead (1851).

[156] *Record*, 23 January 1882, p. 3.

[157] Ibid.

[158] Ibid.

[159] Ibid.

very serious".[160] On the issue of the lower cost of these schools, he suggested that this was a conscious effort on the part of the Ritualists "to undermine the attachment of our middle classes to the principles of the Reformation, by offering to their children the bribe of a higher education at a cheaper rate as the condition of their accepting anti-Protestant teaching".[161] An Evangelical response to the current crisis was required: "This is a very important and very serious question, and it urgently calls for immediate and decisive action."[162] Just in case the reader had not understood the message, the following challenge was put forward:

> Unquestionably the battle of the future is to be fought on the field of education, and it would be a fatal act of supineness if we were to permit some of the very best of the youth of England to be drawn aside from the familiar and well-tried paths of Evangelical truth as taught in the Prayer-book and Thirty-nine Articles of England, that they might be trained in the morality of the Confessional, and in a form of religion which is indistinguishable from the Romish Mass.[163]

The Evangelical gloves were off.

This was an issue on which Evangelicals involved in the setting up of schools at Ramsgate and Long Eaton, were bound to comment. On 30 January 1882, J. B. Whiting, one of the founders of the South-Eastern College, weighed in to the debate. Commenting on the Woodard schools, he said "The scheme has succeeded; 100,000*l* has been expended on it, whilst Evangelical churchmen have been asleep".[164] He went on: "An appeal for help to inaugurate a network of schools over the country is met by a response of 5*l* or 10*l*. But, as Mr. Everard has shown, thousands are wanted."[165] A letter to *The Record* from "J. M." on 17 February 1882 suggested that there were other reasons why it was difficult to found Evangelical schools as "Men of this stamp mostly decline to give themselves up to educational work, feeling that their call is to pastoral ministrations."[166] He believed that one of the reasons why the Church Association's Evangelical Middle-Class Education scheme of 1868[167] had failed was because wealthy

---

[160] *Record*, 27 January 1882, p. 2.
[161] Ibid., p. 3.
[162] Ibid., p. 2.
[163] Ibid.
[164] *Record*, 30 January 1882, p. 2.
[165] Ibid.
[166] *Record*, 17 February 1882, p. 2.
[167] See ch. 7 above.

Evangelicals had declined to give towards the erection of new schools: they believed that their money was better spent supporting "the direct preaching of the Gospel" at home and overseas.[168] This was too much for Revd J. E. Campbell Colquhoun,[169] a Trustee and the Honorary Treasurer of the South-Eastern College at Ramsgate. He reminded the readers of *The Record* that "we have already founded a school of this character at Ramsgate...we have found an educationalist such as is described by "J. M."...and that we have not yet been daunted by the many difficulties we have met with in endeavouring to make our effort permanent."[170] It was clearly very frustrating for those involved in the South-Eastern College that there was so much talk in the Evangelical press on the subject of middle-class education, with so little reference to the efforts at Ramsgate. The Treasurer could not pass up this opportunity to make an appeal to the national readership of *The Record*, suggesting that the Ramsgate school went a long way to addressing the problem which had been the subject of so much debate—a national response to the Woodard schools; "With the Dean of Canterbury as our President, and many tried members of the Evangelical body as our faithful supporters, the Trustees of the South-Eastern College, Ramsgate, appeal for much wider pecuniary help from all parts of England to make their school...a national institution for the promotion of Protestant and Evangelical truth in connection with the Church of England."[171]

Correspondence on this topic peaked in late February 1882, and after this middle-class education began to appear on the meeting agendas of Clerical and Lay Associations around the country. Dr E. H. Perowne, Chairman of the Clerical and Lay Association for the Northern Home Counties District and Master of Corpus Christi College, Cambridge,[172] held the annual meeting for 1882 at Corpus Christi on the 19th and 20th of April. The first subject for discussion was "The Duty of Evangelical Churchmen in reference to the Educational movements of the times."[173] Revd A. T. Field, Vicar of Holbrooke, Derbyshire, opened the proceedings by stating that "What was needed for the children of Evangelical parents were schools started upon the Woodard system, with low fees" and he suggested that "a body like the Clerical and Lay Association might far better than individuals undertake the erection and management of such

---

[168] *Record*, 17 February 1882, p. 2.
[169] Son of the MP, John Campbell Colquhoun, and listed in Appendix 1.
[170] *Record*, 24 February 1882, p. 3.
[171] Ibid.
[172] Perowne was Vice-Chancellor of Cambridge 1879–1881.
[173] *Supplement to The Record*, 28 April 1882, p. 141.

organizations."[174] Revd E. Latham then described his attempts to start a middle-class school at Matlock Bath in Derbyshire. However, it was corporate not individual effort which was being called for, and Walter Walsh[175] concluded the discussion with a statement that the Central Committee of the Union of Clerical and Lay Associations "were taking the matter into consideration", and he "urged upon all the immense importance" of such schools. It appeared that at long last one of the Evangelical organizations, for which the party was famous, was about the take some initiative.

On the afternoon of Wednesday 24 May 1882, a meeting of the Central Committee of the Union of Clerical and Lay Associations was held in the drawing room of Mr H. Smith-Bosanquet. The main topic at hand was Evangelical middle-class education, and the Dean of Canterbury opened proceedings by referring to the "educational advantages" offered by the Woodard schools, and the need to establish a "similar system based upon the Evangelical principles of the Church of England".[176] It was suggested that there was an urgent need "to raise funds and appoint influential trustees" for these proposed schools. A paper was circulated outlining the research that one of the committee members had undertaken into the Woodard schools. Entitled *A Brief Statement of the History and Growth of the Schools connected with "The Corporation of SS. Mary and Nicholas, Lancing"*, it became the basis for the new initiative in which the members of the Union were called to "expend their time, their energy, their substance"[177] in devising and promoting Evangelical efforts to combat the Woodard schools.

The report of this meeting in *The Record* was followed by a letter from Lord Fortescue in which he reminded the readers that the Devon County School had been founded in 1858 as a means of providing for the middle classes "an unritualist, but decidedly Christian, education" which—to the undoubted horror of the Evangelical Anglican readers—included both Protestant Churchmen and Protestant *Dissenters* amongst its supporters. He also mentioned the two other institutions which had been founded by Prebendary Brereton:[178] Norfolk County School and Cavendish College at Cambridge. The editor of *The Record*

---

[174] Ibid.

[175] Walter Walsh had developed a notable career as an anti-Ritualist journalist. He was the author of *The Secret History of the Oxford Movement* and other polemical works. For particulars of Walsh, see the *Free Church Chronicle* 1 (1899): 57–8.

[176] *Record*, 2 June 1882, p. 285.

[177] Ibid.

[178] See ch. 2 above.

suggested in the next issue that "We are thus confronted by three separate and, to a certain extent, antagonistic systems of middle-class education". This was "Canon Woodard's schools, the Evangelical schools, at present represented by the South-Eastern College at Ramsgate, and Lord Fortescue's County schools".[179] He suggested that one of the reasons for the success of the Woodard schools was in their "definiteness" of religious teaching, and that this was one of the weaknesses of the County schools. He also deprecated the County schools for their lack of distinctiveness in religious instruction—pointing out that in the County schools "religious instruction is given which…encourages Dissenters to send their sons to the schools with confidence that their religious feelings and convictions will be respected."[180] This was clearly not the sort of school to which serious members of the Evangelical party could put their name.

The lack of mention of Trent College in all of these discussions, which had by now been in existence for some 16 years, bears some explanation. Canon Scott Robinson wrote a lengthy article to *The Churchman*, a new Evangelical periodical, in which he explained that Trent College, with fees of as much as £60 per annum,[181] could not be classed as a middle-class school, "in the proper sense of the term",[182] as its fees were equivalent to some of the older public schools.[183] He explained that for a large number of middle-class parents:

> The monetary consideration is, and must be, a primary one. It should also be an issue for those considering starting up such schools, for if the Church of England is to maintain any hold upon the great bulk of the Middle Classes, we must face the difficult task of providing boarding schools in which definite and distinct Church teaching may be secured, and at which the total expense to the parent may not exceed £18 or £21, in third grade schools; nor be more than £40 to £50 per annum in those of the second grade.

His subdivision of schools into first-, second- and third-grade is worth noting, for it was typical of the period to categorize everything according to means or income,[184] for "such *nuances* of social status …render educational questions complex and difficult."[185] He explained

---

[179] *Record*, 16 June 1882, p. 337.
[180] Ibid.
[181] In fact the advertised fees were never more than £40 per annum at this time.
[182] W. A. Scott Robertson, "Middle Class Education", *Churchman* 36 (September 1882): 443.
[183] Although, they were nothing like those of Eton, which, according to the same author, were as high as £210 per annum in 1882.
[184] See ch. 2 above for a full discussion of this topic.
[185] Scott Robertson, "Middle Class Education", p. 443.

that "Practical men...can always be made to understand by figures such distinctions (whether relating to the Upper or the Middle Classes) as must ultimately be brought to the monetary test." The following summary of his classification system is revealing of the period as much as it is of the state of English education in 1882.

First-grade, or public schools, as they were commonly called, "abound".[186] When a new one is started "upon reasonably low terms, there is invariably a tendency to increase the charges as time goes on".[187] Under this system, "Canon Woodard's school at Lancing" would have been regarded as a first-grade school as its fees were from £60 to £100 per annum[188]. Evangelicals had a first-grade school "which forms a parallel to Lancing"[189] in Trent College at Long Eaton. They also had a second-grade school at South-Eastern College at Ramsgate, where "distinctive Church teaching is a primary feature in the course; and the total cost to parents varies from £45 to £50 per annum." Furthermore:

> This school, if Churchmen come forward to make it permanent, will form only one small parallel, to the three large schools which Canon Woodard and his friends have established (at a cost exceeding £100,000) for nearly 700 boys at Hurstpierpoint, Denstone, and Taunton. In those three schools a very good education is given, coupled with the advanced Sacramental teaching of Canon Woodard and his coadjutors, at a total [cost] to parents of about £40 to £60 per annum. These are really "Middle Class" schools. [190]

This suggests, of course, that Trent College, with fees of from £40 to £50 per annum, could be regarded as belonging to the same category. Examples of 'Third-grade Schools' could not be found where "distinct Church teaching should form a marked feature of the school course."[191] Yet "Canon Woodward had been able to establish such schools", for example "at Ardingly for 500 boys, and at Ellesmere for 200".[192] In each of these institutions the total cost of a boarder's education was estimated to range between £18 to £25 per annum. This was considerably less than any of the Evangelical middle-class schools that were either in existence, or proposed.

---

[186] Ibid., p. 444.
[187] Ibid.
[188] Ibid.
[189] Ibid.
[190] Ibid.
[191] Ibid., p. 445.
[192] Ibid.

The proprietary, or joint stock company, principle had been used to found a number of new public schools such as Cheltenham College earlier in the century (1841), and it was also the device which Canon J. W. Brereton utilized in his scheme for establishing his "County Schools".[193] Canon Scott Robinson categorized these schools as falling into the second grade of his system,[194] for the cost of board and education at these schools averaged £35 to £45 per annum. According to him, in these schools "religious teaching was given upon a "Protestant" basis; but of such a character that Nonconformists and Churchmen can alike accept it without offence."[195] This was very unsatisfactory to the majority of Evangelicals, who subscribed to "the distinctive teaching of the Church". Nevertheless, "Successful county schools of this nature"[196] were established in Devon, Suffolk, Surrey, Bedford, Norfolk, and in Dorset. Lord Fortescue's advocacy of a "neutral Protestant platform"[197] for the County schools for which he was Patron, was of great concern to these hard-line Evangelicals. Scott Robinson referred to "the effect of neutral Protestant teaching upon our lads",[198] and he recalled a recent meeting at which the Bishop of Ballarat "begged that the Church at home would refrain from sending out to his Australian diocese any clergymen who were either mentally or physically 'flabby'." He argued that if the religious training in a middle-class school "be such that it can be accepted by Churchmen and non-Churchmen alike, must it not be of that nature which the Bishop of Ballarat characterised...?".[199] Evangelicals at home as well as abroad were equally keen to avoid 'flabby lads'.

Canon Robinson urged the setting up of a central fund for the support of local effort in Evangelical middle-class education, such as that at Ramsgate in the Diocese of Canterbury: "A central fund must be gathered around that local effort, first, and then extend its operations into other dioceses, which can commence like local efforts. The central fund must, however, be rapidly raised, or the opportunity will be lost."[200] Robinson also focused on the other perceived threat to the Established Church: that of Nonconformity. His article provided a comprehensive (if convoluted) survey of the growth of Nonconformist schools in Britain, especially schools of the Society of Friends, of

---

[193] See ch. 2 above.
[194] Ibid., p. 448.
[195] Ibid.
[196] Ibid.
[197] Ibid., p. 451.
[198] Ibid., p. 452.
[199] Ibid.
[200] Ibid., p. 449.

which he listed twelve.²⁰¹ Robinson called upon the "various Clerical and Lay Associations, throughout England, to show their vitality by following up this movement for giving distinctive Church education to the Middle Classes." Once they had set the South-Eastern College upon a firm foundation, "they must, from a central fund, do the same in other unwilling dioceses."²⁰² There was to be no going back.

Letters such as this and the initiative which the Clerical and Lay Association (Western District) took in establishing a middle-class schools committee in November 1882, led to the establishment in London of a "central committee…which will co-operate with the Council of the Western Lay and Clerical Association"²⁰³ to raise money for a school in the West of England. Although it was necessary to continue to make constant appeals like this, by now the idea had caught on. The Northern Home Counties branch of the Union of Clerical and Lay Associations had already passed a resolution in support of the movement at a meeting in Cambridge on 19 April 1882, and as late as 1890 a proposal was made to build one in Yorkshire.²⁰⁴ In March 1883, the London Central Committee for Middle-Class Schools advertised that it intended to raise £10,000 for the proposed Dean Close Memorial School—the subject of chapter 9 below.

The Church Pastoral Aid Society

The Church Pastoral Aid Society (CPAS) was founded in 1836 for the purpose of funding additional parish clergy and lay parish workers, particularly in industrial towns and cities experiencing rapid population growth.²⁰⁵ It arose out of discussions between a group of London laymen, among whom Frederic Sandoz²⁰⁶ was "the leading spirit"²⁰⁷ and who had inserted a paragraph in *The Record* in March 1835 which called attention to the want of a 'Church Home Missionary

---

[201] At Ackworth, Saffron Walden, Sidcot (Somerset), Wigton, Rawden, Penketh, Sibford, Ayton, Waterford, Mountmellick, Lisburn, and Brookfield. Altogether they accommodated 1,152 children, mainly boarders. Ibid., p. 453. Cf. W. A. Campbell Stewart, *Quakers and Education*, London 1953.

[202] Ibid., p. 450.

[203] *Rock*, 16 March 1883, p. 174.

[204] *Record*, 13 June 1890, p. 578.

[205] See P. B. Coombs, "A History of the Church Pastoral-Aid Society, 1836–1861", MA thesis, Bristol University 1960.

[206] Frederick Sandoz was a philanthropist and a key lay figure in the Evangelical network based in London in the 1830s. He was the chief organizer of the CPAS. Nothing has been published about Sandoz's early life or education.

[207] Balleine, *History of the Evangelical Party*, p. 139.

Society'.[208] This resulted in "a plan for extending the means of grace in and to necessitous parishes in strict conformity with the spirit, constitution, and discipline of our venerated Church"[209] which was submitted at a meeting, chaired by Lord Ashley,[210] on 19 February 1836. In this way a new Evangelical society was instituted "...for the purpose of benefiting the population of our own country by increasing the number of working clergymen in the Church of England, and encouraging the employment of pious and discreet laymen as helpers to the clergy in duties not ministerial."[211]

In spite of strong High Church opposition to the Society for operating independently of episcopal control[212] and "stiff Churchmen" resistance to the use of lay workers,[213] the CPAS achieved considerable success and in the first year and was able to make grants for 58 additional curates and 13 lay assistants.[214] In 1841 nearly 1,700 clergymen were members of the Society[215] and "the Gorham case[216]...added another 200 clergymen, papal aggression, another

---

[208] *Record*, 12 March 1835, p. 13.

[209] 'Letter of Invitation' circular, cited by E. J. Speck, *Church Pastoral-Aid Society: Sketch of its Origin and Progress*, London 1881, b2 [sic].

[210] Better known by his later title of Lord Shaftesbury.

[211] Speck, *Church Pastoral-Aid Society*, b.

[212] Henry Phillpotts (1778–1869), Bishop of Exeter 1830–69, declared the project "contrary to the practice of all Christian antiquity and of our own branch of Christ's Church in particular, anomalous, pregnant with mischief and perils of the gravest kind." *A Letter to the Archdeacons of the Diocese on the Proposed Scripture Readers*, cited by Balleine, *History of the Evangelical Party*, p. 141. See J. R. Wolffe, "Bishop Henry Phillpotts and the Administration of the Diocese of Exeter 1830–1869", *Report and Transactions of the Devonshire Association for the Advancement of Science, Literature and Art* 114 (1982): 99–113.

[213] Leading to the formation in 1837 by W. E. Gladstone and others, of the Additional Curates' Society (initially called the Clergy Aid Society). The ACS was an explicitly High Church response to the CPAS and unlike the CPAS, restricted its support to clergy rather than to subsidising lay agency. The ACS never equalled its rival in income or influence. See F. W. B. Bullock, *Voluntary Religious Societies, 1520–1799*, St Leonards-on-Sea 1963.

[214] 16 went to Yorkshire, 12 to Lancashire, 6 to London, and 5 to Wales. Balleine, *History of the Evangelical Party*, p. 140.

[215] Chadwick, *The Victorian Church* part 1, p. 446.

[216] In 1850 Bishop Phillpotts of Exeter had refused to institute to the living of Bramford Speke the Evangelical, Revd G. C. Gorham (1787–1857), believing him to be unsound on the doctrine of baptismal regeneration. See Appendix 1 and A. Lentin, "Anglicanism, Parliament and the Courts" in Parsons (ed.), *Religion in Victorian Britain II: Controversies*, pp. 96–7.

200."[217] By 1858 the CPAS had funded 378 curates and 162 lay agents[218] and in 1879 total receipts since the formation of the Society had reached £1,680,811.[219] The Society is today based in Warwick, where new offices were built in 1990, following the sale of its London offices.

Following the Archbishop of Canterbury's judgement on the ritualist practices of the Bishop of Lincoln in 1890,[220] the Church Association decided to abandon its policy of prosecution, and instead support the work of organizations such as the Church Pastoral Aid Society. This was partly due to a letter written by Revd A. J. Robinson, Rector of Holy Trinity, Marylebone, which was published in *The Record* on 12 August 1892. He suggested that the best way to defend the doctrines of the Reformation was to make the parishes in which they were taught "thoroughly efficient". This plea was supported by the Editor in his leading article:

> The wise course lies plainly before us. It is by doing good rather than by preventing evil that the Evangelical body exert a real influence in the Church of England. The repression of illegal and disloyal practices in parish churches is primarily the duty of the authorities; their responsibility will, perhaps, be more readily recognized, and...more easily discharged when it is not attempted to be shared by volunteers. But, on the other hand, Evangelical work...is heaped up around us, waiting to be done. It would, for instance, be a satisfactory and logical result of the Privy Council Judgment if the Church Pastoral Aid-Society were to find its resources suddenly reinforced by the energy and efforts of active Evangelicals.[221]

From this suggestion sprang the 'Forward Movement' of the Society in 1893, which not only strengthened the work of many of the largest and poorest parishes, but also supported the provision of new middle-class schools.

On Thursday 15 December 1892 a memorial was presented to the committee of the Church Pastoral Aid Society by Revd W. H. Barlow "and many other influential and trusted members and friends of the C.P.A.S.".[222] It made a number of suggestions which were later to

---

[217] Speck, *Church Pastoral-Aid Society*, p. 75.
[218] See http://www.special-coll.bham.ac.uk/catalogue_AM_archmiss_misssoc_CMS.html (accessed March 2004); the web address of the Church Missionary Society Archives, located at the University of Birmingham Library.
[219] Speck, *Church Pastoral-Aid Society*, p. 204.
[220] For the Lincoln Judgement, see above, p. 38, fn. 197.
[221] *Record*, 12 August 1892, p. 820.
[222] *Church and People* 4, 31 (February 1893): 269. *Church and People* (1889–) is the official organ of the CPAS.

form the basis of the activities of the CPAS Forward Movement. The suggestions ranged from increasing parish 'pastoral and evangelistic work', to an increase in the number and value of grants for additional clergy and lay agents, to the provision of homes and training institutions for these lay agents, to the provision of middle- and upper-class schools and theological colleges, and finally, to "the presentation to livings [and] the acquiring of advowsons."[223] In short, it identified that the CPAS needed to concentrate its activities on education, evangelism, patronage and training. Already the Forward Movement had attracted the attention of the Evangelical press: an article in *The Rock* of 16 December 1892 anticipated their support for the purchase of Trent College by the Church of England Evangelical College and School Company:

> Amongst the proposals which we expect the memorialists would press upon the kindly consideration of the Pastoral-Aid Committee are education and literacy. To enlarge the sphere of Evangelical influence in the Press will need care and talent. Much simpler and less remote is the fostering of education. The scheme of the Evangelical College and School Company is simple, direct, and feasible. Here our friends are not rushing into untried pastures new. At Ramsgate, at Cheltenham, at Combe Down, and at Trent there are schools worthy of the most frank and energetic countenance.[224]

A conference was held by the committee on 6 January 1893 to discuss the Memorial's suggestions. It was at this meeting that the expression "Forward Movement" was used (but not coined)[225] by the Chairman, Revd F. E. Wigram, to explain how the "suggestions of the memorialists" could be used as a means of "extension of the Society's usefulness."[226] One of the suggestions was in reference to education; "That the Society be invited to consider what steps can be taken, in the interests of Evangelical Churchmanship, to further—(a) the education of middle and upper classes…"[227] Present at the meeting were four members of the Board of the Church of England Evangelical College and School Company,[228] which had been formed two years previously in order to purchase Monkton Combe School near Bath and which had

---

[223] Ibid., p. 270.

[224] *Rock*, 16 December 1892, p. 9.

[225] A Forward Movement was founded in 1885 by Wesleyan Methodists, including Hugh Price Hughes. Its title was adopted by other denominations including the Church of England. It was concerned with the advancement of the Kingdom of God. D. P. Hughes, *The Life of Hugh Price Hughes*, London 1904, p. 167.

[226] *Church and People* 4, 31 (February 1893): 271.

[227] Ibid.

[228] H. W. Webb-Peploe, G. F. Whidbourne, S. Gedge, and P. V. Smith.

recently agreed to purchase Trent College from Francis Wright.[229] The question of how Evangelicals could counter the work of the Woodard schools had been a subject of debate for some years. The Editor of *The Rock*, in his lead article of 27 October 1893, suggested that this "question of religious teaching in middle and upper schools" had become "part of the 'Forward Movement' of the C.P.A.S." He stated that "At Cheltenham, Trent, and Ramsgate there are schools which are doing excellent work. But we greatly doubt whether these schools are supported as they ought to be and might be." He then contrasted the work of the Evangelicals with that of the Anglo-Catholics: "There is one party in the Church of England which has shown that it appreciates the importance of religious teaching given to children of the middle classes. It has rallied around a number of wealthy men, who have provided fine buildings and given a start to schools where the doctrine is distinctly High Church, if not of actually Romanising tendency [and] is instilled into the minds of the pupils."[230] The Forward Movement of the CPAS was seen as the answer to the issue of Evangelical provision of middle-class education.

On 26 April 1894 the General Committee of the CPAS passed a number of resolutions, including one which called for the setting up of "several new agencies…in connection with the Forward Movement",[231] for which "special contributions would be invited", including for "An Education Fund for aiding Evangelical Schools of the Middle and Upper Classes for securing the efficiency of the Religious Instruction given in them, and for promoting the provision of suitable Theological Literature."[232] A 'Religious Education Sub-Committee' was formed which made the following recommendations to the General Committee in May 1894:

1. That a scheme be drawn up by which Evangelical Schools, such as Trent College, the South-Eastern College at Ramsgate, the Dean Close Memorial School at Cheltenham, and others similarly constituted, may be drawn into closer co-operation.

2. That a Capital Fund be established, from which grants may be made to assist Schools already existing, and to found similar ones in other places.

---

[229] See ch. 10 below.
[230] *Rock*, 27 October 1893, p. 8.
[231] *Church and People* 6, 3 (June 1894): 50.
[232] Ibid., p. 51.

3. That an Exhibition Fund be set on foot to assist the education of children of Evangelical parents during their residence in such schools, and to help them at the Universities.

4. That a Register be kept at the Society's office of earnest and suitable masters wishing to serve in such schools.

5. That it is desirable that a Committee should be constituted under the auspices of the Church Pastoral-Aid Society for promoting the cause of Religious education in Upper and Middle-class Schools.[233]

The Sub-Committee further recommended the appointment of a Board of Education to consult together and implement the above recommendations. This Board would include representatives from the Evangelical schools mentioned above,[234] as well as the Evangelical theological colleges: Wycliffe Hall, Ridley Hall and the London College of Divinity. This Board of Education was duly formed and had its first meeting in the following month.

Like many other Evangelical initiatives, the CPAS Board of Education suffered from a perception by Evangelicals that money is better spent in direct evangelism than in the education of Evangelical children. The accounts of the CPAS Forward Movement Fund, which were published in the *Sixty-fourth Annual Report* of 1899, showed that only £88 was spent on the Education Fund, whereas over £3,000 was spent in that year on grants for curates and parishes. By 1900, the Forward Movement fund had been subsumed into the CPAS's general accounts, and no further reference is made to the Board of Education or the Education Fund. However, two Anglican organizations whose members had strong connections with the CPAS, continued to promote middle-class education. They were the Church Schools Company,[235] which had been founding middle-class schools for girls since 1883, and the Evangelical Church Schools Company,[236] which was responsible since 1891 for the promotion of middle-class schools for boys. The Memorandum of Association of The Church of England Evangelical College and School Company (1891) stated that one of the

---

[233] *Report of the Committee, Read at the Fifty-Ninth Annual Meeting on the 3rd May, 1894...*, London 1894. Church of England Record Centre

[234] The Board of Governors of Dean Close School appointed the Headmaster, W. H. Flecker, and a governor, T. H. Clark, representatives to the CPAS Board of Education. General Committee Minute Book 1893–94, Dean Close School Archives.

[235] See ch. 2 above.

[236] See ch. 10 below.

objects for which the company was established was "To provide by establishment and maintenance of schools in England and Wales...for boys *and* girls of classes above those ordinarily attending public elementary schools".[237] It would seem that even though the CPAS failed to provide direct support for middle-class education, the initiative was to be retained by two organizations which were made up of leading CPAS members. The Evangelical Church Schools Company, whose board included four members of the CPAS committee, continued to do this until 1966. It frequently met in the CPAS Board Room. The Church Schools Company, whose committee of management included a founding member of the Evangelical Company, Mr P. V. Smith, still meets today. However, it was an Evangelical organization, now defunct, that was to set up a middle-class school first: the South-Eastern Clerical and Lay Church Alliance was responsible for founding South-Eastern College in Ramsgate, today known as St Lawrence College.

---

[237] Memorandum of Association of Evangelical Church Schools Limited [my italics]. Trent College Archives.

CHAPTER 8

The South-Eastern Clerical and Lay Church Alliance and South-Eastern College, Ramsgate

Although the roots of Evangelicalism in the West of England are well documented[1] and can be traced back to the previous century and even earlier, Anglican Evangelical activity in the South-East was a relatively recent phenomenon. It was centred on the fashionable spa town of Tunbridge Wells, where Canon Edward Hoare (1812–1894)[2] had, since 1860, both hosted and for most of his life, presided over, the 'great organization' which he had founded known as The Aggregate Clerical Meeting. An obituary records that "He made Tunbridge Wells the Canterbury of West Kent, and he was the unofficial primate."[3] Hoare was a CMS stalwart and active in the CPAS. He was regarded as one of the great Evangelical leaders of his time and was a regular guest speaker at Evangelical conferences and meetings.

From its modest beginning, invitations were sent by Canon Hoare to members of seven local Clerical and Lay Societies in the region to assemble in the month of June 1860 for a series of meetings. In this way the Aggregate Clerical Meeting quickly expanded, and by 1870 nearly five hundred clergy (and laymen who had been "introduced by a clergyman") were attending from all parts of the south-east of England; although primarily they were drawn from the counties of Kent, Sussex, and Surrey. These annual meetings provided an excellent opportunity for like-minded Evangelicals to discuss and debate the tenets of the faith, to study the Bible, and to meet for fellowship.

Out of this annual meeting a new society known as the South-Eastern Clerical and Lay Church Alliance was founded in 1871, its main maxims being "Sincere and loyal attachment to the true

---

[1] See especially Kent, "Anglican Evangelicalism in the West of England"; L. P. Fox, "The Work of Revd Thomas Tragenna Biddulph with special reference to his Influence on the Evangelical Movement in the West of England", PhD thesis, Cambridge University 1953; and Munden, "The Church of England in Cheltenham 1826–1856 with particular reference to Revd. Francis Close".
[2] See Appendix 1.
[3] *Record,* 13 July, 1894.

Principles of the English Reformed Church, as distinguished on the other hand from doctrines and practices of a Romanizing tendency and from the Rationalistic free handling of Revelation on the other."[4] The new alliance had as its president the Dean of Canterbury, Robert Payne Smith (1819–1895),[5] and on its committee, Evangelical leaders such as Canon Hoare of Tunbridge Wells; Revd Nathaniel Dimock (1825–1909), Vicar of St Paul's, Maidstone;[6] Revd J. Bradford Whiting (1828–1914), Vicar of St Luke's, Ramsgate;[7] Mr (later Sir) John Deacon of the London banking family;[8] and Mr R. J. Fremlin of the Kent brewing family.

The first of 15 Rules[9] of the Society made clear that the full name of the organization was "The South-Eastern Clerical and Lay Church Alliance on the Principles of the Reformation". The same rule explains that it was to be governed by a central committee "elected by its Members". The central committee was to comprise "not more than twelve Clergymen and twelve Laymen".[10] The elected officers were: a president and vice-president, lay and clerical secretaries; and the secretaries of sub-committees. A Branch Association could be formed by twelve or more members, and if it numbered more than twenty-five it had the power to elect a representative to the central committee, or two representatives when the number exceeded fifty. Clearly the Society expected great things. The combining of its annual meeting with that of the five-hundred strong[11] Tunbridge Wells Aggregate Clerical Meeting from 1888, meant that these expectations were more than adequately met, for by this year the number of members of the South-Eastern Clerical and Lay Alliance totalled 273.[12] The Report of 1888 lists also the members of the Branch Associations, so to this number may be added the members of the branches of Rochester (not given), St Paul's, Maidstone (150), the Isle of Thanet and Neighbourhood (7), and Folkestone (82): making a grand total of over 500 members.

---

[4] *Register of St Lawrence College 1879 to 1934*, 3rd edn, London 1934, p. vi.
[5] See Appendix 1.
[6] Ibid.
[7] Ibid.
[8] Williams, Deacon and Co. was established in 1771 and merged in 1970 with Glyn, Mills and Co. (1853) to become Williams and Glyn's Bank, which in turn became part of the Royal Bank of Scotland in 1985.
[9] Printed in the *Seventeenth Annual Report,* London 1890, p. 6.
[10] Rule 5, ibid., p. 7.
[11] Townsend, *Edward Hoare*, p. 185.
[12] A figure obtained by adding up all of the members' names listed in the *Seventeenth Annual Report.*

The Seventeenth Annual Meeting and Conference of the South-Eastern Clerical and Lay Alliance took place on Wednesday 20 June 1888 in Tunbridge Wells. The sessions were held in connection with the local Aggregate Clerical Meeting, which took place on the previous day. Holy Communion was held at Holy Trinity Church and the conference sessions were held in the Great Hall.[13] The morning session included the committee's report and the president's address, together with the election of the office-holders. Thereafter followed two more sessions: afternoon and evening. The afternoon session included a report from the Headmaster of a school that had been founded by the Association some nine years earlier. For in 1879, Revd J. B. Whiting, one of the organization's leading clerics and vicar of the relatively new parish of St Luke's, Ramsgate, had an idea which would ensure that the work of the Association lasted not just for his generation, but in perpetuity. That idea was South-Eastern College, Ramsgate.

Early in the nineteenth century, the seaside town of Ramsgate was a fashionable watering place and health resort,[14] situated as it is on the warm south-eastern tip of the Isle of Thanet. One of the results of this expansion was that new parishes needed to be created to serve the increasing population,[15] and in 1875 a new church was built in the parish of St Luke. The first vicar was Revd J. Bradford Whiting, a well-known Evangelical.[16] His tenure extended over thirty years, ending only upon his retirement from the ministry in 1905. Bradford Whiting was said to have had an "inextinguishable zeal for education...on Evangelical lines", and as a member of the Committee of the South-Eastern Clerical Alliance, was one of those people responsible in 1879 for the founding by the Alliance of a school "with the object of affording a sound and useful education based upon the

---

[13] This "parish room...of red brick, in a simple Gothic style" was built by the previous incumbent, E. A. Eardley-Wilmot, at a cost of £1,000. See *The Rock* 9 December 1892, p. 1.

[14] The *Times* regularly recorded 'the persons of note' at the town's Grand Balls, and some of the first Victorian 'bathing machines' were used on its beaches. Princess Victoria (and later as Queen) visited Ramsgate many times between the ages of 4 and 23 and her last holiday in Ramsgate was in 1842. Victoria stayed at three different houses in Ramsgate: Townley House, Albion House, and West Cliff House. Albion House now contains the offices of Thanet District Council. See S. Margetson, *Leisure and Pleasure in the Nineteenth Century*, London 1971, pp. 84–8.

[15] New parishes in Ramsgate included St George's 1827, Holy Trinity 1845, Christ Church 1847 and St Luke's, 1875. The parish of St Luke (a village when Ramsgate was just a fishing hamlet, and now an area within Ramsgate town) was based on an ancient parish founded in 1275.

[16] See Appendix 1.

Protestant and Evangelical doctrines and principles of the Church of England."[17]

The South-Eastern College took its name from the organization which initiated it, and the site of the school was selected within the parish of St Luke,[18] "with express reference to the fact that the patronage of the said St Luke's Church, Ramsgate, was vested in the hands of Evangelical Trustees".[19] One Old Boy wrote that there was little doubt that the school owed its genesis to the "fertile brain and restless energy of Revd J. B. Whiting".[20] Whiting continued to be involved in the development of the school[21] until his death, when "An Old S. E. C. Master" wrote to *The Record*: "I have often said, "No J. B. W., no S. E. C.", that is, humanly speaking, St. Lawrence College, Ramsgate (as it is now called), would never have come into existence apart from Mr. Whiting. His interest in the college never flagged. He had many disappointments over it, yet his optimism never failed."[22] He became a shareholder of the newly incorporated college in 1892, but perhaps the best measure of his confidence in the school was the fact that he sent his son, J. M. Whiting, to the College from Lent Term, 1880 to Summer Term, 1886.[23] But Whiting was not the only member of the South-Eastern Clerical and Lay Alliance whose interest extended beyond the normal duties of membership. There were two other men who were particularly influential in the founding of the school. The first of these was the Dean of Canterbury, Robert Payne Smith. The second was the banker, John Deacon, who lived at Mabledon, near Tonbridge.

Dr Robert Payne Smith had been Regius Professor of Divinity at Oxford, 1865–71, before becoming Dean of Canterbury, 1871–95.[24] He took a great interest in education, so much so that it was once said

---

[17] *Memorandum and Articles of Association, The Corporation of the South-Eastern College,* St Lawrence College Archives, p. 13.

[18] Dumpton Park was proposed as an alternative site for the school, but this was in a parish that was not regarded as sufficiently Evangelical. See *Register of St Lawrence College 1879 to 1953,* 4th edn.

[19] *Memorandum and Articles of Association, The Corporation of the South-Eastern College,* pp. 13–4. The trustee of the advowson of St Luke's was Mr John Deacon, a member of the College Council (see below).

[20] "A Brief Historical Sketch of the College", by an Old Boy. In *Old Lawrentian Society Annual Report and List of Members 1929–30,* p. 4.

[21] He was chaplain to the Corporation which governed the school.

[22] *Record,* 28 August 1914, p. 836; part quoted in The *Lawrentian* 26, No 1 (Easter, 1915): 9.

[23] D. A. Scales, *Emile Cornet d'Auquier (1859–1894) Sketch of the First Headmaster's Life,* 1994, p. 17.

[24] See Appendix 1.

of him that "in future times the epithet *scholasticus* would be put after his name".[25] During the years 1855–57, he was Headmaster of the Kensington Proprietary School, from whence he returned to Oxford to take up the sub-librarianship of the Bodleian Library, a post he held until his appointment as Professor of Divinity. Later, he was *ex officio* Chairman of the King's School on the Canterbury Cathedral foundation, and was also Chairman of Faversham's Grammar School,[26] in which he "took an unusually keen interest". He was "instrumental" in founding the Simon Langton Schools in Canterbury, where through his influence a school for girls as well as for boys was founded. Among the other schools at Canterbury in which he was involved were the Clergy Orphan School,[27] the higher elementary Church schools,[28] and the Wesleyan School. Together with John Deacon, he was also connected with the founding of Wycliffe Hall at Oxford. However, South-Eastern College was his greatest educational endeavour. As one contemporary wrote in October 1884: "Everyone is aware that the Dean of Canterbury is associated with great educational movements, but we imagine that he has never furthered a scheme so large and so important as the one whose consummation was celebrated in this town last week. On Friday the Dean of Canterbury opened the new building of the South-Eastern College, a public school, founded five years ago by the South-Eastern Clerical Alliance."[29]

The Dean was the first President of South-Eastern College, where he was "an untiring and ever ready supporter". He acted also as Trustee, "his co-trustees being Revd. J. E. Campbell Colquhoun,[30] Mr C. J. Plumptre, Mr Deacon, and Mr G. C. Courthope.[31] It was said that the Dean's last public act was to attend a School Council meeting in London on Thursday, 28 March 1895. An obituary by the School Captain suggests that he gave to the school not only his energy and vision, but also his religious conviction, for "His heart and soul were

---

[25] R. Payne Smith, *Sermons on the Pentateuch*, p. 60.
[26] Queen Elizabeth Grammar School, Faversham. See Munden, *Education in Faversham*, pp. 40–2, 127.
[27] Now called St Edmund's School, Canterbury.
[28] A successor to the higher elementary Church schools is the elementary school on Broad Street, Canterbury, known as the Diocesan and Payne Smith Church of England School.
[29] *Kent Coast Times*, October 2 1884, part quoted in *SECM* 1 No 1 (December 1884): 2.
[30] Son of J. C. Colquhoun (see Appendix 1).
[31] *Register of St Lawrence College*, 3rd edn., vi. The Trustees were given the responsibility of holding in trust the school property, and were *ex officio* members of the School Council. *Constitution of the South-Eastern College*, point no. 3. St Lawrence College Archives.

for the furtherance of Evangelical principles, and it was because he recognised the vital importance of this being done among the young, that he gave us the support, the time, the interest, the advice, which have helped us forward so much."[32]

John Deacon (1825–1901)[33] became the second president of the Council of South-Eastern College. He was described as having "untiring zeal in the cause of Religious Education".[34] He was one of the original founders and a "great benefactor" of the South-Eastern College, and was associated with the founding of Dean Close School in Cheltenham in 1882, of which he was the first president. Like Dean Payne Smith, he saw the importance of founding not just schools, but also theological colleges of Evangelical conviction, so that together with the Dean of Canterbury and some other Evangelicals, he was involved in the building of Wycliffe Hall in Oxford. He is also recorded as one of the founders of Ridley Hall in Cambridge.[35] The South-Eastern College was, from the very first, "one of the great interests of his life. He watched over it, he rejoiced in its prosperity, and the whole School...bears eloquent witness to his devotion and munificence."[36] There is a direct connection between the location of the school in the parish of St Luke, and Deacon's "lively interest" in the school, for he was patron of the living of St Luke, and a large contributor towards the erection of the new parish church.

---

[32] [T. L. Kember], Obituary, *South-Eastern College Magazine* 6, 1 (August 1895): 17.

[33] See Appendix 1.

[34] *SECM* 12, 1 (April 1901): 8.

[35] Deacon initially gave £1,000 towards the erection of both colleges, and this was followed by "Many other large gifts, extending over a number of years." Bullock, *History of Ridley Hall* vol. 1, p. 107. Bullock was Vice-Principal of Ridley Hall 1931–36.

[36] *Register of St Lawrence College* 3rd edn, p. vii.

Robert Payne Smith (1819–1895)

John Deacon was from a very wealthy family[37] and lived in considerable style;[38] however, like his spiritual and business ancestors in the Clapham Sect,[39] he was keen to share his good fortune with others. The school magazine records that Deacon gave "thousands of pounds towards the cost of necessary buildings and land"[40] for the school. The Headmaster's speech to the school announcing his death in 1901 noted: "...of the large sum—more than £100,000—that has been spent in founding, developing and consolidating the School, he has contributed more than one-third."[41] When he died he was succeeded as President of the College Council by his son, Mr J. F. W. (Frank) Deacon (1859–1941), who by all accounts continued the family tradition of "sympathy, interest and munificence".[42] John Deacon's death was a great loss to the Evangelical cause, for he was not just president of two of its leading schools, but also treasurer, for much of his life, of the Church Missionary Society, the Church Pastoral Aid Society,[43] and the London Society for Promoting Christianity amongst the Jews (LSPCJ).[44] He is remembered today by the school's Deacon

---

[37] John Deacon's father, John Deacon snr (1780–1851) founded the London bank which was the source of the family's wealth.

[38] Edward Benson, Archbishop of Canterbury 1883–1896, stayed with the Deacons "in their beautiful home" after a confirmation service at Tunbridge Wells in May 1883, writing afterwards in his diary, "there is something in Evangelicalism...which is very concordant with wealth." A. C. Benson, *The Life of Edward White Benson*, vol. 2, London 1899, p. 12. The Deacon family seat, Mabledon Park near Tonbridge, was bequeathed to the CPAS in 1941 by John Deacon's son and heir, John F. W. Deacon, who was then President of the organization.

[39] For example, Samuel Thornton (1755–1838) became a Director of the Bank of England at the age of 25, and his brother, Henry Thornton (1760–1815), gave away sixth-sevenths of his considerable income, reducing this to one-third after his marriage. Both were members of what was later dubbed 'The Clapham Sect'. See E. M. Howse, *Saints in Politics*, London 1952.

[40] [J. Bradford Whiting], Obituary, *SECM* 12 No.1 (April 1901): 6–9.

[41] Reprinted in *SECM* 12 No. 1 (April 1901): 9–10. The splendour of the school buildings attest to the expenditure of what was an enormous sum in those days.

[42] *Register of St Lawrence College* 3rd edn, p. vii.

[43] Treasurer 1863–1901, also a Trustee and Life Member of CPAS. He was succeeded as Treasurer of CPAS by his son, J. F. W. Deacon.

[44] Founded in 1808, the LSPCJ organized lectures and schools for London Jewry and established its own church in Palestine Place in 1814. After 1815, the Society was re-established as a solely Anglican foundation, and it was influential in helping to establish the new bishopric of Jerusalem. See W. T. Gidney, *The History of the London Society for Promoting Christianity Amongst the Jews, From 1809 to 1908*, London 1908; and R. Turnbull, "The Emergence of the Protestant Evangelical Tradition", *Churchman* 107, 4 (1993): 345–7.

Memorial Tower, which was opened by the Archbishop of Canterbury in 1905.

The first printed mention of the South-Eastern College was an advertisement in *The Record* on 28 July 1879, inviting applications for the Headmastership of a Middle-Class School in Ramsgate.

> MIDDLE-CLASS SCHOOL, RAMSGATE
> On the principles of the Reformation.
> THE COMMITTEE of the South-Eastern Clerical and Lay Church Alliance - President, the Dean of Canterbury - are prepared to receive applications from Graduates for the HEAD MASTERSHIP of a School about to be opened immediately. An Income of 300*l.* per annum with residence will be guaranteed. Applications to be sent in, on or before August 15, 1859 [*sic*], to Revd. J. E. Campbell-Colquhoun, Chartwell, Westerham, from whom, or from Revd. J. B. Whiting, or Revd. J. E. Brenan,[45] of Ramsgate, further information can be obtained.[46]

Applications for the position were said to be very numerous. Thirty-three candidates were selected as being of special excellence[47] and of those, the unanimous choice of the Council fell on Emile Cornet d'Auquier (1850–1894), a 28-year old Frenchman whose father had been a minister of the Protestant Church in La Bouverie, France.[48] D'Auquier was a firm Evangelical, although his family had converted from Roman Catholicism only in the previous generation. He came to England when he was about 16, in 1866 or 1867, eventually ending up at Ellerslie School in Manchester, where he was French Master until 1876. In that year d'Auquier went up to Cambridge to study Theology, where he was admitted to Clare College on 7 October 1876, graduating with a Bachelor of Arts (Hons) in June 1879, having taken a second class in the special examination in Theology.

D'Auquier was by this time engaged to Alice Maud Cope, who was the daughter of Richard Cope, a Manchester merchant. Soon after he had been appointed Headmaster of the South-Eastern Middle-Class

---

[45] James Eustace Brenan was Vicar of Christchurch, Ramsgate 1873–92. He was Secretary of the London Society for Promoting Christianity among the Jews 1869–73 and later, Vicar of Emmanuel, Clifton and Canon of Gloucester Cathedral. He died in 1901. See Gidney, *History of LSPCJ*, pp. 583–4.

[46] *Record,* 28 July 1879, p. 1.

[47] Extract from "An appreciation of the first Headmaster upon his resignation, 1889." Reprinted in *The Lawrentian* centenary edition, 1979, p. 16.

[48] Much of the biographical information here on Emile Cornet d'Auquier is based on research conducted by Derek Scales, Director of Studies at St Lawrence College. See Scales, *Emile Cornet d'Auquier*, pp. 2–4.

School, Ramsgate (as it was then known), he applied to become a naturalised British citizen, and this was granted on 7 October 1879. He married Alice Maud Cope in Manchester the next day. Like most schoolmasters (and especially headmasters) of the period, he also sought to be ordained. He underwent a preliminary examination in 9 January 1880. As a result of this, he "was warned that it was very doubtful whether he could pass the examination".[49] In the final examination for deacons he achieved a better standard, although his sermon was described as "confused".[50] He passed, and was made deacon by the Archbishop of Canterbury, A. C. Tait, on 22 February 1880. Five years later he sought, with J. B. Whiting's help, to be priested. Whiting wrote to Archbishop E. W. Benson on 15 August 1885, presenting d'Auquier as a special case: "Mr d'Auquier has been partly influenced by a high sense of the functions required of a Priest...He now feels withal that the Pastoral Charge of 200 boys requires his taking Priest's orders."[51] The Archbishop refused his request and, unusually for the time, Emile Cornet d'Auquier never proceeded to full orders.[52]

The first site for the College was a rented house[53] in the middle of the new housing estate of Dane Park being developed north-east of St Luke's church. Dane Park House,[54] as it came to be called, was later to become the Junior School[55] and the 1881 census referred to the College as Dane Park School.[56] For a short while d'Auquier was in an unusual position, for "There was a short interval between the formal opening of the College and the arrival of our first *two* boarders, during which interval I stood in the anomalous position of being Head Master without any pupils."[57] These first two pupils duly arrived on 27

---

[49] Tait Papers 396, ff. 229. Lambeth Palace Library.

[50] Ibid., p. 230.

[51] E. W. Benson Papers 21, ff 64. Lambeth Palace Library.

[52] Fourteen years later, Archbishop F. W. Temple agreed to ordain Masters of the school "if the Master when ordained will have to give religious instruction in the School". Draft letter to Revd J. B. Whiting from Archbishop F. W. Temple, 6 March 1899. F. Temple Papers 27ff 1. Lambeth Palace Library.

[53] The house was in the parish of St Luke.

[54] The house had been built the previous year. It is now demolished, but is thought to have been originally located on what is now known as Cecilia Road. Scales, *Emile Cornet d'Auquier* , p. 20, n 37.

[55] Privately owned by d'Auquier until October 1890, when it was sold to four members of the College Council, who then sold it on to the Council in January 1896.

[56] Public Record Office RG 11/990, 21. Cited by Scales, *Emile Cornet d'Auquier*, p. 20, fn. 37.

[57] *SECM* 1, 9 (December 1887): 267.

October 1879. Their names were H. Kitto[58] and W. W. M. Kitto, and their father later became the Vicar of St Martin-in-the-Fields, London.[59] Three other pupils joined the college that term, one of whom, J. M. Bradley, was d'Auquier's nephew.[60] d'Auquier was the sole member of staff at this time.

Although the College had been open for only three months and at this stage had only nine pupils, the Local College Committee decided that they felt "very strongly that it [was] necessary that some special effort be made to provide Permanent Buildings for the College."[61] In 1880 the Council acquired the right to purchase sixteen acres of land in St Luke's Parish, and the first site and ground plan[62] was drawn up in December 1880 by the Local Committee.[63] A rough plan for the school building was made by d'Auquier in March 1881,[64] but it would be another three years before the first brick was laid. Further land was purchased in the same year, in order to provide proper playing-fields and to "protect" the College,[65] so that the estate then owned by the School covered 160 acres of adjoining open country.

The number of boys at the school steadily rose, so that within two years of opening, there were 56 pupils.[66] At this stage the school was

---

[58] Harold Kitto returned to the school to teach Classics in 1893 and he was Assistant Master 1899–1908. See the 1899 Prospectus for South-Eastern College in the F. Temple papers, vol. 27 p. 3, Lambeth Palace Library. Kitto later became Headmaster of Faversham's Grammar School (see above, p. 261).

[59] Scales, *Emile Cornet d'Auquier*, p. 5. See *SECM* 2, 2 (August 1889): 46; 5, 2 (July 1894): 56; *The Lawrentian* 37, 1 (Easter 1926): 10. The Kitto brothers were at the College from Michaelmas 1879 to Michaelmas 1881, after which they went to Marlborough. It was not unusual in the early days of the school for parents to use the College as a preparatory school. For example, Revd A. J. Tait, Principal of Ridley Hall Cambridge 1908–27, was a pupil at South-Eastern College before going on to Merchant Taylors' School. A similar practice occurred at Monkton Combe School.

[60] His brother, R. W. Bradley, joined the College in 1880. The Bradley family was to be dogged by tragedy: both parents died while the boys were at school (the father in 1880, and the mother in 1884), and on 3 August 1887, J. M. Bradley was killed in a fall in Switzerland while holidaying there with the d'Auquier family. The younger brother was also killed at the age of 35 in the Jamaican earthquake of 1907. D. A. Scales, *Emile Cornet d'Auquier*, p. 20.

[61] Local Committee Minutes (hereafter 'LCM'), January 31, 1880.

[62] To the north west of St Luke's church and south of a lane which is now called College Road.

[63] LCM, December 18, 1880.

[64] LCM, March 19 and 26, 1881.

[65] Because of the encroachment of housing sub-developments which continued in the surrounding district at a rapid pace.

[66] *Register of St Lawrence College* 3rd edn, vii. St Lawrence College Archives

described by one old boy as "a motley collection of villas, bungalows, cottages and 'tin' buildings."[67] The bungalows were local houses[68] rented by the school and the 'tin' buildings were various temporary structures made of corrugated iron which, it was hoped, could be removed to the new site where permanent buildings were being erected.[69] The playing fields were also of a provisional nature, described by the same writer as, "two mudheaps on a slope, very nice for leg-break bowling, but not for being brought down at Rugger".[70] By Christmas 1883, the number of pupils had reached over 100[71] and by 1844, the staff consisted of twelve masters.[72] By this time sufficient capital had been raised[73] for work to start on the permanent school buildings.

---

[67] "A Brief Historical Sketch of the College" in *Old Lawrentian Society Annual Report*, p. 4.

[68] At one time there were as many as six rented houses, the largest of which were known as 'Danecot' and 'Cotswold'. See *The Lawrentian* 37, 1 (Easter 1926): 10. Another was called "Sunnyside".

[69] These temporary structures did not come cheaply: the corrugated iron school room cost £117, which was the equivalent of a term's tuition fees for twenty boys. LCM, 19 March 1881; cf. LCM, 9 April 1881.

[70] "A Brief Historical Sketch of the College", p. 4.

[71] The "List of Students" in the College archives gives the number of pupils in the Michaelmas Term of 1883 as 101, rising to 103 for the Lent Term of 1884.

[72] *Kent Coast Times*, 2 October 1884, quoted by *SECM* 1 no.1 (Dec. 1884): 3.

[73] This was helped in no small way by the Headmaster's willingness to pay for, out of his own pocket, new staff, and even the rent of new playing grounds, until the Council could afford to do the same.

South-Eastern College, 1884

On 17 March 1884, the first bricks were laid[74] of a very impressive new building which was to become the nucleus of the new school site. It was six storeys high and cost more than £10,000. What was later to form the East Wing of the completed building, was finished by September of the same year, in time for the return of 112[75] boys from their summer holidays. The new building was officially opened by the President of the College, the Dean of Canterbury, on Friday 26 September. At a dinner afterwards hosted by the Headmaster and his wife, the Vicar of St Luke's, Revd J. B. Whiting, spoke[76] of the events leading up to the opening of the new building, especially the work of the South-Eastern Clerical and Lay Alliance in founding a school, "which had prospered so well, and which he trusted would result in the sending forth into the world highly-educated men, imbued from their early years with the pure truth of the Gospel, and the sound doctrines of the Reformation."[77] Clearly the founders had not lost sight of the Evangelical motivation for such a foundation.

---

[74] Brick Day, March 17, was observed as a school holiday. A foundation stone was never laid.
[75] "List of Students", St Lawrence College Archives.
[76] There were no less than sixteen speeches and replies issuing in toasts over the course of the evening.
[77] *Kent Coast Times*, 2 October 1884, cited by *SECM* 1, 1 (December, 1884): 5.

September 1884 was a busy month for the Headmaster of South-Eastern College, not just because of the opening of the new college building. For recently d'Auquier had "found a fresh sphere for enterprise and activity",[78] and at his own expense had decided to "take on Dane Park House", which the College had just vacated, and "furnish it for a Junior School".[79] In this month the South-Eastern College Junior School opened as a private school, with Mr R. E. Fiske[80]—who had joined the College staff in 1881—as its Headmaster. Within a year the junior school buildings were completely full,[81] and d'Auquier purchased a piece of land adjacent to the College, upon which in November 1885 he began building a swimming bath, cottages for the masters, and a new building for the junior school.[82] The Junior School moved into its new home a year later in September 1886.[83] Although some on the Council must have been alarmed by the irregularity of this approach to founding a new junior school (and probably saw the potential problems that private ownership of such an integral part of the College's pupil intake could present), the Junior School pupils would later reflect on the wisdom of such a decision: "But for the energy and farsighted policy of Mr d'Auquier, the Junior School would probably not have been built for some years, and we feel that many Old Juniors will be grateful to him for what has been accomplished."[84] The Vicar of St Luke's was also a great supporter of the project, and was willing to have his name attached to the venture in the following advertisement which appeared in *The Rock* on 19 March 1886 and also in the *Church of England Yearbook* for 1887:

---

[78] *SECM* 2, 2 (August 1889): 47.
[79] *The Lawrentian* 37, 1 (Easter 1926): 10.
[80] Robert Elwyn Fiske (1858–1938) was educated at Marlborough College and Keble College, Oxford, where he gained Fourth Class Honours in Jurisprudence in 1881.
[81] The school magazine lists 31 pupils in the Junior School for the Michaelmas Term of 1885. *SECM* 1, 1 (November 1885): 115.
[82] At the same time, he launched into the building of the College tuck-shop, workshop, gymnasium, chapel and chapel organ... "in fact, all the appliances which render this College one of the most complete of any in England." SECM 2, 2 (August 1889): 47.
[83] *SECM* 1, 1 (December 1884): 28; 1, 3 (June 1985): 90; 1, 4 (November 1885):115; 1, 5 (April 1886): 139; 1, 6 (July 1886): 169; 1, 7 (December 1886): 190–191, 207; and *The Lawrentian* 27, 1 (Easter 1926):10.
[84] *The Lawrentian* 37, 1 (Easter 1926): 10.

SOUTH-EASTERN COLLEGE JUNIOR SCHOOL,
Under the immediate supervision of
Revd. E. D'Auquier and Revd. J. B. Whiting.
INCLUSIVE TERMS, 50 GUINEAS.
Head Master—R. E. FISKE, M.A., Oxon.[85]

Revd Ernest Boys, whose two sons were pupils at South-Eastern College, wrote a feature article in 1885 edition of the *Churchman's Penny Magazine* of which he was editor. It was (as one would expect of a parent) fulsome in its praise of the school, pointing out that although the school was "worked upon the lines of the best public schools", the "objectionable features of public schools—fagging and bullying—are quite unknown." He was also at pains to point out that the religious teaching in the school "is all that can be wished":

> It is distinctly Evangelical, and the boys attend the ministry of Revd. John B. Whiting, at St Luke's Church. Mr. Whiting and his curate also give religious instruction in the school. There is a daily Bible-lesson given to all the boys. Family prayer is conducted by the headmaster every morning in the dining-room, with the servants present, so bringing out, as far as possible, the idea of *home*. Every evening a short service is held in the chapel just before bed-time. The private *personal* religion of the boys is also assisted as far as man can do it. Every boy is expected to spend a short time in Bible-reading and prayer, morning and evening, in the bedrooms, while rigid silence is maintained. And the effect of this on the boys, as far as one could judge of it, is eminently good.[86]

The Headmaster also acted as an honorary curate for J. B. Whiting, and he "was energetically involved in a large number of parochial activities, especially in relieving the poor of the parish".[87] Until the temporary chapel[88] was erected in 1884, the boys used to attend morning service in St Luke's Church. On Sundays the uniform

---

[85] *Rock*, 19 March 1886, p. 1; *Church of England Year Book 1887*, p. 722.
[86] E. Boys, "South-Eastern College, Ramsgate", *Churchman's Penny Magazine* 1885, p. 59.
[87] Scales, *Emile Cornet d'Auquier*, p. 8. He was also a director of the 'Coffee Tavern Company' in Ramsgate. *SECM* 2, 2 (August 1889): 47–48; cf. *The Thanet Advertiser*, 19 May 1894, p. 8.
[88] It continued to be used for this purpose until the present chapel was built in 1927. This had been the corrugated iron dining room on the Dane Park site, and was known by a variety of names—'The Tin Church', 'The Iron Church' and 'The Tin Tabernacle'. The last title was the most popular.

consisted of top hats and black "tails" for the Senior School, while the Junior School boys wore top hats and Eton collars.

On Friday 19 March 1886, *The Rock* newspaper published an article on South-Eastern College by the College President, the Dean of Canterbury. In it, he alluded to previous articles he had written about the school which had been founded by the 'South-Eastern Lay and Clerical Alliance' [*sic*] "...for the purpose of giving, at a moderate cost, a first-class education on distinctly Evangelical principles, in accordance with the Thirty-nine articles, which the founders regard as the expression of the mind of the Church of England—not only against the corruptions of the Church of Rome, but also against mediæval superstitions."[89] He went on to appeal for the funds necessary—£10,000—to complete the school buildings. The Dean declared that the school "has liabilities amounting in all to 19,000*l*." and concluded with the following words: "Let this [debt] be wiped off, and the school will become, with God's blessing, a great instrument of hearty work for Christ."[90] Clearly the College Council, and its president in particular, were feeling the financial pressure.

A few weeks later an anonymous author wrote a lengthy article on the same subject, but this time giving "a more detailed account of this Institution".[91] Once again, an appeal was made to Evangelical sympathies: "We consider that it is one of the most important works ever undertaken by the Evangelical party, and destined to have a permanent influence on the thought and religious spirit of the rising generation. The work of training the young, so as to make them have an intelligent appreciation and love of those Evangelical principles which are dear to us, is one the importance of which cannot be overestimated." The following had been written in the school magazine in the previous year: "...we hope that the Trustees will soon see their way to putting up the second and third wings, and so complete the buildings as originally planned."[92] It would take the death in July 1894 of Canon Hoare of Tunbridge Wells—a previous Vicar of Christ Church, Ramsgate, and a well-known Evangelical—and the dedication of the proposed new wing of the College to his memory, to cause a major influx of donations. The Canon Hoare Memorial Wing was opened two years later, in 1896. The boys and staff would have to 'make do' for

---

[89] *Rock*, 19 March 1886, p. 3.
[90] Ibid.
[91] Much of it repeated the *Penny Magazine* article by Revd E. Boys. It is possible that he was the author of this article as well as the one in his own magazine.
[92] *SECM* 1, 4 (November 1885): 115.

Edward Hoare (1812–1894)

some time with a half-finished accommodation building and 'tin sheds' for classrooms, the dining room, and the chapel.

To ensure the Evangelical conviction of its teachers, the College Council drafted a declaration that all staff were required to sign. It is not clear when or even whether it was used, for the archives contain only a draft version, with hand-written changes. Whatever the case, its wording gives a very telling picture of the expectations of the school management towards the religious convictions of all those in school's employ:

> I..............................do hereby declare that I am in full Communion with the Church of England, and that I bona fide and cordially hold Evangelical Principles and by these I signify the Principles and Tenets of the Protestant Faith based upon Holy Scriptures and embodied in the Thirty-nine Articles and Formularies of that Church as settled at the Reformation.
>
> ....
> ....18.......[93]

South-Eastern College enrolments peaked in the Easter term of 1888, when 190 pupils were in the College and 58 pupils in the Junior School: making a total of 248.[94] This was the year of the Seventeenth Annual Meeting of the Clerical and Lay Church Alliance. At this meeting, the Headmaster reported to the Alliance that the high number of pupils was greatly in excess "of the accommodation at our disposal", and the extra pupils were being housed in masters' and servants' quarters. He was anxious to impress upon the meeting that the religious life of the College continued to be the same, with the first half hour of every day's work devoted to the study of religion. "Mr Whiting continues, as before, to take a class, and his spiritual help is much valued by the boys and by myself. The rule about boys reading their Bible and saying their prayers morning and evening is strictly adhered to. About 150 are members of Scripture Union.[95] The daily evening services in the Chapel continue, with the addition of a new

---

[93] St Lawrence College Archives.
[94] "List of Students", St Lawrence College Archives.
[95] At the annual meeting of the South-Eastern Clerical and Lay Alliance in 1886, the Headmaster "alluded to one little incident which showed that the boys, after leaving, did not forget the teaching they had received." For, like the Scripture Union meetings at school, some of the old boys who had gone up to Cambridge, "had formed themselves into a kind of society, which met once a week for prayer and mutual help and edification." *Rock,* 8 October 1886, p. 7.

feature by the introduction of short weekly addresses on the Wednesday evenings."[96]

A year later, when d'Auquier gave notice of his resignation, the numbers had dropped to 161 College and 41 Junior School pupils: a total of 202. Following his departure in the Michaelmas term of 1889, a worrying total[97] of 102 was recorded. Revd E. H. Askwith[98] was appointed as his replacement; however, within two years of his tenure, numbers had dropped to a new low of fifty-nine.[99] Askwith was followed by Revd F. W. Tracy,[100] who was appointed the school's third Headmaster in 1892, and it was under his able leadership that the school began to make a slow recovery. The South-Eastern Clerical and Lay Association continued to administer the estate and to have control of the School until 1892, when the school was incorporated as a Public School Foundation under the "Corporation of the South-Eastern College." Mr Tracy's first step was to arrange for this incorporation, and for the recognition of the College as a Public School. This was followed by the re-organization of the form-system on "the usual Public School plan",[101] and the division of the School into four Houses. He was also responsible for the building of the Canon Hoare Memorial Wing, the new permanent chemical laboratory, and for the purchase of a further sixty acres of land. Under his leadership, pupil numbers rose to 160 in the Upper School.[102] In 1899 Tracy resigned and Mr C. Morris was appointed Headmaster, a position he held for seven years.

The new century was a difficult one for small public schools like South-Eastern College, and in May 1903 a Conference of Representatives of all the Evangelical public schools was held at Lord Wimborne's house in London, "when the question of amalgamation or

---

[96] *Seventeenth Annual Report of the South-Eastern Clerical and Lay Church Alliance...* 1889, St Lawrence College Archives, p. 38.

[97] This included the boys at the Junior School, which the College now owned.

[98] Revd Edward Harrison Askwith (1864–1946) was Assistant Master of Westmorland School before being appointed Headmaster of South-Eastern College 1890–92. He later went on to become Chaplain of Trinity College Cambridge 1894–1909, Vicar of Kirkby Lonsdale with Lupton 1909–17 and Rector of Dickleburgh 1917–24. He wrote a number of books on theology and mathematics and was admitted a Cambridge DD in 1902.

[99] Forty-three of whom had given notice to leave at the end of the next term! Holmes, *The Lawrentian* centenary edition, p. 18.

[100] Before taking up his appointment at Ramsgate, Francis William Tracey was Assistant Master of King William's College on the Isle of Man 1880–4 and Headmaster of King Edward VI School, Totnes 1887–91.

[101] *Register of St Lawrence College* 4th edn, vii.

[102] "A Short History of Our Times", *SECM* 10, 1 (March 1899): 12.

federation was discussed".[103] In November 1903, the governors of South-Eastern College were approached by the directors of the Church of England Evangelical College and School Company[104]—who owned Trent College and Weymouth College and the freehold to Monkton Combe School—with a view to amalgamation.[105] At a meeting of College Council in the next month, this was considered to "present too much difficulty". In 1906 the name of the School was changed to "St Lawrence College", this name being taken from the parish of St Lawrence, in which the greater portion of the College estate was located. The final rumblings of union with another school of Evangelical foundation were recorded thirty years later in the Council Minutes of 26 May 1939. Here it was suggested that St Lawrence College might consider amalgamation with Monkton Combe School, which was having serious financial problems. A delegation went to Monkton Combe in June, which later reported back to the Committee, but it was decided not to proceed.[106] What had been founded as a local public school for the south-east of England, remains one to this day. The school's religious heritage has also been maintained, for many current members of the school staff and Council would be happy to call themselves Evangelical.

It can be seen from the development of South-Eastern College in 1879 to St Lawrence College Ramsgate in 1906, that over a period of twenty-seven years, a local Evangelical foundation was transformed into a middle-class public school and thus entered the twentieth century as a modified educational enterprise. It was the first of two Evangelical schools to be founded through corporate, as opposed to individual, effort; the other 'corporate' school being Dean Close School. Founded in 1882, it is the subject of the next chapter.

---

[103] Council Minute Book 1, 3 December 1903. St Lawrence College Archives
[104] See ch. 10 below.
[105] Executive Committee Minute Book 2, 19 November 1903, St Lawrence College Archives.
[106] Executive Committee Minute Book [9: 1939–1949], 26 May 1939, St Lawrence College Archives.

CHAPTER 9

The Western District Clerical and Lay Association and Dean Close Memorial School

Founded in 1858 in Gloucester as part of a "more comprehensive plan for a general organized association",[1] the 'Western District' was the first Church of England Clerical and Lay Association for the Maintenance of Evangelical Principles.[2] By 1860 it had 320 members.[3] The objects of the Association were:

> first and principally, for general conference with a view to mutual recognition, counsel and communion, at stated periods. Next... to afford opportunities for general consultation on all questions affecting the interests of Religion and of the Established Church; and lastly, to establish and maintain such an organization as may tend, as far as possible, to promote unity in action in every case, wherein such action may seem desirable.[4]

The first meeting recorded in the Association's Minute Book took place on 23 March 1858. The Chairman was Revd Alan Gardner Cornwall (1798–1872), Rector of Newington Bagpath cum Owlpen 1827–71, and Beverstone cum Kingscote 1839–71.[5] Although

---

[1] 'Presbyter', *Church of England Clerical and Lay Association: A letter to a Clergyman of the Church of England*, London 1860, title page. Private possession.
[2] "Standing Rules of the Church of England Clerical and Lay Association..." pasted into the first Minute Book of the Church of England Clerical and Lay Association (hereafter known as the 'General Committee Minute Book'). These Rules were revised at a special meeting on 10 October 1871. See *Report of the Twentieth Annual Conference of the Church of England Clerical and Lay Association Held at Cheltenham, June 5th and 6th, 1877*, Stroud 1877, iii.
[3] Wellings, "Aspects of Late Nineteenth-Century Evangelicalism", p. 178.
[4] Rule 1, Objects of the Association, *Report of the Third Annual Conference of the Church of England Clerical and Lay Association (Western District) held at the Victoria Rooms, Clifton, June 5th and 6th, 1860*. London 1860, p. 6.
[5] These were adjoining rural parishes in the southern Cotswolds a few miles north of Wotton-under-Edge, with a combined annual income of £1,070. His rectory was listed in Crockford's as 'Ashcroft House, Wotton-under-Edge'. Cornwall

Cornwall claimed the idea of the Association as his own, another clergyman present at the first meeting also claimed the title of founder: this was Revd Daniel Capper, Rector of Huntley, near Gloucester, 1839–65.[6] In due course Capper was elected the Honorary Secretary of the Association, a position he shared with Revd John Emeris, Perpetual Curate of St. James', Gloucester 1848–72. By 1860 the Association's General Committee consisted of thirty elected members[7] and they were holding quarterly meetings in rotation at Bristol, Cheltenham, Gloucester and Stroud.

This first committee meeting divided the Association into thirteen districts: Gloucester, Bristol, Cheltenham, Stroud, Wotton-under-Edge, Fairford, Swindon, Chippenham, Wickwar, Newnham, Newland, Stow-on-the-Wold, and Tewkesbury. Each district was linked to the central committee by 'corresponding members', whose duties were "to correspond with the Secretaries"[8] of the Association, and "confer with members resident in their several districts, and to report what subjects they would suggest, and recommend, for investigation during the ensuing year".[9] The plan was to organize annual general meetings or conferences at which members from the different districts could discuss issues of local and personal concern, as well as organize common responses to matters at a national Anglican level. It was also an opportunity for fellowship and mutual support. The Association meetings were to be modelled on those of existing Evangelical clerical societies and conferences[10] and the Islington Clerical Meeting.[11] The following recommendations were included in the minutes of the first meeting as instructions to corresponding members: "These conferences should meet after the manner of Clerical Meetings with Prayer and Reading of the Scriptures and discussion of the Subjects selected for the Consideration of the Association at large and that minutes of each

---

was Rural Dean 1839–66 and secretary of the Tyndale Memorial, a commemorative stone tower erected at Nibley Knowle in the Vale of Berkeley. His *Times* obituary described him as "one of the leaders of the Evangelical party in the diocese".

[6] Daniel Capper (1805–1886) was a Rural Dean 1839–66 and rebuilt Huntley parish church at his own cost in 1863. Kent, "Anglican Evangelicalism in the West of England", p. 180.

[7] Articles of Association, Church of England Clerical and Lay Association, p. 1.

[8] General Committee Minute Book, p. 2.

[9] Ibid.

[10] See above, ch. 7.

[11] See above, p. 37.

meeting be kept."[12] Regrettably, only the minutes of the first Clerical and Lay Association have survived.[13]

The first annual general meeting of the Western District Clerical and Lay Association was held at Christ Church School Room, the Spa, Gloucester, on 8 and 9 June 1858. Sixty-eight members dined at the King's Head Hotel on 8 June, and twenty-one members attended the 8.00 a.m. Holy Communion service at Christ Church on 9 June.[14] The conference discussed four topics which had been chosen by the standing committee[15] two months before from a list of forty-one. They were, first, the issue of "Unity of Action", or how they were to form themselves into a single coherent voice. Secondly, they discussed the issue of how they could support "Christian Missions". Thirdly, the following questions were debated: "Has the Church of England in this diocese[16] that influence among the masses of the population which as an Established Church it ought to have? If not, how is it to be accounted for, and what remedies may be applied?" Finally, discussion centred around "The duty and the importance of Unity and Individuality, of Diversity and Uniformity—separately and relatively considered—in relation to the maintenance of Evangelical principles."[17] This question of Evangelical unity, and how best it could be achieved, had become a favourite item for Evangelical debate.

All Association members were encouraged to unite in a general observance of 17 November 1858[18] as a commemoration of the tercentenary of the Reformation in England. An anonymous pamphleteer used the threat of Ritualism and 'Neologianism'[19] to encourage membership of existing—and the formation of more—Clerical and Lay Associations:

---

[12] General Committee Minute Book, p. 3.
[13] These are now in private ownership. The Minute Book last belonged to T. W. Boyce, Curate of St Werburgh's, Bristol, and the local secretary for the Association's Bristol branch. The last recorded meeting of the Association was the Annual General Meeting of 10 June 1903.
[14] Kent, "Anglican Evangelicalism in the West of England", p. 181.
[15] This comprised the president, the secretaries to the Association, the secretaries to the General Committee, and the treasurer. General Committee Minute Book, p. 3.
[16] The Diocese of Gloucester and Bristol.
[17] The second meeting of the Association, held on 27 April 1858 at Davis's Library in Gloucester. General Committee Minute Book, pp. 9–10.
[18] The anniversary of the death of Queen Mary I and the accession of Queen Elizabeth I.
[19] A name coined by Evangelicals for 'Broad Church liberalism'. Stock reports that "between 1864–5, [an Evangelical] alliance against Neology was formed". Stock, *History of the CMS*, vol. 2, p. 346.

> Now that the Church of England seems called upon to choose, whether she will give her allegiance to Christ, or to Anti-Christ either as Roman or Neologian or a compromise of both—now that hundreds have actually passed away to Rome, and also so considerable a number of the younger Clergy are more or less under the seductive influence of her errors so as to render it difficult to meet with like-minded men as fellow-helpers,—now that the State, hitherto bound up with the Church, apparently either contemplates casting her adrift or reducing her to a condemnation of political servitude,—under these, our present exigencies, the desire for union becomes more intense and irresistible. We want to know each other's thoughts and feelings. We are in great need of mutual information and counsel. We thirst for sympathy and encouragement. We want to act together as one man.[20]

By the time of the annual meeting in 1859, the printed membership of the Western District included fourteen corresponding branches with a total of 234 members. According to John Kent,[21] in the following year, when Bath became part of the Association with 28 members, the total membership of the Western District reached 318, to which 42 additional members described as 'residing at a distance' could be added.[22] By 1865, membership had increased to 383, with another 91 'residing at a distance'. Membership numbers were maintained for the next fifteen years. However, in the 1880s, they began to decline so that by 1887, the numbers had fallen to 228. This decline continued, and by 1901, membership was just 197. It has been suggested that the beginning of the decline in membership numbers in the 1880s coincided with a period of general "dissatisfaction about the inability of Anglican Evangelicals to combine effectively at the national level".[23] This was despite the formation of a 'Central Union of Clerical and Lay Associations' in January 1881.[24] Clearly "organization was no substitute for deeper unity",[25] and the fact that this initiative was being directed from London perhaps explains why a regionally-centred association, such as the Western District, declined to join the new Union; although it was happy to work with the Union in the founding of a new middle-class school at Cheltenham.

---

[20] 'Presbyter', *Church of England Clerical and Lay Association*, pp. 6–7.
[21] Kent, "Anglican Evangelicalism in the West of England", pp. 183–4.
[22] Although the first annual report lists the total members present at the meeting as 170, and the total number of members as: Western District, 320 and Midland District, 105 (making a grand total of 425).
[23] Kent, "Anglican Evangelicalism in the West of England", p. 184.
[24] See above, p. 246.
[25] Kent, ibid.

Despite the interest of other branches of the Clerical and Lay Associations in education,[26] nearly a quarter of a century would pass before the issue of middle-class schools became a topic for discussion at one of the Western District's annual conferences. The matter had been raised regularly in the Evangelical newspapers, but just when some momentum was being gained on the topic, the *Endowed Schools Act* of 1869[27] deterred Church involvement in middle-class education for at least another ten years. Eventually, in 1882, the list of 30 "Subjects for Selection Preparatory to the Annual Conference at Clifton" included the following as subject 17: "The Duty of Evangelical Churchmen in reference to the Educational movements of the time—especially middle-class schools."[28] The first mention of schools in the Association's Minute Book was made in June 1882, when a letter was read at a General Committee meeting from Revd J. P. Jose[29] "calling attention to the proposed Sub-Committee on Middle-Class Education and suggesting the name of Revd T. H. Clark[30] for Secretary".[31] The Committee agreed to thank Mr Jose for his communication and to "act upon it".[32] The next time they met, it was to receive a report from the Sub-Committee on Middle-Class Education.

Evangelicals had expressed concern on this issue since letters began appearing in *The Record* in January that year.[33] In May 1882, the Dean of Canterbury, Robert Payne Smith, led a discussion on the topic at a meeting of the Central Committee of the Union of Clerical and Lay Associations in London. A paper on the Woodard schools was circulated at this meeting,[34] and 'middle-class education' began to appear on the meeting agendas of Clerical and Lay Associations around the country. For example, the first subject for discussion at the Northern Home Counties District Clerical and Lay Association's annual meeting for 1882 was "The Duty of Evangelical Churchmen in reference to the Educational movements of the times."[35] Canon

---

[26] See chs 7 and 8 above.
[27] See above, pp. 86–7.
[28] Pasted into the Church of England Clerical and Lay Association General Committee Minute Book.
[29] Stephen Prust Jose was Vicar of Churchill, Bristol.
[30] Thomas Humphris Clark was Warden of St Lucy's Home, Gloucester 1869–91 at the time. Later he became Rector of Chilfrome, Dorset 1891–93 and Vicar of Heybridge, Essex 1894–1906.
[31] General Committee Minute Book.
[32] Ibid.
[33] See above, pp. 241–43.
[34] See above, pp. 245–46.
[35] *Supplement to The Record*, 28 April 1882, p. 141.

Robinson's *Churchman* article of September 1882 also articulated the same opinion when he urged the setting up of a central fund for the purpose of founding Evangelical Schools. As shown above, schools of this type had already been started in Weymouth, Long Eaton, Monkton Combe and Ramsgate. The fast-growing middle-class suburb of Clifton, high above Bristol's river valley, seemed the perfect place for such an Evangelical venture, for Clifton College, which had opened in 1862, was largely a High Church foundation.[36]

On 2 November 1882 the cumbersomely titled Clerical and Lay Association (Western District) Middle-Class Schools Committee met in Clifton to launch an appeal for an Evangelical day and boarding school.[37] The committee was chaired by Reverend Talbot Greaves, who in 1881 had moved from the parish of Melcombe Regis to Christ Church, Clifton. Both were under the patronage of the Simeon Trust, and Greaves was well-known in Evangelical circles for his leadership of the Weymouth branch of the Church Association. Talbot Greaves was also one of the founders of Weymouth College in Dorset.[38] The Schools Committee met at the house of another local clergyman, Thomas Henry Clark, who was appointed Honorary Secretary.[39] The names of 20 men (11 clergy and 9 laity) who were "willing to act" were listed under the headings of Bath, Bristol, Cheltenham and 'Somerset'. Reference was then made to the "report on Middle-Class Schools recently presented at the Diocesan Conference, and to existing schools in Bristol".[40] The minutes record that "It was considered however that there was room for such a school as that proposed."[41] The following recommendations were agreed to:

---

[36] See ch. 2 above.

[37] Minute Book of the Clerical and Lay Association (Western District) Middle-Class Schools Committee. Dean Close School Archives. The same minute book was used to record minutes of the various other committees that sprang from this original committee. They include the Schools Committee, (also known as the Local Committee and the Cheltenham Local Committee), a 'Preparatory Meeting', the Executive Committee, the various sub-committees of the Executive Committee, and the Annual Meeting of the Life Governors. To avoid confusion, from this point forward the minute book will be referred to as the 'Schools Committee Minute Book' or 'SCMB'.

[38] See ch. 4 above.

[39] T. H. Clark is recorded as one of the early benefactors of Dean Close School, together with A. Peache (who donated £200 in 1883) and W. D. Cruddas (£500 in 1899). In 1907, Clarke left a legacy to the school of £1,000.

[40] SCMB.

[41] Ibid.

1. That a General Meeting of the Association be summoned to discuss the suggestions of the Committee that Clifton or the immediate neighbourhood be the locality for a Middle-Class School.

2. That it should, if possible, be in, or very near a parish in which the church is in the hands of Evangelical Trustees.

3. That the school be for Day Scholars and Boarders.

4. That a moderately sized house be secured and rented as a commencement.

5. That the terms of the school should be about the same as those adopted at the College at Ramsgate.[42]

6. That the Association appoint a Council for the control of the School, the vacancies to be filled up at the Annual Conference;

7. That the Master be appointed by the Council;

8. That a small Standing Committee be appointed at the three Centres to interest themselves in the Cause of Middle-Class education.

9. That a circular be approved appealing for donations to the amount of about £500 to be extended over two years, after which time it is hoped that the School will be self-supporting.

10. They consider that a similar Middle-Class School for girls be desirable.[43]

The Clerical and Lay Association's General Committee met on 1 December 1882 in Bath and accepted a report from its Sub-Committee on Middle-Class Education. To ensure an Evangelical heritage for the proposed school, a resolution was passed by the General Committee which was identical to the one proposed by the Middle-Class Schools Committee, viz. "that, if a School be instituted, it be, if possible, located in a parish, the Patronage of which is in Evangelical hands."[44] It was also resolved that the proposed school's fees "should not exceed 36*l* for Boarders, and for Day boys a charge not beyond those

---

[42] South-Eastern College. A pencilled note here, deleted, says: "Woodward [sic] schools £45; Not to exceed £30".
[43] General Committee Minute Book.
[44] Ibid.

demanded at the Bristol Grammar School."[45] The committee members were keeping a close eye on the perceived competition. This meeting also set out the administrative structure of the school: the Council was to include, "in addition to the President for the Year and the President of the Association", nine clergymen and nine laymen, whose names were listed. It was also decided at this meeting that the school would be called the 'Western College', after the 'Western District' that had founded it.

The location of such a school in the Bristol area had a great deal of support from other Evangelicals in the West. Revd W. F. Lanfear[46] of Weston-super-Mare, was described by Revd T. H. Clark as the 'originator of the scheme'.[47] Canon Richard Brooke, Rector of Bath Abbey (another Simeonite living)[48] was an active supporter, as was James Inskip, a solicitor from Clifton active in the Y.M.C.A. movement.[49] On 8 December, a second meeting of the Schools Committee met to confirm agreement of the proposals made at the General Committee meeting the previous week. It was decided to issue the circular (with a few small alterations) appealing for funds and to "seek promises from influential men".[50] Members of the Council were also encouraged to "make enquiries with the view to obtaining a

---

[45] Ibid.

[46] William Francis Lanfear graduated from Queens' College Cambridge in 1845 and prior to his appointment as Vicar of Christchurch, Weston-super-Mare 1855–75, had been Vicar of St John's, Southall Green, London, and Chaplain of St Marylebone Schools, Southall.

[47] Although Clark was referred to as the "mainspring of the movement", having "raised considerable sums by lectures which he gave throughout the country on the subject of 'Wycliffe'". *Supplement to The Rock*, Friday 14 August, 1885.

[48] Richard E. Brooke was appointed Rector of Bath Abbey in 1875. He was an Honorary Canon of Manchester Cathedral.

[49] Later, he was MP for Bristol. James Inskip's son was Sir Thomas W. H. Inskip, who became the first Viscount Caldecote in 1939. He was Attorney General 1928–9, 1932–6, and a committed Evangelical who successfully opposed the introduction of the new Prayer Book in 1928. His son, the second Viscount Caldecote, was President of the Dean Close School 1960–90. His elder brother, James Theodore Inskip, was one of the early graduates of Ridley Hall and became Bishop of Barking 1919–48, after making Jesmond Parish Church in Newcastle a "centre for Evangelicalism in the north of England". The bishop was a close friend of the Headmaster of Trent College, J. S. Tucker, and was elected a governor of Trent College and also Weymouth College in the early 1920s. See J. T. Inskip, *A Man's Job*, London 1948, p. 108 and A. F. Munden, *Jesmond Parish Church Newcastle Upon Tyne*, Newcastle 1981, p. 21. Revd Dr O. D. Inskip, Headmaster of Framlington College 1887–1913, was a cousin to T. I. and T. W. H. Inskip.

[50] SCMB.

suitable Head Master".[51] The plan was to rent a house in Clifton until sufficient funds and a suitable site were found. However, the publication of the circular and all further discussion of a school in Bristol came to an immediate halt when it was announced that on 17 December 1882, Francis Close, lately Dean of Carlisle, had died.

Francis Close had made his reputation in Cheltenham during the years 1826 to 1856, during which time he was not only the leading clergyman of the town, but also a founder of educational institutions and a national spokesman for education.[52] When he left Cheltenham in 1856, it was suggested that "the Francis Close institution"[53] should be erected to mark his achievements. The members of the committee clearly had not forgotten this desire, and in the weeks that immediately followed his death, there was a great deal of discussion amongst the Association members on this issue. The Middle Class Committee's Minute Book comprises some informal notes made by the Secretary about this period. He begins with the statement that "Just as the Circular was about to be issued, Dean Close died".[54] He also recorded that a "member of the Association...had suggested when the Dean was *in extremis* that this effort should be connected with his name".[55] Around this time the Secretary communicated on the subject of a memorial to Dean Close with the President of the Middle-Class Schools Committee, the President of the General Committee, and the President of the "Central Committee in London".[56] The Secretary's notes finish with the following statement: "As all approved and Mrs [Mary] Close entered warmly into the scheme, contributing £1000 anonymously, the matter was referred to a meeting of the General Committee held on Feb 1st, 1883, and it was resolved that the effort should take the form of a memorial to Dean Close."[57]

Letters began appearing in the Evangelical press in support of the idea of a memorial to Dean Close. The Rector of Cheltenham, Canon Charles Bell (1818–1898),[58] wrote to *The Record* on 5 January 1883 to "commend...the proposed memorial to Dean Close." He commented on the recent call for subscriptions to the "the Pusey Memorial", and complained of apathy and indifference on the part of Evangelicals to similar schemes for their own number. He was particularly concerned

---

[51] Ibid.
[52] See ch. 3 above.
[53] *Cheltenham Journal*, 8 November 1856, p. 1.
[54] SCMB.
[55] Ibid.
[56] A sub-committee of the Union of Clerical and Lay Associations.
[57] SCMB.
[58] See Appendix 1.

about the lack of interest in Evangelical middle-class schools: "The Woodard schools are inoculating the middle classes with a High Church leaven. Shall not we who believe we have God's truth on our side endeavour to counteract such teaching, and raise schools where the teaching shall be scriptural and in accordance with that of our Reformed Church?"[59] Like the man it was honouring, the new school would attempt to articulate an Evangelical response to what was seen as 'the Tractarian threat '.

Before the General Committee of the Clerical and Lay Association met in early February, Canon Bell chaired a "Preparatory Meeting" for the new school on 12 January at Cheltenham Rectory.[60] The main purpose of the meeting was to confirm the siting of the proposed Memorial School in Cheltenham, and to appoint a new local committee to oversee its foundation. The first resolution of the meeting was essentially a statement of purpose, in which the "great want throughout this country of Church of England Middle-Class Schools conducted on sound Protestant & Evangelical principles" was proclaimed. The second resolution followed on from this: "That as a step towards supplying this want it is desirable that a Middle-Class School should be erected as a memorial to the late Dean Close who was a most faithful champion of Evangelical Truth and also involved himself in a remarkable manner in the cause of Scriptural education."[61] The meeting also declared that "the site of the proposed school should be in Cheltenham, or the neighbourhood" and that a local committee be formed "to act in communion with the Council appointed by the General Committee of the Western Division of the Clerical and Lay Association and also with the Central Committee in London".[62] The nominated members of this local committee were all clergy. They included Canon C. Bell, G. W. Chamberlain, G. P. Griffiths, and J. F. S. Gabb. The final decision of the meeting was to launch an appeal "for at least £20,000…and that support be solicited from all throughout the country who were attracted to Evangelical principles, especially from those residing in the West of England." Canon Bell signed the minutes of the meeting. Like his predecessor in the parish, he was a man of action, and he was not going to risk the school being situated

---

[59] *Record,* 5 January, 1883, p. 16.
[60] From 1863, the incumbent was called 'rector'.
[61] Middle Class Committee Minute Book.
[62] Ibid.

Francis Close (1797–1882)

anywhere but in Cheltenham. Other leading members of the Cheltenham community were also present at this meeting. They included such dignitaries as the Mayor, Mr G. Parsonage, Major General Sir Frederick Abbott,[63] Mr W. H. Gwinneth,[64] and Mr W. N. Skillicorn.[65]

The clerical members of the local committee included men who had had some connection with Francis Close during his long ministry in Cheltenham. The Rector of Cheltenham, Canon Bell, chaired the committee. An Irishman, Bell had known the Dean while he was the Vicar of Ambleside, Westmorland 1861–72, and his dignity of Honorary Canon in 1869 was attached to Carlisle Cathedral, where Close had been Dean. Other members included George Griffiths, Vicar of St Mark's in Cheltenham[66] and a keen supporter of the local Clerical and Lay Association. He had grown up in Cheltenham at the time when Close was Perpetual Curate. The appointment of Canon Charles Money (1818–1893)[67] to St Luke's, Cheltenham was a welcome addition to their number, as Money had once been the great man's curate. It was also natural that Talbot Greaves[68] should be part of the new committee, as he had also begun his career as an assistant to Close during the last two years of his Cheltenham ministry. Greaves had chaired the Western District's Middle-Class Schools Committee, the parent of the Cheltenham local committee. He also brought to the committee his experience of setting up Weymouth College. Thus, under the leadership of Charles Bell, the Cheltenham clergy had taken the bit between their teeth and had formed their own committee for the express purpose of building a school in memory of Dean Close in Cheltenham.

The General Committee of the Clerical and Lay Association (Western District) met in Bath on 1 February 1883 to discuss the proposed school. The president, Canon Brooke, chaired the meeting and Canon Bell and T. H. Clark from the Cheltenham committee were

---

[63] Frederick Abbott (1805–1892) had been lieutenant-governor of Addiscombe military college 1851–61.

[64] Mr Gwinneth was also a supporter of the Cheltenham Grammar School, where both he and Francis Close are recognised by the Gwinneth-Close scholarship.

[65] W. N. Skillicorn's father, Captain Skillicorn, had been an early promotor of Cheltenham spa in the late eight-eenth and early nineteenth centuries.

[66] George Pruen Griffiths had been Vicar of St Mark's, which was located very near Dean Close School, since 1862. Prior to this he was Curate of St Mark's 1860–61 and before this, Curate of St Peter's, Cheltenham 1857–59. He was largely responsible for building St Mark's church. In 1899 he was made an honorary Canon of Gloucester Cathedral.

[67] See Appendix 1.

[68] See ch. 4 above.

both in attendance. It resolved that the circular originally authorised to be printed in December was to be changed so that instead of "asking assistance towards the renting of a house in Clifton", it was altered to "An Appeal for a Dean Close Memorial Middle Class School to be erected in the West of England".[69] Advertisements were placed in *The Record* and *The Rock*. The Honorary Secretary of the Cheltenham Local Committee wrote a letter to the second newspaper which was published on 16 March under the heading "Dean Close Memorial School":

> Sir, Allow me to draw attention to the advertisement of the above which appears in another column. We are anxious to obtain 5000*l*, at least by the first of May in promises. As schools of a more or less Romanising character are being spread over the land, it is important that those who value the sound Protestant teachings of the Reformed Church of England for the rising generation of the middle classes should embrace the present opportunity of providing such instruction.[70]

The editor of *The Rock* wrote optimistically that he hoped "that the movement now set on foot...in the West of England...will rapidly develop into a scheme for covering the whole of England with a network of such institutions".[71] A letter from Canon Bell calling for donations to the 'Dean Close Memorial School' was published in the next issue. Using a tone that would have been worthy of his predecessor, Francis Close, he wrote: "It is quite clear that Canon Woodard is part of a conspiracy of Anglo-Catholics to win England back to Catholicism."[72] By 11 June, £6,700 had been paid or promised.[73]

The first formal meeting of the Cheltenham Local Committee was held at Bath on 12 June 1883 where, after a short discussion, "It was decided...that the School should be in or near Cheltenham and that a committee at that place should select a site." The next meeting of the Committee took place on 7 July at which it was resolved that some "influential laymen" be asked to join the Committee. Present at the meeting were two such men: T. E. Williams of Salterley Grange,[74] a local barrister, and Major General Sir F. Abbott. Williams was asked to advertise for a suitable site for the school, and later appointed

---

[69] General Committee Minute Book.
[70] *Rock*, 16 March 1883, p. 142.
[71] Ibid., p. 173.
[72] *Rock*, 22 March 1883, p. 185.
[73] SCMB
[74] Located behind Leckhampton Hill, Cheltenham.

treasurer when the formal appeal for funds was launched. T. H. Clark wrote to *The Rock* on 13 July that "it has now been decided that the school be in Cheltenham, and that one or two sites are under consideration."[75] Helped by Mrs Close's donation and the £6,700 which had been raised jointly by the London and the local committees, nearly £8,000 was collected by the end of the year.[76] The area off Lansdown Road was regarded as a suitable site for a school, lying as it did between the elegant Regency villas of The Park and the newly laid tracks of the Birmingham-Gloucester branch line to the Cotswolds. The Committee received an offer of a 9.5 acre field on the western side of a private thoroughfare called Shelburne Road, which was near to Lansdown Road. Three Trustees for the purchase were proposed: Mr J. Inskip, Mr L. Valpy and Mr T. E. Williams. The total price asked for the site was £1,880, with £27 10s 0d as half the price for the enfranchisement of the copyhold.[77] One of the owners of the property, from the prominent Cheltenham family of Winterbotham,[78] offered to remit this fee as his contribution to the scheme. The price was accepted, and the purchase was completed in April 1884.

At the same time it was decided to incorporate the school under the *Companies Act*, and a sub-committee was formed to draw up a constitution.[79] A copy of the Trust deed of the South-Eastern College at Ramsgate was obtained, as the Central Committee in London had decided "after mature considerations...that...the Ramsgate scheme should be followed"[80] with regards the constitution of the school. This draft constitution was submitted to the Central Committee [for middle-class education] in London, which now met at the National Club. The school's constitution was presented and accepted on 28 December 1883, promulgated by the Charity Commission on 1 February 1886, and enrolled in the High Court of Justice on 4 March 1886. It stated that the name of the institution would be "The Dean Close Memorial School", and that its chief object was "to educate Boys of Parents of limited means for the spheres they [were] to occupy upon Scriptural, Evangelical and Protestant principles in conformity with the Articles of the Church of England as now by law established".[81] In anticipation of

---

[75] *Rock*, 13 July 1883, p. 493. A list of donors to the school was also published in this issue on p. 496.
[76] *Rock*, 30 November 1883, p. 120.
[77] An ancient form of land tenure abolished by legislation in 1925.
[78] The School's Deed of Constitution lists John Winterbotham and James Winterbotham as the vendors.
[79] SCMB
[80] SCMB
[81] Deed of Constitution, p. 4.

possible changes to this theological position, the Trustees wrote into the constitution that the religious teaching was to be in accordance with the Thirty-nine Articles, "in their literal and grammatical sense and that these principles shall for ever be preserved as a most sacred trust at any sacrifice of pecuniary loss or temporal interest".[82] Furthermore, the Life Governors were empowered "at a general meeting of their body specially called for that purpose" to remove any officer of the school "who in the judgement of a majority of Life Governors present shall have ceased to belong to the Church of England...or shall have ceased to hold Scriptural Evangelical and Protestant principles".[83] As a further security, the Life Governors and Executive Committee members were required to sign the following statement:

> I_____ of _____ hereby declare that I am cordially and sincerely attached to the teaching of the thirty-nine Articles of the Church of England as now by Law established in their strictly Scriptural Evangelical and Protestant sense and further that I will make it my first object in the selection of Head Master and in the general government of the School to secure its strictly Scriptural Evangelical and Protestant character.[84]

The Headmaster was required to sign a similar declaration.

According to the constitution, the officers of the institution were to consist of "a President; any number of Vice-Presidents not exceeding twenty, who shall be *ex-officio* Life Governors; any number of Life Governors not exceeding fifty and not less than twenty, half of whom should be clergymen and half laymen; and an Executive Committee, consisting of the Treasurer and Secretary for the time being, and not more than twenty-four persons and not less than twelve, half of them being clergymen and half laymen."[85] The first Ordinary Life Governors included five clergymen and five laymen nominated by the "London Central Committee of the Clerical and Lay Association", and "the remainder by the Committee of the Clerical and Lay Association Western Division".[86] One of these was Canon Charles Money,[87] who had been a member of the founding committee of the Union of Clerical

---

[82] Ibid., p. 17.
[83] Ibid., p. 8.
[84] Ibid., p. 20.
[85] McNeile, *Dean Close School*, Shrewsbury, p. 4.
[86] Ibid., p. 6.
[87] His efforts are commemorated in a plaque in the school chapel which states: "In memory of Revd. Canon C. F. S. Money MA, who as founder in 1884 chose the site for this school". Four of his sons were educated at the school.

and Lay Associations in 1881. Another was Charles Bousefield, who was later appointed a vice-president. It has been suggested in previous accounts of the school's history that Dean Close School was primarily a foundation of the Western District branch of the Clerical and Lay Association.[88] The evidence suggests, however, that the school was *jointly* founded by the Western District Clerical and Lay Association (represented by the Cheltenham Local Committee) *and* the Central Committee in London of the Union of Clerical and Lay Associations . One of the reasons for this was that the funds collected for the foundation of Dean Close School had been raised independently by each of these organizations. The School Prospectus for 1899 accurately records on its front cover that Dean Close School was "Founded under the Auspices of the Central Committee and Western Branch of Clerical and Lay Associations for the maintenance of Evangelical Principles".[89]

There was always a close relationship between the two organizations; however, members of the Western District had declined the central union's offer to merge with it. The Western District was, after all, the *original* Clerical and Lay Association, and preceded the Central Committee by 23 years. The list of vice-presidents in the school constitution included leading representatives from each organization. The Central Committee was represented, among others, by Bishop Perry, Dean Fremantle and Canon Hoare—all founding members of the Union of Clerical and Lay Associations. Members of the General Committee of the Western District who were also vice-presidents of the new school included Canon Brooke (president of the local Association) and Revd Talbot Greaves. The printed list of Life Governors for the new school reads like a *Who's Who* of leading Evangelicals at the end of the nineteenth century. It includes Arthur Peache, a relative of Alfred Peache, a benefactor of Monkton Combe School and the London School of Divinity, and Eugene Stock, author of the three-volume *History of the Church Missionary Society*. Dean Close Memorial School was to be a national rallying point for Evangelicals concerned about education, and it represented for many a united response to the rise of Anglo-Catholicism in the Church of England.

The first elected President of Dean Close School, John Deacon, was a member of the central Union of Clerical and Lay Associations, as well as a major benefactor. He was also the second president of South-

---

[88] See especially McNeile, *Dean Close School*, and R. J. W. Evans, "Town, Gown and Cloth: an essay on the Foundation of the School", in M. A. Girling and L. Hooper (eds), *Dean Close School: The First Hundred Years*, Cheltenham 1986, pp. 1–39.

[89] *Prospectus*, Dean Close Memorial School, Cambridge 1899.

Eastern College (from 1895), during which time he was president of both schools. Deacon was not asked to be President of Dean Close School until February 1886, by which time at least four other people had also been approached to take on this role. In 1884, the Local Committee asked the Earl of Shaftesbury, who was then eighty-three years old. Although he accepted the honorific title of president, he could not come to Cheltenham and he died before the school was opened. In late 1885, the third Earl of Chichester, a long-time president of the Church Missionary Society and an Ecclesiastical Commissioner, was approached, but he declined the honour on account of his age. The Mayor of Cheltenham, George Parsonage, was then asked to take on this position,[90] although he did not feature in any early lists. He was an early supporter of the school, attending the "Preparatory Meeting" at the Cheltenham Rectory on 12 January 1883[91] and laying the cornerstone on 11 November 1884. The Mayor was also a great supporter of Francis Close, having been a member of one of his Bible classes when he was in Cheltenham. It was also suggested by the School Committee, when it met on 16 February 1886, that the Earl of Harrowby be approached to be president. This was abandoned, however, once the name of John Deacon was suggested. When the final version of the constitution was drawn up in March 1886, "John Deacon Esquire" was named the first president and he continued in this role until 1908.

The powers of the Life Governors and Executive Committee were laid down at length in the constitution. In broad terms, the Life Governors had control of all the finances, the property, mortgages and sales, and all the external business of the School. The Executive Committee was given control over all the internal management, with full power "to do or cause to be done all such things as they may think necessary or expedient in connection with the development and management of the Institution".[92] They could also make any new rules and regulations, in accordance with the principles laid down, provided that "such new Rules or Regulations shall require to be confirmed at the next Meeting of the Life Governors but shall in the meantime be in operation".[93] The disposal and expenditure of the capital and income arising from the property were therefore vested in the Executive Committee, whose first duty was "To take all necessary steps to

---

[90] Evans, "Town, Gown and Cloth", p. 16.
[91] It was at this meeting that he moved the first motion on "the great want...of Church of England Middle-Class Schools conducted on sound Protestant Evangelical Principles."
[92] Deed of Constitution, p. 11.
[93] Ibid., p. 12.

procure the erection with all convenient speed...of one or more Master's houses and all such School and other buildings as they shall consider necessary or appropriate",[94] and to furnish them all; to fix the time for opening; to appoint the Head Master; and to "determine the system of education to be adopted".[95]

In March 1884, when completion of the purchase was imminent, it was decided by the Cheltenham Local Committee "to erect when there were sufficient funds a portion of the building to accommodate 70 with power of extension at a cost of £6,100".[96] A Mr Knight was engaged as architect, his plans were accepted, and "he was instructed to reduce the cost as much as possible".[97] Perhaps in response to this instruction, the original building could accommodate only 40 boys. It comprised part of the Headmaster's house, the room which was afterwards used as a library, the adjoining classroom, and a dormitory above. In addition there was "a short passage at right angles which led to the bootroom and lavatories, and lastly the detached building which served the purpose of gymnasium and carpenter's shop".[98] A meeting was held on 8 April at Cheltenham between the Local Committee and the General Committee of the Clerical and Lay Association at which the constitution of the school and the purchase of the land was approved. However, it was decided at this meeting that "the building for the boys should not be commenced until a considerable addition to the funds had been obtained."[99] On 9 May, a meeting "on behalf of the school" was held at the National Club in London, at which a report was given of the "progress made up to the present time."[100] Many of the people present at this meeting recommended "an early commencement of the building."[101] However, this did not get under way until 11 November, when the cornerstone was ceremonially laid by the Mayor, George Parsonage.

The sub-committee, formed to organize the whole event, was instructed to make the appropriate arrangements for the ceremony of the laying of the cornerstone, the service which preceded it at the nearby St Mark's Church,[102] and the luncheon at the Queen's Hotel

---

[94] Ibid., pp. 12–13.
[95] Ibid., p. 13.
[96] SCMB.
[97] Ibid.
[98] McNeile, *Dean Close School*, p. 6.
[99] SCMB.
[100] Ibid.
[101] Ibid.
[102] The school was erected in the (Evangelical) Parish of St Mark. During the early period of the school the pupils worshipped at this church.

which followed. They were requested to invite "the Clergy of the town – all Subscribers of £10 and upwards – the Church Wardens of the Parish Church and of St. Mark's – all the Life-Governors, those holding leading positions in the town, and some of the leading tradesmen."[103] They were also asked "to invite Ladies to the Luncheon" and also to provide a "workmen's dinner". It has been noted that "no intoxicants were supplied" to the workmen,[104] presumably something with which the Dean—a teetotaller—would have been pleased. Some 80 guests dined at the Queen's Hotel, including the Dean's widow and his son, Admiral F. Close, who acknowledged "the generous manner in which his father's memory had been honoured".[105] William R. Fremantle, The Dean of Ripon, preached the sermon at St Mark's[106] and a short service was also held at the site where the blessing was pronounced by the Rector of Cheltenham. Handbills for both the service at St Mark's and the ceremony of the laying of the cornerstone[107] each contained the clearly printed statement that "A collection will be made after the service." The total cost for the day's festivities amounted to over £55; however, this was more than compensated for by the donations received on the day.

Canon Bell suggested in his speech at the luncheon that both the College and the Grammar School in Cheltenham had "moved from their original statutes to become imperfect guardians of Christian tradition and Close's legacy".[108] Both the College and the Grammar School were in a period of temporary decline in the 1880s: the College finding that competition from similar institutions was starting to bite, and the Grammar School preparing to close for a period of two years in order to demolish its cramped Elizabethan accommodation on High Street and build afresh. Bell noted in his speech that "Cheltenham had not been very forward in welcoming this school"[109] and it was true that his critique of the existing educational facilities was not shared by all the residents of Cheltenham. The *Cheltenham Mercury*, a radical journal and no friend of Close, had announced that it was "never in

---

[103] SCMB.
[104] Evans, "Town, Gown and Cloth", p. 16.
[105] SCMB.
[106] Later published as *Sermon Preached in St Mark's Church, Cheltenham, by the Very Revd. The Dean of Ripon on the Occasion of the Laying of the Corner Stone of the Dean Close Memorial School, Tuesday; November 11th, 1884*, Cheltenham 1884.
[107] Pasted in the SCMB.
[108] Evans, "Town, Gown and Cloth", p. 16.
[109] Ibid.

favour of the school, as Cheltenham was already well supplied".[110] However, differences of opinion could not stem the tide of progress and development in a growing town like Cheltenham. One of the owners of the land on which Dean Close buildings were now being erected, James Winterbotham, had recently been elected the chairman of governors of the reconstituted Grammar School. A Mr Knight, the architect of Dean Close School, was also contracted in 1887 to draw up plans for the new Grammar School buildings, as well as the Cheltenham Public Library.

Two meetings in July 1885 discussed at length the question of including some form of technical education in the new school's curriculum. A report was received about the Department of Applied Science and Engineering at King's College, London, and a letter was produced from the Science Master at Uppingham School who described their various shops—"the carpenters [sic], the forge and the metal workshop".[111] The Committee thought that "a blacksmiths and joiner's shop would suffice for the school". Some provision was made for the latter, but the school's first historian, R. F. McNeile, reports that "the smithy was never realised till very much later in the School's history."[112] It is interesting to note that, unlike the Grammar School, Science was not included in the curriculum until 1892.

Throughout the period from December 1883, (when it was accepted by the Charity Commissioners), to December 1885, (when the final draft was enrolled in the High Court), the exact wording of the school's constitution, which was being formally drawn up by the Committee's honorary solicitor, Charles Pidcock, was a subject of much discussion at meetings of both the Local Committee and the General Committee. The constitution's preamble spoke of answering a need for "sound Scriptural Evangelical and Protestant Principles", and in March and June 1885 the committee members engaged in a debate on the retention or omission of the word 'Liturgy' in the articles. One proposal (not adopted, because the chairman, Talbot Greaves, was absent) said: "In the event of changes taking place in the laws of the Church of England which would imperil the maintenance of Scriptural, Protestant and Evangelical teaching in accordance with the trust deed of the school, the Life Governors should have power to arrange for the maintenance of such teaching and should not be bound to be members of the Church as then altered."[113] Later it was agreed that the Life Governors should still be called upon to sign the declaration, but the

---

[110] Ibid.
[111] SCMB.
[112] McNeile, *Dean Close School*, p. 6.
[113] SCMB.

word 'liturgy' could be omitted if desired. This resolution was revised in July 1885 so that the word 'liturgy' was dropped from the declaration altogether, and replaced by "attachment to the teaching of the 39 articles".

An advertisement for a suitable headmaster was drafted at a committee meeting on 6 August 1884, and the following appeared in *The Guardian* and *The Record*: "A Head Master, of decidedly Evangelical and Protestant principles, is required, for the Dean Close Memorial School, Cheltenham. Applicants should be Graduates in Honours and in Holy Orders. A stipend of 300*l* a year guaranteed, with house and the boarding of pupils. Apply, with references and testimonials, to Revd. T. H. Clark, hon. sec., 66, Pembroke-road, Clifton, Bristol."[114] Thirteen applications were received to the first advertisement, of which Revd F. T. Harrison, second master at Weymouth College, seemed the most promising. It was decided to invite him for an interview. However, Talbot Greaves had received a letter which "led the Committee to decide that it would not be desirable to appoint him".[115] What was in the letter is not recorded, although it has been suggested that he may have had some Anglo-Catholic sympathies—something which would clearly have been unacceptable. The Committee wrote to Harrison that "they do not feel that they have had before them a sufficient number of applications to enable them to select a head master".[116] A re-advertisement at the beginning of 1886 was placed in *The Times* and the *Scholastic Journal* as well as *The Record* and the High-Church *Guardian*. At the October 1885 meeting, Talbot Greaves had suggested that the wording of the second advertisement be changed to discourage applicants who were sympathetic to the "Woodard Middle and other schools",[117] suggesting that some of the early applications were from men of this ilk. This advertisement yielded eighteen applications and a short list of two: Revd E. H. Kinder, chaplain of Trent College and an Oxford graduate from the same college as Clark,[118] and Revd W. H. Flecker (1859–1941), Headmaster of the City of London College School and a graduate in mathematics from Durham University.[119] Both candidates were interviewed by the Committee on the 26 January 1886. This included asking the candidates questions about their "theological views". After a short discussion, Flecker was selected "as suitable for

---

[114] Pasted into the SCMB.
[115] SCMB.
[116] Ibid.
[117] Ibid.
[118] Brasenose College.
[119] Flecker was also "a well-known Evangelical and speaker at the May Meetings".

the post", and he was officially appointed the school's first Headmaster on 16 February 1886.[120]

The new Headmaster offered "on his own accord" to board the boys for £27 a year, in addition to £3 for laundry. The fees to be paid were fixed at £42 a year for boys under twelve, and £45 a year for those over that age. The equivalent fees for day boys were £12 and £15. These fees were consistent with those suggested by the General Committee of the Clerical and Lay Association, which resolved in December 1881 that the proposed school's fees "should not exceed 36*l* for Boarders".[121] The Governors of Dean Close School set fees which were more than Cheltenham's Grammar School, but considerably cheaper than the College. It was hoped that parents of strong Protestant conviction would consider the fees a small price to pay in exchange for an education which was described in the School's first prospectus as "based upon Scriptural, Evangelical and Protestant principles in accordance with the Articles and Liturgy of the Church of England".[122] The Committee set Friday 7 May 1886 for the opening of the school, and it was resolved to advertise the School as widely as possible in the public press. The following notice appeared: "The object of the school is to give a thoroughly useful education, based upon the Scriptural, Evangelical, and Protestant principles of the Church of England. The school buildings, which include workshops, are situated in nine acres of ground, and are fitted with every requisite for health and comfort."[123] Plans were also made by the Committee for an official opening ceremony to occur on Thursday 13 May 1886, at which the President of Corpus Christi College was invited to preach.[124]

In his *Supplement to The Rock* of 14 August 1885, the editor described "The edifice of a new public school, which is rapidly rising at Cheltenham" and compared it with South-Eastern College at Ramsgate. He made a favourable comparison with the Woodard schools, a scheme which "has had a remarkable expansion" and went on in a surprisingly non-partisan tone to say: "There is no desire to raise any antagonism against it; but it is very desirable that all the new middle-class schools should not be upon the Woodard pattern. This is a distinctly High Church or Ritualistic pattern, and there are multitudes of parents who…would prefer that their sons should be educated at schools conducted on Evangelical principles."[125] Two years later, the

---

[120] SCMB.
[121] General Committee Minute Book.
[122] Pasted in the SCMB.
[123] Newspaper clipping pasted in the SCMB.
[124] The preacher was later changed to Canon Hoare of Tunbridge Wells.
[125] *Supplement to The Rock*, 14 August 1885.

Rector of Cheltenham, Charles Bell, would be less conciliatory: "Funds have not been wanting to Canon WOODARD and his friends. Their zeal is admirable, and deserves recognition—this we must acknowledge though we are compelled to place ourselves in an attitude of antagonism to their schools."[126]

The buildings that were completed in May 1886 were only a portion of the intended block, comprising the Headmaster's house and the library. For an outlay of £10,757, Messrs. Jones of Gloucester constructed a block described by the *Cheltenham Examiner* as " a simple and economical adaptation of the Elizabethan, in brick, relieved by strings of moulded work".[127] Much was made of the "health, comfort and convenience of the inmates", especially the heating system, which yielded a temperature of 55°F[128] in the winter by the "ingenious introduction of fresh air through special ducts." The newspaper also gave a long description of the design of the drains, encouraged no doubt by the late Victorian preoccupation with proper hygiene and sanitation for schoolboys. The picture on page 302 gives some idea of the scale of the school buildings in 1886. They included the Headmaster's house, the dining hall, and what was later called "Class-room No. 5", with dormitories above the latter two rooms, and the workshops.

It was hoped that, in the course of time, these buildings would eventually be supplemented "so as to provide for one hundred"[129] boys. The school was to open in May, and for the new Headmaster, the first few days of that month dwelt vividly in his mind: "The east wind howled through the unfurnished building; workmen swarmed everywhere, putting finishing touches to their work—no blinds, no gas, no beds! And on the fifth of the month the boys were due to come. Outside on the playing fields a few blades of grass were struggling up amongst a mass of weeds."[130] The first eight boys duly arrived from Flecker's previous school in London, accompanied by the Second Master, Mr J. H. Harvey, "a warm friend of Mr. Flecker".[131] These, together with two other boarders and three day boys living in the town, raised the total to thirteen pupils for the first day of school. By the end of the term, numbers had increased to seventeen and the school had

---

[126] *Rock,* 22 April, 1886, p. 4.
[127] The *Cheltenham Examiner,* 19 May 1886, p. 3.
[128] A chilly 13°C!
[129] W. H. Flecker, "Notes on the History of the School, since its Foundation in May, 1886", *Dean Close Memorial School Magazine,* January 1892, p. 3.
[130] Ibid.
[131] McNeile, *Dean Close School,* p. 9.

fielded its first cricket team, which managed to beat the second eleven of the Grammar School.

In his report on the school's official Opening Day, the editor of the *Cheltenham Examiner* described the institution as of "no ordinary kind", for although "intended to be conducted on sound commercial principles, its *raison d'étre* [sic] is essentially of a religious and not a proprietary nature". He compared it with another school of a similar foundation, then with those of the other camp: "It is, in fact, a companion school to the large Evangelical College at Ramsgate, whose establishment may be regarded as an answer to the movement initiated by Canon Woodard for educating boys of the middle class upon catholic or High Church principles."

Encapsulating the high hopes of the Evangelical party for more of such schools, he went on to explain how that party, "though somewhat tardy in its reply, would now appear to have recognised the full importance of distinctive training for the maintenance of what it holds to be vital in doctrine and historical in the religious life of England." In a final flourish, he proposed that "The Dean Close Memorial School will probably therefore not be the last of such institutions which the zeal of Evangelicals will raise for the promotion of their cause, a cause for which so much strength of piety and nobility of intellect have been associated, and which will never be without witness in the world while time shall last."[132] As will be seen, Dean Close Memorial School was destined to be the last of these new institutions. However, the other speakers on the Opening Day were just as optimistic (if perhaps not as grandiose) in their predictions for the school. Although Dean Close School—the word 'Memorial' was dropped from the school name in the late 1920s—was to be the last nineteenth-century Evangelical public school, it quickly became one of the most prestigious, for in 1896 Flecker was admitted to the Headmasters' Conference, and two years later the School appeared in the *Public Schools' Year Book*. In January 1923, the conference held its fiftieth general meeting at Dean Close School, an honour which was not bestowed on the schools at Ramsgate or Long Eaton until much later.

---

[132] *Cheltenham Examiner*, 19 May 1886, p. 3.

W. H. Flecker (1859–1941)

The main feature of the Opening Day was a special service at St Mark's Church with a sermon by Canon Hoare of Tunbridge Wells. He was a particularly suitable person, being the long-serving vicar of a watering-place not unlike Cheltenham and a prominent preacher and writer on a wide range of topics, much like Close himself. Together with many of the other clergy associated with the school—Bell,[133] Fremantle,[134] Money,[135] and even Flecker the Headmaster[136]—he was an Evangelical 'man of letters' and a popular and well-known author.

---

[133] Canon Bell wrote over a dozen books, including *Night Scenes of the Bible; Hills that Bring Peace; The Saintly Calling; Voices of the Lakes and other Poems; Songs in the Twilight; Our Daily Life, its Dangers and its Duties; Henry Martyn; The Choice of Wisdom; Hymns for the Church and the Chamber; Angelic Beings;* and *Living Truth for Hand and Heart.*

[134] William R. Fremantle co-edited *Ecclesiastical Judgments of the Privy Council,* 1865, and wrote *The Gospel of the Secular Life,* 1882; *The World as the Subject of Redemption* (the Bampton Lecture for 1883), 1885; and *Church Reform,* 1888.

[135] Canon Money wrote *Paraphrase on the Lord's Prayer; Formation of God's Image in the Soul; Retirement and Prayer; Revolution in China and its bearing upon Missionary Efforts.*

[136] His books included the *Student's Prayer Book,* 1903, and *Morning Prayer for Schools,* 4th edn 1907. Flecker himself was the subject of two biographies: C.

Dean Close School, 1886

Canon Hoare called for the School to further the "entrance of the Word into the nation" and he spoke at length on the national neglect of "the education of the middle classes".[137] His address echoed the words of the Dean of Ripon in the same pulpit eighteen months earlier, who had stated in his sermon at the 'cornerstone' service that "In England...to a great extent middle-class education has been sadly neglected." It was also exactly the language of Woodard, and though hardly true towards the end of a period which had seen the foundation of over one hundred new public schools,[138] it suggested that the "clarion call of Victorian clerical pedagogy"[139] still sounded shrilly in the ears of Evangelicals, and that the "middle classes of England" would find to their "infinite advantage ...a sound Scriptural, Protestant, Evangelical training in the Word of the living God".[140] This emphasis on the Bible was also

---

Williams, *Flecker of Dean Close*, London 1946, and L. M. J. Kramer, *Another Look at Dr. W. H. Flecker*, [privately printed]; and of chapters in two books: R. F. McNeile, *Three Decanian Worthies*, Winchester 1951; and J. Sherwood, *No Golden Journey*, London 1973.

[137] The *Cheltenham Examiner*, 19 May 1886, p. 3.

[138] By my count, Dean Close School was seventy-ninth of the 103 public schools founded in the Victorian era.

[139] Evans, "Town, Gown and Cloth", p. 17.

[140] The *Cheltenham Examiner*, 19 May 1886, p. 3.

reflected in the motto chosen for the school, *Verbum Dei Lucerna*.[141] The closing words of Canon Hoare's sermon were followed by a collection for the school's Building Fund, and "thither through mud and rain" the assembled company repaired for another dedicatory service, followed by lunch.

The second service at the school was much shorter and once again those attending included the men who had worked on the school building. Canon Money spoke of "the need which existed for schools of this character to counteract on the one hand the Romanistic and on the other hand the Agnostic tendencies of the age".[142] The service concluded with the hymn, "O God our Help in Ages Past" and the first-ever luncheon in the School building was served in the Dining Hall (later to become the kitchen). Under "an admirable portrait in oils of Dean Close",[143] the President of the Clerical and Lay Association (Western District), Canon Brooke, proposed the toast to "The cherished memory of Dean Close." He said that education was the life work of the late Dean—"the education of the upper middle classes, the education of the poor, the training of teachers" and that "This School was intended to be one of many in which a thoroughly Scriptural, Evangelical, and Protestant training would be given to the middle classes of the country" and that this was a work which the Dean would have greatly loved if he were still alive. The Dean's son, Admiral Close, rose to assert that the School "was what was called an Evangelical school, a school in which the Bible and not priestcraft was chosen as a guide."[144] This was an assertion which, as R. J. W. Evans has pointed out, a columnist for the *Cheltenham Mercury* lost no time in lampooning by suggesting that 'priestcraft' signified rather what the Evangelicals themselves practised.[145] As has been suggested before, this sort of political point-scoring was very much part of the Cheltenham newspaper culture, and, just as during the tenure of the late Dean, one could always rely on conservative newspapers such as the *Cheltenham Examiner* to provide the final word; which was, in this case, that the day's arrangements had "given great and general satisfaction".[146]

---

[141] From Psalm 119.105: "Your word is a lamp to my feet and a light for my path." The original motto, *Ad Maiorem Dei Gloriam*, "for the greater glory of God", was dropped when it was realised that this was the slogan of the Jesuits.

[142] Ibid.

[143] This hangs today in the school's entrance hall.

[144] Ibid.

[145] 'Man-in-the-Moon', a columnist in the *Cheltenham Mercury*. Cited by Evans, "Town, Gown and Cloth", p. 19.

[146] Ibid.

The final toast was to Revd G. P. Griffiths, the chairman of the Local Committee, which, since the appointment of Life Governors, was now calling itself the 'Sub-Committee'. Griffiths was a stalwart of the local Clerical and Lay Association, and as vicar of nearby St Mark's had a vested interest in the school, which he described as falling within his "pastoral charge". This toast was made by a representative of the London Union of Clerical and Lay Associations, Revd H. W. Webb-Peploe. It alluded to a recent conversation over dinner between Mrs Flecker and one of the masters of Cheltenham College, in which he had asked why another school should be opened in a town already well-supplied. She remarked on the new school's Evangelical character. "Oh, Evangelicalism!", he exclaimed, "that's as dead as a doornail."[147] Webb-Peploe spoke for the wider Evangelical community when he stated that "they could point to this School as an evidence that their party so far from being dead was alive and vigorous, ready as ever to do battle for the cause of truth."[148] Indeed, Webb-Peploe was to be involved in the next stage of this battle as a leading member of the Church of England Evangelical College and School Company, the subject of the next chapter.

---

[147] Williams, *Flecker of Dean Close*, p. 45.
[148] Ibid.

Chapter 10

The Church of England Evangelical College and School Company

When A. Leslie Wright decided *c.*1885 that he wished to divest himself of the freehold of Monkton Combe School,[1] the Union of Clerical and Lay Associations was the natural choice as a possible new landlord. By the mid-80s, the Clerical and Lay Associations had become the key Evangelical organizations involved in middle-class education. The South-Eastern Clerical and Lay Association, a member of the Union, had successfully founded South-Eastern College in 1879, and Dean Close Memorial School, a joint initiative of the Western District Clerical and Lay Union and the Union of Clerical and Lay Associations, was just about to open. Before his death in 1880, Henry Wright had "expressed his earnest desire that the school should be placed in the hands of Evangelical trustees".[2] In all, he had spent about £8,000 on the school land and buildings. Ten years later and while still a student at Cambridge, his son, A. Leslie Wright, offered the school to the Central Committee of the Union of Clerical and Lay Associations for £6,000. The Central Committee of the Union immediately set about raising the money required, stating in a circular, "They [felt] that it [was] most important that the work of educating boys in accordance with the principles of the Reformation, so well carried on also at Trent College, the South Eastern College at Ramsgate, and the Dean Close Memorial School at Cheltenham, should be extended as widely as possible, and that such an opportunity as that now presenting itself at Monkton Combe should not be lost."[3] This circular was issued by the Principal of Monkton Combe School, Revd R. G. Bryan, to the parents and supporters of the School, and he obtained "from both Donors and Shareholders a considerable sum towards the purchase of the property".[4]

---

[1] See above, p. 213.
[2] See "Monkton Combe School", an undated appeal to buy the school from Mr Wright by the Clerical and Lay Union, p. 1. Monkton Combe School Archives.
[3] Ibid.
[4] Printed letter from R. G. Bryan to S. Gedge, 21 February 1894. Monkton Combe School Archives.

Articles began appearing in the Evangelical press calling for money for the purchase of Monkton Combe[5] School. An entry in the 'Notes and Comments' section of *The Rock* for 23 May 1890, stated that "Evangelicals will be the laughing stock...of our Ritualistic friends if we cannot raise 3000*l.* to secure...this place for middle-class and higher education."[6] Although the closure of the appeal was given as July 1890, this was later extended to the end of September. The article assured the reader that "the school [would] be Protestant and Reformed" and suggested that "Canon Woodard would have no trouble in raising many times this sum, nor should we, if we were sufficiently organized".[7] Two months later, another list was published in the same newspaper that gave the names of the people who had contributed to the Monkton Combe appeal for funds. Always alert to the value of good publicity, the principal submitted an article to *The Rock* later that year which talked about the school "coming out well" in the number of mathematical distinctions in the Oxford and Cambridge Schools' Examination for Higher Certificates for the years 1889 and 1890.[8] A list of other public schools—Eton, Rossall, Marlborough, Rugby, Cheltenham, Weymouth—was included for comparison.

The first subscribers to the Monkton Combe appeal were Mr R. C. L. Bevan and Prebendary F. E. Wigram[9] with £500 each. Bevan was a Monkton Combe parent whose son, E. R. Bevan, later became a distinguished scholar.[10] Wigram was married to Henry Wright's sister and had taken over as Honorary Secretary of the Church Missionary Society a few months after his brother-in-law's death. He was a "leader among the Evangelical clergy in the diocese of Winchester"[11] and as a "man of private fortune", was a great benefactor[12] of the work

---

[5] Frequently misspelt 'Moncton', 'Monckton' and also 'Coombe' instead of Combe.

[6] *Rock,* 23 May 1890, p. 3.

[7] Ibid.

[8] *Rock,* 7 November 1890, p. 10.

[9] See Appendix 1.

[10] R. C. L. Bevan was also a major benefactor of Ridley Hall, Cambridge; donating £1100 towards the cost of the new buildings. F. W. B. Bullock, *History of Ridley Hall*, vol. 1, p. 194.

[11] Stock, *History of the CMS,* vol. 3, p. 260.

[12] In 1880 Wigram and his wife offered to act as guarantors to the Society for the amount of £10,000 above the agreed budget of £185,000. In 1883 they donated £10,000 towards new buildings for the CMS Missionaries' Children's Home which moved from Highbury to Limpsfield in Surrey in 1887. Between 1915 and 1996 (when it closed), it was an independent boarding school known as St Michael's School.

of the CMS. Other subscribers included A. S. L. Melville with £100, and F. S. Clayton, R. T. Fremlin and Canon Bernard with £25 each. As well as announcing these pledges, the Committee wrote in the circular that "they earnestly ask the friends of Evangelical Religion throughout the country to enable them, by liberal subscriptions, to complete the purchase without delay."[13] However, the property was not finally sold by the Wright family until April 1891, when it was bought by the Church of England Evangelical College and School Company Limited, a body which had been formed in December 1890 by the Central Committee of the Union of Clerical and Lay Associations; "in order to promote institutions in which the rising generation should receive, together with a thoroughly good general education, religious instruction in accordance with the Evangelical principles of the Church of England."[14]

The Memorandum of Association of The Church of England Evangelical College and School Company stated the objects for which the company was established as:

1. To purchase or acquire the Boys' School at Monckton [sic] Combe, in the county of Somerset, now carried on by Reverend Reginald Guy Bryan, and known as Monckton Combe School, and the goodwill thereof, and the lands belonging thereto or occupied therewith, and to carry on the same school in accordance with the Protestant and Evangelical principles of the Church of England.

2. To provide by establishment and maintenance of schools in England and Wales, education in accordance with the aforesaid principles, for boys and girls of classes above those ordinarily attending public elementary schools.

3. To provide, by the establishment and maintenance in England and Wales of colleges hostels and halls at the Universities, education in accordance with the aforesaid principles.[15]

The seven founding company Directors included two well-known Evangelical clergy—Revd J. W. Marshall,[16] Vicar of St John's Blackheath, and Revd G. F. Whidbourne, Vicar of St George's,

---

[13] "Monkton Combe School" undated circular, p. 2. Monkton Combe School Archives.
[14] *Rock,* 18 November 1892, p. 6.
[15] Memorandum of Association of Evangelical Church Schools Limited. Trent College Archives.
[16] At that time he was secretary of both the Clerical and Lay Union and the Protestant Churchmen's Alliance.

Battersea[17]—as well as Sydney Gedge.[18] Mr Leslie L. Gedge, nephew and articled clerk to Sydney Gedge, was initially appointed company secretary by the Clerical and Lay Union,[19] although he was soon replaced by another clerk from his uncle's law firm.[20] The first meeting of the Board of Directors on 12 January 1891 fixed the capital of the company at £25,000, divided into 25,000 shares of £1 each. Like many other Evangelical business ventures, the bankers 'Messrs. Williams, Deacon, and Co.' were appointed to the Company. The first meeting was held at Church Missionary House, Salisbury Square, London. The Honorary Secretary of the Church Missionary Society, Revd F. E. Wigram, was invited to join the Board of Directors; however, he declined on account of "other occupations".[21] Two other Evangelical clergymen were added to the Board of Directors at this first meeting: Canon Brooke,[22] and Prebendary H. W. Webb-Peploe, who was "now an acknowledged party leader".[23] Wigram and Webb-Peploe were at Cambridge together in the 1850s, where they were members of the Cambridge University Prayer Union,[24] one of the

---

[17] Prior to this, George Ferris Whidbourne was curate to H. W. Webb-Peploe at Hanley in Staffordshire 1866–88.

[18] See Appendix 1. Sydney Gedge was Chairman of the Board of Directors from 19 February 1891 to 12 July 1895, when Edmund Hanbury replaced him.

[19] By now the name "Clerical and Lay Union" was being used interchangeably with "Union of Clerical and Lay Associations" (see, for example, the article announcing the formation of the Evangelical College and School Company in *The Rock* of 13 February 1891), despite the fact that the Church Association first used this name for the sub-committee it formed in 1870. The Clerical and Lay Union severed its connection with the Church Association in 1873 when Edward Garbett (see Appendix 1) and some other members of the Union Committee formed the 'Evangelical Union of the Church of England' for the promotion of Church Reform. Although Shaftesbury was nominated as president, within a few years this organization, as Anne Bentley has stated, "faded quietly out of sight, and, probably, out of existence". It seemed that by 1890, the word, 'Union', no matter how it was used, was identified with Clerical and Lay Associations rather than the Church Association.

[20] Mr Stuart Trotter.

[21] Church of England Evangelical College and School Company Ltd Minute Book A, p. 2. Trent College Archives. Hereafter, refered to as 'Minute Books A, B, C', etc.

[22] Brooke was Rector of Bath Abbey. He resigned from the Board on 10 February 1893 because of ill-health.

[23] Bentley, "The Transformation of the Evangelical Party", p. 93.

[24] The Cambridge University Prayer Union (CUPU) was founded in 1848 as The Cambridge Union for Private Prayer. See Bullock, *History of Ridley Hall,* vol. 1, pp. 57–59. Sydney Gedge was one of the early members (he joined in 1850). Later members of the Prayer Union included F. E. Wigram (1856), F. B. Wright

predecessors of the Cambridge Inter-Collegiate Christian Union (CICCU).[25]

The minutes of the first meeting of The Church of England Evangelical College and School Company records that "Messrs Wigram, Marshall and Whidbourne" had entered into, on behalf of the Clerical and Lay Union, "a conditional agreement...for the purchase of Monkton Combe School at the price of £6000".[26] It was resolved "that the agreement dated 30 December 1890 which was made with Mr Alexander Leslie Wright, the Owner, with these gentlemen, be approved and adopted by this Company".[27] An advertisement was drafted, and appeared in *The Rock* newspaper on 13 February 1891. The advertisement mentioned that the Company was considering purchasing Ayerst Hall in Cambridge, which was "established and conducted on the same principles" as Monkton Combe School. This is why the word 'College' is included in the name of the organization. The proposal was not discussed by the board until a later meeting, when a number of possible sites for an Evangelical university college were suggested at both Cambridge and Oxford.

The purchase of Ayerst Hall, Cambridge,[28] "a hostel in connection with the University"[29] had been "under consideration" since the Company was first formed. On 19 February 1891, a letter from Mr Harry Chisbit regarding the sale of Ayerst Hall was read to the Board. Following this, it was resolved "that the Board consider it desirable to establish a hostel at Cambridge and with that view to purchase Ayerst Hall".[30] However, a number of conditions were laid down by the Board, which needed to be met before the purchase could go ahead. On 26 February 1891, the Board received a letter from the principal of Ayerst Hall, Revd William Ayerst, and also letters from the Master of Corpus Christi College, Revd Dr E. H. Perowne, and Revd H. W. Webb-Peploe. Soon after each of these were read, "it was resolved that negotiations for the acquisition of Ayerst Hall be suspended, and that

---

(1856) and H. W. Webb-Peploe (1857). All four of these men, who were clearly friends, were later involved in the Evangelical Church Schools Company.

[25] See F. D. Coggan (ed.), *Christ and the Colleges: A History of the Inter-Varsity Fellowship of Evangelical Unions*, London 1934; J. C. Pollock, *A Cambridge Movement*, London 1953; D. Johnson, *Contending for the Faith: A History of the Evangelical Movement in the Universities and Colleges*, Leicester 1979; and O. R. Barclay *From Cambridge to the World*, Leicester 2002.

[26] Minute Book A, p. 2.

[27] Ibid.

[28] Founded in 1884. See above, p. 233, fn. 88.

[29] *Rock*, 13 February 1891, p. 1.

[30] Minute Book A, p. 7.

Mr Ayerst be informed of this decision."[31] Clearly something in one or all of these letters had caused the Board to change its mind regarding the purchase of Ayerst Hall, but what it was is not recorded in the minutes.

In April 1893, another letter from Mr Ayerst was received by the Board. He had originally asked for £12,000 for the buildings and land at Parkers Piece, but his latest offer was £2,500 for the College's new buildings on Mount Pleasant. The proposal was fully discussed by the Board; the Chairman was requested to visit Cambridge to "examine the ground and make general enquiries."[32] This was duly done but the final decision was that the proposal "could not be entertained". Other suggestions of suitable sites for an Evangelical university college included Cavendish College[33] on a site between the Round Church and the River Cam, and in Oxford, on a plot of ground belonging to Balliol College. However, in the end, the Evangelical College and Schools Company decided to concentrate its energies and resources on schools, not university colleges. Eventually, the word 'College' was dropped from the Company's name.[34]

Concern was raised that the work of the Church of England Evangelical College and Schools Company would affect the enrolments at Trent College. A letter from Dr W. O. Derby to Revd G. F. Whidbourne outlining these concerns was read to the Board in March 1891. Mr Whidbourne was requested to reply "that the new Company have no intention of injuring Trent College and that the Directors think that there is plenty of room for that College and our scheme."[35] By now the Board was receiving a steady flow of letters from individuals, mostly owners of private schools, requesting that the Company consider purchasing their school. These schools included:

>Still House College, London

>Old Hall, Wellington ("Mr Cranage's School")

>Christ's College, Finchley (founded 1857)

>Schorne School (no address given)

---

[31] Ibid., p. 2.
[32] Ibid., p. 93.
[33] Founded in 1876. See above, p. 120.
[34] Although it remained the registered company name until June 1919. Copy of *Memorandum of Association*, Trent College Archives.
[35] Minute Book A, pp. 13–14.

A School for Young Ladies at Brownhill near Stroud

Clarence School in Weston-Super-Mare

Norfolk County School ("Mr Nichol's school").[36]

In each case, the Board declined the invitation, with the standard reply being either "that the Company does not see its way to entertaining the proposal", or "at present the Company was not in a position to adopt the suggestion". One of the more interesting proposals came from the Church Missionary Society in December 1891, who were considering re-locating their Training College at Islington to Cavendish College in Cambridge. The Honorary Secretary had suggested to the Chairman through an "informal communication...that it might be more convenient if this Company would buy it, & the Society take a lease or agree to place a certain number of men there".[37] The Chairman agreed to go to Cambridge to "ascertain upon what terms the College might be obtained, & inspect it, and report to the next meeting of the Board".[38] Like all of the other suggestions listed above, this was not one which was taken up by the Board.

Negotiations continued with the Principal of Monkton Combe School regarding the form of management which should take place following the Company's purchase of the "freehold of the School and surrounding Lands". On 3 April 1891, the Chairman of the Board of Directors, Mr Gedge, wrote to Mr Bryan that "There is every desire on the part of the Board to work with you".[39] Bryan replied with an invitation for a Director to visit Monkton Combe "to look into...several local matters" including the possible purchase of a cricket field of eleven acres which was "owned by a Roman Catholic sort of Company". He saw this as a question to be considered "before any new buildings should be built on the School property so beautifully situated on the overlooking hill".[40] This letter was read out at the next Board meeting in April, and "Mr Gedge was requested to reply to it."[41] Several letters of correspondence between Mr Bryan and Mr Gedge were recorded for the month of April in which Bryan was

---

[36] Founded in 1874. See above, p.121 and Honey, *Tom Brown's Universe*, pp. 70–2.
[37] Minute Book A, p. 47.
[38] Ibid.
[39] Printed letter from Bryan to Gedge, 21 February 1894, p. 3. Monkton Combe School Archives.
[40] Ibid. Bryan was referring here to Monkton Combe Junior School.
[41] Minute Book A, p. 20.

given notice that the Board wished to end his tenancy as Headmaster.[42] This suggestion appears to have been withdrawn after Bryan refused to hand over his pupils. In a letter to Mr Bryan of 29 April 1891, Mr Gedge wrote, "It is clear that you do not propose to part with your goodwill."[43] The Board replied to Bryan's suggestions regarding proposed new Junior School buildings that "The Directors approve generally of the suggestions which [you] made for the erection of an Upper School, and carrying on the Junior School in the present buildings."[44] The principal of Monkton Combe was a guest of the next Board meeting at which he proposed that he continued "in sole control of the Lower School in the present buildings".[45] After a three day visit to Monkton Combe School on Whitsuntide 1891, Mr Gedge suggested to the Board that "the School do continue for the present to be carried on by Revd R. G. Bryan as [before], but that the Company shall make such alterations & modifications therein at their own expense as may be desirable having reference to the fact that at Michaelmas 1892 they probably themselves will become the owner of the School."[46] The issue was discussed in detail at the Board meeting of 19 November 1891, when a list of detailed proposals by Mr Bryan "for the future management of Monkton Combe School & Property" was presented in person by Mr Bryan, who was also interviewed by the Board. The Board's proposal that he remain Master of the Junior School only was met with determined resistance by Bryan, to which the Board replied "that Mr Bryan be requested to reconsider his determination and to write to the Chairman again on the subject".[47] This dispute between the Board of Directors and the principal of Monkton Combe School was never completely resolved, despite a long correspondence between the two parties which culminated in a printed record of these letters being published by Mr Bryan on 21 February 1894. In this, Bryan admits that the issue had degenerated into a conflict, "one party striving to obtain, the other to retain, the management of the School",[48] and although his printed letter had a conciliatory tone, the issue of the management of

---

[42] Printed letter from Bryan to Gedge, p. 3.
[43] Cited in ibid.
[44] Ibid. The "Upper School" referred to here was the existing Junior School, which was situated in two houses on top of the hill; that is, the word 'upper' referred to the location, not the grade level, of the school.
[45] Ibid. Similarly, "Lower School" referred to the Senior School, which was down the hill.
[46] Minute Book A, p. 27. The rest of the sentence—"selecting their Head and other masters"—is crossed out on the archive copy.
[47] Ibid., p. 43.
[48] Printed letter from Bryan to Gedge, p. 4.

the school was completely resolved only when the Monkton Combe School Company bought out the Evangelical Church Schools Company in 1907.[49]

A special Board Meeting was called on Friday 15 July 1892 in order to consider two important proposals that had been received by each Board member. The first was from the Council of the South-Eastern College who wished to form a new Evangelical Collegiate Body for the purpose of promoting middle-class education "in accordance with the Protestant and Evangelical principles of the Church of England". It was resolved that "however desirable the object may be", the proposal from South-Eastern directors was "too indefinite for the Board to pass an opinion upon it".[50] Despite this, the idea of forming an alliance between the Evangelical schools continued to be discussed at regular intervals by the Company until well in to the next century.

The second proposal was a most unexpected one. The Chairman of the Board of Trent College, Francis Beresford Wright, had written to the Evangelical Church Schools Company on 7 July 1892 to suggest that the Company purchase Trent College. Unlike all previous proposals of this nature, the Board was "favourably disposed" to this suggestion. A sub-committee was formed to "consider the proposal in detail and to confer with Mr Beresford Wright".[51] They were empowered to arrange a provisional agreement for the purchase of the school, and to issue a prospectus and "to take other necessary steps to obtain the money which [would] be required".[52] On 23 July 1892, Mr Gedge and General Hutchinson inspected Trent College and by the 14th of October an 'organizing secretary', Mr Mathen, had been appointed to obtain subscriptions for the purchase of Trent College. Advertisements for these were placed in the *Record, Rock, English Churchman, Guardian, Christian*, and the *Life of Faith*. H. W. Webb-Peploe wrote a letter to the editor of *The Rock* on 18 November 1882 which outlined the work of the Evangelical Church School & Colleges Company, and their desire to purchase Trent College in the Midlands. He also mentioned "how successful their high-church friends had been in similar endeavours",[53] and commended the work of the Church Schools Company.[54] The money was eventually raised and Trent

---

[49] See above, p. 215. On 23 October 1907, the Evangelical Church Schools Company sold the freehold of Monkton Combe School to the Monkton Combe School Company for £5,796.
[50] Minute Book A, p. 59.
[51] Ibid., p. 60.
[52] Ibid.
[53] *Rock*, 18 November 1892, p. 6.
[54] See above, p. 100–2.

College was purchased by the Evangelical Church Schools Company on 13 January 1893 for £4,720.

Soon after the purchase of Trent College was concluded, a scholarship fund was begun in a rather unusual way. In 1893, a Miss Reyneth sold her diamond necklace at Christie's for £356, and this money, which she donated to the school, became the seed capital for the Prize Scholarship Fund. Soon after, Revd F. E. Wigram donated £1,000 for a scholarship, and a Scholarships Deed was drawn up to help administer the fund. As suggested elsewhere,[55] Trent College was regarded as the most prestigious of the Evangelical middle-class schools—something which was also suggested by its fees, which at £60 in 1894 were considerably higher than South Eastern, Weymouth, Monkton Combe and Dean Close schools. Scholarships continued to be founded over the ensuing years. On 15 June 1894, Mr Whidborne (a Board member) and his wife gave £1,000 to Ridley Hall, Cambridge and purchased £1,000 in debentures in the school, in order to establish a Bursary Fund for Trent College boys at Ridley Hall which was to be administered by the Trustees.[56] On 12 March 1897, the Church Pastoral Aid Society offered to pay a university scholarship to Trent College. On 12 January 1900, upon the death of one of the founding Board members, Major General G. Hutchinson, a prize funded by the Major General's estate was offered for the best essay on a missionary subject.

In June 1893, a Council of Management of Trent College was formed which had eleven members including a number of Board members as well as the ex-president of the College, Francis Beresford Wright, and Mr C. W. Moule of Corpus Christi College, Cambridge.[57] In order to maintain the link between the school and its founding body, Revd J. W. Marshall wrote to the Midland Clerical and Lay Union to invite representation on the Council of Management. The first meeting of the College Council was held at Trent College on 23 June 1893. One of their early decisions, in October 1893, was to appoint a Bursar, Revd I. A. Smith. However, he was to last only five weeks, departing for Cheltenham Training College on 8 December 1893 and leaving in his wake a trail of accounting irregularities. Thereafter followed a period of financial instability for Trent College, which one school historian described as the period of "The Sinking Ship".[58] There were also some changes in the organization which founded the Evangelical

---

[55] See above, pp. 184–5.
[56] Bullock, *History of Ridley Hall*, vol. 1, p. 313.
[57] C. W. Moule was the brother of H. C. G. Moule and a Fellow and Tutor of Corpus Christi College.
[58] Tarver, *Trent College*.

Church Schools Company, for in 1893 the Union of Clerical and Lay Associations amalgamated with the Protestant Churchmen's Alliance to form the National Protestant Church Union. Perhaps in order to show their continuing support for the scheme, the NPCU sent a donation of £19.12.6 on 31 August 1894 to the Evangelical Church Schools Company which was "to meet any future expenses at Monkton Combe".

Advertisements for the newly managed Trent College were lodged in overseas newspapers such as the *Home News*, the Calcutta *Englishman, Bombay Gazette, Pioneer of Allababad,* and *Irish Times*; as well as local papers such as the *Daily Express* and the *Christian*. Education of the Middle Classes re-appeared in the Evangelical press as an item for discussion in the 1890s.[59] The editorial for *The Rock* on Friday 27 October 1893 complained about Evangelicals having to send their children to High-Church Woodard schools because of the lack of Evangelical equivalents. It mentioned 'Cheltenham, Trent and Ramsgate' as schools which are doing "excellent work", and included a plea for Evangelical parents to take more seriously the decision of where their children go to school. It also suggested that the middle classes were the ones being missed in the "education question".[60] Soon after this, at a Board Meeting on 12 January 1894, a letter was read from the Headmaster of South-Eastern College in which he suggested the two schools should advertise jointly in the *Record, Rock, Guardian, Daily Graphic, Army & Navy Stores Circular,* and the Calcutta *Englishman* newspapers. The Board decided to invite Dean Close School to advertise as well. Pamphlets were to be printed and applications made to the Church Missionary Society and the Church Pastoral Aid Society "for leave to circulate this leaflet with their publications".[61] Later that year, the Headmaster of South-Eastern College visited Trent College "for the purposes of giving the result of his experience" at the South-Eastern College on staffing. Leave was also granted on 23 November 1894 for the company secretary to visit the South-Eastern College at Ramsgate. It would seem that the Evangelical middle-class schools were starting to work together for their common good.

Perhaps arising out of this, the Minute Books of Dean Close School record that from 1893–94, the Church Pastoral Aid Society sought school representatives for a branch that would "further the work of

---

[59] There was also a close relationship between some members of the Evangelical press and the Company, for from August 1894 the Company's Secretary rented an office from *The Rock* newspaper.

[60] *Rock,* 27 October 1893, pp. 8–9.

[61] Minute Book A, p. 114.

Evangelical Schools". The Rector of Clifton, T. H. Clark, and W. H. Flecker, the Headmaster of Dean Close, were appointed to this organization. An article in *The Rock* entitled "Religious Teaching in Higher Class Schools" stated that "the question of religious teaching in middle and upper schools" is part of the "Forward Movement of the C.P.A.S.", which would examine the religious teaching of "the very large intermediate class" which has been largely neglected.[62] This was contrasted with the well-advanced work of the Tractarians, for "There is one party in our Church which has shown that it appreciates the importance of the religious teaching given to children of the middle classes. It has rallied round it a number of wealthy men, who have provided fine buildings and given a start to schools where doctrine of distinctly High Church, if not actually a Romanising tendency, is instilled into the minds of the pupils."[63]

The issue of education for the children of the middle classes once again became a topic for discussion and debate in Evangelical circles. On Friday 14 December 1894, *The Rock* carried an article entitled "Evangelical Education: Important Movement" which ran to two full columns. It reported on "two important meetings of well known Evangelical Churchmen" which were held in the previous week in London. They had partly been called to "further the project for commemorating the late Canon Hoare[64] by building a much-needed additional wing to the South-Eastern College, Ramsgate", but the ultimate aim was claimed as "the promotion of a representative and comprehensive scheme for the general development and expansion of higher education on an Evangelical religious basis."[65] The movement was quoted as having the support of the CPAS; the Earl of Harrowby, D. F. S. Ryder; the Principal of Ridley Hall, H. C. G. Moule; the Archeacon of London, W. M. Sinclair; and the Bishop of Liverpool, J. C. Ryle.

Lord Harrowby was reported as urging "the great importance of the subject in its bearing upon the maintenance of the Protestant character of the Church of England, and expressed the earnest hope that 'our excellent South-Eastern College' might be fully equipped, but that additional colleges and schools might in due course be founded and endowed."[66] Quotations also followed from the Bishop of Liverpool, who wrote: "The Ritualistic body are compassing sea and land to get hold of the children of the middle classes. Our own friends seem to me

---

[62] See above, p. 253.
[63] *Rock*, 27 October 1893, p. 8.
[64] Edward Hoare, Vicar of Tunbridge Wells, had died in July 1894.
[65] *Rock*, 14 December 1894, p. 6.
[66] Ibid.

J. C. Ryle (1816–1900)

only half awake about the matter. They forget that to get a hold upon the young and to instil into them unsound theological opinion has always been the favourite weapon of the Jesuits and their followers in our own Church."[67] A letter from Handley C. G. Moule, the Principal of Ridley Hall, Cambridge, was also quoted in the article. In it, he commended the work of the South-Eastern College and stated:

> The phenomenon of the Woodard Schools is at one of the most stimulating as an example, and most formidable as a fact [*sic*]. They are educating a large generation of young minds to take it for granted that sacerdotalism is Christianity. It will be a disastrous mistake if no worthy effort is made henceforth to train a generation in the intelligent conviction that Evangelical truth, as our Church teaches it, is Christianity.[68]

While this statement reflected his legendary conservatism in theological matters,[69] it is also likely that Moule regarded these schools as a good source of potential students for Ridley Hall.

---

[67] Ibid.

[68] Ibid.

[69] His grandnephew, C. F. D. ("Charlie") Moule, Vice-Principal of Ridley Hall 1936–44, was more liberal in his approach. According to John Stott, who was a student there in the 1940s, Ridley Hall students would wait for signs of this divergence in his lectures, then wag their fingers, saying: "Charlie, what would

The Dean of Norwich, William Lefroy (1836–1909),[70] used statistics to back up his argument. He noted that "the comparative neglect of our work in this department was the more amazing when we thought of what the Church had done for the humbler classes".[71] He quoted numbers to illustrate how Church schools had kept pace with Board schools, but then made the contrast with three Evangelical middle-class schools: Trent College, Dean Close Memorial School, and South-Eastern College. Like the other protagonists, he was keen to compare the work of the Evangelicals with the High Church party, using statistical evidence to show that the three schools listed above had "an aggregate accommodation for only 550 boys, and at a total cost of 69,000*l*. Compare this with what High Churchmen have done in the Woodard schools, with nine such establishments accommodating 2,500 boys (before long 3,000 boys) at a cost of 320,000*l*".[72] He had a point: on the middle-class schools front, the Anglo-Catholics were whipping the Evangelicals.

Sydney Gedge, the Chairman of the Board of the Evangelical Church Schools Company, responded. He made some practical suggestions for helping Evangelical schools, and with reference to the work of the Anglo-Catholics, he said: "I do not think we could do better than to follow the example so successfully set by Canon Woodard. You have a body which is answerable for the general working, if not for the direct management, of these schools, answerable for them also being maintained on the footing of our great public schools".[73] In answering his own question of how Evangelicals could undertake a similar "working", he suggested that they should "strengthen the things that we have", including to the South-Eastern College and Dean Close School. Somewhat predictably, he also called for increased support for the Company's school: "Trent College certainly needs some money, but it more particularly wants boys... At present...the Church of England Evangelical College and School Company, which purchased it about two years ago...are losing money every day...if the school does not increase largely in the next two years or so, we shall be in danger of having to close it..."[74] He then alluded to the "other school system which has not been mentioned"—the Church Schools Company—stating, "although its schools do not

---

Uncle Handley have said?" T. Dudley-Smith, *John Stott: The Making of a Leader*, Leicester 1999, p. 201.

[70] See Appendix 1.
[71] *Rock*, 14 December 1894, p. 6.
[72] Ibid.
[73] Ibid.
[74] Ibid.

Sydney Gedge (1829–1923)

give quite the same direct Evangelical teaching as we could wish, yet so long as on the Council are our friends,[75] Archdeacon Emery and Mr. P. V. Smith, I think we may be sure that there will be nothing in the teaching to which we can object".[76] Mr Gedge then concluded by moving a resolution, which was unanimously adopted, for those present to sign the following declaration:

> That we, the undersigned, taking a deep interest in the subject of the Higher Education for boys and girls, and believing that such education should be based upon Christian principles in accordance with the teaching of the Reformed Church of England, hereby express our willingness to meet as occasion shall arise, for the purpose of consulting upon and endeavouring to forward the best means of promoting this object; and that the Church Pastoral-Aid Society, the National Protestant Church Union, and the National Club, be asked to allow their Secretaries to act for the purpose of convening such meetings and to grant the use of their rooms.[77]

It would seem that the Evangelicals were at last coming together to support a cause that was close to their hearts and their homes: the education of their sons.

A second meeting on the same subject was held the following Wednesday evening in the Christ Church Lecture-room at Hampstead, with the Vicar, Revd G. F. Head,[78] presiding. Mr F. A. Bevan reminded those present of the recent meeting in Brighton,[79] "when the subject of the Woodard schools was agitating the Evangelical world," and he suggested that "long ago Evangelicals should have taken example from the other side, and placed good schools in various parts of the country"; wistfully hinting at what might have been, "had such

---

[75] The editor of *The Rock* newspaper was evidently of the same opinion, as he regularly reported the General Meetings of the Church Schools Company. See, for example, his article in *The Rock* 9 March 1888 p. 15, which provided a synopsis of the Sixth Ordinary General Meeting of the Company, and mentioned the fact that "two new centres have been decided upon at Guildford and Leicester".

[76] *Rock,* 14 December 1894, p. 6.

[77] Ibid.

[78] George Frederick Head was Vicar of Christ Church Hampstead, Middlesex from 1885 until 1897, when he was appointed Vicar of Clifton, Bristol: a Simeon Trustee living. He was the first Vicar of St John's, Carlisle 1867–73, when Francis Close was Dean of Carlisle 1856–81.

[79] An anti-Ritualist meeting in Brighton on 13 September 1894 had degenerated into a public demonstration at which extensive criticism had been levelled at the Woodard schools. Brighton was well known as "an area of intense Ritualist dispute". Machin, *Politics and the Churches in Great Britain*, p. 249.

tactics been energetically adopted". Revd F. W. Tracey, Headmaster of South-Eastern College, recommended that Evangelicals buy the two official books published by the Woodard organization: *The Calendar of the Corporation of St. Nicolas and St. Mary and its Allied Societies* and Canon Lowe's *A Record of Thirty Years Work*, for they "afforded a most magnificent object lesson in the way of carrying out a great work by foresight, self-denial, and incessant industry".[80] Copies of these books can today be found in the archives of the Evangelical schools, just as the reports of some of the Evangelical organizations administering Dean Close and South-Eastern College are located in the Lancing College archives. It obviously paid to keep an eye on the competition.

A meeting was held a few weeks later at the National Club on Friday 5 January 1895, "in connection with the great cause of the Evangelical training for the boys of the upper classes."[81] While it was primarily a fundraiser for the Canon Hoare Memorial Wing at South-Eastern College, the wider question of Evangelical secondary education was also discussed.[82] A few months later, another meeting was held at the National Club to raise funds for South-Eastern College, at which Revd E. N. Coulthard[83] suggested that "the Woodard schools furnish us with a magnificent imagination".[84] The President of the National Club, Mr T. A. Denny, saw things slightly differently.

> I tell you we have been fast asleep for forty or fifty years, and judgement has been going against us by default, and we have simply let things slide. In the meantime, the High Churchmen, and more than High Churchmen—the Romanists and Jesuits, have been hard at work, and the country has been sapped, undermined and honeycombed by traitors and Jesuits within and without, so that it's hard to know where we are in these latter days.[85]

---

[80] *Rock*, 14 December 1894, p. 6.
[81] *Rock*, 12 July 1895, p. 3.
[82] See, for example, the article in *The Rock* 19 July 1895 entitled "Evangelical Education", pp. 10–11; and an editorial in the same issue entitled "Protestants and Education", p. 9.
[83] Ernest Newton Coulthard was a pupil at Monkton Combe School in the 1870s, from where he won an Exhibition to St John's College, Cambridge. He was one of the original eight students at Ridley Hall, Cambridge. He was Curate of St Mary, Kilburn, 1881–88, Metropolitan Secretary of CPAS 1888–93, then Vicar of St James, Bermondsey 1893–1908. Coulthard was followed as Vicar of St James by Revd G. R. Balleine (1873–1966), the author of *A History of the Evangelical Party in the Church of England*.
[84] *Rock*, 19 July 1895, p. 10.
[85] Ibid., p. 11.

The editor of *The Rock*, writing in the same edition, went even further, stating that "the Sacerdotalists are fully alive...and the result is that they have that powerful organization, commonly known as the Woodard schools, spread over the country, and in various ways they have acquired an influence over the youth of the Church which serves their cause marvellously".[86]

A year later, two small articles appeared in *The Rock* on Friday 15 May on the need for Evangelical Schools. The first one began with a quote from the Midland Lay and Clerical Union, who were "calling on their people to work as zealously as the Woodard parishioners did"[87] for the establishment of Evangelical schools. The editor of *The Rock* then writes to commend Trent College, asking his readers to support it and claiming that it could go on to be "a great public school".[88] The school certainly went on to represent Evangelical practice, for any hint of Anglo-Catholicism was dealt with quickly by the Board. On 17 June 1898, the Directors heard that "the Headmaster ha[d] introduced the practice of intoning the services in chapel."[89] The Chairman was requested to inform the Headmaster that "under no circumstances can the Board sanction such changes in the services of the chapel".[90] Four years later, the Headmaster of newly purchased Weymouth College asked "what the Board wished respecting the cross on the Communion table" in the school Chapel. The reply came back that he was to remove it "if it could be legally done".[91] The schools also became venues for Evangelical meetings and 'house parties'. For example, in 1898 Trent College Council agreed to let the college buildings to the British College Christian Union, during the summer holidays. Evangelicals were beginning to see the advantages that instititions such as these could have on the wider work of the party.

Much of the business at the Company board meetings was concerned with the constant shortage of funds. In February 1899, a letter was sent to the National Protestant Church Union to ask for their assistance in the issuing of an appeal for funds, and the Company's overdraft at the bank was frequently extended by the personal guarantee of different Board members, particularly the Chairman. Because of this, any extra purchases of land and buildings at each of the schools was privately done by members or friends of the Board.

---

[86] Ibid., p. 9.
[87] *Rock*, 15 May 1896, p. 315.
[88] Ibid.
[89] Minute Book A, p. 233.
[90] Ibid., pp. 233–4.
[91] Minute Book B, p. 42.

For example, Edmund Hanbury[92] purchased land for a cricket field at Trent College in March 1902, and Colonel Robert Williams purchased an "adjoining house"[93] at Weymouth College in May 1902. In October 1902, the Headmaster of Trent College, Revd J. S. Tucker, met with the Board to report that the two fields below the one purchased by Hanbury were for sale, and that "owing to the townspeople using them as a recreation ground they were a very great annoyance as the language used was horrible & could be heard plainly from the cricket field."[94] Because of the Company's restricted financial position, it was decided that "nothing could be done at once", and, as had been the case for a number of other purchases, the Directors were asked to consider "if it was possible" for any of them to buy the fields themselves.

By the close of the century, the composition of the board of the Church of England Evangelical College and School Company had changed considerably from its first meeting in January 1891. Edmund Hanbury succeeded Sydney Gedge in 1895 as chairman of the governing body. Henry Wace, later Dean of Canterbury (1903–24), agreed to join the Board in 1901 and, following Edmund Hanbury's sudden death, chaired its meetings from 1913. Throughout this period, Prebendary Webb-Peploe retained his seat on the Board, and his considerable influence. The Bishop of Durham, H. C. G. Moule and the Bishop of Liverpool, F. J. Chavasse (1846–1928),[95] were also listed as governors of the school, however they rarely attended meetings in person, choosing instead to send a proxy. On 21 March 1902, the Directors of the Company decided to purchase Weymouth College at a cost of £7000 plus £1500 in shares in the Company "to be taken immediately by the vendors or their friends".[96] While Edmund Hanbury had a long-standing involvement in Weymouth College, the sale of the school was initiated and facilitated by the President of Weymouth College and local Member of Parliament, Colonel Robert Williams,[97] who in April 1902 personally guaranteed £500 towards the outstanding expenses of the college. Sydney Gedge, now 73 years of age, acted as the solicitor—presumably because of his personal contact with Colonel Williams in the House of Commons. The sale was completed on 8 May 1902. Two years later in their Annual Report, the

---

[92] Later, he was chairman of the Board, 1895–1913.
[93] Ibid., p. 47. This was later identified as "Radipole Cottage", which became part of the Junior School.
[94] Ibid., p. 53.
[95] See Appendix 1.
[96] Minute Book B, p. 34.
[97] Williams was the member for West Dorset, which included Monkton Combe. He opened the new buildings at Monkton Combe Junior School in 1907.

company directors wrote that they had purchased Weymouth College "to save it from falling into the hands of other parties, who might be opposed to Evangelical principles."[98] They also referred to the "excessive activity" in the south of England of "a large number of the teaching order of Roman Catholics" who had been expelled from France and had migrated to England. The Evangelical Church Schools Company, as the cumbrously titled Church of England Evangelical College and School Company Limited began calling itself,[99] was now landlord of Monkton Combe School[100] as well as being responsible for the management of two other schools: Trent College and Weymouth College. The Board of Directors dealt with each of these schools in turn at their monthly meetings. From *circa* 1910, the monthly Directors' meetings were made up of four sub-committees: the Meeting of Directors, the Trent College Council, the Weymouth College Council, and the General Purposes Committee.

For financial reasons, various attempts were made to merge the different organizations which ran the Evangelical schools. In 1902, Edmund Hanbury of the Evangelical Church Schools Company met with J. F. W. Deacon of South-Eastern College to discuss "the question of an amalgamation of the three schools".[101] There was also talk about joining with Dean Close School. On 14 January 1903, the Treasurer reported that he had been present at a meeting of the Evangelical Church Schools Company, where although "they had decided to retain this organization as a Company...this....would not prevent [their] joining with the Dean Close School, [or] be a barrier to [their] uniting with the South-Eastern College".[102] The minutes of the Directors' meetings of Monkton Combe School Limited record "a scheme for affiliating various evangelical schools"[103] which was discussed at a meeting held in London in 1903. These plans for amalgamation never came to anything,[104] and as the key Evangelicals on the Board such as Prebendary Webb-Peploe and Dean Wace resigned, the management

---

[98] *Evangelical Church Schools Annual Report* 1904, p. 12. Monkton Combe School Archives.

[99] The Company officially changed to this name on 18 June 1919. Copy of *Memorandum of Association*, p. 1. Trent College Archives.

[100] It remained so until 1907.

[101] Minute Book B, p. 34.

[102] Minute Book C, p. 7.

[103] Minutes of the Directors' Meetings, Monkton Combe School Ltd. p. 22. Monkton Combe School Archives.

[104] Again, this was mainly because of financial obstacles. It was also despite another, unsuccessful attempt to form a "Federation of Evangelical Schools" in November 1919. Governors Executive Committee Minute Book, Dean Close School Archives.

no longer represented this party, or indeed any party. Weymouth College closed in 1940,[105] and when in 1966 the name of the parent company for Trent College was changed from Evangelical Church Schools Limited to Trent College Limited,[106] the connection with Evangelicals was largely severed. However, until recently there remained a physical connection between the current management of Trent College and the old Company in the form of a brass plaque on the door of the old Bursar's office, which announced the "Evangelical Schools Board". It remained until 1986, when the door of what had become the Wright Housemaster's flat, was demolished.

In their Annual Report for 1904, the Church of England Evangelical College and School Company (abbreviated to "Evangelical Church Schools" on the front cover), announced that "In December last the total of the two schools reached 171" and that numbers had since then gone up, so that "the present total of the two schools [was] nearly 200." By this time, the "object of these Schools" had been reduced to two main purposes:

(1). To provide a good, sound religious education on public school lines, and on the principles of the Reformation.

(2). To afford to the sons of poor clergy and deserving laymen an opportunity for securing, at a moderate cost, as good an education as is given in any of the more expensive public schools of the day.[107]

The need for more funds was also raised in the Report, in which the governors stated their hope that, "legacies will be left by kind friends...as has been the case in the Woodard Schools", who had set a "noble example" in this respect, for "[we] cannot believe that the friends of the Evangelical cause will be less generous to [sic] those of other Schools of theology whose educational plans have gained so much by legacies."[108] While not begrudging the success of the "Sacerdotal party"[109] in founding schools, the Evangelicals were acutely aware of the consequences the lack of financial support would have on the future of their party as much as the schools themselves. For while the "Ritualists and Romanists are vying with each other in this question of education", the Evangelical party lacked the same activity and earnestness in the cause of education. For many

---

[105] See ch. 4 above.
[106] By special resolution dated 24 November 1966. Copy of *Memorandum of Association*, Trent College Archives.
[107] *Evangelical Church Schools Annual Report* 1904, p. 3. Monkton Combe School Archives.
[108] Ibid., p. 3.
[109] Ibid., p. 9.

Evangelicals, the future of the nation, as well as education, was at stake:

> England has been lifted up among the nations of this world, owing to the value she has hitherto attached to a simple, Evangelical religion, and, if she is to retain her position, it behoves every Englishman who values his country, to see that the rising generation are brought up to value those principles which did so much to make our forefathers great, and that there shall always be educated men holding Evangelical principles, capable of filling any position, however responsible, in the affairs of the nation.[110]

In their report, the governors of the Evangelical Church Schools Company were not just representing a party position, but they were also articulating what was regarded by some Evangelicals as the critical provision of schools for their sons and daughters.

The Evangelical Church Schools Company was the most successful corporate response to the perceived need for Evangelical middle-class schools, both in terms of the number of schools it administered, and the length of time the Company was associated with a school. From 1940, when Weymouth College closed, the Evangelical Church Schools Company managed just one school, Trent College. Although the other Evangelical schools, particularly Dean Close and St Lawrence's, frequently discussed the idea of amalgamation in the early years of the twentieth century, this was soon abandoned as each school concentrated on its own specialties in sport, academic subjects and religion. While this was happening, the membership of the Company Board was becoming progressively less Evangelical, so that it would be difficult today to find the sort of 'distinctive Churchmanship' on the school board which was characteristic of the nineteenth-century founders of the Company. However, unlike some of their colleagues, the members of the original board of directors were less interested in the work of Nathaniel Woodard and more interested in providing a means of educating the Evangelical middle-class.

---

[110] Ibid., p. 7.

Conclusion

The Church of England Evangelical College and School Company was typical of the more moderate and less partisan Evangelical organizations, in that it regarded its main role as providing support for Evangelicals—in this case parents of boys about to complete their secondary education—rather than becoming enmeshed in the religious politics of the day. There is no evidence to support the idea that the members of this Company were working to combat the enormous success of the Woodard Corporation, although there are indications that they may have been inspired and encouraged by Woodard's achievements to provide a similar system of schools for Evangelicals. However, a great deal of the publicity surrounding the foundation and development of these new schools was extremely partisan, with newspaper reporters and local supporters of the schools taking every opportunity to criticise Woodard and the Anglo-Catholics; also referred to as Tractarians, Ritualists and Romanists. The late nineteenth century was a period of deep division within the Church of England as the different Church parties—High Church, Broad Church and Evangelical—began to identify and fight for their particular theological positions. They were all united in regarding the survival and growth of the Church of England into the twentieth century as being dependent on the survival and growth of their particular party.

Other corporate responses by Evangelicals to the need for middle-class schools were either more, or less, concerned with the effect that such schools would have on the growth and development of the Evangelical party. The Church Association's 'Middle Class Schools Provisional Committee', true to the aims of the organization to which it was attached, was very concerned about the effect that the Woodard schools would have on the strength of the party. They regarded the founding of Evangelical schools as essential for the survival of Evangelicalism and a means of slowing the growth of Anglo-Catholicism. Despite forming a Committee on middle-class education and publishing tracts on the dangers of the Woodard schools, the Church Association was not directly associated with the foundation of any new schools. This initiative was to pass to the more moderate and less zealous Clerical and Lay Associations, with some later support from the home-mission-minded Church Pastoral Aid Society. It is likely, however, that the Church Association's concerns about the growth of the Woodard system, and calls for funds for the setting up of five Evangelical schools of the same *genre*, had the effect of spurring its members into some type of response, even if it was not directed at this organization. In 1869, the Church Association had a huge subscription base of over 8,000 members. As the century progressed, many of these men were becoming increasingly uncomfortable with its policy of prosecuting Ritualist clergy. Some of these members would have been motivated by the Association's concern about middle-class education, but they would not have seen the Church Association as the most appropriate body to set up such schools.

Until this study, very little was known about the Clerical and Lay Associations which met "to take counsel together" at various regional locations around the country. The first Clerical and Lay Association was formed in Bristol in 1858, and by the end of the century there were at least 18 such organizations meeting at regular intervals during the year for fellowship and Bible study, and holding annual conferences. Some of these organizations included 'the middle-class schools issue' as a topic of discussion at their annual conferences. St Lawrence College (originally 'South-Eastern College') in Ramsgate was founded by the South-Eastern Clerical and Lay Church Alliance which held its annual conferences at Tunbridge Wells. The idea of a middle-class boys school in the English Midlands was first raised by the Midland Clerical and Lay Association, although it only became a reality through the initiative of one of its leading members, Francis Wright. Dean Close School in Cheltenham was the result of discussions between the Western District Clerical and Lay Association and the central committee of the Union of Clerical and Lay Associations in London. As with the schools already mentioned, it owed much to efforts of individual Evangelicals, but the organization which raised the capital, built, and governed the school was an association which drew its membership from a wide domain.

The death of Francis Close in December 1882 provided the catalyst for the establishment of a new Evangelical middle-class school in Cheltenham. It was a project that had already been under way since the Clerical and Lay Association (Western District) Middle-Class Schools Committee had met in Clifton, Bristol, the year before to launch an appeal for an Evangelical day and boarding school. It had already been decided that the school should be founded in an Evangelical parish and well-known Evangelical clergy at Bristol, Bath, Weston-super-Mare and Cheltenham actively supported the scheme. Although it was originally intended that the school would be established in Bristol, following Close's death it was decided to site the school in Cheltenham as a memorial to the famous Incumbent of St Mary's parish. Of all the Evangelical middle-class schools which were

Conclusion

founded in the nineteenth century, Dean Close Memorial School was probably the only one that was a direct response to the "Tractarian threat" which the Woodard schools presented. This was most likely a reflection of the hardening of party positions later in the century, and Dean Close School was the latest and last of these middle-class schools which were set up during this period. Canon Charles Bell, the Rector of Cheltenham, was—like his recently deceased predecessor in the parish—an outspoken critic of Anglo-Catholicism. He saw the project as a means of counteracting the work of the High Church. The Secretary of the Cheltenham Local Committee wrote a letter to *The Record* in which he compared the Dean Close Memorial School with those "of a more or less Romanising character", which were "being spread over the land". A letter from Canon Bell was published in the same issue in which he stated that "Canon Woodard is part of a conspiracy of Anglo-Catholics to win England back to Catholicism". The publicity surrounding the respective foundation, fundraising, building and opening of Dean Close Memorial School was a source of Evangelical vituperation of both Anglo-Catholicism and the Woodard schools.

St Lawrence College at Ramsgate was founded three years earlier by a group of men associated with the South-Eastern Clerical and Lay Church Alliance. Like Dean Close School, it was to be situated in a parish which was under 'Evangelical patronage', and the local Vicar, J. Bradford Whiting, was one of the key people involved in the project. Like its sister school in Cheltenham, the establishment of St Lawrence College was the result of group effort, with a number of other key Evangelicals who were active members of the South-Eastern Alliance, closely associated with the project. One of these, Dr Robert Payne Smith, Dean of Canterbury and Regius Professor of Divinity at Oxford, was also closely associated with a number of other educational efforts both in Kent and beyond. Contemporary accounts accord to him the status of a leading educationalist, and he would make an ideal subject for further research if the diocesan archives at Canterbury were able to offer up more material than they have to date. Payne Smith was a firm Evangelical and in an article he wrote for *The Rock* newspaper in 1886, he referred to the school founders' desire to provide a school which would work against "the corruptions of the Church of Rome, [and] also against mediæval superstitions." The founders of St Lawrence were keen to provide an Evangelical alternative to those schools which were seen as an attempt by the High Church party to increase their strength.

This sort of approach had a long history, and could be traced back to an earlier period of Evangelicalism. At the beginning of the Victorian era, Francis Close made a name for himself as an outspoken critic of all things to do with Roman Catholicism, as well as (for good measure), the breaking of the Sabbath, the theatre and the races. But his interest in education resulted in the establishment of schools of every kind in Cheltenham, all of which were to sport the 'Evangelical' tag because of his powerful influence. Cheltenham College, founded by retired army officers for the purpose of educating their upper-middle class sons, quickly became one of Close's educational projects. His position as Clerical Vice-President and Chairman of the College Board ensured that while he was at Cheltenham, no Tractarian or Roman Catholic would be employed by the College, and the unique (but ultimately short-lived) position of theological tutor was held by an Evangelical. Close also used the many opportunities this position gave him, to make public statements about the College's "Protestant evangelical religion" and the Boards' Evangelical and anti-Catholic stance. Even after he had left Cheltenham, Close's concerns about the growing influence of "Tractarians" in educating the middle class led to his 1861 publication *High-Church Education Dangerous and Delusive*, in which he criticised what he described as Woodard's opposition to Scripture, and his "Romeward direction". Cheltenham College retained its Evangelical ethos for only about twenty years, from which time forward the declining number of Evangelicals on the Board and on the staff (particularly after the position of theological tutor was abolished) saw it become more closely associated with the High Church party. Close was also associated with a number of other middle-class education ventures, including the re-founding of Cheltenham's Grammar School, the founding of an Evangelical teacher training college, and (to a lesser extent) the establishment of a middle-class school for girls. Only the training college retained its Evangelical ethos, largely because of the care which Close put into its charter of foundation. However, the involvement of Evangelicals in the training of teachers is beyond the scope of this study, and furthermore, it has been documented in some detail by others.

Three other schools that were founded in the 1860s were also largely the result of the efforts of individual Evangelicals. Talbot Greaves, who also later became involved in the founding of Dean Close School, was the prime mover in establishing a middle-class boys school at Weymouth in Dorset. As the Evangelical incumbent of the adjacent parish of Melcombe Regis, in 1859 Greaves founded one of the new 'middle schools' which were being supported by the National Society. In 1862 this was re-founded as Weymouth Grammar School, eventually changing its name to Weymouth College in 1875. Despite Talbot Greaves' excellent Evangelical credentials—he assisted Francis

Conclusion 331

Close at Cheltenham 1854–56 before moving to Weymouth—there is no record of any anti-Catholic or anti-Woodard statements from either Greaves or the other men involved in the schools' foundation. A second school of this type was founded by Francis Wright in Long Eaton in 1866. Although Wright and his extended family were well-known Evangelicals, there is no evidence that Francis Wright founded Trent College in opposition to the schools which were being established by Nathaniel Woodard, including Denstone College at nearby Uttoxeter. The evidence suggests that the school's later supporters, reporters and even its first historian, M. A. J. Tarver, were the ones motivated by an anti-High Church party feeling. On the other hand, Woodard's letters during this period suggest that he and his deputy, E. C. Lowe, were very concerned about an Evangelical school which was being built on *their* doorstep.

The third school resulting from individual Evangelical effort was founded in Monkton Combe, a small village just outside of Bath, in 1868. Francis Pocock had retired early from the mission field due to ill health, and within five years of becoming Vicar of Monkton Combe, he had started a middle-class school in which he had initially hoped to train boys to become missionaries. Unlike the other schools which are part of this study, Monkton Combe School was privately owned for the first 23 years of its life; firstly by Francis Pocock, then by Alfred Peache, then by Henry Wright, and lastly by Leslie Wright. Its adherence to a particularly firm Evangelicalism came about more from the convictions of its second principal, R. G. Bryan, than its founder. There is no record of any negative feeling towards the work of Nathaniel Woodard, although the school's religious teaching was described as "Protestant and Evangelical" in an 1895 school *Prospectus*. In keeping with the sympathies of its founder, many of its past pupils went on to become missionaries with the Church of England, and although the school's missionary 'honour board' is no longer kept up to date, today it has a large number of pupils whose parents are overseas missionaries. Like Weymouth College and Trent College, Monkton Combe School eventually became the property of the Church of England Evangelical College and School Company, although unlike the other two schools, this relationship was short-lived, for in 1901 a locally-based Evangelical body became the new governors of the school.

This study began with a survey of the nineteenth-century Church of England, and finishes with the review of an organization, the 'Church of England Evangelical College and Schools Company', which was keen to promote its allegiance to the Established Church. A brief survey of the distinctive features of the nineteenth-century Church of

England showed that Evangelicals came to be regarded by contemporaries as an essential part of the mainstream Church. This was despite the fact that some of their more outspoken members would have seen themselves as representing the only true Reformed Church of England, and saw the innovations of the Oxford Movement as dangerous in the extreme. Just as the history of Evangelicalism has been largely ignored by church historians, the history of Evangelical Anglican involvement in education deserves more than the occasional reference which is all it has received until now. The schools described above are examples of the important contribution by Anglican Evangelicals to the development of middle-class education in the nineteenth century.

While the analysis of what is meant by the term, 'middle-class', continues to be the subject of much sociological and historical debate, nineteenth-century middle-class education has been extensively studied by historians of education. Recent leaders in this field have been John Roach and David Allsobrook. In describing the *Anglican* contribution to this sector, they have drawn heavily on the prior work of Brian Heeney and John Honey. During their lifetimes (Brian Heeney died in 1983 and John Honey in 2001), these two men made some important historical discoveries about the involvement of Anglicans in nineteenth-century middle-class education: Heeney concentrated on the High Church and Honey largely on the Broad Church. The present book attempts to go some way to completing the picture. An examination of the influence of *Evangelical* Anglicans in nineteenth-century middle-class education shows that their significant contribution has, until now, been largely overlooked.

APPENDICES

APPENDIX 1

Biographical Notes* on Some Key Nineteenth-Century Evangelicals

Auriol, Edward (1805–1880). Rector of St Dunstan's-in-the-West (a Simeon Trustee living) 1842–80, and a prebendary of St Paul's Cathedral. Although shy and retiring, his counsel was widely sought. He was described as "The Nestor of the Evangelical party" and "the wisest of all the Evangelical clergy" by Eugene Stock, the CMS historian. He was the archetypal committee man, and was on the CMS committee and various CMS subcommittees. Auriol was also a Simeon Trustee and a council member of Wycliffe Hall, Oxford, and on the joint committee of Wycliffe Hall and Ridley Hall, Cambridge. He was a very active member of the Council of the Church Association.

Barlow, William Hagger (1833–1908). Rector of St Ebbe's, Oxford 1873–75; Principal of the CMS Training College, Islington 1875–82; Vicar of St James's, Clapham 1882–87; Vicar and Rural Dean of Islington 1887–1901; Dean of Peterborough 1901–1908. Barlow was

---

* The most frequently referenced sources of information for these short biographies are: L. Stephens and S. Lee, *Dictionary of National Biography* 22 vols, Oxford 1917–96; D. M. Lewis (ed.), *The Blackwell Dictionary of Evangelical Biography 1730–1860* 2 vols, Oxford 1995; T. Larsen (ed.), *Biographical Dictionary of Evangelicals*, Leicester 2003; F. Boase, *Modern English Biography* 6 vols, London 1965; J. A. Venn and J. Venn (eds), *Alumni Cantabrigienses Part II: 1752–1900* 6 vols, Cambridge 1922–54; J. Foster (ed.), *Alumni Oxonienses 1715–1886* (series 2), Nendeln, Liechtenstein 1968; P. Townend (ed.), *Burke's Genealogical and Heraldic History of the Peerage, Baronetage and Knightage*, London 1963; *Crockford's Clerical Directory*, London 1869–1900; E. Stock, *The History of the Church Missionary Society* 4 vols, London 1899–1916; F. W. B. Bullock, *The History of Ridley Hall Cambridge* 2 vols, Cambridge 1941; G. R. Balleine, *A History of the Evangelical Party in the Church of England*, London 1951 (1908); J. S. Reynolds, *The Evangelicals at Oxford 1735–1871*, Oxford 1975 (1953); and N. A. D. Scotland, *Evangelical Anglicans in a Revolutionary Age 1789–1901*, Carlisle 2004. The material obtained from these works has not been identified, except occasionally through the use of quotation marks. Other sources of more detailed biographical information, including biographies and memoirs, are listed after each entry.

awarded a Cambridge BD in 1875, and both a BD and DD of Oxford in 1895. He was an original member of the council of Wycliffe Hall (1877) and became a member of the Council of Ridley Hall in 1881. It was said that "in the Evangelical School of the Church of England, during the last thirty years of the nineteenth century, no one had greater influence, or a larger share in its work and development." It was also said that "Dr. Barlow dispensed more patronage than any man in England." Balleine writes that "Dr Barlow was the man of affairs, the strong counsellor behind the scenes, to whom others constantly turned to for advice on practical matters, who led committees and guided policies and was popularly supposed to be all-powerful on the patronage trusts." See M. Barlow (ed.) *The Life of William Hagger Barlow, D.D.*, London 1910; and the obituary notice by Sydney Gedge in the 1908 *C.U.P.U. Report*, pp. 13–14.

Bell, Charles Dent (1818–1898). Appointed an Honorary Canon of Carlisle Cathedral in 1869, made DD in 1878 and is notable for writing 23 popular hymns. Bell was Rector of Cheltenham from 1872 (succeeding Francis Close, q.v.) until his sudden death at the National Club in 1898. See J. Julian (ed.), *A Dictionary of Hymnology*, London 1915, p. 133.

Bickersteth, Edward (1786–1850). Deputation secretary to the CMS 1816–30; Rector of Watton, Hertfordshire, 1830–50; and in 1842 succeeded Josiah Pratt as principal secretary of the CMS. Bickersteth was a prolific author and a missionary "statesman", becoming in the 1830s "perhaps the leading Anglican evangelical spokesman to the nation." Bickersteth was invited by CMS in 1815 to lead an investigation into its mission work in Sierra Leone. After returning home, he became head of its missionary training college, which in 1820 moved to Barnsbury House, Islington. Bickersteth was a "tireless pastor, and promoter of church societies, a founder of the London Central Mission, the CPAS, the Evangelical Alliance, the Irish Church Mission and the Parker Society." His son, Edward Henry, became Bishop of Exeter (q.v.) and nephew, Robert, became Bishop of Ripon (q.v.). See T. R. Birks, *Memoir of the Revd Edward Bickersteth*, 2 vols, London 1851; and M. Hennell, *Sons of the Prophets*, London 1979, pp. 29–49.

Bickersteth, Edward Henry (1825–1906). Vicar of Christ Church, Hampstead 1855–85; Dean of Gloucester from January 1885; and Bishop of Exeter from May 1885 until September 1900. His pastoral ministry was described as "a perpetual gentle force that made for holiness" and he was a committed parish visitor, often meeting with church wardens and Sunday School teachers as well as clergy. Bickersteth was a great supporter of mission and was three times speaker at the annual meeting of CMS and preached the annual sermon in 1888. He had an important national profile through his writing, which included a commentary on the New Testament; an epic poem in 12 books; and a number of well-loved hymns as well as a collection of hymns. His *Hymnal Companion to the Book of Common Prayer* (1870) became a favourite amongst Evangelicals, so that by 1877 it was being used in over a thousand churches. His father was Edward Bickersteth the elder (q.v). His son, also Edward, became Bishop of South Tokyo. See F. K. Aglionby, *The Life of Edward Henry Bickersteth: Bishop and Poet*, London 1907.

Bickersteth, Robert (1816–1884). Bishop of Ripon 1857–1884. While at Ripon, Bickersteth was an uncompromising opponent of Ritualism, biblical criticism and secularism, and was an ardent advocate of popular preaching, religious education and church building. He was deeply concerned about the religious welfare of the English labouring poor. He took a keen interest in education and was a leading influence in the founding of the Diocesan Training College in 1860. See M. C. Bickersteth, *A Sketch of the Life and Episcopate of the Right Reverend Robert Bickersteth, D.D.*, London 1887; and D. N. Hempton, "Bickersteth, Bishop of Ripon: the Episcopate of a Mid-Victorian Evangelical" *Northern History* 17 (1981): 183–202.

Boultbee, Thomas Pownall (1818–1884). After ordination and a college fellowship, Boultbee was curate to Francis Close from 1849, theological tutor at Cheltenham College from 1853, and the first Principal of London College of Divinity from 1863. The college arose out of a paper he read before the Clerical and Lay Association (Western District) in 1860. Eugene Stock claimed, "He and Mrs Boultbee made St. John's Hall quite an important social centre...for London Evangelicals." Boultbee made a significant contribution to the theological education of Evangelicals and gave papers on ordination training at church congresses. He was made a prebendary of St Paul's Cathedral and awarded an LLD in 1872.

Boyd, Archibald (1803–1883). Perpetual Curate of Christ Church, Cheltenham 1842–59; Vicar of St James's, Paddington 1859–67; Dean of Exeter from 1867. Boyd was "a born orator, a scholarly and eloquent preacher" and a "firm but moderate Evangelical." While Vicar of St James's, Paddington, he preached to large congregations and he was a Canon of Gloucester from 1857. See Contem Ignotus, *The Golden Decade of a Favoured Town*, London 1884, pp. 70–102.

Champneys, William Weldon (1807–1875). Vicar of St Mary's Whitechapel 1837–60; Vicar of St Pancras, London 1860–7; Dean of Lichfield, 1867–75. St Mary's parish had a population of over 30,000 and contained some of East London's worst slums. Champneys became perhaps the most effective 'slum clergyman' of the mid-century, so that attendances of 100 on a Sunday before his arrival rose to a remarkable 10,000 (including Sunday Schools and district churches) by the time of the 1851 Religious Census. He was a "convinced but not militant" Evangelical having been a "pioneer of the modern type of parochial organization" at St Mary's, Whitechapel, and a member of the Church Association council from its formation in 1865. Champneys was a Canon of St Paul's Cathedral 1851–68. See C. Bullock, 'Biographical Sketch', in *The Story of the Tentmaker: W. Weldon Champneys*, London 1875.

Chavasse, Francis James (1846–1928). Rector of St Peter-le-Bailey, Oxford 1878–89; Examining Chaplain to Bishop of Exeter (E. H. Bickersteth) 1885–1900; Principal of Wycliffe Hall 1889–1900; Bishop of Liverpool 1900–1923. Chavasse was Vice-President of South-Eastern College 1895–1928, and was awarded a DD in 1900. See J. B. Lancelot, *Francis James Chavasse*, London 1929.

Close, Francis (1797–1882). Close's father, Henry Jackson Close (1753–1806), Rector of Hitcham, Suffolk, died when he was aged nine. At this time his elder brother, J. M. Close, became his guardian. Close spent the next seven years at boarding schools, and in 1812 went to Hull Grammar School as a private pupil of John Scott (1777–1834), the Headmaster and a leading Evangelical. In January 1816, Close entered St John's College, Cambridge, taking letters of introduction from his brother and his tutor to Charles Simeon (q.v.), Fellow of Kings College and Vicar of Holy Trinity church. In time, Simeon became a mentor to Close, his influence lasting throughout Close's lifetime. After his graduation in 1820, Close married Anne Diana Arden (1791–1877), and later that year was ordained Deacon to the curacy of Church Lawford, Warwickshire; after another year he was ordained Priest. In 1822, Close moved from Church Lawford to become Assistant Curate at Willesden and Kingsbury, Middlesex; his brother living at the nearby village of Kilburn. Inspired perhaps by the business activities of his elder brother, Francis Close set about increasing the number of schools in Kingsbury, where, unlike Church Lawford and Willesden, there were no schools. In his first year, Close opened a temporary day and Sunday school; during the next year he

Appendix 1

secured a site from All Souls College, Oxford, which owned the estate, and raised £153, including a grant from the National Society. A building was completed by September 1823 and for the rest of his time in the parish, Close took a keen interest in the work of the school. The experience he gained from establishing this school in Kingsbury was important for his later work in Cheltenham. Living on the outskirts of London made it possible for Close to become involved with Evangelicals in the capital; however, there were still few Evangelical clergy in London. One of the ways in which their numbers began to increase was through Evangelicals purchasing advowsons. In the autumn of 1816, Charles Simeon had purchased the patronage to the parish church of St Mary, Cheltenham, from Joseph Pitt. At that time, Charles Jervis (1782–1826) was the Evangelical incumbent. In 1824, at the age of 27, Francis Close was appointed Curate of Holy Trinity church, erected in 1823 as a 'chapel of ease' to St Mary's. While Curate of Holy Trinity, Close gained a reputation as a popular preacher; he also published sermon series on the Liturgy and on Genesis. But he was not to remain there for long, for on 25 September 1826, just two years and six months after he had arrived in Cheltenham, Charles Jervis died and Simeon appointed Close to the living of Cheltenham parish church. It was a substantial promotion, and one that was to have important consequences for both Close and the town of Cheltenham. Refer to Chapter 3 for further information about Close, and see especially A. F. Munden, *A Cheltenham Gamaliel: Dean Close of Cheltenham*, Cheltenham 1997; and M. Hennell, *Sons of the Prophets: Evangelical Leaders of the Victorian Church*, London 1979.

Colquhoun, John Campbell (1803–1870). Radical MP for Dumbartonshire 1832–35 and a Conservative MP for Kilmarnock Burghs 1837–41 and Newcastle-under-Lyme 1842–47. As well as being on the Council of the Church Association since its formation, he was Chairman of the National Club, which became a focus for religiously based Conservatism, and Chairman of the Church of England Education Society. He was also "an active parliamentary representative of the Evangelical party in the Church of Scotland" and an original member of the Oxford Evangelical Trust. His son, John Erskine Campbell-Colquhoun, was Vicar of Southwold, Suffolk, 1870–2. See J. Wolffe, *The Protestant Crusade in Great Britain 1829–1860*, Oxford 1991, p. 76.

Deacon, John (1825–1901). Son of John Deacon the elder of Battersea, who was a great friend of Wilberforce. Deacon the younger was educated at Oriel College, Oxford, before becoming a very successful London banker and "a great supporter of Evangelicalism in the Church of England". He was one of the founders of Ridley and Wycliffe Halls, and was Honorary Treasurer of their joint councils, remaining on as Treasurer of Ridley Hall after their separation 1893. He was suceeded both as Treasurer and Trustee of the two Halls by his son, J. F. W. ("Frank") Deacon (1859–1941).

Dimock, Nathaniel (1825–1909). Vicar of Wymynswold, Kent 1872–76, and St Paul's Maidstone 1876–87; then English Chaplain at San Remo 1887–8. Sometimes using the pseudonym 'An English Presbyter', he wrote over 20 books and pamphlets on theology and liturgy from an Evangelical perspective. He was regarded as a "profound student of sacramental questions, including the doctrine and ritual of Holy Communion," and his book, *The Doctrine of the Sacraments* (1871) was regarded as a valuable Evangelical contribution to the Eucharistic debate.

Emery, William (1825–1910). Archdeacon of Ely 1864–1907 and made a Canon of Ely Cathedral in 1870. At various and frequently the same times he was also Bursar, Dean and Tutor at Corpus Christi College, Cambridge; Permanent Honorary Secretary of the Church Congress; Honorary Secretary of the Ely Diocesan Conference; Chairman of the Hunstanton Convalescent Home and Honorary Secretary of the Central Council of Diocesan Conferences. He was Chairman of the Council of the Church Schools Company (Ltd) 1883–1903. Emery "was a born inaugurator of movements. He started the Volunteer Movement at Cambridge in 1859, and in 1861 his efforts brought about the first Church Congress." He was described by Owen Chadwick as the "father of the Church Congresses", being present at every Church Congress from the 1st – 47th, and their chief organizer. See M. F. G. Donovan, *After the Tractarians*, Glasgow 1933, p. 79.

Fremantle, William R. (1807–1895). Coxswain of the first Oxford University boat in 1829; Rector of Pitchcott, Buckinghamshire 1832–1841; Vicar of Steeple Claydon, Buckinghamshire, 1841–68; Rector of Middle Claydon with East Claydon; Rural Dean 1841–76 and Dean of Ripon 1876–95. He was brother to Sir Thomas Francis Fremantle MP, the first Lord Cottesloe, and brother-in-law to Henry Wright, the CMS Secretary. His son was Colonel Francis E. Fremantle, MP for St Albans. His predecessor at Ripon was another well-known

Appendix 1

Evangelical, Revd Hugh McNeile (q.v.) and successor, William Henry Fremantle, a nephew and a noted theological 'liberal'. As a "well-known protagonist of Evangelical issues in word and print", William Fremantle was on the founding committee for both Wycliffe and Ridley Halls, and later the council of Wycliffe Hall. As Dean of Ripon, he was remembered (amongst other things) for providing a meal for all the visiting "country people" attending the parish services at the Minster on Sundays. His influence among Evangelicals was described as being "very great". See W. R. Fremantle, *Recollections of Dean Fremantle, Chiefly by Himself*, London 1921.

Garbett, Edward (1817–1886). Vicar of St Stephen's, Birmingham; Perpetual Curate of St Bartholomew's, Gray's Inn Road, 1854–63; Vicar of Christ Church, Surbiton, 1863–77; Rector of Barcombe, Lewes 1877–78. Garbett was Chaplain to Lord Shaftesbury as well as Boyle Lecturer 1860–63 and Bampton Lecturer 1867. He was a member of the Church Association general committee from its formation in 1865. Garbett was active on a national scale as editor of *The Record* (1853–67) and for some time of *The Christian Advocate*, as well as speaking regularly at Church Congresses (1866, 1870–4 and 1879).

Gedge, Sydney (1829–1923) of Mitcham Hall, Surrey. Liberal Member of Parliament for Stockport and afterwards for Walsall. Vice-president of the CMS from 1886 and, "for many years", chairman of the Committee. Gedge was a board member of the National Protestant Church Union, and founding board member of the Church of England Evangelical College & Schools Company (see Chapter 10). He was also one of the four original Trustees of both Wycliffe and Ridley Halls. His father, Sydney Gedge (1802–1883), was also a noted Evangelical, having been a member of the CMS Committee until his death; he was also involved in schools, having been second master of King Edward's School, Birmingham for most of his life (1835–59).

Greaves, Aden Ley [Talbot] (1826–1899). The fourth son of William Greaves, MD, of Mayfield, Staffordshire. After graduating in 1850 from St John's College, Cambridge, Greaves was ordained Deacon and subsequently appointed curate to the family living at Mayfield, becoming vicar in 1854. Greaves assisted Francis Close at Cheltenham 1854–6, and was Rector of Melcombe Regis, Dorset, 1856–81. He was Vicar of Clifton, Bristol, 1881–91 and Priest-in-Charge of Holy Trinity Chapel, Torquay 1891–6, where "he built a new church, himself subscribing a third of the cost". He purchased the advowson of Holy Trinity, Torquay and two other livings in that town. He died in February 1899 from an accident while riding. Talbot Greaves was from a large family of well-known Evangelicals. See "The Greaves Family: Some Clarifications", *Notes and Queries* 28 (October 1981): 405–8; and C. A. G. Greaves, *Records of My Life 1831–1911*, London 1912.

Hathaway, Edward Penrose (1818–1897). Rector of St Ebbe's, Oxford, 1868–73, where he "restored Evangelical teaching". Hathaway was instrumental in obtaining patronage of St Aldate's, Oxford, in 1858. He was founder and an original trustee of the Oxford Evangelical Trust, which was set up in 1864 to administer the Oxford advowsons of St Peter-le-Bailey, St Ebbe's and St Clement's, then later also Holy Trinity and St Matthew's, Grandpont. Prior to being ordained at age 50, Hathaway had been a lawyer. Following his wife's accidental death in 1872, he resigned from St Ebbe's and retired from parish ministry for nine years. By 1877 he was living at Clifton, Bristol. In 1882 Hathaway became Vicar of St Andrew-the-Less, Clifton, then Rector of Holbrook, Suffolk 1885–92. In 1893 he presided at a meeting which founded the (continuing) Oxford Pastorate, to provide additional spiritual guidance for undergraduates attached to local Evangelical parishes. A "capable administrator, a self-effacing Christian, a devoted pastor, Hathaway was a determined upholder of Evangelicalism."

Hoare, Edward (1812–1894). Grandson of the London banker Samuel Hoare (1751–1825), he was the Incumbent of Christ Church, Ramsgate 1847–53, then Holy Trinity, Tunbridge Wells from 1853–94, being appointed Honorary Canon of Canterbury Cathedral in 1868. Hoare was a pupil of Charles Perry (q.v.) while at Cambridge, and "widely famed for his pastoral gifts and notable Evangelical ministry." He was a CMS Committee stalwart and active in the CPAS and other societies. An important local Evangelical leader, he was also a well-known missioner and a significant participant in national church affairs. He spoke out against Ritualism and 'holiness' teaching. He was an early premillennialist and a widely read author of doctrinal, eschatological and homiletical works. See J. H. Townsend, *Edward Hoare, M.A., A Record of His Life based upon a Brief Autobiography*, London 1897.

Appendix 1 343

Kinnaird, Arthur Fitzgerald (1814–1887), the tenth Baron Kinnaird. After an early diplomatic career, he became a banker and served as Liberal MP for Perth, 1837–39 and 1852–78, before he was elevated to be the eleventh Baron Kinnaird. He became D.L. and J.P. for Perthshire and Kent, and J.P. for London. He was a prominent Evangelical parliamentarian, and a familiar figure at the May meetings, being a key supporter of the CMS and Ridley Hall, Cambridge, where he was on the College Council from 1881 and a Trustee from 1885. He was involved in the London Missionary Society, the CMS, the Malta Protestant College, the London City Mission, the Ragged Schools Union, and the YMCA. His wife, Lady Mary Jane Kinnaird, was also a leading Evangelical. See K. Heasman, *Evangelicals in Action*, London 1962.

Lefroy, William (1836–1909). Originally a broadchurchman, Lefroy was influenced by the evangelical preaching of D. L. Moody of Northfield, USA. J. C. Ryle, The first Bishop of Liverpool, made him an honorary canon in 1880, Rural Dean of South Liverpool in 1884, and Archdeacon of Warrington in 1887. From 1876, he was a prominent member of the Liverpool school board in the 'voluntary' interest. He was Dean of Norwich 1889–1909.

McNeile, Hugh (1795–1879). Rector of St Jude's, Liverpool 1834–48; St Paul's, Prince's Park, Liverpool 1848–67; and Dean of Ripon 1868–75. McNeile was a "big, impetuous, eloquent Irishman" and regarded by Eugene Stock, the CMS historian, as "unquestionably the greatest Evangelical preacher and speaker in the Church of England" during the nineteenth century. Between 1834 and 1868, when he departed to be Dean of Ripon, he exercised an "unrivalled influence" on the town of Liverpool, immersing himself in the civil and religious life of the town. Soon after arriving in Liverpool, he successfully led the opposition to the town council's decision to remove religious instruction from the corporation schools, boldly appealing for funds to open rival schools, which ultimately led to a mass exodus from the corporation schools. The council conceded defeat and "from that moment his power and authority in municipal life were prodigious". Although he exerted a wider influence through his writings and as Dean of Ripon, McNeile's supreme achievement was at Liverpool. See G. H. Francis, *Orators of the Age*, New York 1847, pp. 308–14; J. Murphy, *The Religious Problem in English Education*, Liverpool 1959; and A. Wardle, "The Life and Times of the Revd Dr Hugh McNeile, 1795–1879", MA thesis, University of Manchester 1981.

Money, Charles Forbes Septimus (1818–1893). Curate to Francis Close at Cheltenham 1845–46. Before studying at Cambridge, he worked for the Colonial Office, and while he was serving curacies in London he was an associate secretary for the CMS, specializing in African affairs. He was Vicar of St John's, Deptford from 1855–83, where he was "one of the leading Evangelicals in the diocese", and became a Canon of Rochester Cathedral in 1875 and Rural Dean of Deptford from 1879. He returned to Cheltenham in 1883 to be the third Incumbent of St Luke's Church until 1888, departing at 70 years of age to take up two more incumbencies at Holy Trinity, Kilburn and All Saints' Birling, Kent, before his death. See A. F. Munden, *A History of St Luke's Church, Cheltenham 1854–2004*, Cheltenham 2004.

Moule, Handley Carr Glynn (1841–1920). Although raised to the episcopate (as Bishop of Durham) in 1901, for over 20 years before this, he made a distinctive contribution to the life of Evangelicals as a teacher, theologian, writer and leader. He was made Fellow of Trinity College, Cambridge in 1865; Assistant Master, Marlborough College 1865–67; worked as an assistant curate to his father at Fordington 1867–72 and 1877–80; Senior Dean, Trinity College 1873–77; first Principal of Ridley Hall, Cambridge 1880–1899; honorary chaplain to Queen Victoria 1899–1901 and King Edward VII 1901; and finally Bishop of Durham 1901–20. He was a prolific author, writing for the layman as well as the theologian. Some of his important works include *Outlines of Christian Doctrine* (1889); four commentaries in the *Cambridge Bible for Schools* series; four *Expositor's Bible* commentaries; six volumes of sermons; a large number of smaller devotional works; as well as over 30 tracts and papers. He also wrote a biography, *Charles Simeon* (1892); and a church history, *The Evangelical School in the Church of England* (1901); and several religious and non-religious poems, for which he won the Seatonian Prize from Cambridge University five times between 1869 and 1876. Moule was also an active speaker: he was Select Preacher at Cambridge for thirteen years, spoke regularly at Keswick Conventions and addressed the annual Anglican Church Congress eighteen times. See J. B. Harford & F. C. MacDonald, *Handley Carr Glyn Moule, Bishop of Durham*, London 1922; C. F. D. Moule *Memories of Ridley Hall*; and M. L. Loane, *Makers of Our Heritage*, London 1967, pp. 57–98.

Appendix 1 345

Moule, Walter Stephen (1864–1949). A student at Monkton Combe School 1887–91, W. S. Moule graduated from Corpus Christi College, Cambridge in 1886 and Ridley Hall in 1887. He was a CMS missionary in China from 1888–1925, where his appointments included Examining Chaplain to the Bishop of Cheking; Archdeacon of Cheking; and Principal of Trinity College, Nangpo. On returning home, he was Vicar of Abbotsbury, Dorset, from 1925–42. His father, Arthur Moule, was also a CMS missionary in China, where he was Archdeacon to George Moule, the Bishop of Mid-China. He married one of the daugters of Henry Wright (q.v.).

Peache, Alfred (1818–1900). Perpetual Curate of Mangotsfield with Downend, Bristol 1859–74, and Vicar of Downend 1874–78. In 1857, he and his sister, Kezia Peache (1820–1899) inherited an annual income of £50,000 from their father's estate. Encouraged by T. P. Boultbee and Joseph Ditcher, he gave a sum of this magnitude to establish the London College of Divinity, and with his sister eventually gave over £120,000 to the College. Most of the Peache fortune was used for educational purposes. As well as the London College of Divinity, Peache was a generous benefactor to the Clergy Daughters' School, established in Gloucester (1831) and later moved to Bristol (1836); Monkton Combe School (see Chapter 6 above); Ridley Hall, Cambridge; and Huron College, London, Ontario (now part of University of Western Ontario), where he endowed the chair of Divinity, and from which he recieved a DD in 1885 and was made Chancellor. Peache established a patronage trust soon after he came into his fortune, and this eventually included 23 livings and is known today as the Peache Trust. See G. C. B Davies, *Men for the Ministry*, London 1963 and A. F. Munden, *The History of St John's College, Nottingham, Part One: Mr Peache's College at Kilburn*, Nottingham 1995, pp. 10–18.

Perry, Charles (1807–1891). Born at Moor Hall in Essex, his father was a shipbuilder with works at Blackwall. Perry was educated at Harrow and Trinity College, Cambridge, where he was one of the eight men who first rowed an eight-oared boat on the Cam. He became a Fellow and Tutor of his college 1832–40. He was ordained in 1836, having previously experienced a period of religious doubt. Perry was appointed the first Bishop of Melbourne on the advice of Henry Venn in 1847. He secured the passage of the 1854 Church Assembly Act in Victoria, which provided for lay representation in synod, and under its auspices summoned the first legally authorized synod in the colonies in 1856. Perry retired in 1876, returning to Britain where he took up residence in his deceased sister's house in Regent's Park in London. From this central base, he maintained an active interest in Evangelical church committees, especially the CMS for which he was a vice-president. Perry was one of the founders of Ridley Hall in Cambridge (1881), earning the title "Father of Ridley Hall" because of his pioneering work. As early as February 1841, he published a paper on the need for a new approach to theological education entitled *Clerical Education, considered with an especial reference to the Universities.* See G. Goodman, *The Church in Victoria during the Episcopate of the Right Reverend Charles Perry*, London 1892; A. de Q. Robin, *Charles Perry Bishop of Melbourne*, Nedlands 1967; and the entry for Perry in B. Dickey (ed) *The Australian Dictionary of Evangelical Biography*, Sydney 1994.

Ryder, Henry (1777–1836). Bishop of Gloucester 1815–24, and Lichfield & Coventry 1824–36. Widely regarded as the "first Evangelical bishop", Ryder was an energetic diocesan, rarely preaching less than twice on a Sunday and often three times, besides giving a weekly lecture in one of the Gloucester churches. On Sunday afternoons he examined and instructed children in the Gloucester National School, and in 1816 he established the Gloucester Diocesan Society for the education of the poor, and was instrumental in founding the female penitentiary. At Lichfield he plunged into evangelistic work and church building, and "Evangelicalism made particularly rapid advance in Birmingham", which was part of this diocese. See G. C. B. Davies, *The First Evangelical Bishop: Some Aspects of the Life of Henry Ryder*, London, Tyndale Press, 1958; and W. J. Baker, "Henry Ryder of Gloucestershire", *Transactions of the BCAS* (1971):130–144.

Ryle, John Charles (1816–1900). Rector of Helmingham from 1844–45; Vicar of Stradbroke from 1861–80; and the first Bishop of Liverpool 1880–1900. While he was incumbent of the parish of Helmingham in Suffolk, he gained a national profile through his publications. These included the hymn books *Spiritual Songs* (1849) and *Hymns for the Church on Earth* (1850); biographies of Latimer, Baxter and Whitefield entitled *The Bishop, The Pastor*, and *The Preacher* respectively; and his well-known *Expository Thoughts on the Gospels* (1856–73). Ryle also wrote over 200 tracts, which were at times free or otherwise sold for a penny and had a "remarkable circulation at home and in overseas colonies". Ryle gave a lead to the Evangelicals by his active participation in the newly instituted church congresses, he helped to establish an annual diocesan conference in Norwich, and he supported the move to revive Convocation. He was closely associated with the founding of Wycliffe Hall, Oxford, in 1877; and of Ridley Hall, Cambridge in 1879. His later publications included *Knots Untied* (1874), *Old Paths* (1877) and *Practical Religion* (1878). Ryle was extremely active at the parish and the diocesan level. When appointed to the new see of Liverpool in 1880, "he had to lay essential foundations and build for the future from ground level". During his episcopate, the number of incumbents in the diocese increased from 170 when he started, to 205 by 1897; the number of curates rose from 120 to 220; and confirmations increased 4500 to 8300 by 1890. Twenty-seven churches and forty-eight mission halls were built between 1880 and 1890, and paid Scripture Readers—laymen who would assist ordained ministers in teaching, organization and diaconal work—were widely used; fifty readers being active by 1890. Ryle's moderate Calvinism led to his opposition of the doctrine regarding the pursuit of holiness that was taught by the founders of the Keswick Movement. As a result of this, Ryle and his supporters became increasingly marginalised towards the end of the century. See P. Toon and M. Smout, *John Charles Ryle: Evangelical Bishop*, Cambridge 1976; M. L. Loane, *John Charles Ryle 1816–1900*, London 1983; I. D. Farley, "J C Ryle: Episcopal Evangelist: A Study in late Victorian Evangelicalism." PhD thesis, Durham University 1988; and I. D. Farley, *J. C. Ryle: First Bishop of Liverpool*, Carlisle 2000.

Shaftesbury, Anthony Ashley-Cooper (1801–1885) was known by the courtesy title of Lord Ashley until he became the seventh Earl of Shaftesbury in 1851. Shaftesbury's parliamentary career spanned—almost continuously—more than 50 years. Among other organizations, he was involved in the CPAS (being a 'founder' in 1836 and president from this time until his death in 1885), the London Society for Promoting Christianity amongst the Jews, the British and Foreign Bible Society, the Protestant Alliance, the Ragged School Union, the Society for Improving the Condition of the Labouring Classes, and the Lunacy Commission. He was the chairman or president of many of these bodies. Other key political activities included his involvement in the Factory Acts of 1833 to 1847, which set limits on the ages of employees and the length of working days; and the establishment of a Royal Commission into conditions in British mines, which led to improvements in employee conditions. Throughout his life, Shaftesbury was at pains to stress the Protestantism of the Church of England, and as Palmerston's step-son-in-law, was able to yield considerable influence in the years 1855–65 to promote bishops of a similar Evangelical persuasion. Shaftesbury's long career elevated him to the position of the leading lay Evangelical of his day, and a figure of national stature. See G. F. A. Best, *Shaftesbury*, London 1964; G. B. A. M. Finlayson, *The Seventh Earl of Shaftesbury, 1801–1885*, London 1981; J. Pollock, *Shaftesbury: The Poor Man's Earl*, London 1985.

Simeon, Charles (1759–1836). Son of a successful lawyer, Simeon was educated at Eton and King's College, Cambridge, where he remained a Fellow for the rest of his life. He was the leading Evangelical of his day, and influenced many undergraduates who attended the sermon and 'conversation' parties he hosted in his rooms, or the services at which he preached as the Incumbent of Holy Trinity Church from 1783. He was closely involved in the formation of many of the leading Evangelical societies such as the CMS, the Bible Society, and the London Society for Promoting Christianity amongst the Jews. In order to extend the influence of Evangelicals in the Church of England, in 1816 Simeon began to purchase the advowsons of livings so that 'serious' clergy, especially those with the ability to preach, should be appointed. This lead to the formation of the Simeon Trust in 1817. At the time of his death in 1836 Simeon had the right to appoint the clergymen to 42 livings and perpetual curacies. See W. Carus, *Memoirs of Charles Simeon*, Cambridge 1847; H. C. G. Moule, *Charles Simeon*, London rev. edn. 1948; C. Smyth, *Simeon and Church Order*, Cambridge 1940; A. Pollard and M. Hennell (eds), *Charles Simeon, 1759–1836*, London 1959; and especially H. E. Hopkins, *Charles Simeon of Cambridge*, London 1977.

Smith, Robert Payne; known as Robert **Payne Smith** (1819–1895). Assistant Master at Edinburgh Academy 1847–53; Headmaster of Kensington Proprietary School 1853–57; Sub-Librarian at the Bodleian 1857–65; Regius Professor of Divinity at Oxford 1865–71; Bampton Lecturer in 1869; and Dean of Canterbury 1871–95. An orientalist, he wrote a number of books "of notably accurate scholarship" on Syriac studies, and his Syriac dictionary "started a new era in the study of Syriac". Payne Smith was a voluminous writer on controversial theology, "in which he favoured the conservative and evangelical side". From 1865 till his death in 1895, all his publications, apart from the *Thesaurus Syriacus*, as his dictionary was called, were in defence of the Evangelical point of view. He was a founding member of the councils of Wycliffe Hall, Oxford, and Ridley Hall, Cambridge; having presented an important paper at the Church Congress at Nottingham in 1871 on the subject of 'clerical education'. He remained the Chairman of the Council of Wycliffe Hall Council for the rest of his life. He was made DD 1865 and Hon DLitt 1892. His son, William

Henry Payne Smith, was Vice-Principal of Wycliffe Hall 1880–3 and Assistant Master of Rugby School 1884–1907. Robert Payne Smith was one of the founders of South-Eastern College, now St Lawrence College, Ramsgate.

Stowell, Hugh (1799–1865). Appointed Curate in Charge of St Stephen's, Salford, Manchester in 1828, where he stayed until his death in 1865. It was his love of children which initially drew him into municipal life. The Lancashire Public School Association, which had been formed to agitate for secular education, tried to persuade a town hall meeting to send a petition to parliament. Stowell made a masterly speech of over two hours with such effect that it carried an amendment asking that no system of general education should be sanctioned of which the Christian religion was not the basis. From that time he was widely respected by local politicians. "His authority grew with the passing years, until it became comparable with that of McNeile in Liverpool, and Close in Cheltenham." See J. B. Marsden, *Memoirs of Revd. Hugh Stowell*, London 1868; and C. Bullock, *Hugh Stowell: A Life and Its Lessons*, London 1881; and S. E. Maltby, *Manchester and the Movement for National Elementary Education, 1800–1870*, Cambridge 1918.

Sumner, Charles Richard (1790–1874). Bishop of Llandaff 1826–27 and Winchester 1827–69. Younger brother of John Bird Sumner (q.v.), he showed particular concern, as a bishop, for education and providing schools for the poor. He was a great church builder, and formed a Diocesan Building Society in 1837. During his Winchester episcopate, 201 new churches were built and 119 restored or rebuilt, at a cost of over £2,000,000. Visitation of the diocese was given a great priority, including (for perhaps the first time since the Reformation) the clergy of the Channel Islands. "He was a pronounced Evangelical who rigorously contended against the Oxford Movement." See G. H. Sumner, *Life of Charles Richard Sumner*, London 1876; and N. A. D. Scotland, *Good and Proper Men*, Cambridge 2000, p 210.

Sumner, John Bird (1780–1862), elder brother to Charles Sumner. Bishop of Chester 1828–48 and the first "avowed Evangelical" Archbishop of Canterbury 1848–62. While at Chester, Sumner proved an outstanding pastor and gifted administrator. He was responsible for a massive increase in church building and accommodation, so that by 1839 he had consecrated 161 new churches. He was a great supporter of the church's missionary work and oversaw the revival of the Convocations of Canterbury and York, despite the fact that he had originally been in opposition to this development. He was an able theologian and his *Apostolic Preaching Considered* (1814) and *Treatise on the Records of Creation* (1816) both went through many editions. "His archiepiscopate was marked by mild and statesmanlike policies, an almost total lack of factionalism, and wise and temperate leadership." See N. A. D. Scotland, *John Bird Sumner: Evangelical Bishop*, Leominster 1995.

Thornton, Henry (1760–1815). Youngest son of John Thornton (1720–1790), the "wealthiest merchant in Europe but one", Henry Thornton entered the family business of banking where he rose to become a director of the Bank of England. In 1782, he was elected MP for Southwark, a seat he held for the remainder of his life. Thornton's residence at Clapham became the focal point for the "Clapham sect", and he worked hard for its causes alongside his cousin, Wilberforce (q.v.). He became the first treasurer of the British and Foreign Bible Society and the CMS. Until his marriage he gave away six-sevenths of his considerable income for Christian and charitable causes, including £2,000 a year to distribute Bibles. See S. Meacham, *Henry Thornton of Clapham 1760–1815*, London 1964.

Venn, John (1759–1813). Rector of Clapham 1792–1813. Son of the distinguished Henry Venn of Huddersfield (1725–1797). A man of "good culture, good judgement and perseverance", he organised his parish on vigorous Evangelical lines. He was one of the first clergymen to introduce parish schools; he boldly started a Sunday evening service; he organised a system of district visiting; published a collection of psalms and hymns for use in the parish; and was active in the work of the Society for Bettering the Condition of the Poor at Clapham. He was a member of the Eclectic Society and combined with Simeon to draft a set of initial rules for the Society for Missions in Africa and the East (the future CMS). Above all, he was the personal friend and spiritual guide of perhaps the most notable congregation in the whole of England during his generation: the Clapham Sect. See M. Hennell, *John Venn and the Clapham Sect*, London 1958.

Venn, Henry (1796–1873). The son of John Venn (q.v.) and the grandson of Henry Venn of Huddersfield. Henry Venn the younger was educated at Queens' College, Cambridge, where he was a Fellow from 1819 to 1829. From 1834 to 1847, he was Incumbent of St John's, Upper Holloway, and from 1841 until 1872, Honorary Clerical Secretary of the CMS. In this capacity "he orchestrated its missionary strategy and was a key figure in the re-invigoration of the society." The

Appendix 1 351

CMS and the church of the day owed much to "the depth and profundity of his thinking, and his vision and broad sympathy", giving him a significance which extends beyond the nineteenth century. See M. Hennell, *Sons of the Prophets: Evangelical Leaders of the Victorian Church*, London 1979, pp. 68–90; and T. E. Yates, *Venn and the Victorian Bishops Abroad*, London 1978.

Venn, John (1802–1890). The second son of his namesake (q.v.), Venn was educated at Queens' College, Cambridge, where he was a Fellow 1828–33. From 1833 until 1870 he was Vicar of St Peter's with St Owen, Hereford, and a prebendary of Hereford Cathedral 1843–68. He was a trustee of the Simeon Trust for much of this time.

Villiers, Henry Montagu (1813–1861). Bishop of Carlisle 1856–60 and Durham 1860–61. As a bishop he was a strong pastor who worked hard to raise clerical incomes. He was a vigorous opponent of the Oxford Movement and attacked the use of the Confessional. He actively supported Evangelical societies, revived the office of Rural Dean and created 18 new rural deaneries within his archdeaconries of Carlisle and Westmorland. Under Villiers' Carlisle episcopate, the number of graduate clergy increased, and he conducted 11 ordination services. He travelled extensively throughout his diocese and set himself a target of preaching in every church. Villiers was translated from Carlisle to Durham where he fell seriously ill and died just as he was beginning to prepare for his Primary Visitation. See A. F. Munden, "The First Palmerston Bishop: Henry Montagu Villiers, Bishop of Carlisle, 1856–1860 and Bishop of Durham, 1860–1861", *Northern History* 26 (1990): 186–206.

Wace, Henry (1836–1924). Dean of Canterbury 1903–1924, Wace held a number of distinguished positions, including Boyle Lecturer 1874–75; Professor of Ecclesiastical History at King's College London 1875–88; Bampton Lecturer at Oxford in 1879; prebendary of St Paul's 1881–1903; Principal of King's College London 1883–97; Examining Chaplain to the Archbishop of Canterbury (Benson) 1883–96 and 1896–1903 (F. Temple); Honorary Chaplain to Queen Victoria 1884–89; and Honorary Chaplain to King Edward VII 1901–1903. Wace was awarded a DD in 1883; he was a Trustee of the Oxford Evangelical Trust 1898–1924; President of London College of Divinity 1909–24; President St John's Hall, Durham 1909–19; and Chairman of Governors of Weymouth & Trent Colleges 1913–24. Wace was also Chairman of the Council of the National Church League for many years and was a frequent speaker at its meetings. During the whole of his ministry, Wace was an avowed Evangelical, but it was during the last 30 years of his life that he exercised the most profound and widespread influence. For some years he edited the *Churchman*, frequently making contributions to it, as well as to *The Record*, the *Quarterly Review*, and *The Times*—for which he wrote lead articles for over twenty years. His other writing activities included being the co-editor of *A Select Library of Nicene and Post-Nicene Fathers of the Christian Church* and of *Luther's Primary Works*, and producing a collection of essays on the teaching of the Reformers entitled *Principles of the Reformation*. However, Wace was no 'stay-at-home scholar'; he worked on behalf of King's College Hospital, held the chairmanship for many years of the Clergy Mutual Insurance Society, and gave countless addresses to conferences and meetings throughout the land. He was hailed by many Evangelicals as a champion for their cause, and he was "one of the most potent and respected voices within Evangelicalism for three decades or more." See G. Johnson, "Dean Wace", *Churchman* (April 1924): 95–101.

Webb-Peploe, Hanmer William (1837–1923). Vicar of St Paul's, Onslow Square, London 1876–1919 and a prebendary of St Paul's Cathedral from 1893. Before this, he succeeded his father as Vicar of King's Pyon with Birley 1866–76. Eugene Stock said that Webb-Peploe was universally recognized as "the leading Evangelical clergyman in London, and one of the first half-dozen in the whole country." He was "an active supporter of CMS and regarded as a 'prophet' of the annual Keswick Convention". He became a member of Ridley Hall Council in 1883 (replacing Alfred Peache, q.v.), and was one of the founding directors of the Church of England Evangelical College and School Company (see Chapter 10 above), as well as being a popular parochial 'missioner' and speaker at the annual Islington Clerical Meeting, where he "rapidly rose to the position of a principal leader." Webb-Peploe was one of the four senior vice-presidents of the Cambridge Inter-Collegiate Christian Union which was created in February 1911 after CICCU disaffiliated from the Student Christian Movement in 1910. See S. Barabas, *So Great Salvation: The History and Message of the Keswick Convention*, London 1952, pp. 165–9.

Weeks, John Wills (*c*.1800–1857). CMS missionary and Bishop of Sierra Leone 1855–57. Originally a carpenter by trade, after receiving training as a schoolmaster he was sent in 1824 to Sierra Leone as a CMS schoolteacher to work in the villages settled by re-captives freed from the slave ships. One of his pupils was the future Bishop of Niger and the first black bishop, Samuel Adjai Crowther. In 1845 he returned with his wife to the then impoverished parish of Lambeth; his Sierra Leone congregation sending him a contribution to relieve the Lambeth poor. In 1855 he succeeded Bishop Vidal as second Bishop of the newly created diocese of Sierra Leone. See C. Fyfe, *A History of Sierra Leone*, London 1962.

Whiting, John Bradford (1828–1914). Vicar of St Luke's, Ramsgate 1875–1905. Prior to this he was Curate of Saffron Walden 1851–56; Associate Secretary of CMS 1856–61; and Vicar of Broomfield, Essex 1861–74. Whiting was a well-known Evangelical, being chaplain to Bishop J. C. Wigram of Rochester from 1864–67 (q.v.), and chaplain to the Isle of Thanet [Clerical and Lay] Union from 1876–78. In 1881, Whiting travelled on behalf of CMS, with the Lay Secretary, Mr E. Hutchinson, to the island of Madeira to "confer of the affairs of the Mission". This was later known as the "Madeira Conference" and was widely reported. Whiting was also on the General Committee of the Church Association.

Wigram, Frederick E. (1834–1897). Honorary Secretary of the CMS 1880–95. Wigram was made a prebendary of St Paul's Cathedral in 1896 and was on the Council of Ridley Hall, Cambridge 1882–97. Two of his sons went to Ridley: E. F. E. Wigram became a CMS missionary in Pakistan and Principal of St John's CMS Divinity School 1896–1910; H. F. E. Wigram migrated to Australia. The Wigram family included such well-known Evangelicals as J. C. Wigram (q.v.), Bishop of Rochester 1860–67, and W. B. Wigram, Secretary to the General Committee of the Western District Clerical and Lay Association. The family's connection with Monkton Combe School was maintained into the next century when D. R. Wigram was appointed the seventh Headmaster in 1946. See the Cambridge University Prayer Union Report of 1898, viii, at Cambridge University Library.

Wigram, Joseph Cotton (1798–1867). Sixth Wrangler at Cambridge 1819; Rector of Tisted, Hampshire 1839–50; Rector of St Mary's Southampton 1850–60; Archdeacon of Surrey 1847–60; and Bishop of Rochester 1860–67. Wigram was involved in various educational projects during his lifetime: he was Secretary of the National Society from 1828 to 1839, and in 1861 he agreed to give his support to Nathaniel Woodard's scheme for middle-class boarding schools at a public meeting in the Sheldonian Theatre in Oxford. This support was subsequently withdrawn when it became clear to Wigram that "doctrines that ran counter to Protestantism" were being taught in

Woodard's schools. Wigram was a conscientious bishop who worked hard to raise his clergy's stipends and encouraged them to use lay helpers, including 'Mission Women', in their parishes. In 1862 Wigram published *The Cottager's Family Prayers*, a manual for family devotions wherein he advocated that there should be a fixed time, every day, morning and evening when every person in the house should assemble to pray. Wigram was responsible for making baptisms a more public occasion by encouraging his clergy to incorporate these into normal Sunday services. Along with other Evangelical bishops, Wigram advocated more frequent services of Holy Communion and established a new emphasis on pastoral care and the bishop as the manager of the diocese. Wigram once denounced his clergy for wearing moustaches, smoking and playing cricket on village greens, leading to him being dubbed the 'Bishop of Little Things' by a secular newspaper in 1860. See the *Gentleman's Magazine* 1867, vol. 1, p. 669 and N. A. D. Scotland, *Good and Proper Men*, Cambridge, 2000.

Wilberforce, William (1759–1833). Wilberforce experienced various Evangelical influences in his childhood, including being sent as a day-boy to Hull Grammar School and hearing the preaching of John Newton. In the 1780s he became involved in the movement for the abolition of the slave trade, and this cause was to occupy his talents, time and energies for the remainder of his life. From 1787 onwards Wilberforce and a small band of followers dedicated themselves to this 'glorious enterprise' and to other aims of national and international importance, consistent with and expressive of their Evangelical faith. An inner circle of the band lived in the same neighbourhood and subsequently became known as the 'Clapham Sect'; a few like Wilberforce were members of Parliament, where they were collectively designated 'the Saints'. See R. Isaac and S. Wilberforce, *The Life of William Wilberforce* 5 vols, London 1858; R. Coupland, *Wilberforce: A Narrative*, Oxford 1923; R. Furneaux, *William Wilberforce*, London 1974; and J. Pollock, *Wilberforce*, Berkhamstead 1977.

Wilson, Daniel (1778–1858). Assistant Tutor at St Edmund Hall, Oxford 1807–12 and Vice-Principal 1807–12; Vicar of Islington 1824–32; Founder of the London Clerical Education Society and Islington Clerical Conference; First Bishop of Calcutta 1832–58 and Metropolitan of India. Wilson died when he fell ill during his first journey back to England. He was a "strong churchman [who] established episcopacy on a firm basis". See J. Bateman, *The Life of*

Appendix 1

the Right Revd. Daniel Wilson, Boston, Mass., 1860; and M. Loane, *Oxford and the Evangelical Succession*, London 1950, pp. 247–96.

Wright, Henry (1833–1880). Ordained in 1857, he "laboured for a time among the miners and iron-workers of the Butterley estate belonging to his family" before becoming Vicar of St Nicholas, Nottingham. He was Clerical Secretary of the Church Missionary Society from 1872 and during this time he was Minister of St John's Chapel Downshire Hill, Hampstead, and a prebendary of St Paul's Cathedral. Henry Wright is regarded as the 'founder' of Wycliffe Hall at Oxford and he was a major benefactor of Monkton Combe School near Bath (see Chapter 6 above). He drowned while bathing in Lake Coniston on Friday 13 August 1880.

APPENDIX 2

Church Association Register of Evangelical Schools

(from the *Church Intelligencer*, August 1912, p. 127)

List of Schools, &c., where Religious Instruction is a Special Feature and of a Strictly Evangelical Character

Name of School and Situation	Principal	Boys or Girls	Fees per Annum	
			Boarders	Day Scholars
St George's College, Eastbourne	W. Davies, Esq.,	Boys	50 to 60 Gs.	...
The High School, Baldslow Road, Hastings	J Hooper, Esq., MA, LL.B	Boys	40 to 50 Gs.	7 to 10 Gs.
Upper Mount, Southsea	Miss S E Davies	Girls	60 to 100 Gs.	12 to 30 Gs.
Dean Close Memorial School, Cheltenham	Revd. Dr. Flecker	Boys	£48 tp £50	...
Trafalgar House Boys' School, Lee-on-the-Solent, Hants	W.W. Webb, Esq., B.A. & H.J. Webb, Esq.	Boys	60 to 78 Gs.	...
Welby House, North Foreland, near Broadstairs	Miss Hibbs	Girls	£110	
Brook Green College, 45, 47, 53 & 55, Aynhoe Rd W.	Miss Biddlecombe	Girls	40 to 50 Gs.	6 to 18 Gs.
Brean Down House, Esplanade, Burnham, Somerset	Miss Jones, LL.A	Girls	40 to 70 Gs.	5 to 35 Gs.
Westfield College, Hampstead, N.W.	Miss C.L. Maynard (Girt Col)	Girls (over 18)	£105	...
Rhianva College, Hunstanton Chilton Rectory, Sudbury, Suffolk	Mrs Hackney	Girls	40 to 50 Gs.	15 Gs.
Chilton Rectory, Sudbury, Suffolk	Revd. J. Milner, MA (Cantab)	Boys (8–12 yrs)	60 to 80 Gs.	...
Monkton Combe School, nr. Bath	Revd. J.W. Kearnes MA	Boys	55 to 65 Gs.	15 to 25 Gs.

List of Schools, &c., where Religious Instruction is a Special Feature and of a Strictly Evangelical Character

Name of School and Situation	Principal	Boys or Girls	Fees per Annum Boarders	Fees per Annum Day Scholars
Trent College, Derbyshire	Revd. J.S. Tucker, MA	Boys	£50 to £75	...
Weymouth College, Dorsetshire	H.C. Barnes Lawrence, Esq. MA	Boys	£50 to £75	£25 to £30
Weymouth College, Junior School Boys		Boys	£44 to £60	£16 to £21
'Winterdyne', Hesketh Park, Southport	Miss Clough	Boys (6–14 yrs)	45 to 50 Gs.	12 to 21 Gs.
Queen's School, Dalby Square, Cliftonville, Margate	Mrs J.W. Walton, LL.A	Girls	£45	10 Gs.
Alberbury Vicarage, Salop	Rev. Ellis, G. Roberts MA (Oxon)	Backward / delicate boys (over 15)	£90 to £120 52 Gs	...
Woolston, Kirtleton Avenue, Weymouth	Mrs Kirby, LL.A.	Both (under 15)	39 to 48 Gs.	6 to 15 Gs.
Egerton House School, Exeter	Miss Gardiner	Girls	42 to 48 Gs.	7.s to 12 Gs.
Cheltenham House School, Cromer	H.M. Padley, Esq., BA	Boys (8–15 yrs)	£68 to £80	21 to 24 Gs.
St Lawrence College, St Lawrence-on-Sea, Ramsgate	Revd. E.C. Sherwood, MA (Oxon)	Boys		
The Mount, Folkston	Miss Ruspini	Girls (8 yrs onwards)	50 to 90 Gs.	12 Gs.

For terms upon which Schools are admitted to this list apply to the Secretary of the Church Association, J.W.D. Barron, 13 & 14, Buckingham St., Strand, London.

APPENDIX 3

Middle-Class Schools Referred to in this Book

Name of School	Location	Foundation
Leicester and Leicestershire Collegiate School	Leicester	1836 (closed 1866)
The Proprietary School for the Town and County of Leicester	Leicester	1837
Cheltenham Diocesan Boys' School	Cheltenham	1839
Cheltenham Proprietary College	Cheltenham	1841
West Somerset County School (later, Wellington School)	Wellington, Somerset	1842
College of St Columba	Rathfarnham (near Dublin)	1843
Cheltenham Commercial and Classical Proprietary School on Church of England Principles	Cheltenham	1845
St Andrew's College	Harrow Weald, Middlesex	1846 (closed 1860)
St Peter's College (later, Radley College)	Radley, Abingdon (near Oxford)	1847
St Nicolas College	Shoreham, Sussex	1847
Shoreham Grammar School and Collegiate Institute (later, SS. Mary and Nicolas Grammar School, then Lancing College)	Shoreham, then Lancing, Sussex	1848

Middle-Class Schools Referred to in this Book (cont.)

Name of School	Location	Foundation
St John's Middle School (later, Hurstpierpoint)	Shoreham, then Hurstpierpoint, Sussex	1849
St Andrew's College	Bradfield, Berkshire	1850
St Mary's College	Harlow, Essex	1851
Cheltenham Ladies' College	Cheltenham	1854
Devon County School	West Buckland	1858
St Saviour's School (later, Ardingly)	Shoreham, Sussex	1858
East Devon County School (formerly Sampford Peverall Proprietary School)	Sampford Peverall, Devon	1860 (closed 1886)
Melcombe Regis 'Middle School'	Weymouth, Dorset	1860
Surrey County School	Cranleigh	1862
Weymouth College (originally Weymouth Grammar School, then Weymouth Collegiate School)	Weymouth, Dorset	1863 (closed 1940)
St Edward's School	Oxford	1863
Dorset County School	Dorset	1864

Middle-Class Schools Referred to in this Book (cont.)

Name of School	Location	Foundation
Framlingham College (originally, Albert Middle Class College, then Suffolk County School)	Framlingham, Suffolk	1865
Bedford County School	Bedford	1866
Monkton Combe School	Monkton Combe (near Bath)	1868
St Chad's Middle School (later, Denstone College)	Denstone	1868
Trent College	Long Eaton, Nottinghamshire	1868
Norfolk County School	Elmham, Norfolk	1874
South-Eastern College (later, St Lawrence College)	Ramsgate, Kent	1879
Dean Close Memorial School (later, Dean Close School)	Cheltenham	1882
North-Eastern County School	Barnard Castle	1882

Bibliography

Primary Sources

Books, Tracts and Pamphlets   362
Newspapers, Journals and Magazines   370
Reports, Minutes and Papers   372

Secondary Sources

Books and Monographs   380
Journals   407
Theses and Dissertations   412

Primary Sources: Books, Tracts and Pamphlets

Acland, Arthur H. D., ed. *Memoir and Letters of the Right Honourable Sir Thomas Dyke Acland.* London: [privately printed], 1902.

Acland, Thomas D. *Middle-Class Education. Scheme of the West of England Examination and Prizes; for June 1857. With Introductory Remarks Addressed to Members of the Universities.* London: J. Ridgeway, 1857.

Adams, W. E. *Memoirs of a Social Atom.* New York: A. M. Kelley, 1968.

Arnold, Matthew. *A French Eton; or, Middle Class Education and the State.* London: Macmillan & Co, 1864.

———. *Friendship's Garland: Being the Conversations, Letters and Opinions of the Late Arminius, Baron von Thunder-Ten-Tronckh.* London: Smith, Elder & Co., 1871.

———. *Matthew Arnold on Education.* Edited with an introduction by Gillian Sutherland. Harmondsworth: Penguin Education, 1973 (1910).

Arnold, Thomas. *The Miscellaneous Works of Thomas Arnold.* Ed. Arthur Penrhyn Stanley. London: B. Fellowes, 1845.

Atkinson, J. A. *Rural Deans and Ruri-Decanal Chapters.* Manchester: Hale & Rowarth, 1864.

Barlow, Margaret, ed. *Life of William Haggar Barlow, D. D.* London: George Allen and Sons, 1910.

Bartley, George C. T. *Schools for the People.* London: Bell & Daldy, 1871.

Barton, Cecil Edward. *John Barton: A Memoir.* London: Hodder & Stoughton, 1910.

Bateman, James. *The Tractarian Tendencies of Diocesan Theological Colleges.* London: Seeleys, 1853.

———. *The Church Association: Its Policy and Prospects Considered in a Letter to the Chairman.* London: William Ridgeway, 1880.

Bateman, Josiah. *Life of the Right Revd. Daniel Wilson, D. D., Late Lord Bishop of Calcutta and Metropolitan of India.* 2 vols. London: John Murray, 1860.

Battersby and Battersby, eds. *Memoir of T. D. Harford-Battersby, Late Vicar of St. John's, Keswick and Honorary Canon of Carlisle.* London: Seeley & Co., 1890.

Bibliography

Biber, George E. *Bishop Blomfield and his Times. An Historical Sketch.* Reprinted from the *Churchman's Magazine.* London: Harrison, 1857.

Bickersteth, Montagu Cyril. *A Sketch of the Life and Episcopate of the Right Reverend Robert Bickersteth, D. D.* London: Rivingtons, 1887.

Bickersteth, Samuel. *Life and Letters of Edward Bickersteth, Bishop of South Tokyo.* London: John Murray, 1905.

Birks, T. R. *A Memoir of the Revd. Edward Bickersteth.* 2 vols. 3rd edn. London: L. Seeley, 1852.

Brereton, J. L. *County Education: A Letter Addressed to the Right Honourable the Earl of Devon.* London: James Ridgeway, 1861.

———. *Principles and Plan of a Farm and County School.* London: n.p., 1861.

———. *The County College: An Educational Proposal Addressed to the University of Cambridge.* Cambridge: n.p., 1872.

———. *County Education: A Contribution of Experiments, Estimates and Suggestions.* London: Bickers and Son, 1874.

———. *County Education: The Reports of the Devon and Norfolk County School Assocations for the Year 1874, with a Few Remarks by the Revd. J. L. Brereton.* London: Bickers & Son, 1875.

———. *County Education: Accounts of the Devon and Norfolk County School Assocations for 1875, with a Few Remarks on the New College for Junior Students in Cambridge.* London: Bickers & Son, 1876.

Brown, Abner William. *Recollections of the Conversation Parties of the Revd. Charles Simeon, M. A., Senior Fellow of King's College, and Perpetual Curate of Trinity Church, Cambridge.* London: Hamilton Adams, 1863.

Bullock, C. *The Story of the Tentmaker W. Weldon Champneys.* London: n.p., 1875.

———. *Hugh Stowell: A Life and Its Lessons.* London: n.p., 1881.

Calendar of S. Nicolas College, Shoreham, for the Year of our Lord 1850. Shoreham: S. Nicolas College, 1850.

Calendar of The College of S. Nicolas, Lancing, for the Year of our Lord 1859. London: John Henry & James Parker, 1859.

Carlisle, N. *A Concise Description of the Endowed Grammar Schools in England and Wales.* 2 vols. London: Baldwin, Cradock & Joy, 1818.

Cartaret-Bisson, F. S. de. *Our Schools and Colleges: Being a Complete Compendium of Practical Information upon all Subjects Connected* with *Education and Examination Recognized in the United Kingdom at the Present Day.* 4th edn. London: Simpkin, Marshall & Co., 1879.

Carus, William, ed. *Memoirs of the Life of the Revd. Charles Simeon. M. A., late Senior Fellow of King's College, and Minister of Trinity Church, Cambridge.* 3rd edn. London: J. Hatchard & Son, 1848.

Cawood, John. *Is the Revision of the Prayer-Book Desirable at the Present Time? Being the Substance of a Paper Read Before the Ludlow, Leominster, and Tenbury Lay and Clerical Church Association, at Ludlow, etc.* London: Seeley, Jackson & Halliday, 1869.

Cecil, Richard. *Memoirs of the Revd. John Newton, Late Rector of the United Parishes of St. Mary Woolnoth and St. Mary Woolchurch.* London: J. Seeley, 1817.

Chandler, George. *An Address Delivered at the Opening of the Church of England Metropolitan Commercial School, Rose Street, Soho Square, January 28, 1839.* London: John W. Parker, 1839.

Charlesworth, Samuel Beddome. *Memorials of a Blessed Life: A Brief Record of the Work of Mrs Maria Amelia Charlesworth.* London: Seeley, Jackson & Halliday, 1882.

Chavasse, F. J. *Plain Words on Some Present Day Questions.* London: Henry Frowde, 1899.

Churton, E., ed. *Memoir of Joshua Watson.* 2 vols. London: James Parker, 1861.

Close, F. *A Letter Addressed to the Inhabitants of Cheltenham on the Subject of the Races.* London: n.p., 1830.

———. *Sermon on the Occasion of the Visit of the Chartists to Cheltenham Parish Church.* London: n.p., 1840.

———. *The Restoration of the Churches is the Restoration of Popery: Proved and Illustrated from the Authenticated Publications of the 'Cambridge Camden Society'. A Sermon, Preached in the Parish Church, Cheltenham, on Tuesday, November 5th, 1844.* London: Hatchard and Son, 1844.

———. *The Roman Antichrist and Lying Spirit.* London: Hatchard & Son, 1846.

———. *National Education: Training Schools for Masters and Mistresses. Speech of the Revd Francis Close, at a Public Meeting, held at Ipswich, on Monday, 25 October 1847.* Colchester: n.p., 1847.

———. *Semper Idem; Or, Popery Everywhere and Always the Same.* London: Hatchard, 1851.

———. *High-Church Education Delusive and Dangerous: Being an Exposition of the System Adopted by Revd. W. Sewell*. London: Hatchard, 1855.

———. *A Letter to the Proprietors of Cheltenham College and to those Parents who have Sons at the School*. Carlisle: n.p., 1862.

———. *The Footsteps of Error Traced Through Period of Twenty-Five Years; or Superstition: The Parent of Modern Doubt*. London: Hatchard & Co., 1863.

———. *The Catholic Revival*. London: Hatchard & Co., 1866.

———. *"The English Church Union": A Ritualistic Society. Proved and Illustrated in a Series of Letters Originally Published in the 'Rock' Newspaper*. London: Hatchard & Co., 1868.

———. *Further Evidence of the True Character of the English Church Union, being the Substance of a Speech Delivered at the Annual Meeting of the Church Association in Carlisle, September 10th 1869*. London: Hatchard & Co., 1869.

———. *The Stage, Ancient and Modern; Its Tendencies on Morals and Religion: A Lecture by Francis Close*. London: Hatchard, 1877.

Colquhoun, J. C. *William Wilberforce: His Friends and Times*. London: Longmans, Green, Reader, and Dyer, 1866.

———. *Shall Protestant Churchmen Take Part in Convocation and Diocesan Synods?* London: Hatchards, 1869.

Conybeare, W. J. *Essays Ecclesiastical and Social. Reprinted, with Additions, from the Edinburgh Review*. London: Longman, Brown, Green & Longmans, 1855.

Curteis, G. H. *Bishop Selwyn of New Zealand, and of Lichfield: A Sketch of his Life and Work*. London: Kegan Paul, Trench & Co.: London, 1889.

Davidson, R. T. and Benham, W. *Life of Archibald Campbell Tait, Archbishop of Canterbury*. London: Macmillan & Co., 1891.

Denison, E. B., ed. *The Life of John Lonsdale, Bishop of Lichfield*. London: John Murray, 1868.

Denison, G. A. *The School of the "Church Schools Company." A Letter to the Clergy and People of the Archdeaconry of Taunton*. 2nd edn. Oxford: Parker & Co., [1883].

Duppa, Baldwin Francis. *County Colleges of Agriculture*. London: Central Society of Education, 1839.

Dury, T. *On the Parties in the Church of England*. London: n.p., 1850.

Fitzgerald, J. P. *Familiar Sketches of the late Revd. John Charlesworth*. London: n.p., 1865.

Fortescue, Lord Hugh. *The Devon County School: Its Objects, Costs and Studies.* Exeter: n.p., 1862.

———. *Public Schools for the Middle Classes (A letter to the Bishop of Exeter).* London: William Ridgeway, 1880 (1862).

———. *Public Schools for the Middle Classes.* London: Longman, Green, Roberts & Green, 1864.

Foster, Joseph. *Oxford Men and Their Colleges.* Oxford: Parker & Co., 1893.

Fremantle, W. R. *Recollections of Dean Fremantle, Chiefly by Himself.* London: Cassell and Company, 1921.

Garbett, E. *Union Among Evangelical Churchmen.* London: William Hunt & Co., 1870.

———. ed. *Evangelical Principles: A Series of Doctrinal Papers Explanatory of the Positive Principles of Evangelical Churchmanship.* London: William Hunt & Co., 1875.

Gladstone, William E. *Gleanings of Past Years, 1843–78.* 7 vols. London: John Murray, 1879.

Goding, John. *Norman's History of Cheltenham.* Cheltenham: Norman, 1863.

Goodman, G. *The Church in Victoria During the Episcopate of the Right Reverend Charles Perry.* London: Seeley and Co., 1892.

Gregory, Robert. *Do our National Schools Provide for All Whom They Ought to Train? A Letter to His Grace, the Archbishop of Canterbury.* London: Rivingtons, 1865.

Greaves, C. A. G. *Records of My Life, 1831–1911.* London: Essex Hall, 1912.

Grier, R. M. *John Allen, Vicar of Prees and Archdeacon of Salop: A Memoir.* London: Rivingtons, 1889.

Hadden, R. H., ed. *Reminiscences of William Rogers, Rector of St Botolph's, Bishopsgate.* London: Kegan Paul, Trench & Co., 1888.

Hare, Augustus J. C. *Memorials of a Quiet Life.* 2 vols. London: Daldy, Isbister & Co., 1877.

Hodder, E. *The Life and Work of the Seventh Earl of Shaftesbury.* 3 vols. London: n.p., 1886.

Hook, Walter Farquhar. *Letter to the Right Reverend the Lord Bishop of Ripon, on the State of the Parties in the Church of England.* London: J. G. F. and J. Rivington, 1841.

Hunter, A. A., ed. *Cheltenham College Register, 1841–1889.* London: G. Bell & Sons, 1890.

Hussey, Robert. *A Letter to Thomas Dyke Acland Esq., M. P., on the System of Education, to be Established in the Diocesan Schools for the Middle Classes.* London: J. G. F. & J. Rivington, 1839.

Ignotas, Contem [Richard Glover]. *A Voice from the People; Or, Thoughts on Education, Especially with Reference to the Peculiar Wants of the Middle Class.* London: Joseph Masters, 1857.

———. *The Golden Decade of a Favoured Town: Being Biographical Sketches and Personal Recollections of the Celebrated Characters who have been Connected with Cheltenham from 1843 to 1853.* London: Elliot Stock, 1884.

James, Samuel. *Some Thoughts, Observations, and Hints on Middle Class Education.* London: Longman, Brown, Green and Longmans, 1853.

———. *The Church and Society. I Middle Classes. II Lower Classes. III Upper Classes. Being Papers Read at Meetings of the Clerical Society of Maidenhead and Taplow Deaneries, with an Appendix on Middle Class Education.* London: Windsor [printers], [1869].

Jameson, T. *A Treatise on Cheltenham Waters, and Biliary Diseases.* London: Longman, 1809.

Lankester, E., ed. *The Natural History of Dee Side and Braemar.* London: [privately printed], 1855.

Lawrence, A. E. Barnes. *A Churchman to Churchmen: A Series of Lectures on Matters of Controversy at the Present Day.* London: Simpkin, Marshall & Co., 1893.

Lowe, Edward C. *St Nicolas College and its Schools. A Record of Thirty Years' Work in the Effort to Endow the Church of England with a System of Self-Supporting Public Boarding Schools for the Upper, Middle and Lower Middle Classes.* London: James Parker and Co., 1878.

Mallet, Charles. *Herbert Gladstone, a Memoir.* London: Hutchinson & Co., 1932.

Marsden, J. B. *Memoirs of the Life and Labours of the Revd. Hugh Stowell, M. A.* London: Hamilton, Adams & Co., 1868.

[Mathison, G. F.] *How Can the Church Educate the People? The Question Considered with Reference to the Incorporation and Endowment of Colleges for the Middle and Lower Classes of Society in a Letter Addressed to the Lord Archbishop of Canterbury.* London: Francis and John Rivington, 1844.

Maurice, Frederick. *The Life of Frederick Denison Maurice Chiefly Told in his Own Letters.* 2 vols. London: Macmillan & Co., 1884.

Milner, Mary. *The Life of Isaac Milner, D. D., F. R. S., Dean of Carlisle.* London: J. W. Parker, 1842.

Montgomery, R. *The Three Parties: Or, Things as they are in the Church of England; Being an Extract from the Revd. R. Montgomery's Gospel Before the Age.* London: C. Mitchell, 1845.

Mozley, T. *Reminiscences Chiefly of Oriel College and the Oxford Movement.* London: Longmans & Co., 1882.

Norton, Lord. *High and Low Church.* London: Percival & Co., 1892.

Palmer, William. *A Narrative of Events Connected with the Publication of the Tracts for the Times.* London: n.p., 1843.

Payne Smith, Robert. *Sermons on the Pentateuch.* London: S.P.C.K., 1896.

Perceval, A. P. *A Collection of Papers Concerning the Theological Movement of 1833.* London: J. G. F. & J. Rivington, 1842.

Raikes, Elizabeth R. *Dorothea Beale of Cheltenham.* London: A. Constable, 1908.

Reid, Wemyss. *Memoirs and Correspondence of Lyon Playfair.* London: Cassell and Company, 1899.

Ryder, Thomas Dudley. *A Memoir of the Hon. and Rt. Revd. Henry Ryder, D. D.* London: n.p., 1886.

Ryle, H. E. *On the Church of England.* London: Macmillan & Co., 1904.

Ryle, J. C. *We must Unite!* London: William Hunt & Sons, 1868.

———. *Knots Untied.* London: William Hunt & Sons, 1874.

———. *Old Paths,* London: William Hunt & Sons, 1877.

———. *Our Diocesan Conference. What good is it likely to do? And what dangers must it try to avoid?* London: William Hunt & Sons,, 1879.

———. *The Upper Room: Being a Few Truths for the Times.* Edinburgh: The Banner of Truth Trust, 1888 (reprinted 1970).

———. *Home Truths,* London: William Hunt & Sons, (eight series 1851–1871).

Scott, R. P., ed. *What is Secondary Education?* London: Rivingtons, 1899.

Seeley, Robert. B. *Essays on the Church.* London: Seeley & Burnside, 1834.

Selwyn, G. A. *The Work of Christ in the World: Four Sermons Preached Before the University of Cambridge on the Four Sundays Preceding Advent in the Year of Our Lord 1854.* Cambridge: Macmillan & Co., 1855.

Skinner, James. *The Church in the Public School: A Sermon Preached at the Annual Commemoration Festival at St Mary's College, Harlow, Essex, with a Letter to the Revd. the President of the College.* London: J. H. and Jas. Parker, 1861.

Smellie, Alexander. *Evan Henry Hopkins: A Memoir.* London: Marshall Brothers, 1920.

Smith, Gerard E., ed. *Recollections of the Late Francis Wright of Osmaston Manor, Derbyshiret, Esq.* London: Bemrose & Sons, 1873.

Stephen, Caroline Emelia, ed. *The Right Honourable Sir James Stephen: Letters with Biographical Notes.* Gloucester: [privately printed], 1906.

Straton, N. D. J. *Why Should We Join the Protestant Churchmen's Alliance?* London: n.p., 1889.

Stretton, C. E. *History of the Midland Railway.* London: Methuen & Co., 1901.

Sumner, G. H. *Life of Charles Richard Sumner.* London: John Murray, 1876.

Tait, A. C. *Middle Class Education. A Speech delivered at The Devon County School, West Buckland, by the Lord Bishop of London.* London: Longmans, Green, Roberts & Green, 1865.

Thornton, F. V. *The Education of the Middle Classes in England. A Lecture Delivered to Members of the Mechanics' Institute, Romsey, 20 December, 1861.* London: n.p., 1861.

Townsend, J. H. *Edward Hoare, M. A. A Record of His Life Based upon a Brief Autobiography.* London: Hodder & Stoughton, 1897.

Trollope, Anthony. *Rachel Ray.* London: Oxford University Press, 1988 (1863).

Tuckwell, W. *Reminiscences of Oxford.* London: Cassell & Company, 1900.

Vaughan, Robert. *Religious Parties in England.* London: n.p., 1838.

Vibart, H .M. *Addiscombe: Its Heroes and Men of Note.* Westminster: A. Constable and Co., 1894.

Walsh, Walter. *The Secret Work of the Ritualists.* London: n.p., 1894.

———. *The Secret History of the Oxford Movement.* London: Swan Sonnenschein and Co., 1899.

[Ward, Paul]. *Reminiscences of Cheltenham College.* London: Bemrose & Sons, 1868.

Wigram, J. C. *The Cottager's Family Prayers.* Chelmsford: T. B. Arthy, 1863.

Wilberforce, R. G. *The Life of the Right Reverend Samuel Wilberforce, D. D.* 3 vols. London: John Murray, 1881.

Wilberforce, Robert I. and Samuel, eds. *Life of William Wilberforce.* 5 vols. London: John Murray, 1838.

Williams, E. *Life and Letters of Rowland Williams.* vol 2. London: Henry S. King and Co., 1874.

Wilson, Henry Bristow. "The National Church." In *Essays and Reviews*, 173–248. 11th edn. London: Green, Longman, Roberts and Green, 1863.

Woodard, Nathaniel. *A Plea for the Middle Classes*, New Shoreham: n.p.,1848.

———. *St Nicolas College: Directions to Chaplains.* New Shoreham: n.p., 1848.

———. *Public Schools for the Middle Classes. A Letter to the Clergy of the Diocese of Chichester.* London: n.p., 1851.

———. *St Nicolas College: St Saviour's Lower Middle Class School, for the Sons of Small Shopkeepers, Artizans, Clerks, and Others of Limited Means.* Brighton: J. F. Eyles [printer], 1859.

———. *The Scheme of Education of St Nicolas College with Suggestions for the Permanent Constitution of that Society in a Letter to the Most Noble Marquis of Salisbury, D.C.L., Chancellor of the University of Oxford.* London: James Parker & Co, 1869.

———. *The Society and Schools of St Mary and St Nicolas College.* London: n.p., 1878.

Primary Sources: Newspapers, Journals and Magazines

Blackwood's Edinburgh Magazine
British Critic, Quarterly Theological Review and Ecclesiastical Record
British Quarterly Review
Carlisle Journal
Cassell's Family Magazine
Cheltenham Chronicle
The Cheltenham Examiner
Cheltenham Free Press
Cheltenham Journal
Cheltenham Mercury
Christian Observer

Church Intelligencer (previously called the *Monthly Intelligencer*)
Church Review
Church Times
The Churchman
The Churchman's Penny Magazine
Contemporary Review
Derbyshire Advertiser
Dorset County Chronicle
The Edinburgh Review
English Churchman
English Churchman and St. James's Chronicle
The English Journal of Education
Fraser's Magazine
Free Church Chronicle
The Guardian
Illustrated London News
Illustrated Sporting and Dramatic News
Kent Coast Times
Long Eaton Advertiser
Looker On
Lynn Advertiser
Macmillan's Magazine
Monthly Intelligencer (later, the *Church Intelligencer*)
Morning Post
The National Review
Protestant Churchman
The Record, and *Supplement to The Record*
The Rock
Salford Chronicle
Southern Times
Sun-Herald
The Times

Specific Newspaper Articles

Bowen, C. S. C. "The English Evangelical Clergy." *Macmillan's Magazine* 3 (1860): 113–121.

Conybeare, W. J. "Church Parties." *Edinburgh Review* 98 (1853): 273–342.

———. "Bishop Phillpotts." *Edinburgh Review* 95 (1852): 54–94.

Gladstone, W. E. "The Evangelical Movement; Its Parentage, Progress, and Issue." *British Quarterly Review* 139 (July 1879): 1–26.

Kebble, T. E. "The Middle Classes." *The National Review* 1 (1883).

"Middle-Class Education." *The English Journal of Education* (1 July 1861): 228–236.

"On the Position of the Evangelical Party in the Church of England." *Fraser's Magazine* 73 (January 1878): 22–31.

"On the Present Position of the Evangelical Party in the Church of England." *Christian Observer* 73 (February 1873): 83–96.

Plumptre, E. H. "Church Parties, Past, Present and Future." *Contemporary Review* 7 (1868).

Saunders, W. M. "Cavendish College, Cambridge." *Cassell's Family Magazine* (1885): 300–2.

Scott Robertson, W. A. "Middle Class Education." *The Churchman* 36 (September 1882): 442–450.

Stephen, L. "The Broad Church." *Fraser's Magazine* 1 [new series] (March 1870): 313–25.

Thorold, Anthony W. "The Evangelical Clergy of 1868." *Contemporary Review* 8 (1868): 569–596.

"What has Become of the Middle Classes?" *Blackwood's Edinburgh Magazine* (August 1885): 175–180.

Primary Sources: Reports, Minutes and Papers

Minute Books, Reports and Manuscript in Private Possession

Minutes of the General Committee for the Clerical and Lay Association (Western District).

Report of the Second Annual Meeting, Held 7th and 8th June, 1859 at the St James' Schoolroom, Cheltenham. Gloucester: [Davies and Son, printer],1859.

Report of the Third Annual Conference of the Church of England Clerical and Lay Association (Western District), held at the Victoria Rooms, Clifton, June 5th and 6th, 1860. [1860].

Report of the Fourth Annual Conference of the Church of England Clerical and Lay Association (Western District), Held at Bath, 4th and 5th June 1861. London: Seeley, Jackson & Halliday, 1861.

Report of the Seventh Annual Conference of the Church of England Clerical and Lay Association (Western District), Held at Bath, 31st May and 1st June, 1864. Stroud: [J Elliott, printer], 1864.

Report of the Eighth Annual Conference of the Church of England Clerical and Lay Association (Western District), Held at Cheltenham, May 30th and 31st, 1865. Stroud: [J. Elliott, printer], 1865.

Report of the Ninth Annual Conference of the Church of England Clerical and Lay Association (Western District), Held at Bristol, June 5th and 6th, 1866. Stroud: [J Elliott, printer], 1865.

Report of the Tenth Annual Conference of the Church of England Clerical and Lay Association (Western District), Held at Bath, June 4th,5th, 1867. Stroud: [J Elliott, printer], 1867.

Report of the Twentieth Annual Conference of the Church of England Clerical and Lay Association, Held at Cheltenham, June 5th and 6th, 1877. Stroud: [J Elliott, printer],1877.

Report of the Proceedings of the 41st Annual Meeting, Held at Bath, 24th and 25th May 1898. Bath: n.p., 1898.

Midland Clerical and Lay Association. *Report of the First Meeting of the Midland District of the Clerical and Lay Association Held in Derby on 19th and 20th June, 1860.* [1860].

Midland Clerical and Lay Association. *Report of the Proceedings at the First Annual Conference, Held at Derby, on 19th and 20th June, 1860.* [1860].

Midland Clerical and Lay Association. *Report of the Proceedings of the Fourth Annual Conference, Held at Nottingham on June 2nd and 3rd, 1863.* [1863].

Church of England Clerical and Lay Association: A Letter to a Clergyman of the Church of England. [signed 'Presbyter'.] 2nd edn. London: Seeley, Jackson and Halladay, 1860.

D. A. Scales, "Stemma of the *English Churchman*."

Francis Close,"Autobiography" [1860]

The British Library

Schemes of the West of England Examination and Prizes, 1857.

The Hertfordshire Almanac for 1914.

Lloyd's Register, 1858.

Prospectus of Surrey County School at Cranleigh, 1863.

Report of the United Conference of the Western, North-Western, and Midland Districts of the Church of England Clerical and Lay Association, Held in Birmingham, June 4th and 5th, 1878. London: n.p., 1878.

Cambridge University Library

Cambridge University Prayer Union Report of 1898

Haddon Willmer, "Evangelicalism 1785–1835" Hulsean Prize essay, 1962.

James Scholefield, "Sermon on the Death of the Revd. Charles Simeon." *The Pulpit* 29 (1837): 200–205.

E. Boys, "South-Eastern College, Ramsgate." *Churchman's Penny Magazine* (March 1885): 58–60.

Cheltenham College Archives

Minutes of the Board of Directors of the Proprietary College

Rules and Regulations of Cheltenham College, Instituted 1840, 1859.

Cheltenham College Annual Reports, 1841–

Report of the Committee Appointed at a Special General Meeting of the Proprietors of Cheltenham College, on 13 November 1861.

Cheltenham Public Library

Report of a Committee appointed at a Vestry Meeting held on the 6th Nov. 1828, to meet a Deputation from the College of Corpus Christi, published in *The Grant of Richard Pate, Esq. by which he founded The Free Grammar School and Hospital, in the Town of Cheltenham, in the Year 1578*, Cheltenham: n.p., 1833.

Report of the First Annual Examination and Distribution of Prizes; Also the Substance of a "Familiar Discourse" Delivered to the Scholars, in Accordance with the Will of the Founder, by the Revd F. Close A. M. on June 23, 1853. Cheltenham: [G. Norman, printer], 1853.

Pate's Grammar School, Cheltenham. Detailed Report of the Committee Appointed, by the Parish, in Vestry Assembled, on Easter Tuesday 1848. Cheltenham: [Rowe & Norman, printers], 1849.

Report of a Committee Appointed at a Vestry Meeting Held on the 6th November, 1828, [1833].

A. Miles, "History of Cheltenham and District," 10 vols. 1930–32.

Church Pastoral Aid Society Archives

Annual Reports

Occasional Papers

Church and People: Echoes of Church Pastoral-Aid Work

Church Society Archives at Lambeth Palace Library

Minutes of the Council, 1–21 (1867–1950).

Minutes of the General Committee, 1867–95.

Minutes of the Clerical and Lay Union, 1870–73.

Annual Reports

"Appeal for Protestant Middle Class Schools"

Articles of Association, Church of England Clerical and Lay Association

Letter on Church Questions, from J. C. Colquhoun, Esq., to Colonel Savile and the Members of the Conference at Clifton, October, 1869. London: Hatchards, 1869.

Objects and Working of the Church Association [proof copy, 1898]

The Church Association: What Is It? London: Church Association, 1905.

[E. P. Hathaway and W. F. Stubbs] *The Woodard Schools.* 2nd edn. London: Church Association, 1868.

Church Association Tracts, vol 1.

Church of England Record Centre

Report of the Committee, Read at the Fifty-Ninth Annual Meeting on the 3rd May, 1894. London: S.P.C.K., 1894.

35th Annual Report of the Norwich Diocesan Society.

8th Annual Report of the Exeter Diocesan Board.

Official Yearbook of the Church of England, 1883–1887.

Corpus Christi College Archives

Scheme for the Administration of the Charity School known as Pate's Grammar School and Hospital Charity, Cheltenham. Cheltenham: n.p., 1900.

Letter from Francis Close to Dr Norris, 5 July 1853.

Dean Close School Archives

Minute Book of the Clerical and Lay Association (Western District) Middle-Class Schools Committee. [This Minute Book was also used to record minutes of the various other committees which sprang from this original committee. They include the Schools Committee, (also known as the Local Committee and the Cheltenham Local Committee), a 'Preparatory Meeting', the Executive Committee, the various sub-committees of the Executive Committee, and the Annual Meeting of the Life Governors.]

The First School Minute Book

General Committee Minute Book

Dean Close Memorial School *Deed of Constitution*, 1886.

Dean Close Memorial School *Prospectus*, 1899.

Dean Close Memorial School Magazine 1–9 (January 1892–August 1894)

The Decanian, 1895–

W. H. Flecker, "Notes on the History of the School, Since its Foundation in May, 1886." *The Dean Close Memorial School Magazine* 1 (January 1892): 3–7.

R. F. McNeile, "The First Ten Years 1886–1896." *The Decanian* 195 (1956): 6–8.

"H. Elder's Memoirs"

"Notes on Francis Close"

Lambeth Palace Library

Archbishop F. Temple Papers

Archbishop Tait Papers

Archbishop E. W. Benson Papers

Lancing College Archives

(a) Correspondence

Letter from James Bateman to Nathaniel Woodard, 30 October 1868.

Letter from Nathaniel Woodard to Julius Hare, 9 December 1851.

Letter from Nathaniel Woodard to Lord Cranborne, 21 November 1866.

Letter from the Bishop of Lichfield and New Zealand to the Revd G. R. Mackarness, 23 January 1868.

Letter from the Revd William Allen to Mr Bird, 12 October 1868.

Letter from James Bateman to Nathaniel Woodard, n.d., ['Tuesday'].

Letter from the Revd G. R. Mackarness to Nathaniel Woodard, 20 June 1868.

Letter from G. A. Denison to N. Woodard, 21 October 1879.

(b) Other documents

Prospectus and List of Shareholders of the Church Schools Company Limited, for Boys and Girls, 1 February 1884.

B. Handford, *Nathaniel Woodard: Printed Notes of a Lecture Delivered at Hurstpierpoint College, 5 November 1974.*

Monkton Combe School Archives

(a) Correspondence

Letter from R. G. Bryan to S. Gedge, 21 February 1894.

Letter from G. R. F. Prowse to Mr Powell, 11 February 1928.

Letter from G. R. F. Prowse to A .T. Wicks, 28 August 1937.

Letter from W. S. Moule to A. F. Lace (undated).

Letter from M. E. Relton to H. J. Powell (undated).

(b) Other documents

Minutes of the Directors' Meetings

A Call for Consecrated Educational Talents

Evangelical Church Schools Annual Report

A. T. Wicks and A. F. Lace, eds. *Monkton Combe Register, 1868–1964*. 35th edn. [Monkton Combe: Monkton Combe School], 1965.

A. G. Whitehouse, ed. *Monkton Combe School Register 1968–1994*. 37th edn. [Monkton Combe: Monkton Combe School], 1994.

Monkton Combe School *Prospectus*, Summer 1895.

Old Monktonian Gazette

D. L. Pitcairn, "Memorial Sermon on the Revd. Francis Pocock", 23 March 1919.

"Brief Notes taken down from Mr Pocock."

T. Wicks, "Notebook 1".

A. F. Lace, "Notes".

"Reminiscences", *The Old Monktonian Gazette* (May 1959):106.

L. H. Gamlen, "O.M. Reminiscences", 1940.

National Society Archives at the Church of England Record Centre

Minute Book of the General Committee

Minute Book of the Committee of Inquiry and Correspondence

Minute Book of the Middle Class Schools Committee

Minutes of the Committee of Council on Education

Annual Report of the National Society, vols 1–89 (1811–1900)

National Society Middle Class Schools Committee Report

St Lawrence College Archives

Minutes of Council of South-Eastern College

Minutes of the Executive Committee of the Council of the Corporation of the South-Eastern College

Minutes of the Local Committee [of the South-Eastern Clerical and Lay Church Association], held at Dane Park School House.

Constitution of the South-Eastern College

Memorandum and Articles of Association, The Corporation of the South-Eastern College, 1893.

Seventeenth Annual Report of the South Eastern Clerical and Lay Church Alliance on The Principles of the Reformation, for 1888. Canterbury: [J. A. Jennings, printer], 1889.

South Eastern College Magazine (SECM), 1884–1914.

The Lawrentian, 1914–

"List of Students"

Register of St Lawrence College. London: The Old Lawrentian Club, 1912; 2nd edn. [Ramsgate]: Old Lawrentian Club, 1925; 3rd edn. [Ramsgate]: Old Lawrentian Society, 1934; 4th edn. n.p., 1955.

"A Brief Historical Sketch of the College, by an Old Boy." In *Old Lawrentian Society Annual Report and List of Members 1929–30.*

D. A. Scales, *Emile Cornet D'Auquier (1850–1894): A Sketch of the First Headmaster's Life*, [privately printed], 1994.

St Lawrence College Year Book. Ramsgate: St Lawrence College, Old Lawrentian Society, 1945.

"A Short History of Our Times", *SECM* 10, 1 (March 1899): 12.

Trent College Archives

Minute Books of the Evangelical Church Schools Company, vols A–F (January 1891–December 1912).

Minutes of Sub-Committees appointed by the Board, 27 February 1895–20 November 1899.

Minutes of the Meetings of Directors, Weymouth College Council and Trent College, 19 November 1913–8 December 1915.

Trent College *Prospectus* for 1887, 1890 and 1895.

Frank Lott, "Early Records: Trent College", 1869–73.

Memorandum of Association of Evangelical Church Schools Limited

Report of the Inspection of Trent College, Long Eaton, Derbyshire. London: Board of Education, 1929.

Trent College Chronicle, April 1874–July 1874.

Trent College Magazine,1874–5.

Trident , December 1890–

Weymouth College Archives at the Weymouth Public Library

The O. W. Budget

The Clavinian

Weymouth College Magazine, 1901–1943.

The Dorset Yearbook, 1923.

E. V. Tanner, "Weymouth College, 1902–1940" [a photograph album].

"A Great Proprietary School. The Story of Weymouth College." *St James's Budget* 18 May, 1894.

J. B. Kerridge, *Weymouth and Melcombe Regis Local Rakings.* London: n.p., 1866.

Bibliography

Parliamentary Statutes and Reports

(a) Statutes

3 & 4 Vict. 1847: Cap. 77. *An Act for Improving the Condition and Extending the Benefits of Grammar Schools, 1847.*

32 & 33 Vict. 1869: 197–208. Cap. 56. *Endowed Schools Act, 1869.*

3 and 4 Vict. 1874: Cap. 86. *The Public Worship Regulation Act, 1874.*

(b) Reports, Returns & Minutes

Annual Reports of the Charity Commissioners (Brougham Enquiry), 1818–37.

Minutes of the Committee of Council on Education, 1846–1849.

Report of Her Majesty's Commissioners Appointed to Inquire into the State of Popular Education in England (Newcastle Commission), 6 vols, 1861.

Report of Her Majesty's Commissioners on Revenues and Management of Certain Colleges and Schools (Clarendon Commission), 4 vols, 1864.

Report of Her Majesty's Commissioners Appointed to Inquire into the Education Given in Schools not Comprised within Her Majesty's Two Former Commissions (SIC or Taunton Commission), 21 vols, 1867–8.

Report of Endowed Schools Commissioners to Committee of Council on Education, 1872.

Report of Royal Commission on Elementary Education Acts (Cross Commission), 2nd Report, 1887.

Report of Royal Commission on Secondary Education (Bryce Commission), vol 9, 1895.

Return of the Pupils in Public and Private Secondary and Other Schools in England, 1987.

Secondary Sources: Books and Monographs

Acland, Arthur H. D. and H. Llewellyn Smith, eds. *Studies in Secondary Education.* London: Percival & Co., 1892.

Adamson, J. W. *An Outline of English Education, 1789–1902.* Cambridge: Cambridge University Press, 1930.

Addleshaw, G. W. O. *The High Church Tradition.* London: Faber & Faber, 1941.

Aglionby, Francis Keyes. *The Life of Edward Henry Bickersteth: Bishop and Poet.* London: Longmans, Green & Co., 1907.

Aldrich, Richard. *School and Society in Victorian Britain: Joseph Payne and the New World of Education.* New York: Garland Pub., 1995.

Aldrich, R. and P. Gordon. *Dictionary of British Educationists.* London: Woburn, 1989.

All Saints' School, Bloxham, 1860–1960: Brief History of the School and its Progress. [All Saints' School], 1960.

Allen, W. O. B. and E. McClure. *Two Hundred Years: The History of The Society for Promoting Christian Knowledge, 1698–1898.* London: S.P.C.K., 1898.

Allister, D. S. "Anglican Evangelicalism in the Nineteenth Century." In *The Evangelical Succession in the Church of England,* ed. D. N. Samuel, 64–81. Cambridge: James Clarke, 1979.

Allsobrook, David Ian. *Schools for the Shires: The Reform of Middle-Class Education in Mid-Victorian England.* Manchester: Manchester University Press, 1986.

Altholz, Josef L. "The Mind of Victorian Orthodoxy: Anglican Responses to 'Essays and Reviews', 1860–1864." In *Religion in Victorian Britain 4: Interpretations,* ed. Gerald Parsons, 28–40. Manchester: Manchester University Press, 1988.

———. *The Religious Press in Britain, 1760–1900.* London: Greenwood Press, 1989.

———. *Anatomy of a Controversy: The Debate over "Essays and Reviews", 1860–1864.* Aldershot: Scholar Press, 1994.

Anderson, Perry. "The Figures of Descent." In *English Questions,* ed. Perry Anderson, 121–92. London: Verso, 1992.

Annan, Noel. *Roxburgh of Stowe.* London: Longmans, 1965.

Archer, R. L. *Secondary Education in the Nineteenth Century.* Cambridge: Cambridge University Press, 1921.

Arnold, F. *Our Bishops and Deans.* 2 vols. London: Hurst & Blackett, 1875.

Arnstein, Walter L. *Protestant versus Catholic in Mid-Victorian England.* London: University of Missouri Press, 1982.

Avis, Paul. *Anglicanism and the Christian Church.* Edinburgh: T. & T. Clark, 1988.

———. "What is Anglicanism?" In *The Study of Anglicanism,* eds Stephen Sykes and John Booty, 405–24. London: S.P.C.K., 1988.

Bailey, Peter. *Leisure and Class in Victorian England: Rational Recreation and the Contest for Control, 1830–1885.* London: Routledge & Kegan Paul, 1978.

Balleine, G. R. *A History of the Evangelical Party in the Church of England.* London: Longmans, Green, & Co., 1908.

———. *A History of the Evangelical Party in the Church of England.* 2nd edn. [Includes a Postscript by the author.] London: Longmans, Green & Co, 1933.

———. *A History of the Evangelical Party in the Church of England.* 3rd edn. [The Postscript is replaced in this edn. by an Appendix by G. W. Bromiley.] London: Church Book Room Press, 1951.

Bamford, T. W. *Thomas Arnold.* London: Cresset Press, 1960.

———. *Rise of the Public Schools: A Study of Boys' Public Boarding Schools in England and Wales from 1837 to the Present Day.* London: Thomas Nelson & Sons Ltd, 1967.

Banks, J. A. *Prosperity and Parenthood.* London: Routlege & Kegan Paul, 1954.

Banks, Olive. *Parity and Prestige in English Secondary Education.* London: Routledge & Kegan Paul, 1955.

Barabas, S. *So Great Salvation.* London: Morgan & Scott, 1952.

Barclay, Oliver R. *From Cambridge to the World.* Leicester: Inter-Varsity Press, 2002.

Barnard, H. C. *A Short History of English Education, 1760–1944.* London: University of London Press, 1947.

B[arry], D. T. *CMS Register of Missionaries and Native Clergy from 1804 to 1904.* London: [privately printed], 1906.

Battersby and Battersby, eds., *Memoir of T. D. Harford-Battersby Late Vicar of St. John's, Keswick and Honorary Canon of Carlisle.* London, 1890.

Battiscombe, Georgina. *John Keble: A Study in Limitations.* London: Constable, 1963.

———. *Shaftesbury: A Biography of the Seventh Earl 1801–1885*. London: Constable & Company, 1974.

Baxter, R. Dudley. *National Income: The United Kingdom*. London: Macmillan & Co, 1868.

Beale, Miss [Dorothy]. *History of the Cheltenham Ladies' College*. Cheltenham: n.p., [1904].

Beales, D. *From Castlereagh to Gladstone 1815–1885*. London: Nelson, 1969.

Bebbington, D. W. *Evangelicalism in Modern Britain*. London: Unwin Hyman, 1989.

———. *Holiness in Nineteenth-Century England*. Carlisle, 2000.

Beechey, St. Vincent. *The Rise and Progress of Rossall School: A Jubilee Sketch*. London: Skeffington & Son, 1894.

Bell, Arthur. *Tudor Foundation: A Sketch of the History of Richard Pate's Foundation in Cheltenham*. Chalfont St Giles, Buckinghamshire: Richard Sadler Ltd, 1974.

———. *Pleasure Town: Cheltenham 1830–1860*. London: Richard Sadler, 1981.

Bell, E. Moberly. *A History of the Church Schools Company 1883–1958*. London: S.P.C.K., 1958.

Benson, Arthur Christopher. *The Life of Edward White Benson, Sometime Archbishop of Canterbury* 2 vols. London: MacMillan & Co., 1899.

Bentley, James. *Ritualism and Politics in Victorian England: The Attempt to Legislate for Belief*. Oxford: Oxford University Press, 1978.

Beresford, W. *Diocesan Histories: Lichfield*. London: S.P.C.K., [n.d.]

Berry, M. H. A. "The Canterbury Diocesan Training School, 1840–9." In *Canterbury Chapters: A Kentish Heritage for Tomorrow*, eds M. H. A. Berry and J. H. Higginson, 123–31. Liverpool: Dejall & Meyorre International Publishers, 1976.

Best, G. F. A. *Shaftesbury*. London: B. T. Batsford, 1964.

———. *Temporal Pillars: Queen Anne's Bounty, the Ecclesiastical Commissioner, and the Church of England*. Cambridge: Cambridge University Press, 1964.

———. "Popular Protestantism in Victorian Britain." In *Ideas and Institutions of Victorian Britain*, ed. R. Robson. London: Bell, 1967.

Bevan, Edwyn R. *Wilmot Eardley Bryan: A Memoir*. Bath: Fyson & Co., 1935.

Bibliography

Birchenough, Charles. *History of Elementary Education in England and Wales from 1800 to the Present Day.* 3rd edn. London: University Tutorial Press, 1938.

Blackie, John. *Bradfield, 1850–1975.* Bradfield: The Warden & Council of Bradfield College, 1976.

Blake, Steven T. *Cheltenham's Churches and Chapels AD 773–1883.* Cheltenham: Cheltenham Borough Council Art Gallery & Museum Service, 1979.

———. *Pittville 1824–1860.* Cheltenham: Cheltenham Art Galleries & Museums, 1988.

Bloesch, D. G. *The Evangelical Renaissance.* London: Hodder & Stoughton, 1973.

Blumenau, Ralph. *A History of Malvern College, 1865 to 1965.* London: Macmillan, 1965.

Boase, F., ed. *Modern English Biography.* 6 vols. London: Cass, 1965.

Boddy, Maureen and Jack West. *Weymouth: An Illustrated History.* Wimborne: Dovecote, 1983.

Book of Records of Weymouth College, Sometime known as Weymouth Grammar School and also as Weymouth Collegiate School [Compiled by an Old Weymouthian]. London: Relfe Brothers, 1897.

Booth, John. *Framlingham College: The First Sixty Years.* Ipswich: The Society of Old Framlinghams, 1925.

Bowen, Desmond. *The Idea of the Victorian Church.* Montreal: McGill University Press, 1968.

Bowley, A. L. *Wages and Income in the United Kingdom since 1860.* Cambridge: Cambridge University Press, 1937.

Boyd, A. K. *The History of Radley College 1847–1947.* Oxford: Basil Blackwell, 1948.

Bradbury, John L. *Chester College and the Training of Teachers, 1839–1975.* Chester: Governors of Chester College, 1975.

Bradley, A. G., A. C. Champneys and J. W. Barnes. *A History of Marlborough College During Fifty Years from its Foundation to the Present Time.* London: John Murray, 1893.

Bradley, Ian. *The Call to Seriousness: The Evangelical Impact on the Victorians.* London: Jonathan Cape, 1976.

———. *The English Middle Classes are Alive and Kicking.* London: Collins, 1982.

Bready, J. Wesley. *England: Before and After Wesley; The Evangelical Revival and Social Reform.* New York: Russell & Russell, 1938.

Brent, Richard. *Liberal Anglican Politics: Whiggery, Religion and Reform, 1830–1841*. Oxford: Clarendon Press, 1987.

Briggs, Asa. *The Age of Improvement, 1783-1867*. London: Longmans, Green & Co., 1959.

———. *A Social History of England*. London: Penguin, 1994.

Briggs, Asa and John Saville. *Essays in Labour History*. London: Macmillan, 1967.

Brilioth, Yngve. *The Anglican Revival: Studies in the Oxford Movement*. London: Longmans, Green & Co., 1933.

Britten, James. *A Prominent Protestant (Mr John Kensit)*. London: Catholic Truth Society, 1898.

Brose, Olive J. *Church and Parliament. The Reshaping of the Church of England, 1828–1860*. London: Oxford University Press, 1959.

Brown, C. K. Francis. *The Church's Part in Education, 1833–1941*. London: S.P.C.K., 1942.

———. *A History of the English Clergy, 1800–1900*. London: The Faith Press, 1953.

Brown, F. K. *Fathers of the Victorians*. Cambridge: Cambridge University Press, 1961.

Brown, J. R. *Number One Millbank: The Story of the Ecclesiastical Commissioners*. London: S.P.C.K., 1944.

Bryans, E. *A History of St. Peter's College, Radley, 1847–1924*. Oxford: n.p., 1926.

Bullock, F. W. B. *The History of Ridley Hall, Cambridge*. 2 vols. Cambridge: Council of Ridley Hall, 1941.

———. *A History of Training for the Ministry of the Church of England and Wales from 1800 to 1874*. St Leonard's-on-Sea: Budd & Gillatt, 1955.

———. *Evangelical Conversion in Great Britain, 1696–1845*. St-Leonards-on-Sea: Budd & Gillatt, 1959.

———. *Voluntary Religious Societies, 1520–1799*. St Leonards-on-Sea: Budd & Gillatt, 1963.

Burgess, H. J. *Enterprise in Education*. London: S.P.C.K., 1958.

Burn, W. L. *The Age of Equipoise*. London: Allen & Unwin, 1964.

Burns, A. "W. J. Conybeare: 'Church Parties'." In *From Cranmer to Davidson: A Church of England Miscellany*, ed. Stephen Taylor. Woodbridge: Boydell, 1999.

———. *The Diocesan Revival in the Church of England, c. 1800–1870*. Oxford: Clarendon Press, 1999.

Bury, Charles A. *The Church Association.* London: William Macintosh, 1873.

Butler, P. *Gladstone, Church, State and Tractarianism: A Study of his Religious Ideas and Attitudes 1809–1859.* Oxford: Oxford University Press, 1982.

———. *Pusey Rediscovered.* London: S.P.C.K., 1983.

———. "From the Early Eighteeenth Century to the Present Day." In *The Study of Anglicanism,* eds S. Symonds and J. T. Lang. London: S.P.C.K., 1988.

Butler, Tim and Mike Savage, *Social Change and the Middle Classes.* London: UCL Press, 1995.

Butterfield, H. *The Whig Interpretation of History.* London: G. Bell & Sons, 1951.

Canton, William. *History of the British and Foreign Bible Society.* 5 vols. London: John Murray, 1904.

Carpenter, S. C. *Church and People, 1789–1889: A History of the Church of England from William Wilberforce to 'Lux Mundi'.* London: S.P.C.K., 1933.

Chadwick, Owen. *The Mind of the Oxford Movement.* London: Adam & Charles Black, 1960.

———. *The Victorian Church.* Part 1. London: A & C Black, 1966.

———. *The Victorian Church.* Part 2. London: A & C Black, 1970.

———. *The Spirit of the Oxford Movement: Tractarian Essays.* Cambridge: Cambridge University Press, 1990.

Chandler, Arthur R. *Alleyn's: The Coeducational School.* Henley on Thames: Gresham Books, 1998.

Chandos, John. *Boys Together: English Public Schools 1800–1864.* London: Hutchison, 1984.

Christian, Roy. *Butterley Brick: 200 Years in the Making.* London: Henry Melland, 1990.

Christie, O. F. *A History of Clifton College, 1860–1934.* Bristol: J. W. Arrowsmith, 1935.

Church, R. W. *The Oxford Movement: Twelve Years, 1833–1845.* London: Macmillan & Co., 1891.

Church Schools Company, 1883–1933. London: Cowley, 1934.

Clark, G. Kitson. *The Making of Victorian England: Being the 1961 Ford Lectures Delivered Before the University of Oxford.* London: Methuen, 1962.

———. *Churchmen and the Condition of England 1832–1885: A Study in the Development of Social Ideas and Practice from the Old Regime to the Modern State*. London: Methuen, 1973.

Clark, J. C. D. *English Society, 1688–1832*. Cambridge: Cambridge University Press, 1985.

———. *Revolution and Rebellion: State and Society in England in the Seventeenth and Eighteenth Centuries*. Cambridge: Cambridge University Press, 1986.

Clarke, Amy Key. *A History of the Cheltenham Ladies' College, 1853–1953*. London: Faber & Faber, 1953.

Clarke, C. P. S. *The Oxford Movement and After*. London: A. R. Mowbray, 1932.

Clarke, M. L. *Classical Education in Britain, 1500–1900*. Cambridge: Cambridge University Press, 1959.

Clarke, W. K. L. *A History of the S.P.C.K.* London: S.P.C.K., 1959.

Cliff, Philip B. *The Rise and Development of the Sunday School Movement in England 1780–1980*. Nutfield, Redhill, Surrey: 1986.

Cockshut, A. O. J. *Anglican Attitudes: A Study of Victorian Religious Controversies*. London: Collins, 1959.

Coggan, F. D., ed. *Christ and the Colleges: A History of the Inter-Varsity Fellowship of Evangelical Unions*. London: The Inter-Varsity Fellowship of Evangelical Unions, 1934.

Cole, G. D. H. *Studies in Class Structure*. London: Routledge & Kegan Paul, 1955.

Coleman, B. I. *The Church of England in the Mid-Nineteenth Century: A Social Geography*. London: Historical Association, 1980.

Connell, W. F. *The Educational Thought and Influence of Matthew Arnold*. London: Routledge & Kegan Paul, 1950.

———. *The Foundations of Secondary Education*. Melbourne: Australian Council for Educational Research, 1967.

Conway, Robert Russ. *Weymouth College 1901–1927*. London: Sherren & Son [printer], [1947].

Coombs, J. *George Anthony Denison: The Firebrand, 1805–1896*. London: The Church Literature Association, 1984.

Cornish, F. Warre. *A History of The English Church in the Nineteenth Century*. 2 vols. London: Macmillan & Co., 1933.

Corsi, P. *Science and Religion: Baden Powell and the Anglican Debate, 1800–1860*. Cambridge: Cambridge University Press, 1988.

Coupland, Reginald. *Wilberforce: A Narrative*. Oxford: Clarendon Press, 1923.

Cowie, Leonard W. and Evelyn E. Cowie. *That One Idea: Nathaniel Woodard and his Schools.* Ellesmere: Woodard Corporation, 1991.

Cox, J. *The English Churches in a Secular Society: Lambeth, 1870–1930.* Oxford: Oxford University Press, 1982.

Crafts, N. F. R. *British Economic Growth During the Industrial Revolution.* Oxford: Clarendon Press, 1985.

Creighton, Louise. *G. A. Selwyn, D.D., Bishop of New Zealand and Lichfield.* Longmans, Green & Co.: London, 1923.

Crockford's Clerical Directory. Oxford: Oxford University Press, 1869–1900.

Crook, Zena and Brian Simon. "Private Schools in Leicester and the County, 1780–1840." In *Education in Leicestershire, 1540–1940*, ed. Brian Simon, 122–29. Leicester: Leicester University Press, 1968.

Cross, F. L. *The Oxford Movement and the Seventeenth Century.* London S.P.C.K., 1933.

Cross, F. L. and E. A. Livingstone, eds. *Oxford Dictionary of the Christian Church.* Oxford: Oxford University Press, 1983.

Crowther, M. A. *Church Embattled: Religious Controversy in Mid-Victorian England.* London: David & Charles, 1970.

———. "Church Problems and Church Parties." In *Religion in Victorian Britain 4: Interpretations*, ed. Gerald Parsons, 4–27. Manchester: Manchester University Press, 1988.

Curtis, S. J. *History of Education in Great Britain.* London: University Tutorial Press, 1965.

Dahrendorf, Ralf. *Class and Class Conflict in an Industrial Society.* Stanford: Stanford University Press, 1959.

Davies, G. C. B. *Henry Phillpotts, Bishop of Exeter, 1778–1869.* London: S.P.C.K., 1954.

———. *The First Evangelical Bishop.* London: Inter-Varsity Press, 1958.

———. *Men for the Ministry.* London: Hodder & Stoughton, 1963.

Dent, H. C. *The Training of Teachers in England and Wales, 1800–1975.* London: Hodder & Stoughton, 1977.

Dewey, Clive. *The Passing of Barchester.* London: Hambledon, 1991.

Dickey, Brian, ed. *The Australian Dictionary of Evangelical Biography.* Sydney: Evangelical History Association, 1994.

———. "'Going about and doing good': Evangelicals and Poverty c.1815–1870", In *Evangelical Faith and Public Zeal: Evangelicals and Society in Britain 1780–1980*, ed. J. Wolffe, 38–58. London: S.P.C.K., 1995.

Digby, Anne and Peter Searby. *Children, School and Society in Nineteenth-Century England.* London: Macmillan, 1981.

Ditchfield, G. M. *The Evangelical Revival.* London: UCL Press, 1998.

Dix, John R. *Pen Pictures of Popular English Preachers.* London: Partridge & Oakey, 1852.

Donovan, Marcus F. G. *After the Tractarians.* Glasgow: Philip Allan, 1933.

Dowland, David A. *Nineteenth-Century Anglican Theological Training: The Redbrick Challenge.* Oxford: Clarendon Press, 1997.

Downer, A. C. *A Century of Evangelical Religion at Oxford.* London: Church Book Room Press, 1938.

Dudley-Smith, Timothy. *John Stott: The Making of a Leader.* Leicester: Intervarsity Press, 1999.

Edwards, David L. *Leaders of the Church of England 1828–1944.* London: SCM Press Ltd., 1971.

———. *Christian England.* Rev'd. edn. London: William Collins & Sons, 1989.

Egan, H. *Ealing College 1820–1970.* Gloucester: The British Publishing Company Ltd, 1969.

Elliott-Binns, L. E. *The Evangelical Movement in the English Church.* London: Methuen & Co., 1928.

———. *The Early Evangelicals: A Religious and Social Study.* London: Lutterworth, 1953.

———. *Religion in the Victorian Era.* 3rd ed. London: Lutterworth, 1953.

Ellis, Ieuan. *Seven Against Christ: A Study of "Essays and Reviews".* Leiden: E. J. Brill, 1980.

Ellsworth, L. E. *Charles Lowder and the Ritualist Movement.* London: Darton, Longman & Todd, 1982.

Elwell Walter A. ed. *Evangelical Dictionary of Theology* Carlisle: Paternoster Press, 1984

Evans, R. J. W. "Town, Gown and Cloth: An Essay on the Foundation of the School." In *Dean Close School: The First Hundred Years,* eds M. A. Girling and L. Hooper, 1–39. Cheltenham: Dean Close School, 1986.

Evennett, H. O. *The Catholic Schools of England and Wales.* Cambridge: Cambridge University Press, 1944.

Every, George. *The High Church Party, 1688–1718.* London: S.P.C.K., 1956.

Faber, G. *Oxford Apostles.* Harmondsworth: Penguin, 1954.

Fairweather, E. R. *The Oxford Movement.* Oxford: Oxford University Press, 1964.

Falkner, Charles G. *The Book of Records of Weymouth College, Sometime known as Weymouth Grammar School and Weymouth Collegiate School.* 2nd edn. Manchester: Richard Johnson & Sons, 1913.

——. *The Book of Records of Weymouth College, Sometime known as Weymouth Grammar School and Weymouth Collegiate School.* 3rd edn. Manchester: Richard Johnson & Sons, 1923.

——. *History of Weymouth College to 1901.* London: The Old Weymouthian's Club, [1937].

Farley, Ian D. *J. C. Ryle: First Bishop of Liverpool.* Carlisle: Paternoster, 2000.

Findlay, J. J., ed. *Arnold of Rugby: His School Life and Contribution to Education.* Cambridge: Cambridge University Press, 1914.

Finlayson, Geoffrey B. A. M. *The Seventh Earl of Shaftesbury, 1801–1885.* London: Eyre & Methuen, 1981.

Forbes, Duncan. *The Liberal Anglican Idea of History.* Cambridge: Cambridge University Press, 1952.

Foster, Joseph, ed. *Alumni Oxonienses, 1715–1886 (Series 2).* Nendeln, Liechtenstein: Kraus Reprint, 1968.

Francis, G. H. *Orators of the Age: Comprising Portraits, Critical, Biographical, and Descriptive.* New York: Harper & Brothers, 1847.

Fraser, Derek. *Urban Politics in Victorian England: The Structure of Politics in Victorian Cities.* Leicester: Leicester University Press, 1976.

Furneaux, R. *William Wilberforce.* London: Hamish Hamilton, 1974.

Furness, W., ed. *The Centenary History of Rossall School.* Aldershot: Gale & Polden, 1945.

Furnivall, Frederick James. *Early History of the Working Men's College. Reprinted from the Working Men's College Magazine, etc.* London: n.p., 1891.

Fyfe, C. *A History of Sierra Leone.* London: n.p., 1962.

Gardner, Brian. *The Public Schools.* London: Hamilton, 1973.

Gash, Norman. *Reaction and Reconstruction in English Politics, 1832–1852.* Oxford: Clarendon Press, 1965.

———. *Sir Robert Peel: The Life of Sir Robert Peel After 1830.* London: Longman, 1972.

Gidney, W. T. *The History of the London Society for the Promoting Christianity amongst the Jews, from 1809 to 1908.* London: London Society for Promoting Christianity amongst the Jews, 1908.

Gilbert, A. D. *Religion and Society in Industrial England: Church, Chapel and Social Change.* London: Longman, 1976.

Gilley, Sheridan. *Newman and His Age.* London: Darton, Longman & Todd, 1990.

Giley, S. and W. J. Shiels, *A History of Religion in Britain.* Oxford: Basil Blackwell, 1994.

Girling, M. A. and L. Hooper, eds. *Dean Close School: The First Hundred Years.* Cheltenham: Dean Close School, 1986.

Gordon, Peter. *Selection for Secondary Education.* London: Woburn Press, 1980.

Goldthorpe, John H. *Social Mobility and Class Structure in Modern Britain.* Oxford: Clarendon Press, 1980.

Gordon, J. *Evangelical Spirituality.* London: SPCK, 1991.

Graber, Gary W. *Ritual Legislation in the Victorian Church of England: Antecedents and Passage of the Public Worship Regulation Act, 1874.* New York: The Edwin Mellen Press, 1993.

Grave, W. W. *Fitzwilliam College, Cambridge 1869–1969.* Cambridge: The Fitzwilliam Society, 1983.

Guggisberg, F. G. *The Shop: The Story of the Royal Military Academy.* London: Cassell & Co., 1900.

Haig, Alan. *The Victorian Clergy.* London: Croom Helm, 1984.

Hammond, J. L. *Lord Shaftesbury.* London: Constable, 1924.

Handford, Basil. *Lancing: A History of SS. Mary and Nicolas College, Lancing 1848–1930.* Oxford: Basil Blackwell, 1933.

———. *Lancing College: History and Memoirs.* Chichester, Sussex: Phillimore & Co., 1986.

Hans, N. *New Trends in Education in the Eighteenth Century.* London: Routledge & Kegan Paul Ltd., 1951.

Harding, Frederick A. J. *The Social Impact of the Evangelical Revival.* London: The Epworth Press, 1947.

Harford, J. B. and F. C. Macdonald. *Handley Carr Glyn Moule, Bishop of Durham.* London: Hodder & Stoughton, 1922.

Harper, Alfred, ed. *History of the Cheltenham Grammar School, from its Remodelling Under the Chancery Deed of 1851. As Collected from the Newspaper Reports.* Cheltenham: A. Harper [printer], 1856.

Harrison, J. F. C. *Learning and Living, 1790–1960: A Study in the History of the English Adult Education Movement.* London: Routledge & Kegan Paul, 1961.

Hart, G. *A History of Cheltenham.* Leicester: Leicester University Press, 1965.

Hartford, J. B. and F. C. MacDonald. *Handley Carr Glyn Moule.* London: Hodder & Stoughton, 1922.

Heasman, Kathleen. *Evangelicals in Action: An Appraisal of their Social Work in the Victorian Era.* London: Geoffrey Bles Ltd, 1962.

Heeney, B. *Mission to the Middle Classes: The Woodward Schools 1848–1891.* London: S.P.C.K., 1969.

———. *A Different Kind of Gentleman: Parish Clergy as Professional Men in Early and Mid-Victorian England.* Hamden, Conn.: Archon Books, 1976.

Heiser, F. B. *The Story of St Aiden's College, Birkenhead 1897–1947.* Chester: Philipson & Golder, 1947.

Hempton, David N. *Religion and Political Culture in Britain and Ireland: From the Glorious Revolution to the Decline of the Empire.* Cambridge: Cambridge University Press, 1996.

Hennell, Michael. *John Venn and the Clapham Sect.* London: Lutterworth, 1958.

———. *Sons of the Prophets: Evangelical Leaders of the Victorian Church.* London: S.P.C.K., 1979.

Hennock, E. P. *Fit and Proper Persons: Ideal and Reality in Nineteenth-Century Urban Government.* London: Edward Arnold, 1973.

Hibbert, Christopher. *No Ordinary Place.* London: John Murray, 1997.

Hilton, Boyd. *The Age of Atonement: The Influence of Evangelicalism on Social and Economic Thought, 1795–1865.* Oxford: Clarendon Press, 1988.

Hindmarsh, B. *John Newton and the Evangelical Tradition*, Oxford, Clarendon Press, 1996.

History of All Saints' School, Bloxham, 1860–1910, with Supplement, 1910–1925. 2nd edn. Bloxham: All Saints School, 1926.

Hobsbawm, E. J. "The Labour Aristocracy in Nineteenth-Century Britain." In *Democracy and the Labour Movement,* ed. J. Saville. London: Lawrence & Wishart, 1954.

Hole, Charles. *The Early History of the Church Missionary Society for Africa and the East to the end of 1814.* London: Church Missionary Society, 1896.

———. *A Manual of English Church History.* London: Longmans, Green & Co., 1910.

Holmes, Geoffrey. *Augustan England: Professions, State and Society, 1680–1730.* London: George Allen & Unwin, 1982.

Honey, J. R. de S. *Tom Brown's Universe: The Development of the Victorian Public School.* London: Millington, 1977.

Hooper, Arthur. *Sketches of Long Eaton & District: Some Events, Happenings and Records Relative to the Growth of Long Eaton from a Village to Township.* n.p., 1954.

Hope, Valerie. *The First Hundred Years of the Church Schools Company.* London: The Church Schools Company, 1984.

Hopkins, Hugh Evan. *Charles Simeon of Cambridge.* London: Hodder & Stoughton, 1977.

Howse, E. M. *Saints in Politics: The Clapham Sect and the Growth of Freedom.* London: George Allen & Unwin, 1952.

Hudson, D. J. and M. K. Swales. *Discovering Denstone.* Denstone: n.p., 1979.

Hughes, D. P. *The Life of Hugh Price Hughes.* London: Hodder & Stoughton, 1904.

Hughes, Thomas. *Tom Brown's Schooldays.* London: Methuen, 1904 (originally 1857).

Humphris, E.. *The Life of Adam Lindsay Gordon.* London: Eric Partridge, 1912.

Hunt, Margaret R. *The Middling Sort: Commerce, Gender, and the Family in England, 1680–1780.* Berkeley: University of California Press, Ca., 1995.

Hurt, John. *Education in Evolution: Church, State, Society and Popular Education, 1800–1870.* London: Rupert Hart-Davis, 1971.

Hylson-Smith, Kenneth. *Evangelicals in the Church of England.* Edinburgh: T & T Clark, 1988.

———. *High Churchmanship in the Church of England. From the Sixteenth Century to the Late Twentieth Century.* Edinburgh: T & T Clark, 1993.

Inglis, K. S. *The Churches and the Working Classes in Victorian England.* London: Routledge & Kegan Paul, 1963.

Inskip, J. T. *A Man's Job.* London: Skeffington & Son, 1948.

Jagger, Peter J. *Gladstone, Politics and Religion: A Collection of Founder's Day Lectures Delivered at St. Deiniols' Library, Hawarden, 1967.* London: Macmillan, 1984.

———. *Gladstone: The Making of a Christian Politician.* Alison Park, Pa.: Pickwick Publications, 1991.

James, Lionel. *A Forgotten Genius: Sewell of St Columbia's and Radley.* London: Faber & Faber Ltd., 1945.

James, Norman G. Brett. *A History of Mill Hill School, 1807-1907.* London: Andrew Melrose, [n.d.].

Jay, Elizabeth. *The Religion of the Heart: Anglican Evangelicalism and the Nineteenth-Century Novel.* Oxford: Clarendon Press, 1979.

———, ed. *The Evangelical and Oxford Movements.* Cambridge: Cambridge University Press, 1983.

Johnson, D. *Contending for the Faith: A History of the Evangelical Movement in the Universities and Colleges.* Leicester: Inter-Varsity Press, 1979.

Johnson, Malcolm. *Bustling Intermeddler? The Life and Work of Charles James Blomfield.* Leominster: Gracewing, 2001.

Jones, Gareth Stedman. *Languages of Class: Studies in English Working Class History, 1832–1982.* Cambridge: Cambridge University Press, 1983.

Jones, Peter d'A. *The Christian Socialist Revival, 1877–1914.* Princeton: Princeton University Press, 1968.

Joyce, Patrick. *Work, Society and Politics.* Brighton: Harvester Press, 1980.

———. *Visions of the People: Industrial England and the Question of Class, 1848–1914.* Cambridge: Cambridge University Press, 1991.

Julian, John, ed. *A Dictionary of Hymnology.* 2nd edn. London: John Murray, 1915.

Kamm, Josephine. *Indicative Past. A Hundred Years of the Girls' Public Day School Trust.* London: Allen & Unwin, 1971.

Kandel, I. L. *History of Secondary Education.* Boston: Houghton Mifflin Company, 1930.

Kazamias, Andreas M. *Politics, Society and Secondary Education in England.* Philadelphia: University of Pennsylvania Press, 1966.

Kent, J. *Holding the Fort: Studies in Victorian Revivalism.* London: Epworth Press, 1978.

———. *The Unacceptable Face: The Modern Church in the Eyes of the Historian.* London: S.C.M., 1987.

———. "Anglican Evangelicalism in the West of England, 1858–1900." In *Protestant Evangelicalism: Britain, Ireland, Germany and America c.1780–c.1950: Essays in Honour of W. R. Ward,* ed. Keith Robbins, 179–200. Oxford: Basil Blackwell (for The Ecclesiastical History Society), 1990.

Kirk, K. E. *The Story of the Woodard Schools.* Abingdon-on-Thames: Abbey Press, 1952.

Knight, Frances. *The Nineteenth-Century Church and English Society.* Cambridge: Cambridge University Press, 1995.

Koditschek, Theodore. *Class Formation and Urban-Industrial Society: Bradford, 1750–1850.* Cambridge: Cambridge University Press, 1990.

Kramer, L. M. J. *Another Look at Dr. W. H. Flecker.* [privately printed], [n.d.].

Lace, A. F. *A Goodly Heritage: A History of Monkton Combe School 1868 to 1967.* Bath: Monkton Combe School, 1968.

Lancelot, B. *Francis James Chavasse.* Oxford: Basil Blackwell, 1929.

Laqueur, T. W. *Religion and Respectability: Sunday Schools and Working Class Culture, 1780–1850.* London: Yale University Press, 1976.

Lawson, John. *A Town Grammar School Through Six Centuries.* London: Oxford University Press, 1963.

Leach, A. F. *A History of Winchester College.* London: Duckworth & Co., 1899.

———. *A History of Bradfield College.* London: H. Frowde, 1900.

———. *Early Yorkshire Schools.* vol. 2. Yorkshire Archaeological Society Record Series 23. Leeds [printed for the Society], 1903.

Leadbetter, F. W. B. *A Celebration of Trent College 1866–2002.* Nottingham: Trent College, 2002.

Leinster-Mackay, D. P. *The Rise of the English Prep School.* Lewes: Falmer Press, 1984.

———. *The Educational World of Edward Thring.* London: Falmer Press, 1987.

———. *Alleyn's and Rossall Schools: The Second World War, Experience and Status.* Educational Administration and History Monograph, no. 18. Leeds: University of Leeds, 1990.

Lentin, Antony. "Anglicanism, Parliament and the Courts." In *Religion in Victorian Britain 2: Controversies,* ed. Gerald Parsons, 88–106. Manchester: Manchester University Press, 1988.

Levine, Philippa. *The Amateur and the Professional: Antiquarians, Historians and Archaeologists in Victorian England, 1838–86.* Cambridge: Cambridge University Press, 1986.

Lewis, Donald M., ed. *The Blackwell Dictionary of Evangelical Biography, 1730–1860.* Oxford: Basil Blackwell, 1995.

———. *Lighten their Darkness: The Evangelical Mission to Working-Class London. 1828–1860,* Carlisle: Paternoster Press, 2001.

Little, Brian. *The Colleges of Cambridge, 1286–1973.* Bath: Adams & Dart, 1973.

Loane, Marcus L. *Oxford and the Evangelical Succession.* London: Lutterworth Press, 1950.

———.*Cambridge and the Evangelical Succession.* London: Lutterworth Press, 1952.

———. *Archbishop Mowll. The Biography of Howard West Kilvinton Mowll, Archbishop of Sydney and Primate of Australia.* London: Hodder & Stoughton, 1960.

———. *Makers of Our Heritage.* London: Hodder & Stoughton, 1967.

———. *John Charles Ryle 1816–1900.* London: Hodder & Stoughton, 1983.

[Loder, J.]. *Trent 1868–1978.* London: Trent College, [1968].

MacDonald, Alec. *A Short History of Repton.* London: Ernest Benn, 1929.

Machin, G. I. T. *Politics and the Churches in Great Britain, 1832 to 1868.* Oxford: Clarendon Press, 1977.

———. *Politics and the Churches in Great Britain, 1869–1921.* Oxford: Clarendon Press, 1987.

Mack, Edward C. *Public Schools and British Opinion: 1780 to 1860.* London: Methuen & Co., 1938.

MacLeish, J. *Evangelical Religion and Popular Education.* London: Metheun, 1969.

Magnus, L. *The Jubilee Book of the Girls' Public Day School Trust, 1873–1923.* Cambridge: Cambridge University Press, 1923.

Maltby, S. E. *Manchester and the Movement for National Elementary Education, 1800–1870.* Cambridge: University Press, 1918.

Mangan, J. A. *Athleticism in the Victorian and Edwardian Public School: The Emergence and Consolidation of an Educational Ideology.* Cambridge: Cambridge University Press, 1981.

Mann, Michael. *The Sources of Social Power, vol. 2: The Rise of Classes and Nation States, 1760–1914.* Cambridge: Cambridge University Press, 1993.

Margetson, S. *Leisure and Pleasure in the Nineteenth Century.* London: Victorian Book Club, 1971.

Marsh, D. C. *The Changing Social Structure of England and Wales, 1871–1951.* London: Routledge & Kegan Paul, 1958.

Marsh, P. T. *The Victorian Church in Decline: Archbishop Tait and The Church of England 1869–1882.* London: Routledge & Kegan Paul, 1969.

Massie, J. W. *The Evangelical Alliance: Its Origins and Development. Containing Personal Notices of its Distinguished Friends.* London: John Snow, 1847.

Mathias, Peter. "The Industrial Revolution: Concept and Reality." In *The First Industrial Revolutions,* eds Peter Mathias and John A. Davis, 1–24. Oxford: Basil Blackwell, 1989.

Mayor, Stephen. *The Churches and the Labour Movement.* London: Independent Press Ltd., 1967.

McAdam, M. A. and H. R. Holloway. *Hurstpierpoint College, 1865–1965.* New Shoreham: Hurstpierpoint, 1965.

McCann, Phillip and Francis Young. *Samuel Wilderspin and the Infant School Movement.* London: Croom Helm, 1982.

McClatchey, Diana. *Oxfordshire Clergy, 1777–1869.* Oxford: The Clarendon Press, 1960.

McCrum, Michael. *Thomas Arnold, Headmaster: A Reassessment.* Oxford: Oxford University Press, 1989.

McLachlan, H. *English Education Under the Test Acts: Being the History of the Nonconformist Academies, 1662–1830.* Manchester: Manchester University Press, 1931.

McLeod, Hugh. *Class and Religion in the Late Victorian City.* London: Croom Helm, 1974.

———. *Religion and Irreligion in Victorian England: How Secular was the Working Class?* Bangor: Headstart History, 1993.

McNeile, R. F. *Dean Close School Alumni, 1886 to 1948.* Winchester: The Old Decanian Society, 1950.

———. *Three Decanian Worthies.* Winchester: The Wykeham Press, 1951.

———. *A History of Dean Close School.* Shrewsbury: Wilding & Son, 1966.

Meacham, Standish. *Henry Thornton of Clapham, 1760–1815.* Cambridge, Mass.: Harvard University Press, 1964.

———. *The Lord Bishop: The Life of Samuel Wilberforce, 1805–1873.* Cambridge, Mass.: Harvard University Press, 1970.

Megahey, A. J. *A History of Cranleigh School.* London: William Collins, 1983.

Moorman, J. R. H. *A History of the Church of England.* 3rd edn. London: A & C Black, 1980.

More, Charles. *Training of Teachers, 1847–1947: History of the Church Colleges at Cheltenham.* London: P. Hambledon, 1992.

———. *A Splendid College: An Illustrated History of Teacher Training in Cheltenham, 1847–1990.* London: Cambridge University Press, 1992.

Morgan, Michael C. *Cheltenham College: The First Hundred Years.* Chalfont St. Giles: The Cheltonian Society, 1968.

Morris, J. "The Regional Growth of Tractarianism: Some Reflections." In *From Oxford to the People: Reconsidering Newman and the Oxford Movement,* ed. Paul Vaiss. Leominster: Gracewing, 1996.

Morris, R. J. *Class and Class Consciousness in the Industrial Revolution, 1780–1850.* London: Macmillan, 1979.

———. *Class, Sect and Party; The Making of the British Middle Class: Leeds, 1820–50.* Manchester: Manchester University Press, 1990.

Mottram, R. H. and C. Coote. *Through Five Generations: The History of the Butterley Company.* London: Faber & Faber, [1950].

Moule, H. C. G. *Charles Simeon.* London: Methuen & Co., 1892.

———. *The Evangelical School in the Church of England.* London: James Nisbet & Co., 1901.

———. *Memories of a Vicarage.* London: The Religious Tract Society, 1914.

———. *Charles Simeon.* London: The Inter-Varsity Fellowship, 1948.

Munden, A. F. *Eight Centuries of Education in Faversham.* Faversham: Faversham Society, 1972.

———. *Jesmond Parish Church, Newcastle Upon Tyne.* Newcastle Upon Tyne: Clayton, 1981.

———. *English Church History, 1815–1914.* 3 vols. Bramcote, Nottingham: St John's Theological College, 1995.

———. *The History of St John's College, Nottingham, Part One: Mr Peache's College at Kilburn.* Nottingham: St John's College, 1995.

———. *A Cheltenham Gamaliel: Dean Close of Cheltenham.* Cheltenham: Dean Close School, 1997.

———. *Wearing the giant's armour: Edward Walker (1823 – 1872) The first Rector of Cheltenham*, Cheltenham: Cheltenham Local History Society 2003.

———. *A History of St Luke's Church, Cheltenham 1854–2004*, Cheltenham: St Luke's Church, 2004.

Munden, A. F. and N. Pollard. *Anglican Theological, Missionary and Educational Institutions*. Coventry: [privately published], 1988.

Murphy, James. *The Religious Problem in English Education: The Crucial Experiment*. Liverpool: Liverpool University Press, 1959.

———. *Church, State and Schools in Britain, 1800–1970*. London: Routledge & Kegan Paul, 1971.

Musgrave, P. W. *The Sociology of Education*. London: Methuen, 1965.

———. *Society and Education in England Since 1800*. London: Methuen, 1968.

Neale, R. S. *Class in English History 1680–1850*. Oxford: Basil Blackwell, 1981.

Newman, J. H. *Apologia Pro Vita Sua*. New York: Penguin Books, 1994.

Newsome, David H. *A History of Wellington College, 1859–1959*. London: John Murray, 1959.

———. *Godliness and Good Learning*. London: John Murray, 1961.

———. *The Parting of Friends: A Study of the Wilberforces and Henry Manning*. London: John Murray, 1966.

———. *The Convert Cardinals: John Henry Newman and Henry Edward Manning*. London: John Murray, 1993.

Nockles, Peter B. "New Perspectives on the High Church Tradition: Historical Background, 1730–1830." In *Tradition Renewed: The Oxford Movement Conference Papers,* ed. D.G. Rowell, 24–50. London: Darton, Longman & Todd, 1986.

———. "Church Parties in the Pre-Tractarian Church of England, 1750–1833: The 'Orthodox'—Some Problems of Definition and Identity." In *The Church of England, c.1689–c.1833: From Toleration to Tractarianism,* eds J. Walsh *et. al.* Cambridge: Cambridge University Press, 1993.

———. "Pusey and the Question of Church and State." In *Pusey Rediscovered,* ed. P. Butler, 255–97. London: S.P.C.K., 1983.

———. *The Oxford Movement in Context: Anglican High Churchmanship, 1760–1857*. Cambridge: Cambridge University Press, 1994.

Noll, Mark A., David W. Bebbington and George A. Rawlyk eds. *Evangelicalism: Comparative Studies of Popular Protestantism in*

North America, The British Isles, and Beyond, 1700–1990. Oxford: Oxford University Press, 1994.

Norman, E. R. *Anti-Catholicism in Victorian England.* London: George Allen & Unwin, 1968.

———. *Church and Society in England, 1770–1970.* Oxford: Clarendon Press, 1976.

———. *The Victorian Christian Socialists.* Cambridge: Cambridge University Press, 1987.

O'Day, R. "The Clerical Renaissance in Victorian England and Wales." In *Religion in Victorian Britain 1: Traditions,* ed. Gerald Parsons, 185. Manchester: Manchester University Press, 1988.

———. "The Men from the Ministry." In *Religion in Victorian Britain 2: Controversies,* ed. Gerald Parsons, 259–79. Manchester: Manchester University Press, 1988.

Obelkevich, James. *Religion and Rural Society: South Lindsey, 1825–1875.* Oxford: Clarendon Press, 1976.

Ogilvie, Vivian. *The English Public School.* London: B. T. Batsford, 1957.

Ollard, S. L. *A Short History of the Oxford Movement.* London: A. R. Mowbray & Co., 1915.

———. *The Anglo-Catholic Revival.* London: A. R. Mowbray & Co., 1925.

Ollard, S. L. and Gordon Crosse. *A Dictionary of English Church History.* London: Mowbray & Co., 1912.

Orr, J. Edwin. *The Second Evangelical Awakening in Britain.* London: Marshall, Morgan & Scott, 1949.

Otter, Sir John. *Nathaniel Woodard: A Memoir of His Life.* London: John Lane The Bodley Head, 1925.

Overton, J. H. *The English Church in the Nineteenth Century (1800–1833).* London: Longmans, Green & Co., 1894.

Owen, David. *English Philanthropy, 1660–1960.* Cambridge, Mass.: Harvard University Press, 1965.

Park, Trevor. *St. Bees College, 1816–1895.* Barrow-in-Furness: St. Bega Publications, 1982.

Parry, J. P. *Democracy and Religion: Gladstone and the Liberal Party, 1867–1875.* Cambridge: Cambridge University Press, 1986.

Parry, J. P. and Stephen Taylor, eds. *Parliament and the Church, 1529–1960.* Edinburgh: Edinburgh University Press, 2000.

Parsons, Gerald, James R. Moore and John Wolffe, eds. *Religion in Victorian Britain*. 5 vols. Manchester: Manchester University Press, 1988–1997.

Patten, J. A. *These Remarkable Men*. London: Lutterworth Press, 1945.

Paz, D. G. *Popular Anti-Catholicism in Mid-Victorian Britian*. Stanford, Cal.: Stanford University Press, 1992.

Pearce, Tim. *Then and Now: An Anniversary Celebration of Cheltenham College 1841–1991*. Aldershot, Hants: The Cheltonian Society, 1991.

Percival, Alicia C. *The Origins of the Headmasters' Conference*. London: John Murray, 1969.

Perkin, H. *The Origins of Modern English Society*. London: Routledge & Kegan Paul, 1969.

Perry, R. *Ardingly, 1858–1946. A History of the School*. London: Old Ardinians Society, 1951.

Pigg, C. H., ed. *Cheltenham College Register 1841–1919. Additions and Corrections, 1919–1951*. Cheltenham: Cheltenham College, 1953.

Piggin, S. *Firestorm of the Lord: The History and Prospects for Revival in the Church and the World*. Carlisle: Paternoster Press, 2000.

Pitcairn, Revd. D. L. and Revd. A. Richardson. *Historical Guide to Monkton Combe, Combe Down and Claverton*. London: n.p., 1924.

Pollard, Arthur and Michael Hennell, eds. *Charles Simeon (1759–1836): Essays Written in Commemoration of his Bicentenary by Members of the Evangelical Fellowship for Theological Literature*. London: S.P.C.K., 1959.

Pollock, J. C. *A Cambridge Movement*. London: John Murray, 1953.

———. *The Keswick Story*. London: Hodder & Stoughton, 1964.

———. *Wilberforce*. London: Constable, 1977.

———. *Shaftesbury: The Poor Man's Earl*. London: Hodder & Stoughton, 1985.

Poole-Connor, E. J. *Evangelicalism in England*. London: Henry E. Walter, 1966.

Port, M. H. *Six Hundred New Churches: A Study of the Church Building Commission, 1818–1856, and its Church Building Activities*. London: S.P.C.K., 1961.

Price, A. C. *A History of the Leeds Grammar School from its Foundation to the End of 1918*. Leeds: R. Jackson, 1919.

Price, C. and Randall, I. *Transforming Keswick.* Carlisle: O M Publishing, 2000.

Prideaux, E. B. R. *A Survey of Elementary English Education.* Glasgow: Blackie, 1914.

Proby, W. H. B. *Annals of the 'Low' Church Party in England down to the Death of Archbishop Tait.* 2 vols. London: J. T. Hayes, 1888.

Randall, I. and Hilborn, D. *One Body in Christ* Carlisle: Paternoster Press, 2001.

Ralls, W. "The Papal Aggression of 1850: A Study in Victorian Anti-Catholicism." In *Religion in Victorian Britain 4: Interpretations*, ed. Gerald Parsons. Manchester: Manchester University Press, 1988.

Reardon, B. M. G. *Religious Thought in the Nineteenth Century.* Cambridge: Cambridge University Press, 1966.

Reed, John Shelton. *Glorious Battle: The Cultural Politics of Victorian Anglo-Catholicism.* London: Vanderbilt University Press, 1996.

Reynolds, J. S. *The Evangelicals at Oxford, 1735–1871.* Oxford: Marcham Manor Press, 1975 (originally 1953).

Rich, R. W. *The Training of Teachers in England and Wales during the Nineteenth Century.* Cambridge: University Press, 1933.

Roach, John. *Public Examinations in England, 1850–1900.* Cambridge: Cambridge University Press, 1971.

———. *A History of Secondary Education in England, 1800–1870.* London: Longman, 1986.

———. *Secondary Education in England, 1870–1902: Public Activity and Private Enterprise.* London: Routledge, 1991.

Roberts, David. *Paternalism in Early Victorian England.* London: Croom Helm, 1979.

Roberts, G. Bayfield. *History of the English Church Union 1859–1894.* London: Church Printing Co., 1895.

Robin, A. de Q. *Charles Perry, Bishop of Melbourne.* Nedlands, W.A.: The University of Western Australia Press, 1967.

Rosman, Doreen M. *Evangelicals and Culture.* London: Croom Helm, 1984.

Rowell, Geoffrey. *Hell and the Victorians: A Study of the Nineteenth-Century Theological Controversies Concerning Eternal Punishment and the Future Life.* Oxford: Clarendon Press, 1974.

———. *The Vision Glorious: Themes and Personalities of the Catholic Revival in Anglicanism.* Oxford: Oxford University Press, 1983.

———, ed. *Tradition Renewed: The Oxford Movement Conference Papers.* London: Darton, Longman & Todd, 1986.

Royle, Edward. "Evangelicals and Education." In *Evangelical Faith and Public Zeal: Evangelicals and Society in Britain 1780–1980*, ed. J. Wolffe, 117–137. London: S.P.C.K., 1995.

Rusk, R. R. *A History of Infant Education.* London: University of London Press, 1933.

Russell, George W. E. *A Short History of the Evangelical Movement.* London: A. R. Mowbray & Co., 1915.

Sanders, Charles R. *Coleridge and the Broad Church Movement.* Durham, N.C.: n.p., 1942.

Sanderson, Michael. *Education, Economic Change and Society in England, 1780–1870.* London: Macmillan, 1983.

———. *Educational Opportunity and Social Change in Britain.* London: Faber, 1987.

Savage, Mike. *Property, Bureaucracy and Culture: Middle Class Formation in Contemporary Britain.* London: Routledge, 1992.

Scheme for the Administration of the Charity School known as Pate's Grammar School and Hospital Charity, Cheltenham. Cheltenham: Norman, Sawyer & Co. [printer], 1900.

Scotland, Nigel A. D. *John Bird Sumner: Evangelical Archbishop.* Leominster: Gracewing, 1995.

———. *Good and Proper Men: Lord Palmerston and the Episcopal Bench.* Cambridge: James Clark & Co., 2000.

———. *Evangelical Anglicans in a Revolutionary Age.* Carlisle: Paternoster Press, 2004.

Scrimgeour, R. M., ed. *The North London Collegiate School, 1850–1950.* Oxford: Oxford University Press, 1950.

Searby, Peter. *The Training of Teachers in Cambridge University: The First Sixty Years, 1879–1939.* Cambridge: Cambridge University Department of Education, 1982.

———, ed. *Educating the Victorian Middle Class: Proceedings of the 1981 Annual Conference of the History of Education Society of Great Britain.* Leicester: History of Education Society, 1982.

Seeley, M. *The Later Evangelical Fathers.* London: Seeley, Jackson & Halliday, 1879.

Sewell, Brocard. *My Dear Time's Waste.* London: St Albert's Press, 1966.

Sharp, R. "New Perspectives on the High Church Tradition: Historical Background, 1730–1780." In *Tradition Renewed: The Oxford Movement Conference Papers,* ed. D.G. Rowell, 4–23. London: Darton, Longman & Todd, 1986.

Sherwood, John. *No Golden Journey: A Biography of James Elroy Flecker.* London: Heinemann, 1973.

Shrosbee, Colin. *Public Schools and Private Education: The Clarendon Commission, 1861–64, and the Public Schools Acts.* Manchester: Manchester University Press, 1988.

Simms, T. H. *Homerton College, 1695–1978, Cambridge.* Cambridge: Trustees of Homerton College, 1979.

Simon, Brian. *Studies in the History of Education, 1780–1870.* London: Lawrence & Wishart, 1960.

———. *Education and the Labour Movement, 1870–1920.* London: Lawrence & Wishart, 1965.

Simon, Brian and Ian Bradley, eds. *The Victorian Public School: Studies in the Development of an Educational Institution.* London: Gill and Macmillan, 1975.

Simpson, W. J. Sparrow. *The History of the Anglo-Catholic Revival from 1845.* London: George Allen & Unwin, 1932.

Smail, John. *The Origins of Middle-Class Culture: Halifax, Yorkshire, 1660–1780.* Ithaca, NY: Cornell University Press, 1994.

Smith, Frank. *History of English Elementary Education, 1760–1902.* London: University of London Press, 1931.

Smount, M. *Bishop Ryle: Ritualism and Reaction in Protestant Liverpool.* Liverpool: Newsham Publications, 1974.

Smyth, Charles H. E. *Simeon and Church Order: A Study of the Origins of the Evangelical Revival in Cambridge in the Eighteenth Century.* Cambridge: Cambridge University Press, 1940.

———. *The Church and the Nation: Six Studies in the Anglican Tradition.* London: Hodder & Stoughton, 1962.

———. "The Evangelical Discipline." In *Ideas and Beliefs of the Victorians,* ed. H. Grisewood, 97–104. London: E. P. Dutton, 1966.

Soloway, R. A. *Prelates and People: Ecclesiastical Social Thought in England, 1783–1852.* London: Routledge & Kegan Paul, 1969.

Speck, E. J. *Church Pastoral-Aid Society: Sketch of its Origin and Progress.* London: Seeley, Jackson & Halliday, 1881.

Spence-Jones, H. D. M. *The Church of England: A History for the People.* 4 vols. London: Cassell & Company, 1904.

Stamp, J. C. *British Incomes and Property: The Application of Official Statistics to Economic Problems.* London: P. S. King & Son, 1916.

Stephen, [Sir] James. *Essays in Ecclesiastical Biography.* 2 vols. 3rd ed. London: Longman, Brown, Green & Longmans, 1853.

Stephens, L. and S. Lee, eds. *Dictionary of National Biography.* 22 vols. Oxford: Oxford University Press, 1917–96.

Stephens, W. B. *Sources for English Local History.* Cambridge: Cambridge University Press, 1981.

Stewart, Robert. *The Politics of Protection: Lord Derby and the Protectionist Party, 1841-1852.* Cambridge: Cambridge University Press, 1971.

Stewart, W. A. C. *Quakers and Education as Seen in their Schools in England.* London: Epworth Press, 1953.

Stewart, W. A. C. and W. P. McCann. *The Educational Innovators, 1750–1880.* London: Macmillan, 1967.

Stock, Eugene. *The History of the Church Missionary Society: its Environment, its Men and its Work.* 4 vols. London: Church Missionary Society, 1899–1916.

———. *My Recollections.* London: James Nisbet & Co., 1909.

———. *The English Church in the Nineteenth Century.* London: Longmans, Green & Co., 1910.

Sykes, Stephen and John Booty, eds. *The Study of Anglicanism.* London: S.P.C.K., 1988.

Symondson, Anthony, ed. *The Victorian Crisis of Faith.* London: S.P.C.K., 1970.

Symons, R. G., ed. *A Century at Monkton Combe Junior School.* Bath: Monkton Combe School, 1988.

Tait, Arthur J. *Charles Simeon and His Trust.* London: S.P.C.K., 1936.

Talboys, R. St. C. *A Victorian School: Being the Story of Wellington College.* Oxford: Basil Blackwell, 1943.

Tarver, M. A. J. *Trent College.* London: G. Bell & Sons, 1929.

Telford, John. *A Sect That Moved the World.* London: Charles H. Kelly, 1907.

Tompson, Richard S. *Classics or Charity? The Dilemma of the Eighteenth-Century Grammar School.* Manchester: Manchester University Press, 1971.

Toon, Peter. *Evangelical Theology 1833–1856: A Response to Tractarianism.* London: Marshall, Morgan & Scott, 1979.

———, ed. *J. C. Ryle: A Self-Portrait.* Swenger, Pa.: Reiner Publications, 1975.

Toon, Peter. and M. Smout. *John Charles Ryle, Evangelical Bishop.* Cambridge: James Clarke, 1976.

Bibliography

Townend, Peter, ed. *Burke's Genealogical and Heraldic History of the Peerage, Baronetage and Knightage.* London: Burke's Peerage, 1963.

Trafford, Robert S. *The Revd Francis Close and the Foundation of the Training Institution at Cheltenham 1845-78.* Cheltenham: Park Published Papers, 1997.

Tropp, Asher. *The School Teachers: The Growth of the Teaching Profession in England and Wales from 1800 to the Present Day.* Melbourne: Heinemann, 1957.

Turner, John Munsey. *Conflict and Reconciliation: Studies in Methodism and Ecumenism in England, 1740-1982.* London: Epworth Press, 1985.

Unwin, Robert W. "The Established Church and the Schooling of the Poor: the Role of the S.P.C.K. 1699-1720." In *The Churches and Education,* ed. Vincent McClelland, 14-32. Evington, Leicester: History of Education Society, 1984.

Varley, E. A. *The Last of the Prince Bishops: William Van Mildert and the High Church Movement of the Early Nineteenth Century.* Cambridge: Cambridge University Press, 1992.

Venn, J. A. and John Venn, eds. *Alumni Cantabrigienses.* Part 2 (1752-1900), 6 vols. Cambridge: Cambridge University Press, 1922-54.

Virgin, Peter N. *The Church in an Age of Negligence: Ecclesiastical Structure and Problems of Church Reform, 1700-1840.* Cambridge: James Clarke, 1989.

Vlaeminke, Meriel. *The English Higher Grade Schools.* London: Woburn Press, 2000.

Wahrman, Dror. *Imagining the Middle Class: The Political Representation of Class in Britain, c. 1780-1840.* Cambridge: Cambridge University Press, 1995.

Wainwright, David. *Liverpool Gentlemen: A History of Liverpool College, an Independent Day School, from 1840.* London: Faber & Faber, 1960.

Walker, J. H. C. *Three Score Years and Ten: A Short History of Monkton Combe Junior School.* Bath: Fyson & Co Ltd., 1956.

Wallis, J. P. R., ed. *The Zambezi Expedition of David Livingstone 1858-1863.* London: Chatto & Windus, 1956.

Walsh, John, Colin Haydon and Stephen Taylor, eds. *The Church of England, c.1689-c.1833: From Toleration to Tractarianism.* Cambridge: Cambridge University Press, 1993.

Walsh, W. *The History of the Romeward Movement in the Church of England, 1833–1864*. London: John Nisbet & Co., 1900.

Ward, W. R. *Religion and Society in England 1790–1850*. London: B. T. Batsford Ltd., 1972.

———. *The Protestant Evangelical Awakening*. Cambridge: Cambridge University Press, 1992.

Waterman, A. M. C. *Revolution, Economics and Religion: Christian Political Economy, 1798–1833*. Cambridge: Cambridge University Press, 1991.

Webster, A. B. *Joshua Watson: The Story of a Layman, 1771–1855*. London: S.P.C.K., 1954.

Welsby, Paul A. and Henry J. Burgess. *A Short History of the National Society*. London: National Society, 1961.

White, James F. *The Cambridge Movement: The Ecclesiologists and the Gothic Revival*. London: Cambridge University Press, 1962.

Wickenden, T. D. *William Ellis School, 1862–1962: The History of a School and Those Who Made it*. London: William Ellis School, 1962.

Williams, C. *Flecker of Dean Close*. London: The Canterbury Press, 1946.

Wolffe, John. *The Protestant Crusade in Great Britain, 1829–1860*. Oxford: Oxford University Press, 1991.

———. *God and Greater Britain: Religion and National Life in Britain and Ireland, 1843–1945*. London: n.p., 1994.

———. "Anglicanism." In *Nineteenth-Century English Religious Traditions: Retrospect and Prospect*, ed. D. G. Paz, 1–31. Westport, Conn.: Greenwood, 1995.

———, ed. *Evangelical Faith and Public Zeal: Evangelicals and Society in Britain, 1780–1980*. London: S.P.C.K., 1995.

Woodroofe, Kathleen. *From Charity to Social Work in England and the United States*. London: Routledge & Kegan Paul, 1962.

Worrall, B. G. *The Making of the Modern Church: Christianity in England Since 1800*. London: S.P.C.K., 1988.

Yates, Nigel. *The Oxford Movement and Anglican Ritualism*. London: n.p., 1983.

———. *Buildings, Faith, and Worship: The Liturgical Arrangement of Anglican Churches, 1600–1900*. Oxford: Clarendon Press, 1991.

———. *Anglican Ritualism in Victorian Britain, 1830–1910*. Oxford: Oxford University Press, 1999.

Yates, T. E. *Venn and Victorian Bishops Abroad.* London: S.P.C.K., 1978.

Secondary Sources: Journals

Aldridge, Richard. "Uncertain Vintage: the Origins of the Church of England Education Society." *History of Education Society Bulletin* 18 (Autumn 1976): 41–43.

Altholz, Josef L. "The Mind of Victorian Orthodoxy: Anglican Responses to 'Essays and Reviews', 1860–1864." *Church History* 51, no. 2 (1982): 186–97.

———. "Alexander Haldane, *The Record* and Religious Journalism." *Victorian Periodicals Review* 20 (1987): 23–30.

Arnstein, W. L. "The Myth of the Triumphant Victorian Middle Class." *The Historian* 37 (1975): 205–21.

Ashton, O. "Clerical Control and Radical Responses in Cheltenham." *Midland History* 8 (1983): 137.

Avis, P. "The Tractarian Challenge to the Identity of Anglicanism." *King's Theological Review* 9 (1986): 14–17.

Bahlman, D. W. R. "Politics and Church Patronage in the Victorian Age." *Victorian Studies* 22, no. 3 (Spring 1979): 253–295.

Baker, W. J. "Henry Ryder of Gloucester, 1815–24, England's First Evangelical Bishop." *Transactions of the Bristol and Gloucestershire Archeological Society for 1970* 89 (1971): 130–144.

Balda, Wesley D. "Simeon's 'Protestant Papists': A Sampling of Moderate Evangelicalism within the Church of England, 1839–1865." *Fides et Historia* 16, no. 1 (Fall–Winter 1983): 55–67.

Balls, F. E. "The Endowed Schools Act 1869 and the Development of the English Grammar Schools in the Nineteenth Century—I The Origins of the Act." *The Durham Research Review* 5, no. 19 (1967): 207–16.

———. "The Endowed Schools Act 1869 and the Development of the English Grammar Schools in the Nineteenth Century—II The Operations of the Act." *The Durham Research Review* 5, no. 20 (1968): 219–29.

Bamford, T. W. "Public School Towns in the Nineteenth Century." *British Journal of Educational Studies* 6, no. 1 (November 1957): 25–36.

———. "Public Schools and Social Class." *British Journal of Sociology* 12 (1961).

Baron, G. "The Origins and Early History of the Headmasters' Conference, 1869–1914." *Educational Review* 7 (1954–5): 223–34.

Berwick, G. T. "Close of Cheltenham: Parish Pope. A Study in the Evangelical Background to the Oxford Movement." *Theology* 39 (September and October 1939): 193–201, 276–285.

Best, G. F. A. "The Evangelicals and the Established Church in the Early Nineteenth Century." *Journal of Theological Studies* 10 [new series] (1959): 63–78.

———. "The Mind and Times of William Van Mildert." *Journal of Theological Studies* 14, no. 2 (1963): 355–70.

Briggs, Asa. "Middle-Class Consciousness in English Politics, 1790–1846." *Past and Present* (April 1956): 65–72.

Cahill, Gilbert A. "The Protestant Association and the Anti-Maynooth Agitation of 1845." *Catholic Historical Review* 43, no. 3 (1957): 273–308.

Cannell, George. "Resistance To The Charity Commissioners: The Case of St. Paul's Schools, 1860–1904." *History of Education* 10, no.4 (1981): 245–262.

Clegg, Herbert. "Evangelicals and Tractarians [in 3 parts]." *Historical Magazine of the Protestant Episcopal Church* 35 (1966): 111–153; 35 (1966): 237–294; and 36 (1967): 127–178.

Cole, G. D. H. "The Conception of the Middle Classes." *British Journal of Sociology* 1 (1950): 275–90.

Cowie, L. W. "Exeter Hall." *History Today* (June 1968): 390–397.

Cruickshank, Marjorie A. "The Anglican Revival and Education: A Study of School Expansion in the Cotton Manufacturing Areas of North-West England, 1840–1850." *Northern History* 15 (1979): 176–90.

Culbertson, Eric. "Victorian Evangelical Theology." *The Churchman* 106, no. 4 (1992): 308–322.

Dell, Robert S. "Social and Economic Theories and Pastoral Concerns of a Victorian Archbishop." *Journal of Ecclesiastical History* 16 (1965): 196–208.

Fores, M. "The Myth of a British Industrial Revolution." *History* 66 (1981): 181–98.

Fryer, W. R. "The High Churchmen of the Earlier Seventeenth Century." *Renaissance and Modern Studies* 5 (1961): 106–48.

Gibson, W. T. "Disraeli's Church Patronage, 1868–1880." *Anglican and Episcopal History* 61 (1992): 197–210.

Gomez, F. G. "The Endowed Schools Act, 1869—A Middle-Class Conspiracy? The South-West Lancashire Evidence." *Journal of Educational Administration and History* 6, no. 1 (1974): 9–18.

Harrison, B. "Religion and Recreation in Nineteenth Century England." *Past and Present* 38 (1967): 98–125.

Hearl, Trevor. "Military Academies and English Education: A Review of some Published Material." *History of Education Society Bulletin* 2 (1968): 11–20.

———. "Military Education and the School Curriculum, 1800–1870." *History of Education* 5, no. 3 (1976): 251–264.

Heeney, B. "Tractarian Pastor: Edward Monro of Harrow Weald I. The Practice of the Parish Ministry." *Canadian Journal of Theology* 13, no. 4 (1967): 241–53.

———. "The Theory of Pastoral Ministry in the Mid-Victorian Church of England." *Historical Magazine of the Protestant Episcopal Church* 42 (1974): 215–30.

Hempton, D. N. "Evangelicalism and Eschatology." *Journal of Ecclesiastical History* 31, no. 2 (1980): 179–94.

———. "Bickersteth, Bishop of Ripon: The Episcopate of a mid-Victorian Evangelical." *Northern History* 17 (1981): 183–202.

Higginson, J. H. "The Evolution of 'Secondary Education'." *British Journal of Educational Studies* 10, no. 2 (1972): 165–77.

Holloday, J. D. "Nineteenth Century Evangelical Activism: from Private Charity to State Intervention, 1830–50." *Historical Magazine of the Protestant Episcopal Church* 50 (1982): 53–79.

Houghton, E. R. and J. L. Altholz. "The British Critic, 1824–1843." *Victorian Periodicals Review* 24, no. 3 (1991): 111–8.

Johnson, G. "Dean Wace." *Churchman* (April 1924): 95–101.

Johnson, Richard. "Educational Policy and Social Control in Early Victorian England." *Past and Present* 49 (1970): 96–119.

Kent, J. "The Role of Religion in the Cultural Structure of the later Victorian City." *Transactions of the Royal Historical Society* 23 (1973): 153–173.

———. "Church on Fire: The Story of Anglican Evangelicals." *Expository Times* 110, no. 3 (December 1998): 91.

Knight, Frances. "From Diversity to Sectarianism: The Definition of Anglican Identity in Nineteenth-Century England." *Unity and Diversity in the Church*, Studies in Church History 32 (1996).

Leinster-Mackay, D. P. "English Proprietary Schools." *Educational Research* 8, no. 1 (1981): 44–56.

———. "Pioneers in Progressive Education: Some Little-Known Proprietary and Private School Exemplars." *History of Education* 9, no. 3 (1980): 213–7.

———. "The Endowed Schools Legislation, 1869–1874: Some Differences of Interpretation." *Educational Studies* 13, no. 3 (1987): 223–38.

Lewis, H. "The Present Condition of the Evangelicals." *Nineteenth Century and After* 62 (July-December 1907): 228–37.

Lilley, R. C. "Attempts to Implement the Bryce Commission's Recommendations—and the Consequences." *History of Education* 11, no. 2 (1982): 99–111.

Machin, G. I. T. "The Last Victorian Anti-Ritualist Campaign, 1895–1906." *Victorian Studies* 25 (1982): 277–302.

Mallia, S. "The Malta Protestant College." *Melita Historica* 10, no. 3 (1990): 257–282.

Mather, F. C. "Georgian Churchmanship Reconsidered: Some Variations in Anglican Public Worship, 1714–1830." *Journal of Ecclesiastical History* 36 (1985): 255–83.

McClatchey, Diana. "The Church and Education." *Modern Churchman* 36, no. 7–12 (1947): 352–60.

McLeod, H. "Recent Studies in Victorian Religious History." *Victorian Studies* 21, no. 2 (1978): 245–256.

Meacham, S. "The Evangelical Inheritance." *Journal of British Studies* 3 (1963): 88–104.

Morris, R. J. "Voluntary Societies and British Urban Elites, 1780–1850: An Analysis." *Historical Journal* 26 (1983): 95–118.

Munden, A. F. "Evangelical in the Shadows: Charles Jervis of Cheltenham." *Churchman* 96, no. 2 (August 1982): 142–151.

———. "The First Palmerston Bishop: Henry Montagu Villiers, Bishop of Carlisle 1850–60 and Bishop of Durham 1860–1." *Northern History* 26 (1990): 186–206.

———. "Nigel Scotland's *The life and work of John Bird Sumner.*" *Anvil* 13, no. 3 (1996): 299–300.

———. "The Munificient Friend of Israel: Jane Cook of Cheltenham (1775–1851)." *Cheltenham Local History Journal* 17 (2001): 38.

Musgrove, Frank. "Middle-Class Families and Schools." *The Sociological Review* 7 (1959): 169–78.

———. "Middle-Class Education and Employment in the Nineteenth Century." *Economic History Review* 12 (August 1959): 99–111.

Neale, R. S. "Class and Class-Consciousness in Early Nineteenth-Century England: Three Classes or Five?" *Victorian Studies* 12, no. 1 (1968): 5–32.

Nockles, Peter B. "Recent Studies of John Henry Newman." *Anglican and Episcopal History* 63, no. 1 (1994): 73–86.

O'Neill, M. C. "St Columba's College." *The Irish Tatler and Sketch* 65 (April 1956): 49–51.

Parry, J. P. "Religion and the Collapse of Gladstone's First Government." *Historical Journal* 25 (1982): 71–101.

Pollard, Arthur. "A Trap to Catch Calvinists (or Bishop Marsh's Eighty-Seven Questions)." *Church Quarterly Review* 162 (1961): 447–54.

———. "Trollope and the Evangelicals." *Nineteenth-Century Fiction* 37 (1982): 329–39.

———. "The Evangelical Revival: The Triumphant Phase (1790–1830)." *The Churchman* 107, no. 3 (1993): 254–266.

Roach, John. "Middle-Class Education and Examinations: Some Early Victorian Problems." *British Journal of Educational Studies* 10, no. 2 (May 1962): 176–193.

Roberts, J. T. "The Genesis of the Cross Commission." *Journal of Educational Administration and History* 17, no. 2 (1985): 30–8.

Samuel, David N. "Roots and Reformations." *The Churchman* 104, no. 3 (1990): 197–213.

Scotland, Nigel A. D. "The Centenary of Dean Close School and the Contribution of Francis Close to Education." *History of Education Society Bulletin* 40 (Autumn 1987): 29–40.

———. "The College of St. Paul and St. Mary, Cheltenham: A Unique Evangelical Enterprise in Anglican Higher Education." *History of Education Society Bulletin* 44 (Autumn 1989): 26–30.

———. "John Bird Sumner, 1780–1862: Claphamite Evangelical Pastor and Prelate." *Bulletin of the John Rylands* (University Library of Manchester) 74, no. 1 (1992): 57–73.

Searby, P. "Joseph Lloyd Brereton and the Education of the Victorian Middle Class." *Journal of Educational Administration and History* 11, no. 1 (1979): 4–14.

Simon, Brian. "Education: Owen, Mill, Arnold and the Woodard Schools." *Victorian Studies* 13, no. 4 (1970): 403–7.

Smyth, Charles H. E. "The Evangelical Movement in Perspective." *Cambridge Historical Journal* 7 (1943): 160–74.

Spring, David. "The Clapham Sect: Some Social and Political Aspects." *Victorian Studies* 5 (1961–2): 35–48.

Stone, L. "Social Mobility in England, 1500–1700." *Past and Present* 33 (1966): 16–55.

Storch, R. D. "The Policeman as Domestic Missionary: Urban Discipline and Popular Culture, 1850–1880." *Journal of Social History* 9, no. 4 (1976): 481–509.

Stunt, T. C. F. "John Henry Newman and the Evangelicals." *Journal of Ecclesiastical History* 21, no. 1 (January 1970): 65–74.

———. "The Greaves Family." *Notes and Queries* (October 1981): 405–8.

Toon, Peter. "The Parker Society." *Historical Magazine of the Protestant Episcopal Church* 46, no. 3 (1977): 323–332.

Welch, P J. "Contemporary Views on the Proposals for the Alienation of Capitular Property in England, 1832–1840." *Journal of Ecclesiastical History* 5 (1954): 184–195.

Wellings, M. "The Oxford Movement in Late Nineteenth-Century Retrospect: R. W. Church, J. H. Rigg and Walter Walsh." *Studies in Church History* 33 (1997): 511–15.

Williams, Sarah J. "The Language of Belief: An Alternative Agenda for the Study of Victorian Working Class Religion." *Journal of Victorian Culture* 1 (1996): 303–17.

Wolffe, J. R. "Bishop Henry Phillpotts and the Administration of the Diocese of Exeter, 1830–1869." *Transactions of the Devonshire Association* 114 (1982): 99–113.

———. "The Evangelical Alliance in the 1840s." *Studies in Church History* 23 (1986): 334–5.

———. "The First Century of *The Churchman*." *The Churchman* 102, no. 3 (1988): 197–214.

Secondary Sources: Theses and Dissertations

Balda, Wesley. "Spheres of Influence: Simeon's Trust and its implications for Evangelical Patronage." PhD thesis, Cambridge University, 1981.

Bentley, Anne. "The Transformation of the Evangelical Party in the Church of England in the Later Nineteenth Century." PhD thesis, Durham University, 1971.

Best, G. F. A. "Church and State in English Politics, 1800–1833." PhD thesis, Cambridge University, 1955.

Bradley, I. C. "The Politics of Godliness: Evangelicals in Parliament, 1784–1835." DPhil thesis, Oxford University, 1974.

Bibliography

Brown, Raymond. "Evangelical Ideas of Perfection." PhD thesis, Cambridge University, 1964.

Burgess, Henry J. "The Work of the Established Church in the Education of the People, 1833–1870." PhD thesis, London University, 1954.

Burns, R. A. "The Diocesan Revival in the Church of England c. 1825–1865." DPhil thesis, Oxford University, 1990.

Casson, J. S. "John Charles Ryle and the Evangelical Party in the Nineteenth Century." MPhil thesis, University of Nottingham, 1969.

Coombs, P. B. "A History of the Church Pastoral-Aid Society, 1836–1861." MA thesis, Bristol University, 1960.

Ervine, W. J. C. "Doctrine and Diplomacy: Some Aspects of the Life and Thought of Anglican Evangelical Clergy, 1797–1837." PhD thesis, Cambridge University, 1967.

Evershed, W. A. "Party and Patronage in the Church of England, 1800–1945: A Study of Patronage Trusts and Patronage Reform." DPhil thesis, Oxford University, 1985.

Farley, I. D. "J. C. Ryle: Episcopal Evangelist: A Study in Late Victorian Evangelicalism." PhD thesis, Durham University, 1988.

Fong, W. J. "The Ritualist Crisis: Anglo-Catholics and Authority, with Special Reference to the English Church Union, 1859–1882." PhD thesis, University of Toronto, 1977.

Fox, L. Pamela. "The Work of the Revd Thomas Tragenna Biddulph with Special Reference to his Influence on the Evangelical Movement in the West of England." PhD thesis, Cambridge University, 1953.

Hardman, Bryan E. "The Evangelical Party in the Church of England, 1855–65." PhD thesis, Cambridge University, 1963.

Heeney, W. B. D. "The Established Church and the Education of the Victorian Middle Classes. A Study of the Woodard Schools, 1847–1891." DPhil thesis, Oxford University, 1961.

Herring, G. W. "Tractarianism to Ritualism: A Study of Some Aspects of Tractarianism Outside Oxford from the Time of Newman's Conversion in 1845 until the First Ritual Commission in 1867." DPhil thesis, Oxford University, 1984.

Honey, J. R. de S. "The Victorian Public School, 1828–1902: The School as Community." DPhil thesis, Oxford University, 1970.

Hylson-Smith, K. "The Evangelicals in the Church of England, 1900–1939." PhD thesis, University of London, 1982.

James, M. G. "The Clapham Sect—its History and Influence." DPhil thesis, Oxford University, 1950

Jay, E. J. "Anglican Evangelicalism and the Nineteenth Century Novel." DPhil thesis, Oxford University, 1975.

Leinster-Mackay, D. P. "The English Private School, 1830–1914, with Special Reference to the Private Preparatory School." PhD thesis, Durham University, 1972.

Martin, R. H. "The Pan-Evangelical Impulse in Britain, 1795–1830, with Special Reference to Four London Societies." DPhil thesis, Oxford University, 1974.

Munden, A. F. "The Anglican Evangelical Party in the Diocese of Carlisle in the Nineteenth Century, with Particular Reference to the Ministries of Bishop Samuel Waldegrave and Dean Francis Close." PhD thesis, Durham University, 1987.

———. "The Church of England in Cheltenham, 1826–1856, with particular reference to the Revd. Francis Close." MLitt thesis, Birmingham University, 1980.

Newell, "Studies in Evangelical Prose Literature: Its Rise and Decline." PhD thesis, Liverpool University, 1976.

Nockles, P. B. "Continuity and Change in Anglican High Churchmanship in Britain, 1792–1850." DPhil thesis, Oxford University, 1982.

Orchard, S. C. "English Evangelical Eschatology 1790–1850." PhD thesis, Cambridge University, 1968.

Pugh, R. K. "The Episcopate of Samual Wilberforce, Bishop of Oxford 1845–1869, and of Winchester 1869–1873, with Special Reference to the Administration of the See of Oxford." DPhil thesis, Oxford University, 1957.

Rennie, Ian S. "Evangelicalism and English Public Life, 1823–50." PhD thesis, University of Toronto, 1962.

Rosman, Doreen M. "Evangelicals and Culture in England, 1790–1833." PhD thesis, Keele University, 1978.

Toon, P. "The Evangelical Anglican Response to Tractarian Teaching, 1833–56." DPhil thesis, Oxford University, 1977.

Wellings, Martin. "Aspects of Late Nineteenth-Century Evangelicalism." 2 vols. DPhil thesis, Oxford University, 1989.

Whisenant, James C. "Anti-Ritualism and the Division of the Evangelical Party in the Nineteenth-Century Church of England." PhD thesis, Vanderbilt University, 1998.

Wolffe, J. R. "Protestant Societies and Anti-Catholic Agitation in Great Britain, 1829–1860." DPhil thesis, Oxford University, 1984.

Wright, W. H. "The Voluntary Principle in Education: The Contribution to English Education made by the Clapham Sect and its Allies and the Continuance of Evangelical Endeavour by Lord Shaftesbury." MEd thesis, Durham University, 1964.

Young, Howard Van Jr. "The Evangelical Clergy in the Church of England, 1790–1850." PhD thesis, Brown University, 1958.

Index

A

Aggregate Clerical Meeting, 235, 257–58
Allsobrook, David, 77, 115, 117, 118
Altholz, Josef, 23, 40, 46
Anglo-Catholic historiography, 16–18, 21
Arnold, Matthew, 77, 79
Arnold, Thomas, 43–47, 118, 119, 210
Auriol, Edward, 225, 230, 335
Avis, Paul, 13
Ayerst Hall, 233, 309–10

B

Balda, Wesley, 31
Balleine, G. R., 24–25, 237
Barlow, Revd W. H., 37, 205–6, 252, 335
Bebbington, D. W., 28
Bell, Canon Charles, 285–89, 301, 329, 336
Best, Geoffrey, 17, 48
Bickersteth, Revd E. H., 186, 336
Boultbee, Thomas, 142, 337
Bowen, Desmond, 15, 58
Bradley, Ian, 27, 31
Brereton, Revd J. L., 115, 117–21, 124
Briggs, Asa, 65, 67, 68
Brilioth, Y., 18
British Reformation Society, 37, 223
Broad Church, 4, 5, 13, 43–47, 115. *See* Latitudinarianism

Brooke, Canon Richard, 284, 288, 303, 308
Brose, Oliver, 48
Browne, Revd John, 135–36
Bryan, Revd R. G., 201–6, 209–14, 232, 311, 312
Bryce Commission, 76, 96, 99
Burns, Arthur, 13, 14, 20, 44, 51

C

Chadwick, Owen, 11, 14, 50, 52, 53
Chavasse, Francis J., 40, 323, 338
Cheltenham College, 132–43, 150, 154, 295, 330
Cheltenham Grammar School, 143–53, 295
Christian Socialists, 45, 55, 57, 58, 59
Church Association, 2, 6, 38, 41, 184, 219–34, 238, 252
Church Building Commission, 21
Church of England Education Society, 98
Church of England Evangelical College and School Company, 189, 214, 253, 255, 305–11, 318, 322, 323, 325. *See* Evangelical Church Schools Company
Church of England League, 39
Church parties, 11–16, 47, 49
Church Pastoral Aid Society, 250, 251, 252, 315

Church Schools Company, 99–102, 255
Church Society, 2, 39, 223, 226
Church, R. W., 16
Clapham Sect, 21, 30, 264
Clapton Sect, 21. *See* Hackney Phalanx
Clarendon Commission, 80
Clark, J. C. D., 18, 19, 61
Clerical and Lay Associations, 232, 234–38, 245
  Midlands, 174, 181, 236, 238
  South-Eastern Alliance, 257–60, 274
  Union of, 213, 238–50, 292, 305, 307, 315
  Western District, 277–88, 292
Clerical and Lay Union, 231, 309. *See* Clerical and Lay Associations, Union of
Close, Francis, 42, 127–56, 285, 338. *See* also ch. 9
Colquhoun, J. C., 98, 219, 339
Conybeare, Revd W. J., 13, 43
County Schools Movement, 118–24, 247, 249
CPAS Forward Movement, 252–55
Crowther, M. A., 15, 44, 52
Cruddas, W. D., 189

D

D'Auquier, Emile Cornet, 265, 266, 270, 271
Dahrendorf's five-class model, 69
Daubeny, Archdeacon, 20
Deacon, John, 262, 264, 292, 340
Dean Close Memorial School (Dean Close School), 131, 285–300, 303
Dewey, C., 20
Drummond, Henry, 30
Dudley Baxter, R., 70, 72

E

Ealing College. *See* Hermosa School
Elementary education, 62
Ellis, Revd John, 160, 161
Endowed Schools Act, 86, 87, 281
Endowed Schools Commission, 229
Ervine, William, 31
Essays and Reviews, 45
Evangelical Church Schools Company, 256, 313, 314, 324, 326. *See* Church of England Evangelical College and School Company

F

Flecker, Revd W. H., 297, 300, 301
Fortescue, Lord, 246
Framlingham College, 84, 122
Francis Brown, C. K., 52
Fremantle, William R., 292, 295, 301, 340

G

Garbett, Revd Edward, 230, 341
Gedge, Sydney, 168, 308, 311, 312, 318, 320, 341
Gilbert, Alan, 53
Gladstone, W. E., 24, 61, 89, 92, 102, 109, 251
Goode, William, 33
Grammar schools, 78, 79, 145

Index 419

Greaves, Revd Talbot, 157–60, 166, 282, 288, 297, 330, 341

H

Hackney Phalanx, 21–23
Haldane, Alexander, 41
Hanbury, Edmund, 189, 323
Harford-Battersby, T. D., 29
Heeney, Brian, 52, 110
Hempton, D. N., 30
Hermosa School, 234
High Church, 13, 18, 19, 22
Hilton, Boyd, 27, 54
Hoadly, Bishop, 20
Hoare, Canon Edward, 225, 257, 272, 301, 302, 316, 341
Honey, John, 5, 117
Hopkins, Evan Henry, 29
Howley, William, 22
Humphreys, Edward R., 147–52
Hurstpierpoint College, 105, 111, 112, 248
Hylson-Smith, Kenneth, 25

I

Islington Clerical Meeting, 37, 235

J

Jay, Elizabeth, 27
Joint stock company principle, 249
Jowett, Benjamin, 46

K

Kent, John, 12, 26–27, 47, 49
Keswick Convention, 29
Knight, F., 11, 15, 20

L

Lace, A. F., 198
Lancing College, 111

Latitudinarianism, 13, 20, 43, 46. *See* Broad Church
Leinster-Mackay, Donald, 83
Litton, E. A., 33
London Society for Promoting Christianity amongst the Jews (LSPCJ), 264, 347, 348
Low Church, 13, 20, 31
Lowder, Charles, 36

M

Machin, G. I. T., 34, 60
Manners-Sutton, Charles, 22
Maurice, F. D., 57, 59
McNeile, Hugh, 30, 343
Melcombe Regis School, 163
Middle class, 65–76
  Education levels, 74–76
  Income ranges, 70–71
  Occupations, 71–74
Middle-Class Schools Association, 228
Miller, Revd J. A., 163, 165, 167
Money, Canon Charles, 291, 301, 303, 344
Monkton Combe School, 193–216, 276, 305, 306, 309, 311–13
Moule, Handley, 317, 344
Munden, A. F., 42, 99, 127, 135, 339, 344, 351
Musgrove, Frank, 70

N

National Church League, 38
National Club, 37
National Protestant Church Union, 315
National Schools, 96, 97
National Society, 21, 23, 89, 91, 93, 95, 97
Neale, R. S., 69

Newman, J. H., 16, 18
Nockles, P., 14, 16, 18, 20
Nonconformist schools, 249
Norman, Edward, 15, 54
Norris, Henry H., 22, 23

O

O'Day, Rosemary, 53
Ollard, S. L., 17
Osmaston Manor, 173, 174
Overton, J. H., 17
Oxford Movement, 14, 16, 17, 19. *See* Tractarians

P

Parker Society, 32
Parsons, G., 11, 13
Parsons, Gerald, 29, 50, 52, 62
Pate Foundation, 143, 144, 148, 152, 153
Peache, Revd Alfred, 202–4, 345
Perry, Charles, 239, 345
Pitt, Joseph, 129
Pocock, Revd Francis, 193–204
Price, Charles, 29
Private schools, 78, 82, 88
Proprietary schools, 83, 84, 85
Protestant Alliance, 38
Protestant Churchmen's Alliance, 38, 315
Public schools, 80, 81, 82

R

Radley College, 104, 105, 106
Randall, Ian, 29
Reed, J. S., 18, 19
Rennie, Ian, 31
Repton School, 178
Revival movements, 29
Ridley Hall, 42
Ritualism, 15, 18, 19, 34, 36, 38, 40, 220

Roach, John, 77, 81, 83
Rogers, Revd William, 115, 116, 117, 124
Rosman, Doreen, 27
Ryle, J. C., 40, 225, 227, 237, 317, 346

S

Scholarships, 314
School curricula, 134, 147–49, 164, 296
School fee levels, 244, 247, 248, 298, 314, 356, 357
Scotland, Nigel, 29
Searby, Peter, 117
Selwyn, Bishop George, 53
Sewell, Revd William, 102, 104, 106
Shaftesbury, Lord, 30, 38, 347
Simeon Trust, 31, 282
Simeon, Charles, 26, 348
Smith, Robert Payne, 260, 262, 272, 348
Society for Promoting Christian Knowledge (SPCK), 23
Society for the Propagation of the Gospel (SPG), 23
South-Eastern Clerical and Lay Alliance. *See* Clerical and Lay Associations
South-Eastern College, 245, 260–76, 290, 313, 316
South-Eastern College Junior School, 270
St Andrew's College, Bradfield, 106
St Chad's College, Denstone, 180–83
St Edward's School, 108
St John's Middle School. *See* Hurstpierpoint College
St Lawrence College. *See* South-Eastern College

Index

Stephens, W. B., 12
Stock, Eugene, 24
Suffolk County School. *See* Framlingham College
Sumner, Charles, 51, 349
Sumner, John Bird, 56, 59, 349
Surrey County School, 123

T

Tarver, M. A. J., 190
Taunton Commission, 73, 74, 85, 86
Temple, Frederick, 47
Thirty-nine Articles, 27, 291
Thompson, Kenneth, 49, 50
Toon, Peter, 26
Tractarians, 13, 15, 23, 29, 32, 33, 139. *See* Oxford Movement
Trent College, 6, 176–91, 243, 247, 248, 254, 313–15, 318, 322, 323, 325

V

Van Mildert, William, 22
Virgin, Peter, 49

W

Wace, Henry, 190, 351
Wahrman, Dror, 66, 67
Watson, Archdeacon J. J., 22
Watson, Joshua, 22, 23
Webb-Peploe, Revd H. W., 304, 308, 352

Weymouth College, 162–71
Weymouth Grammar School, 159–62. *See* Weymouth College
Weymouth Middle School, 158–63. *See* Melcombe Regis School
Whiting, Revd J. B., 259, 260, 353
Wigram, Frederick E., 353
Wigram, Prebendary F. E., 306
Wilberforce, Samuel, 50
Wilson, Daniel (the elder), 37
Wolffe, John, 12, 27, 32, 37, 45, 47, 54, 61
Woodard schools, 110, 112, 113, 221, 222, 226, 242–46, 298, 318, 321
Woodard, Nathaniel, 73, 104, 111, 114, 180, 182, 184
Worrall, B. J., 46
Wright, A. Leslie, 213, 305
Wright, Francis, 173–80, 186, 188, 190, 328
Wright, Francis Beresford, 188, 313
Wright, Henry, 188, 206, 207, 208, 355
Wycliffe Hall, 42

Y

Yates, Nigel, 14, 15, 18, 19, 33

Studies in Evangelical History and Thought
(All titles uniform with this volume)
Dates in bold are of projected publication

Andrew Atherstone
Oxford's Protestant Spy
The Controversial Career of Charles Golightly
Charles Golightly (1807–85) was a notorious Protestant polemicist. His life was dedicated to resisting the spread of ritualism and liberalism within the Church of England and the University of Oxford. For half a century he led many memorable campaigns, such as building a martyr's memorial and attempting to close a theological college. John Henry Newman, Samuel Wilberforce and Benjamin Jowett were among his adversaries. This is the first study of Golightly's controversial career.
***2006** / 1-84227-364-7 / approx. 324pp*

Clyde Binfield
Victorian Nonconformity in Eastern England
Studies of Victorian religion and society often concentrate on cities, suburbs, and industrialisation. This study provides a contrast. Victorian Eastern England—Essex, Suffolk, Norfolk, Cambridgeshire, and Huntingdonshire—was rural, traditional, relatively unchanging. That is nonetheless a caricature which discounts the industry in Norwich and Ipswich (as well as in Haverhill, Stowmarket and Leiston) and ignores the impact of London on Essex, of railways throughout the region, and of an ancient but changing university (Cambridge) on the county town which housed it. It also entirely ignores the political implications of such changes in a region noted for the variety of its religious Dissent since the seventeenth century. This book explores Victorian Eastern England and its Nonconformity. It brings to a wider readership a pioneering thesis which has made a major contribution to a fresh evolution of English religion and society.
***2006** / 1-84227-216-0 / approx. 274pp*

John Brencher
Martyn Lloyd-Jones (1899–1981) and Twentieth-Century Evangelicalism
This study critically demonstrates the significance of the life and ministry of Martyn Lloyd-Jones for post-war British evangelicalism and demonstrates that his preaching was his greatest influence on twentieth-century Christianity. The factors which shaped his view of the church are examined, as is the way his reformed evangelicalism led to a separatist ecclesiology which divided evangelicals.
2002 / 1-84227-051-6 / xvi + 268pp

Jonathan D. Burnham
A Story of Conflict
The Controversial Relationship between Benjamin Wills Newton and John Nelson Darby
Burnham explores the controversial relationship between the two principal leaders of the early Brethren movement. In many ways Newton and Darby were products of their times, and this study of their relationship provides insight not only into the dynamics of early Brethrenism, but also into the progress of nineteenth-century English and Irish evangelicalism.
2004 / 1-84227-191-1 / xxiv + 268pp

Grayson Carter
Anglican Evangelicals
Protestant Secessions from the Via Media, c.1800–1850
This study examines, within a chronological framework, the major themes and personalities which influenced the outbreak of a number of Evangelical clerical and lay secessions from the Church of England and Ireland during the first half of the nineteenth century. Though the number of secessions was relatively small—between a hundred and two hundred of the 'Gospel' clergy abandoned the Church during this period—their influence was considerable, especially in highlighting in embarrassing fashion the tensions between the evangelical conversionist imperative and the principles of a national religious establishment. Moreover, through much of this period there remained, just beneath the surface, the potential threat of a large Evangelical disruption similar to that which occurred in Scotland in 1843. Consequently, these secessions provoked great consternation within the Church and within Evangelicalism itself, they contributed to the outbreak of millennial speculation following the 'constitutional revolution' of 1828–32, they led to the formation of several new denominations, and they sparked off a major Church–State crisis over the legal right of a clergyman to secede and begin a new ministry within Protestant Dissent.
2007 / 1-84227-401-5 / xvi + 470pp

J.N. Ian Dickson
Beyond Religious Discourse
Sermons, Preaching and Evangelical Protestants in Nineteenth-Century Irish Society
Drawing extensively on primary sources, this pioneer work in modern religious history explores the training of preachers, the construction of sermons and how Irish evangelicalism and the wider movement in Great Britain and the United States shaped the preaching event. Evangelical preaching and politics, sectarianism, denominations, education, class, social reform, gender, and revival are examined to advance the argument that evangelical sermons and preaching went significantly beyond religious discourse. The result is a book for those with interests in Irish history, culture and belief, popular religion and society, evangelicalism, preaching and communication.
2005 / 1-84227-217-9 / approx. 324pp

Neil T.R. Dickson
Brethren in Scotland 1838–2000
A Social Study of an Evangelical Movement
The Brethren were remarkably pervasive throughout Scottish society. This study of the Open Brethren in Scotland places them in their social context and examines their growth, development and relationship to society.
2003 / 1-84227-113-X / xxviii + 510pp

Crawford Gribben and Timothy C.F. Stunt (eds)
Prisoners of Hope?
Aspects of Evangelical Millennialism in Britain and Ireland, 1800–1880
This volume of essays offers a comprehensive account of the impact of evangelical millennialism in nineteenth-century Britain and Ireland.
2004 / 1-84227-224-1 / xiv + 208pp

Khim Harris
Evangelicals and Education
Evangelical Anglicans and Middle-Class Education in Nineteenth-Century England
This ground breaking study investigates the history of English public schools founded by nineteenth-century Evangelicals. It documents the rise of middle-class education and Evangelical societies such as the influential Church Association, and includes a useful biographical survey of prominent Evangelicals of the period.
2004 / 1-84227-250-0 / xviii + 422pp

Mark Hopkins
Nonconformity's Romantic Generation
Evangelical and Liberal Theologies in Victorian England

A study of the theological development of key leaders of the Baptist and Congregational denominations at their period of greatest influence, including C.H. Spurgeon and R.W. Dale, and of the controversies in which those among them who embraced and rejected the liberal transformation of their evangelical heritage opposed each other.

2004 / 1-84227-150-4 / xvi + 284pp

Don Horrocks
Laws of the Spiritual Order
Innovation and Reconstruction in the Soteriology of Thomas Erskine of Linlathen

Don Horrocks argues that Thomas Erskine's unique historical and theological significance as a soteriological innovator has been neglected. This timely reassessment reveals Erskine as a creative, radical theologian of central and enduring importance in Scottish nineteenth-century theology, perhaps equivalent in significance to that of S.T. Coleridge in England.

2004 / 1-84227-192-X / xx + 362pp

Kenneth S. Jeffrey
When the Lord Walked the Land
The 1858–62 Revival in the North East of Scotland

Previous studies of revivals have tended to approach religious movements from either a broad, national or a strictly local level. This study of the multifaceted nature of the 1859 revival as it appeared in three distinct social contexts within a single region reveals the heterogeneous nature of simultaneous religious movements in the same vicinity.

2002 / 1-84227-057-5 / xxiv + 304pp

John Kenneth Lander
Itinerant Temples
Tent Methodism, 1814–1832

Tent preaching began in 1814 and the Tent Methodist sect resulted from disputes with Bristol Wesleyan Methodists in 1820. The movement spread to parts of Gloucestershire, Wiltshire, London and Liverpool, among other places. Its demise started in 1826 after which one leader returned to the Wesleyans and others became ministers in the Congregational and Baptist denominations.

2003 / 1-84227-151-2 / xx + 268pp

Donald M. Lewis
Lighten Their Darkness
The Evangelical Mission to Working-Class London, 1828–1860

This is a comprehensive and compelling study of the Church and the complexities of nineteenth-century London. Challenging our understanding of the culture in working London at this time, Lewis presents a well-structured and illustrated work that contributes substantially to the study of evangelicalism and mission in nineteenth-century Britain.

2001 / 1-84227-074-5 / xviii + 372pp

Herbert McGonigle
'Sufficient Saving Grace'
John Wesley's Evangelical Arminianism

A thorough investigation of the theological roots of John Wesley's evangelical Arminianism and how these convictions were hammered out in controversies on predestination, limited atonement and the perseverance of the saints.

2001 / 1-84227-045-1 / xvi + 350pp

Lisa S. Nolland
A Victorian Feminist Christian
Josephine Butler, the Prostitutes and God

Josephine Butler was an unlikely candidate for taking up the cause of prostitutes, as she did, with a fierce and self-disregarding passion. This book explores the particular mix of perspectives and experiences that came together to envision and empower her remarkable achievements. It highlights the vital role of her spirituality and the tragic loss of her daughter.

2004 / 1-84227-225-X / xxiv + 328pp

Donald J. Payne
The Theology of the Christian Life in J.I. Packer's Thought
Theological Anthropology, Theological Method, and the Doctrine of Sanctification

J.I. Packer has wielded widespread influence on evangelicalism for more than three decades. This study pursues a nuanced understanding of Packer's theology of sanctification by tracing the development of his thought, showing how he reflects a particular version of Reformed theology, and examining the unique influence of theological anthropology and theological method on this area of his theology.

2005 / 1-84227-397-3 / approx. 374pp

July 2005

Ian M. Randall
Evangelical Experiences
A Study in the Spirituality of English Evangelicalism 1918–1939
This book makes a detailed historical examination of evangelical spirituality between the First and Second World Wars. It shows how patterns of devotion led to tensions and divisions. In a wide-ranging study, Anglican, Wesleyan, Reformed and Pentecostal-charismatic spiritualities are analysed.
1999 / 0-85364-919-7 / xii + 310pp

Ian M. Randall
Spirituality and Social Change
The Contribution of F.B. Meyer (1847–1929)
This is a fresh appraisal of F.B. Meyer (1847–1929), a leading Free Church minister. Having been deeply affected by holiness spirituality, Meyer became the Keswick Convention's foremost international speaker. He combined spirituality with effective evangelism and socio-political activity. This study shows Meyer's significant contribution to spiritual renewal and social change.
2003 / 1-84227-195-4 / xx + 184pp

James Robinson
Pentecostal Origins
Early Pentecostalism in Ireland in the Context of the British Isles
Harvey Cox describes Pentecostalism as 'the fascinating spiritual child of our time' that has the potential, at the global scale, to contribute to the 'reshaping of religion in the twenty-first century'. This study grounds such sentiments by examining at the local scale the origin, development and nature of Pentecostalism in Ireland in its first twenty years. Illustrative, in a paradigmatic way, of how Pentecostalism became established within one region of the British Isles, it sets the story within the wider context of formative influences emanating from America, Europe and, in particular, other parts of the British Isles. As a synoptic regional study in Pentecostal history it is the first survey of its kind.
2005 / 1-84227-329-1 / xxviii + 378pp

Geoffrey Robson
Dark Satanic Mills?
Religion and Irreligion in Birmingham and the Black Country
This book analyses and interprets the nature and extent of popular Christian belief and practice in Birmingham and the Black Country during the first half of the nineteenth century, with particular reference to the impact of cholera epidemics and evangelism on church extension programmes.
2002 / 1-84227-102-4 / xiv + 294pp

Roger Shuff
Searching for the True Church
Brethren and Evangelicals in Mid-Twentieth-Century England
Roger Shuff holds that the influence of the Brethren movement on wider evangelical life in England in the twentieth century is often underrated. This book records and accounts for the fact that Brethren reached the peak of their strength at the time when evangelicalism was at it lowest ebb, immediately before World War II. However, the movement then moved into persistent decline as evangelicalism regained ground in the post war period. Accompanying this downward trend has been a sharp accentuation of the contrast between Brethren congregations who engage constructively with the non-Brethren scene and, at the other end of the spectrum, the isolationist group commonly referred to as 'Exclusive Brethren'.
2005 / 1-84227-254-3 / xviii+ 296pp

James H.S. Steven
Worship in the Spirit
Charismatic Worship in the Church of England
This book explores the nature and function of worship in six Church of England churches influenced by the Charismatic Movement, focusing on congregational singing and public prayer ministry. The theological adequacy of such ritual is discussed in relation to pneumatological and christological understandings in Christian worship.
2002 / 1-84227-103-2 / xvi + 238pp

Peter K. Stevenson
God in Our Nature
The Incarnational Theology of John McLeod Campbell
This radical reassessment of Campbell's thought arises from a comprehensive study of his preaching and theology. Previous accounts have overlooked both his sermons and his Christology. This study examines the distinctive Christology evident in his sermons and shows that it sheds new light on Campbell's much debated views about atonement.
2004 / 1-84227-218-7 / xxiv + 458pp

Kenneth J. Stewart
Restoring the Reformation
British Evangelicalism and the Réveil at Geneva 1816–1849
Restoring the Reformation traces British missionary initiative in post-Revolutionary Francophone Europe from the genesis of the London Missionary Society, the visits of Robert Haldane and Henry Drummond, and the founding of the Continental Society. While British Evangelicals aimed at the reviving of a foreign Protestant cause of momentous legend, they received unforeseen reciprocating emphases from the Continent which forced self-reflection on Evangelicalism's own relationship to the Reformation.
2006 / 1-84227-392-2 / approx. 190pp

Martin Wellings
Evangelicals Embattled
Responses of Evangelicals in the Church of England to Ritualism, Darwinism and Theological Liberalism 1890–1930
In the closing years of the nineteenth century and the first decades of the twentieth century Anglican Evangelicals faced a series of challenges. In responding to Anglo-Catholicism, liberal theology, Darwinism and biblical criticism, the unity and identity of the Evangelical school were severely tested.
2003 / 1-84227-049-4 / xviii + 352pp

James Whisenant
A Fragile Unity
Anti-Ritualism and the Division of Anglican Evangelicalism in the Nineteenth Century
This book deals with the ritualist controversy (approximately 1850–1900) from the perspective of its evangelical participants and considers the divisive effects it had on the party.
2003 / 1-84227-105-9 / xvi + 530pp

Haddon Willmer
Evangelicalism 1785–1835: An Essay (1962) and Reflections (2004)
Awarded the Hulsean Prize in the University of Cambridge in 1962, this interpretation of a classic period of English Evangelicalism, by a young church historian, is now supplemented by reflections on Evangelicalism from the vantage point of a retired Professor of Theology.
2006 / 1-84227-219-5 / approx. 350pp

Linda Wilson
Constrained by Zeal
Female Spirituality amongst Nonconformists 1825–1875

Constrained by Zeal investigates the neglected area of Nonconformist female spirituality. Against the background of separate spheres, it analyses the experience of women from four denominations, and argues that the churches provided a 'third sphere' in which they could find opportunities for participation.

2000 / 0-85364-972-3 / xvi + 294pp

Paternoster
9 Holdom Avenue,
Bletchley,
Milton Keynes MK1 1QR,
United Kingdom
Web: www.authenticmedia.co.uk/paternoster

July 2005

www.ingramcontent.com/pod-product-compliance
Lightning Source LLC
Chambersburg PA
CBHW071224290426
44108CB00013B/1283